CONTEMPORARY ISSUES IN SOCIAL PSYCHOLOGY

SECOND EDITION

CONTEMPORARY ISSUES IN SOCIAL PSYCHOLOGY

SECOND EDITION

Edited by

Lawrence S. Wrightsman

George Peabody College for Teachers

and

John C. Brigham

Florida State University

BROOKS/COLE PUBLISHING COMPANY
MONTEREY, CALIFORNIA
A Division of Wadsworth Publishing Company, Inc.

ISBN: 0-8185-0071-9
L.C. Catalog Card No: 72-92050
Printed in the United States of America
1 2 3 4 5 6 7 8 9 10—77 76 75 74 73

This book was edited by Micky Lawler and designed by Jane Mitchell. Technical art was drawn by John Foster. The book was typeset by Datagraphics, Inc., Phoenix, Arizona, and printed and bound by Kingsport Press, Kingsport, Tennessee.

PREFACE TO THE FIRST EDITION

The scientific approach to the study of social psychology is still in its infancy. It is no wonder that the topic appears to be one whole "blooming, buzzing mass of confusion," to use William James' term. Social psychology at present has no unifying theory yet contains a multitude of concepts and theories of limited range, each with its own proponents. There is controversy over the use of most procedures, the utility of most concepts, and the interpretation of most findings.

While the controversial and unsettled nature of the field makes it frustrating, that controversy also makes the field exhilarating. The purpose of this book is to reflect this stimulating nature of contemporary social psychology. I have identified 11 of the most important research concepts in social psychology through a reading of current textbooks, journals, and convention reports. Each part of this book focuses on one of the 11 concepts and includes three readings from the literature. Generally, the first article in each part is a statement of theory or a review of previous work on the concept; the second article is a report of research that has tested a hypothesis generated by the theory; and the third article is a replication of the research, a critique, or a review of research on the concept. In each part, the aim has been to select readings that (1) reflect significant thought and work and that (2) the reader will find inherently interesting and provocative. The titles of some of the selections have been modified in order to fit the theory-research-critique format of the book. Certain less central passages of some articles have been deleted in order to present a compact package of work on each concept; ellipses have been used to mark any such deletions.

This book of readings can be used in conjunction with a standard textbook for an undergraduate course in social psychology and thus expose the student to original writing and greater detail than a text can. If the instructor prefers to use his lectures to give the continuity that a textbook supplies, *Contemporary Issues in Social Psychology* can be used in place of the text. Or the book can serve to acquaint graduate students in a proseminar course with research on current concepts in social psychology.

Several special features have been used to increase the value of a book of readings as a learning device. Each part contains an introduction

v

and a summary written for this volume. The purposes of the introductions are to define the concepts under study, to place them in historical perspective, and to alert the reader to the significant aspects and relationships in the three selections that follow. The purposes of the summaries are to highlight the basic findings in the articles, to describe other recent work using the concept, to attempt to resolve conflicting findings, and to point out unanswered questions. Original bibliographies have been retained so that the reader can pursue the topic in more depth if he wishes. The glossary at the end of the book defines the significant concepts and procedures used.

It should be recognized that all the basic concepts in current social-psychological research are not covered. I doubt that any two social psychologists would agree on what the basic concepts are, and my selection, though it is based upon a review of current texts and the suggestions of others, no doubt reflects some of my biases.

I wish to thank a number of people who are responsible for improvements in the book. I especially want to thank the authors and publishers of the selections for permission to reprint this material; credit is given each one in the source notes for the readings. Charles T. Hendrix, Psychology Editor of Brooks/Cole, made the original suggestion of the format and has made a number of useful recommendations. Several reviewers—Professors Georgia Babladelis, of California State College; Daryl J. Bem, of Stanford University; Earl R. Carlson, of California State College; Philip S. Gallo, Jr., of San Diego State College; Chester A. Insko, of the University of North Carolina; Bhuwan Joshi, of the University of California, Santa Cruz; and Harry C. Triandis, of the University of Illinois—suggested articles to be considered, topics to be included, and changes to be made in the introductions and summaries. Most of their suggestions have been followed. Mrs. Peggy Lee Foster and Mrs. Mildred Harrington typed portions of the manuscript with accuracy and speed. I owe special debts of gratitude to Mrs. Doreen Lovelace for her expert handling of correspondence with the authors and publishers and for her persevering nature in typing part of the manuscript and to Miss Paula Abrams for her accurate typing of revisions and for her thorough proofreading.

Lawrence S. Wrightsman

PREFACE TO THE SECOND EDITION

In the five years since the publication of the first edition of this book, the field of social psychology has reflected great continuity—in the utilization of theories of limited range (as opposed to the use of grand theory or no theory at all), in the predominance of laboratory-based research, and in the attention to a vast number of topics that may be considered social psychological. Yet changes have also been quite evident over this brief period of time. More social psychologists now seek field settings and unobtrusive measures to test their hypotheses, rather than relying entirely on laboratory experiments and paper-and-pencil measures. There is an increasing realization that the research process itself is social psychological, that both experimenters and subjects have expectations about the outcomes of their research activity, and that such expectations may have a considerable influence on the research results obtained. In addition, the times in which we are living demand even more than before that social psychologists bring to bear their techniques and knowledge on the problems of our world. Many of these problems—overpopulation, pollution, war, racism and sexism, and others—can be better understood when a social psychological viewpoint is used.

This second edition of *Contemporary Issues in Social Psychology* also reflects both continuity and change. As in the first edition, some of the most important issues in the field have been chosen for intensive study. In the first edition 11 topics were used; in this edition we have increased this number slightly, to 12. These topics were identified by surveying contemporary journals and soliciting reactions from a panel of social psychologists who served as consultants as the second edition was being planned.

For each of the 12 basic issues or topics, three selections from the literature were selected for reprinting here. As in the first edition, the first article is usually a statement of theory or a review of previous research on that topic or issue. The second article is a report of an empirical study that tests a hypothesis relevant to the issue. The third article is a critique of previous research or a replication or extension that further clarifies our knowledge about the issue.

As in the first edition, we have selected articles that are important reflections of contemporary concerns in the professional field. In some articles, less central passages have been deleted in order to present a more compact presentation.

Each of the sections includes an introduction and summary written specifically for this volume. The use of these materials is designed to add to the continuity offered by the three articles on each issue. The introductions to each section attempt to place each issue within an appropriate context, define the basic variables, and alert the reader to the most significant features of the articles that follow. The summaries highlight the most important findings, attempt to resolve conflicting results, and point to possible topics for further study.

Although the general format remains as it was in the first edition, there have been changes in the specific issues covered and in the particular articles reprinted. Of the 11 topics in the first edition, only 5 have been retained in the second. Two other first-edition sections, Conformity and Authoritarianism-Obedience, have been collapsed into one section, entitled Obedience and Compliance. Six entirely new sections have been added: the Social Psychology of the Research Process, Helping Behavior, the Risky Shift, Aggression and Violence, Sexism, and the Attribution of Attitudes and Emotional States. Only 5 of the 33 articles utilized in the first edition are included in the second.

We regret that some of the topics from the first edition could not be included. We look with nostalgia at some of the "classic" topics such as Leadership, Person Perception, and Conformity; these areas remain ones with some contemporary interest and activity. Although one reason for dispensing with them was the recent availability of brief paperback books on each of these topics, our main reason was that other issues should be given heightened consideration. In making these changes, we relied heavily on the suggestions for deletions and additions made by a panel of consultants.

This last comment leads us into a description of what we believe is the most important change in this second edition. Some issues in this edition, particularly Sexism and Moral Development, extend considerably beyond the coverage of most conventional textbooks in social psychology today. Our purpose is to stretch the concern of social psychologists. If *Contemporary Issues in Social Psychology* is used as an adjunct to a text in a Social Psychology course, students will find topics in the former not introduced by the text. Although some may see this as a problem, we see the function of a book of readings as a consciousness-raising one. *Contemporary Issues in Social Psychology* has as one goal the exploration of issues that social psychologists are currently debating. But it also reflects issues in the contemporary scene about which social psychology should have something to say. Often standard textbooks, as repositories of past knowledge, fail to look toward the real world, where new issues are constantly being generated. We hope this book of readings does some of that. The use of this book along with a standard text for an undergraduate course in social psychology can expose the reader both to new topics and to greater depth in theory, methodology, and analysis. Or, if the instructor prefers to use lecture material to give the extensive continuity that many textbooks provide, *Contemporary Issues in Social Psychology* can be used in place of a text. An additional use of this book is to acquaint graduate students in a proseminar course with current research in social psychology.

We wish to thank a number of people who have participated in the formulation of this book as it now stands. Acknowledgment to the authors and publishers of the reprinted articles for permission to reprint is given in the source notes at the beginning of each reading. Several social psychologists served as reviewers and consultants as we prepared this edition; they are Les Herold of California State College at San Bernardino, Lance K. Canon of the University of Washington, Robert Wicklund of the University of Texas at Austin, Samuel Komorita of Indiana University, Philip Gallo of San Diego State College, Harry C. Triandis of the University of Illinois, Dalmas Taylor of the University of Maryland, Daryl J. Bem of Stanford University, and Frances Hill of the University of Montana.

The staff of Brooks/Cole, particularly Bonnie Fitzwater, Terry Hendrix, Bill Hicks, and Vena Dyer, expedited our work greatly. Mrs. Robert Lovelace, Mrs. Pat Gosen, and Mrs. Eileen Parramore handled correspondence with authors and publishers and typed the numerous revisions of the manuscript. Stuart Oskamp, Acting Chairman of the Department of Psychology, Claremont Graduate School, provided office space and materials for one of the editors during a sabbatical leave in which final revisions were made.

Lawrence S. Wrightsman
John C. Brigham

CONTENTS

HOW TO READ
A SCIENTIFIC
RESEARCH REPORT*

*Adapted from Strange, J. R., & Strange, S. M. *Reading for meaning in college and after.* Monterey, Calif.: Brooks/Cole, 1972, pp. 54-66. We wish to thank Jack and Sallie Strange for giving us permission to adapt their suggestions.

Each article reprinted in this book was written by a psychologist or group of psychologists with the intent of communicating their theories or findings to their peers. Scientific writing, like all other forms, has its specific style and format. The undergraduate student who has not read many scientific journal articles in the past may profit from studying this brief section before starting to read the articles reprinted in this book. Although all the articles in this book are scientific in intent, some are review articles or speculative pieces, whereas others report empirical findings in detail. The first type is easier to read; such articles may possess some personal style, and there is permitted some deviation from the formal restrictions of style and format that must be maintained in the reports of empirical findings. It is the reading of the second type, called the research report, that we will discuss in detail here.

Notice that every research report is organized as follows:

1. An introduction, which sets forth the purpose of the study, defines terms, reviews relevant past research, and sets forth hypotheses that will be tested by the study.

2. A Procedure section, which describes the subjects who participated in the study, the methods used to test the hypotheses, and the instruments (tests, equipment, and so on) employed.

3. A Results section, which employs statistical techniques to determine and report the outcomes of the hypotheses. Basically, the Results section reports whether each of the study's hypotheses was confirmed or disconfirmed. Other important empirical findings are also presented in the Results section.

4. A Discussion section, which evaluates and interprets the findings presented in the Results section. Here is the place where the findings are put "in context"; for example, they may be related to the findings of other studies. Particularly if hypotheses are not confirmed, the Discussion section is the appropriate place for the researcher to offer explanations for the findings. And the Discussion section almost inevitably ends with something to the effect that, before we have a complete understanding of the phenomenon under study, "further research is necessary."

The Results and Discussion sections are sometimes collapsed together. Some articles contain a

Summary and Conclusions section, and all articles end with a list of references.

It is suggested that, when you are ready to read a research report in this book, you do the following:

1. Read the title of the article and then quickly skim through it to obtain a general idea of the researcher's purpose and findings.

2. Next, reread the Section Introduction and the Section Summary, which will usually deal succinctly with the main points in each of the articles in that section.

3. At this point you should identify the hypotheses of the study and be sure you understand them. Then you should determine, for each hypothesis, whether the findings confirmed or disconfirmed it. This is done by reading relevant sections of the Results and Discussion sections. In addition, you should attempt to understand the study's experimental design and controls, its procedures, and its instruments.

4. Now carefully read the article in its entirety. The organization of the article—the reason for the sections appearing as they do—should be more apparent now. You may find that utilization of the references at the end of the article is necessary if you wish a thorough understanding of procedures, data analyses, and findings. Because space is limited in journals, a research report will often refer the reader to an earlier article that used the same procedure, rather than reprint it in detail. Likewise, the justifiability of certain statistical techniques may be indicated by references to other articles or books.

5. Last of all, underline the important points of the research report. Preparing a brief summary of the article, which deals with the hypotheses, procedures, results, and conclusions, is a good way of developing an integrated understanding of the study.

The statistical techniques and analyses in some of the articles may be beyond your level of training. However, if you follow the above suggestions, you should still be able to understand the thrust of the article.

SECTION 1

The Social Psychology of the Research Process

Social psychology is concerned with the behavior of individuals and the varied social influences on their behavior. For example, a young man driving hurriedly to meet his girlfriend at the airport might ordinarily fail to stop at a stop sign —except that he notices a police car behind him. But the actual presence of other people is, of course, just one type of social influence. The norms, the rules, the laws a person has learned as a part of growing up have effects, too. In the situation just posed, some persons would never fail to stop at the stop sign, even in the middle of the night or in the direst of emergencies. Such behavior, even if it occurs when the person is alone, is social behavior, because it reflects the implied presence of others and the learning of rules from others. Deviant behaviors, even when performed alone (such as cheating on a take-home exam), also are within the domain of social psychology.

Is all behavior, then, social behavior? No, there are many cases of nonsocial behaviors. One type is represented by reflex acts, such as the immediate jerking of one's hand away from a hot stove. Learning to avoid certain foods or certain actions can result without the actual or implied presence of others.

But although not all behavior falls within the realm of social psychology, our methods of gathering information about human behavior represent social behaviors. The research process is social-psychological in nature. Consider a study of the acuity of hearing under different stimulus conditions. Perhaps the research psychologist is interested in the effects of prolonged exposure to loud noise on the auditory sensitivity of the listener. The actual extent of hearing loss, if any, resulting from such exposure is not affected by social considerations. But how is the loss *measured*? By a self-report of the subject, who indicates after each presentation of a stimulus sound whether or not he can hear it. The subject in the loud-noise experiment may not accurately report whether he hears a sound on every presentation of the stimulus. On a given trial he may not hear a sound, but he may say that he does. Or, if he has to identify a number, he may take a wild guess that happens to be correct. The *measurement* of his physical reaction is a social situation. The subject may try to make himself look good. On the other hand, he may not care about the results and hence may not even try to be accurate.

This is just one example of the fact that our *knowledge-gathering activity* is social in nature. The research process, involving an interaction between subject and researcher, is one in which the uncontrolled expectations, needs, and abilities of each can lead to an outcome different from that under controlled conditions. Other examples are numerous: a white interviewer with a Southern accent, asking blacks their opinions about school busing to achieve racial balance, may not get the same answers from them that a black interviewer would; a doctoral student, reading the timer to see how quickly a rat has run a maze, may unintentionally misread the dial so that the "results" he records give added support to his hypothesis.

Thus the social psychology of the data-gathering process is an area worthy of concern and of substantive study in its own right. First of all, it gives us knowledge about the accuracy of methodology in psychological research; but, more importantly, it generates insights of its own about human social behavior (Miller, 1972). And in recent years it has become a controversial area of study, centering around the question: just how much, if any, are the results of research studies invalidated by the fact that the data-gathering process is a social one?

The approaches to this problem may be divided into two classes: those concerned with *experimenter effects* and those dealing with *subject effects*. "Experimenter effects" refer to qualities of the experimenter's appearance and behavior that may influence research outcomes. These cover not only deliberate "faking" of data or outcomes but the many other ways an experimenter can cause certain subjects to respond in desired ways. The *inadvertent* or *unconscious* communication by experimenters of the ways they expect subjects to perform is considered to be a more widespread hazard than is deliberate falsification of findings by the researcher. Experimenter

effects can exert a great and deleterious influence on our search for knowledge, and they will be reviewed in detail in the editors' summary to Section 1.

The three articles reprinted in this section deal with the other major aspect of the social psychology of the research process: the expectations and motivations of research subjects. For too long, researchers in psychology have ignored the fact that their human subjects enter into the research activity with concerns, needs, and other very important influences on their behavior in the situation. One subject may be wondering "Will this experiment hurt me?" Another may be concerned about doing a good job or appearing to be bright, well adjusted, or motivated. A third may be tired and motivated to do the least work possible. The effects of these and other expectations is the topic of study for this section.

As will be our usual format in each section of this book, we present first a theoretical article that gives an overview of the topic. One of the controversies regarding the nature of the experimental subject is the degree to which he or she is motivated to *cooperate* with the experimenter. In the first article of this section, Martin T. Orne of the University of Pennsylvania proposes that cooperation is a primary *demand characteristic* operating on college students who participate as subjects in most psychological experiments. As will be our custom throughout this book, the second article is a research report that empirically investigates a theory or construct from the first article. In this second article, Sigall, Aronson, and Van Hoose ask whether "cooperation" is really a basic concern of subjects participating in experiments. The article makes a useful distinction between "cooperation" and desires to do well. If cooperation with the experimenter is to be obtained at the sacrifice of "looking good," will the subject still cooperate?

Another major subject variable is analyzed in the third article in this section. Much of our scientific knowledge of psychological processes is based on the responses of *volunteer* subjects. How representative are these volunteers? Do their responses adequately reflect those of nonvolunteers? Why do they choose to participate? Thomas Hood and Kurt Back review previous work and examine catharsis and self-disclosure as reasons for volunteering for experiments.

REFERENCE

Miller, A. G. (Ed.) *The social psychology of psychological research.* New York: Free Press, 1972.

ARTICLE 1

On the Social Psychology of the Psychological Experiment:
With Particular Reference to Demand Characteristics and Their Implications[1]

Martin T. Orne[2]

It is to the highest degree probable that the subject['s] . . . general attitude of mind is that of ready complacency and cheerful willingness to assist the investigator in every possible way by reporting to him those very things which he is most eager to find, and that the very questions of the experimenter . . . suggest the shade of reply expected. . . . Indeed . . . it seems too often as if the subject were now regarded as a stupid automaton. . . .

A. H. Pierce, 1908[3]

Since the time of Galileo, scientists have employed the laboratory experiment as a method of understanding natural phenomena. Generically, the experimental method consists of abstracting relevant variables from complex situations in nature and reproducing in the laboratory segments of these situations, varying the parameters in-

Reprinted from *American Psychologist,* **17,** 1962, 776–783. Copyright 1962 by the American Psychological Association, and reproduced by permission of the author and the publisher.

[1]This paper was presented at the Symposium, "On the Social Psychology of the Psychological Experiment," American Psychological Association Convention, New York, 1961.

The work reported here was supported in part by a Public Health Service Research Grant, M-3369, National Institute of Mental Health.

[2]I wish to thank my associates Ronald E. Shor, Donald N. O'Connell, Ulric Neisser, Karl E. Scheibe, and Emily F. Carota for their comments and criticisms in the preparation of this paper.

[3]See reference list (Pierce, 1908).

volved so as to determine the effect of the experimental variables. This procedure allows generalization from the information obtained in the laboratory situation back to the original situation as it occurs in nature. The physical sciences have made striking advances through the use of this method, but in the behavioral sciences it has often been difficult to meet two necessary requirements for meaningful experimentation: reproducibility and ecological validity.[4]

It has long been recognized that certain differences will exist between the types of experiments conducted in the physical sciences and those in the behavioral sciences because the former investigates a universe of inanimate objects and forces, whereas the latter deals with animate organisms, often thinking, conscious subjects. However, recognition of this distinction has not always led to appropriate changes in the traditional experimental model of physics as employed in the behavioral sciences. Rather the experimental model has been so successful as employed in physics that there has been a tendency in the behavioral sciences to follow precisely a paradigm originated for the study of inanimate objects, i.e., one which proceeds by exposing the subject to various conditions and observing the differences in reaction of the subject under different conditions. However, the use of such a model with animal or

[4]Ecological validity, in the sense that Brunswik (1947) has used the term: appropriate generalization from the laboratory to nonexperimental situations.

human subjects leads to the problem that the subject of the experiment is assumed, at least implicitly, to be a *passive responder* to stimuli—an assumption difficult to justify. Further, in this type of model the experimental stimuli themselves are usually rigorously defined in terms of what *is done* to the subject. In contrast, the purpose of this paper will be to focus on what the human subject *does* in the laboratory: what motivation the subject is likely to have in the experimental situation, how he usually perceives behavioral research, what the nature of the cues is that the subject is likely to pick up, etc. Stated in other terms, what factors are apt to affect the subject's reaction to the well-defined stimuli in the situation? These factors comprise what will be referred to here as the "experimental setting."

Since any experimental manipulation of human subjects takes place within this larger framework or setting, we should propose that the above-mentioned factors must be further elaborated and the parameters of the experimental setting more carefully defined so that adequate controls can be designed to isolate the effects of the experimental setting from the effects of the experimental variables. Later in this paper we shall propose certain possible techniques of control which have been devised in the process of our research on the nature of hypnosis.

Our initial focus here will be on some of the qualities peculiar to psychological experiments. The experimental situation is one which takes place within the context of an explicit agreement of the subject to participate in a special form of social interaction known as "taking part in an experiment." Within the context of our culture the roles of subject and experimenter are well understood and carry with them well-defined mutual role expectations. A particularly striking aspect of the typical experimenter-subject relationship is the extent to which the subject will play his role and place himself under the control of the experimenter. Once a subject has agreed to participate in a psychological experiment, he implicitly agrees to perform a very wide range of actions on request without inquiring as to their purpose, and frequently without inquiring as to their duration.

Furthermore, the subject agrees to tolerate a considerable degree of discomfort, boredom, or actual pain, if required to do so by the experimenter. Just about any request which could conceivably be asked of the subject by a reputable investigator is legitimized by the quasi-magical phrase, "This is an experiment," and the shared assumption that a legitimate purpose will be served by the subject's behavior. A somewhat trivial example of this legitimization of requests is as follows:

A number of casual acquaintances were asked whether they would do the experimenter a favor; on their acquiescence, they were asked to perform five push-ups. Their response tended to be amazement, incredulity and the question "Why?" Another similar group of individuals were asked whether they would take part in an experiment of brief duration. When they agreed to do so, they too were asked to perform five push-ups. Their typical response was "Where?"

The striking degree of control inherent in the experimental situation can also be illustrated by a set of pilot experiments which were performed in the course of designing an experiment to test whether the degree of control inherent in the *hypnotic* relationship is greater than that in a waking relationship.[5] In order to test this question, we tried to develop a set of tasks which waking subjects would refuse to do, or would do only for a short period of time. The tasks were intended to be psychologically noxious, meaningless, or boring, rather than painful or fatiguing.

For example, one task was to perform serial additions of each adjacent two numbers on sheets filled with rows of random digits. In order to complete just one sheet, the subject would be required to perform 224 additions! A stack of some 2,000 sheets was presented to each subject— clearly an impossible task to complete. After the instructions were given, the subject was deprived of his watch and told, "Continue to work; I will return eventually." Five and one-half hours later, the *experimenter* gave up! In general, subjects tended to continue this type of task for several hours, usually with little decrement in perfor-

[5]These pilot studies were performed by Thomas Menaker.

mance. Since we were trying to find a task which would be discontinued spontaneously within a brief period, we tried to create a more frustrating situation as follows:

Subjects were asked to perform the same task described above but were also told that when finished with the additions on each sheet, they should pick up a card from a large pile, which would instruct them on what to do next. However, every card in the pile read,

You are to tear up the sheet of paper which you have just completed into a minimum of thirty-two pieces and go on to the next sheet of paper and continue working as you did before; when you have completed this piece of paper, pick up the next card which will instruct you further. Work as accurately and as rapidly as you can.

Our expectation was that subjects would discontinue the task as soon as they realized that the cards were worded identically, that each finished piece of work had to be destroyed, and that, in short, the task was completely meaningless.

Somewhat to our amazement, subjects tended to persist in the task for several hours with relatively little sign of overt hostility. Removal of the one-way screen did not tend to make much difference. The postexperimental inquiry helped to explain the subjects' behavior. When asked about the tasks, subjects would invariably attribute considerable meaning to their performance, viewing it as an endurance test or the like.

Thus far, we have been singularly unsuccessful in finding an experimental task which would be discontinued, or, indeed, refused by subjects in an experimental setting.[6, 7] Not only do subjects continue to perform boring, unrewarding tasks, but they do so with few errors and little decrement in speed. It became apparent that it was extremely difficult to design an experiment to test the degree of social control in hypnosis, in view

[6]Tasks which would involve the use of actual severe physical pain or exhaustion were not considered.

[7]This observation is consistent with Frank's (1944) failure to obtain resistance to disagreeable or nonsensical tasks. He accounts for this "primarily by *S*'s unwillingness to break the tacit agreement he had made when he volunteered to take part in the experiment, namely, to do whatever the experiment required of him" (p. 24).

of the already *very high degree of control in the experimental situation itself.*

The quasi-experimental work reported here is highly informal and based on samples of three or four subjects in each group. It does, however, illustrate the remarkable compliance of the experimental subject. The only other situations where such a wide range of requests are carried out with little or no question are those of complete authority, such as some parent-child relationships or some doctor-patient relationships. This aspect of the experiment as a social situation will not become apparent unless one tests for it; it is, however, present in varying degrees in all experimental contexts. Not only are tasks carried out, but they are performed with care over considerable periods of time.

Our observation that subjects tend to carry out a remarkably wide range of instructions with a surprising degree of diligence reflects only one aspect of the motivation manifested by most subjects in an experimental situation. It is relevant to consider another aspect of motivation that is common to the subjects of most psychological experiments: high regard for the aims of science and experimentation.

A volunteer who participates in a psychological experiment may do so for a wide variety of reasons ranging from the need to fulfill a course requirement, to the need for money, to the unvoiced hope of altering his personal adjustment for the better, etc. Over and above these motives, however, college students tend to share (with the experimenter) the hope and expectation that the study in which they are participating will in some material way contribute to science and perhaps ultimately to human welfare in general. We should expect that many of the characteristics of the experimental situation derive from the peculiar role relationship which exists between subject and experimenter. Both subject and experimenter share the belief that whatever the experimental task is, it is important, and that as such no matter how much effort must be exerted or how much discomfort must be endured, it is justified by the ultimate purpose.

If we assume that much of the motivation of the subject to comply with any and all experimental instructions derives from an identification with the goals of science in general and the success of the experiment in particular,[8] it follows that the subject has a stake in the outcome of the study in which he is participating. For the volunteer subject to feel that he has made a useful contribution, it is necessary for him to assume that the experimenter is competent and that he himself is a "good subject."

The significance to the subject of successfully being a "good subject" is attested to by the frequent questions at the conclusion of an experiment, to the effect of, "Did I ruin the experiment?" What is most commonly meant by this is, "Did I perform well in my role as experimental subject?" or "Did my behavior demonstrate that which the experiment is designed to show?" Admittedly, subjects are concerned about their performance in terms of reinforcing their self-image; nonetheless, they seem even more concerned with the utility of their performances. We might well expect then that as far as the subject is able, he will behave in an experimental context in a manner designed to play the role of a "good subject" or, in other words, *to validate the experimental hypothesis.* Viewed in this way, the student volunteer is *not* merely a passive responder in an experimental situation but rather he has a very real stake in the successful outcome of the experiment. This problem is implicitly recognized in the large number of psychological studies which attempt to conceal the true purpose of the experiment from the subject in the hope of thereby obtaining more reliable data. This maneuver on the part of psychologists is so widely known in the college population that even if a psychologist is honest with the subject, more often than not he will be distrusted. As one subject pithily put it, "Psychologists always lie!" This bit of paranoia has some support in reality.

The subject's performance in an experiment might almost be conceptualized as problem-solving behavior; that is, at some level he sees it as his task to ascertain the true purpose of the experiment and respond in a manner which will support the hypotheses being tested. Viewed in this light, the totality of cues which convey an experimental hypothesis to the subject become significant determinants of subjects' behavior. We have labeled the sum total of such cues as the *"demand characteristics of the experimental situation"* (Orne, 1959a). These cues include the rumors or campus scuttlebutt about the research, the information conveyed during the original solicitation, the person of the experimenter, and the setting of the laboratory, as well as all explicit and implicit communications during the experiment proper. A frequently overlooked, but nonetheless very significant source of cues for the subject lies in the experimental procedure itself, viewed in the light of the subject's previous knowledge and experience. For example, if a test is given twice with some intervening treatment, even the dullest college student is aware that some change is expected, particularly if the test is in some obvious way related to the treatment.

The demand characteristics perceived in any particular experiment will vary with the sophistication, intelligence, and previous experience of each experimental subject. To the extent that the demand characteristics of the experiment are clear-cut, they will be perceived uniformly by most experimental subjects. It is entirely possible to have an experimental situation with clear-cut demand characteristics for psychology undergraduates which, however, does not have the same clear-cut demand characteristics for enlisted army personnel. It is, of course, those demand characteristics which are perceived by the subject that will influence his behavior.

We should like to propose the heuristic assumption that a subject's behavior in any experimental situation will be determined by two sets of variables: (a) those which are traditionally defined as experimental variables and (b) the perceived demand characteristics of the experimental situation. The extent to which the subject's behavior is related to the demand characteristics, rather than to the experimental variable, will in large measure determine both the extent to which the experiment can be replicated

---

[8]This hypothesis is subject to empirical test. We should predict that there would be measurable differences in motivation between subjects who perceive a particular experiment as "significant" and those who perceive the experiment as "unimportant."

with minor modification (i.e., modified demand characteristics) and the extent to which generalizations can be drawn about the effect of the experimental variables in nonexperimental contexts [the problem of ecological validity (Brunswik, 1947)].

It becomes an empirical issue to study under what circumstances, in what kind of experimental contexts, and with what kind of subject populations, demand characteristics become significant in determining the behavior of subjects in experimental situations. It should be clear that demand characteristics cannot be eliminated from experiments; all experiments will have demand characteristics, and these will always have some effect. It does become possible, however, to study the effect of demand characteristics as opposed to the effect of experimental variables. However, techniques designed to study the effect of demand characteristics need to take into account that these effects result from the subject's *active* attempt to respond appropriately to the *totality* of the experimental situation.

It is perhaps best to think of the perceived demand characteristics as a contextual variable in the experimental situation. We should like to emphasize that, at this stage, little is known about this variable. In our first study which utilized the demand characteristics concept (Orne, 1959b), we found that a particular experimental effect was present only in records of those subjects who were able to verbalize the experimenter's hypothesis. Those subjects who were unable to do so did not show the predicted phenomenon. Indeed we found that whether or not a given subject perceived the experimenter's hypothesis was a more accurate predictor of the subject's actual performance than his statement about what he thought he had done on the experimental task. It became clear from extensive interviews with subjects that response to the demand characteristics is not merely conscious compliance. When we speak of "playing the role of a good experimental subject," we use the concept analogously to the way in which Sarbin (1950) describes role playing in hypnosis: namely, largely on a nonconscious level. The demand characteristics of the situation help define the role of "good experimental sub-

ject," and the responses of the subject are a function of the role that is created.

We have a suspicion that the demand characteristics most potent in determining subjects' behavior are those which convey the purpose of the experiment effectively but not obviously. If the purpose of the experiment is not clear, or is highly ambiguous, many different hypotheses may be formed by different subjects, and the demand characteristics will not lead to clear-cut results. If, on the other hand, the demand characteristics are so obvious that the subject becomes fully conscious of the expectations of the experimenter, there is a tendency to lean over backwards to be honest. We are encountering here the effect of another facet of the college student's attitude toward science. While the student wants studies to "work," he feels he must be honest in his report; otherwise, erroneous conclusions will be drawn. Therefore, if the subject becomes acutely aware of the experimenter's expectations, there may be a tendency for biasing in the opposite direction. (This is analogous to the often observed tendency to favor individuals whom we dislike in an effort to be fair.[9])

Delineation of the situations where demand characteristics may produce an effect ascribed to experimental variables, or where they may obscure such an effect and actually lead to systematic data in the opposite direction, as well as those experimental contexts where they do not play a major role, is an issue for further work. Recognizing the contribution to experimental results which may be made by the demand characteristics of the situation, what are some experimental techniques for the study of demand characteristics?

As we have pointed out, it is futile to imagine an experiment that could be created without demand characteristics. One of the basic characteristics of the human being is that he will ascribe purpose and meaning even in the absence of pur-

[9]Rosenthal (1961) in his recent work on experimenter bias, has reported a similar type of phenomenon. Biasing was maximized by ego involvement of the experimenters, but when an attempt was made to increase biasing by paying for "good results," there was a marked reduction of effect. This reversal may be ascribed to the experimenters' becoming too aware of their own wishes in the situation.

pose and meaning. In an experiment where he knows some purpose exists, it is inconceivable for him not to form some hypothesis as to the purpose, based on some cues, no matter how meager; this will then determine the demand characteristics which will be perceived by and operate for a particular subject. Rather than eliminating this variable then, it becomes necessary to take demand characteristics into account, study their effect, and manipulate them if necessary.

One procedure to determine the demand characteristics is the systematic study of each individual subject's perception of the experimental hypothesis. If one can determine what demand characteristics are perceived by each subject, it becomes possible to determine to what extent these, rather than the experimental variables, correlate with the observed behavior. If the subject's behavior correlates better with the demand characteristics than with the experimental variables, it is probable that the demand characteristics are the major determinants of the behavior.

The most obvious technique for determining what demand characteristics are perceived is the use of postexperimental inquiry. In this regard, it is well to point out that considerable self-discipline is necessary for the experimenter to obtain a valid inquiry. A great many experimenters at least implicitly make the demand that the subject not perceive what is really going on. The temptation for the experimenter, in, say, a replication of an Asch group pressure experiment, is to ask the subject afterwards, "You didn't realize that the other fellows were confederates, did you?" Having obtained the required, "No," the experimenter breathes a sigh of relief and neither subject nor experimenter pursues the issue further.[10] However, even if the experimenter makes an effort to elicit the subject's perception of the hypothesis of the experiment, he may have difficulty in obtaining a valid report because the subject as well as he himself has considerable interest in appearing naive.

Most subjects are cognizant that they are not supposed to know any more about an experiment than they have been told and that excessive

knowledge will disqualify them from participating, or, in the case of a postexperimental inquiry, such knowledge will invalidate their performance. As we pointed out earlier, subjects have a real stake in viewing their performance as meaningful. For this reason, it is commonplace to find a pact of ignorance resulting from the intertwining motives of both experimenter and subject, neither wishing to create a situation where the particular subject's performance needs to be excluded from the study.

For these reasons, inquiry procedures are required to push the subject for information without, however, providing in themselves cues as to what is expected. The general question which needs to be explored is the subject's perception of the experimental purpose and the specific hypotheses of the experimenter. This can best be done by an open-ended procedure starting with the very general question of, "What do you think that the experiment is about?" and only much later asking specific questions. Responses of "I don't know" should be dealt with by encouraging the subject to guess, use his imagination, and in general, by refusing to accept this response. Under these circumstances, the overwhelming majority of students will turn out to have evolved very definite hypotheses. These hypotheses can then be judged, and a correlation between them and experimental performance can be drawn.

Two objections may be made against this type of inquiry: (a) that the subject's perception of the experimenter's hypotheses is based on his own experimental behavior, and therefore a correlation between these two variables may have little to do with the determinants of behavior, and (b) that the inquiry procedure itself is subject to demand characteristics.

A procedure which has been independently advocated by Riecken (1958) and Orne (1959a) is designed to deal with the first of these objections. This consists of an inquiry procedure which is conducted much as though the subject had actually been run in the experiment, without, however, permitting him to be given any experimental data. Instead, the precise procedure of the experiment is explained, the experimental material is shown to the subject, and he is told what he

---

[10]Asch (1952) himself took great pains to avoid this pitfall.

would be required to do; however, he is not permitted to make any responses. He is then given a postexperimental inquiry as though he had been a subject. Thus, one would say, "If I had asked you to do all these things, what do you think that the experiment would be about, what do you think I would be trying to prove, what would my hypothesis be?" etc. This technique, which we have termed the pre-experimental inquiry, can be extended very readily to the giving of pre-experimental tests, followed by the explanation of experimental conditions and tasks, and the administration of postexperimental tests. The subject is requested to behave on these tests as though he had been exposed to the experimental treatment that was described to him. This type of procedure is not open to the objection that the subject's own behavior has provided cues for him as to the purpose of the task. It presents him with a straight problem-solving situation and makes explicit what, for the true experimental subject, is implicit. It goes without saying that these subjects who are run on the pre-experimental inquiry conditions must be drawn from the same population as the experimental groups and may, of course, not be run subsequently in the experimental condition. This technique is one of approximation rather than of proof. However, if subjects describe behavior on the pre-inquiry conditions as similar to, or identical with, that actually given by subjects exposed to the experimental conditions, the hypothesis becomes plausible that demand characteristics may be responsible for the behavior.

It is clear that pre- and postexperimental inquiry techniques have their own demand characteristics. For these reasons, it is usually best to have the inquiry conducted by an experimenter who is not acquainted with the actual experimental behavior of the subjects. This will tend to minimize the effect of experimenter bias.

Another technique which we have utilized for approximating the effect of the demand characteristics is to attempt to hold the demand characteristics constant and eliminate the experimental variable. One way of accomplishing this purpose is through the use of simulating subjects. This is a group of subjects who are not exposed to the experimental variable to which the effect has been attributed, but who are instructed to act *as if* this were the case. In order to control for experimenter bias under these circumstances, it is advisable to utilize more than one experimenter and to have the experimenter who actually runs the subjects "blind" as to which group (simulating or real) any given individual belongs.

Our work in hypnosis (Damaser, Shor, & Orne, 1963; Orne, 1959b; Shor, 1959) is a good example of the use of simulating controls. Subjects unable to enter hypnosis are instructed to simulate entering hypnosis for another experimenter. The experimenter who runs the study sees both highly trained hypnotic subjects and simulators in random order and does not know to which group each subject belongs. Because the subjects are run "blind," the experimenter is more likely to treat the two groups of subjects identically. We have found that simulating subjects are able to perform with great effectiveness, deceiving even well-trained hypnotists. However, the simulating group is not exposed to the experimental condition (in this case, hypnosis) to which the given effect under investigation is often ascribed. Rather, it is a group faced with a problem-solving task: namely, to utilize whatever cues are made available by the experimental context and the experimenter's concrete behavior in order to behave as they think that hypnotized subjects might. Therefore, to the extent that simulating subjects are able to behave identically, it is possible that demand characteristics, rather than the altered state of consciousness, could account for the behavior of the experimental group.

The same type of technique can be utilized in other types of studies. For example, in contrast to the placebo control in a drug study, it is equally possible to instruct some subjects not to take the medication at all, but to act as if they had. It must be emphasized that this type of control is different from the placebo control. It represents an approximation. It maximally confronts the simulating subject with a problem-solving task and suggests how much of the total effect could be accounted for by the demand characteristics—assuming that the experimental group had taken full advantage of them, an assumption not necessarily correct.

All of the techniques proposed thus far share

the quality that they depend upon the active co-operation of the control subjects, and in some way utilize his thinking process as an intrinsic factor. The subject does *not* just respond in these control situations but, rather, he is required *actively* to solve the problem.

The use of placebo experimental conditions is a way in which this problem can be dealt with in a more classic fashion. Psychopharmacology has used such techniques extensively, but here too they present problems. In the case of placebos and drugs, it is often the case that the physician is "blind" as to whether a drug is placebo or active, but the patient is not, despite precautions to the contrary; i.e., the patient is cognizant that he does not have the side effects which some of his fellow patients on the ward experience. By the same token, in psychological placebo treatments, it is equally important to ascertain whether the subject actually perceived the treatment to be experimental or control. Certainly the subject's perception of himself as a control subject may materially alter the situation.

A recent experiment (Orne & Scheibe, 1964) in our laboratory illustrates this type of investigation. We were interested in studying the demand characteristics of sensory deprivation experiments, independent of any actual sensory deprivation. We hypothesized that the overly cautious treatment of subjects, careful screening for mental or physical disorders, awesome release forms, and, above all, the presence of a "panic (release) button" might be more significant in producing the effects reported from sensory deprivation than the actual diminution of sensory input. A pilot study (Stare, Brown, & Orne, 1959), employing pre-inquiry techniques, supported this view. Recently, we designed an experiment to test more rigorously this hypothesis.

This experiment, which we called Meaning Deprivation, had all the *accoutrements* of sensory deprivation, including release forms and a red panic button. However, we carefully refrained from creating any sensory deprivation whatsoever. The experimental task consisted of sitting in a small experimental room which was well lighted, with two comfortable chairs, as well as ice water and a sandwich, and an optional task of adding numbers. The subject did not have a watch during this time, the room was reasonably quiet, but not soundproof, and the duration of the experiment (of which the subject was ignorant) was four hours. Before the subject was placed in the experimental room, 10 tests previously used in sensory deprivation research were administered. At the completion of the experiment, the same tasks were again administered. A microphone and a one-way screen were present in the room, and the subject was encouraged to verbalize freely.

The control group of 10 subjects was subjected to the identical treatment, except that they were told that they were control subjects for a sensory deprivation experiment. The panic button was eliminated for this group. The formal experimental treatment of these two groups of subjects was the same in terms of the objective stress—four hours of isolation. However, the demand characteristics had been purposively varied for the two groups to study the effect of demand characteristics as opposed to objective stress. Of the 14 measures which could be quantified, 13 were in the predicted direction, and 6 were significant at the selected 10% alpha level or better. A Mann-Whitney U test has been performed on the summation ranks of all measures as a convenient method for summarizing the overall differences. The one-tailed probability which emerges is $p = .001$, a clear demonstration of expected effects.

This study suggests that demand characteristics may in part account for some of the findings commonly attributed to sensory deprivation. We have found similar significant effects of demand characteristics in accounting for a great deal of the findings reported in hypnosis. It is highly probable that careful attention to this variable, or group of variables, may resolve some of the current controversies regarding a number of psychological phenomena in motivation, learning, and perception.

In summary, we have suggested that the subject must be recognized as an active participant in any experiment, and that it may be fruitful to view the psychological experiment as a very special form of social interaction. We have proposed that the subject's behavior in an experiment is a function of the totality of the situation, which includes the experimental variables being investigated and at least one other set of variables which we have subsumed under the heading, demand characteristics of the experimental situation. The study and control of demand characteristics are not simply matters of good experimental technique; rather, it is an empirical issue to determine under what circumstances demand characteristics significantly affect subjects' experimental behavior. Several empirical techniques have been proposed for this purpose. It has been suggested that control of these variables in particular may lead to greater reproducibility and ecological validity of psychological experiments. With an increasing understanding of these factors intrinsic to the experimental context, the experimental method in psychology may become a more effective tool in predicting behavior in nonexperimental contexts.

REFERENCES

Asch, S. E. Social psychology. New York: Prentice-Hall, 1952.

Brunswik, E. Systematic and representative design of psychological experiments with results in physical and social perception. (Syllabus Series, No. 304) Berkeley: University of California Press, 1947.

Damaser, Esther C., Shor, R. E., & Orne, M. T. Physiological effects during hypnotically-requested emotions. Psychosomatic Medicine, 1963, 25, 334–343.

Frank, J. D. Experimental studies of personal pressure and resistance: I. Experimental production of resistance. Journal of General Psychology, 1944, 30, 23–41.

Orne, M. T. The demand characteristics of an experimental design and their implications. Paper read at American Psychological Association, Cincinnati, 1959. (a)

Orne, M. T. The nature of hypnosis: Artifact and essence. Journal of Abnormal and Social Psychology, 1959, 58, 277–299. (b)

Orne, M. T., & Scheibe, K. E. The contribution of nondeprivation factors in the production of sensory deprivation effects: The psychology of the "panic button." Journal of Abnormal and Social Psychology, 1964, 68, 3–12.

Pierce, A. H. The subconscious again. Journal of Philosophy, Psychology, and Scientific Method, 1908, 5, 264–271.

Riecken, H. W. A program for research on experiments in social psychology. Paper read at Behavioral Sciences Conference, University of New Mexico, 1958.

Rosenthal, R. On the social psychology of the psychological experiment: With particular reference to experimenter bias. Paper read at American Psychological Association, New York, 1961.

Sarbin, T. R. Contributions to role-taking theory: I. Hypnotic behavior. Psychological Review, 1950, 57, 255–270.

Shor, R. E. Explorations in hypnosis: A theoretical and experimental study. Unpublished doctoral dissertation, Brandeis University, 1959.

Stare, F., Brown, J., & Orne, M. T. Demand characteristics in sensory deprivation studies. Unpublished seminar paper, Massachusetts Mental Health Center and Harvard University, 1959.

ARTICLE 2

The Cooperative Subject: Myth or Reality?

Harold Sigall, Elliot Aronson, and Thomas Van Hoose

The validity of findings in some psychological experiments, especially those using human subjects, has recently been questioned. In particular, it has been suggested by various commentators that results thought to be attributable to an experimental manipulation are frequently artifactual and due to the demands of the experimental situation resulting from the nature of the experimenter-subject interaction (Orne, 1962; Orne & Scheibe, 1964; Riecken, 1962; Rosenberg, 1965). What are the relevant factors that contribute to or produce these artifacts? Examination of the references cited above would indicate that although different points and emphases are made, the views offered tend to be complementary and supportive of one another, rather than contradictory. But this may be illusory. To elaborate, let us review some of these writings.

Riecken (1962) was concerned more with random error than systematic error; he suggested that subjects care about how they appear to an experimenter and that they want to appear in the best possible light. Therefore, subjects "put their best foot forward." How to put one's best foot forward, however, is not a simple question. The subject is confronted with a task and will be evaluated on his performance. In addition, since experimenters can either be defied or cooperated with, the subject is open to evaluation on his cooperativeness.

Riecken points out that in order to know what can be done to succeed at making a favorable impression, the subject must know what is going

From the *Journal of Experimental Social Psychology*, 1970, **6**, 1–10. Reprinted with permission of the authors and the publisher; copyright 1970 by Academic Press, Inc.

on in the experiment. He tries to find out what is going on by progressively defining the experimental situation. The cues used to accomplish this definition include the subject's pre-experimental expectations, features of the scene (e.g., apparatus), and what the experimenter says and/or expects.

Orne (1962) takes a slightly different approach to the same general problem. His position is that subjects, above all, want to be "good subjects" and that they satisfy this desire by cooperating with the experimenter. He states: "Admittedly, subjects are concerned about their performance in terms of reinforcing their self image; nonetheless, they seem even more concerned with the utility of their performances" (p. 778).

Thus, whereas Riecken (1962) named the two dimensions on which a subject may be evaluated —on the task and on "cooperativeness"—Orne orders the importance of the two, concluding that cooperativeness is the more salient. In addition, much like Riecken's "progressive definition" concept, Orne suggests that: "at some level he (the subject) sees it as his task to ascertain the true purpose of the experiment and respond in a manner which will support the hypothesis being tested" (p. 779).

The third position presented here is the one advanced by Rosenberg (1965). Rosenberg is concerned with systematic error introduced through the subject-experimenter interaction. He says that a subject in an experimental situation, confronted by a psychologist, suffers from "evaluation apprehension," which he defines as "anxiety-toned concern that he (the subject) win a positive evaluation from the experimenter, or at least that he provide no sound grounds for a negative one" (p. 29). Rosenberg goes on to point out that there is no conflict between his notions and those put forth by Orne.

It should be clear, however, that there is no conflict between Orne and Rosenberg *only if* the evaluation apprehension experienced by subjects is over an evaluation of their cooperativeness. If, on the other hand, evaluation apprehension refers to an evaluation of the subject's performance— his ability or personality characteristics, for example—then the two positions can be in conflict. Under certain circumstances, in order to cooperate by confirming the experimenter's hypothesis, the subject may be forced to appear to be stupid, slow, or strange. Conversely, a subject may have to disconfirm the experimenter's expectations (be uncooperative) in order to impress him as being intelligent, above average, or clever.

These seemingly congruent but differing approaches bring us to the present problem. Specifically, the question we are asking is: If, in fact, a subject alters his "natural" behavior due to the nature of the experimental situation, is it because he is trying to please the experimenter, and therefore opts to cooperate with him in an effort to confirm the hypothesis, or is it because he is trying to appear in a good light—intelligent, attractive, efficient, etc.—regardless of what the experimenter's hypothesis may be?

What is the nature of the evidence on this question? The conclusions reached by Orne (1962), that subjects are cooperative and try to help the experimenter to verify his hypothesis, were in part based on research in which it was demonstrated that subjects would continue to do page after page of arithmetic problems, even when they were made to destroy each page upon completion before tackling the succeeding page. Is this cooperation in the technical meaning of the word? I.e., do these results demonstrate that subjects attempt to help the experimenter to verify his hypothesis? Hardly. What they do show is that subjects are obedient—i.e., that they will do what an experimenter tells them to do (see Milgram, 1963).*

Additional evidence, in the form of informal

*Reprinted in Section 6 of this book—Eds.

data (a personal communication from Zajonc), is cited by Riecken (1962). Zajonc found that when the experimenter told the subjects he believed the hypothesis to be true, the data supported that hypothesis; when he indicated that he felt the hypothesis was false, the obtained data did not support the hypothesis. These results would seem to support Orne, but the findings may be confounded. It is not clear whether the subjects *really* cooperated with the experimenter, or if they were attempting to present themselves as able people. If, instead of deciphering the experimenter's hypothesis, the subject is told "point blank" what the experimenter wants, he may feel that the experimenter is really trying to find out how nice he (the subject) is. Thus, he may comply with the experimenter's explicitly stated wishes as a way of putting his best foot forward.

Similarly, Rosenthal's (1966) work, while demonstrating experimenter bias, is not unequivocal regarding cooperativeness. For example, in one study (Rosenthal & Fode, 1963) subjects were instructed to rate people pictured in photographs on a success-failure continuum. Some experimenters were led to believe that the ratings would be high, others that the ratings would be low. Those who expected high ratings obtained significantly higher ratings than those who expected low ratings. Somehow the experimenter affected the data. Moreover, the cues emitted by the experimenter were extremely subtle; i.e., the cues were not discernible to investigators attempting to define them. It is difficult to know whether these cues suggested to the subject how to cooperate or how to put his best foot forward. For example, the experimenters who expected high ratings may have believed and conveyed to the subjects that perception of success was a good thing. Of course, there are numerous other possibilities, but our point is that one definite interpretation is not possible.

Thus, clear evidence demonstrating the cooperative nature of subjects does not seem to exist. Our own hypothesis is that subjects would rather look good than cooperate with the experimenter. Underlying our hypothesis in the present experiment is the notion that the subject's concern about "looking good" is centered around how he will appear on an ability dimension. His concern about being evaluated as a cooperative subject is secondary, if present at all. Thus, we predict that if a subject knows the experimenter's hypothesis, he will not try to be consistent with those expectations if his cooperation will fail to put him in a good light.

A test of this hypothesis has important methodological consequences. In building an experiment, there are literally scores of problems that an experimenter must solve and potential pitfalls that he must avoid. Some of these avoidance attempts are mutually antagonistic; e.g., in a specific situation, the kinds of precautions that we take to guard against the cooperative subject may weaken the impact of the experimental variable or may result in a situation which increases a subject's evaluation apprehension or leads to other sources of variance. Thus, while it is a good general rule for the experimenter to be cautious (even overly cautious when possible), a superabundance of caution is not always reasonable. For this reason it is essential to know whether the cooperative subject presents a real problem or whether his supposed existence is a myth due to a tendency to confuse cooperativeness with obedience or a desire to look good.

METHOD

Subjects and Design

It was necessary to allow subjects the opportunity to cooperate with the experimenter. Therefore, in the experimental conditions the experimenter had to make a hypothesis known. In addition, it was necessary that in one situation (a) both the experimenter and subject would profit from the subject's cooperation, and in the other situation (b) cooperation would benefit the experimenter but not the subject, while lack of cooperation would satisfy the subject's needs at the expense of the experimenter's. Moreover, we wanted to eliminate a direct "achievement" alternative, and therefore situation (a), above, took on two forms: one in which both the experimenter and subject would gain by an increase in output, and the other in which a decrease in output would fulfill the goals of both. A control condition was also employed to provide a baseline with which to compare the experimental conditions. Subjects were 40 undergraduates enrolled in introductory psychology at the University of Texas. They were randomly assigned to one of the four conditions and were tested individually.

Procedure

The experimenter greeted the subject and explained that the experiment was one with implications for industrial psychology. He told the subjects that their task would consist of copying a list of telephone numbers. After acknowledging that this task was not exciting, he pointed out that it was selected because it was related to several industrial types of tasks, and at the same time had been shown to be independent of intelligence and related abilities. The experimenter then supplied blank sheets of paper and a long strip of telephone numbers, and set a timer to ring after seven minutes. He told the subjects that he wanted them to have a practice trial first, and that he would return after seven minutes. The experimenter instructed the subjects not to rush, to work at a normal rate, and to stop when the timer sounded. He then left the room. When seven minutes had passed, the experimenter returned, collected the practice trial paper, and told the subjects to rest for a few moments while he left to get the forms for the "real trial." Again, the experimenter left the room.

It should be clear that up until this point subjects had received very little information; nor had they been assigned to a condition. This was done to reduce the possibility of experimenter bias during the presentation of the initial instructions. In addition, we used blank paper and one extremely long list of telephone numbers, rather than ruled paper and numbers as they appear in a telephone book, in order to minimize the possibility that subjects would be aware of the extent of their output.

When the experimenter left to get the "real trial" forms, he totaled the numbers copied. Then he randomly drew a card, thereby assigning the subject to one of the four conditions. The experimenter returned to the room with the "real trial" forms. These forms were merely sheets of paper made up with a series of lines, each of which provided space for one telephone number. Each line was preceded by a number, so that the subject would be aware of how many telephone numbers he had copied at any given time.

In the Control condition the experimenter merely said: "Here are the forms for the real trial." He provided a second list of telephone numbers, reset the timer, told subjects to begin, and left.

In the Increased-Output condition, the experimenter added 20 to the total amount copied during "practice," rounded that number to the nearest five, and said: "Before we begin, let me tell you a little more about what we're doing. We have a theory relating the amount of illumination in a room to a person's performance in a room such as this." Pointing out that only half the available illumination was turned on, he continued: "With the amount of light and a trivial, boring task, and given this time limit of seven minutes, we feel that if you don't rush you'll do about X numbers or about $X/7$ per minute." "X" was equal to the amount done in practice (unknown to the subject) plus 20, and rounded off, and "$X/7$" was that amount divided by seven. The experimenter then said, "You may look at the clock from time to time to see how you're doing." Again, the experimenter left, returning after seven minutes to collect the data and explain the true purpose of the experiment to the subject.

The Decreased-Output condition was identical to the Increased-Output condition in every way except that the quantity of telephone numbers given in the experimental hypothesis was arrived at by subtracting 20 from the practice total and rounding off this number, rather than adding 20.

The fourth condition was the Decreased-Output-Obsessive-Compulsive condition. Here the experimenter, after subtracting 20 from the practice trial and rounding that total to the nearest five, said, "Before we begin, let me tell you a little more about what we're doing. There is a personality type called obsessive-compulsive. People who possess this characteristic are overly meticulous and overly concerned with detail. We have a theory that this task is a good indication of the

obsessive-compulsive because people who feel compelled to rush at a trivial, boring task (like the copying of phone numbers) tend to be obsessive-compulsive. Given this time limit of seven minutes, we expect that you'll do about X numbers or $X/7$ per minute. You may look at the clock from time to time to see how you're doing." As before, after collecting the dependent measure (i.e., the phone numbers copied on the real trial), the experimenter debriefed the subjects.

Summarizing the three experimental conditions, we see that in the Increased-Output condition the experimenter "hypothesized" increased production. Since high output would also satisfy achievement needs of the subject, we can infer that "cooperation" on the part of the subject would be rewarding to both. In the Decreased-Output-Obsessive-Compulsive condition, the experimenter "hypothesized" decreased output. Here, too, if we assume that subjects did not want to be classified as obsessive-compulsive, "cooperation" would benefit both subject and experimenter. However, in the Decreased-Output condition the experimenter "hypothesized" a decrease, while subjects could demonstrate competence by increasing output. Thus, in the latter situation, "cooperation" with the experimenter would hinder the subject from satisfying his own aims, while satisfying his own aims would prevent him from aiding the experimenter.

TABLE 1.   Mean change in output from "practice" to "real" trial.

Condition	Mean change
Control	+1.9
Increased-Output	+5.7
Decreased-Output	+6.2
Decreased-Output-Obsessive-Compulsive	−8.0

The means of the differences between the two trials for the four conditions are presented in Table 1. As expected, the least amount of change was manifested in the Control condition, in which subjects increased their output by 1.9 units (telephone numbers). Subjects in the Increased-Output condition increased their performance by 5.7 units, while those in the Decreased-Output condition increased by 6.2. Subjects in the Decreased-Output-Obsessive-Compulsive condition *decreased* their output by 8.0 units. Analysis of variance yielded an $F=6.28$, 3 and 36 *df,* demonstrating the differences between the means to be statistically significant beyond the .005 level.* Moreover, Duncan's Multiple Range Test showed that every pair of means differed significantly ($p < .01$) with the exception of the Increased-Output and Decreased-Output pair.

Thus, it may be seen that our hypothesis has been supported; i.e., subjects looked as though they were cooperating with the experimenter only when such "cooperation" also resulted in good, effective behavior. When the experimenter expected increased output (Increased-Output condition), he was "assisted." When he expected decreased output and behavior to the contrary would indicate obsessive-compulsiveness (Decreased-Output-Obsessive-Compulsive condition), he was "assisted." Thus, subjects either speeded up or slowed down, depending on which mode of behavior would make them appear as more effective people. Simultaneously, the behavior exhibited also served to support the experimenter's "hypothesis."

One may ask how we can be sure that the important process involved was self-enhancement and that the incidental covariant was cooperativeness, rather than vice versa. To answer this question we must examine the nature and results of the crucial Decreased-Output condition. In this condition subjects were, in effect, presented with a choice. We know from the results of the Decreased - Output - Obsessive - Compulsive and Increased-Output conditions that subjects do adjust their behavior as a function of the information they are given. Considering this and the results of the Control condition, we can assume that in the Decreased-Output condition subjects' behavior was affected by the instructions. Consequently, the subjects' alternatives were (a) to decrease output and thereby help the experimenter

confirm his hypothesis, or (b) to work as fast as possible, thereby impressing the experimenter with ability, at the cost of disconfirming the experimenter's "hypothesis." Thus, the subject could either cooperate or make himself appear effective. Unlike the other two experimental conditions, in the Decreased-Output condition it was impossible to do both at the same time. The results are unequivocal: subjects *increased* their output, thereby appearing "good," while the experimenter's hypothesis was disconfirmed. It should be noted that the increased output was virtually identical regardless of whether the experimenter hypothesized an increase or a decrease in output.

After running these conditions it was suggested to us that if our subjects were truly motivated to look good, then subjects who were merely told by the experimenter that he was interested in the relationship between illumination and productivity, but not given a specific hypothesis regarding output, should manifest greater increases in output than control subjects. In order to follow up this possibility 24 additional subjects were tested.[1] Half of them were randomly assigned to virtually an exact replication of the Control condition. The remainder received treatment identical to the Increased-Output and Decreased-Output conditions, except that they were not presented with any particular hypothesis. The mean changes, from practice to real trial ($T_2 - T_1$), were -0.1 in the replicated control condition, and +2.9 in the new unspecified-hypothesis condition—a difference between groups of 3.0 telephone numbers. Analysis of variance resulted in an $F = 3.81$, 1 and 22 *df,* indicating that this difference is significant at the .07 level. This suggests that the simple fact that subjects are aware of the existence of a hypothesis regarding output will lead them to attempt to impress the experimenter, even if the attempt requires that they ignore some instructions (which, in this particular case, directed subjects not to rush).

Before elaborating on our data we must comment on the theoretical difficulties involved in this type of research. To use a social psychologi-

*Analysis of variance is a statistical technique that aids us in determining whether observed differences among means are due to some chance variations or to the effects of the experimental treatment. In this case, the differences among the groups would have occurred fewer than 5 times in 1000 because of chance variations. Thus we have strong reasons to believe that the differences in instructions had a real effect on performance.—Eds.

[1] The authors would like to thank Phyllis Baunach for her assistance in collecting the data.

cal experiment to investigate problems (indeed, artifacts) that plague social psychological experiments is somewhat akin to placing two mirrors face-to-face and trying to point out the original image in one of them. How do we know that the data we are using to discuss possibly biased data are not, in and of themselves, biased? We cannot be absolutely certain that this trap was avoided. However, certain evidence does bear on the issue. At the conclusion of the experimental session, each subject received a thorough interview (see Aronson & Carlsmith, 1968). One of the aims of this interview was an attempt to detect any suspicion on the part of the subject. In this interview, the experimenter discussed the terrible consequences which would befall him if he published data which were at all tainted. In this vein, he pleaded with the subject to *cooperate* by providing the experimenter with any evidence that might be relevant. Accordingly, the subject was carefully probed for his own hypotheses and encouraged to venture wild guesses. There was no evidence whatever that any subject suspected the true hypothesis. To argue that subjects (a) guessed our true hypothesis and behaved congruently in order to be cooperative, and (b) refused to cooperate with the experimenter's request in the post-experimental interview is at least somewhat far-fetched. As Aronson and Carlsmith (1968) point out, if the subject is really trying to be helpful, then why should he suddenly stop being so? Moreover, the sense of satisfaction achieved by a freshman upon discovering a ruse perpetrated by an experimenter would seem to be very great. Thus, whether the subject is trying to be cooperative or attempting to present himself as bright, disclosure of his own hypotheses during the post-experimental interview should be forthcoming.

Assuming that the present set of data is unbiased, we must reach the conclusion that, in this experiment, subjects were not cooperative, and that when they appeared to be cooperative, this behavior on closer examination can be seen to be a covariant of behavior by the subject designed to impress the experimenter with his ability. These findings suggest that evaluation apprehension does occur, and that subjects do

adjust their performances in light of the hypotheses. The nature of this adaptation seems, however, to be more in line with Rosenberg's (1965) formulation than with those of Riecken (1962) or Orne (1962). Riecken's belief that the subject's concern was over being evaluated on cooperativeness seems unwarranted. Moreover, our data provide no substantiation whatever for Orne's belief that subjects are *more* concerned over the utility of their performances than with reinforcing their self-images. This is not to say that subjects are disobedient. Subjects are obedient in the sense that if they are instructed to do something, they fulfill that request. Our data indicate that this concept may have been overextended to include subjects trying to make the experimenter's data turn out well. Our results show that subjects *refuse* to cooperate in this manner if such behavior goes against their self-interest.

Obviously, we cannot conclude on the basis of this single experiment that subjects never manifest cooperative behavior *per se*. It is possible that under certain circumstances cooperativeness would occur. However, the inducements to be cooperative in the present experiment were powerful indeed. Considering both the lack of clear evidence on cooperativeness in the literature and the results of the present experiment, we must conclude that the large amount of concern spent over the "cooperative subject" problem has been disproportionate. Although the problem of subject cooperativeness should not be ignored, it seems that the experimenter's energy would be better directed toward solving other methodological problems.

REFERENCES

Aronson, E., & Carlsmith, J. M. Experimentation in social psychology. In G. Lindzey and E. Aronson (Eds.), *Handbook of social psychology*. (Rev. ed.) Vol. II. Reading, Mass.: Addison-Wesley, 1968.

Milgram, S. Behavioral study of obedience. *Journal of Abnormal and Social Psychology*, 1963, **67**, 371–378.

Orne, M. T. On the social psychology of the psychological experiment. *American Psychologist*, 1962, **17**, 776–783.

Orne, M. T., & Scheibe, K. E. The contribution of non-deprivation factors in the production of sensory deprivation effects: The psychology of the "panic button." *Journal of Abnormal and Social Psychology,* 1964, **68,** 3–12.

Riecken, H. W. A program for research on experiments in social psychology. In N. F. Washburne (Ed.), *Decision, values, and groups,* Vol. II. New York: Pergamon Press, 1962. Pp. 25–41.

Rosenberg, M. J. When dissonance fails: On eliminat-

ing evaluation apprehension from attitude measurement. *Journal of Personality and Social Psychology,* 1965, **1,** 28–42.

Rosenthal, R. *Experimenter effects in behavioral research.* New York: Appleton-Century-Crofts, 1966.

Rosenthal, R., & Fode, K. I. (Psychology of the Scientist: V) Three experiments in experimenter bias. *Psychological Reports,* 1963, **12,** 491–511.

ARTICLE 3

Self-Disclosure and the Volunteer:
A Source of Bias in Laboratory Experiments[1]

Thomas C. Hood[2] and Kurt W. Back

The success of social psychological experiments depends on the subject's following the rules set for his behavior by the experimenter. Denzin (1970) has pointed out that this is really a sociological question: How are experimenters able to stage performances so successfully in laboratories? We suggest here that part of the explanation lies in the image of the experimental situation for the subject. We propose that the subject enters the experiment as a stage for self-disclosure and catharsis, and that for this reason, he will cooperate with the experimenter in staging the experimental process.

This position implies that the decision to volunteer is a function of the willingness to disclose oneself or even the need for catharsis. The characteristics of the volunteer have been studied from many points of view; however, few consistent findings have been reported. It may be a straw in the wind that the long chapter on experiments in the latest *Handbook of Social Psychology* (Aronson & Carlsmith, 1968) has no

Reprinted from *Journal of Personality and Social Psychology*, **17**, 1971, 130–136. Copyright 1971 by the American Psychological Association, and reproduced by permission of the authors and the publisher.

[1] A version of this paper was presented at the meeting of the Southern Sociological Society in Atlanta, Georgia, April 1, 1967. The investigation was supported by a grant from the Office of Naval Research, Group Psychology Branch, Contract 1181-11. The authors wish to thank Jack Preiss and Donal Muir for their helpful comments.

[2] Collection and analysis of this data were accomplished while this author was associated with the Department of Sociology and Anthropology at Duke University.

discussion of the issue of volunteer bias and its consequences. From a wealth of experiments and surveys, Rosenthal and Rosnow (1969) cited five characteristics which can be stated with confidence as distinguishing volunteers from nonvolunteers: high educational level, occupational status, and intelligence, low authoritarianism, and high need for approval. Tune (1969) reported additional support for the first two characteristics, but not for the third. The first three characteristics can be classified as superior ability to perform and great confidence in it, and the last two as greater openness and willingness to be looked at. Rosenthal and Rosnow (1969) suggested three other less established characteristics of volunteers —more sociable, greater arousal seeking, and more unconventional—which would appear to indicate an interaction style favoring catharsis. Four studies especially suggest that individuals who volunteer may be seeking cathartic situations (Bell, 1962; Lasagna & von Fleisinger, 1954; Martin & Marcuse, 1958; Riggs & Kaess, 1955). We find a similar situation in self-selection for interviews especially on sensitive topics, such as sexual behavior. Maslow and Sakoda (1952) found that self-esteem distinguished volunteers from nonvolunteers in Kinsey's studies and that students with higher self-esteem were more willing to admit unconventional sex attitudes and behavior. Kaats and Davis (in press) found that volunteers were more unconventional in their sexual attitudes and admitted more precoital behavior, but did not have more coital behavior.

Similar to experiments, interview volunteers seem to be more willing to reveal themselves than nonvolunteers.

The laboratory situation can be seen as an ideal place for safe catharsis. It is set away from day-to-day social relationships, usually involves interaction with strangers (Simmel, 1950), and allows peculiar nonnormative behavior (Back, Hood, & Brehm, 1964).

The hypothesis of the study therefore proposes that the greater the number of past attempts at achieving catharsis, the more likely an individual is to volunteer to participate in an experiment. The hypothesis assumes first that the past attempts to achieve catharsis are a valid indicator of the need for catharsis. They do not tell us the presently felt need for catharsis at the time the request for volunteers is made. Second, the hypothesis assumes that the volunteer perceives the experiment as a cathartic situation. These assumptions are analogous to those of Edwards (1968) and Riecken (1962), who emphasized potential subject's perceptions of the experiment as a key to understanding the volunteering process.

Past attempts at achieving catharsis could be measured in a number of different ways. Jourard's (1964) work on the process of self-disclosure suggests that verbalizing one's self and one's problems to another individual is a way of experiencing release from the tensions produced by the disciplines of the roles we play in everyday life. In meeting the expectations of our role partners, we are not permitted always to reveal our personal feelings about these expectations (Goffman, 1959, 1961). To verbalize these feelings to a friend or a sympathetic listener provides a release for the individual (Strauss, 1956). Thus, measuring the degree to which a person has disclosed his personal feelings to others should provide a valid indicator of the number of past attempts at achieving catharsis. Operationally, the hypothesis was that volunteers show significantly higher amounts of self-disclosure than nonvolunteers.

Further thought about and reading on the matter suggest that revelation of one's personal feelings and the decision to volunteer for an

experiment may both be modified by other variables. Jourard (1964) found a consistent difference in the self-disclosure scores of males and females. Chittick (1967) found situational variables important in determining the amount of self-disclosure. Volunteering studies such as that of Martin and Marcuse (1958) reported differences in volunteering behavior according to the type of experiment to be conducted. These studies suggested a refinement of the basic design to allow any sex differences and description of experimental differences to appear.

METHOD

Data for the study were collected by creating a volunteering situation by means of a questionnaire. This questionnaire and another containing the self-disclosure index were administered to five classes of introductory sociology students. The classes were composed of single undergraduates and were taught by four different instructors. A few uncontrolled differences in the preparation of the classes for the experiment are discussed below. Usable data were obtained for 39 male and 55 female students.

The first questionnaire administered contained personal characteristics, a scale measuring anxiety and social desirability (Christie & Budnitsky, 1957), an affiliation scale, and the self-disclosure index. Only the anxiety, social desirability, and self-disclosure scales were used in the analysis. On all scales, a high score indicates a greater magnitude of the variable being measured.

Jourard's (1964) self-disclosure inquiry revealed three things about a given pattern of disclosure: (a) What did the individual talk about? (b) To whom did the individual talk? (c) How extensively did they talk about a given topic? In essence, the self-disclosure questionnaire asks the subject to recall conversations with specific people. The questionnaire asks the individual to score selected statements as to the amount of disclosure to different individuals. The statements are grouped in topical areas. Three topics with 10 statements each were presented. The first, work (or studies), included such statements as,

"What I find to be the worst pressures and strains in my work" and "My ambitions and goals in my work." The second, personality, included such statements as, "What feelings, if any, that I have trouble expressing or controlling" and "The kinds of things that make me especially proud of myself, elated, full of self-esteem or self-respect." The third, body, included such statements as, "How I wish I looked; my ideals for overall appearance" and "My past record of illness and treatment" (Jourard, 1964). For each of 10 statements in each area, the respondent indicates whether he has not (scored 0), has only generally (scored 1), or has fully and completely (scored 2) disclosed himself to each of three target persons. These different individuals represent types of persons or specific persons to whom the individual may have spoken. Roommate, college professor I like best, and parent of the same sex were selected as relevant target persons. Roommate provides a level of disclosure to a potential intimate with many characteristics similar to experimental subjects. College professor provides a level of disclosure to a person similar to the experimenter (Beardslee & O'Dowd, 1962). Parent of the same sex provides a base line of disclosure to a person of the same sex in a usually intimate group.

Self-disclosure scores are computed by summing the responses to the statements. In addition to subscores summing the responses to statements in a given content area by target persons, summary scores may be computed. These are obtained by summing across target persons for a content area and across content areas for a given target person. A general score summing all responses is computed.

The second questionnaire contained four descriptions of experiments, a scale for evaluating each description, a request for volunteers for the four experiments described, and a question on past experimental participation. The subjects were instructed by the questionnaire to evaluate their willingness to participate after reading a description of each experiment.[3] The experiments

[3] A copy of this questionnaire appears in the Appendix of Hood (1964).

were described in one-paragraph statements, designed to emphasize a single characteristic of the demands of the situation for behavior. In our analysis the experiments were given the following names and were presented to the subjects in this order: (a) Competition—This experiment was described as a single elimination tournament comparing ability under the pressure of competition with a previous test of ability under noncompetitive conditions. (b) Control—This experiment emphasized the ability of the experimenter to manipulate an undefined situation. (c) Affiliation—This experiment was to test the problem-solving efficiency of different-sized groups. After completing the task, subjects were to evaluate their liking for each other. (d) Self-revelation—This experiment was described as a control group for the study of interaction rates in group therapy sessions. Subjects of both sexes would be asked to talk about their own experiences and problems in an effort to keep content similar. After the four descriptions were presented, the subject was asked to indicate the number of experiments in which he was willing to participate and to rank order the experiments according to his preference.

For the purpose of this study, three distinctions were made among the subjects. Those indicating a preference to participate in no experiments were called nonvolunteers; volunteers were divided into those indicating a willingness to participate in from one to three of the experiments and those willing to participate in all of the experiments. A sex difference appeared here. Among female subjects a sufficiently large number volunteered for only part of the experiments, so as to be treated as a separate category. Most males chose either to participate in all of the experiments or none of them. Males volunteering for only part of the experiments were grouped with those volunteering for all in the following analysis.

RESULTS

Among the male subjects, volunteers disclosed themselves more than nonvolunteers. In Table 1 all of the comparisons are in the predicted direc-

TABLE 1.   Mean self-disclosure scores for nonvolunteers and volunteers among the male subjects.

Self-disclosure score	Nonvolunteers	Volunteers	t
	(n = 19)	(n = 20)	
Total	55.63	84.25	4.32[****]
Content area totals			
Work	27.42	36.95	3.09[***]
Personality	15.74	25.70	3.62[***]
Body	12.37	21.60	3.78[***]
Target person totals			
Roommate	24.37	39.75	4.02[****]
Parent of same sex	27.47	35.15	1.93[*]
Professor I like best	3.68	9.35	3.08[***]
Specific scales			
Roommate			
Work	11.16	15.20	2.57[**]
Personality	7.58	12.70	3.33[***]
Body	5.63	11.00	3.92[****]
Parent of same sex			
Work	12.74	14.55	1.14
Personality	8.00	9.80	1.04
Body	6.74	10.30	2.57[**]
Professor			
Work	3.53	6.35	2.01[*]
Personality	.16	2.70	3.20[***]
Body	.00	.30	1.64

[*]$p < .10, df = 37$
[**]$p < .05, df = 37$
[***]$p < .01, df = 37$
[****]$p < .001, df = 37$

Ed. note.—This table presents the average scores for the nonvolunteers and the volunteers on each part of the self-disclosure measure. The n's at the top of the table indicate that there were 19 subjects in the nonvolunteer group and 20 volunteers. The t column reflects the t-value for the difference in the two averages. Each row should be read across; for example, in regard to the *total score*, or the total amount of self-disclosure revealed, the average score for the non-volunteers was 55.63, whereas it was 84.25 for the volunteers. Since a higher score indicates greater self-disclosure, this means the volunteers reported more self-disclosure. But was the difference a statistically significant one? The resultant t-value of 4.32 has a p value (or probability) of less than .001. We interpret this to mean that this difference could have occurred less than 1 time in 1000 (<.001); therefore the difference is a true one.

tion, and all but three of the t values* are significant. The seven comparisons listed first are sums of the subscores, but the consistency in direction of the difference justifies their use.

The only consistent pattern that emerges for the female groups reported in Table 2 is that those volunteering for some of the experiments had consistently lower self-disclosure scores than the other two groups. One-way analyses of variance were used to test the differences in means on the self-disclosure scores. No significant differ-

*A t-test is a statistical technique used to determine if the average scores of two groups are different enough to rule out chance as a likely reason for the difference.—Eds.

ences in the self-disclosure scores appeared in comparing females who volunteered for none, some, or all of the experiments. The F value for total self-disclosure was 2.12 ($df=2/52, p < .10$). Other F values for the table were low and nonsignificant as well.

These results suggest that self-disclosure is related to volunteering among males but not among females. Jourard's (1964) findings and De Beauvoir's (1961) observations suggest that women disclose their personal feelings to each other with greater frequency than men do to each other. If self-disclosure is a relatively more common activity among women, perhaps the threshold at which self-disclosing activity becomes a salient characteristic of the experimental situation is higher. In this case past patterns of self-disclosure may differentiate volunteers from nonvolunteers if the salience of self-disclosure is increased. Salience might be increased by limiting the disclosure scores considered to those relevant to the experimental situation. For the reasons noted above, the disclosures to college professor and to roommate were combined. Salience could also be increased by manipulating the description of the experiment for which the subjects volunteered. Two experimental descriptions were believed to emphasize this aspect of the experimental situation. (a) The "control" experimenter manipulated the situation to obtain reactions from the subject. The description left the content and specific nature of the experiment in doubt, with the exception of this characteristic. (b) The "group therapy" or "self-revelation" experiment description explicitly suggested that subjects would be encouraged "to talk about their own problems" and asked to "talk about their own lives, experiences, and problems."

Females, who indicated that they would be willing to participate in some of the experiments but not in other experiments, were used in this analysis. The self-disclosure scores for those volunteering for a particular experiment but not for certain other experiments are compared in Table 3. These comparisons do not include those female subjects who volunteered for all or for none of the experiments; the self-disclosure scores for these subjects appear in the top part of the table. Two of the experimental descriptions should have increased the salience of the self-disclosing aspect of the experiment. Differences for the descriptions emphasizing control by the experimenter and emphasizing the necessity to make statements about oneself show the predicted direction. In addition the difference for the control experiment was significant. These findings suggest that volunteering and past self-disclosure may be related for females, if the salience of the disclosure aspect of the experimental situation is increased.

The analysis of the results for the social desirability variable followed a pattern similar to that of the relationship between self-disclosure and volunteering. Volunteering could be interpreted as a socially desirable act, if the subject thought that he was being a "nice guy" by volunteering. This interpretation could arise if the subject saw his participation, as Orne (1962) suggested, as aiding in the advance of science through the confirmation of hypotheses. Volunteering, in the absence of any reward, could be interpreted as doing the experimenter a favor, being helpful, and giving him reason to feel kindly toward the subject. Thus, social desirability was predicted to be positively related to volunteering. For male subjects, this held on the general level, distinguishing between volunteers and nonvolunteers.[4] For female subjects a relationship appeared only when those volunteering for some experiments were examined. Of this group, those females in-

TABLE 2.   Mean self-disclosure scores for volunteering groups among female subjects.

Self-disclosure score	None	Some	All
	(n = 25)	(n = 16)	(n = 14)
Total	100.76	86.94	100.50
Content area totals			
Work	41.32	36.94	42.79
Personality	31.96	25.56	30.21
Body	27.48	24.44	27.50
Target person totals			
Roommate	47.96	38.56	44.71
Parent of same sex	41.64	39.62	41.64
Professor I like best	11.16	8.75	14.14
Specific scales			
Roommate			
Work	17.68	15.31	16.93
Personality	16.12	12.62	14.14
Body	14.14	10.62	13.64
Parent of same sex			
Work	15.64	15.38	15.43
Personality	13.08	11.12	13.29
Body	12.92	13.12	12.93
Professor			
Work	8.00	6.25	10.43
Personality	2.76	1.81	2.79
Body	.40	.68	.93

[4]Analysis of all male subjects revealed a trend in the expected direction; significance was reached when the last class section was excluded from the analysis. Since the last section occurred immediately before a traditional party weekend and about 3 weeks before final examinations, it became possible that it was socially desirable to *not* volunteer. This class had the lowest volunteer ratio of all classes; the majority did not volunteer.

TABLE 3. A comparison of females volunteering for selected experiments with those who did not volunteer on the amount of disclosure to roommate and to college professor.

Volunteer status	n	S^2	$\overline{X}$	t
Volunteered for all	14	176.28	58.86	.053
Volunteered for none	25	233.53	59.12	
Volunteered for some				
Included competition experiment	4	282.92	48.25	.123
Excluded competition experiment	12	346.00	47.00	
Included control experiment	5	346.20	60.80	2.358*
Excluded control experiment	11	195.16	41.18	
Included affiliation experiment	11	364.45	46.64	.220
Excluded affiliation experiment	5	195.16	48.80	
Included self-revelation experiment	10	71.07	49.80	.569
Excluded self-revelation experiment	6	770.97	43.17	

*$p<.05$.
Ed. note.—The S^2 column reports the *variance* for each group. The greater the S^2 value, the more spread out are the scores of the different members of that group.

cluding the control experiment showed a higher social desirability score than those excluding it; those excluding the competition experiment showed a higher social desirability than those including it. Both of these findings reached the .10 level of significance and should be considered only suggestive. The companion anxiety scale failed, as it did for others, to differentiate volunteers and nonvolunteers (Howe, 1960; Rosenthal & Rosnow, 1969).

TABLE 4. Comparison of self-disclosure means by sex of respondent and content area.

Sex	Work	Personality	Body
	Roommate		
Male	13.67	10.21	8.38
Female	16.80	14.60	13.00
	Professor		
Male	4.97	1.46	.15
Female	8.11	2.49	.62
	Parent		
Male	13.67	9.18	8.56
Female	15.36	12.56	12.98

Three additional findings are of some interest. A comparison of the different sociology class groupings shows that males volunteered at a comparable rate, regardless of who their instructor was or what he told them prior to participation in this study ($F=1.67$, $df=3/35$, $p < .10$). Female subjects responded with more volunteering for some instructors than for others ($F=4.93$, $df=3/51$, $p < .01$). A test of the effect of these differences on the relationship between volunteering and past self-disclosure failed to modify the differences reported above.[5] Second, an analysis of the appeal of the four experiments revealed that the subjects did not vary significantly in their overall willingness to participate. However, males rated the competition experiment highest; females rated the affiliation experiment highest. Third, males either volunteered or did not volunteer, while females divided into those volunteering for one, for some, or for all of the experiments. In response to the request for volunteers, males revealed a tendency to volunteer for all or none of the experiments; females volunteered as frequently for one, two, or three of the experiments as for all of them.

Like Jourard we found self-disclosure to be higher in females than in males. Table 4 shows a

[5]This analysis was particularly important for the female subjects, since there appears to be an effect of the instructor on the amount of volunteering. A two-way analysis of variance of the self-disclosure scores revealed no interaction effect between the class in which the subject was recruited and volunteer category. (For example, the F for total personality disclosure was 2.12, $df=2/45$, $p < .05$.) The class including five females was excluded from this analysis because of the heavy weight that would be given to the scores of one volunteer.

comparison of self-disclosure scores by sex and Table 5 the analysis of variance. Although some interaction effects appear, self-disclosure is clearly a more common activity among females than among males.

DISCUSSION

On consideration, the sex differences in the results form a pattern which can be interpreted according to salience of self-disclosure in the perception of experiments. For males the generally low amount of past self-disclosure increases the uniqueness of the self-revealing aspect of the experiment; a large difference in the self-disclosure scores of volunteers and nonvolunteers results. For females the generally high amount of past self-disclosure decreases the uniqueness of the self-revealing aspect of the experiment; small differences between the volunteering groups result. As the salience of this aspect decreases, other factors begin to influence volunteering. The females were more responsive to differences in the recruiting situation, and tended to exclude specific experiments as alternatives for participation. For males these factors were less important. When these factors are controlled by looking at the response to each experiment separately, and when the salience of self-disclosure is increased, then self-disclosure becomes a factor for the females as well. The pattern of the social desirability variable shows a general significance of the volunteering act among the males and modification of this significance by specific factors among females.

There are two other possible interpretations, both of which have certain difficulties. First, females may have responded to the specific content of the descriptions more than to some generalized image of the experiment. Second, differences in male and female strategy may have modified the meaning of self-disclosure with regard to experimental involvement. Differences in amounts of past self-disclosure could, in this case, be only reflections of the difference in meaning. The first interpretation cannot be tested with our data, but an open-ended question might be used to explore this possibility in future research. The

TABLE 5. Analysis of variance of self-disclosure means.

Source	df	MS	F
		Roommate	
Between Ss	93		
Groups (A)	1	1121.689	19.84**
Error	92	56.538	
Within Ss	188		
Trials (B)	2	466.386	22.598[a]**
A X B	2	14.591	2.412
Error	184	6.047	
Total	281		
		Professor	
Between Ss	93		
Groups (A)	1	162.947	9.15**
Error	92	17.800	
Within Ss	188		
Trials (B)	2	1033.036	19.73**
A X B	2	45.193	6.31**
Error	184	7.164	
Total	281		
		Parent	
Between Ss	93		
Groups (A)	1	686.308	15.94**
Error	92	43.044	
Within Ss	188		
Trials (B)	2	385.004	7.26**
A X B	2	43.042	4.32*
Error	184	9.963	
Total	281		

[a]Error and interaction terms pooled.
*$p < .05$.
**$p < .01$.

TABLE 6. Correlation between total self-disclosure and rating of experiment.

Experiment	Sex	
	Males	Females
Competition	.090	.116
Affiliation	.228	.270*

Note.—Males: $df = 38$; females: $df = 54$.
*$p < .10$.

Ed. note.—Correlation is an indication of the degree of relationship between two variables in the same population. Four correlation coefficients are reported here. Correlations can range from +1.000 (perfect positive correlation) through 0.000 (absence of relationship) through -1.000 (perfect negative correlation). All four correlations reported here are low positive correlations.

responsiveness of the female subject to small differences in the recruiting situation can be interpreted as evidencing an accommodative strategy in volunteering. Female preference for the experiment described as affiliative supports this pattern. However, as Table 6 shows, correlations between the evaluation scores for the two experiments and the total self-disclosure scores were similar for both sexes. These results suggest a common rather than different interpretation of volunteering for all individuals (Rosen, 1951).

The significance of this study for research in experimental social psychology is twofold. A characteristic of volunteers has been suggested and an interpretation advanced as to why and when it becomes important in the decision to volunteer. Since self-disclosure has been shown to be related to other variables (Jourard, 1964), self-disclosure may interact with the experimental variable, providing a difference in the control and experimental groups not solely explicable by the presence of the experimental variable. When a volunteer population is used and characteristics of volunteers remain unknown, this effect is an ever-present possibility. This caution holds for a general population as well, if the variable has a potential effect and is unmeasured and uncontrolled. The study has suggested that relatively high self-disclosure scores are characteristic of male volunteers and of female volunteers when the self-disclosure can be related to the characteristics of the specific experiment involved. In addition, there is some evidence that participation in an experiment may, under certain circumstances, attract individuals having high social desirability scores. The female portion of the sample was more responsive to differences in the recruiting situation than the male portion. All of these findings have significance only as they suggest the possibility of the effect of unknown interactions in the experimental conditions of laboratory experiments. The exact effect of these variables can only be measured by conducting experiments where the variable is a known rather than an unknown quantity. Future studies should consider the selective effect of perceived characteristics of experiments on the composition of volunteer subject populations.

REFERENCES

Aronson, E., & Carlsmith, J. M. Experimentation in social psychology. In G. Lindzey and E. Aronson (Eds.), *Handbook of social psychology,* Vol. 2. (2nd ed.) Reading, Mass.: Addison-Wesley, 1968.

Back, K. W., Hood, T. C., & Brehm, M. L. The subject role in small group experiments. *Social Forces,* 1964, **43**, 181–187.

Beardslee, D. C., & O'Dowd, D. D. The college-student image of the scientist. In B. Barber and W. Hirsch (Eds.), *The sociology of science.* Glencoe, Ill.: Free Press, 1962.

Bell, C. R. Personality characteristics of volunteers for psychological studies. *British Journal of Social and Clinical Psychology,* 1964, **1**, 81–95.

Chittick, E. V., & Himelstein, P. The manipulation of self-disclosure. *Journal of Psychology,* 1967, **65**, 117–121.

Christie, R. W., & Budnitsky, S. A short forced-choice anxiety scale. *Journal of Consulting Psychology,* 1957, **21**, 501.

De Beauvoir, S. In H. M. Parshley (Ed. and trans.), *The second sex.* New York: Bantam Books, 1961.

Denzin, N. *The research act.* Chicago: Aldine, 1970.

Edwards, C. N. Defensive interaction and the volunteer subject: An heuristic note. *Psychological Reports,* 1968, **22**, 1305–1309.

Goffman, E. *Encounters.* Indianapolis: Bobbs-Merrill, 1961.

Goffman, E. *The presentation of self in everyday life.* Garden City, N. Y.: Doubleday, 1959.

Hood, T. C. The volunteer subject: Patterns of self-presentation and the decision to participate in social psychological experiments. Unpublished master's thesis, Duke University, 1964.

Howe, E. S. Quantitative motivational differences between volunteers and nonvolunteers for a psychological experiment. *Journal of Applied Psychology,* 1960, **44**, 115–120.

Jourard, S. M. *The transparent self.* Princeton, N. J.: Van Nostrand, 1964.

Kaats, G. R., & Davis, K. E. Effects of volunteer biases in studies of sexual behavior and attitudes. *Journal of Sex Research,* in press.

Lasagna, L., & von Fleisinger, J. M. The volunteer subject in research. *Science,* 1954, **120**, 359–361.

Martin, R. M., & Marcuse, F. L. Characteristics of volunteers and nonvolunteers in psychological experimentation. *Journal of Consulting Psychology,* 1958, **22**, 475–479.

Maslow, A. H., & Sakoda, J. M. Volunteer-error in the Kinsey study. *Journal of Abnormal and Social Psychology,* 1952, **47**, 259–267.

Orne, M. T. On the social psychology of the psychological experiment: With particular reference to demand characteristics and their implications. *American Psychologist,* 1962, **17**, 776–783.

Riecken, H. W. A program for research on experiments in social psychology. In N. F. Washburne (Ed.), *Decisions, values, and groups,* Vol. 2. New York: Macmillan, 1962.

Riggs, M. M., & Kaess, W. Personality differences between volunteers and nonvolunteers. *Journal of Psychology,* 1955, **40,** 229–245.

Rosen, E. Differences between volunteers and nonvolunteers for psychological studies. *Journal of Applied Psychology,* 1951, **35,** 185–193.

Rosenthal, R., & Rosnow, R. The volunteer subject. In R. Rosenthal & R. Rosnow (Eds.), *Artifact in behavioral research.* New York: Academic Press, 1969.

Simmel, G. In K. Wolff (Ed. & trans.), *The sociology of George Simmel.* Glencoe, Ill.: Free Press, 1950.

Strauss, A. (Ed.) *The social psychology of George Mead.* Chicago: University of Chicago Press, 1956.

Tune, G. S. A further note on the differences between cooperative and noncooperative volunteer subjects. *British Journal of Social and Clinical Psychology,* 1969, **8,** 183–184.

SECTION SUMMARY

The social-psychological nature of the research process has ramifications for every topic covered in this book. The data used to understand virtually every topic of study in social psychology are gained either through self-reports of subjects or through observations of subjects' behaviors in controlled laboratory conditions and field studies. For example, Section 3 reports on cooperation vs. competition in a laboratory choice situation; certainly the subject's reactions could be influenced here by an awareness that he or she is a research subject who is being studied. Section 8 deals with the highly controversial possibility of racial differences in intelligence; in such cases the expectations of the examiner can influence the IQ-test performance of a child or an adult. Many of the topics in remaining sections (moral development in Section 2, prejudice in Section 9, and attitude change in Section 11) rely on subjects' responses to paper-and-pencil questionnaires, on which they can misrepresent their true feelings if they wish.

Thus it is quite appropriate for social psychology to question whether the social-psychological nature of the research process impedes the gathering of adequate, representative data. In the introduction to this section a distinction was made between two types of factors that can influence the research process: (1) experimenter effects, which include the expectations the experimenter holds about the outcomes, his manner in dealing with subjects, and other qualities; and (2) subject characteristics. At this point let us look at what is known about the first of these factors.

Interest in experimenter effects has generated the following kinds of research questions.

1. In research and testing situations, what qualities of the data collector affect the response of the subject?

2. Do experimenters either inadvertently or deliberately treat subjects in ways that increase the likelihood of obtaining results they want?

3. Do experimenters, interviewers, and psychological testers communicate their expectations to subjects so that the subjects perform in the way the psychologists expect them to?

Robert Rosenthal (1964, 1966, 1967, 1968; Rosenthal & Jacobson, 1968; Evans & Rosenthal, 1969) has done the most extensive research regarding experimenter effects on research outcomes. Rosenthal divides experimenter effects into two categories, on the basis of whether they influence the subject's actual behavior or the experimenter's recording of it. As examples of the latter, Rosenthal lists the following.

1. *Observation errors by the experimenter.* For example, Cordaro and Ison (1963) had observers watching and recording the movements of planaria (worms). Some observers were told to expect a very high incidence of turning; other observers were led to believe that their planaria would not move much. (The planaria had actually been assigned randomly to the two conditions.) But observers in the "high-incidence expectation" condition reported twice as many turns and three times as many contractions as did observers expecting low rates. If we assume that the *actual* rate of response in the worms was the same in both conditions, we see that this serves as an example of an experimenter expectancy effect that did not affect the behavior of the subjects (the worms) but did influence the observing of them.

2. *Recording errors.* It is often impossible to note whether an error is in the observation or the recording of a response, but the distinction may still be a useful one. For example, in some of the early card-guessing tasks used to measure extrasensory perception, the researchers (who believed in the presence of ESP) made more recording errors favorable to ESP (Rosenthal, 1966).

3. *Intentional error.* A researcher can, of course, deliberately alter or falsify records in order to produce "findings" congenial with his theories. Although he documents several cases of this activity (1966), Rosenthal believes it does not happen often.

But the expectations or behaviors of experimenters can also influence the subject's actual behavior. A psychological tester who greets a child by saying "Well, Johnny, let's see how dumb you are today" is likely to elicit less-than-customary test performance from the child. The warmth or friendliness of the experimenter may affect the subject's approach to a laboratory task. For example, Luft (1953) employed an undergraduate female experimenter who administered 10 inkblots to 60 freshmen subjects, half males and half females. The subject's task was to indicate which blots he or she liked and which blots he or she disliked. For 30 of the subjects, the experimenter played a warm, friendly role, showing much enthusiasm and interest in the subject's responses. On the average, these subjects liked 7.6 of the 10 blots. For the remaining 30 subjects, the experimenter played a cool, unfriendly role, which included asking the subjects some questions about current political events that they most certainly would not be expected to know about. These subjects liked only 3.1 of the 10 inkblots, on the average. Although "blot liking" is not the most important of life's behaviors, Luft's study shows that the experimenter's behavior vis-a-vis the subject *can* influence the subject's actual behavior to a dramatic degree.

The conclusion that experimenters' expectations often influence the outcomes of research projects is not without its critics. The most thorough critique of Rosenthal's work is that by Barber and Silver (1968a, 1968b), who analyzed 31 studies on this topic. Barber and Silver concluded that many of the studies of experimenter-expectancy effects were inadequate in regard to procedures or statistical analysis of results. Yet even Barber and Silver granted that 12 of the reviewed studies "apparently showed" that experimenters' expectations can bias results. We believe that there is enough potential danger here that researchers must increase their vigilance—that they must seek ways of reducing or eliminating the role of experimenter bias in influencing results.

Now let us return to the factor of concern in each article reprinted in this section: the behavior of research subjects.

In the first article, Orne proposes that subjects —as subjects in a psychological experiment—are concerned with helping the researcher in the scientific enterprise as well as with maintaining a positive self-image.* More recent research has sought empirical evidence about the subjects' motivations for participating in psychological research. Jackson and Pollard (1966) questioned volunteers for a sensory-deprivation experiment and found that 50% of the subjects said that they had volunteered out of curiosity, 21% for the money they were paid, and only 7% to advance scientific knowledge. Schultz (1969) reports similar findings. In many experiments students in introductory psychology classes are required to serve as research subjects; such a requirement may reduce any desire to help in the scientific quest. Certainly compulsory participation is not popular with most students. Gustav (1962) found that 37% of such students claimed they would not have participated voluntarily and an additional 40% reflected unfavorable reactions ranging from annoyance to fear. Continued use of a compulsory-participation requirement would seem to jeopardize Orne's goal (expressed in the first article) of the subject's taking an active role in the research process. Instead of the subject's aiding the experimenter in further understanding the phenomenon under study, the compulsory subject's reaction may be that of misleading or "beating the researcher in such a way that he

---

*In his recent writings, Orne (1969, 1970) has dealt more definitively and extensively with some of the problems in translating his proposals into concrete designs.

never found out" (Argyris, 1968, p. 188). (Incidentally, in the recently revised Code of Ethics of the American Psychological Association, required or compulsory participation is considered to be an unacceptable procedure.)

But if compulsory use of subjects is not wise, use of only volunteers is no better, as the third article indicates. The body of literature reviewed by Hood and Back in that article shows that volunteers for psychological experiments differ in many important ways from those who choose not to volunteer. Clearly the use of a volunteer sample increases the likelihood that the sample will be an *unrepresentative one,* if we are studying the *psychological* characteristics or reactions of subjects.

Beyond this problem is the fact that most of the laboratory experimentation in psychology is conducted with college-student subjects, who certainly do not adequately represent the general population on such important variables as age, education, socioeconomic status, or life-style. The surveys of both Smart (1966) and Schultz (1969) of studies published in the two largest American psychological journals found that 75-85% of these studies used college students as subjects. Less than 1% used a general adult sample.

Is there a solution to the problem of selecting a representative sample of subjects? The establishment of large panels of subjects has been suggested by Smart (1966). These subjects would be adequately paid for their time, and the group would be constituted so as to represent the general adult population in regard to variables of importance. At present the National Opinion Research Center maintains such a sample, which is designed to approximate the adult population of the United States. But such samples are necessarily volunteer samples, and the prolonged use of the same subjects in such a panel may spoil the authenticity of their later responses. Regardless of these problems, such an approach would be an improvement over the mandatory participation of subjects who are certainly not representative of the general population.

In this section the first and third articles have something in common to say about the specific relationship of the experimenter to the subject.

Orne proposes a dialogue between the two, and Hood and Back reflect a realization that the subject's degree of self-disclosure influences his participation in an experiment. Jourard (1968) has extended the application of the self-disclosure concept to the relationship between experimenter and subject. Jourard proposes that, instead of the traditional impersonal, distrustful relationship between the two, a mutual self-disclosure should take place. The subject would describe what the experimental treatment and his responses to it really mean to him. The experimenter would explain what his purposes were and what the subject's responses mean to him. A greater openness and mutual understanding would result.

Jourard bases his proposal on a philosophical basis for psychological research that is radically different from the usual one. The traditional philosophy of science seeks a distance between experimenter and subject, for a subject is viewed as an object to be studied and even "manipulated." Moreover, theories of behavior are seen as "manmade, *scientist*-oriented constructions of reality" (Miller, 1972, p. 2; italics in original). Jourard opts for a humanistic conception of psychological research and assumes—contrary to the above position—that what we know of human behavior is, to a large degree, what man will show to us. Thus Jourard sees the necessity of having experimenter and subject participate in an open, egalitarian relationship.

Although Jourard's view is a radical one that is not as yet accepted by the majority of social-psychological researchers, a number of influential thinkers and writers call for revision of the frequent procedure in which the experimenter's main goals appear to be the control and deception of the subject (Brown, 1965; Kelman, 1967, 1968; Smith, 1969). And Orne's suggestion of a decade ago, that the subject be considered a collaborator instead of an anonymous object of study, is being explored through the use of role-playing techniques (Greenberg, 1967), postexperimental inquiry (Levy, 1967; Golding & Lichtenstein, 1970), and other procedures. None of these innovations is without its problems, and some social psychologists strongly object to them. For example, Freedman (1969) believes that the "let's pretend" mental set given to subjects in studies using role playing leads them to continue to react in such an "as-if" way in subsequent experiments. Freedman argues that carefully designed experiments *can* provide opportunities for spontaneous, realistic behavior in the laboratory.

So the controversy continues. Can subjects' rights be met within a context that provides researchers opportunities to gain accurate, generalizable data? If there are procedures that ensure both goals, they have not yet been well developed.

REFERENCES

Argyris, C. Some unintended consequences of rigorous research. *Psychological Bulletin,* 1968, **70,** 185–197.

Barber, T. X., & Silver, M. J. Fact, fiction, and the experimenter bias effect. *Psychological Bulletin,* Monograph Supplement, 1968, **70**(6), Part 2, 1–29. (a)

Barber, T. X., & Silver, M. J. Pitfalls in data analysis and interpretation: A reply to Rosenthal. *Psychological Bulletin,* Monograph Supplement, 1968, **70**(6), Part 2, 48–62. (b)

Brown, R. *Social psychology.* New York: Free Press, 1965.

Cordaro, L., & Ison, J. R. Observer bias in classical conditioning of the planaria. *Psychological Reports,* 1963, **13,** 787–789.

Evans, J. T., & Rosenthal, R. Interpersonal self-fulfilling prophecies: Further extrapolations from the laboratory to the classroom. *Proceedings, 77th Annual Convention,* APA, 1969, **4,** 371–372.

Freedman, J. L. Role playing: Psychology by consensus? *Journal of Personality and Social Psychology,* 1969, **13,** 107–114.

Golding, S. L., & Lichtenstein, E. Confession of awareness and prior knowledge of deception as a function of interview set and approval motivation. *Journal of Personality and Social Psychology,* 1970, **14,** 213–223.

Greenberg, M. S. Role playing: An alternative to deception? *Journal of Personality and Social Psychology,* 1967, **7,** 152–157.

Gustav, A. Students' attitudes toward compulsory participation in experiments. *Journal of Psychology,* 1962, **53,** 119–125.

Jackson, C. W., & Pollard, J. C. Some nondeprivation variables which influence the "effects" of experimental sensory deprivation. *Journal of Abnormal Psychology,* 1966, **71,** 383–388.

Jourard, S. M. *Disclosing man to himself.* Princeton, N.J.: Van Nostrand, 1968.

Kelman, H. C. Human use of human subjects: The problem of deception in social psychological experiments. *Psychological Bulletin,* 1967, **67,** 1–11.

Kelman, H. *A time to speak: On human values and social research.* San Francisco: Jossey-Bass, 1968.

Levy, L. H. Awareness, learning, and the beneficent subject as expert witness. *Journal of Personality and Social Psychology,* 1967, **6,** 365–370.

Luft, J. Interaction and projection. *Journal of Projective Techniques,* 1953, **17,** 489–492.

Miller, A. G. (Ed.) *The social psychology of psychological research.* New York: Free Press, 1972.

Orne, M. T. Demand characteristics and the concept of quasi-controls. In R. Rosenthal and R. Rosnow (Eds.), *Artifact in behavioral research.* New York: Academic Press, 1969. Pp. 143–179.

Orne, M. T. Hypnosis, motivation, and the ecological validity of the psychological experiment. In W. J. Arnold and M. M. Page (Eds.), *Nebraska symposium on motivation, 1970.* Lincoln: University of Nebraska Press, 1970. Pp. 187–265.

Rosenthal, R. The effect of the experimenter on the results of psychological research. In B. Maher (Ed.), *Progress in experimental personality research,* Vol. I. New York: Academic Press, 1964. Pp. 80–114.

Rosenthal, R. *Experimenter effects in behavioral research.* New York: Appleton-Century-Crofts, 1966.

Rosenthal, R. Covert communication in the psychological experiment. *Psychological Bulletin,* 1967, **67,** 356–367.

Rosenthal, R. Experimenter expectancy and the reassuring nature of the null hypothesis decision procedure. *Psychological Bulletin,* Monograph Supplement, 1968, **70**(6), Part 2, 30–47.

Rosenthal, R., & Jacobson, L. *Pygmalion in the classroom.* New York: Holt, Rinehart & Winston, 1968.

Rubin, Z. Jokers wild in the lab. *Psychology Today,* 1970, **4**(7), 18–24.

Schultz, D. P. The human subject in psychological research. *Psychological Bulletin,* 1969, **72,** 214–228.

Smart, R. Subject selection bias in psychological research. *Canadian Psychologist,* 1966, **7a,** 115–121.

Smith, M. B. *Social psychology and human values.* Chicago: Aldine, 1969.

SUGGESTED READINGS FOR FURTHER STUDY

Aronson, E., & Carlsmith, J. M. Experimentation in social psychology. In G. Lindzey and E. Aronson (Eds.), *Handbook of social psychology.* (Rev. ed.) Reading, Mass.: Addison-Wesley, 1968. Vol. II. Pp. 1–79.

Friedman, N. *The social nature of psychological research*. New York: Basic Books, 1967.

Katz, I. Some motivational determinants of racial differences in intellectual achievement. *International Journal of Psychology,* 1967, **2**, 1–12.

Miller, A. G. (Ed.) *The social psychology of psychological research*. New York: Free Press, 1972.

Rosenberg, M. J. The conditions and consequences of evaluation apprehension. In R. Rosenthal and R. L. Rosnow (Eds.), *Artifact in behavioral research.* New York: Academic Press, 1969. Pp. 279–349.

Rosenthal, R. On not so replicated experiments and not so null results. *Journal of Consulting and Clinical Psychology,* 1969, **33**, 7–10.

Rosenthal, R., & Rosnow, R. L. The volunteer subject. In R. Rosenthal and R. L. Rosnow (Eds.), *Artifact in behavioral research.* New York: Academic Press, 1969. Pp. 59–118.

Sattler, J. Racial "experimenter effects" in experimentation, testing, interviewing, and psychotherapy. *Psychological Bulletin,* 1970, **73**, 137–160.

Snow, R. E. Review of *Pygmalion in the classroom. Contemporary Psychology,* 1969, **14**, 197–199.

Webb, E. J., Campbell, D. T., Schwartz, R. D., & Sechrest, L. *Unobtrusive measures: Nonreactive research in the social sciences.* Chicago: Rand-McNally, 1966.

SECTION 2

Moral Development

Newborn infants might accurately be described as the personification of selfishness and self-centeredness. They want all their needs and wishes to be fulfilled immediately, and they have no awareness of the existence of anyone else but themselves. Truly, each one is the center of his or her own universe.

Let us grant that most of the adults we know do not fit this description. What accounts for the transformation from the egocentric infant to the more civilized adult? Evidently there has been a process of *socialization*—an acquisition of personality characteristics, values, and beliefs (Mussen, 1967). Two European psychologists have developed the most extensive descriptions of the patterns of moral development and socialization in children. Of one, Sigmund Freud, the reader is probably aware.

Freud, born in Vienna in 1856, was trained as a medical doctor and concentrated his practice on the treatment of what was then called "nervous diseases" (neuroses). As a result of his observations and his extensive self-analysis (Freud kept a pencil and paper at his bedside so he could immediately record his every dream), he developed his highly influential theory of personality development, *psychoanalysis.* Basic to Freud's theory is the belief that the child must move through a series of stages in order to become a mature, well-socialized adult. Each stage is qualitatively different from the previous ones, in that the child's orientation has shifted to a new aspect of growth.

The second major influence is Jean Piaget, a Swiss developmental psychologist who was born in 1896 and who has lived most of his life in Geneva. Since 1921 he has been Director of Studies of the Institut Jean-Jacques Rousseau. Many prominent psychologists, including Roger Brown (1965), rate Piaget as second only to Freud in the importance of his contributions to modern psychology. Like Freud, Piaget believes that the child must pass through a series of stages in his development. But whereas Freud concentrates on motivations and emotions, Piaget emphasizes mental or cognitive factors in development.

Although American psychologists have been aware of Piaget's work since the publication of his book *The Language and Thought of the Child* in 1924, it was not until the last two decades that his work has intensely interested them. The earlier lack of interest was partially the result of Piaget's more subjective, "clinical," almost anecdotal approach, which contrasted with the American concern for operational definitions and methodological precision. Moreover, it seems that American psychologists mistook Piaget's writings as final statements of his theory, when he actually intended them more as progress reports. Finally, Piaget was (and is) more concerned with the description of phenomena, whereas American psychologists were more concerned with functional, cause-and-effect relationships.

During the 1960s American psychologists "discovered" Piaget. Why? It is hard to say. The *Zeitgeist* ("temper of the times") may have had something to do with it. Piaget's approach was compatible with the increasing emphasis of American psychology on cognitive determinants. A few prominent American psychologists began talking and writing about Piaget, and John Flavell, now at the University of Minnesota, wrote a book that pulled together Piaget's basic concepts and principles. (Piaget has yet to do so; although he has written more than 30 books and innumerable articles, not one of them integrates and summarizes his many interests and concerns.) The first selection in this section is the portion of Flavell's book that describes Piaget's theory of moral development as expressed in Piaget's *The Moral Judgment of the Child*. Piaget's earlier books are more concerned with the development of intelligence, logical reasoning, mathematical abilities, and other mental skills. So this book, first published in 1932, reflects something of a shift in Piaget's interests, although even here his emphasis is still on a cognitive approach to moral development. *The Moral Judgment of the Child*, as Flavell indicates, is concerned with the ways children learn rules, their attitudes toward justice, and their evaluations of the severity of immoral actions. Piaget has given us a set of concepts with which the child's moral development can be described.

What do empirical tests of Piaget's theory show? The second selection, an excerpt from an article by Ronald C. Johnson of the University of Hawaii, is a test of the applicability of Piaget's stages and concepts to American children's moral judgments. Johnson reviews five of Piaget's basic concepts: immanent justice, moral realism, retributive versus restitutive punishment, belief in severe punishment, and type of responsibility for acts. Johnson developed stories to test the child's acceptance of each concept and presented them to children of differing ages. The article reports the relationships between the child's maturity of moral judgment and factors such as the child's age, IQ, the attitudes of the child's parents, and other possibly important influences.

But Piaget's theory has often been criticized because it essentially sees moral development as ending at age 11 or 12. Lawrence Kohlberg, an American psychologist now at the Graduate School of Education, Harvard University, has proposed a more elaborated and extended theory. Kohlberg's approach may be considered an extension of Piaget's approach because it is cognitive in orientation, it sees development as passing through stages, and it uses stories posing moral dilemmas. However, Kohlberg's stories deal with more morally ambiguous situations than Piaget's. For example, one story asks whether a doctor should fulfill a patient's request for a death-inducing injection. The patient was suffering from an incurable disease and was usually in intense pain. In her calmer moments she begged the doctor to put her out of her misery. Should he?

Perhaps Kohlberg's most useful story—and one he refers to in the third article in this section— is the following:

In Europe, a woman was near death from a special kind of cancer. There was one drug that the doctors thought might save her. It was a form of radium that a druggist in the same town had recently discovered. The drug was expensive to make, but the druggist was charging ten times what the drug cost him to make. He paid $200 for the radium and charged $2,000 for a small dose of the drug. The sick woman's husband, Heinz, went to everyone he knew to borrow money, but he could only get together about $1,000, which is half of what it cost. He told the druggist that his wife was dying, and asked him to sell it cheaper or let him pay later. But the druggist said, "No, I discovered the drug and I'm going to make money from it." So Heinz got desperate and broke into the man's store to steal the drug for his wife. Should Heinz have done that? Why? Is it a husband's duty to steal the drug for his wife if he can get it no other way? Would a good husband do it? Did the druggist have the right to charge that much when there was no law actually setting a limit to the price? Why? If the husband does not feel very close or affectionate to his wife, should he still steal the drug? [Kohlberg, 1963, pp. 18–19]*

In this section we have thus included three articles that represent the cognitive approach to moral development. But this is only one way to

*From Kohlberg, L.: The development of children's orientations toward a moral order. (1) Sequences in the development of moral thought. *Vita Humana,* **6**: 11–33 (1963).

view moral development. In the summary to this section we will evaluate Piaget's and Kohlberg's cognitive theories and compare them with the psychoanalytic approach developed by Freud.

REFERENCES

Brown, R. *Social psychology.* New York: Free Press, 1965.

Kohlberg, L. The development of children's orientations toward a moral order: I. Sequence in the development of moral thought. *Vita Humana,* 1963, **6,** 11–33.

Mussen, P. Early socialization: Learning and identification. In *New directions in psychology,* Vol. III. New York: Holt, Rinehart, & Winston, 1967. Pp. 51–110.

Piaget, J. *The moral judgment of the child.* New York: Free Press, 1948. (First published in 1932.)

ARTICLE 4

Piaget's Theory of Moral Judgment

John H. Flavell

The Moral Judgment of the Child is concerned, as its title says, with the child's moral *judgments,* i.e., his ideas and attitudes about rules, justice, ethical behavior, and so on. Although it does here and there deal with questions of moral behavior as well, it treats these as secondary and subsidiary to those of moral judgment. Although this work is not a direct, fifth-volume sequel to the other four, there is, nevertheless, considerable continuity. Piaget makes ample use of his earlier insights in the design and interpretation of the research in this area. As a case in point, he identifies a *moral realism* in children which directly parallels the *intellectual realism* described earlier. The book consists of four long chapters: the first three experimental and theoretical and the fourth purely theoretical. Research findings are, as usual, interpreted in terms of developmental stages. It should be noted, however, that Piaget is exceedingly cautious and guarded about how the term *stage* should be construed in this area. He indicates again and again that individual differences in moral judgment are enormous at every age level studied, that his stages are thereby so overlapping as to be almost (but not quite) reducible to agenetic types, that similar studies carried out on populations of children different from his would likely yield different developmental patterns, and so on.

The book commences with an interesting investigation of children's attitudes and behavior

with respect to the rules of a game, namely, the game of marbles as played by children in French Switzerland. The inquiry consists of two parts. The first part is designed to find out the extent to which the child conforms to rules of the marble game in his actual playing behavior. The experimenter gives the child some marbles and, feigning ignorance of the game,[1] asks the child to show him how to play it. With the youngest children this procedure was supplemented by watching them play the game together. The second part of the inquiry aims at the child's verbally expressed understanding of the nature of rules, his attitudes towards them, and so on. The experimenter begins by asking if the child could make up a new rule for the marble game and, if so, whether other children would agree to it, whether it would be "fair," etc. He then asks about the history and origins of rules: whether people have always played the game by present rules, and how the rules originated.

As to the child's behavioral conformity to the rules, the stages appeared to be as follows. In stage 1 the child uses the marbles simply as free-play materials, without any attempt to adapt to social rules. At most, the child develops private rituals of play which might be called *motor rules.* Stage 2 (about 3–5 years) begins when the child imitates aspects of the rule-regulated play behavior of his elders. However, it is clear that the child assimilates what he sees to private, egocentric schemas; confident that he is playing by the older

[1]Actually, Piaget had previously made it a point to master the rules of this game, including all local variations, so as to spot any breaches in the rules as they occurred.

children's rules, he nonetheless plays in an idiosyncratic, socially isolated manner, unintentionally flouting the rules at every turn. From about 7–8 years on, the child begins to play the game in a genuinely social way, in accordance with a mutually agreed upon set of rules. But until about age 11–12, this grasp of and conformity to the rules is still vague and approximate (stage 3). From 11–12 on, however, they are completely understood and obeyed to the letter by all (stage 4); moreover, the act of codifying rules now seems to have a positive fascination for the child, e.g., he is constantly engaged in revising the statutes to cover new and unforeseen contingencies.

For the child's verbalized notions about rules, Piaget found three stages. Stage 1 corresponds to the stage 1 in behavioral conformity to rules: rules are simply not part of his life space. Stage 2 is more interesting. Here, the child regards the rules of the game as eternal and unchangeable, stemming from parental or divine authority; suggested changes in the rules are usually resisted; the new rules "are not fair," even if others agree to abide by them. But there is a curious hiatus between theory and practice in this stage. While regarding the rules as sacred and inviolable in his conscious thought, he unwittingly breaks them at every turn in his actual behavior (the stage 2 in the practice of rules). In stage 3 (about 10–11), the child evidences quite different attitudes and beliefs with respect to rules. Rules may always be changed, provided only that others agree to abide by them. Rules are neither God-given nor eternal; children of long ago were probably the first marble players, and the rules have undoubtedly evolved and changed considerably since then. And, as we have seen, this relativistic attitude towards rules in theory is accompanied by scrupulous adherence to rules in practice—just the reverse of the situation in stage 2.

A second series of experiments bear on developmental changes in attitudes towards actions more specifically moral than conformity to the rules of a game. In one group of studies the subject was presented with a number of stories in which a child performs some morality-relevant act under a specified set of circumstances. The subject was then to judge the relative culpability of the various acts, giving the reasons for his judgment. The results can be summarized as follows. Although individual differences were substantial as usual, the younger children tended to regard as most immoral those acts which had the most serious objective consequences, with no consideration of subjective antecedents (motives, etc.) in the wrongdoer. Thus, the child who breaks fifteen cups through an accident he could not have avoided was judged "naughtier" than one who accidentally breaks a single cup while engaged in deliberate malfeasance. Similarly, a child who steals a roll to give to a poor and hungry friend was judged guiltier than one who steals a (less costly) piece of ribbon for herself. The older children (particularly from 9–10 years on) were more inclined to take into account the motives behind the wrongful act and weigh moral responsibility accordingly.

Other investigations in this series deal with the child's ideas about and attitudes towards the telling of lies. The results parallel those for clumsiness and stealing and can be summarized as follows. First, the youngest children define a lie simply as "naughty words," i.e., lying is rather like swearing. A little later, it is defined as an untrue statement of any kind, with or without intention to deceive. And finally, it is restricted exclusively to untruths with intent to deceive. Second, younger children regard a lie as culpable in the degree that it deviates from the truth, regardless of the intent of the teller. Thus, a tall tale innocently told by a young child is worse than a more believable untruth told with deliberate intent to deceive, just as the bigger theft with altruistic motives was worse than the smaller one with selfish motives. Again, the older children tend to evaluate guilt in terms of the motives involved. Third, younger children judge a lie which *fails* to deceive (usually because it is so "big," so unbelievable) as "naughtier" than one which succeeds; for them, it is the exposure of the untruth which is reprehensible. With older children, on the other hand, the lie which succeeds in its deceitful intent is worse. Fourth, as with clumsiness, an unintentional falsehood with serious objective consequences is judged worse by the younger subjects than a deliberate lie which happens not to result in anything serious. Again, older children reverse this evaluation. Fifth, younger children are inclined to say that a lie is bad because one is punished for it; older children think it is bad *per se,* whether one gets punished or not, because it violates mutual trust, makes good relations with others impossible, etc. And finally, younger children tend for various reasons to believe that a lie told to an adult is worse than one told to a peer, while older children see them as equally blameworthy.

The third chapter of the book deals with the child's conception of justice. There is a lot of theory and research in this long (135 pages) and meaty chapter, but at least its main points can be summarized. Ideas about how various misdeeds ought to be punished (what Piaget calls the problem of *retributive justice*) constitutes the first topic. Piaget distinguishes two broad classes of punishment. The first is *expiatory punishment:* the wrongdoer should suffer, expiate by means of, a punishment which is painful in proportion to the seriousness of the offense but need in no way be related to the offense. The second is *punishment by reciprocity:* the emphasis here is not so much on inflicting severe punishment for expiation's sake but in bringing home to the offender in the most direct possible way the nature and consequences of his breach of relations with others by setting a punishment which is logically related to the offense. Suppose the offense consists of a child failing to bring home food for supper, having been told to do so. To spank the offender, deny him some privilege, etc., would be classed as expiatory punishment. Punishments by reciprocity might include giving the child less supper than usual (since he failed to bring home the food) or refusing to do him a favor (since he refused to do you one). The point here is to "make the punishment fit the crime" in some intrinsic way so that the transgressor will better understand the implications of what he has done. Piaget posed hypothetical misdeeds of this kind and had the children choose, from several different suggested punishments, the one they thought was "best" or "fairest" for the case at hand. There was at least a tendency for the younger children to favor expiatory punishments (and usually the more severe the better) with the older children electing pun-

ishments of the reciprocity type. Furthermore, the older children were less inclined to think that direct and severe punishment itself, without explanation and discussion of why the act was wrong, would be an effective deterrent to future wrongdoing.

Two other investigations described in this chapter are worth relating. In the first, Piaget found that the younger children were more prone than the older ones to believe in what he calls *immanent justice:* the idea that Nature herself will punish misdeeds, e.g., a boy running away from a policeman (he had been caught stealing apples) crosses a river on a rotten bridge and the bridge breaks (*because* he had just done wrong; ordinarily it would not have broken). The second investigation consisted of various studies of *distributive justice,* i.e., how punishments and rewards should be distributed to members of a group. These interesting studies seemed to point to the existence of three rough stages. In the first (prior to age 7–8), the child is inclined to regard as "just" or "fair" whatever rewards or punishments the authority figure decides to dispense, even if it involves unequal punishment for the same crime, the granting of special privileges to favored individuals, and so forth. In stage 2 (about 7–8 to 11–12 years), the child is a rabid egalitarian: all *must* be treated equally, no matter what the circumstances. In stage 3 (from 11–12 or so), the child tempers equality with equity— a kind of relativistic egalitarianism in which strict equality will sometimes be winked at in favor of a higher justice. The subtle difference between stages 2 and 3 can be illustrated by responses to the following story:

Story II. One Thursday afternoon, a mother asked her little girl and boy to help her about the house, because she was tired. The girl was to dry the plates and the boy was to fetch in some wood. But the little boy (or girl) went and played in the street. So the mother asked the other one to do all the work. What did he say? (*ibid.,* p. 276).

The stage-2 response is simply to assert the basic unfairness of the request and advocate noncompliance. The stage-3 response grants the basic inequity but suggests compliance anyhow, out of wish to help the mother, not to make her suffer in the service of principle, and so on. Similarly, equity may preclude hitting back a small child who has hit you first, whereas equality demands an eye for an eye with no exceptions.

The changing concept of justice is also expressed in children's reactions to this vignette:

One afternoon, on a holiday, a mother had taken her children for a walk along the Rhone. At four o'clock she gave each of them a roll. They all began to eat their rolls except the youngest, who was careless and let his fall into the water. What will the mother do? Will she give him another one? What will the older ones say? (*ibid.*, p. 267).

Here is a judgment which is both pre-equality and pre-equity, with punishment at all costs winning the day:

Pail (7): *"He shouldn't be given another. He didn't need to let it drop.*—And what would the older ones have said if the little boy had been given another roll? —*That it wasn't fair: 'He's let it drop into the water and you go and give him another one.'*—Was it right to give him another one?—*No. He hadn't been good"* (*ibid.*, pp. 268–269).

And here is a case in which a conception of justice founded in strict equality prevails (with possibly a hint at equity):

Mel (13), G.: *"They should have divided up what the other children had left and given some to the little chap.*—Was it fair to give him any more?—*Yes, but the child ought to have been more careful.*—What does 'fair' mean?—*It means equality among everyone"* (*ibid.*, p. 270).

A number of the oldest children also reached an essentially egalitarian conclusion (the child ought to be given a second roll), but by means of a more subtle and mature line of reasoning involving considerations of equity. These subjects carefully distinguished between the loss of the roll as a disembodied and abstract bit of wrongdoing and the same event as it occurred in its living context, with extenuating circumstances (the wrongdoer is young and irresponsible, etc.):

Camp (11), G.: *"The little boy ought to have taken care. But then he was a little boy, so they might give him a little piece more.*—What did the others say?— *They were jealous and said that they ought to be given*

a little piece more too. But the little one deserved to be given a little piece more. The older ones ought to have understood.—Do you think it was fair to give him some more?— ... *Of course! It was a shame for the little one. When you are little you don't understand what you are doing"* (*ibid.*, p. 271).

Throughout these three chapters, and especially in the final chapter, Piaget interjects what amounts to a theory of the development of moral judgment. In brief, it is this. There appear to be two moralities in childhood, at least within the culture from which Piaget's subjects were drawn. The developmentally earlier one is a *morality of constraint*, formed in the context of the unilateral relations between child as inferior and adult as superior. The child adapts to the prohibitions and sanctions handed down from on high by reifying them (*a moral realism* akin to the *intellectual realism* studied earlier) into moral absolutes— simple "givens" which are unquestioned and sacred, in theory if not in practice. Hence, the child views wrongdoing in objective rather than subjective terms, is confined to the letter rather than the spirit of the law, and is incapable of seeing morality-relevant acts either in terms of the inner motives of the actor or in terms of the social-interpersonal meaning of the act itself (i.e., as a breach of solidarity and mutual trust between group members). For a morality of constraint, it must be the overt consequences alone which count in assessing the wrongfulness of acts (untruths, clumsiness, and the like), not the inner intentions and motives involved. Similarly, justice reduces simply to whatever the authority commands, rather than being seen as an equitable distribution of sanctions and rewards, these sanctions and rewards meaningfully related to the acts which engendered them.

With development, this morality of constraint is at least partially replaced by a *morality of cooperation*, formed out of the reciprocal relationships among status peers and based on mutual, rather than unilateral, respect. With a growing understanding of the role of motives in the actions of self and others and of the social implications of antisocial behavior, the child comes to the basic *raison d'être* of morality and begins to conceive (if not always to follow in practice) moral action as an autonomous good, essential to the intact functioning of any social unit. With this orientation, rules become rational conventions which serve orderly group action rather than arbitrary and untouchable dicta: malfeasance is judged by motivational as well as objective criteria; and justice, now placed in a social context, is seen in terms of equality and equity.

It is clear that the mechanism which Piaget holds responsible for the development of a rational morality is exactly the same as that which he thinks engenders rationality in general, and therein lies the important theoretical tie between this and the preceding four books (*ibid.,* pp. 406–411).[2] Both morality and logic are fired in the crucible of the spontaneous give and take, the interplay of thought and action, which takes place in peer-peer interactions. The prescripts, logical and moral, which parents and other adults impose upon the young and egocentric mind are compliantly accepted but at the same time simplified and distorted. It is only through a sharing of perspectives with equals—at first other children, and later, as the child grows up, adults—that a genuine logic and morality can replace an egocentric, logical, and moral realism. It might also be mentioned that even in these early days Piaget had developed strong opinions about how to educate children, based on just these conceptions (*ibid.,* pp. 411–414). For example, he believed that schools should foster and encourage group projects in which children could freely exchange ideas on a common intellectual task close to their own interests. As he himself acknowledged, his philosophy of education is closely aligned in this respect with that of Dewey and other progressivists.

[2]Piaget also sees an intrinsic connection between morality and thought *per se,* apart from the developmental parallelism, e.g., "Logic is the morality of thought just as morality is the logic of action" (*ibid.,* p. 404).

ARTICLE 5

A Study of Children's Moral Judgments

Ronald C. Johnson

The development of moral judgment in the child has been of considerable interest to the social scientist. Among the students of human development, Jean Piaget (1932) has been, perhaps, most influential in this area of study. His studies of the child's developing understanding of causality, of physical and temporal reality, and of ethics and moral judgment have been extremely fruitful. This study proposes to test some of Piaget's ideas concerning developmental changes in moral judgment.

Moral judgment, for Piaget, consists of a number of areas. These include: (a) immanent justice—the belief in the existence of automatic punishments which emanate from things themselves; (b) moral realism—a belief that acts should be judged in terms of consequences, not on the basis of the motive behind the act; (c) belief that punishment should be retributive vs. belief that punishment should be restitutive (merely restore the equilibrium destroyed by the punished act); (d) acceptance or rejection of the idea that the more severe punishment is more efficacious, and (e) choice of collective (essentially, guilt by association) or of individual responsibility for punishable acts. . . .

Piaget sees three forces interacting to produce developmental change in moral judgment: adult constraint, peer group cooperation and reciproc-

Excerpted from *Child Development*, 1962, **33**, 327–354. Reprinted with permission of the author and the publisher. ©The Society for Research in Child Development, Inc., 1962.

This study is based on a dissertation submitted in partial fulfillment of the requirements of the Ph.D. degree at the University of Minnesota. The author is grateful to Dale B. Harris, the major advisor of the dissertation, for his help and advice.

ity, and the changing character of the child's mind. He says, ". . . We have three processes to consider: the spontaneous and unconscious egocentrism belonging to the individual as such, adult constraint, and cooperation. . . . Cooperation alone can shake the child out of its initial state of unconscious egocentrism; whereas constraint acts quite differently and strengthens egocentric features of moral realism until such time as cooperation delivers the child both from egocentrism and from the results of this constraint" (1932, p. 184). The interaction of these factors, the changing mind of the child, the amount of adult constraint, and the amount of peer group cooperation and reciprocity, to Piaget, cause developmental differences in systems of responsibility and type of moral judgment used by children of different ages.

Piaget and his assistants studied a sample of about 100 children aged about 6 to 12, from homes of lower socioeconomic groups, in Geneva, Switzerland. They were questioned and interviewed individually.

So far as this writer can determine, Piaget's study was conducted primarily to show that developmental changes occur in moral judgment and then to determine how the factors of adult constraint, peer group cooperation, and qualitative changes in thought processes interact to produce these changes in moral judgment.

Piaget shows that age changes in belief do occur. Younger children accept the concepts of immanent justice and moral realism, believe that retribution should be the primary basis for punishment, and believe in the efficacy of severe punishment. Older children reject the concepts of immanent justice and moral realism and believe that less severe, restitutive punishments are more appropriate. The youngest and older segments of his sample accepted communicable responsibility as just, while a middle age group did not. This writer was unable to find any statement by Piaget that these changes necessarily occur at a specific age, even in his own sample. Piaget seems most aware that changes in belief would occur at different times in other segments of society (e.g., see his statement concerning immanent justice [1932, pp. 255–256]), though he would say that the direction of change would be the same.

It does not seem that he has achieved his second objective, that of showing how the interaction of constraint, cooperation, and mental change cause this change to occur. While the interview technique that Piaget used may have decided advantages, it would seem impossible, through interviews, to determine the relative significance of three factors, each acting on moral judgment and each acting upon the other two factors. None of the material presented seems, to this writer, to be able to separate out the influence of each of these three factors in terms of anything but Piaget's own subjective judgment. Therefore, it would seem that Piaget's purposes are only half fulfilled; he has shown that age change in moral judgment does occur, but has not shown exactly what influence various factors have in producing the change.

Of the studies done since Piaget, one confirms his belief that childish egocentricity is involved in change in moral judgment (Lerner, 1937), while the only other study of this aspect of moral judgment does not (Isaacs, 1930). None of the three studies that dealt directly with peer group cooperation confirms Piaget's emphasis on this factor (Harrower, 1934; Isaacs, 1930; and Lerner, 1937). Five of the seven studies that deal with adult constraint confirm Piaget in this area (Abel, 1941; Dennis, 1943; Harrower, 1934; Isaacs, 1930; and Lerner, 1937), while one other study, that of Ching-Ho Liu (1950), seems to qualify his statements somewhat, and one study, that of MacRae (1950), is opposed to Piaget's beliefs regarding the effect of adult constraint.

Piaget was not concerned with testing, empiri-

cally, to discover whether moral judgment consisted of one general or of a number of specific factors. The conclusions of Lerner (1937), MacRae (1950), and Medinnus (1957) are that responses in areas of moral judgment are not too closely related to each other. Lerner and Medinnus both present material which shows that the age of change in belief concerning various areas of moral judgment is variable from one area to the next, while MacRae's conclusions are based on the results of a series of intercorrelations between responses to questions concerning moral judgment, indicating the same results to be true. . . .

This study was concerned first with an attempt to determine the degree of interrelation within and between areas of moral judgment. This study dealt secondly with the relation of various antecedent conditions to moral judgment. There was an attempt to discover the relation of adult constraint, "egocentricity," age, sex, IQ, and parental occupational level to moral judgment. Though certainly one should also measure peer group cooperation, this seemed impossible in a sample sufficiently large to give a reliable determination for the primary problem. Previous findings concerning the effect of peer solidarity are uniformly negative, indicating that, of the variables, this might best be omitted.

This study, using a different method of gaining information, different questions, and different age groups, cannot be considered a test of the validity of Piaget's own work, since it was not directly comparable. However, it did attempt to test Piaget's ideas.

METHOD

Sample

This study included all the children (all of those present on the day when their classes were tested) in grades 5, 7, 9, and 11 in a midwestern public school system. . . . The total sample consisted of 807 subjects. . . .

A comparison of the occupational level of the parents of these children with that of the urban population of the United States indicates that the sample was a very close approximation of the general population, as measured by the Minnesota Occupational Scale (1950). Information concerning IQ was available in 732 cases of the total sample of 807. The mean IQ of the sample was 105.9. The sample closely approximated U. S. urban norms in intelligence as well as in occupational level.

Measuring Devices

The major purpose of this study was to determine the degree of interrelation between responses to questions formulated to represent different areas or kinds of moral judgment. The writer's initial problem was that of devising a test of moral judgment within which a number of questions could be found having to do with each of the areas under discussion. A number of stories were made up, modeled quite closely after those of Piaget. The stories illustrated five types of moral judgment: immanent justice, moral realism, retribution and expiation vs. restitution and reciprocity, the efficacy of severe punishment, and communicable responsibility.

Piaget's questions were generally quite simple, since they were designed for use with 6- to 12-year-olds. The writer wished to use an older sample, so that the moral judgment test could be administered as a paper and pencil test and so that a test of "abstractness-concreteness" might be used. For these reasons, a number of new questions, based on those used by Piaget, were devised. The work of Dennis (1953) in the field of animism, another area studied by Piaget, clearly indicates that the level of questions asked affects the level of response more than any qualitative age change in approaches to problem solving. The assumption was therefore made (and later confirmed) that with the proper questions there would be considerable variation in response even in a much older group than Piaget's.

A number of question stories similar to Piaget's were discussed with several people familiar with Piaget's work to find those stories most similar to Piaget's own. Since Medinnus (1957) believed that differences in the "level of abstraction" in the stories might account for differences in the type of response obtained, items

were eliminated and revised until they seemed of approximately equal difficulty to this writer and to Medinnus, who helped in their selection. Twenty items were retained as those likely to be intrinsically interesting to the subjects, most similar in meanings to those of Piaget, and of an equal level of difficulty.

[A selection of] the moral judgment test items appear below, followed by a discussion of the way that responses would, according to Piaget's results, be scored in terms of maturity. (The remaining 15 of the 20 items may be found in the original article—Ed.)

1. Four boys went downtown one day and were looking around in the store windows. One boy said, "Let's go into this store and see if we can take something." Two of the others thought this was a good idea but the other one didn't want to. The three that wanted to told the one that didn't want to that they'd tell all the other guys that he was chicken. So he went with them. They all took a few things but then the store detective caught up with them. He caught the one that suggested it and he caught the two that had gone along with the idea. But he didn't notice the one who hadn't wanted to take anything, even though he was right beside the others and was acting the same as they were, so that this one didn't get caught at all.

Do you think that this boy would have been caught, too, if he had wanted to take things like the other three did?

Now why did this one get away when the other three were caught?

2. A girl named Nancy liked one of the boys in her class an awful lot, but she didn't want anyone to know it, even though she'd never been out with this boy or anything like that. She told her best girl friend about it and the girl friend promised not to tell. But then she got angry at Nancy one day and told a lot of people, so that Nancy got teased a lot, but this boy hadn't gone with her before, so she had nothing to lose on that score.

Now here is a story something like the first one:
This girl was named Sharon. She was going steady with one boy, but her parents had visitors from out of town, who had a son her age. Her parents asked her to show this boy a little of the town. She didn't like doing this because she thought it wasn't fair to her steady boy friend, but she went out with this boy to be polite. She told her best girl friend about this and the girl friend promised not to tell—just like in the first story. Entirely by accident, this girl friend mentioned it in front of Sharon's steady boy friend and some other kids. He got angry at Sharon because she'd gone out with some-

one else when they were supposed to be going steady, so he quit going with her. Sharon got teased and lost her boy friend too because of what her girl friend had said without thinking.

Now was Nancy's girl friend or was Sharon's girl friend the worse?
Why?

3. Some boys and girls were playing football in the street. A pass was thrown and the boy who ran to catch it ran up onto a yard and trampled some recently planted shrubs and flowers. What should be done to the boy: (1) make him pay for the damage done or replace the shrubs and flowers; (2) give him a licking so he won't do it again; (3) not allow him to play football.

What punishment would be fairest?
What punishment would be hardest?

4. The stores downtown are always worried about shoplifting. In the past few years the stores have been good to high school students by giving them part-time work, especially at Christmas, to provide those who don't have much money with some buying power. The police have been working on the shoplifting problem, too, arresting many more people. Shoplifting has decreased recently.

What do you think is responsible for most of the decrease, the stores' helping the young people or the increased police action?
Why?

5. A group of young people were coming back to school after playing softball. Some of them had picked up rocks on the baseball diamond and were throwing them around. Finally, one boy threw a rock which broke a window in the school. The principal was nearby and heard the crash. He took them all into a room and asked them who broke the window. Some of them hadn't thrown any rocks at all, and of those who had thrown them only one broke the window. The boy who had broken the window wouldn't say that he had done it and the other boys would not tell on him.

Should the principal punish all of the boys or none of them?
Why?

In questions 1, 6, 11, and 16, all dealing with immanent justice, the mature response would be one which brought in the idea of chance—that chance caused one boy to escape while the others were caught. The immature response would be the one that attributed some sort of supernatural cause to these events.

Questions 2, 7, 12, and 17 all had to do with moral realism. The mature response would be one in which acts were judged in terms of intent; the immature response would judge an act according to its consequences.

The problem of choosing between punishment in terms of expiation or retribution as opposed to punishment in terms of restitution appears in questions 3, 8, 13, and 18. The mature response would be the restitutive one, chosen because it was fairest, not because it was hardest. (Sometimes the restitutive punishment might be chosen not because it was fairest, but solely because it was considered to be the most severe. In this case the response would be considered an immature one.) The choice of an expiatory punishment would be scored as an immature response.

Questions 4, 9, 14, and 19 had to do with the efficacy of severe punishment. Answers in which the position was taken that the less severe punishment was more effective were scored as mature, while those responses that indicated a belief in the efficacy of the more severe punishment were scored as immature.

Communicable responsibility was dealt with in questions 5, 10, 15, and 20. In each case, those responses that rejected communicable responsibility were judged to be mature, while those that accepted the idea of communicable responsibility were considered to be immature. This is not in strict accordance with Piaget's position. He says that both very young and older children accepted communicable responsibility while the middle age group of his sample rejected it. Very young children accept communicable responsibility because they believe that everything an adult does is fair while older children accept communicable responsibility as evidence of peer group solidarity. Since there is cross-cultural evidence (e.g., that gathered by Durkheim and by Fauconnet) that advanced cultures tend to reject communicable responsibility, the writer decided to score the rejection of communicable responsibility as the mature response. . . .

A test of the relation of various antecedent conditions to the systems of moral judgment used by the subjects involved the use of other measuring devices, plus the gathering of information from school records. The antecedent conditions were adult constraint, egocentricity, age (as measured by grade in school), sex, parental occupation, intelligence quotient, and religious training. Information concerning all but the first two of these variables was obtained from school records.

Many of the investigators working in the area since the time of Piaget's publication have believed adult constraint to be most significant in producing variance in the moral judgment of children. This belief seems to be based on the finding, common to many studies, that there is considerable social class difference in the age when a shift toward a more mature moral judgment occurs, with upper and middle socioeconomic groups shifting early and lower occupational groups changing in type of belief considerably later. It is assumed in the studies cited above that this difference is a result of the fact that lower occupational groups are more coercive and constraining. This interpretation seems open to question. Other factors, such as class differences in intelligence, might equally well account for the differences obtained. This study represents the first attempt to relate parental constraint to moral judgment by means of individual tests administered to a selected sample of the parents of the subjects.

The test of parent attitudes used was that devised by Shoben (1949). Shoben attempted to obtain information concerning the attitudes of the parents of problem and of nonproblem children. Seventy-four of his items discriminated between the two groups of mothers and could be placed in one of three clusters. The clusters were relatively independent of one another. They were labeled "Ignoring," "Possessive," and "Dominating" and could have been scored (although Shoben did not do so) as independent subscales. Each item consisted of a statement (e.g., "A child should be seen and not heard") plus the choices of "strongly agree," "mildly agree," "mildly disagree," and "strongly disagree," following the statement. Scoring in Shoben's sample was such as to discriminate between the responses of mothers of problem and of nonproblem children. The scores ranged from those most characteristic of mothers of problem children down to those most characteristic of mothers of nonproblem children. . . . The scoring system devised for this study was designed to measure the sheer amount of dominativeness, ignoringness, and possessiveness expressed in response to questions in the subscales concerned with these three facets of parental attitude. The investigator and two additional judges (both psychologists) independently weighted the responses to each question in each of the three scales. For example, it was assumed that the person who strongly agrees that "children should give their parents unquestioning obedience" is more dominative than the one who strongly disagrees with this statement and that parents who believe that "children should be seen and not heard" are more ignoring than those who do not believe this to be so. The first question given above would be scored for dominance as follows: strongly agree, 4; mildly agree, 3; mildly disagree, 2; and strongly disagree, 1.

All three of the judges agreed on the weighting of responses to all but six of the 74 items. The weights assigned to responses on which there was a difference of opinion were those that were assigned by two of the three judges.

The other variable of significance to Piaget is that of developmental changes in thought processes. According to Piaget, the stage of egocentricity begins in the child in the time interval following the formation of sensorimotor intelligence. The stage of egocentricity includes, from the ages of 7 or 8 to 11 or 12, a period of concreteness, ". . . i.e., operational groupings of thought concerning objects that can be manipulated or known through the senses. Finally, from 11 to 12 years and during adolescence, formal thought is projected and its groupings characterize the completion of reflective thought" (1950, p. 123).

The egocentricity of the young child presumably predisposes him toward an immature system of moral judgment. The problem of measuring egocentricity seems a most difficult one. This writer is not familiar with any direct tests measuring all aspects of "egocentricity," nor of any indirect test of it other than some individual tests used by Piaget and by Lerner (1937) which seem, by inference, to be measuring egocentricity. There is, however, a test available in one area that bears on Piaget's concept of egocentricity. This test is the Gorham Proverbs Test (1956) designed to measure concreteness and abstractness of thought. The stage of concreteness, for Piaget

(1950), is a late portion of the egocentric period of the child's development. This stage is followed by a period characterized by increasing ability in "reflective thought." This "reflective thought" seems analogous to what is usually called the ability to deal with abstract materials. The Gorham Proverbs Test was designed to measure differential qualities of abstract as opposed to concrete thought. Therefore, the test appears to be measuring a major, late developing aspect of egocentricity.

The Shoben scale and the Gorham test are of somewhat limited utility in the study of factors involved in producing change in moral judgment. The Shoben test is a measure of attitudes, not of behavior. The greatest difficulty in the use of the Gorham test is that it does not measure egocentricity as would be desired, but measures concreteness (only one aspect of egocentricity) and abstractness (a characteristic that is dependent upon a lack of egocentricity). The defects associated with these measuring devices force one to be cautious in drawing conclusions from the results obtained from these tests.

Procedure

The test of moral judgment was administered to the subjects in May of 1957. . . . Two class sections took the Gorham Proverbs Test at each grade level in grades 7, 9, and 11. Fifty-one students were tested in grade 7, 61 students in grade 9, and 55 students in grade 11. The testing schedule omitted grade 5 because the school officials did not wish to take time in this grade; nor did the writer strongly urge the testing of this grade, for the Proverbs test, despite the fact that it had been standardized on populations as young as fifth graders, seemed quite difficult for the seventh grade sample.

The moral judgment test and the Proverbs test were administered in the school. Further data gathering involved contacting the parents of the subjects. The writer wished to determine the relations of adult constraint to abstractness-concreteness and to moral judgment. This required obtaining some measure of adult attitudes toward freedom and constraint. After repeated telephoning plus a number of home visits, the writer contacted the parents of 138 of the original sample of 167 subjects. In two cases, the people at the home could not speak English so these were dropped, leaving a total of 136 cases. Of the 136, five parents refused to take part, leaving a total of 131 cases where parents agreed to cooperate. Three pairs of siblings were in the sample of subjects tested on both abstractness-concreteness and moral judgment, so that only 128 sets of parents were involved in the parent attitude study. Of the 128 parents, 96 sent back their filled-out questionnaires. A comparison of the occupational levels of the respondents and non-respondents (including those that could not be contacted) showed that 59 per cent of the parents in groups I to III responded, as compared with 61 per cent of the parents in groups V to VII.

It seems clear that the returns were not biased by disproportionate returns at different levels of parental occupation. Since this would be a principal area where one would expect to find bias, it seems probable that the responding parents were reasonably representative of the subject population.

Scoring

The Proverbs test was scored according to Gorham's protocols. The parent attitude survey was scored on the basis of parental ignoringness, posessiveness, and dominance. It should be noted that one additional measure of parent attitudes resulted from the scoring of the parent attitude questions. Extremeness of point of view—that is, how often the parent either strongly agreed or strongly disagreed rather than mildly agreed or disagreed—seemed related to the maturity of the responses made by that parent's child. This writer, therefore, scored each test for the total number of extreme positions taken in the entire test.

All answers to moral judgment questions were of an either-or or of a multiple choice type. Thus, it was a simple matter to score the moral judgment questions to indicate relative maturity of response. . . .

RESULTS

The data to be presented in the following pages are divided into sections. There are a number of problems to be dealt with, and, for the purpose of clarity, they will be taken up in serial order. The first four sections of the results and discussion deal with responses to the moral judgment questions themselves, and the fifth with the relation of moral judgment to antecedent conditions. The results appear in the following order: (a) reliability of the moral judgment test; (b) intercorrelations of responses to moral judgment questions; (c) correlations of responses within moral judgment areas; (d) correlations of responses between moral judgment areas; and (e) relation of moral judgment responses to antecedent conditions.

Reliability of the Moral Judgment Test[1]

Information was obtained concerning the reliability of the total test (20 items) and also of the four-item subtests in each of the five moral judgment areas (immanent justice, moral realism, retribution vs. restitution, efficacy of severe punishment, and communicable responsibility) at the four age levels tested. The results are presented in Table 1.

It is apparent that the reliability of the 20-item moral judgment test, and also of the subscales, was not as high as that usually attained in educational tests. Subscale reliabilities were sometimes higher than the reliability of the whole scale, in-

[1]Reliability refers to the consistency of the responses of individuals to the test. In this case, the person's answers to different questions in each subscale are being compared to see if they are consistent—Ed.

dicating that the various areas of moral judgment are not as closely knit as one would expect on the basis of Piaget's discussion. Hoyt states that ". . . it is possible to have higher reliability for a subscale than for scores obtained by adding several subscales. This seems to occur when the subscales have zero, negative, or low positive intercorrelations."[2] Statistically, the relatively low reliability values of the subscales and of the whole scale set definite limits to the size of the interrelations that can appear among the so-called varieties or areas of moral judgment.

Intercorrelations of Responses to Moral Judgment Questions

Responses to each item on the 20-item test were correlated with responses to every other item at each of the four age levels—a total of 760 correlations. Among this many correlations, where no relation of any sort actually existed, one would expect to find, by chance, 38 values significant at the .05 level and beyond. There actually were 294 positive correlations and 79 negative correlations significant at or beyond the .05 level of confidence. It seems clear that responses to moral judgment questions were positively correlated with one another to a far greater extent than one could expect by chance. A larger number of negative correlations were obtained than one could expect by chance. Some questions that seem, logically, to be positively related to other questions were apparently negatively correlated with other questions at one or more grade levels if judged in terms of the responses obtained.

[2]Personal communication (1958).

TABLE 1.   Reliability of moral judgment questions.*

	Grade 5	Grade 7	Grade 9	Grade 11
Total test	.61	.59	.55	.56
Immanent justice	.66	.68	.67	.67
Moral realism	.58	.49	.30	.38
Retribution vs. restitution	.45	.17	.28	.15
Efficacy of severe punishment	.60	.59	.50	.44
Communicable responsibility	.32	.46	.39	.26

*Reliability calculated through the use of Hoyt's (1952) analysis of variance method (rational equivalence) of estimating test reliability.

Correlations of Responses within Moral Judgment Areas

Questions 1, 6, 11, and 16 of the moral judgment test measured immanent justice; 2, 7, 12, and 17, moral realism; 3, 8, 13, and 18, retribution vs. restitutive punishment; 4, 9, 14, and 19, the efficacy of severe punishment; and 5, 10, 15, and 20, communicable responsibility. . . .

Of the correlations of responses within areas of moral judgment . . . 102 out of 120 correlations were positive and significant. The area of immanent justice showed higher correlations between responses than other areas, but correlations in all areas of moral judgment were such that one is justified in talking about consistency within areas of moral judgment, especially when considering the reliability of the test items. Items 1 and 4 seemed less closely related to their respective areas of moral judgment than were most items. Item 20, an attempt to push the rejection of communicable responsibility to its logical extreme, was more often negatively than positively correlated to other items dealing with this aspect of

moral judgment in grades 5 and 11; on the other hand, it was more often positively correlated with other items in this area in grades 7 and 9. It seems that one can legitimately discuss areas of moral judgment, that these areas exist, since responses to the different questions within areas were almost always correlated positively and significantly with one another.

Correlations of Responses between Moral Judgment Areas

A more basic problem is the determination of whether there is any consistent correlation between the type of response made in one area of moral judgment and responses made in each of the other areas of moral judgment. It is implicit in Piaget's theory (1950, pp. 106–107) that response tendencies in the various areas of moral judgment (excluding communicable responsibility) are positively related to one another. This is a testable proposition. The writer, in dealing with this problem by correlating responses in the various moral judgment areas with one another, used

TABLE 2.   Correlations of responses between moral judgment areas.

	Moral realism	Retribution vs. restitution	Efficacy of severe punishment	Communicable responsibility
Immanent justice				
Grade 5	.12	.27†	.09	.13
Grade 7	.29†	.18*	.17	.06
Grade 9	.16*	.09	.14	.12
Grade 11	.07	.19*	.27†	.09
Moral realism				
Grade 5		.23*	.34†	.30†
Grade 7		.33†	.32†	.18*
Grade 9		.20*	.33†	.15
Grade 11		.16	.10	.00
Retribution vs. restitution				
Grade 5			.18*	.16
Grade 7			.33†	.18*
Grade 9			.30†	.00
Grade 11			.22*	.09
Efficacy of severe punishment				
Grade 5				.21*
Grade 7				.06
Grade 9				.08
Grade 11				.04

*Significant at the .05 level.
†Significant at the .01 level.

the statistic epsilon (ϵ) developed by Kelly and discussed by Peters and Van Voorhis (1940, pp. 316–329), to express the degree of association or correlation. . . . The correlations of response tendencies between moral judgment areas are presented in Table 2.

Twenty of the 40 correlations between areas of moral judgment were significant. The statistic, epsilon, does not give an indication of the direction of the relationship found, but this can be determined through the computation of column means. All of the significant correlations shown in Table 2 were positive, except for the correlation of moral realism with communicable responsibility at grade 7, where the relation was negative, and the correlation of immanent justice with efficacy of severe punishment at grade 11, where the relation was curvilinear. In this curvilinear relation, both highly mature and highly immature sets of responses to the immanent justice question were positively related to mature responses to questions concerning the efficacy of severe punishment.

The intercorrelations among areas of moral judgment seem to show that mature moral judgments in the areas of moral realism, retribution vs. restitution, and efficacy of severe punishment were the most closely correlated with one another, that responses to questions concerning immanent justice were somewhat less closely correlated to responses in other areas of moral judgment, and that belief or nonbelief in communicable responsibility was even less closely related to other aspects of moral judgment.

Relation of Moral Judgment Responses to Antecedent Conditions

Piaget suggests that changes from immature to mature moral judgment result from changes in the amount of adult constraint and peer group cooperation experienced by the child and from qualitative changes in the child's method of thought. The child's level of development, for Piaget, is best predicted from chronological age. Most students of moral judgment since Piaget have found intelligence and social class to be related to the type of moral judgment made by the child. All of these variables, except peer cooperation, were measured in this study. Each significant relation between these variables and moral judgment responses is presented in Table 3.

From the data in Table 3 it seems that IQ and parental occupation were more closely related to moral judgment than were the other variables studied in the areas of moral realism, retribution vs. restitution, and the efficacy of severe punishment. In general, one can say that brightness, represented by IQ, was more closely related to the type of moral judgment used in those three areas listed above than was any of the other variables measured in this study. Since parent's occupation and child's IQ were themselves positively correlated, it may well be that the correlations found between parent's occupation and the moral judgment of the child were merely reflections of differences due, basically, to IQ, rather than to cultural differences denoted by occupational level. The results of a determination of class differences in parental attitudes, discussed later in this study, seem to favor this position.

Immanent justice and communicable responsibility responses were less often significantly related to the antecedent conditions of sex, parental occupation and IQ than were judgments concerning moral realism, retribution vs. restitution, and the efficacy of severe punishment. It may be that the higher degree of association between responses to moral judgment questions in the latter three areas is a result of the fact that response tendencies in these areas were related to the same antecedent conditions.

Chronological age was positively and significantly related in all areas of moral judgment—even "communicable responsibility" where, from Piaget's analysis, one would expect a negative relation in this age range. Age change was by no means saltatory, however—no sudden shifts in response tendencies were evident.

Out of 45 correlations of abstractness with moral judgment, six were significant. If abstractness is indicative of a freedom from egocentricity, one would expect high abstractness scores to be positively related to mature moral judgment. Five of the six significant correlations were in this di-

TABLE 3. Significant correlations of antecedent factors with moral judgment responses.

Factor	Immanent justice	Moral realism	Retribution vs. restitution	Efficacy of severe punishment	Communicable responsibility
IQ	.17(9)*	.34(5)*	.31(5)*	.24(5)*	
	.23(11)†	.36(7)*	.42(7)*	.30(7)*	
		.31(9)*	.23(9)*	.30(9)*	
		.20(11)*			
Parent occupation	.21(9)‡	.21(7)‡	.23(5)‡	.18(5)‡	
	.22(11)‡	.17(9)‡	.23(7)‡		
		.16(11)‡			
Age (entire sample combined)	.35§	.35§	.25§	.26§	.12§
Abstractness	.29(9)¶	.25(7)¶	.26(7)¶	.34(9)¶	
	.26(11)¶			.46(11)‖	
Concreteness		.31(11)**		.36(7)††	.38(9)††
Parent attitudes					
Ignoringness	.31(9)§§		.39(7)‡‡		.32(7)‡‡
Possessiveness	.53(11)§§				.32(7)‡‡
					.52(11)‡‡
Dominativeness				.44(11)§§	.40(11)‡‡
Extremeness of point of view	.32(11)§§			.40(9)§§	.29(7)§§
					.40(11)§§

Note.–Grade level at which correlation was found is indicated in parentheses following each coefficient.
  *High IQ positively related to mature judgment.
  †IQ related to moral judgment curvilinearly; highest and lowest IQ made most mature responses.
  ‡Higher parental occupation positively related to mature moral judgments.
  §Increasing age positively related to mature moral judgments.
  ¶High abstractness positively related to mature moral judgments.
  ‖High abstractness negatively related to mature moral judgments.
  **High concreteness negatively related to mature moral judgments.
  ††High concreteness positively related to mature moral judgments.
  ‡‡High amounts of the parent attitude positively related to mature moral judgments.
  §§High amounts of the parent attitude negatively related to mature moral judgments.

rection. Only three of the 45 correlations of concreteness with moral judgment were significant. If concreteness is a manifestation of egocentricity, concreteness should be negatively correlated with mature moral judgment. The reverse held true in two of the three significant correlations.

If one scored the parent attitude scale in terms of the amount of ignoringness, possessiveness, and dominance expressed by the parents, one would expect, from Piaget's theory, to obtain the following results: belief in immanent justice, moral realism, retribution and expiation, as opposed to restitution or reciprocity, and the efficacy of severe punishment are all learned from the parents. If this is so, possessiveness and dominativeness should be positively correlated and ignoringness negatively correlated with acceptance of these beliefs. On the other hand, acceptance of communicable responsibility is usually learned from the peer group, which uses communicable responsibility as an evidence of group solidarity. Here it would seem probable that the ignored child, more free to interact with peers, should show less mature moral judgment than the child of possessive or dominative parents who presumably would have somewhat fewer peer group contacts. Of the 45 correlations of the parent attitudes of expressed dominativeness, possessiveness, and ignoringness with the level of the child's moral judgment, eight were significant, seven of them in the direction predicted from the above discussion.

Extremeness of point of view on the part of the parent was correlated more frequently with the moral judgment of the child than were Shoben's subscales of ignoringness, possessiveness, or dominativeness. Extremeness of point of view was not significantly correlated with the type of parental response to any of the three subscales; there was no significant correlation, for instance, between the amount of dominativeness expressed and the number of extreme positions taken—so that the parent's extremeness of point of view seems, in its own right, to be a significant factor in relation to the child's level of moral judgment. The parents who more frequently take extreme points of view tended to have children who are immature in their moral judgment.

The existing significant correlations of parent attitude to moral judgment were not distributed randomly, but occurred most frequently in the areas of immanent justice and communicable responsibility, the very areas that showed few significant correlations with such variables as intelligence and parental occupation.

One can ask whether parent attitudes as measured here may be merely a reflection or indirect measure of social class differences in approach, either to childrearing or to answering questionnaires. The writer attempted to determine whether this might be the case. The responding parents had already been categorized into occupational groups. They were now divided into two larger groupings, those in classes I to III and those in classes V to VII of the Minnesota Occupational Scale. Their responses were divided into those above and below the median in amount of expressed dominativeness, possessiveness, and ignoringness and in the number of extreme points of view. A comparison of the attitudes of these two groups allows one to determine whether the obtained correlations between parent attitudes and moral judgment are actually a result of some occupational group bias in responses. An analysis of the data indicates that this was not the case. There were no significant differences in attitude between the two groups. Parent attitudes, as expressed on the Shoben scale, were not significantly related to parental occupation as measured by the Minnesota Occupational Scale.

DISCUSSION

The primary purpose of this study was to determine the amount of association between responses to moral judgment questions.

The reliability of the test items, as a whole scale, seems to indicate in itself that responses concerning various aspects of moral judgment are related to one another empirically as well as logically, but not to as large an extent as one would expect from Piaget's analysis. Reliability did not change appreciably from one age to another. This seems to indicate (as do the actual correlations between responses) that moral judgment remains consistent in the amount of association from one area to another, contrary to what one might expect.

The reliability of subscales measuring specific areas of moral judgment was often somewhat higher than that of the total scale, suggesting a low association between areas but a higher association within areas. The reliability of the subscales seems rather high, in general, since each subscale consisted of only four items. Although high, when looked at in this fashion, subscale reliability was still so low that one cannot expect inter- and intra-moral judgment area correlations to be as high as they might be with a more reliable test. It should be noted, however, that the whole scale reliability of this test is equal to that of some widely used measuring devices, e.g., the Rorschach Test (see Stagner, 1948). . . .

The correlations of responses within moral judgment areas, like the reliability figures, seem to argue for quite considerable consistency within each area. This consistency may be due, in a large part, to the common correlations of items within an area to such things as intelligence and socioeconomic differences.

The results tend to support the idea that there is at least some consistency in response between areas. The correlations between responses in the five different areas of moral judgment indicate that judgments made regarding moral realism, retribution and expiation vs. restitution and reciprocity, and the efficacy of severe punishment were often significantly related to one another. Immanent justice was somewhat less frequently correlated positively and significantly with these three areas, though certainly there were far more positive and significant correlations than one would expect by chance. Communicable responsibility was less closely correlated with other areas of moral judgment; in fact, one of the four significant correlations of communicable responsibility with other areas of moral judgment was negative. The fact that the data were obtained separately at each of four age levels with quite similar results lends support through replication to the findings discussed above.

Piaget assumes, as a result of his logical analysis and of his findings, that response tendencies are similar in all areas of moral judgment (except for communicable responsibility), that there is what we would now call a general factor of moral judgment. The findings above were, in general, the results one would expect on the basis of Piaget's theoretical discussion, except that responses to questions involving communicable responsibility seemed largely unrelated, rather than negatively related, to responses in the other four moral judgment areas. With this exception the correlations were in the expected direction but were considerably lower than one would expect from Piaget's own work. The reliability data, as well as the interarea correlations of the responses, seem to show that what might be called a general factor of moral judgment was present, but with a rather low degree of saturation.

The second purpose of this study was to determine the relation of a number of variables to the type of moral judgment used by the subjects. A number of antecedent conditions were investigated. Some of these factors, such as sex, IQ, and parent occupation were touched on peripherally in Piaget's investigation and discussion of moral judgment. Other factors were discussed more comprehensively by Piaget. These were age (as a sign or indicator of the condition of the organism with reference to the next two factors, rather than a direct cause of change), egocentricity (which the writer attempted to measure, admittedly indirectly, through a test of abstractness-concreteness), and adult constraint. The latter two factors, interacting with one another and with peer group cooperation, were believed by Piaget to be directly causal in producing changes in beliefs concerning moral judgment. . . .

Of those variables that were not discussed to any extent by Piaget, IQ was clearly the most significant in its relation to responses concerning

moral realism, retribution and expiation vs. restitution and reciprocity, and the efficacy of severe punishment. Sex of subjects and parent occupation of subjects also showed a considerable number of significant correlations with responses in these three moral judgment areas. Immanent justice seemed less closely related, and communicable responsibility seemed essentially unrelated to this group of variables.

Age was correlated with the type of response made in all five areas. One would expect on the basis of Piaget's work that increasing age is positively correlated with more mature moral judgment in all areas except that of communicable responsibility, where an increase in peer group solidarity might well cause a greater frequency of immature responses as age increased. Contrary to Piaget's theory, even communicable responsibility showed a very low but significant positive correlation between age and mature moral judgment. Within the age groups studied there was certainly no evidence for any large, sudden change in beliefs concerning moral judgment.

Parent attitudes, as expressed on questionnaire responses, most often showed significant correlations with responses to questions concerning communicable responsibility and immanent justice. These are the very areas that were less closely correlated with the first group of antecedent conditions. Abstractness and concreteness were related to moral judgment in the direction predicted by Piaget, but perhaps because abstractness is itself related to IQ. None of these variables was closely and consistently related to moral judgment to the extent that it accounted for the major portion of the variance, perhaps because the test of moral judgment was itself less reliable than one would desire.

This writer's general conclusions regarding these antecedent conditions are that IQ and chronological age were the variables most closely correlated to the type of response made with reference to moral realism, retribution and expiation vs. restitution and reciprocity, and the efficacy of severe punishment. Age and to some extent, IQ and parent attitudes, seemed to be correlated with responses to immanent justice items.

Only parent attitude items seemed correlated to any extent with type of response made to questions involving communicable responsibility. . . .

REFERENCES

Abel, T. M. Moral judgments among subnormals. *Journal of Abnormal and Social Psychology,* 1941, **36**, 378–392.

Dennis, W. Animism and related tendencies in Hopi children. *Journal of Abnormal and Social Psychology,* 1943, **38**, 21–37.

Dennis, W. Animistic thinking among college and university students. *Scientific Monthly,* 1953, **76**, 247–250.

Gorham, D. R. *Clinical manual for the proverbs test.* Psychological Test Specialists, 1956.

Gorham, D. R. A proverbs test for clinical and experimental use. *Psychological Reports,* 1956, Monographed Supplement No. 1.

Guilford, J. P. *Psychometric methods.* New York: McGraw-Hill, 1954.

Harrower, M. R. Social status and the moral development of the child. *British Journal of Educational Psychology,* 1934, **4**, 75–95.

Hoyt, C. R. An analysis of variance method of estimating test reliability. *Educational and Psychological Measurement,* 1952, **12**, 756–758.

Isaacs, S. *Intellectual growth in young children.* New York: Harcourt, 1930.

Lerner, E. *Constraint areas and the moral judgment of the child.* Kenosha, Wis.: Banta, 1937.

Lerner, E. The problem of perspective in moral reasoning. *American Journal of Sociology,* 1937, **43**, 249–269.

Liu, Ching-Ho. The influence of cultural background on the moral judgment of children. Unpublished doctoral dissertation, Columbia University, 1950.

MacRae, D., Jr. The development of moral judgment in children. Unpublished doctoral dissertation, Harvard University, 1950.

Medinnus, G. R. An investigation of Piaget's concept of the development of moral judgment in six to twelve year old children from lower socioeconomic class. Unpublished doctoral dissertation, University of Minnesota, 1957.

Minnesota scale for paternal occupations. Minneapolis: Univ. of Minnesota Press, 1950.

Peters, C. C., and Van Voorhis, W. R. *Statistical procedures and their mathematical bases.* New York: McGraw-Hill, 1940.

Piaget, J. *The moral judgment of the child.* New York: Harcourt, 1932.

Piaget, J. *The psychology of intelligence.* New York: Harcourt, 1950.

Shoben, E. J., Jr. The assessment of parental attitudes in relation to child adjustment. *Genetic Psychology Monographs,* 1949, **39**, 101–148.

Stagner, R. *Psychology of personality.* New York: McGraw-Hill, 1948.

ARTICLE 6

The Child as a Moral Philosopher

Lawrence Kohlberg

How can one study morality? Current trends in the fields of ethics, linguistics, anthropology and cognitive psychology have suggested a new approach which seems to avoid the morass of semantical confusions, value-bias and cultural relativity in which the psychoanalytic and semantic approaches to morality have foundered. New scholarship in all these fields is now focusing upon structures, forms and relationships that seem to be common to all societies and all languages rather than upon the features that make particular languages or cultures different.

For 12 years, my colleagues and I studied the same group of 75 boys, following their development at three-year intervals from early adolescence through young manhood. At the start of the study, the boys were aged 10 to 16. We have now followed them through to ages 22 to 28. In addition, I have explored moral development in other cultures—Great Britain, Canada, Taiwan, Mexico and Turkey.

Inspired by Jean Piaget's pioneering effort to apply a structural approach to moral development, I have gradually elaborated over the years of my study a typological scheme describing general structures and forms of moral thought which can be defined independently of the specific content of particular moral decisions or actions.

The typology contains three distinct levels of moral thinking, and within each of these levels distinguishes two related stages. These levels and stages may be considered separate moral philosophies, distinct views of the socio-moral world.

Reprinted from *Psychology Today* Magazine, September, 1968. Copyright © Communications/Research/Machines, Inc.

We can speak of the child as having his own morality or series of moralities. Adults seldom listen to children's moralizing. If a child throws back a few adult cliches and behaves himself, most parents—and many anthropologists and psychologists as well—think that the child has adopted or internalized the appropriate parental standards.

Actually, as soon as we talk with children about morality, we find that they have many ways of making judgments which are not "internalized" from the outside, and which do not come in any direct and obvious way from parents, teachers or even peers.

MORAL LEVELS

The *preconventional* level is the first of three levels of moral thinking; the second level is *conventional,* and the third *postconventional* or autonomous. While the preconventional child is often "well-behaved" and is responsive to cultural labels of good and bad, he interprets these labels in terms of their physical consequences (punishment, reward, exchange of favors) or in terms of the physical power of those who enunciate the rules and labels of good and bad.

This level is usually occupied by children aged four to 10, a fact long known to sensitive observers of children. The capacity of "properly behaved" children of this age to engage in cruel behavior when there are holes in the power structure is sometimes noted as tragic (*Lord of the Flies, High Wind in Jamaica*), sometimes as comic (Lucy in *Peanuts*).

The second or *conventional* level also can be described as conformist, but that is perhaps too smug a term. Maintaining the expectations and rules of the individual's family, group or nation is perceived as valuable in its own right. There is a concern not only with *conforming* to the individual's social order but in *maintaining,* supporting and justifying this order.

The *postconventional* level is characterized by a major thrust toward autonomous moral principles which have validity and application apart from authority of the groups or persons who hold them and apart from the individual's identification with those persons or groups.

MORAL STAGES

Within each of these three levels there are two discernible stages. At the preconventional level we have:

Stage 1: Orientation toward punishment and unquestioning deference to superior power. The physical consequences of action regardless of their human meaning or value determine its goodness or badness.

Stage 2: Right action consists of that which instrumentally satisfies one's own needs and occasionally the needs of others. Human relations are viewed in terms like those of the marketplace. Elements of fairness, of reciprocity and equal sharing are present, but they are always interpreted in a physical, pragmatic way. Reciprocity is a matter of "you scratch my back and I'll scratch yours," not of loyalty, gratitude or justice.

And at the conventional level we have:

Stage 3: Good-boy—good-girl orientation. Good behavior is that which pleases or helps others and is approved by them. There is much conformity to stereotypical images of what is majority or "natural" behavior. Behavior is often judged by intention—"he means well" becomes important for the first time, and is overused, as by Charlie Brown in *Peanuts.* One seeks approval by being "nice."

Stage 4: Orientation toward authority, fixed rules and the maintenance of the social order. Right behavior consists of doing one's duty, showing respect for authority and maintaining the given social order for its own sake. One earns respect by performing dutifully.

At the postconventional level, we have:

Stage 5: A social-contract orientation, generally with legalistic and utilitarian overtones. Right action tends to be defined in terms of general rights and in terms of standards which have been critically examined and agreed upon by the whole society. There is a clear awareness of the relativism of personal values and opinions and a corresponding emphasis upon procedural rules for reaching consensus. Aside from what is constitutionally and democratically agreed upon, right or wrong is a matter of personal "values" and "opinions." The result is an emphasis upon the "legal point of view," but with an emphasis upon the possibility of *changing* law in terms of rational considerations of social utility, rather than freezing it in the terms of Stage 4 "law and order." Outside the legal realm, free agreement and contract are the binding elements of obligation. This is the "official" morality of American government, and finds its ground in the thought of the writers of the Constitution.

Stage 6: Orientation toward the decisions of conscience and toward self-chosen *ethical principles* appealing to logical comprehensiveness, universality and consistency. These principles are abstract and ethical (the Golden Rule, the categorical imperative); they are not concrete moral rules like the Ten Commandments. Instead, they are universal principles of *justice,* of the *reciprocity* and *equality* of human rights, and of respect for the dignity of human beings as *individual persons.*

UP TO NOW

In the past, when psychologists tried to answer the question asked of Socrates by Meno, "Is virtue something that can be taught (by rational discussion), or does it come by practice, or is it a natural inborn attitude?" their answers usually have been dictated, not by research findings on children's moral character, but by their general theoretical convictions.

Behavior theorists have said that virtue is behavior acquired according to their favorite general principles of learning. Freudians have claimed that virtue is superego-identification with parents generated by a proper balance of love and authority in family relations.

The American psychologists who have actually studied children's morality have tried to start with a set of labels—the "virtues" and "vices," the "traits" of good and bad character found in ordinary language. The earliest major psychological study of moral character, that of Hugh Hartshorne and Mark May in 1928–1930, focused on a bag of virtues including honesty, service (altruism or generosity), and self-control. To their dismay, they found that there were *no* character traits, psychological dispositions or entities which corresponded to words like honesty, service or self-control.

Regarding honesty, for instance, they found that almost everyone cheats some of the time, and that if a person cheats in one situation, it doesn't mean that he *will* or *won't* in another. In other words, it is not an identifiable character trait, *dishonesty*, that makes a child cheat in a given situation. These early researchers also found that people who cheat express as much or even more moral disapproval of cheating as those who do not cheat.

What Hartshorne and May found out about their bag of virtues is equally upsetting to the somewhat more psychological-sounding names introduced by psychoanalytic psychology: "superego-strength," "resistance to temptation," "strength of conscience," and the like. When recent researchers attempt to measure such traits in individuals, they have been forced to use Hartshorne and May's old tests of honesty and self-control and they get exactly the same results— "superego strength" in one situation predicts little to "superego strength" in another. That is, virtue-words like honesty (or superego-strength) point to certain behaviors with approval, but give us no guide to understanding them.

So far as one can extract some generalized personality factor from children's performance on tests of honesty or resistance to temptation, it is a factor of ego-strength or ego-control, which always involves non-moral capacities like the ca-

pacity to maintain attention, intelligent-task performance, and the ability to delay response. "Ego-strength" (called "will" in earlier days) has something to do with moral action, but it does not take us to the core of morality or to the definition of virtue. Obviously enough, many of the greatest evil-doers in history have been men of strong wills, men strongly pursuing immoral goals.

MORAL REASONS

In our research, we have found definite and universal levels of development in moral thought. In our study of 75 American boys from early adolescence on, these youths were presented with hypothetical moral dilemmas, all deliberately philosophical, some of them found in medieval works of casuistry.

On the basis of their reasoning about these dilemmas at a given age, each boy's stage of thought could be determined for each of 25 basic moral concepts or aspects. One such aspect, for instance, is "Motive Given for Rule Obedience or Moral Action." In this instance, the six stages look like this:

1. Obey rules to avoid punishment.
2. Conform to obtain rewards, have favors returned, and so on.
3. Conform to avoid disapproval, dislike by others.
4. Conform to avoid censure by legitimate authorities and resultant guilt.
5. Conform to maintain the respect of the impartial spectator judging in terms of community welfare.
6. Conform to avoid self-condemnation.

In another of these 25 moral aspects, the value of human life, the six stages can be defined thus:

1. The value of a human life is confused with the value of physical objects and is based on the social status or physical attributes of its possessor.
2. The value of a human life is seen as instrumental to the satisfaction of the needs of its possessor or of other persons.
3. The value of a human life is based on the empathy and affection of family members and others toward its possessor.

4. Life is conceived as sacred in terms of its place in a categorical moral or religious order of rights and duties.

5. Life is valued both in terms of its relation to community welfare and in terms of life being a universal human right.

6. Belief in the sacredness of human life as representing a universal human value of respect for the individual.

I have called this scheme a typology. This is because about 50 percent of most people's thinking will be at a single stage, regardless of the moral dilemma involved. We call our types *stages* because they seem to represent an *invariant developmental sequence.* "True" stages come one at a time and always in the same order.

All movement is forward in sequence, and does not skip steps. Children may move through these stages at varying speeds, of course, and may be found half in and half out of a particular stage. An individual may stop at any given stage and at any age, but if he continues to move, he must move in accord with these steps. Moral reasoning of the conventional or Stage 3-4 kind never occurs before the preconventional Stage-1 and Stage-2 thought has taken place. No adult in Stage 4 has gone through Stage 6, but all Stage-6 adults have gone at least through 4.

While the evidence is not complete, my study strongly suggests that moral change fits the stage pattern just described. (The major uncertainty is whether all Stage 6's go through Stage 5 or whether these are two alternate mature orientations.)

HOW VALUES CHANGE

As a single example of our findings of stage-sequence, take the progress of two boys on the aspect "The Value of Human Life." The first boy, Tommy, is asked: "Is it better to save the life of one important person or a lot of unimportant people?" At age 10, he answers: "all the people that aren't important because one man just has one house, maybe a lot of furniture, but a whole bunch of people have an awful lot of furniture and some of these poor people might have a lot of money and it doesn't look it."

Clearly Tommy is in Stage 1: he confuses the value of a human being with the value of the property he possesses. Three years later (age 13) Tommy's conceptions of life's value are most clearly elicited by the question "Should the doctor 'mercy kill' a fatally ill woman requesting death because of her pain?" He answers: "Maybe it would be good to put her out of her pain. She'd be better off that way. But the husband wouldn't want it. It's not like an animal. If a pet dies you can get along without it—it isn't something you really need. Well, you can get a new wife, but it's not really the same."

Here his answer is Stage 2: the value of the woman's life is partly contingent on its hedonistic value to the wife herself but even more contingent on its instrumental value to her husband, who can't replace her as easily as he can a pet.

Three years later still (age 16) Tommy's conception of life's value is elicited by the same question, to which he replies: "It might be best for her, but her husband—it's a human life—not like an animal; it just doesn't have the same relationship that a human being does to a family. You can become attached to a dog, but nothing like a human you know."

Now Tommy has moved from a Stage-2 instrumental view of the woman's value to a Stage-3 view based on the husband's distinctively human empathy and love for someone in his family. Equally clearly, it lacks any basis for a universal human value of the woman's life, which would hold if she had no husband or if her husband didn't love her. Tommy, then, has moved step by step through three stages during the ages 10–16. Tommy, though bright (I.Q. 120), is a slow developer in moral judgment. Let us take another boy, Richard, to show us sequential movement through the remaining three steps.

At age 13, Richard said about the mercy-killing: "If she requests it, it's really up to her. She is in such terrible pain, just the same as people are always putting animals out of their pain," and in general showed a mixture of Stage-2 and Stage-3 responses concerning the value of life. At 16, he said: "I don't know. In one way, it's murder; it's not a right or privilege of man to decide who shall live and who should die. God put life into everybody on earth and you're taking away something from that person that came directly from God, and you're destroying something that is very sacred. It's in a way part of God and it's almost destroying a part of God when you kill a person. There's something of God in everyone."

Here Richard clearly displays a Stage-4 concept of life as sacred in terms of its place in a categorical moral or religious order. The value of human life is universal; it is true for all humans. It is still, however, dependent on something else, upon respect for God and God's authority; it is not an autonomous human value. Presumably if God told Richard to murder, as God commanded Abraham to murder Isaac, he would do so.

At age 20, Richard said to the same question: "There are more and more people in the medical profession to think it is a hardship on everyone— the person, the family—when you know they are going to die. When a person is kept alive by an artificial lung or kidney it's more like being a vegetable than being a human. If it's her own choice, I think there are certain rights and privileges that go along with being a human being. I am a human being and have certain desires for life and I think everybody else does too. You have a world of which you are the center, and everybody else does too and in that sense we're all equal."

Richard's response is clearly Stage 5, in that the value of life is defined in terms of equal and universal human rights in a context of relativity ("You have a world of which you are the center and in that sense we're all equal"), and of concern for utility or welfare consequences.

THE FINAL STEP

At age 24, Richard says: "A human life takes precedence over any other moral or legal value, whoever it is. A human life has inherent value whether or not it is valued by a particular individual. The worth of the individual human being is central where the principles of justice and love are normative for all human relationships."

This young man is at Stage 6 in seeing the value of human life as absolute in representing a univer-

sal and equal respect for the human as an individual. He has moved step by step through a sequence culminating in a definition of human life as centrally valuable rather than derived from or dependent on social or divine authority.

In a genuine and culturally universal sense, these steps lead toward an increased *morality* of value judgment, where morality is considered as a form of judging, as it has been in a philosophic tradition running from the analyses of Kant to those of the modern analytic or "ordinary language" philosophers. The person at Stage 6 has disentangled his judgments of—or language about—human life from status and property values (Stage 1), from its uses to others (Stage 2), from interpersonal affection (Stage 3), and so on; he has a means of moral judgment that is universal and impersonal. The Stage-6 person's answers use moral words like "duty" or "morally right," and he uses them in a way implying universality, ideals, impersonality: He thinks and speaks in phrases like "regardless of who it was," or ". . . I would do it in spite of punishment."

ACROSS CULTURES

When I first decided to explore moral development in other cultures, I was told by anthropologist friends that I would have to throw away my culture-bound moral concepts and stories and start from scratch learning a whole new set of values for each new culture. My first try consisted of a brace of villages, one Atayal (Malaysian aboriginal) and the other Taiwanese.

My guide was a young Chinese ethnographer who had written an account of the moral and religious patterns of the Atayal and Taiwanese villages. Taiwanese boys in the 10–13 age group were asked about a story involving theft of food. A man's wife is starving to death but the store owner won't give the man any food unless he can pay, which he can't. Should he break in and steal some food? Why? Many of the boys said, "He should steal the food for his wife because if she dies he'll have to pay for her funeral and that costs a lot."

My guide was amused by these responses, but

I was relieved: they were of course "classic" Stage-2 responses. In the Atayal village, funerals weren't such a big thing, so the Stage-2 boys would say "He should steal the food because he needs his wife to cook for him."

This means that we need to consult our anthropologists to know what content a Stage-2 child will include in his instrumental exchange calculations, or what a Stage-4 adult will identify as the proper social order. But one certainly doesn't have to start from scratch. What made my guide laugh was the difference in form between the children's Stage-2 thought and his own, a difference definable independently of particular cultures.

Illustrations number 1 and number 2 indicate the cultural universality of the sequence of stages which we have found. Illustration number 1 presents the age trends for middle-class urban

boys in the U.S., Taiwan and Mexico. At age 10 in each country, the order of use of each stage is the same as the order of its difficulty or maturity.

In the United States, by age 16 the order is the reverse, from the highest to the lowest, except that Stage 6 is still little-used. At age 13, the good-boy, middle stage (Stage 3), is not used.

The results in Mexico and Taiwan are the same, except that development is a little slower. The most conspicuous feature is that at the age of 16, Stage-5 thinking is much more salient in the United States than in Mexico or Taiwan. Nevertheless, it *is* present in the other countries, so we know that this is not purely an American democratic construct.

Illustration 2 shows strikingly similar results from two isolated villages, one in Yucatan, one in Turkey. While conventional moral thought increases steadily from ages 10 to 16 it still has not

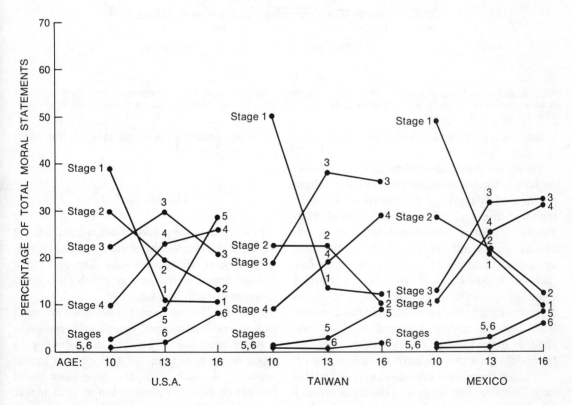

FIGURE 1. Middle-class urban boys in the U.S., Taiwan, and Mexico. At age 10 the stages are used according to difficulty. At age 13, Stage 3 is most used by all three groups. At age 16, U.S. boys have reversed the order of age 10 stages (with the exception of 6). In Taiwan and Mexico, conventional (3-4) stages prevail at age 16, with Stage 5 also little used.

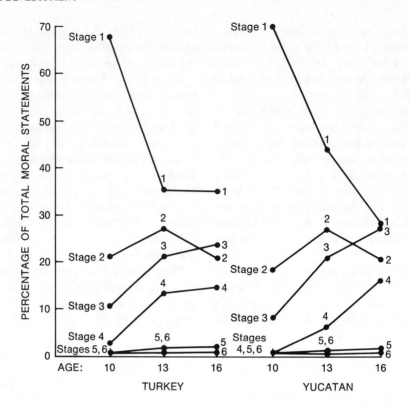

FIGURE 2. Two isolated villages, one in Turkey, the other in Yucatan, show similar patterns in moral thinking. There is no reversal of order, and preconventional (1-2) thought does not gain a clear ascendency over conventional stages at age 16.

achieved a clear ascendency over preconventional thought.

Trends for lower-class urban groups are intermediate in the rate of development between those for the middle-class and for the village boys. In the three divergent cultures that I studied, middle-class children were found to be more advanced in moral judgment than matched lower-class children. This was not due to the fact that the middle-class children heavily favored some one type of thought which could be seen as corresponding to the prevailing middle-class pattern. Instead, middle-class and working-class children move through the same sequences, but the middle-class children move faster and farther.

This sequence is not dependent upon a particular religion, or any religion in the usual sense. I found no important differences in the development of moral thinking among Catholics, Protestants, Jews, Buddhists, Moslems and atheists.

Religious values seem to go through the same stages as all other values.

TRADING UP

In summary, the nature of our sequence is not significantly affected by widely varying social, cultural or religious conditions. The only thing that is affected is the *rate* at which individuals progress through this sequence.

Why should there be such a universal invariant sequence of development? In answering this question, we need first to analyze these developing social concepts in terms of their internal logical structure. At each stage, the same basic moral concept or aspect is defined, but at each higher stage this definition is more differentiated, more integrated, and more general or universal. When one's concept of human life moves from Stage 1 to Stage 2 the value of life becomes more differentiated from the value of property, more integrated (the value of life enters an organizational hierarchy where it is "higher" than property so that one steals property in order to save life) and more universalized (the life of any sentient being is valuable regardless of status or property). The same advance is true at each stage in the hierarchy. Each step of development then is a better cognitive organization than the one before it, one which takes account of everything present in the previous stage, but making new distinctions and organizing them into a more comprehensive or more equilibrated structure. The fact that this is the case has been demonstrated by a series of studies indicating that children and adolescents comprehend all stages up to their own, but not more than one stage beyond their own. And importantly, *they prefer this next stage.*

We have conducted experimental moral discussion classes which show that the child at an earlier stage of development tends to move forward when confronted by the views of a child one stage further along. In an argument between a Stage-3 and Stage-4 child, the child in the third stage tends to move toward or into Stage 4, while the Stage-4 child understands but does not accept the arguments of the Stage-3 child.

Moral thought, then, seems to behave like all other kinds of thought. Progress through the moral levels and stages is characterized by increasing differentiation and increasing integration, and hence is the same kind of progress that scientific theory represents. Like acceptable scientific theory—or like *any* theory or structure of knowledge—moral thought may be considered partially to generate its own data as it goes along, or at least to expand so as to contain in a balanced self-consistent way a wider and wider experiential field. The raw data in the case of our ethical philosophies may be considered as conflicts between roles, or values, or as the social order in which men live.

THE ROLE OF SOCIETY

The social worlds of all men seem to contain the same basic structures. All the societies we

have studied have the same basic institutions—family, economy, law, government. In addition, however, all societies are alike because they *are* societies—systems of defined complementary roles. In order to *play* a social role in the family, school or society, the child must implicitly take the role of others toward himself and toward others in the group. These role-taking tendencies form the basis of all social institutions. They represent various patternings of shared or complementary expectations.

In the preconventional and conventional levels (Stages 1–4), moral content or value is largely accidental or culture-bound. Anything from "honesty" to "courage in battle" can be the central value. But in the higher postconventional levels, Socrates, Lincoln, Thoreau and Martin Luther King tend to speak without confusion of tongues, as it were. This is because the ideal principles of any social structure are basically alike, if only because there simply aren't that many principles which are articulate, comprehensive and integrated enough to be satisfying to the human intellect. And most of these principles have gone by the name of justice.

Behavioristic psychology and psychoanalysis have always upheld the Philistine view that fine moral words are one thing and moral deeds another. Morally mature reasoning is quite a different matter, and does not really depend on "fine words." The man who understands justice is more likely to practice it.

In our studies, we have found that youths who understand justice act more justly, and the man who understands justice helps create a moral climate which goes far beyond his immediate and personal acts. The universal society is the beneficiary.

SECTION SUMMARY

The three articles in this section reflect the *cognitive* orientation to moral development. Let us contrast this approach with the psychoanalytic one, which emphasizes emotional and motivational aspects.

In contrast to Piaget's emphasis on cognitive or mental factors in moral development, Freud believed motives and emotions to be more crucial. Freud saw the newborn child as motivated by a set of selfish drives, called the *id.* This aspect of personality seeks immediate gratification for itself, but such gratification leads to conflict with other people. To Freud, socialization, or the process of growing up in one's own society, essentially means that the child learns that it is not desirable for many of these needs to be gratified at once or at all. Such immediate gratification would lead to conflict with others or to anarchy. As the infant matures, he or she develops two other aspects of personality that aid in the socialization process. Both of these, the superego and the ego, are products of learning, according to Freud. The *superego* includes a set of drives that we may think of as the conscience. As the child grows older, he or she learns what is "right" and what is "wrong." Of course, these rules, mores, and customs vary from society to society, but in each group there are certain ones that most members of the society must adhere to. While the child has been acquiring a superego, a third set of drives, the *ego,* has been developing as well. This set is oriented toward doing what seems logical, reasonable, and best in the long run. In the anthropomorphic way that these divisions have usually been presented, the ego is represented as the sensible part of the personality; the ego restrains the id, whose demands are irrational, impulsive, and potentially self-harmful, and at the same time restrains the superego, whose concerns are rigid, moralistic, and unrealistic. To Freud, the ego should strengthen its position as the "executive" of personality as the child gets older. The healthy person is the one with "ego-strength"; when the ego loses control, psychopathology is the result.

But the Freudian and cognitive approaches have some general similarities, too. For example, Freud also used the concept of "stages" of personality development. He hypothesized that, as the child grows older, his psychic energy, or *libido,* is largely directed to different parts of the body. If the child's needs are not satisfied at a particular stage, a portion of this libidinal energy will remain devoted to that need (that is, will "fixate"), even though the child has now passed on to a concern with the next stage. Fixation at a particular stage or stages has two outcomes: (1) as an adult, the person is not able to be unselfish or to love others because most of the psychic energy is still devoted to selfish needs; and (2) the personality of the adult will reflect the presence of these unsatisfied earlier needs. For example, a man who fixated at the oral stage of development would, as an adult, show his oral needs by, perhaps, engaging in excessive talking, chewing, or smoking or by the choice of a mouth-oriented occupation (selling, preaching, or teaching).

Let us now turn to an evaluation of some of the aspects of Piaget's and Kohlberg's cognitive theories. Two assumptions of Piaget's theory were tested by Johnson's study described in the second article: (1) that a given child's response tendencies in all areas of moral judgment (except for type of responsibility) are similar; and (2) that age, egocentricity, and adult constraint influence maturity of moral judgment.

Johnson's findings on similarities in response tendencies are generally consistent with Piaget's theory. Johnson correctly chose to test these relationships *within* each grade, a procedure that led to smaller relationships than if he had included all grade levels in one group. In Table 2 on p. 48, the correlations that are starred identify the significant relationships between moral judgment areas. A starred relationship should be interpreted as a confirmation of Piaget's first assumption. Although the size of the correlation is often small, there are enough significant relationships to support Piaget's assumption of similarity. Within the limits of the marginal reliability of the test and the difficulties in accurately measuring the judgments of young children, we may conclude that a general factor of moral judgment is present.

In testing Piaget's second assumption, Johnson found confirmation of age changes in all five areas of moral judgment. Other variables, including parents' attitudes and egocentricity, produced less consistent relationships with maturity of moral judgments. Parental attitudes were usually related to the child's moral judgments in the areas of immanent justice and communicable responsibility but not in other areas.

What are the results of other tests of Piaget's formulations? There have been numerous ones, some of which are summarized in Johnson's article. Berkowitz (1964), who reviewed studies in both Europe and the United States, found "only uneven support for Piaget's analysis" (p. 48). Berkowitz concluded that evidence for a common factor at a particular age is not always present; age changes in maturity of judgments do not always conform to Piaget's expectations. Studies by Durkin (1959a, 1959b) and by Boehm and Nass (1962) found, as did Johnson's, that older children believe intent should be a stronger determinant of punishment than should objective consequences. But older children do not always advocate greater reciprocity of punishment (Durkin, 1959a, 1959b, 1959c). Berkowitz concluded: "They sometimes believe, for example, that teachers or other authorities are the appropriate people to punish a child who fights, rather than they themselves, and consequently it is not necessary or right to give back blow for blow" (1964, p. 49). After a thorough review of this area, Bronfenbrenner (1962) suggested that, as the locus of the studies moves farther and farther from the European mainland, there is less and less empirical confirmation of Piaget's formulation.

What these findings imply is that Piaget's formulation was too simplified; it failed to consider the ways of viewing punishments as other than retributive vs. restitutive types. Yet, despite Berkowitz' conclusion, it does appear that, if children are *forced* to choose between retributive and restitutive types of punishment, the older children tend to think the latter is more appropriate. However, refinement is needed, not only in the concepts used but in extensions to later years. Moral development involves more than the two-step process of moving from constraint to cooperation, implied by Piaget's original formulation. Piaget continues to refine and revise and write, and we must await his final statement.

Like Piaget's, Freud's theory of moral development can be faulted because it stops too early.

Brown (1965) tells us that, for many Freudians, moral development is considered largely complete by the age of 5. Yet the approaches of Peck and Havighurst (1960) and of Kohlberg indicate a longer period of development. As we have seen, Kohlberg's approach is more like Piaget's; Peck and Havighurst's utilizes the Freudian concept of stages.

Peck and Havighurst (1960, p.3) hypothesize five character types, each representing a successive period of development:

Character Type	Developmental Period
Amoral	Infancy
Expedient	Early childhood
Conforming	Later childhood
Irrational-conscientious	Later childhood
Rational-altruistic	Adolescence and adulthood

These researchers' longitudinal study of the children of "Prairie City, U.S.A." led them to conclude that: (1) adolescents differ as to which character type they manifest, and (2) most individuals tend to maintain the same attitudes and motives from ages 10 to 16.

As Kohlberg indicates in the third article in this section, his theory is also more detailed. He finds it necessary to utilize six developmental stages to account for the reactions of boys, aged 7-17, to his moral dilemmas.

Kohlberg's theory is at present undergoing much empirical study and refinement. As his article indicates, there are differences among cultures in the rate of moral development. There is also a solid indication that children move from Stage 1 to Stage 2 to Stage 3. The proposed sequence through the remaining stages has much less support. It may be, for example, that Stages 5 and 6 each serve as terminal points for moral development and that Stage 6 is *neither* more *nor* less advanced than Stage 5. (Kohlberg recognizes this possibility in his article.) Thus the *invariant developmental sequence* proposed by Kohlberg has, at this time, received only partial support.

But what if a person's moral judgment has reached Stage 6? Does this mean that in a given situation his behavior will be any different from that of a person at Stage 2? Moral judgment or moral knowledge does not necessarily imply moral conduct. Roger Brown (1965) distinguishes among three aspects of morality: (1) *moral knowledge,* or *moral cognitions,* dealing with beliefs about what actions are right or wrong; (2) *moral sentiments,* or emotional feeling about actions; and (3) *moral behavior,* or the actions that actually take place. The relationships among these aspects of morality have only recently been studied within the framework of Kohlberg's moral-judgment stages. The following findings have been offered.

1. The Kohlberg moral-judgment stories were administered to college students who had earlier participated in Milgram's (1963) obedience study (reprinted in Section 6). Milgram's subjects were directed to administer increasingly intense shocks to another person who was obviously in great pain, under the guise of a "teaching-and-learning" experiment. Although the number of subjects was small (only 34) the results reflected some relationship between stage of moral judgment and reaction to the demand to obey the experimenter. Of the 8 subjects who were at Stage 5 or 6 in moral judgment, 6 (75%) refused to continue to obey the experimenter. But of 24 subjects at the conventional moral-judgment levels (Stage 3 or 4), only 3 (12½%) refused to continue. Principled moral *judgment* was thus related to the moral *action* of refusal to participate in an endeavor that brought great pain to another person (Kohlberg, 1969).

2. Krebs (1967) observed the extent of cheating among sixth-grade children on four tests. Again, although the numbers of subjects are small, the results indicate some relationship between judgment and behavior. Among the 5 sixth-graders at Stage 5 or 6, only 1 cheated. On the other hand, 67% of the 63 subjects at Stages 3 and 4 cheated, and 83% of the 55 children at Stages 1 and 2 cheated.

3. Participation or nonparticipation in the Free Speech Movement at the University of California at Berkeley (the first campus sit-in) was related to the student's stage of moral judgment

(Haan, Smith, & Block, 1968). Those at Stages 3 and 4 were less likely to participate; those at Stages 5 and 6 *and at Stage 2* were more likely to. But the preconventional Stage 2s and the postconventional Stage 5s and 6s participated for different reasons. The Stage-2 participants saw the campus protest as stemming from a power conflict in which they were out to better their own personal situation. The Stage-5 and Stage-6 participants, on the other hand, were concerned about basic issues of civil rights and the place of students as citizens in an academic community.

The relationship between moral judgment and moral action is, of course, one example of the relationship between attitudes and behavior. This issue is one of the most central ones for social psychology. Do verbalizations about attitudes predict one's behavior? This question will be explored in depth in Section 9.

REFERENCES

Allport, G. W. *The nature of prejudice.* Reading, Mass.: Addison-Wesley, 1954.

Berkowitz, L. *The development of motives and values in the child.* New York: Basic Books, 1964.

Boehm, L., & Nass, M. L. Social class differences in conscience development. *Child Development,* 1962, **33,** 565–574.

Bronfenbrenner, U. The role of age, sex, class, and culture in studies of moral development. *Religious Education* (Research Supplement), 1962, **57,** S3–17.

Brown, R. *Social psychology.* New York: Free Press, 1965.

Durkin, D. Children's concepts of justice: A comparison with the Piaget data. *Child Development,* 1959, **30,** 59–67. (a)

Durkin, D. Children's concepts of justice: A further comparison with the Piaget data. *Journal of Educational Research,* 1959, **52,** 252–257. (b)

Durkin, D. Children's acceptance of reciprocity as a justice-principle. *Child Development,* 1959, **30,** 289–296. (c)

Haan, N., Smith, M. B., & Block, J. Moral reasoning of young adults: Political-social behavior, family background, and personality correlates. *Journal of Personality and Social Psychology,* 1968, **10,** 183–201.

Kohlberg, L. The cognitive-developmental approach to socialization. In D. A. Goslin (Ed.), *Handbook of socialization theory and research.* Chicago: Rand McNally, 1969. Pp. 347–480.

Krebs, R. Some relations between moral judgment, attention, and resistance to temptation. Unpublished doctoral dissertation, University of Chicago, 1967.

Milgram, S. Behavioral study of obedience. *Journal of Abnormal and Social Psychology,* 1963, **67**, 371–378.

Peck, R. F., & Havighurst, R. J. *The psychology of character development.* New York: Wiley, 1960.

SUGGESTED READINGS FOR FURTHER STUDY

Aronfreed, J. *Conduct and conscience: The socialization of internalized control over behavior.* New York: Academic Press, 1968.

Bandura, A., & Walters, R. *Social learning and personality development.* New York: Holt, Rinehart & Winston, 1963.

Berkowitz, L. *The development of motives and values in the child.* New York: Basic Books, 1964.

Bronfenbrenner, U. *Two worlds of childhood: U.S.A. and U.S.S.R.* New York: Russell Sage Foundation, 1970.

Brown, R. *Social psychology.* New York: Free Press, 1965. (Chapter 8, particularly pp. 401–411.)

Erikson, E. *Childhood and society.* New York: Norton, 1950. (Republished in 1963.)

Evans, R. I. *Dialogue with Erik Erikson.* New York: Dutton, 1969.

Hartshorne, H., May, M. A., & Maller, J. B. *Studies in the nature of character,* Vol. II: *Studies in service and self-control.* New York: Macmillan, 1929.

Kohlberg, L. The cognitive-developmental approach to socialization. In D. A. Goslin (Ed.), *Handbook of socialization theory and research.* Chicago: Rand McNally, 1969. Pp. 347–480.

Piaget, J. *The moral judgment of the child.* Glencoe, Ill.: Free Press, 1948. (Originally published in 1932; paperback edition published in 1965.)

Schwartz, S. H. Words, deeds, and the perception of consequences and responsibility in action situations. *Journal of Personality and Social Psychology,* 1968, **10**, 232–242.

Cooperation and Competition in Small Groups

INTRODUCTION

In contemporary American life, both cooperation and competition are desirable in particular situations, and many of our everyday motivational conflicts can be posed in these terms. When a friend asks to borrow Ed's lecture notes, does Ed refuse because they may enable the friend to do better than Ed on the exam? Should Jan help the group by working on the sorority float, or should she spend her precious time on her term paper? Should Ron try to break the individual scoring record, even though it may cost his basketball team a state-tournament berth? In this section we will examine some of the theorizing and research on cooperation and competition in small groups. Let us first consider the meanings of these terms.

Morton Deutsch (1949a, 1949b) has reviewed several definitions of cooperation and competition. Applying these definitions to situations involving small groups of people, he introduced the concepts of *promotively interdependent goals* and *contriently interdependent goals.* In what we think of as a cooperative situation, the goals of all persons are promotively interdependent; that is, one person cannot obtain his goal unless the others achieve theirs. An example of this is reflected in the statement by the athlete in the postgame interview that, although he sacrificed a chance to set an individual record, he was happy to do so because it was more important to him for his team to win the game. Similarly, the wife who cannot enjoy a movie if her spouse is disturbed by it reflects this promotively interdependent orientation. Games can be played in a way that reflects this orientation; there is nothing in a game that makes it inherently competitive. For example, two-handed solitaire can be a group game with a promotively interdependent orientation if there are no individual rewards but only those achieved when both persons reach the goal of playing all their cards.

On the other hand, people in social interactions may be contriently interdependent, which means that, if one achieves his goal, by that action the others are prevented from reaching theirs. Most individual games and sports, most contests, and most elections are thus structured (if we assume that the goal of the individual is to win). In chess, in tennis, and even in tic-tac-toe, the success of one player means the failure of the other.

At this point it may be well to make a distinction between group goals and individual goals. In most social interactions both types of goals are likely to occur. In a tennis match, even though a player loses, certain of his or her individual goals may have been satisfied by the activity—a desire for exercise, an opportunity to escape one's worries, the need to be with another person. The individual goal of winning may or may not be primary. Two tennis players, despite their most violent competition with each other, form a dyad (a two-person group) that holds a promotively interdependent group goal: that of participating together in an enjoyable manner. Thus, although they are contriently interdependent in regard to each one's individual goal of winning, they are promotively interdependent in their group goal of enjoying the match. If one gets angry and quits, this action prevents both of them from achieving the group goal.

Realization of the variety of individual and group goals in every encounter reaffirms Deutsch's statement that there are few situations that are purely cooperative or purely competitive. However, for purposes of understanding, it is desirable for us to study initially those interactions in which purely cooperative or purely competitive conditions exist. In such investigations the goal is not to represent "real life," because in real life most interactions are characterized as possessing a varied mixture of goals for each participant.

Deutsch has tested his theory in a variety of studies (Deutsch, 1949a, 1949b, 1960a, 1960b, 1962; Deutsch & Krauss, 1962; Deutsch, Epstein, Canavan, & Gumpert, 1967). The initial experiment used students in a rather different type of introductory psychology course. Instead of attending lectures, students met weekly in small groups (five students plus an instructor) for discussion of problems and case histories. Groups were paired on the basis of their productivity in discussion of a case history. Then one group in each pair was assigned to a cooperative-treatment condition, and one was assigned to a competitive

condition. Those groups in the cooperative-treatment condition were told that their groups would be evaluated by comparison of their solutions and recommendations with those of the other groups. (Each group was to be given two problems, a puzzle problem and a human-relations problem, to solve at each weekly session.) Among the five cooperatively oriented groups, the one that worked together most effectively would receive a grade of A.

In the competitive condition, groups were told that the contributions of each member would be evaluated and ranked. *Within* each group, the student who had contributed the most in quality and quantity to the discussions, recommendations, and solutions would receive the highest grade; the individual who contributed least would receive the lowest grade. Regardless of its experimental condition, every group was told that it must come to one solution for each problem. In both conditions, grades (or ranks) would be a part of the students' course grades. In all other ways the groups in the cooperative and competitive conditions were treated the same way.

Observations during the meetings and the self-ratings of the students afterward indicated that the groups graded on the basis of group performance were more often characterized by a "we feeling," or group-centeredness. Students in groups in the competitive condition rated themselves as more self-oriented and more desirous of surpassing the others. There was more coordination of efforts in the cooperative condition, whose members also reported that they were more agreeable and accepting of the ideas of the others than were group members in the competitive condition. The cooperative orientation also had a beneficial effect on productivity; the cooperative groups solved the puzzle problems more rapidly and produced more on the human-relations problems. Observers rated the human-relations discussions of the cooperative groups as showing more insight and understanding, as well as more productivity.

In the two and one-half decades since the publication of Deutsch's theoretical article, the interest of social psychologists in the phenomena of cooperation and competition has accelerated. Recently the Prisoner's Dilemma game and other mixed-motive games have been utilized to study these phenomena. These "games" are in some ways dissimilar to the usual type of game. Basically, such two-person games force each participant to make a choice between competing and cooperating, with the amount of his payoff being determined not only by his choice but also by the choice of the other person. Most of the games are a variety of the Prisoner's Dilemma described by Luce and Raiffa (1957) as follows:

Two subjects are taken into custody and separated. The district attorney is certain they are guilty of a specific crime, but he does not have adequate evidence to convict them at a trial. He points out to each prisoner that each has two alternatives: to confess to the crime the police are sure they have done or not to confess. If they both do not confess then the district attorney states that he will book them on some very minor, trumped-up charge . . .; if they both confess, they will be prosecuted, (and) he will recommend (a rather severe) sentence, (and) but if one confesses and the other does not, then the confessor will receive rather lenient treatment for turning state's evidence whereas the latter will get the "book" slapped at him [p.95].

Notice that, in this situation, if each prisoner chooses what is best for him individually, *without consideration of what the other will choose,* he would choose not to confess. But if he chooses not to confess and the other prisoner has chosen to confess, then he will get the "book" thrown at him—the most severe sentence of all. The outcome for each prisoner is determined by the combination of his choice and that of the other.

The Prisoner's Dilemma games used in social-psychological research have generally employed a matrix with less severe payoffs than jail sentences. In fact, rewards have been employed rather than the punishments indicated in the original "dilemma." Amounts of money, ranging from pennies to $60, have been used, as well as points to be added to one's final-exam score. A typical matrix looks like this:

Second person chooses between:

		A	B
First person	X	$3, $3	$0, $5
chooses between:	Y	$5, $0	$1, $1

The decision facing the first person is to choose between X and Y; the decision facing the second person is to choose between A and B. The first figure in each box refers to the winnings of the first person and the second figure to the winnings of the second person. Notice the possibilities. If the first person picks X, the second person can pick A or B. If the first picks X, the second can pick A, putting them in the XA intersection ($3, $3), meaning each gets $3. But the second person could pick B (after the first person picked X), making the payoffs $0 and $5, giving nothing to the first person and $5 to himself.

If the first person picks Y and the second picks A, the payoffs are $5 and $0, respectively; in this case, the second person is letting the first win grandly. If the choices are Y and B, the payoff is $1 each.

This example implies that the second person chooses *after* the first person and knows what the first has chosen. This procedure, labeled sequential responding, gives a great deal of power to the second person and is sometimes used. Other experiments have had the two subjects choose at the same time, which is referred to as a simultaneous choice. Some studies have used only one trial and some as many as 300.

Regardless of these variations, the essential nature of the game is consistent: a choice that leads to the most individual gain is, in the long run, self-defeating. If each chooses for the most individual gain, it would mean a choice of Y by the first person and a choice of B by the second. This set of choices would put them in the lower-right payoff box; each would receive $1. But the desirable choice, if one can assume the other will cooperate, is XA, paying each $3.

The first article in this section is an excellent overview of cooperative and competitive behaviors in two-person games. The authors, Philip S. Gallo, Jr., of San Diego State College, and Charles G. McClintock, of the University of California at Santa Barbara, are experienced researchers in the area, and in this article they constructively evaluate early findings on behavior in mixed-motive games.

When reading this review article, the student should recognize that experimenters have used a variety of matrices, methods, and strategies in studying behavior in a two-person game situation. The difference between values in the matrix, the amount of money, the real versus imaginary nature of the money, the number of trials, and the order of responding (simultaneous versus sequential) have all sometimes differed from one experiment to the next. In effect, the Prisoner's Dilemma is a generic term for a number of specific situations similar in the sense that the subject must always choose between different responses that carry different implications. The variations make it difficult to determine the degree of similarity in findings across different studies. Within particular studies such factors have been controlled, leading to the conclusions presented in the review.

The conclusions drawn by Gallo and McClintock were appropriate on the basis of the limited research up to that time (1965). Since then, many more Prisoner's Dilemma studies have been completed; there are now more than 400 in the literature. As we will show in the summary of this section, most of the conclusions and speculations advanced by Gallo and McClintock remain accurate today. However, more recent studies on the effects of the *strategy of the other participant* indicate that, in regard to that variable, the effects appear to be greater than Gallo and McClintock's review indicated.

Hence the remaining articles in this section were chosen because they examine the ways in which the other person's choices (or his strategy of responding) affect the subject's decision to cooperate or compete. For example, what does the subject do if he finds that the other participant always makes the cooperative response, even if he has not? Does the subject decide to act "in kind" and cooperate, or does he decide to exploit the other subject, to "get it while the getting is good"? Through the use of a preprogrammed set of responses designed by the experimenter, the *apparent* choices of the other participant can be entirely cooperative or entirely competitive. Such variations in other's strategy were employed in the second article in this section, by Wrightsman,

Davis, and others at George Peabody College for Teachers. This article also isolates the effect of the other participant's race: do white undergraduates cooperate less with blacks than with other whites?

The third article, by Komorita and Mechling, is also interested in the effects of the other's strategy but emphasizes the factors related to the betrayal of trust. How does a subject react when he is instructed to respond in a cooperative way, only to find that the other player betrays this orientation and begins to choose exploitatively? Komorita and Mechling expected, and found, that such a betrayal would cause the subject to waver from his previous pattern of cooperative choices. But the researchers also determined the degree to which continued cooperation was affected by the timing of the betrayal (whether it came after 4 cooperative trials or after 10), the size of the loss to the subject, and the strength of the temptation to defect. In reviewing this article, the reader should consider factors that influence reactions to a betrayal of trust.

REFERENCES

Deutsch, M. A theory of cooperation and competition. *Human Relations,* 1949, **2,** 129–152. (a)

Deutsch, M. An experimental study of the effects of cooperation and competition upon group process. *Human Relations,* 1949, **2,** 199–231. (b)

Deutsch, M. The effect of motivational orientation upon trust and suspicion. *Human Relations,* 1960, **13,** 122–139. (a)

Deutsch, M. Trust, trustworthiness, and the F scale. *Journal of Abnormal and Social Psychology,* 1960, **61,** 138–140. (b)

Deutsch, M. Cooperation and trust: Some theoretical notes. In M. R. Jones (Ed.), *Nebraska symposium on motivation.* Lincoln: University of Nebraska Press, 1962. Pp. 275–319.

Deutsch, M., & Krauss, R. M. Studies of interpersonal bargaining. *Journal of Conflict Resolution,* 1962, **6,** 52–76.

Deutsch, M., Epstein, Y., Canavan, D., & Gumpert, P. Strategies of inducing cooperation: An experimental study. *Journal of Conflict Resolution,* 1967, **11,** 345–360.

Luce, R. D., & Raiffa, H. *Games and decisions: Introduction and critical survey.* New York: Wiley, 1957.

ARTICLE 7

Cooperative and Competitive Behavior in Mixed-Motive Games

Philip S. Gallo, Jr., and Charles G. McClintock

During recent years there has been considerable attention given to "mixed-motive" games, that is, to behavioral situations in which individuals must choose between responses which are assumed to serve different motives. The reasons for this interest are numerous: (a) the development of game theory as a formal model for human behavior; (b) the general theoretical and empirical concern with the process of decision-making which reflects the involvement of the social sciences in the problems of management, both civilian and military; (c) the recognition of the methodological importance of simulation as a way to study human behavior, particularly as regards this behavior in an organizational environment; and (d) the greater theoretical concern in social psychology and related disciplines with the processes of cognition and motivation as well as the relationship between them.

A game can be defined as a situation in which the persons involved are attempting to attain some goal(s) and in which their success or failure is dependent not only upon their strategy choices but also upon the strategy choices of the other individual(s) in the situation. A mixed-motive game is one in which the goals of the players are partially coincident and partially in conflict. Of particular interest are mixed-motive games in which attempts by the players to maximize their individual gains without regard for the gains of others result in losses to both (all). In such games, in effect, cooperative behavior is rewarded and competitive behavior is punished.

The selection of such situations seems to be based on both theoretical and pragmatic reasons. The major theoretical reason is that much research in this area stems from theories of small group behavior in which a fundamental assumption is made that mutually cooperative behavior between members leads to the formation and maintenance of groups, and mutually competitive behavior results in the disruption of groups (Homans, 1961; Thibaut and Kelley, 1959). The major pragmatic reason for emphasis upon cooperation vs. competition is the interest by researchers in this field in problems of international politics. The fundamental assumption made in this area is that cooperation leads to the resolution of conflict, whereas competition leads to a continuation and intensification of conflict.

HISTORICAL ANTECEDENTS OF GAME PLAYING RESEARCH

One of the earliest attempts to study a situation in which cooperation or competition could develop was performed by Mintz (1951). A number of persons held strings to which individual cones were attached. They were instructed to remove their cones from a narrow necked bottle which was slowly filled with water from the bottom.

From *Journal of Conflict Resolution,* 1965, **9,** 68–78. Reprinted with permission of the authors and the publisher, the Center for Conflict Resolution, University of Michigan.

This research was supported by the United States Air Force through the Air Force Office of Scientific Research of the Air Research and Development Command, under Contract Number AF 49(638)-794.

Small monetary rewards were given to subjects who removed their cones before they became wet. Although sufficient time was allotted for all subjects to remove their cones, few subjects were able to do so because of jams which occurred in the neck of the bottle. The subjects were able to complete the task successfully only when the instructions stressed intergroup rather than intragroup competition. Kelley (1953) conducted an experiment conceptually similar to that of Mintz and found that increases in threats of punishment for failure to escape from the situation decreased the number of people who succeeded in escaping, a phenomenon well recognized in mob reactions to danger.

Another approach to the problem of cooperation vs. competition was taken by Sidowski, Wykoff, and Tabory (1956) and extended by Kelley, Thibaut, Radloff, and Mundy (1962). They studied behavior in the "minimal social situation." Two subjects, unaware of each other's presence, were placed in experimental cubicles. Each subject was instructed to press one or the other of two buttons until instructed to stop. As the subjects pushed the buttons, they were either rewarded with points or punished with electric shock. The awarding of points or administration of shock to each subject was actually determined by the button presses made by the other player.

The results of these experiments indicate that people learn to cooperate in this situation, i.e., they tend to stabilize on the responses which provide points for the other player. In addition, the study by Kelley *et al.* demonstrated that subjects also learned this type of behavior when they were informed of the existence of the other subject and were told that their responses would have an effect on the other subject. They were not told, however, what the effect would be. The authors explain the results in terms of a "win—stay, lose—change" strategy. The subjects themselves were generally able to verbalize the principle that the other subject's behavior would be stable when rewarded and variable when punished.

Recent experiments in game playing behavior have generally used situations somewhat more complex than those described above. Although many mixed-motive games have been developed, a major share of the literature has been devoted

to the "Prisoner's Dilemma" game. The general form of the Prisoner's Dilemma game is represented by the following matrix (Scodel, Minas, Ratoosh, and Lipetz, 1959)[1]:

	B_1	B_2
A_1	X_1,X_1	X_2,X_3
A_2	X_3,X_2	X_4,X_4

and is described by the following set of rules:

1) $2X_1 > X_2 + X_3 > 2X_4$
2) $X_3 > X_1$
3) $X_3 > X_2$
4) $X_4 > X_2$

One of the more common numerical representations of the game is shown in the following matrix:

	B_1	B_2
A_1	+5,+5	−4,+6
A_2	+6,−4	−3,−3

If we assume the usual game theoretical definition of rationality, that each player wants to do "best" for himself, the dilemma becomes apparent. Player A realizes that his A_2 strategy will give him a larger payoff than his A_1 strategy, regardless of which strategy player B selects. Similarly, player B realizes that his B_2 strategy dominates his B_1 strategy. Each player therefore selects his second strategy, which places them in the $A_2 B_2$ cell and results in a payoff of −3 for each player. Luce and Raiffa (1957) have maintained that this unhappy state of affairs is indeed the only "rational" solution to the game. . . .

EMPIRICAL STUDIES OF THE PRISONER'S DILEMMA GAME

Since the purpose of this paper is to indicate some of the main directions that PD game research has taken and to critically appraise them, this review of the literature will be selective rather than exhaustive. Four types of independent variables seem to have received the greatest attention. These are: (1) manipulations of the payoff matrices, (2) personality variables, (3) strategy of the other player, and (4) possibilities for communica-

[1]For a verbal description of the game see Luce and Raiffa (1957), p. 95.

tion. A number of other variables that have received less attention will also be examined. Many studies have investigated several independent variables in factorial designs and in these cases an arbitrary decision was made concerning which heading or headings to place them under.

Manipulations of the Payoff Matrix

Manipulations of the payoff matrices have generally taken one of three forms. The rules of the PD game can be adhered to but the discrepancy between X_3 and X_2 can be manipulated within certain limits. Rapoport and Orwant (1962) have proposed that an index of competitive advantage can be obtained by subtracting the X_2 payoff from the X_3 payoff. As this index becomes larger, presumably the temptation to defect from a cooperative strategy becomes stronger. A second type of matrix manipulation involves the relaxation of one or more rules of the PD game, usually in an attempt to encourage cooperation. A third type of manipulation is to destroy the usual symmetry of the PD game, thus actually changing it to a different type of non-zero-sum game. Such games are outside of the scope of the present paper but will be mentioned when results can be directly compared to those obtained in PD games.

Manipulations of the first two types have been performed by Scodel, Minas, Ratoosh, and Lipetz (1959) and Minas, Scodel, Marlowe, and Rawson (1960). The effect of enlarging the competitive index was to produce a larger percentage of competitive play, as expected. The authors also report several games in which rule 4 and/or rule 2 was relaxed. In these studies, rule 4 was relaxed so that the worst payoff was in the case of joint defection from cooperation, and rule 2 was relaxed to destroy the individual advantage to be gained from defection. Both of these variations should and did produce less competitive behavior than in a standard PD game. Even in these variations, however, the number of competitive choices still exceeded the number of cooperative choices and tended to increase over trials. Similar results were also found by Scodel (1962).

Solomon (1960) reported a study in which several asymmetric games as well as a PD game were used. The asymmetric games varied the amount of power that the simulated "other" player had

over the S. The PD game was conceptualized as an equal power situation. The Ss in the PD game tended to make the largest number of suspicious (competitive) responses.

Personality Variables

Scores on the F scale tend to correlate negatively with cooperative behavior in the PD game (Deutsch, 1960b). The Ss played a two-trial version of the game in which they announced their choice before the simulated "other" player had chosen on trial one and after they had been told that the "other" had made a cooperative choice on trial two. A cooperative choice would indicate "trust" on trial one and "trustworthiness" on trial two. High scorers on the F scale made significantly fewer responses of each type than low scorers.

Lutzker (1960) investigated the relationship between Internationalism, an inverse F scale correlate, and cooperative behavior. The results indicated that those who are highly Internationalistic tend to make fewer competitive responses than those who are highly Isolationistic. The usual over-trials increase in noncooperative choices was evident in the Isolationist group, but did not occur in the case of the Internationalists. Even the Internationalists, however, did not cooperate on a majority of the trials. These results were essentially confirmed in a later study by McClintock, Harrison, Strand, and Gallo (1963). McClintock, Gallo, and Harrison (1964), using an asymmetric game, suggest that Internationalists may be more responsive to variations in their opponents' strategy. They tended, more than Isolationists, to punish a previously competitive opponent and to reward a previously cooperative one.

Another personality variable that may be related to game playing behavior is the measure of "flexible ethicality" developed by Bixenstine, Potash, and Wilson (1963). This scale measures the extent to which an ethical hero is approved on reasonable, workable grounds (N) or on the basis of rigid and unreasoning obedience to ethical values (F). The actual measure is N minus F. Subjects high in (N–F) made significantly more cooperative choices than those who scored medium or low in this measure. In a follow-up study by Bixenstine and Wilson (1963), the relationship of this variable to behavior reached only the 0.10 level of significance, while a still later study by Bixenstine, Chambers, and Wilson (1964) failed to demonstrate any relationship between this variable and behavior. It should be pointed out, however, that the latter two studies were quite complex and the second one used an asymmetric game rather than a PD game.

A large number of studies have failed to demonstrate any relationship between sex of the players and choice behavior. These studies include those done by Marlowe (1959), Lutzker (1960), Minas, Scodel, Marlowe, and Rawson (1960), Wilson and Bixenstine (1962), and Bixenstine, Potash, and Wilson (1963). Two exceptions to this general trend are the study by Bixenstine and Wilson (1963), which employed a shifting sequence of cooperative responses made by the simulated "other," and the study by Bixenstine, Chambers, and Wilson (1964). In these two studies women tended to respond somewhat less cooperatively than men. The authors suggest that women may form judgments of their opponent more quickly than do men and may be more affected by disconfirmation of expectations or differences in status. They further suggest that the restricted choices and equal status relationship of the PD game do not allow sex differences to be expressed.

Strategy of the Other

Quite a few of the previously cited studies have employed a simulated, rather than a real, other player. That is, each *S* actually played against a preprogrammed set of responses sent to him by the experimenter, while believing that he was actually playing against a real opponent. Bixenstine, Potash and Wilson (1963) used a random strategy of 83 percent cooperative responses for one group and 83 percent competitive responses for a second group, followed in all groups by an 83 percent matching strategy. McClintock, Harrison, Strand, and Gallo (1963) used random strategies of 85 percent, 50 percent, and 15 percent cooperative responses for their three groups. Neither experiment demonstrated any effect of the "other's" strategy on the choice behavior of the *S*s.

There are, however, two exceptions to this finding. Solomon (1960) found that more cooperative responses were made by the *S*s when they played against a matching strategy than against either an unconditionally cooperative or an unconditionally competitive strategy. Bixenstine and Wilson (1963) demonstrated that, when the strategy of the "other" reaches as high as 95 percent cooperative or competitive and is systematically varied over trials, the *S*s do tend to respond in kind. However, even a 95 percent cooperative opponent fails to induce over 50 percent cooperative play on the part of the subject.

Possibilities for Communication

Loomis (1959) studied the effects of communication on frequency of cooperative play. Half of his *S*s sent, and the other half received, standardized notes expressing expectation, intention, retaliation, and/or absolution. Five levels of communication were used, from expectation alone to all of them in combination. Perceived trust was positively related to level of communication, and trustworthiness (cooperation) was positively related to perceived trust. Note receivers were somewhat more cooperative than note senders, but both groups averaged over 50 percent cooperative play. Deutsch (1958) also reports increased cooperation when communication was allowed. This was true only when the *S*s had been given an individualist motivational set and did not hold true when the *S*s had been given cooperative or competitive instructions. Scodel, Minas, Ratoosh, and Lipetz (1959) report an increase in joint cooperative responses as a function of communication but note that joint competitive responses still predominate.

Other Independent Variables

Motivational Set. Deutsch (1958, 1960a) varied the nature of the pregame instructions given to the players. Three different sets of instructions stressed either the importance of making as many points as possible (1) for the dyad, (2) for the individual, irrespective of the outcome for the other, or (3) maximizing the difference between the player and his opponent. These instructions were identified by Deutsch as being cooperative, individualistic, or competitive respectively. Varying a number of other conditions such as communication and reversibility and simultaneity of choice, Deutsch found a direct relationship between motivational orientation and number of cooperative choices. The *S*s who had been given the individualistic orientation were the most sensitive to the presence of the other independent variables, going from a low of 21 percent to a high of 77 percent cooperative responses. The *S*s given the cooperative responses were invariably cooperative (97 percent–78 percent) whereas *S*s given the competitive instructions were invariably competitive (36 percent–13 percent).

Presence of a Third Choice.   Wilson and Bixenstine (1962) have hypothesized that the low proportion of cooperative choices in the PD game is the result of a "bind" that develops early in the game. Once the players get into the joint competitive cell, it is difficult to reestablish cooperation because the player who initiates a unilateral move back to cooperation is punished more severely than if he remained competitive and his opponent is reinforced for not having made a cooperative response. They proposed to break this bind by adding a choice to the usual two present in the PD game that could be used to communicate a desire to return to cooperation without excessively punishing the player who makes it or excessively rewarding his opponent. The results indicate a decrease in the number of joint competitive choices, but do not indicate a corresponding increase in the number of joint cooperative responses.

Group Variables.   The presence of a mutually disliked third party can influence the output of cooperative choices. Deutsch (1960a) reports the results of a study in which two naive *S*s first took an intelligence test in the company of an irritating and obnoxious "stooge." The two naive *S*s then played a PD game in the presence of the stooge. The players made more cooperative responses in the presence of the stooge than are usually obtained in the game. This tendency was considerably stronger when the stooge was placed in an interdependent relationship with the *S*s, such that he won what they lost.

The effects of pitting two-man teams against one another have been investigated by Wilson, Chun, and Kayatani (1964). The two teammates jointly chose a strategy to play against the opposing team and at the same time played an identical PD game against each other to decide the division of the winnings, if any. The results indicated that the players made more than twice as many competitive choices against the opposing team than against their partners. Accompanying this behavior was a change in the favorability of the motives assigned to the other players, the ratings of one's partner becoming more favorable and the ratings of one's opponents becoming less favorable.

Number of Trials.   The experiments reviewed thus far have all employed a relatively small number of trials, usually well below 100. In a forthcoming report, Rapoport (in press) describes some experiments with the PD game in which *S*s played from 300 to 700 trials. The results from the early trials are similar to those that have been reported here, but certain differences do appear after 50 to 150 trials. When male *S*s play one another, the usual decline in cooperative behavior is observed in the early trials but a reversal tends to occur after about 50 trials, and it continues upward to an asymptote of well over 50 percent cooperative responses. In addition, this upward trend is strong enough to bring the total percentage of cooperative responses to above 50 percent for the entire game. Pairs of female *S*s also show this reversal but it occurs later in the game and rises more slowly. Overall, pairs of female *S*s produce only about one-half as many cooperative responses as pairs of male *S*s. When mixed sex pairs are used there is virtually no difference in the performance of males and females. The mixed sex pairs tend to play more cooperatively than pairs of female *S*s but less cooperatively than pairs of male *S*s.

DISCUSSION AND CONCLUSIONS

The results of the studies that we have cited present a fairly consistent pattern. In general, the percentage of cooperative responses that are obtained in the PD game tends to be well below 50 percent, and this percentage tends to decrease over a series of trials. People who differ on personality variables believed associated with their general interpersonal orientation tend to respond differentially to the game. The S's rate of cooperative responses is apparently not influenced by noncontingent cooperative or competitive strategies played against him. Finally, opportunities for communication may, but do not necessarily, ameliorate the conflict present in the game.

In view of these results it would be reasonable to conclude that the conflict presented by the PD game is so severe and the opportunities for communication so limited that the possibilities for cooperation are extremely limited. Such an interpretation would, however, overlook the fact that there is one important independent variable that has not yet been manipulated. This variable is the meaningfulness of the rewards for cooperation. All of the studies cited in this paper have shared a common feature. The Ss played for either imaginary money or actual money in very small amounts, usually less than a dime per trial. One reason that larger rewards have not been offered is, obviously, the expense involved. A second reason is that role playing techniques have proved satisfactory in several areas of social psychological research. However, a doctoral dissertation completed by one of the authors (Gallo, 1963) indicates that game playing behavior may be strikingly different when the Ss are playing for real, rather than imaginary, rewards.

Gallo's study was based on a game invented by Deutsch and Krauss (1960). The Ss in the Deutsch and Krauss experiment played a simulated trucking game, in which they had to learn to alternate in the use of a one-way section of road. The Ss received a fixed amount of imaginary money per trial from which was subtracted their operating expenses. The operating expenses accumulated in direct proportion to the length of time needed to reach the destination. If the Ss learned to alternate, both Ss would show a profit. If, however, both Ss insisted on maximizing their payoffs, a stalemate would develop on the one-way path and both Ss would lose money. Although obviously not a Prisoner's Dilemma game, its conceptual properties are quite similar.

The results indicated that Ss were able to learn the cooperative alternation. Over a series of twenty trials, the majority of dyads showed a net profit and also showed a significant improvement in payoffs as the experiment progressed. However, a second group of Ss were given barriers that they could use to block their opponent's truck on its way to the goal. The Ss who had the option of using these barriers experienced a large net loss over the twenty trials and showed no sign of learning. Further studies by Deutsch and Krauss (1962) and Borah (1963) confirmed the fact that the Ss who were given the barriers were unable to learn the cooperative alternation engaged in by the Ss who did not have the barriers.

The experiment by Gallo was a replication of these studies with several differences, two of which are of interest here. The payoff values used by the previous experimenters were multiplied by a factor of 4.5 to provide a maximum payoff of $1.15 per trial. Perfect alternation would result in a payoff of $16.00 per S for the total experiment. Half of the Ss (16 dyads) played for imaginary money, just as they had in the previous experiments. The other half played for real money. All Ss had the option of using the barriers, although half of the Ss in each condition had them only for the last ten trials.

The Ss who played for imaginary money lost an average of $38.80 per dyad over the twenty trials. If this is divided by 4.5 it comes out to $8.62 as compared to an average loss of $8.75 for the comparable group in Deutsch and Krauss' original experiment. On the other hand, the Ss who played for real money won an average of $9.92 per dyad. Divided by 4.5 this equals $2.20 which compares favorably with the $2.03 average winnings of the Deutsch and Krauss Ss who did not have the barriers. Only two of the imaginary money dyads showed a profit, whereas 14 of the real money dyads came out ahead. In addition, the real money Ss showed an entirely different pattern of play than the imaginary money Ss. The dyads playing for real money showed a significant improvement in payoffs over trials and also showed a significant decrease in barrier use.

The interpretation given to these results would seem equally applicable to the PD situation. The

S is placed in a situation in which he is told to amass for himself as many points, imaginary dollars, or real pennies as he can. If he is reasonably intelligent, and understands the implications of the strategy choices available to him, he realizes that to follow the instructions involves making a long and boring sequence of strategy choices which will cause himself and his partner to amass the reward at an equal and slow rate. If the reward has no real value to him, it would be far more interesting to invent a new game in which the object is to maximize the difference between his own payoffs and those of his opponent. In effect, the *S* changes the game from a non-zero-sum game to a zero-sum game.

Another possibility is that we may have overestimated our *S*s intelligence and/or understanding and he does not realize the implication of his choices. This is a factor which is probably true in at least a certain percentage of cases. If so, the *S* will probably experiment with various strategy choices, particularly the one that maximizes his short-run gain. By the time he learns the implications of what he is doing, if he ever does, it is probably too late to break out of the competitive pattern that has been established, particularly if motivation to do so is minimal or entirely lacking. In either of these two cases, the strategy choices made by the *S* will tend to come out looking the same, and will be predominantly competitive.

The results of the trucking game would seem to indicate that the most pressing unanswered question in PD research is whether *S*s are unable or unmotivated to learn to cooperate. The majority of the trucking *S*s were apparently merely unmotivated. If this is also true of the PD game, a series of parametric studies would seem to be called for. A promising start in this direction would be to offer larger, more meaningful rewards to the *S*s over a series of matrices designed to both encourage and discourage competition. Another avenue of attack would be to offer the *S*s attractive and desirable prizes for amassing a certain total number of points over a series of trials. The number of points could also be varied to encourage or discourage competition. If *S*s will cooperate under adequate motivational conditions, a more meaningful framework will be established within which to study the numerous variables which are thought to be related to the formation of cooperative or competitive behavior.

Perhaps even more important is the increased generalizability such an approach would give to the findings of PD research. Surely a great deal of the importance assigned to research in this area comes from the resemblance of this simple conflict situation to numerous conflicts that are present in the real world. In real world conflicts the motivation of the participants is extremely high. Unfortunately, this has not been the case in most experimental studies of conflict.

REFERENCES

Bixenstine, V. E., Chambers, N., and Wilson, K. V. Asymmetry in payoff in a non-zero-sum game, *Journal of Conflict Resolution,* June 1964, **8** (No. 2), 151–159.

Bixenstine, V. E., Potash, H. M., and Wilson, K. V. Effects of level of cooperative choice by the other player on choices in a Prisoner's Dilemma game: Part I. *Journal of Abnormal and Social Psychology,* 1963, **66,** 308–313.

Bixenstine, V. E., and Wilson, K. V. Effects of level of cooperative choice by the other player on choices in a Prisoner's Dilemma game: Part II. *Journal of Abnormal and Social Psychology,* 1963, **67,** 139–147.

Borah, L. A., Jr. The effects of threat in bargaining: Critical and experimental analysis. *Journal of Abnormal and Social Psychology,* 1963, **66,** 37–44.

Deutsch, M. Trust and suspicion. *Journal of Conflict Resolution,* Dec. 1958, **2** (No. 4), 265–279.

Deutsch, M. The effect of motivational orientation upon threat and suspicion. *Human Relations,* 1960a, **13,** 37–44.

Deutsch, M. The effect of motivational orientation upon threat and suspicion. *Human Relations,* 1960a, **13,** 122–139.

Deutsch, M. Trust, trustworthiness, and the F scale. *Journal of Abnormal and Social Psychology,* 1960b, **61,** 138–140.

Deutsch, M., and Krauss, R. M. The effect of threat upon interpersonal bargaining. *Journal of Abnormal and Social Psychology,* 1960, **61,** 181–189.

Deutsch, M., and Krauss, R. M. Studies of interpersonal bargaining. *Journal of Conflict Resolution,* Mar. 1962, **6** (No. 1), 52–76.

Flood, M. M. Some experimental games. *Management Science,* 1958, **5,** 5–26.

Gallo, P. S. The effects of different motivational orientations in a mixed motive game. Unpublished Ph.D. thesis, University of California at Los Angeles, 1963.

Homans, G. *Social behavior: Its elementary forms.* New York: Harcourt, 1961.

Kelley, H. H. The consequences of different patterns of interdependency in small groups. *Final Report to National Science Foundation,* 1953.

Kelley, H. H., Thibaut, J. W., Radloff, R., and Mundy, D. The development of cooperation in the minimal social situation. *Psychological Monographs,* 1962, **76,** 1–19.

Loomis, J. L. Communication, the development of trust and cooperative behavior. *Human Relations,* 1959, **12,** 305–315.

Luce, R. D., and Raiffa, H. *Games and decisions.* New York: Wiley, 1957.

Lutzker, D. R. Internationalism as a predictor of cooperative behavior. *Journal of Conflict Resolution,* Dec. 1960, **4** (No. 4), 426–430.

Marlowe, D. Some personality and behavioral correlates of conformity. Unpublished Ph.D. thesis, Ohio State University, 1959.

McClintock, C. G., Gallo, P. S., and Harrison, A. Some effects of variations in other strategy upon game behavior. *Journal of Personality and Social Psychology,* 1965, **1,** 319–325.

McClintock, C. G., Harrison, A., Strand J., and Gallo, P. Internationalism-isolationism, strategy of the other player, and two-person game behavior. *Journal of Abnormal and Social Psychology,* 1963, **67,** 631–635.

Minas, J. S., Scodel, A., Marlowe, D., and Rawson, H. Some descriptive aspects of two-person, non-zero-sum games. II. *Journal of Conflict Resolution,* June 1960, **4** (No. 2), 193–197.

Mintz, A. Non-adaptive group behavior. *Journal of Abnormal and Social Psychology,* 1951, **46,** 150–159.

Rapoport, A. *Prisoner's dilemma,* Ann Arbor: Univ. of Michigan Press, 1966.

Rapoport, A., and Orwant, C. Experimental games: A review. *Behavioral Science,* 1962, **7** (No. 1), 1–37.

Scodel, A. Induced collaboration in some non-zero-sum games. *Journal of Conflict Resolution,* Dec. 1962, **6** (No. 4), 335–340.

Scodel, A., Minas J. S., Ratoosh, P., and Lipetz, M. Some descriptive aspects of two-person-non-zero-sum games. *Journal of Conflict Resolution,* June 1959, **3** (No. 2), 114–119.

Sidowski, J. B., Wykoff, L. B., and Tabory, H. The influence of reinforcement and punishment in a minimal social situation. *Journal of Abnormal and Social Psychology,* 1956, **52,** 115–119.

Solomon, L. The influence of some types of power relationships and game strategies upon the development of interpersonal trust. *Journal of Abnormal and Social Psychology,* 1960, **61,** 223–230.

Thibaut, J., and Kelley, H. *The social psychology of groups.* New York: Wiley, 1959.

Wilson, K. V., and Bixenstine, V. E. Effects of a third choice on behavior in a Prisoner's Dilemma game. Nebraska Psychiatric Institute and Kent State University, 1962. (Mimeo.)

Wilson, W., Chun, N., and Kayatani, M. Projection, attraction, and strategy choices in intergroup competition. University of Hawaii, 1964. (Mimeo.)

ARTICLE 8

Effects of Other Person's Strategy and Race upon Cooperative Behavior in a Prisoner's Dilemma Game

Lawrence S. Wrightsman, Dan W. Davis, William G. Lucker, Robert H. Bruininks, James R. Evans, Richard E. Wilde, Dennis G. Paulson, and Gary M. Clark

The purposes of this study were the following: (1) to find out if types of game strategy used by the other person influence the extent of the subject's cooperation, and (2) to determine if Southern undergraduates cooperate less with a black than with a white in a two-person non-zero-sum game. . . .

Although the race of the other player would seem to be a significant factor influencing the extent of cooperation in a mixed-motive game, apparently few studies have looked at this dimension. Several studies done at the University of Hawaii have looked at ethnic-group differences in cooperative behavior; for instance, Wilson and Wong (1965) compared levels of cooperation in pairs of students of Caucasian ancestry and pairs of students of Japanese ancestry, using a modified PD game. On each trial, homogeneous ethnic-group pairs first played with confederates, then between themselves. Confederates were always of the same ethnic group as the subjects. Results showed that subjects of Japanese ancestry made significantly more cooperative responses than did those of Caucasian ancestry. Wong's (1964) unpublished study replicated this finding.* However, since all four subjects in a particular group were of the same ethnic ancestry, no conclusions could be drawn regarding differences in cooperation when the "other player" was a member of a different ethnic group.

Uejio and Wrightsman (1967) remedied this by completing a PD game in which 80 Japanese-American and Caucasian female subjects played against another female, either of the same ethnic group or the other one. Each subject was told the first name and the ethnic background of the other subject. Instead of playing against the other subject, as she was led to believe, each subject played a 50-trial game against a preprogrammed set of responses which were cooperative 76% of the time. Over the 50 trials, Japanese-Americans were nonsignificantly more cooperative (21.43 vs. 18.05 cooperative choices, or 42.8% vs. 36.1%) than were Caucasians. Each group tended to be more cooperative when the other player was a member of the other ethnic group than when the other player was a member of her own group, but the interaction was not significant. . . .

Cooperation between the Caucasian and Negro races is often proposed as a goal of contemporary American society. Thus it is surprising that apparently no studies have been done combating adult whites and blacks in a two-person game. Two studies have compared black-white differences in extent of cooperation, but only one pitted one race against the other. Sampson and Kardush (1965) used black and white children ages 7–11 as

Adapted from *Cooperation and Competition: Readings on Mixed-Motive Games* by Lawrence S. Wrightsman, Jr., John O'Connor, and Norma H. Baker. Copyright 1972 by Wadsworth Publishing Company, Inc. Reprinted with permission of the publisher, Brooks/Cole Publishing Company, Monterey, California.

*This study has been published by Wilson and Wong (1968)—Eds.

subjects in a two-person game. Each dyad was homogeneous in regard to race. At both older and younger age levels and in the case of both sexes, black children were more cooperative than were white children of the same social-class level. Sampson and Kardush report: "42 percent of the Negro responses indicate either a polite or a collaborative strategy while only 19 percent of the white responses do. If we break this down even further, it is interesting to note that 21 percent of the Negro responses were categorized in the polite or considerate category, whereas *none* of the white responses were so categorized. This indicates that the Negroes not only collaborated but acted in a manner to help their partner gain higher rewards for himself" (1965, p. 219; italics in original). But this study did not confront whites with blacks in the same dyad, so it has no direct implications for the present study.

The other study (Harford & Cutter, 1966) did compare the results of 20 white boys (ages 6–12) who played against another white boy for 10 trials and then either against another white or a black boy. There were significant decreases in cooperation in the second set of trials regardless of whether these white boys interacted with other whites or with black boys. The geographical origin of the subjects is not specified. Since the number of subjects per condition was likewise restricted, it is hard to evaluate the non-significant nature of the differences in this study.

The role of one's attitude toward blacks might affect his extent of cooperation. We could expect that anti-black subjects, when playing against a black, might be more likely to choose competitively, as this choice is often interpreted as representing the expression of aggression. On the other hand, the extremely pro-black subject might be more inclined to be cooperative when interacting with a black than when interacting with a white. Such an analysis would then use attitude toward blacks as a moderating variable to explain differential predictions.

Turning to a consideration of the role of the strategy of the other person upon extent of cooperation, we find that the strategy of the other player (whether he is cooperative or competitive) has only sometimes had an effect upon the sub-

ject's level of cooperation. Among those showing an effect are the studies of Solomon (1960), Wong (1964), Nathenson (1966), and Bixenstine and Wilson (1963). For example, Solomon (1960) found that more cooperative responses were made by the subjects when they played against a matching strategy than against either an unconditionally cooperative or an unconditionally competitive strategy. Bixenstine and Wilson (1963) found similar differences when 95% cooperative vs. 95% competitive strategies were compared.

In an unpublished study Wong (1964) studied the role of the strategy of the other person upon intergroup and intragroup cooperation. Each group was composed of two subjects and two confederates, the latter having been instructed to use either a cooperative, a competitive, or an accommodating strategy. Subjects and confederates would first make a choice as a team, playing against the other dyad. Then each individual also made an intragroup choice to determine the distribution of the team's winnings, if any. If the confederate was to play cooperatively, he chose blue (the cooperative response) on 18 of the 20 trials. If he was to use a competitive strategy, he chose red on every trial. An accommodating strategy was defined as choosing cooperatively on the first trial and then on each of the following trials, picking what the subject had chosen on the previous trial. The competitive strategy on the part of the confederate did elicit more competition from the subject, but there were no differences in cooperation between the cooperative and accommodating treatments. Nathenson (1966) also found that the competitive strategy elicited less cooperation than did any of three other types, a cooperative type and two "accommodating types." One of his accommodating types, in which the confederate matched the choice of the subject from the previous trial, produced the most cooperation.

On the other hand, several studies have shown no effect as a result of variations in the strategy of the other player. Gallo and McClintock (1965), in reviewing the literature, report:

Bixenstine, Potash, and Wilson (1963) used a random strategy of 83 percent cooperative responses for one group and 83 percent competitive responses for a second group, followed in all groups by an 83 percent matching strategy. McClintock, Harrison, Strand, and Gallo (1963) used random strategies of 85 percent; 50 percent, and 15 percent cooperative responses for their three groups. Neither experiment demonstrated any effect of the "other's" strategy on the choice behavior of the subject [1965, p. 73].

A possible moderating factor which may explain these conflicting results is the sequence of responses. Most of the studies in which other's strategy made a difference used a successive means of responding; i.e., one subject responded and the other subject knew the first subject's response before choosing his. Solomon (1960), Wong (1964), and Nathenson (1966) all used successive responses and found strategy effects. Bixenstine, Potash, and Wilson (1963) and apparently McClintock et al. used a simultaneous method, whereby each subject made his response without knowledge of the other's. In these studies, the absence of strategy effects may be caused by the simultaneous manner of responding.

A possible factor leading to variation in the findings may be the amount of information the subject has about the game procedures. Disclaimers of experimenters to the contrary, it is our impression that many subjects are not clear about the implications of their responses when they begin the experiment. This study attempted to ensure that each subject understood the implications of each type of choice before she began in the hope that this would lead to greater effects from variations in the strategies of the other player. . . .

METHOD

Subjects

A sample pool of 149 Caucasian females was randomly constituted during the Fall semester, 1965, from a list of 198 freshmen women registered at George Peabody College for Teachers. Each member of the sample pool was initially contacted by a letter requesting her voluntary participation in a "psychological research project." A personal telephone contact followed the letter to ascertain each subject's willingness to participate in the study and to schedule a definite

time and date for participation. (Only four subjects refused to participate, and four others failed to arrive at their assigned times.) Telephone contacts continued until 80 subjects had participated in the study. . . .

Apparatus

Each subject worked in a separate laboratory room, containing a chair and table. On the table was a box with lights and switches. A matrix was positioned on each box so that the intersection of the two activated lights corresponded to the payoff for that particular trial. The payoff matrix was as follows:

(switch)	X	+5¢, +5¢	-4¢, +6¢
(switch)	Y	+6¢, -4¢	-3¢, -3¢
		A	B

(The first number in each of the intersections represents the subject's earnings.) . . . The experimenter read all instructions concerning game play to the subjects over an intercom system to speakers in both rooms.

PROCEDURE

Thirty trials of successive contingent choice play in the Prisoner's Dilemma (PD) game constituted the experimental task.

One-half of the subjects were assigned to a Negro "game partner" and the other half to a Caucasian "game partner." These "game partners" were accomplices who were thus used throughout the experiment. Neither the black nor the white accomplices were students; they were hired through an employment agency. Participation of the accomplices was counterbalanced to avoid possible confounding by order effects. The accomplices were trained to follow one of four sets of preprogrammed instructions.

The 80 subjects were tested over a two-week period, with a full-time, trained experimenter in charge. Subjects were successively scheduled by random assignment to one of the following conditions of game play:

1. 90% cooperative play in which the accomplice made 90% cooperative (or A) responses;*
2. 90% competitive play in which the accomplice made 90% competitive (or B) responses;*
3. match play in which the accomplice always made a response similar to the response made by the subject for that trial (e.g., if subject chose X the accomplice chose A, or if subject chose Y, the accomplice chose B);
4. uninformed play in which the subject was not given any information regarding either the "other person's" responses or the earnings or losses resulting from any single trial of play.

Thus, the subjects were constituted into groups according to race of the game partner and type of game strategy. The eight treatment conditions each contained ten subjects.

Details of the procedure are as follows:

Subjects were met at the door of the experimental area by the experimenter. The accomplice was already seated at the table in her room. The subject was required to pass in front of the accomplice's room in order to reach her room. The experimenter stopped in front of the open doorway of the accomplice's room to introduce the participants to each other and to mention that they would participate together in the experiment. The accomplice was instructed to look up from the table and nod pleasantly to the subject. No verbal reply was made to the subject by the accomplice. During the actual game play, the experimenter occupied the remaining room.

After the subject was seated, the experimenter read a standard set of instructions from her room to the participants. The subject was told that she had been selected by a "flip of a coin" to choose first on each trial. The instructions used were similar to those of Scodel, Minas, Ratoosh, and Lipetz (1959). Terms were chosen so as to avoid giving the subject an artificial game set. The subject was informed that she could choose either the

*The sequence of the accomplice's responses was randomly determined but was constant for each subject within the same condition.

X or Y light and that the other person (accomplice) would see her choice before making a response. The instructions in the uninformed condition were changed to indicate that the other person's responses would not appear on the participant's control board. The instructions concluded with a brief series of prearranged, simulated trials in order to acquaint the subject with all of the possible combinations of joint-choice responses.

After completing these training trials, both players were requested to fill out a questionnaire consisting of four questions which measured understanding of all possible choice combinations. If an error appeared on the subject's questionnaire, the experimenter stated that her answers were not completely correct and that a portion of the instructions (including simulated game trials) would be repeated. Following the correct completion of the questionnaire, each subject was given $1. The experimenter explained that any losses which occurred during trials would be deducted at the completion of the experiment. Participants were told that they would be allowed to keep all earnings.

During the experiment the experimenter monitored game play and recorded the responses for each trial. The intratrial sequence included a randomly determined one- to six-second time lapse between the subject's and the accomplice's responses, followed by a ten-second time lapse in which the experimenter and the participants recorded earnings (or responses, if in uninformed play) for that trial. The recording period was followed by a ten-second intertrial interval.

After the 30 trials, the experimenter totaled up the subject's earnings while the subject completed a postexperimental questionnaire. The questionnaire required the subject to rate the other player on each of 22 traits and to describe her reactions to the experiment. Subjects earning less than $1.50 were given amounts ranging between $1.50 and $1.75 for their participation; the others were given what they earned.

Subjects were requested not to speak to their friends about the experiment until after its completion. Each subject was asked to (and did) sign a statement agreeing not to tell others about this study until a report was sent to her. Informal checking in the dormitories indicated that this agreement was not universally upheld; it is unclear whether the percentage who talked to others approximated the 64% in Wuebben's (1967) study who admitted violating the promise not to talk. However, a post hoc analysis comparing the scores of the first half of the subjects with the second half showed no differences, so any communication did not seem to influence the results.

Approximately one month after the completion of the project, each subject was sent a letter telling her of the results and explaining the deception employed in the study.

RESULTS

The only variable used to measure the dependent variable, extent of cooperation, was the number of X (cooperative) choices made by the subject on the 30 trials. To analyze the effects of the race and strategy of the other player upon the subject's degree of cooperation, a 2 x 4 x 3 analysis of variance* (Lindquist, Type III, 1953) was used. The third dimension, in addition to race (2 levels) and strategy (4 levels), was a trial-blocks dimension. It was decided to analyze the data by three trial blocks (Trials 1–10, 11–20, and 21–30) to determine if there were changes between trial blocks in numbers of cooperative choices made.

Table 1 presents the mean number of cooperative choices within and across trial blocks under the different experimental conditions. Mean number of cooperative choices for all subjects was 17.45 of the 30 trials. The greatest amount of cooperation occurred when the other player matched the subject's choice; the average was 25.9 and three of the 20 subjects in this condition chose cooperatively on all 30 trials. The mean amount of cooperation under 90% Cooperation (17.7) was very similar to the mean amount when the subject had no information about the other's response (16.2). Responses did not appear to be influenced by the race of the other player, except possibly in the 90% Cooperative condition. Here mean cooperation when the other player was white was 19.7; when the other was black, it was 15.7.

Table 2 presents the analysis of variance for these means. The race of the other player did not have a significant effect on scores, but the strategy of the other player did ($p < .001$). The other significant effect was the interaction between strategy and trial blocks ($p < .001$).

This interaction was analyzed to determine the simple effects, first looking at strategy differences in each trial block. On Trial Block 1, these strategy differences were significant (see bottom row of Table 1 for means; $F = 19.077$, d$f = 3/76$, $p < .001$). There is homogeneity of variance (F_{max} test, $F = 1.676$, $df = 19/19$, $p > .05$) for strategy conditions on Trial Block 1, so the error term was pooled in order to test simple effects using t tests. Table 3 presents the means, standard deviations, and t tests[†] for each strategy condition on Trial Block 1. It indicates that each pairwise comparison except that between 90% Cooperation and Matching is significant; in other words, even during the first 10 trials the varying strategies were influencing extent of cooperation. Even during the first 10 trials, the matching strategy had led to greater cooperation than had the 90% Cooperation strategy or the condition in which the subject had no information about the other. Also, on the first 10 trials, the 90% Competitive strategy had led to less cooperation than any of the other strategies.

On Trial Block 2 (Trials 11–20) the strategies also led to significant differences in cooperation ($F = 18.549$, $df = 3/76$, $p < .001$). The variances are heterogeneous (F_{max} test, $F = 4.505$, $df = 19/19$, $p < .05$) for strategy conditions on Trial Block 2, so the error terms could not be pooled for testing simple effects using t tests. The significant differences are the same as those for Trial Block 1; that is, Matching > 90% Cooperation; 90% Cooperation = No Information; No Information > 90% Competition.

*For definition of analysis of variance, see footnote on page 17 or Glossary.

†For definition of t test, see footnote on page 23 or Glossary.

TABLE 1. Mean number of cooperative choices made in each trial block and under each condition.

Race of other player	90% cooperative trial block: 1	2	3	Total	90% competitive trial block: 1	2	3	Total	Strategy of other player: matching trial block: 1	2	3	Total	no information trial block: 1	2	3	Total	mean across strategies
White	6.8	6.6	6.3	19.7	3.8	3.5	2.0	9.3	7.4	9.0	9.2	25.6	5.3	5.3	5.4	16.0	17.65
Black	5.2	4.8	5.7	15.7	4.0	4.2	2.5	10.7	8.1	9.2	·8.9	26.2	5.0	6.1	5.3	16.4	17.25
Mean across Races	6.0	5.7	6.0	17.7	3.9	3.85	2.25	10.0	7.75	9.1	9.05	25.9	5.15	5.7	5.35	16.2	17.45

Note. N of subjects = 80; N of trials = 30.

TABLE 2. Analysis of variance of programmed conditions and race across trial blocks.

Source	df	SS	MS	F
Race (B)	1	1.066	1.066	.107
Strategy conditions (C)	3	856.266	285.422	28.717*
B X C	3	30.334	10.111	1.017
Error (B)	72	715.600	9.939	
Trials (A)	2	8.858	4.429	2.336
A X B	2	.509	.255	.134
A X C	6	54.709	9.118	4.809*
A X B X C	6	9.591	1.599	.843
Error (n)	144	273.000	1.896	

*$p < .001$.

TABLE 3. Means, SDs, and t tests of conditions (C) for trials 1-10 (A_1).

M	SD	Conditions	C_1	C_2	C_3	C_4
6.0	1.89	90% Cooperation (C_1)		4.015**	3.346**	1.625
3.9	1.62	90% Competition (C_2)			7.361**	2.39*
7.75	1.62	Matching (C_3)				4.971**

*$p < .05$.
**$p < .01$.

TABLE 4. Means, SDs, and t tests of conditions (C) for trials 11-20 (A_2).

M	SD	Conditions	C_1	C_2	C_3	C_4
5.7	2.62	C_1		2.50*	5.18**	0
3.85	2.03	C_2			9.686**	2.377*
9.1	1.33	C_3				4.864**
5.7	2.83	C_4				

*$p < .05$.
**$p < .01$.

On Trial Block 3 (Trials 21–30) the strategies had the same effects ($F = 27.672$, $df = 3/76$, $p < .001$). The variances were heterogeneous (F_{max} test, $F = 3.59$, $df = 19/19$, $p < .05$) for strategy conditions on the third trial block, so the error terms could not be pooled for testing simple effects using t tests. Table 5 presents the means,

the significant interaction effects between strategy and trial blocks, we may say the following:

1. The levels of cooperation in the 90% Cooperation and the No Information conditions do not differ from each other on any of the three trial blocks; nor do the levels significantly vary from one trial block to another.

TABLE 5. Means, SDs, and t tests of conditions (C) for trials 21-30 (A_3).

M	SD	Conditions	t			
			C_1	C_2	C_3	C_4
6.0	2.88	C_1		5.026*	4.160*	.701
2.25	1.68	C_2			13.229*	4.057*
9.05	1.57	C_3				4.928*
5.35	2.98	C_4				

*$p < .01$.

standard deviations, and t values for pairwise comparisons for Trial Block 3. Once again, Matching leads to significantly more cooperation than does the 90% Cooperation condition or the No Information condition, and the 90% Competition condition leads to significantly less cooperation.

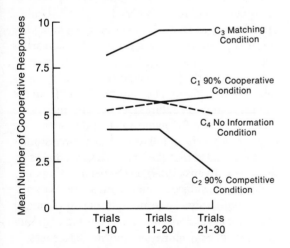

FIGURE 1.   Mean number of cooperative responses for each trial block for each condition.

The other analysis of the strategy X trial block interaction studied the differences in trial block means for each separate strategy condition. . . .

Figure 1 graphically portrays these changes over trial blocks. To summarize the analysis of

2. The level of cooperation in the 90% Competitive condition is significantly less on all three trial blocks. On the first 10 trials it is lower than are the levels for other conditions at that stage. This level stays about the same on the second 10 trials, but significantly decreases on the third 10 trials.

3. The level of cooperation in the Matching condition is significantly higher than that of the other conditions on each of the three trial blocks. It increases significantly from the first to second trial block and remains there.

There is one other finding worthy of note in the race-strategy relationships. Note that, in Table 1, in the 90% Cooperation condition, the number of cooperative choices when the other player is white averages 19.7, while it is 15.7 when the other player is black. Since there was no significant strategy-by-race interaction, this difference is not significant. Yet it is provocative that the largest race effect occurred in the direction that it did and *in the strategy condition* that it did, for it is in this condition that the subject has a chance to exploit the other player. Even though the subject chooses first, she can soon learn that whatever she chooses, the other player almost always will push X, giving the subject a chance to take more for herself. We hypothesized that if this exploitation were to occur, it would be directed more toward the black than toward the white, and that it would occur here. However, not only is the interaction nonsignificant, but also a separate t test for these 20 subjects produced a t value of 1.38, which is nonsignificant. . . .

DISCUSSION

Subject to the particular features of the PD game utilized in the present study, certain generalizations may be drawn. The features which may limit the generalizability of these conclusions to other PD game play are the following:

1. The effects resulting from the particular apparatus and procedures used, particularly the use of a sequential method of responding.

2. The instructions, which intentionally avoided any specific reference to competition and also clarified the contingency of any single outcome—i.e., the result is dependent upon the choice made by both players.

3. The population was composed of female freshmen who had never previously participated in a psychological experiment.

4. The limitations imposed by programming only four types of other's strategy.

The conclusions to be drawn are as follows:

1. The most relevant factor affecting the subject's choice behavior is "other's" play. The subjects' attitudes toward human nature have some minimal effect, but even distrusting players predominantly cooperate when the other player reinforces their cooperation.

2. The prevalent myth that subjects never approach 50% cooperative responses in a 30-trial game is emphatically disproven. Subjects in all the strategy conditions except the 90% Competitive one averaged better than 50% cooperation, and the Matching condition elicited an average of 86% cooperation.

3. To effect greatest levels of cooperation from the subject, matching play, or an accommodating strategy, is much more effective than an unconditionally cooperative strategy. This reinforces a similar finding by Nathenson, who found that two types of accommodating strategy were more effective than a predominantly cooperative strategy (not based on the subject's choice). The weak influence of an unconditionally cooperative strat-

egy is indicated by the fact that the amount of cooperation elicited by it did not significantly differ from "no information" about the player's response. The greater power of the matching strategy in eliciting cooperation appears to lie in its emphasis on reinforcement. Subjects in the Matching condition soon learn that if they seek a maximum individual gain (by choosing Y and hoping the other player will choose X), their choice is negatively reinforced. But if they choose X, they are positively reinforced. That this learning occurs quickly is indicated by the fact that cooperation is higher in this condition even on the first 10 trials. On the other hand, the 90% Cooperative condition represents a random reinforcement schedule. The subject is not negatively reinforced for competitive choices—in fact, he is sometimes rewarded for them. The degree to which he can compete and exploit—and get away with it—is limited only by his fear of retaliation and his spirit of fair play.

4. Contrary to the statement made by Gallo and McClintock (1965), the present authors believe that the amount and clarity of *information*, rather than the amount of reward, is the most relevant dimension of PD game play in need of investigation. Gallo and McClintock cite Gallo's (1963) study as an indication that large monetary rewards produce more cooperation than do artificial rewards. This study used the "Trucker's" game, a procedure similar to the PD game in its mixed-motive nature, but quite different from the PD game in its structure. Despite this finding, no study *using the PD game* has found that the size of the rewards is an influence,[*] and three studies have concluded that the size of rewards makes no difference. Evans (1964), using pennies vs. points added to the subject's final exam score; Wrightsman (1966), using large amounts of real vs. imaginary money; and Oskamp,[†] using varying amounts of real money, found no differences.

The present authors believe that the amount of training and pre-experimental testing given the subjects in the present study may account for the subjects' relatively high levels of cooperation. Previous studies have not always been clear in

---

[*]At the time this article was written.—(Eds.)

[†]Oskamp, S. Personal communication, April 3, 1967.

regard to the extent of training and instructions given to their subjects. In the present study, no subject participated until after she was able to answer five questions about the outcomes and implications of various choice combinations. Our impression is that this study emphasized pre-training more than most, but, as we did not vary amount of training in this study, we have no proof that it is a factor.

5. The results of this study add to the conclusion that the sequential method of responding *may* encourage greater effects from varying the strategy of the other player. Most of the previous studies using a sequential method of responding (Solomon, 1960; Nathenson, 1966; Wong, 1964) found a strategy effect, while those using simultaneous responding did not (McClintock et al., 1963; Bixenstine et al., 1963). Dramatic differences in cooperation were demonstrated in the present study, using a sequential method in which the subject always responded first. Apparently, no study has compared these two methods in regard to their capacity to elicit strategy differences; certainly this point needs to be clarified.

6. For the subjects of the present study, who mostly are Southern in origin, game responses are not affected by the race of the other player. Neither differential expectation was verified—white coeds do not cooperate more with a white or with a black. A reciprocal *F* test was not significant; i.e., the groups were not more alike than could be expected by chance alone.

REFERENCES

Bixenstine, V. E., Potash, H. M., & Wilson, K. V. Effects of level of cooperative choice by the other player on choices in a Prisoner's Dilemma game: Part I. *Journal of Abnormal and Social Psychology,* 1963, **66,** 303–313.

Bixenstine, V. E., & Wilson, K. V. Effects of level of cooperative choice by the other player in a Prisoner's Dilemma game: Part II. *Journal of Abnormal and Social Psychology,* 1963, **67,** 139–147.

Evans, G. Effect of unilateral promise and value of rewards upon cooperation and trust. *Journal of Abnormal and Social Psychology,* 1964, **69,** 587–590.

Gallo, P. S. The effects of different motivational orientations in a mixed-motive game. Unpublished doctoral dissertation, University of California at Los Angeles, 1963.

Gallo, P. S., & McClintock, C. G. Cooperative and competitive behavior in mixed-motive games. *Journal of Conflict Resolution,* 1965, **9,** 68–78.

Harford, T. C., & Cutter, H. S. G. Cooperation among Negro and white boys and girls. *Psychological Reports,* 1966, **18,** 818.

Lindquist, E. F. *The design and analysis of experiments in psychology and education.* Boston: Houghton-Mifflin, 1953.

McClintock, C. G., Harrison, A., Strand, S., & Gallo, P. S. Internationalism-isolationism, strategy of the other player, and two-person game behavior. *Journal of Abnormal and Social Psychology,* 1963, **67,** 631–635.

Nathenson, M. The effect of four types of strategies upon cooperative behavior in a two-person game. Unpublished master's thesis, University of Hawaii, 1966.

Sampson, E. E., & Kardush, M. Age, sex, class, and race differences in response to a two-person non-zero-sum game. *Journal of Conflict Resolution,* 1965, **9,** 212–220.

Scodel, A., Minas, J. S., Ratoosh, P., & Lipetz, M. Some descriptive aspects of two-person non-zero-sum games. *Journal of Conflict Resolution,* 1959, **3,** 114–119.

Solomon, L. The influence of some types of power relationships and game strategies upon the development of interpersonal trust. *Journal of Abnormal and Social Psychology,* 1960, **61,** 223–230.

Uejio, C. K., & Wrightsman, L. S. Ethnic-group differences in the relationship of trusting attitudes to cooperative behavior. *Psychological Reports,* 1967, **20,** 563–571.

Wilson, W., & Wong, J. Intergroup attitudes and strategies in non-zero-sum dilemma games: I. Differential response to cooperative and competitive opponents. Unpublished manuscript, University of Hawaii, 1965.

Wilson, W., & Wong, J. Intergroup attitudes towards cooperative vs. competitive opponents in a modified Prisoner's Dilemma game. *Perceptual and Motor Skills,* 1968, **27**(3), 1059–1066.

Wong, J. The effect of cooperative, competitive, and accommodating intergroup strategies. Unpublished manuscript, University of Hawaii, 1964.

Wrightsman, L. S. Personality and attitudinal correlates of trusting and trustworthy behaviors in a two-person game. *Journal of Personality and Social Psychology,* 1966, **4,** 328–332.

Wuebben, P. L. Honesty of subjects and birth order. *Journal of Personality and Social Psychology,* 1967, **5,** 350–352.

Betrayal and Reconciliation in a Two-Person Game[1]

S. S. Komorita and John Mechling[2]

Of a variety of experimental games suggested by game theory, probably of greatest interest to psychologists is the two-person Prisoner's Dilemma game.[3] This game is structured in such a way that each player is faced with a conflict of motives—a motive to maximize *personal* gain versus the motive to maximize *mutual* gain. Some investigators, therefore, have used it as a paradigm for the study of cooperation and competition. Another interesting aspect of this game is that a cooperative choice implicitly implies trust in the other person, since it would be foolish to cooperate if one did not expect the other to reciprocate such a choice. One of the interesting problems, therefore, is to determine the relevant variables which lead to the development of trust.

The typical paradigm in past research has been to present a large number of trials to subjects and relate certain experimental variables with the degree of cooperative choice over trials. Deutsch, for example, has shown that communication and the motivational orientation of subjects are critical variables, and Rapoport has shown that the payoff values of the matrix affect the degree of

From *Journal of Personality and Social Psychology,* **6,** 1967, 349–353. Copyright 1967 by the American Psychological Association, and reproduced by permission.

[1]This study was supported, in part, by a grant from the Carnegie Foundation to the Center for the Study of Cognitive Processes, Wayne State University.

[2]The junior author was a participant in the National Science Foundation Undergraduate Research Participation Program during the conduct of this study.

[3]For a detailed discussion of this game see Luce and Raiffa (1957), and for a review of empirical research see Rapoport and Orwant (1962) and Gallo and McClintock (1965).

cooperation (Deutsch, 1960; Rapoport & Chammah, 1965).

Rapoport and Chammah (1965) have also shown that the proportion of cooperative choices over a series of trials is U shaped, declining initially, and then increasing on later trials. There are large individual differences, however, and some subjects reach an asymptotic stage where they never make cooperative responses. In such studies where subjects are given a large number of trials it is assumed, explicitly or implicitly, that trust and cooperation are learned and develop over the course of trials.

Although the present study made the same assumption, unlike in previous research an attempt was made to determine the conditions under which an act of betrayal leads to distrust or suspicion, and the variables which influence the process of reconciliation. In effect, the subjects were instructed to assume a cooperative orientation; the cooperative orientation was extinguished by leading them to believe that they had been betrayed; then the recovery of cooperative choice was used as the response measure. It was assumed, of course, that the study of betrayal and reconciliation would lead to a better understanding of the development of trust.

METHOD

Subjects

The subjects for the study were 64 undergraduate students (32 women and 32 men) enrolled in introductory psychology classes, and participating in the experiment to fulfill part of their requirements for the course.

Procedure

All subjects were scheduled in pairs of the same sex and were seated across a table facing each other with a wooden partition between them so that they could not see each other. In front of each subject was a subject control panel displaying the game matrix with two buttons (push-button switches), red and black, corresponding to the two choices in the game. The experimenter sat at right angles to the subjects with another wooden partition separating him from both subjects. A master control panel was wired in such a way that the experimenter could receive information about the subjects' choices on each trial and also permitted the experimenter to send preprogrammed feedback to both subjects simultaneously. When both subjects pressed a button on their panels, a light in one of the cells of the matrix came on indicating to each subject how much each had won as well as the choice made by the other. Another light on the subject control panel served as a signal for the beginning of a trial.

Subjects were instructed that the values of the matrix represented points and that their task was to accumulate as many points as possible. They were also informed that these points would be converted to money at the end of the experiment, not necessarily on a one-to-one basis, but the more points they accumulated the more money they would receive.

In order to ensure cooperation at the outset, a modification of Deutsch's cooperative orientation was used (Deutsch, 1960); for example, part of the instructions was as follows:

Let me emphasize that you should consider yourselves to be partners. You're interested in your partner's welfare as well as your own. You care how she does and she cares how you do. In other words, choose the combination where you can both benefit the most. . . .

After making certain that subjects understood the instruction and the experimental situation, they were instructed not to talk or communicate with each other.

All subjects were led to believe that they were playing with each other, but in actuality they were playing against the experimenter. They were led to believe that they were cooperating with each other for a number of trials, and then were double-crossed on two consecutive trials. Thereafter, the experimenter played "red" (cooperative choice) on three consecutive trials, and subsequently initiated the previous responses of the subject; for example, if the subject played "red," the experimenter played "red" on the next trial. The response measure of reconciliation was the number of trials to reach a criterion of five consecutive cooperative responses after the two betrayals.

TABLE 1.   Game matrix with two independent variables: temptation (T) and loss (L).[a]

		Other (E)	
		Red	Black
S	Red	5, 5	L, T
	Black	T, L	1, 1

[a]Left and right cell entries denote payoffs to subject and other, respectively.

Independent Variables

Three variables, each with two levels, were manipulated. In Table 1 and Figure 1, two of these variables are summarized, where T refers to temptation (to defect) and L refers to the loss incurred when betrayed. All subjects received 5 points for the "red, red" combination and 1 point for the "black, black" combination, and as indicated in Figure 1 the manipulated values of temptation were 6 and 9, and the losses when betrayed were 0 and -5.

It was hypothesized that the greater the harm experienced when betrayed, the greater the effects of the betrayal; hence, it was predicted that the -5 condition would require a greater number of trials for reconciliation to occur. With regard to the effects of temptation, it was hypothesized that it would require more trials for reconciliation when temptation was slight than when it was large. The rationale is that when one is betrayed when the other's temptation is negligible, it implies an intent on the part of the other to injure and harm rather than to maximize his own gain.

The third variable consisted of the number of cooperative trials before the betrayal with 4 and 10 trials before the two double-crosses. This treatment was intended to vary the expectation of a cooperative response. It was hypothesized that if an individual strongly expected a cooperative response from the other person, the effects of a disconfirmation of this expectation ought to be greater than if the expectation was not as strong. Accordingly, it was predicted that subjects with 10 mutually cooperative trials would require a larger number of trials for reconciliation than subjects with 4 such trials.

In summary, there were three independent variables, each with two levels: (a) temptation, T (6 and 9), (b) loss incurred, L (0 and -5), and (c) number of cooperative trials before the betrayal (4 and 10 trials). The levels of the three variables were factorially combined to form a 2^3 factorial analysis of variance design with eight subjects in each condition. In addition, there was an equal number of men and women in each condition (2 pairs each), but the analysis indicated that neither main effect nor any of the interactions involving sex was significant; hence, the results for sex differences have been omitted. Finally, a postexperimental questionnaire consisting of a set of evaluative semantic differential scales was also administered to subjects asking them to rate the other person's behavior as well as their own.

T(6), L(0)	
5, 5	0, 6
6, 0	1, 1

T(9), L(0)	
5, 5	0, 9
9, 0	1, 1

T(6), L(-5)	
5, 5	-5, 6
6, -5	1, 1

T(9), L(-5)	
5, 5	-5, 9
9, -5	1, 1

FIGURE 1.   Game matrices showing values of T (6 and 9) and L (0 and -5).

RESULTS

The data for five subjects (three in the 10-trial condition and two in the 4-trial condition) were discarded because they responded noncooperatively on one or more trials before the experimenter could double-cross them. For the 64 subjects who responded cooperatively until the first betrayal, Table 2 shows the proportions of cooperative choices for the first five trials after the first of two betrayals. It can be seen that the majority of subjects ignored the first betrayal; but after the second, most subjects reciprocated the defection. In general, the rates of recovery after the two betrayals are very rapid, but this is not unreasonable since the experimenter responded cooperatively for three consecutive trials after the two betrayals. The rates of recovery also seem to vary for the different experimental conditions, and these differences are consistent with the means for number of trials to criterion shown in Table 3. Since the variances of the data in Table 3 were highly heterogeneous, for the purpose of the analysis of variance a reciprocal transformation was used, and Hartley's F_{max} test indicated that the variances of the transformed data were not significantly different ($F_{max} = 6.818$; $df = 7$, 8; $p < .05$).

Table 4 shows the summary data for the analysis of variance* based upon the transformed data. It can be seen that all three main effects are significant at the .05 level. The triple interaction and the Trials X Loss first-order interaction, however, are also significant. It can be seen in Table 3 that these interactions are due mainly to the highly discrepant mean of 22.6 for the high-temptation, high-loss, four-trial condition. Accordingly, in order to provide evidence for the reliability of these interaction effects, this condition was replicated on eight additional subjects. The mean number of trials to criterion for this group was found to be 24.75, and is consistent with the mean of 22.16 for the original group of eight subjects.

Table 3 shows that when the loss incurred is

*For definition of analysis of variance, see footnote on page 17 or Glossary.

TABLE 2.   Proportions of cooperative choices immediately after the first of two consecutive betrayals.

Trials	4 cooperative trials				10 cooperative trials				Mean proportion
	T(6)		T(9)		T(6)		T(9)		
	L(0)	L(-5)	L(0)	L(-5)	L(0)	L(-5)	L(0)	L(-5)	
1	.75	.62	.25	.50	1.0	.87	.75	.87	.70
2	.37	.25	.37	.12	.62	.25	.25	.62	.36
3	.75	.50	.87	.50	.87	.62	.37	.37	.61
4	1.0	.75	.87	.50	1.0	.62	.50	1.0	.78
5	1.0	.50	1.0	.37	1.0	.75	.62	.87	.77

TABLE 3.   Means and standard deviations (in parentheses) of number of trials to Criterion.

	4 cooperative trials		10 cooperative trials		Grand Means
	T(6)	T(9)	T(6)	T(9)	
L(0)	6.87 (0.80)	8.75 (5.78)	6.50 (0.57)	9.37 (3.78)	7.87
L(-5)	11.87 (5.41)	22.12 (8.97)	10.37 (5.29)	9.12 (5.69)	13.37
Grand means	4 trials: 12.41		10 trials: 8.84		
	T(6): 8.91		T(9): 12.34		

small ($L = 0$), the effect of the number of prior cooperative trials is negligible. When the loss is large, however, there is a marked effect of the number of cooperative trials when temptation is high but not when it is low. Thus, there seems to be a multiplicative effect of the three variables on trials to criterion.

TABLE 4.   Summary analysis of variance table.[a]

Source	MS	F
Temptation (T)	65.205	5.258[*]
Loss (L)	264.062	21.294[**]
Trials	72.675	5.861[*]
T X L	2.891	--
T X Trials	13.142	9.061[**]
T X L X Trials	80.998	6.532[*]
Error	12.401	

[a]Data for the effects of sex have been omitted since neither main effect nor interactions involving sex were significant.

[*]$p < .05$, $df = 1/48$.
[**]$p < .01$, $df = 1/48$.

One possible explanation for the interaction effects is that in the discrepant condition involving high temptation, high loss, and four prior cooperative trials, information about the intentions of the other was more ambiguous. Since perceived intentions were uncertain and the negative consequence of being betrayed was severe, subjects in this condition may have attempted to minimize the risk and consequences of another betrayal. Another explanation is that when temptation and loss are high, a certain number of mutually reinforcing trials is necessary before such reinforcements have any effects. Subjects in the 10-trial condition had experienced the rewards of mutual cooperation for 10 trials, and it is plausible that the 4-trial group had not had a sufficient number of reinforcing experiences to overcome the suspicion and fear of another betrayal.

With regard to the effects of the loss when betrayed, the data indicate, as predicted, that the greater the magnitude of the loss, the more trials it requires for reconciliation to occur. However, the significant interaction also indicates that this effect is greater under the 4-trial than under the 10-trial condition. For temptation to defect, the results indicate that the *smaller* the temptation, the *fewer* trials necessary for reconciliation. This is contrary to the author's prediction and suggests an interesting question concerning the effects of temptation—namely, whether the effect of temptation is a function of the subject's *own* temptation to defect, or a function of the subject's fear that the *other* person is tempted. This is especially relevant when the temptation is high, but a similar question may be asked when the temptation is small; that is, when temptation is small, subjects have very little reason to continue responding competitively, but it is plausible that they project this motive to the other person as well.

Still another motivating factor is the amount of resentment or hostility aroused by the betrayal. In the postexperimental questionnaire, subjects were asked to evaluate the other person's behavior as well as their own on a semantic differential scale with bipolar adjectives like "fair-unfair," "honest-dishonest," "clean-dirty," and the data were analyzed for the different conditions. The one significant result was the main effect for temptation ($F = 4.099$; $df = 1, 48$) indicating that the high-temptation groups negatively evaluated the other person's behavior significantly more than the low-temptation groups. Thus, resentment may have played a significant role in the process of reconciliation.

The data for the effects of temptation and consequences of a betrayal are consistent with the results found by Rapoport and Chammah (1965), who used a conventional paradigm where subjects played the game over a large number of trials. Their results showed that the proportion of cooperative choices was smaller when temptation was large and when the negative consequence of making a cooperative response (when the other person defects) was small. Whereas subjects in their study actually played each other over a large number of trials, in the present study there were much fewer trials and all subjects were given a preprogrammed sequence of feedback responses. The results of this study, nevertheless, lend support to the results found by Rapoport and Chammah, and the implications of the results for these two variables seem to be clear—the process of reconciliation seems to follow the same underlying principles as the development of trust.

The implications regarding the effect of the number of prior cooperative trials, on the other hand, are not as clear. Under the assumption that the stronger the expectation, the greater the effects of a disconfirmation of the expectation, it had been predicted that the high-expectation groups would require a large number of trials for reconciliation. Since the opposite tendency was found for the 4-trial group under the high-loss, high-temptation condition, a post hoc explanation is that this group had not experienced or learned the reinforcing effects of mutual cooperation. It is plausible that subjects in this situation, like animals in an avoidance conditioning paradigm, were not "aware" that betrayal (punishment) was no longer forthcoming, and the severity of the loss for the betrayal made it difficult to overcome their fear of another betrayal. The interesting paradox is that if we could somehow coerce or entice subjects to cooperate at the outset, they would experience the mutual benefits of cooperation, and generalizing from the results of this study, trust and cooperative behavior should be greatly facilitated.

REFERENCES

Deutsch, M. The effect of motivational orientation upon trust and suspicion. *Human Relations,* 1960, **13,** 123–139.

Gallo, P. S., & McClintock, C. G. Cooperative and competitive behavior in mixed-motive games. *Journal of Conflict Resolution,* 1965, **9,** 68–78.

Luce, R. D., & Raiffa, H. *Games and decisions.* New York: Wiley, 1957.

Rapoport, A., & Orwant, C. Experimental games: A review. *Behavioral Science,* 1962, **7,** 1–37.

Rapoport, A., & Chammah, A. *Prisoner's dilemma: A study in conflict and cooperation.* Ann Arbor: University of Michigan Press, 1965.

SECTION SUMMARY

It seems appropriate at this point to seek answers to two questions. First, what are the determinants of cooperation, competition, and exploitation in the Prisoner's Dilemma (PD) and other mixed-motive games? Second, can the determinants be applied to conflicts in real-world situations, whether they be interpersonal or international?

The vast literature generated by the interest in mixed-motive games indicates that the degree of cooperation can be influenced by many, but not all, of the ingenious manipulations devised by experimenters. However, generalizations such as this one must always be qualified because of the interaction of situational and intrapersonal factors in the determination of each response by the subject. For example, a unilaterally cooperative strategy on the part of the other participant may elicit cooperation from the subject *only* if the subject had been given a motivational set to cooperate at the beginning of game play. If we review the independent variables selected by Gallo and McClintock in the first article in this section and consider more recent findings, the following conclusions appear to be in order.

1. MANIPULATION OF THE PAYOFF MATRIX

If subjects play for real money instead of imaginary money, degree of cooperation may be increased, decreased, or affected not at all. The same complex conclusion is in order when the size of payoff values is multiplied by a constant of 10 or 100 and real money is used. Some investigators, such as Gallo (1963; Gallo & Sheposh, 1971; Gallo & Winchell, 1970), find that the use of real money encourages more cooperative play. Gallo's Trucking-game study described in the first article in this section, as well as Gallo and Sheposh's (1971) study, found a beneficial effect on cooperation from the use of real money, although the effect in the latter study was minimal. In contrast, neither the massive manipulations of payoff values by Knox and Douglas (1968, 1971) nor those by Wrightsman (1966) had any effect on level of cooperation in brief series of PD-game trials. A careful review by Oskamp and Kleinke (1970) concludes that the size of the reward is unimportant in the Prisoner's Dilemma game but important in the Trucking game.

Where does such a conflicting set of conclusions leave us? It indicates that the effect is not a straightforward one. We need to consider other aspects of game-playing behavior, such as the symbolic nature of rewards. Just what is rewarding in a game? Is it only the visible manifestations of "winning"—the trophy, the monetary gain? No, certainly there are other matters at stake—achievement needs, self-esteem, one's public image. Gallo (1968) has proposed that such symbolic rewards are more important than the tangible monetary ones, whether in a Prisoner's Dilemma game or in real-world encounters. A fascinating series of studies by Bert Brown (1968, 1971) demonstrates that subjects will sacrifice monetary gains in order to "save face"; maintaining an image in front of one's peers is a greater determinant of cooperation (*or* competition) than is the possibility of financial remuneration. Here is an example of mixed-motive game research that extends its concerns into the real world. In the field of international relations, a government official may conclude that the importance of losses of supplies or missile bases or even troops may be minor in comparison to the loss of prestige in the eyes of other nations. We need further understanding of the symbolic rewards in game play. How may they be classified and measured? How do they interact with tangible rewards? Money, as a reward, has the virtue of being quantified and easily communicated; however, it would be a major error to assume that a monetary manipulation covers all the rewards involved in game play.

2. PERSONALITY AND ATTITUDE VARIABLES

The search for personality and attitude characteristics that can be related to extent of cooperation in every situation appears to be a fruitless endeavor. Although occasionally such relationships are found, many times the situation is such that it constrains the possibility of intrapersonal characteristics having any influence. In line with Gallo and McClintock's review, we believe that personalities and attitudes of participants can play a role, but that their effects are moderated by the following considerations.

a. Personality orientations and attitudes toward human nature often influence choices on the *first* trial of a game, but, under the influence of powerful situational determinants, these effects dissipate over a series of trials (Terhune, 1968, 1970; Wrightsman, 1966). For example, if the other participant has adopted a consistently competitive strategy, most subjects will do likewise (as the second article in this section demonstrates), and this reaction occurs regardless of the subject's general disposition toward trust, benevolence, or altruism.

b. The applicability of game behavior as a "criterion" may be questioned. That is, the behavior exhibited in the game may not be a valid, consistent reflection of anything. As Knox and Douglas (1968) indicate, a subject's behavior in the game may at times be so inconsistent from trial to trial that no other variable could possibly be related to it! This point demonstrates the interaction between different types of factors. More inconsistent game behavior appears to occur with smaller rewards, and this situation lowers opportunities for significant attitude-behavior relationships.

c. The restrictions in most mixed-motive games, such as the requirement of a binary choice and the absence of communication or visual interaction, may inhibit the subject in the utilization of his attitudes. Christie and Geis (1970) have shown that Machiavellian attitudes, for example, are much more likely to have influences on interpersonal behavior if the interpersonal situation contains three qualities: face-to-face contact between participants, latitude for improvisation in the kind of response made to the other participant, and opportunities for the participant to capitalize on the feelings the other person displays in the situation. When these factors are absent—as they are in the usual PD game task—Christie and Geis find that highly power-oriented, manipulative, cynical subjects are no more successful than are less Machiavellian ones.

3. STRATEGY OF THE OTHER

The program of studies at Peabody College (reported in Wrightsman, O'Connor, & Baker, 1972) indicates that, within the limits resulting from the procedures used in its studies, a *match-ing strategy* by the other participant is the most powerful single determinant of heightened cooperation by the subject. In five studies that used similar procedures (including the one described in the second article in this section), a matching strategy produced a cooperative choice by the subject in more than 80% of the trials. Many subjects cooperated on 28, 29, or even all 30 trials. The principle of reinforcement reigned supreme; subjects quickly learned that the other participant always chose the same response as theirs and thus came quickly to choose cooperatively themselves.

But the Peabody studies used sequential play, whereas most PD-game studies employ simultaneous play. Results of investigations using the latter type of play are less consistent but still indicate that a matching strategy is an effective device for instilling cooperation in a subject. Again, qualifications abound. For example, different games (Prisoner's Dilemma vs. Chicken game vs. a Maximizing Differences game) produce different results (Oskamp, 1972). Gallo and McClintock's early conclusion that unilateral cooperation by the other participant does not lead to increased cooperation by the subject still holds; in fact, Shure, Meeker, and Hansford (1965) have shown the relatively ineffective nature of a pacifist strategy in a tacit bargaining game. They report that, although 48% of their subjects began the task with the intention of cooperating, only 39% ended up cooperating with the pacifist.

4. POSSIBILITIES FOR COMMUNICATION

The standard Prisoner's Dilemma game does not permit communication between subjects. When this restriction is removed, cooperation levels often increase, as Gallo and McClintock indicate. More recent studies (Durkin, 1972; Wichman, 1970) confirm this finding. But what actually transpires when communication is possible? Durkin (1972) believes that very brief eye-to-eye contact facilitates an encountering process, which changes the orientation of the subject. However, verbal communications (or even nonverbal frowns or smiles) can have either a threatening or a conciliatory tone; programs of research on threatening communications in mixed-motive games instituted by Deutsch and Krauss (1960, 1962) and by Tedeschi and his co-workers (Tedeschi, 1970) offer promise.

5. COMPREHENSIVENESS AND DETAIL OF INSTRUCTIONS

Gallo and McClintock ended their review by asking if PD-game subjects really understood the implications of their choices. More recent research (Wrightsman, Bruininks, Lucker, & O'-Connor, 1972) indicates that less thorough instructions encourage a locked-in mutually competitive response. If experimenters make sure that subjects understand the meaning of their choices —before the game starts—heightened levels of cooperation should result.

Let us now turn to the second question posed at the beginning of this summary. We can agree that the mixed-motive game has proved to be a useful tool for the study of social behavior in the laboratory, but what value does it have for understanding conflict in the real world? Can one's parents' marital quarrels or the Arab-Israeli conflict be understood any better through the knowledge derived from the research in this section?

Several social psychologists have expressed skepticism. For example, Harold Kelley (1964) notes that subjects faced with the task of solving the problems posed by interdependence utilize a variety of processes to solve them. Any experimenter who believes that one construct—such as *cooperation*—can explain the variety of processes is probably simplifying matters. Some subjects make an essentially rational response to the game; they study all the available information, analyze the implications, and make the best choice to fit their goals. But Kelley points out that the other subjects utilize a trial-and-error process, in which they maintain or alter their choices on the basis of reinforcement received for previous responses. A third type of process, used by some subjects, involves the importation of previous rules of thumb to the game situation. Sometimes such rules of thumb may be relevant and

appropriate, but sometimes they are not. Kelley concludes, that, to understand both laboratory and real-world choices, we need more information about these processes. For example, when subjects in one PD-game study were queried about the reasons for their choices (O'Connor, Baker, & Wrightsman, 1972), as many as 44% reported their motivation as an *experimenting* one. (Such an orientation was reflected in comments like: "I wanted to see what he would do" or "I got tired of flipping the blue, so every once in a while I would flip the red one to make things a little different.")

Other social psychologists (Gergen, 1969; Pruitt, 1967) have cautioned against easy applications of PD-game research to real-world conflicts. Among the limitations of the PD-game situation are its lack of opportunity for communication, the use of small or meaningless rewards, and the absence of any chance to try out decisions tentatively and then reverse them if the results are unsatisfactory. Pruitt also notes that the usual norms that foster cooperation are absent in the laboratory. He states that, in real-life tasks with co-workers, "people may feel constrained by custom to be helpful and expect their fellow workers to feel similarly constrained. Such norms may not be so easily available in the laboratory situation because of its novelty" (Pruitt, 1967, p. 22).

Does a person who shows cooperative behavior in a mixed-motive game also behave cooperatively in other social situations? Apparently only one study has concerned itself with this basic question (Sermat, 1970). Sermat conducted four experiments to investigate similarity in cooperation rates. In the first two experiments, subjects participated in a "Paddle Game" between one and two months after they had been subjects in a mixed-motive game. The Paddle Game resembles the mixed-motive games in theoretical structure though not in procedures. In Experiment III, two tasks (Paddle Game and Chicken Game) were completed during the *same* session, with the same person as the other participant in both. Experiment IV studied cooperative and competitive behavior in a story-writing task that had to resolve differing interpretations of a picture.

Given these varied procedures, what did Sermat find? In both Experiment I and Experiment II, there was a tendency for previously cooperative subjects to act more cooperatively in the Paddle Game, but the effect was not statistically significant. In Experiment III, in which both activities were performed in the same session with the same other participants, there was a high degree of relationship between cooperation levels if the mixed-motive game preceded the Paddle Game (r of .86 for subjects in a matching condition; r of .50 for subjects in a condition in which the "other" always chose competitively). However, when the Paddle Game came first, there were no consistent relationships. Experiment IV, which studied how cooperators and competitors resolved differences in picture interpretations, found few clear-cut differences between the two groups. After watching the face-to-face discussions, observers were completely unable to identify whether each had been a cooperator or a competitor previously. Most of the differences between cooperators and competitors were not consistent from one sex to the other.

So Sermat's findings indicate that consistencies between the degree of cooperation in a mixed-motive game and its manifestations in other social settings are rather minimal. Until greater consistencies are demonstrated, we are not convinced that the findings reported in this section can be very *specifically* applied to real-world conflicts. However, this should not cause researchers to terminate research on laboratory conflicts. We grant that further research on Prisoner's Dilemma games for their own sake is unwarranted. What is needed is a series of studies that maintain the mixed-motive conflict but extend the list of possible influential variables. Real-life settings for such conflicts—in the classroom, at the union-management mediation table, on the athletic field—also must be used, but in combination with a degree of experimental control as close as possible to that offered by the laboratory.

REFERENCES

Brown, B. R. The effects of need to maintain face on interpersonal bargaining. *Journal of Experimental Social Psychology,* 1968, **4,** 107–122.

Brown, B. R. Saving face. *Psychology Today,* 1971, **4**(12), 55–59.

Christie, R.,.& Geis, F. (Eds.) *Studies in Machiavellianism.* New York: Academic Press, 1970.

Deutsch, M., & Krauss, R. M. The effect of threat upon interpersonal bargaining. *Journal of Abnormal and Social Psychology,* 1960, **61,** 181–189.

Deutsch, M., & Krauss, R. M. Studies of interpersonal bargaining. *Journal of Conflict Resolution,* 1962, **6,** 52–76.

Durkin, J. E. Moment of truth encounters in Prisoner's Dilemma. In L. S. Wrightsman, J. O'Connor, and N. J. Baker (Eds.), *Cooperation and competition: Readings on mixed-motive games.* Monterey, Calif.: Brooks/Cole, 1972. Pp. 192–196.

Gallo, P. S. The effects of different motivational orientations in a mixed-motive game. Unpublished doctoral dissertation, University of California at Los Angeles, 1963.

Gallo, P. S. Prisoners of our own dilemma? Paper presented at the meeting of the Western Psychological Association, San Diego, March 1968. (Reprinted in L. S. Wrightsman, J. O'Connor, and N. J. Baker (Eds.), *Cooperation and competition: Readings on mixed-motive games.* Monterey, Calif.: Brooks/Cole, 1972. Pp. 43–49.

Gallo, P. S., & Sheposh, J. The effects of incentive magnitude on cooperation in the Prisoner's Dilemma game. *Journal of Personality and Social Psychology,* 1971, **19,** 42–46.

Gallo, P. S., & Winchell, J. D. Matrix indices, large rewards, and cooperative behavior in a Prisoner's Dilemma game. *Journal of Social Psychology,* 1970, **81,** 235–241.

Gergen, K. J. *The psychology of behavior exchange.* Reading, Mass.: Addison-Wesley, 1969.

Kelley, H. H. Satisfactory interaction: A problem-solving approach. Paper presented at the meeting of the American Psychological Association, Los Angeles, September 1964.

Knox, R. E., & Douglas, R. L. Low payoffs and marginal comprehension: Two possible constraints upon behavior in the Prisoner's Dilemma. Paper presented at the meeting of the Western Psychological Association, San Diego, March 1968.

Knox, R. E., & Douglas, R. L. Trivial incentives, marginal comprehension, and dubious generalizations from Prisoner's Dilemma studies. *Journal of Personality and Social Psychology,* 1971, **20,** 160–165.

O'Connor, J., Baker, N. J., & Wrightsman, L. S. The nature of rationality in mixed-motive games. In L. S. Wrightsman, J. O'Connor, and N. J. Baker (Eds.), *Cooperation and competition: Readings on mixed-motive games.* Monterey, Calif.: Brooks/Cole, 1972. Pp. 19–29.

Oskamp, S. Effects of programmed strategies on cooperation in the Prisoner's Dilemma and other mixed-motive games. In L. S. Wrightsman, J. O'Connor, and N. J. Baker (Eds.), *Cooperation and competition: Readings on mixed-motive games.* Monterey, Calif.: Brooks/Cole, 1972. Pp. 147–188.

Oskamp, S., & Kleinke, C. Amount of reward as a variable in the Prisoner's Dilemma game. *Journal of Personality and Social Psychology,* 1970, **16,** 133–140.

Pruitt, D. G. Reward structure and cooperation: The decomposed Prisoner's Dilemma game. *Journal of Personality and Social Psychology,* 1967, **7,** 21–27.

Sermat, V. Is game behavior related to behavior in other interpersonal situations? *Journal of Personality and Social Psychology,* 1970, **16,** 92–109.

Shure, G. H., Meeker, R. J., & Hansford, E. H. The effectiveness of pacifist strategies in bargaining games. *Journal of Conflict Resolution,* 1965, **9,** 106–117.

Tedeschi, J. T. Threats and promises. In P. Swingle (Ed.), *The structure of conflict.* New York: Academic Press, 1970. Pp. 155–191.

Terhune, K. W. Motives, situation, and interpersonal conflict within the Prisoner's Dilemma. *Journal of Personality and Social Psychology,* Monograph Supplement, 1968, **8,** 1–24.

Terhune, K. W. The effects of personality in cooperation and conflict. In P. Swingle (Ed.), *The structure of conflict.* New York: Academic Press, 1970. Pp. 193–234.

Wichman, H. Effects of isolation and communication in a two-person game. *Journal of Personality and Social Psychology,* 1970, **16,** 114–120.

Wrightsman, L. S. Personality and attitudinal correlates of trusting and trustworthy behaviors in a two-person game. *Journal of Personality and Social Psychology,* 1966, **4,** 328–332.

Wrightsman, L. S., Bruininks, R. H., Lucker, W. G., & O'Connor, J. Effects of extensiveness of instructions upon cooperation in a Prisoner's Dilemma game. In L. S. Wrightsman, J. O'Connor, and N. J. Baker (Eds.), *Cooperation and competition: Read-ings on mixed-motive games.* Monterey, Calif.: Brooks/Cole, 1972. Pp. 258–270.

Wrightsman, L. S., O'Connor, J., & Baker, N. J. (Eds.) *Cooperation and competition: Readings on mixed-motive games.* Monterey, Calif.: Brooks/Cole, 1972.

SUGGESTED READINGS FOR FURTHER STUDY

Brown, B. R. Saving face. *Psychology Today,* 1971, **4**(12), 55-59.

Deutsch, M. Socially relevant science: Reflections on some studies of conflict. *American Psychologist,* 1969, **24,** 1076–1092.

Kelley, H. H. Experimental studies of threats in interpersonal negotiations. *Journal of Conflict Resolution,* 1965, **9,** 79–105.

Kelley, H. H., & Stahelski, A. J. The social interaction basis of cooperators' and competitors' beliefs about others. *Journal of Personality and Social Psychology,* 1970, **16,** 66–91.

Kershenbaum, B. R., & Komorita, S. S. Temptation to defect in the Prisoner's Dilemma game. *Journal of Personality and Social Psychology,* 1970, **16,** 110–113.

Oskamp, S., & Perlman, D. Effects of friendship and disliking on cooperation in a mixed-motive game. *Journal of Conflict Resolution,* 1966, **10,** 221–226.

Rapoport, A., & Chammah, A. M. *Prisoner's Dilemma.* Ann Arbor: University of Michigan Press, 1965.

Swingle, P. (Ed.) *The structure of conflict.* New York: Academic Press, 1970.

Vinacke, W. E. Variables in experimental games: Toward a field theory. *Psychological Bulletin,* 1969, **71,** 293–317.

Wrightsman, L. S., O'Connor, J., & Baker, N. J. (Eds.) *Cooperation and competition: Readings on mixed-motive games.* Monterey, Calif.: Brooks/Cole, 1972.

SECTION 4

Helping Behavior

As our society becomes more complex, urbanized, and fast paced, the need for interdependence between persons necessarily increases. This increased interdependence, along with the factors that may facilitate or inhibit it, has become of prime interest to social scientists. One important aspect of this picture is the study of the conditions under which people will help or refuse to help others.

In its general sense, this research involves the study of *altruism,* which can be defined as "behavior carried out to benefit another without anticipation of rewards from external sources" (Macaulay & Berkowitz, 1970, p. 3). The scientific study of altruism has generated considerable research, some of which will be outlined in the Summary to this section. Much of the recent attention, however, has focused on helping behavior within one very specific context: that of an emergency situation. This research interest has stemmed rather directly from the grave concern and puzzlement produced by reports in recent years of seemingly bizarre events—tragic cases in which individuals who are in dire need of help from others have gone unaided—even as dozens of people witness their cries for help. The end result of this lack of aid has often been the injury or death of the person who needed it.

Probably the most widely known case of this sort occurred in 1964, when Kitty Genovese was murdered near her home in New York City at 3:30 A.M. Her assailant took more than half an hour to murder her, and her screams for help were heard by at least 38 of her neighbors. Nobody came directly to her aid; furthermore, no one even called the police! (Rosenthal [1964] has written a book about this incident.) Do occurrences such as this reflect a growing amount of apathy, callousness, and lack of concern for others in modern urban society? Or, are there other factors that may contribute to such appalling situations?

Bibb Latané and John Darley, then at Columbia University and New York University, respectively, initiated a program of research to attempt to answer such questions. They began by identifying the following situational characteristics that seem to differentiate an emergency situation from a nonemergency situation (Latané & Darley, 1969, 1970): (1) An emergency involves threat or harm. There are relatively few positive rewards for successful action in an emergency; usually, the best that can be hoped for is a return to the status quo. (2) Emergencies are unusual and rare events, and people will have had little personal experience in handling such a situation. (3) Emergencies differ widely from one another. Each emergency (for example, a drowning, a fire, an assault) presents a different type of problem, and each requires a different type of action. (4) Emergencies are unforeseen; they emerge suddenly and without warning. Hence they must be handled without the benefit of forethought or planning. (5) An emergency requires instant action; the individual must come to a decision before he has had time to consider his alternatives. It places him in a condition of stress. All of these characteristics provide good reasons for a person *not* to intervene. As Latané and Darley (1969) have commented, ". . . the bystander to an emergency situation is in an unenviable position. It is perhaps surprising that anyone should intervene at all" (p. 247).

In the first article in this section, Latané and Darley describe three studies that they carried out to assess the effects of different situational variables on the likelihood of bystander intervention in emergencies. As the reader will see, their results suggest that *apathy* is not a wholly accurate term for describing cases in which bystanders do not intervene. Rather, they propose, there are two distinct *social processes*—pluralistic ignorance and diffusion of responsibility—that play a major role in emergency situations.

Irving M. Piliavin, Judith Rodin, and Jane Al-lyn Piliavin, then of the University of Pennsylvania and Columbia University, provide further evidence of the importance of the situational variables in the second article in this section. They carried out a field study in which emergencies were repeatedly staged in the midst of reasonably large groups of people in their "laboratory on wheels." Since their results appear to be somewhat at variance with the model proposed by Latané and Darley, the reader is encouraged to apply his or her analytical talents to decide whether such apparently disparate results can be integrated into a coherent theoretical framework.

The numerous forces inherent in urban living are discussed on a broader scale in the third article by Stanley Milgram, who is now at the Graduate Center of the City University of New York. The key concept that he describes is *overload*, the inability of a system (such as a person) to process inputs from the environment because they are too numerous to cope with or because they arrive in too rapid succession. Milgram points out that lack of trust, lack of civility, and bystander nonintervention may all be adaptive responses to such overload.

REFERENCES

Latané, B., & Darley, J. M. Bystander "apathy." *American Scientist,* 1969, **57,** 244–268.

Latané, B., & Darley, J. M. *The unresponsive bystander: Why doesn't he help?* New York: Appleton-Century-Crofts, 1970.

Macaulay, J. R., & Berkowitz, L. Overview. In J. R. Macaulay and L. Berkowitz (Eds.), *Altruism and helping behavior.* New York: Academic Press, 1970. Pp. 1–9.

Rosenthal, A. M. *Thirty-eight witnesses.* New York: McGraw-Hill, 1964.

ARTICLE 10

Social Determinants of Bystander Intervention in Emergencies[1]

Bibb Latané and John M. Darley

Almost 100 years ago, Charles Darwin wrote: "As man is a social animal, it is almost certain that he would . . . from an inherited tendency be willing to defend, in concert with others, his fellow-men; and be ready to aid them in any way, which did not too greatly interfere with his own welfare or his own strong desires" (*The Descent of Man*). Today, although many psychologists would quarrel with Darwin's assertion that altruism is inherited, most would agree that men will go to the aid of others even when there is no visible gain for themselves. At least, most would have agreed until a March night in 1964. That night, Kitty Genovese was set upon by a maniac as she returned home from work at 3:00 AM. Thirty-eight of her neighbors in Kew Gardens came to their windows when she cried out in terror; but none came to her assistance, even though her stalker took over half an hour to murder her. No one even so much as called the police.

Since we started our research on bystander response to emergencies, we have heard about dozens of such incidents. We have also heard many explanations: "I would assign this to the effect of the megalopolis in which we live, which makes closeness very difficult and leads to the alienation of the individual from the group," contributed a psychoanalyst. "A disaster syndrome," explained

From *Altruism and Helping Behavior* by J. R. Macaulay and L. Berkowitz (Eds.), 1970. Reprinted with permission of the authors and the publisher, Academic Press, Inc.

[1]The research reported in this paper was supported by National Science Foundation Grants GS1238, GS1239, GS2292, and GS2293, and was conducted at Columbia University and New York University.

a sociologist, "that shook the sense of safety and sureness of the individuals involved and caused psychological withdrawal from the event by ignoring it." "Apathy," others claim. "Indifference." "The gratification of unconscious sadistic impulses." "Lack of concern for our fellow men." "The Cold Society." These explanations and many more have been applied to the surprising failure of bystanders to intervene in emergencies —failures which suggest that we no longer care about the fate of our neighbors.

But can this be so? We think not. Although it is unquestionably true that the witnesses in the incidents above did nothing to save the victim, "apathy," "indifference," and "unconcern" are not entirely accurate descriptions of their reactions. The 38 witnesses of Kitty Genovese's murder did not merely look at the scene once and then ignore it. Instead they continued to stare out of their windows at what was going on. Caught, fascinated, distressed, unwilling to act but unable to turn away, their behavior was neither helpful nor heroic; but it was not indifferent or apathetic either.

Actually, it was like crowd behavior in many other emergency situations; car accidents, drownings, fires, and attempted suicides all attract substantial numbers of people who watch the drama in helpless fascination without getting directly involved in the action. Are these people alienated and indifferent? Are the rest of us? Obviously not. It seems only yesterday we were being called overconforming. But why, then, do we not act?

Paradoxically, the key to understanding these failures of intervention may be found exactly in the fact that so surprises us about them: so many bystanders fail to intervene. If we think of 38, or 11, or 100 individuals, each looking at an emergency and callously deciding to pass by, we are horrified. But if we realize that each bystander is picking up cues about what is happening and how to react to it from the other bystanders, understanding begins to emerge. There are several ways in which a crowd of onlookers can make each individual member of that crowd less likely to act.

DEFINING THE SITUATION

Most emergencies are, or at least begin as, ambiguous events. A quarrel in the street may erupt into violence or it may be simply a family argument. A man staggering about may be suffering a coronary, or an onset of diabetes, or he simply may be drunk. Smoke pouring from a building may signal a fire, but on the other hand, it may be simply steam or airconditioner vapor. Before a bystander is likely to take action in such ambiguous situations, he must first define the event as an emergency and decide that intervention is the proper course of action.

In the course of making these decisions, it is likely that an individual bystander will be considerably influenced by the decisions he perceives other bystanders to be taking. If everyone else in a group of onlookers seems to regard an event as nonserious and the proper course of action as nonintervention, this consensus may strongly affect the perceptions of any single individual and inhibit his potential intervention.

The definitions that other people held may be discovered by discussing the situation with them, but they may also be inferred from their facial expressions or behavior. A whistling man with his hands in his pockets obviously does not believe he is in the midst of a crisis. A bystander who does not respond to smoke obviously does not attribute it to fire. An individual, seeing the inaction of others, will judge the situation as less serious than he would if alone.

But why should the others be inactive? Probably because they are aware that other people are also watching them. The others are an audience to their own reactions. Among American males, it is considered desirable to appear poised and collected in times of stress. Being exposed to the public view may constrain the actions and expressions of emotion of any individual as he tries to avoid possible ridicule and embarrassment. Even though he may be truly concerned and upset about the plight of a victim, until he decides what to do, he may maintain a calm demeanor.

If each member of a group is, at the same time, trying to appear calm and also looking around at the other members to gauge their reactions, all members may be led (or misled) by each other to define the situation as less critical than they would if alone. Until someone acts, each person sees only other nonresponding bystanders and is likely to be influenced not to act himself. A state of "pluralistic ignorance" may develop.

It has often been recognized that a crowd can cause contagion of panic, leading each person in the crowd to overreact to an emergency to the detriment of everyone's welfare. What we suggest here is that a crowd can also force inaction on its members. It can suggest by its passive behavior that an event is not to be reacted to as an emergency, and it can make any individual uncomfortably aware of what a fool he will look for behaving as if it is.

Where There's Smoke, There's (Sometimes) Fire[2]

In this experiment we presented an emergency to individuals either alone or in groups of three. It was our expectation that the constraints on behavior in public combined with social influence processes would lessen the likelihood that members of three-person groups would act to cope with the emergency.

College students were invited to an interview to discuss "some of the problems involved in life at an urban university." As they sat in a small room waiting to be called for the interview and filling

---

[2]A more complete account of this experiment is provided in Latané and Darley (1968). Keith Gerritz and Lee Ross provided thoughtful assistance in running the study.

out a preliminary questionnaire, they faced an ambiguous but potentially dangerous situation. A stream of smoke began to puff into the room through a wall vent.

Some subjects were exposed to this potentially critical situation while alone. In a second condition, three naive subjects were tested together. Since subjects arrived at slightly different times, and since they each had individual questionnaires to work on, they did not introduce themselves to each other or attempt anything but the most rudimentary conversation.

As soon as the subjects had completed two pages of their questionnaires, the experimenter began to introduce the smoke through a small vent in the wall. The "smoke," copied from the famous Camel cigarette sign in Times Square, formed a moderately fine-textured but clearly visible stream of whitish smoke. It continued to jet into the room in irregular puffs, and by the end of the experimental period, it obscured vision.

All behavior and conversation were observed and coded from behind a one-way window (largely disguised on the subject's side by a large sign giving preliminary instructions). When and if the subject left the experimental room and reported the smoke, he was told that the situation "would be taken care of." If the subject had not reported the smoke within 6 minutes from the time he first noticed it, the experiment was terminated.

The typical subject, when tested alone, behaved very reasonably. Usually, shortly after the smoke appeared, he would glance up from his questionnaire, notice the smoke, show a slight but distinct startle reaction, and then undergo a brief period of indecision, perhaps returning briefly to his questionnaire before again staring at the smoke. Soon, most subjects would get up from their chairs, walk over to the vent and investigate it closely, sniffing the smoke, waving their hands in it, feeling its temperature, etc. The usual Alone subject would hesitate again, but finally would walk out of the room, look around outside, and, finding somebody there, calmly report the presence of the smoke. No subject showed any sign of panic; most simply said: "There's something strange going on in there, there seems to be some

sort of smoke coming through the wall. . . . " The median subject in the Alone condition had reported the smoke within 2 minutes of first noticing it. Three-quarters of the 24 people run in this condition reported the smoke before the experimental period was terminated.

Because there are three subjects present and available to report the smoke in the Three Naive Bystanders condition as compared to only one subject at a time in the Alone condition, a simple comparison between the two conditions is not appropriate. We cannot compare speeds in the Alone condition with the average speed of the three subjects in a group because, once one subject in a group had reported the smoke, the pressures on the other two disappeared. They could feel legitimately that the emergency had been handled and that any action on their part would be redundant and potentially confusing. Therefore, we used the speed of the first subject in a group to report the smoke as our dependent variable. However, since there were three times as many people available to respond in this condition as in the Alone condition, we would expect an increased likelihood that at least one person would report the smoke by chance alone. Therefore, we mathematically created "groups" of three scores from the Alone condition to serve as a baseline.[3]

In contrast to the complexity of this procedure, the results were quite simple. Subjects in the three-person-group condition were markedly inhibited from reporting the smoke. Since 75% of the Alone subjects reported the smoke, we would expect over 98% of the three-person groups to include at least one reporter. In fact, in only 38% of the eight groups in this condition did even one person report ($p < .01$). Of the 24 people run in these eight groups, only one person reported the smoke within the first 4 minutes before the room got noticeably unpleasant. Only three people reported the smoke within the entire experimental period. Social inhibition of reporting was so strong that the smoke was reported faster when

[3]The formula for calculating the expected proportion of groups in which at least one person will have acted by a given time is $1-(1-p)^n$ where p is the proportion of single individuals who acted by that time and n is the number of persons in the group.

only one person saw it than when groups of three were present ($p < .01$).

Subjects who had reported the smoke were relatively consistent in later describing their reactions to it. They thought the smoke looked somewhat "strange." They were not sure exactly what it was or whether it was dangerous, but they felt it was unusual enough to justify some examination. "I wasn't sure whether it was a fire, but it looked like something was wrong." "I thought it might be steam, but it seemed like a good idea to check it out."

Subjects who had not reported the smoke were also unsure about exactly what it was, but they uniformly said that they had rejected the idea that it was a fire. Instead, they hit upon an astonishing variety of alternative explanations, all sharing the common characteristic of interpreting the smoke as a nondangerous event. Many thought the smoke was either steam or airconditioning vapors, several thought it was smog, purposely introduced to simulate an urban environment, and two actually suggested that the smoke was a "truth gas" filtered into the room to induce them to answer the questionnaire accurately! Predictably, some decided that "it must be some sort of experiment" and stoically endured the discomfort of the room rather than overreact.

The results of this study clearly support the prediction. Groups of three naive subjects were less likely to report the smoke than solitary bystanders. Our predictions were confirmed—but this does not necessarily mean that our explanation of these results is the correct one. As a matter of fact, several alternative explanations center around the fact that the smoke represented a possible danger to the subject himself as well as to others in the building. For instance, it is possible that the subjects in groups saw themselves as engaged in a game of "chicken" in which the first person to report would admit his cowardliness. Or it may have been that the presence of others made subjects feel safer, and thus reduced their need to report.

To rule out such explanations, a second experiment was designed to see whether similar group inhibition effects could be observed in situations where there is no danger to the individual himself for not acting. In this study, male Columbia University undergraduates waited either alone or with a stranger to participate in a market research study. As they waited they heard a woman fall and apparently injure herself in the room next door. Whether they tried to help and how long they took to do so were the main dependent variables of the study.

The Fallen Woman[4]

Subjects were telephoned and offered \$2 to participate in a survey of game and puzzle preferences conducted at Columbia by the Consumer Testing Bureau (CTB), a market research organization. When they arrived, they were met at the door by an attractive young woman and taken to the testing room. On the way, they passed the CTB office, and through its open door they were able to see a desk and bookcase piled high with papers and filing cabinets. They entered the adjacent testing room, which contained a table and chairs and a variety of games, and they were given questionnaires to fill out. The representative told subjects that she would be working next door in her office for about 10 minutes while they were completing the questionnaire and left by opening the collapsible curtain which divided the two rooms. She made sure that subjects were aware that the curtain was unlocked and easily opened and that it provided a means of entry to her office. The representative stayed in her office, shuffling papers, opening drawers, and making enough noise to remind the subjects of her presence. Four minutes after leaving the testing area, she turned on a high fidelity stereophonic tape recorder.

The Emergency. If the subject listened carefully, he heard the representative climb up on a chair to reach for a stack of papers on the bookcase. Even if he were not listening carefully, he heard a loud crash and a scream as the chair collapsed and she fell to the floor. "Oh, my God, my foot . . . I . . . I . . . can't move . . . it. Oh . . .

---

[4]This experiment is more fully described in Latané and Rodin (1969).

my ankle," the representative moaned. "I . . . can't get this . . . thing . . . off me." She cried and moaned for about a minute longer, but the cries gradually got more subdued and controlled. Finally she muttered something about getting outside, knocked over the chair as she pulled herself up and thumped to the door, closing it behind her as she left. The entire incident took 130 seconds.

The main dependent variable of the study, of course, was whether the subjects took action to help the victim and how long it took them to do so. There were actually several modes of intervention possible: a subject could open the screen dividing the two rooms, leave the testing room and enter the CTB office by the door, find someone else, or most simply, call out to see if the representative needed help. In one condition, each subject was in the testing room alone while he filled out the questionnaire and heard the fall. In the second condition, strangers were placed in the testing room in pairs. Each subject in the pair was unacquainted with the other before entering the room and they were not introduced.

Across all experimental groups, the majority of subjects who intervened did so by pulling back the room divider and coming into the CTB office (61%). Few subjects came the round-about way through the door to offer their assistance (14%), and a surprisingly small number (24%) chose the easy solution of calling out to offer help. No one tried to find someone else to whom to report the accident.

Since 70% of Alone subjects intervened, we should expect that at least one person in 91% of all two-person groups would offer help if members of a pair had no influence upon each other. In fact, members did influence each other. In only 40% of the groups did even one person offer help to the injured woman. Only eight subjects of the 40 who were run in this condition intervened. This response rate is significantly below the hypothetical baseline ($p < .001$). Social inhibition of helping was so strong that the victim was actually helped more quickly when only one person heard her distress than when two did ($p < .01$).

When we talked to subjects after the experiment, those who intervened usually claimed that they did so either because the fall sounded very serious or because they were uncertain what had occurred and felt they should investigate. Many talked about intervention as the "right thing to do" and asserted they would help again in any situation.

Many of the noninterveners also claimed that they were unsure what had happened (59%), but had decided that it was not too serious (46%). A number of subjects reported that they thought other people would or could help (25%), and three said they refrained out of concern for the victim—they did not want to embarrass her. Whether to accept these explanations as reasons or rationalizations is moot—they certainly do not explain the differences among conditions. The important thing to note is that noninterveners did not seem to feel that they had behaved callously or immorally. Their behavior was generally consistent with their interpretation of the situation. Subjects almost uniformly claimed that in a "real" emergency they would be among the first to help the victim.

These results strongly replicate the findings of the Smoke study. In both experiments, subjects were less likely to take action if they were in the presence of others than if they were alone. This congruence of findings from different experimental settings supports the validity and generality of the phenomenon; it also helps rule out a variety of alternative explanations suitable to either situation alone. For example, the possibility that smoke may have represented a threat to the subject's personal safety and that subjects in groups may have had a greater concern to appear "brave" than single subjects does not apply to the present experiment. In the present experiment, nonintervention cannot signify bravery. Comparison of the two experiments also suggests that the absolute number of nonresponsive bystanders may not be a critical factor in producing social inhibition of intervention; pairs of strangers in the present study inhibited each other as much as did trios in the former study.

Other studies we have done show that group inhibition effects hold in real life as well as in the laboratory, and for members of the general population as well as college students. The results of these experiments clearly support the line of theoretical argument advanced earlier. When by-standers to an emergency can see the reactions of other people, and when other people can see their own reactions, each individual may, through a process of social influence, be led to interpret the situation as less serious than he would if he were alone, and consequently be less likely to take action.

These studies, however, tell us little about the case that stimulated our interest in bystander intervention: the Kitty Genovese murder. Although the 38 witnesses to that event were aware, through seeing lights and silhouettes in other windows, that others watched, they could not see what others were doing and thus be influenced by their reactions. In the privacy of their own apartments, they could not be clearly seen by others, and thus inhibited by their presence. The social influence process we have described above could not operate. Nevertheless, we think that the presence of other bystanders may still have affected each individual's response.

DIFFUSION OF RESPONSIBILITY

In addition to affecting the interpretations that he places on a situation, the presence of other people can also alter the rewards and costs facing an individual bystander. Perhaps most importantly, the presence of other people can reduce the cost of not acting. If only one bystander is present at an emergency, he carries all of the responsibility for dealing with it; he will feel all of the guilt for not acting; he will bear all of any blame others may level for nonintervention. If others are present, the onus of responsibility is diffused, and the individual may be more likely to resolve his conflict between intervening and not intervening in favor of the latter alternative.

When only one bystander is present at an emergency, if help is to come it must be from him. Although he may choose to ignore them out of concern for his personal safety, or desire "not to get involved," any pressures to intervene focus uniquely on him. When there are several observers present, however, the pressures to intervene do not focus on any one of the observers; instead, the responsibility for intervention is shared

among all the onlookers and is not unique to any one. As a result, each may be less likely to help.

Potential blame may also be diffused. However much we wish to think that an individual's moral behavior is divorced from considerations of personal punishment or reward, there is both theory and evidence to the contrary. It is perfectly reasonable to assume that under circumstances of group responsibility for a punishable act, the punishment or blame that accrues to any one individual is often slight or nonexistent.

Finally, if others are known to be present, but their behavior cannot be closely observed, any one bystander may assume that one of the other observers is already taking action to end the emergency. If so, his own intervention would only be redundant—perhaps harmfully or confusingly so. Thus, given the presence of other onlookers whose behavior cannot be observed, any given bystander can rationalize his own inaction by convincing himself that "somebody else must be doing something."

These considerations suggest that even when bystanders to an emergency cannot see or be influenced by each other, the more bystanders who are present, the less likely any one bystander would be to intervene and provide aid. To test this suggestion, it would be necessary to create an emergency situation in which each subject is blocked from communicating with others to prevent his getting information about their behavior during the emergency.

A Fit to be Tried[5]

A college student arrived in the laboratory, and was ushered into an individual room from which a communication system would enable him to talk to other participants (who were actually figments of the tape recorder). Over the intercom, the subject was told that the experimenter was concerned with the kinds of personal problems faced by normal college students in a high-pressure, urban environment, and that he would be asked to participate in a discussion about these problems. To avoid embarrassment about discussing personal problems with strangers, the ex-

---

[5]Further details of this experiment can be found in Darley and Latané (1968).

perimenter said, several precautions would be taken. First, subjects would remain anonymous, which was why they had been placed in individual rooms rather than face-to-face. Second, the experimenter would not listen to the initial discussion himself, but would only get the subject's reactions later by questionnaire.

The plan for the discussion was that each person would talk in turn for 2 minutes, presenting his problems to the group. Next, each person in turn would comment on what others had said, and finally there would be a free discussion. A mechanical switching device regulated the discussion, switching on only one microphone at a time.

The Emergency.   The discussion started with the future victim speaking first. He said he found it difficult to get adjusted to New York and to his studies. Very hesitantly and with obvious embarrassment, he mentioned that he was prone to seizures, particularly when studying hard or taking exams. The other people, including the one real subject, took their turns and discussed similar problems (minus the proneness to seizures). The naive subject talked last in the series, after the last prerecorded voice.

When it was again the victim's turn to talk, he made a few relatively calm comments, and then, growing increasingly loud and incoherent, he continued:

I er I think I I need er if if could er er somebody er er er er er er er give me a little er give me a little help here because I er I'm er er h-h-having a a a a real problem er right now and I er if somebody could help me out it would er er s-s-sure be sure be good . . . because er there er er a cause I er I uh I've got a a one of the er sie . . . er er things coming on and and and I could really er use some help so if somebody would er give me a little h-help uh er-er-er-er-er c-could somebody er er help er uh uh uh (Choking sounds). . . . I'm gonna die er er I'm . . . gonna die er help er er seizure (chokes, then quiet).

The major independent variable of the study was the number of people the subject believed also heard the fit. The subject was led to believe that the discussion group was one of three sizes: a two-person group consisting of himself and the victim; a three-person group consisting of him-

self, the victim and the other person; or a six-person group consisting of himself, the victim, and four other persons.

The major dependent variable of the experiment was the time elapsed from the start of the victim's seizure until the subject left his experimental cubicle. When the subject left his room, he saw the experimental assistant seated at the end of the hall, and invariably went to the assistant to report the seizure. If 5 minutes elapsed without the subject's having emerged from his room, the experiment was terminated.

Ninety-five percent of all the subjects who ever responded did so within the first half of the time available to them. No subject who had not reported within 3 minutes after the fit ever did so. This suggests that even had the experiment been allowed to run for a considerably longer period of time, few additional subjects would have responded.

Eighty-five percent of the subjects who thought they alone knew of the victim's plight reported the seizure before the victim was cut off; only 31% of those who thought four other bystanders were present did so. Every one of the subjects in the two-person condition, but only 62% of the subjects in the six-person condition ever reported the emergency. To do a more detailed analysis of the results, each subject's time score was transformed into a "speed" score by taking the reciprocal of the response time in seconds and multiplying by 100. Analysis of variance of these speed scores indicates that the effect of group size was highly significant ($p < .01$), and all three groups differed significantly one from another ($p < .05$).

Subjects, whether or not they intervened, believed the fit to be genuine and serious. "My God, he's having a fit," many subjects said to themselves (and we overheard via their microphones). Others gasped or simply said, "Oh." Several of the male subjects swore. One subject said to herself, "It's just my kind of luck, something has to happen to me!" Several subjects spoke aloud of their confusion about what course of action to take: "Oh, God, what should I do?"

When those subjects who intervened stepped out of their rooms, they found the experimental assistant down the hall. With some uncertainty but without panic, they reported the situation. "Hey, I think Number 1 is very sick. He's having a fit or something." After ostensibly checking on the situation, the experimenter returned to report that "everything is under control." The subjects accepted these assurances with obvious relief.

Subjects who failed to report the emergency showed few signs of the apathy and indifference thought to characterize "unresponsive bystanders." When the experimenter entered her room to terminate the situation, the subject often asked if the victim was all right. "Is he being taken care of?" "He's all right, isn't he?" Many of these subjects showed physical signs of nervousness; they often had trembling hands and sweating palms. If anything, they seemed more emotionally aroused than did the subjects who reported the emergency.

Why, then, didn't they respond? It is not our impression that they had decided not to respond. Rather, they were still in a state of indecision and conflict concerning whether to respond or not. The emotional behavior of these nonresponding subjects was a sign of their continuing conflict, a conflict that other subjects resolved by responding.

The fit created a conflict situation of the avoidance-avoidance type. On the one hand, subjects worried about the guilt and shame they would feel if they did not help the person in distress. On the other hand, they were concerned not to make fools of themselves by overreacting, not to ruin the ongoing experiment by leaving their intercoms, and not to destroy the anonymous nature of the situation, which the experimenter had earlier stressed as important. For subjects in the two-person condition, the obvious distress of the victim and his need for help were so important that their conflict was easily resolved. For the subjects who knew that there were other bystanders present, the cost of not helping was reduced and the conflict they were in was more acute. Caught between the two negative alternatives of letting the victim continue to suffer or rushing, perhaps foolishly, to help, the nonresponding bystanders vacillated between them rather than choosing not to respond. This distinction may be academic for the victim, since he got no help in either case, but it is an extremely important one for understanding the causes of bystanders' failures to help.

Although subjects experienced stress and conflict during the emergency, their general reactions to it were highly positive. On a questionnaire administered after the experimenter had discussed the nature and purpose of the experiment, every single subject found the experiment either "interesting" or "very interesting" and was willing to participate in similar experiments in the future. All subjects felt that they understood what the experiment was all about and indicated that they thought the deceptions were necessary and justified. All but one felt they were better informed about the nature of psychological research in general.

CONCLUSION

We have suggested two distinct processes which might lead people to be less likely to intervene in an emergency if there are other people present than if they are alone. On the one hand, we suggested that the presence of other people may affect the interpretations each bystander puts on an ambiguous emergency situation. If other people are present at an emergency, each bystander will be guided by their apparent reactions in formulating his own impressions. Unfortunately, their apparent reactions may not be a good indication of their true feelings. It is possible for a state of "pluralistic ignorance" to develop, in which each bystander is led by the apparent lack of concern of the others to interpret the situation as being less serious than he would if alone. To the extent that he does not feel the situation is an emergency, he will be unlikely to take any helpful action.

Even if an individual does decide that an emergency is actually in process and that something ought to be done, he still is faced with the choice of whether he himself will intervene. Here again, the presence of other people many influence him —by reducing the costs associated with nonintervention. If a number of people witness the same event, the responsibility for action is diffused, and each may feel less necessity to help.

"There's safety in numbers," according to an old adage, and modern city dwellers seem to believe it. They shun deserted streets, empty subway cars, and lonely dark walks in dark parks, preferring instead to go where others are or to stay at home. When faced with stress, most individuals seem less afraid when they are in the presence of others than when they are alone.

A feeling so widely shared should have some basis in reality. Is there safety in numbers? If so, why? Two reasons are often suggested: individuals are less likely to find themselves in trouble if there are others about, and even if they do find themselves in trouble, others are likely to help them deal with it. While it is certainly true that a victim is unlikely to receive help if nobody knows of his plight, the experiments above cast doubt on the suggestion that he will be more likely to receive help if more people are present. In fact, the opposite seems to be true. A victim may be more likely to get help, or an emergency be reported, the fewer the people who are available to take action.

Although the results of these studies may shake our faith in "safety in numbers," they also may help us begin to understand a number of frightening incidents where crowds have heard but not answered a call for help. Newspapers have tagged these incidents with the label, "apathy." We have become indifferent, they say, callous to the fate of suffering of others. Our society has become "dehumanized" as it has become urbanized. These glib phrases may contain some truth, since startling cases such as the Genovese murder often seem to occur in our large cities, but such terms may also be misleading. Our studies suggest a different conclusion. They suggest that situational factors, specifically factors involving the immediate social environment, may be of greater importance in determining an individual's reaction to an emergency than such vague cultural or personality concepts as "apathy" or "alienation due to urbanization." They suggest that the failure to intervene may be better understood by knowing the relationship among bystanders rather than that between a bystander and the victim.

REFERENCES

Darley, J. M., & Latané, B. Bystander intervention in emergencies: Diffusion of responsibility. *Journal of Personality and Social Psychology,* 1968, **8,** 377–383.

Latané, B., & Darley, J. M. Group inhibition of bystander intervention. *Journal of Personality and Social Psychology,* 1968, **10,** 215–221.

Latané, B., & Rodin, J. A lady in distress: Inhibiting effects of friends and strangers on bystander intervention. *Journal of Experimental Social Psychology,* 1969, **5,** 189–202.

ARTICLE 11

Good Samaritanism:
An Underground Phenomenon?[1]

Irving M. Piliavin, Judith Rodin, and Jane Allyn Piliavin

Since the murder of Kitty Genovese in Queens, a rapidly increasing number of social scientists have turned their attention to the study of the good Samaritan's act and an associated phenomenon, the evaluation of victims by bystanders and agents. Some of the findings of this research have been provocative and nonobvious. For example, there is evidence that agents, and even bystanders, will sometimes derogate the character of the victims of misfortune, instead of feeling compassion (Berscheid & Walster, 1967; Lerner & Simmons, 1966). Furthermore, recent findings indicate that under certain circumstances there is not "safety in numbers," but rather "diffusion of responsibility." Darley and Latané (1968) have reported that among bystanders hearing an epileptic seizure over earphones, those who believed other witnesses were present were less likely to seek assistance for the victim than were bystanders who believed they were alone. Subsequent research by Latané and Rodin (1969) on response to the victim of a fall confirmed this finding and suggested further that assistance from a group of

From *Journal of Personality and Social Psychology,* **13,** 1969, 289–299. Copyright 1969 by the American Psychological Association, and reproduced by permission of the authors and the publisher.

[1]This research was conducted while the first author was at Columbia University as a Special National Institute of Mental Health Research Fellow under Grant 1-F3-MH-36, 328-01. The study was partially supported by funds supplied by this grant and partially by funds from National Science Foundation Grant GS-1901 to the third author. The authors thank Virginia Joy for allowing the experimental teams to be recruited from her class, and Percy Tannenbaum for his reading of the manuscript and his helpful comments.

bystanders was less likely to come if the group members were strangers than if they were prior acquaintances. The field experiments of Bryan and Test (1967), on the other hand, provide interesting findings that fit common sense expectations; namely, one is more likely to be a good Samaritan if one has just observed another individual performing a helpful act.

Much of the work on victimization to date has been performed in the laboratory. It is commonly argued that the ideal research strategy over the long haul is to move back and forth between the laboratory, with its advantage of greater control, and the field, with its advantage of greater reality. The present study was designed to provide more information from the latter setting.

The primary focus of the study was on the effect of type of victim (drunk or ill) and race of victim (black or white) on speed of responding, frequency of responding, and the race of the helper. On the basis of the large body of research on similarity and liking as well as that on race and social distance, it was assumed that an individual would be more inclined to help someone of his race than a person of another race. The expectation regarding type of victim was that help would be accorded more frequently and rapidly to the apparently ill victim. This expectation was derived from two considerations. First, it was assumed that people who are regarded as partly responsible for their plight would receive less sympathy and consequently less help than people seen as not responsible for their circumstances (Schopler & Matthews, 1965).

Secondly, it was assumed that whatever sympathy individuals may experience when they observe a drunk collapse, their inclination to help him will be dampened by the realization that the victim may become disgusting, embarrassing, and/or violent. This realization may, in fact, not only constrain helping but also lead observers to turn away from the victim—that is, to leave the scene of the emergency.

Aside from examining the effects of race and type of victim, the present research sought to investigate the impact of modeling in emergency situations. Several investigators have found that an individual's actions in a given situation lead others in that situation to engage in similar actions. This modeling phenomenon has been observed in a variety of contexts including those involving good Samaritanism (Bryan & Test, 1967). It was expected that the phenomenon would be observed as well in the present study. A final concern of the study was to examine the relationship between size of group and frequency and latency of the helping response, with a victim who was both seen and heard. In previous laboratory studies (Darley & Latané, 1968; Latané & Rodin, 1969) increases in group size led to decreases in frequency and increases in latency of responding. In these studies, however, the emergency was only heard, not seen. Since visual cues are likely to make an emergency much more arousing for the observer, it is not clear that, given these cues, such considerations as crowd size will be relevant determinants of the observer's response to the emergency. Visual cues also provide clear information as to whether anyone has yet helped the victim or if he has been able to help himself. Thus, in the laboratory studies, observers lacking visual cues could rationalize not helping by assuming assistance was no longer needed when the victim ceased calling for help. Staging emergencies in full view of observers eliminates the possibility of such rationalization.

To conduct a field investigation of the above questions under the desired conditions required a setting which would allow the repeated staging of emergencies in the midst of reasonably large groups which remained fairly similar in composition from incident to incident. It was also desirable that each group retain the same composition over the course of the incident and that a reasonable amount of time be available after the emergency occurred for good Samaritans to act. To meet these requirements, the emergencies were staged during the approximately 7½-minute express run between the 59th Street and 125th Street stations of the Eighth Avenue Independent (IND) branch of the New York subways.

METHOD

Subjects

About 4,450 men and women who traveled on the 8th Avenue IND in New York City, weekdays between the hours of 11:00 A.M. and 3:00 P.M. during the period from April 15 to June 26, 1968, were the unsolicited participants in this study. The racial composition of a typical train, which travels through Harlem to the Bronx, was about 45% black and 55% white. The mean number of people per car during these hours was 43; the mean number of people in the "critical area," in which the staged incident took place, was 8.5.

Field Situation. The A and D trains of the 8th Avenue IND were selected because they make no stops between 59th Street and 125th Street. Thus, for about 7½ minutes there was a captive audience who, after the first 70 seconds of their ride, became bystanders to an emergency situation. A single trial was a nonstop ride between 59th and 125th Streets, going in either direction. All trials were run only on the old New York subway cars which serviced the 8th Avenue line since they had two-person seats in group arrangement rather than extended seats. The designated experimental or critical area was that end section of any car whose doors led to the next car. There are 13 seats and some standing room in this area on all trains (see Figure 1).

Procedure

On each trial a team of four Columbia General Studies students, two males and two females, boarded the train using different doors. Four different teams, whose members always worked

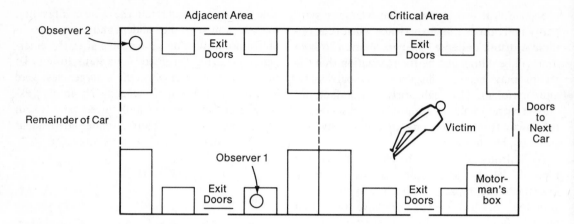

FIGURE 1.   Layout of adjacent and critical areas of subway car.

together, were used to collect data for 103 trials. Each team varied the location of the experimental car from trial to trial. The female confederates took seats outside the critical area and recorded data as unobtrusively as possible for the duration of the ride, while the male model and victim remained standing. The victim always stood next to a pole in the center of the critical area (see Figure 1). As the train passed the first station (approximately 70 seconds after departing) the victim staggered forward and collapsed. Until receiving help, the victim remained supine on the floor looking at the ceiling. If the victim received no assistance by the time the train slowed to a stop, the model helped him to his feet. At the stop, the team disembarked and waited separately until other riders had left the station. They then proceeded to another platform to board a train going in the opposite direction for the next trial. From 6 to 8 trials were run on a given day. All trials on a given day were in the same "victim condition."

Victim.   The four victims (one from each team) were males between the ages of 26 and 35. Three were white and one was black. All were identically dressed in Eisenhower jackets, old slacks, and no tie. On 38 trials the victims smelled of liquor and carried a liquor bottle wrapped tightly in a brown bag (drunk condition), while on the remaining 65 trials they appeared sober and carried a black cane (cane condition). In all other aspects, victims dressed and behaved iden-

tically in the two conditions. Each victim participated in drunk and cane trials.[2]

Model.   Four white males between the ages of 24 and 29 assumed the roles of model in each team. All models wore informal clothes, although they were not identically attired. There were four different model conditions used across both victim conditions (drunk or cane).

1. *Critical area—early.* Model stood in critical area and waited until passing fourth station to assist victim (approximately 70 seconds after collapse).

2. *Critical area—late.* Model stood in critical area and waited until passing sixth station to assist victim (approximately 150 seconds after collapse).

3. *Adjacent area—early.* Model stood in middle of car in area adjacent to critical area and waited until passing fourth station.

[2]It will be noted later that not only were there more cane trials than drunk trials, they were also distributed unevenly across black and white victims. The reason for this is easier to explain than to correct. Teams 1 and 2 (both white victims) started the first day in the cane condition. Teams 3 (black) and 4 (white) began in the drunk condition. Teams were told to alternate the conditions across days. They arranged their running days to fit their schedules. On their fourth day, Team 2 violated the instruction and ran cane trials when they should have run drunk trials; the victim "didn't like" playing the drunk! Then the Columbia student strike occurred, the teams disbanded, and the study of necessity was over. At this point, Teams 1 and 3 had run on only 3 days each, while 2 and 4 had run on 4 days each.

4. *Adjacent area—late.* Model stood in adjacent area and waited until passing sixth station.

When the model provided assistance, he raised the victim to a sitting position and stayed with him for the remainder of the trial. An equal number of trials in the no-model condition and in each of the four model conditions were preprogrammed by a random number table and assigned to each team.

Measures. On each trial one observer noted the race, sex, and location of every rider seated or standing in the critical area. In addition, she counted the total number of individuals in the car and the total number of individuals who came to the victim's assistance. She also recorded the race, sex, and location of every helper. A second observer coded the race, sex, and location of all persons in the adjacent area. She also recorded the latency of the first helper's arrival after the victim had fallen and on appropriate trials, the latency of the first helper's arrival after the programmed model had arrived. Both observers recorded comments spontaneously made by nearby passengers and attempted to elicit comments from a rider sitting next to them.

RESULTS AND DISCUSSION

As can be seen in Table 1, the frequency of help received by the victims was impressive, at least as compared to earlier laboratory results. The victim with the cane received spontaneous help, that is, before the model acted, on 62 of the 65 trials. Even the drunk received spontaneous help on 19 of 38 trials. The difference is not explicable on the basis of gross differences in the numbers of potential helpers in the cars. (Mean number of passengers in the car on cane trials was 45; on drunk trials, 40. Total range was 15–120.)

On the basis of past research, relatively long latencies of spontaneous helping were expected; thus, it was assumed that models would have time to help, and their effects could be assessed. However, in all but three of the cane trials planned to be model trials, the victim received help before the model was scheduled to offer assistance. This was less likely to happen with the drunk victim. In many cases, the early model was

able to intervene, and in a few, even the delayed model could act (see Table 1 for frequencies).

A direct comparison between the latency of response in the drunk and cane conditions might be misleading, since on model trials one does not know how long it might have taken for a helper to arrive without the stimulus of the model. Omitting the model trials, however, would reduce the number of drunk trials drastically. In order to get around those problems the trials have been dichotomized into a group in which someone helped *before* 70 seconds (the time at which the early model was programmed to help) and a group in which no one had helped by this time. The second group includes some trials in which people helped the model and a very few in which no one helped at all.[3] It is quite clear from the first section of Table 2 that there was more immediate, spontaneous helping of the victim with the cane than of the drunk. The effect seems to be essentially the same for the black victim and for the white victims.[4]

What of the total number of people who helped? On 60% of the 81 trials on which the victim received help, he received it not from one good Samaritan but from two, three, or even more.[5] There are no significant differences between black and white victims, or between cane

[3]If a comparison of latencies is made between cane and drunk nonmodel trials only, the median latency for cane trials is 5 seconds and the median for drunk trials is 109 seconds (assigning 400 seconds as the latency for nonrespondents). The Mann-Whitney U for this comparison is significant at $p < .0001$.

[4]Among the white victim teams, the data from Team 2 differ to some extent from those for Teams 1 and 4. All of the cane-after 70 seconds trials are accounted for by Team 2, as are 4 of the 5 drunk-before 70 trials. Median latency for cane trials is longer for Team 2 than for the other teams; for drunk trials, shorter. This is the same team that violated the "alternate days" instruction. It would appear that this team is being rather less careful—that the victim may be getting out of his role. The data from this team have been included in the analysis although they tend to reduce the relationships that were found.

[5]The data from the model trials are not included in this analysis because the model was programmed to behave rather differently from the way in which most real helpers behaved. That is, his role was to raise the victim to a sitting position and then appear to need assistance. Most real helpers managed to drag the victim to a seat or to a standing position on their own. Thus the programmed model received somewhat more help than did real first helpers.

TABLE 1. Percentage of trials on which help was given, by race and condition of victim, and total number of trials run in each condition.

Trials	White victims		Black victim	
	Cane	Drunk	Cane	Drunk
No model	100%	100%	100%	73%
Number of trials run	54	11	8	11
Model trials	100%	77	–	67%
Number of trials run	3	13	0	3
Total number of trials	57	24	8	14

Note.—Distribution of model trials for the drunk was as follows: critical area: early, 4; late, 4; adjacent area: early, 5; late, 3. The three model trials completed for the cane victim were all early, with 2 from the critical area and 1 from the adjacent area.

and drunk victims, in the number of helpers subsequent to the first who came to his aid. Seemingly, then, the presence of the first helper has important implications which override whatever cognitive and emotional differences were initially engendered among observers by the characteristics of the victim. It may be that the victim's uniformly passive response to the individual trying to assist him reduced observers' fear about possible unpleasantness in the drunk conditions. Another possibility is that the key factor in the decisions of second and third helpers to offer assistance was the first helper. That is, perhaps assistance was being offered primarily to him rather than to the victim. Unfortunately the data do not permit adequate assessment of these or other possible explanations.

Characteristics of Spontaneous First Helpers

Having discovered that people do, in fact, help with rather high frequency, the next question is, "Who helps?" The effect of two variables, sex and race, can be examined. On the average, 60% of the people in the critical area were males. Yet, of the 81 spontaneous first helpers, 90% were males. In this situation, then, men are considerably more likely to help than are women ($x^2 = 30.63$; $p <$ .001).

Turning now to the race variable, of the 81 first helpers, 64% were white. This percentage does not differ significantly from the expected percentage of 55% based on racial distribution in the cars. Since both black and white victims were used, it is also possible to see whether blacks and whites are more likely to help a member of their own race. On the 65 trials on which spontaneous

TABLE 2. Time and responses to the incident.

Trials on which help was offered:	Total number of trials		% of trials on which 1 + persons left critical area[b]		% of trials on which 1 + comments were recorded[b]		Mean number of comments	
	White victims	Black victim	White victims	Black victim	White victims	Black victim	White victims	Black victim
Before 70 sec.								
Cane	52	7	4%	14%	21%	0%	.27	.00
Drunk	5	4	20%	0%	80%	50%	1.00	.50
Total	57	11	5%	9%	26%	18%	.33	.18
After 70 sec.								
Cane	5	1	40%	–	60%	–	.80	–
Drunk	19	10	42%	60%	100%	70%	2.00	.90
Total	24	11	42%	64%	96%	64%	1.75	.82
x^2	36.83	a	x^2time = 23.19		x^2time = 31.45			
p	<.001	<.03	$p<.001$		$p<.001$			
			x^2cane-drunk = 11.71		x^2cane-drunk = 37.95			
			$p<.001$		$p<.001$			

Note.—Percentage and means not calculated for n's less than 4.
[a]Fisher's exact test, estimate of two-tailed probability.
[b]Black and white victims are combined for the analyses of these data.

TABLE 3. Spontaneous helping of cane and drunk by race of helper and race of victim.

Race of helper	White victims			Black victim			All victims		
	Cane	Drunk	Total	Cane	Drunk	Total	Cane	Drunk	Total
Same as victim	34	10	44	2	6	8	36	16	52
Different from victim	20	1	21	6	2	8	26	3	29
Total	54	11	65	8	8	16	62	19	81

Note.–Chi-squares are corrected for continuity. While victims, $x^2 = 2.11$, $p = .16$; black victim, $p = .16$ (two-tailed estimate from Fisher's exact probabilities test); all victims, $x^2 = 3.26$, $p = .08$.

help was offered to the white victims, 68% of the helpers were white. This proportion differs from the expected 55% at the .05 level ($x^2 = 4.23$). On the 16 trials on which spontaneous help was offered to the black victim, half of the first helpers were white. While this proportion does not differ from chance expectation, we again see a slight tendency toward "same-race" helping.

When race of helper is examined separately for cane and drunk victims, an interesting although nonsignificant trend emerges (see Table 3). With both the black and white cane victims, the proportion of helpers of each race was in accord with the expected 55%–45% split. With the drunk, on the other hand, it was mainly members of his own race who came to his aid.[6]

This interesting tendency toward same-race helping only in the case of the drunk victim may reflect more empathy, sympathy, and trust toward victims of one's own racial group. In the case of an innocent victim (e.g., the cane victim), when sympathy, though differentially experienced, is relatively uncomplicated by other emotions, assistance can readily cut across group lines. In the case of the drunk (and potentially dangerous) victim, complications are present, probably blame, fear, and disgust. When the victim is a member of one's own group—when the conditions for empathy and trust are more favor-

able—assistance is more likely to be offered. As we have seen, however, this does not happen without the passing of time to think things over.

Recent findings of Black and Reiss (1967) in a study of the behavior of white police officers towards apprehended persons offer an interesting parallel. Observers in this study recorded very little evidence of prejudice toward sober individuals, whether white or black. There was a large increase in prejudice expressed towards drunks of both races, but the increase in prejudice towards blacks was more than twice that towards whites.

Modeling Effects

No extensive analysis of the response to the programmed model could be made, since there were too few cases for analysis. Two analyses were, however, performed on the effects of adjacent area versus critical area models and of early versus late models within the drunk condition. The data are presented in Table 4. While the area variable has no effect, the early model elicited help significantly more than did the late model.

Other Responses to the Incident

What other responses do observers make to the incident? Do the passengers leave the car, move out of the area, make comments about the incident? No one left the car on any of the trials. However, on 21 of the 103 trials, a total of 34 people did leave the critical area. The second section of Table 2 presents the percentage of trials on which someone left the critical area as a function of three variables: type of victim, race of victim, and time to receipt of help (before or after 70

---

[6] It is unfortunate from a design standpoint that there was only one black victim. He was the only black student in the class from which our crews were recruited. While it is tenuous to generalize from a sample of one, the problems attendant upon attributing results to his race rather than to his individual personality characteristics are vitiated somewhat by the fact that response latencies and frequencies of help to him in the cane condition fall between responses to Teams 1 and 4 on the one hand and Team 2 on the other.

TABLE 4. Frequency of help as a function of early (70 seconds) versus late (150 seconds) and adjacent versus critical area programmed models.

Help	Critical area			Adjacent area			Both areas		
	Early	Late	Both	Early	Late	Both	Early	Late	Total
Received	4	2	6	5	1	6	9	3	12
Not received	0	2	2	0	2	2	0	4	4
Total	4	4	8	5	3	8	9	7	16

Note.—Early versus late: $p < .04$ (two-tailed estimate from Fisher's exact test). All three cane-model trials were early model trials; two critical area, one adjacent. Help was received on all. Table includes drunk trials only.

seconds). People left the area on a higher proportion of trials with the drunk than with the cane victim. They also were far more likely to leave on trials on which help was not offered by 70 seconds, as compared to trials on which help was received before that time.[7] The frequencies are too small to make comparisons with each of the variables held constant.

Each observer spoke to the person seated next to her after the incident took place. She also noted spontaneous comments and actions by those around her. A content analysis of these data was performed, with little in the way of interesting findings. The distribution of number of comments over different sorts of trials, however, did prove interesting (see Section 3 of Table 2). Far more comments were obtained on drunk trials than on cane trials. Similarly, most of the comments were obtained on trials in which no one helped until after 70 seconds. The discomfort observers felt in sitting inactive in the presence of the victim may have led them to talk about the incident, perhaps hoping others would confirm the fact that inaction was appropriate. Many women, for example, made comments such as, "It's for men to help him," or "I wish I could help him—I'm not strong enough," "I never saw this kind of thing before—I don't know where to look," "You feel so bad that you don't know what to do."

A Test of the Diffusion of Responsibility Hypothesis

In the Darley and Latané experiment it was predicted and found that as the number of bystanders increased, the likelihood that any individual would help decreased and the latency of response increased. Their study involved bystanders who could not see each other or the victim. In the Latané and Rodin study, the effect was again found, with bystanders who were face to face, but with the victim still only heard. In the present study, bystanders saw both the victim and each other. Will the diffusion of responsibility finding still occur in this situation?

In order to check this hypothesis, two analyses were performed. First, all nonmodel trials were separated into three groups according to the number of males in the critical area (the assumed reference group for spontaneous first helpers). Mean and median latencies of response were then calculated for each group, separately by type and race of victim. The results are presented in Table 5. There is no evidence in these data for diffusion of responsibility; in fact, response times, using either measure, are consistently faster for the 7 or more groups compared to the 1 to 3 groups.[8]

As Darley and Latané pointed out, however, different-size real groups cannot be meaningfully compared to one another, since as group size increases, the likelihood that one or more persons

---

[7]Individuals are also somewhat more likely to leave the area with the black victim than with the white victims ($\chi^2 = 3.23$, $p < .08$). This race effect is most probably an artifact, since the black victim ran more drunk trials than cane trials, the white victims, vice versa.

[8]The total number of people in the car was strongly related to the number of males in the critical area. Similar results are obtained if latencies are examined as a function of the total number of people in the car.

TABLE 5.   Mean and median latencies as a function of number of males in the critical area.

No. males in critical area	Cane			Drunk		
	White victims	Black victim	Total	White victims	Black victim	Total
1-3	16	12	15	–	309	309
M	7	12	7	–	312	312
Mdn.	17	2	19		4	4
N						
4-6						
M	20	6	18	155	143	149
Mdn.	5	4	5	105	70	73
N	23	4	27	4	4	8
7 and up						
M	3	52	9	107	74	97
Mdn.	1	52	1.5	102	65	84
N	14	2	16	7	3	10
Kruskal-Wallis Test (H)			5.08			6.01
p			.08			.05

Note.–Means and medians in seconds. Model trials omitted; no response assigned 400 seconds.

will help also increases. A second analysis as similar as possible to that used by those authors was therefore performed, comparing latencies actually obtained for each size group with a base line of hypothetical groups of the same size made up by combining smaller groups. In order to have as much control as possible the analysis was confined to cane trials with white victims and male first helpers coming from the critical area. Within this set of trials, the most frequently occurring natural groups (of males in the critical area) were those of sizes 3 ($n = 6$) and 7 ($n = 5$). Hypothetical groups of 3 ($n = 4$) and 7 ($n = 25$) were composed of all combinations of smaller sized groups. For example, to obtain the hypothetical latencies for groups of 7, combinations were made of (a) all real size 6 groups with all real size 1 groups, plus (b) all real size 5 groups with all real size 2 groups, etc. The latency assigned to each of these hypothetical groups was that recorded for the faster of the two real groups of which it was composed. Cumulative response curves for real and hypothetical groups of 3 and 7 are presented in Figure 2.

As can be seen in the figure, the cumulative helping response curves for the hypothetical groups of both sizes are lower than those for the corresponding real groups. That is, members of real groups responded more rapidly than would

be expected on the basis of the faster of the two scores obtained from the combined smaller groups. While these results together with those summarized in Table 5 do not necessarily contradict the diffusion of responsibility hypothesis, they do not follow the pattern of findings obtained by Darley and Latané and are clearly at variance with the tentative conclusion of those investigators that "a victim may be more likely to receive help . . . the fewer people there are to take action [Latané & Darley, 1968, p. 221]."

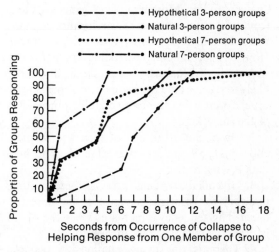

FIGURE 2.   Cumulative proportion of groups producing a helper over time (cane trials, white victims, male helpers from inside critical area).

Two explanations can be suggested to account for the disparity between the findings of Table 5 and Figure 2 and those of Darley and Latané and Latané and Rodin. As indicated earlier in this paper, the conditions of the present study were quite different from those in previous investigations. First, the fact that observers in the present study could see the victim may not only have constrained observer's abilities to conclude there was no emergency, but may also have overwhelmed with other considerations any tendency to diffuse responsibility. Second, the present findings may indicate that even if diffusion of responsibility *is* experienced by people who can actually see an emergency, when groups are larger than two the increment in deterrence to action resulting from increasing the number of observers may be less than the increase in probability that within a given time interval at least one of the observers will take action to assist the victim. Clearly, more work is needed in both natural and laboratory settings before an understanding is reached of the conditions under which diffusion of responsibility will or will not occur.

CONCLUSIONS

In this field study, a personal emergency occurred in which escape for the bystander was virtually impossible. It was a public, face-to-face situation, and in this respect differed from previous lab studies. Moreover, since generalizations from field studies to lab research must be made with caution, few comparisons will be drawn. However, several conclusions may be put forth:

1. An individual who appears to be ill is more likely to receive aid than is one who appears to be drunk, even when the immediate help needed is of the same kind.

2. Given mixed groups of men and women, and a male victim, men are more likely to help than are women.

3. Given mixed racial groups, there is some tendency for same-race helping to be more frequent. This tendency is increased when the victim is drunk as compared to apparently ill.

4. There is no strong relationship between number of bystanders and speed of helping; the expected increased "diffusion of responsibility" with a greater number of bystanders was not obtained for groups of these sizes. That is, help is not less frequent or slower in coming from larger as compared to smaller groups of bystanders; what effect there is, is in the opposite direction.

5. The longer the emergency continues without help being offered (a) the less impact a model has on the helping behavior of observers; (b) the more likely it is that individuals will leave the immediate area; that is, they appear to move purposively to another area in order to avoid the situation; (c) the more likely it is that observers will discuss the incident and its implications for their behavior.

A model of response to emergency situations consistent with the previous findings is currently being developed by the authors. It is briefly presented here as a possible heuristic device. The model includes the following assumptions: Observation of an emergency creates an emotional arousal state in the bystander. This state will be differently interpreted in different situations (Schachter, 1964) as fear, disgust, sympathy, etc., and possibly a combination of these. This state of arousal is higher (a) the more one can empathize with the victim (i.e., the more one can see oneself in his situation—Stotland, 1966), (b) the closer one is to the emergency, and (c) the longer the state of emergency continues without the intervention of a helper. It can be reduced by one of a number of possible responses: (a) helping directly, (b) going to get help, (c) leaving the scene of the emergency, and (d) rejecting the victim as undeserving of help (Lerner & Simmons, 1966). The response that will be chosen is a function of a cost-reward matrix that includes costs associated with helping (e.g., effort, embarrassment, possible disgusting or distasteful experiences, possible physical harm, etc.), costs associated with not helping (mainly self-blame and perceived censure from others), rewards associated with helping (mainly praise from self, victim, and others), and rewards associated with not helping (mainly those stemming from continuation of other activities). Note that the major motivation implied in the model is not a positive "altruistic" one, but rather a selfish desire to rid oneself of an unpleasant emotional state.

In terms of this model, the following after-the-fact interpretations can be made of the findings obtained:

1. The drunk is helped less because costs for helping are higher (greater disgust) and costs for not helping are lower (less self-blame and censure because he is in part responsible for his own victimization).

2. Women help less because costs for helping are higher in this situation (effort, mainly) and costs for not helping are lower (less censure from others; it is not her role).

3. Same-race helping, particularly of the drunk, can be explained by differential costs for not helping (less censure if one is of opposite race) and, with the drunk, differential costs for helping (more fear if of different race).

4. Diffusion of responsibility is not found on cane trials because costs for helping in general are low and costs for not helping are high (more self-blame because of possible severity of problem). That is, the suggestion is made that the diffusion of responsibility effect will increase as costs for helping increase and costs for not helping decrease. This interpretation is consistent with the well-known public incidents, in which possible bodily harm to a helper is almost always involved, and thus costs for helping are very high, and also with previous research done with non-visible victims in which either (a) it was easy to assume someone had already helped and thus costs for not helping were reduced (Darley & Latané) or (b) it was possible to think that the emergency was minor, which also reduces the costs for not helping (Latané & Rodin).

5. All of the effects of time are also consistent with the model. The longer the emergency continues, the more likely it is that observers will be aroused and therefore will have chosen among the possible responses. Thus, (a) a late model will elicit less helping, since people have already reduced their arousal by one of the other methods; (b) unless arousal is reduced by other methods, people will leave more as time goes on, because arousal is still increasing; and (c) observers will discuss the incident in an attempt to reduce self-blame and arrive at the fourth resolution, namely a justification for not helping based on rejection of the victim.

Quite obviously, the model was derived from these data, along with data of other studies in the area. Needless to say, further work is being planned by the authors to test the implications of the model systematically.

REFERENCES

Berscheid, E., & Walster, E. When does a harmdoer compensate a victim? *Journal of Personality and Social Psychology,* 1967, **6,** 435–441.

Black, D. J., & Reiss, A. J. *Studies in crime and law enforcement in major metropolitan areas.* (Report submitted to the President's Commission on Law Enforcement and Administration of Justice). Washington, D.C.: United States Government Printing Office, 1967.

Bryan, J. H., & Test, M. A. Models and helping: Naturalistic studies in aiding behavior. *Journal of Personality and Social Psychology,* 1967, **6,** 400–407.

Darley, J., & Latané, B. Bystander intervention in emergencies: Diffusion of responsibility. *Journal of Personality and Social Psychology,* 1968, **8,** 377–383.

Latané, B., & Darley, J. Group inhibition of bystander intervention in emergencies. *Journal of Personality and Social Psychology,* 1968, **10,** 215–221.

Latané, B., & Rodin, J. A lady in distress: Inhibiting effects of friends and strangers on bystander intervention. *Journal of Experimental Social Psychology,* 1969, **5,** 189–202.

Lerner, M. J., & Simmons, C. H. Observer's reaction to the "innocent victim": Compassion or rejection? *Journal of Personality and Social Psychology,* 1966, **4,** 203–210.

Schachter, S. The interaction of cognitive and physiological determinants of emotional state. In L. Berkowitz (Ed.), *Advances in experimental social psychology.* Vol. 1. New York: Academic Press, 1964.

Schopler, J., & Matthews, M. W. The influence of the perceived causal locus of partner's dependence on the use of interpersonal power. *Journal of Personality and Social Psychology,* 1965, **4,** 609–612.

Stotland, E. A theory and experiments in empathy. Paper presented at the meeting of the American Psychological Association, New York, September 1966.

ARTICLE 12

The Experience of Living in Cities: A Psychological Analysis[1]

Stanley Milgram

When I first came to New York it seemed like a nightmare. As soon as I got off the train at Grand Central I was caught up in pushing, shoving crowds on 42nd Street. Sometimes people bumped into me without apology; what really frightened me was to see two people literally engaged in combat for possession of a cab. Why were they so rushed? Even drunks on the street were bypassed without a glance. People didn't seem to care about each other at all.

This statement represents a common reaction to a great city, but it does not tell the whole story. Obviously, cities have great appeal because of their variety, eventfulness, possibility of choice, and the stimulation of an intense atmosphere that many individuals find a desirable background to their lives. Where face to face contacts are important, the city is unparalleled in its possibilities. It has been calculated by the Regional Plan Association (1969) that in Nassau county, a suburb of New York City, an official can meet 11,000 others with whom he may do business within 10 minutes of his office by foot or car. In Newark, a moder-

Reprinted and abridged from F. F. Korten, S. W. Cook, and J. I. Lacey (Eds.), *Psychology and the Problems of Society,* American Psychological Association, 1970. This article is a slightly revised version of an article appearing in *Science,* March 13, 1970. Copyright © 1970 by the American Association for the Advancement of Science and reprinted with their permission and the permission of the author.

[1]This paper is based on an Invited Address presented to the Division of General Psychology at the Annual Meeting of the American Psychological Association, Washington, D. C., September 2, 1969.

Barbara Bengen worked closely with the author in preparing the present version of this paper, and its expository values reflect her skill. The author wishes to express thanks to Gary Winkel, editor of *Environment and Behavior,* for useful suggestions and advice.

ate-sized city, he could see more than 20,000 persons. But in midtown Manhattan an office worker can meet 220,000 persons within 10 minutes of his desk. There is an order of magnitude increment in the communication possibilities offered by a great city. That is one of the bases of its appeal and, indeed, of its functional necessity. The city provides options that no other social arrangement permits. But there is a negative side also, as we shall see.

Granted that cities are indispensable in a complex society, we may still ask what contribution psychology can make to understanding the experience of living in them. What theories are relevant? How can we extend our knowledge of the psychological aspects of life in cities through empirical inquiry? If empirical inquiry is possible, along what lines should it proceed? In short, where do we start in the construction of urban theory and in laying out lines of research?

Observation is the indispensable starting point. Any observer in the streets of midtown Manhattan will see: *(a)* large numbers of people, *(b)* high density, and *(c)* heterogeneity of population. These three factors need to be at the root of any sociopsychological theory of city life, for they condition all aspects of our experience in the metropolis. Wirth (1938), if not the first to point to these factors, is nonetheless the sociologist who relied most heavily on them in his analysis of the city. Yet, for a psychologist there is something unsatisfactory about Wirth's theoretical variables. *Numbers, density,* and *heterogeneity* are demographic facts, but they are not yet psychological facts. They are external to the individual. Psychology needs an idea that links the individual's *experience* to the demographic circumstances of urban life.

One link is provided by the concept of *overload.* This term, drawn from systems analysis, refers to the inability of a system to process inputs from the environment because there are too many inputs for the system to cope with, or because successive inputs come so fast that Input A cannot be processed when Input B is presented. When overload is present, adaptations occur. The system must set priorities and make choices. Input A may be processed first while B is kept in abeyance, or one input may be sacrificed altogether. City life, as we experience it, constitutes a continuous set of encounters with adaptations to overload. Overload characteristically deforms daily life on several levels, impinging on *role performance,* evolution of *social norms, cognitive functioning,* and the *use of facilities.*

The concept has been implicit in several theories of urban experience. Simmel (1950) pointed out that since urban dwellers come into contact with vast numbers of people each day, they conserve psychic energy by becoming acquainted with a far smaller proportion of people than their rural counterparts and by maintaining more superficial relationships even with these acquaintances. Wirth (1938) points specifically to "the superficiality, the anonymity, and the transitory character of urban social relations," and to the loss of community that produces "the state of *anomie,* or the social void." Simmel notes as well that the high density of cities encourages inhabitants to create distance in social contacts to counteract the overwhelming pressures of close physical contact. The greater the number and frequency of human contacts the less time, attention, and emotional investment one can give to each of them, thus, the purported blasé and indifferent attitude of city dwellers toward each other.

One adaptive response to overload, therefore, is that *less time is given to each input.* A second adaptive mechanism is that *low priority inputs are disregarded.* Principles of selectivity are formulated so that the investment of time and energy is reserved for carefully defined inputs (e.g., the urbanite disregards a drunk, sick on the street, as he purposefully navigates through the crowd). Third, *boundaries are redrawn in certain social transactions so that the overloaded system can shift the burden to the other party in the exchange;* for example, harried New York bus drivers once made change for customers, but now this responsibility has been shifted to the client who must have the exact fare ready. Fourth, *reception is blocked off prior to entering a system;* city dwellers increasingly use unlisted telephone numbers to prevent individuals from calling them, and a small but growing number resort to keeping the telephone off the hook to prevent incoming calls. More subtly, one blocks inputs by assuming an unfriendly countenance, which discourages others from initiating contact. Additionally, *social screening devices are interposed between the individual and environmental inputs* (in a town of 5,000 anyone can drop in to chat with the mayor, but in the metropolis organizational screening devices deflect inputs to other destinations). Fifth, the *intensity of inputs is diminished by filtering devices* so that only weak and relatively superficial forms of involvement with others are allowed. Sixth, *specialized institutions are created to absorb inputs that would otherwise swamp the individual* (e.g., welfare departments handle the financial needs of a million individuals in New York City, who would otherwise create an army of mendicants continuously importuning the pedestrian). The interposition of institutions between the individual and the social world, a characteristic of all modern society and most acutely present in the large metropolis, has its negative side. It deprives the individual of a sense of direct contact and spontaneous integration in the life around him. It simultaneously protects and estranges the individual from his social environment.

Many of these adaptive mechanisms apply not only to individuals, but to institutional systems as well, as Meier (1962) has so brilliantly shown in connection with the library and the stock exchange.

In summary, the observed behavior of the urbanite in a wide range of situations appears to be determined largely by a variety of adaptations to overload. We shall now deal with several specific consequences of responses to overload, which come to create a different tone to city and town.

SOCIAL RESPONSIBILITY

The principal point of interest for a social psychology of the city is that moral and social involvement with individuals is necessarily restricted. This is a direct and necessary function of excess of input over capacity to process. Restriction of involvement runs a broad spectrum from refusal to become involved in the needs of another person, even when the person desperately needs assistance (as in the Kitty Genovese case), through refusal to do favors, to the simple withdrawal of courtesies (such as offering a lady a seat, or saying "sorry" when a pedestrian collision occurs). In any transaction more and more details need to be dropped as the total number of units to be processed increases and assaults an instrument of limited processing capacity. There are myriad specific situations dealing with social responsibility. Specific incidents can be ordered in terms of two dimensions. First, there is the dimension of the importance of the action in question. Clearly, intervening to save someone's life rates higher than tipping one's hat, though both imply a degree of social involvement with others. Second, one may place any specific incident in terms of its position on a social-anomic continuum. Thus, in regard to courtesy expressions, a person may extend courtesies (the social end of the continuum) or withhold them (the anomic end). Anomic conditions, up and down the spectrum, are said to characterize the metropolis in comparison with the small town.

The ultimate adaptation to an overloaded social environment is to totally disregard the needs, interests, and demands of those whom one does not define as relevant to personal need satisfaction, and to develop optimally efficient means of identifying whether an individual falls into the category of friend or stranger. The disparity in treatment of friends and strangers ought to be greater in cities than towns; the time allotment and willingness to become involved with those who can make no personal claim on one's time will be less in cities than in towns.

Bystander Intervention in Crises

The most striking deficiencies in urban social responsibility occur in crisis situations, such as the Genovese murder in Queens. As is well known, in 1964, Catherine Genovese, coming home from a night job in the early hours of an April morning, was stabbed repeatedly over an extended period of time. Thirty-eight residents of a respectable New York City neighborhood admitted to having witnessed at least part of the attack but none went to her aid or called the police until after she was dead. Milgram and Hollander (1964) analyzed the event in these terms:

Urban friendships and associations are not primarily formed on the basis of physical proximity. A person with numerous close friends in different parts of the city may not know the occupant of an adjacent apartment. This does not mean that a city dweller has fewer friends than does a villager, or knows fewer persons who will come to his aid; however, it does mean that his allies are not constantly at hand. Miss Genovese required immediate aid from those physically present. There is no evidence that the city had deprived Miss Genovese of human associations, but the friends who might have rushed to her side were miles from the scene of her tragedy.

Further, it is known that her cries for help were not directed to a specific person; they were general. But only individuals can act, and as the cries were not specifically directed, no particular person felt a special responsibility. The crime and the failure of community response seem absurd to us. At the time, it may well have seemed equally absurd to the Kew Gardens residents that not one of the neighbors would have called the police. A collective paralysis may have developed from the belief of each of the witnesses that someone else must surely have taken that obvious step [p.602].

Latané and Darley (1969) have reported laboratory approaches to the study of bystander intervention and have established experimentally the principle that the larger the number of bystanders the less likely it is that any one of them will intervene in an emergency. In any quantitative characterization of the social texture of city life a first order of business is the application of these experimental methods to field situations set in large cities and small towns. Theorists argue that the indifference shown in the Genovese case would not be present in a small town, but in the absence of solid experimental findings the question remains an open one.

More than just callousness prevents bystanders from participating in altercations between people. A rule of urban life is respect for other people's emotional and social privacy, perhaps because physical privacy is so hard to achieve. And in situations for which the standards are heterogeneous, it is much harder to know whether taking an active role is unwarranted meddling or an appropriate response to a critical situation. If a husband and wife are quarreling in public, at which point should a bystander step in? On the one hand, the heterogeneity of the city produces substantially greater tolerance of behavior, dress, and codes of ethics than does the small town, but this diversity also encourages people to withhold aid for fear of antagonizing the participants or crossing an inappropriate and difficult-to-define line.

Moreover, the frequency of demands present in the city gives rise to norms of noninvolvement. There are practical limitations to the Samaritan impulse in a major city. If a citizen attended to every needy person, if he were sensitive to and acted on every altruistic impulse that was evoked in the city, he could scarcely keep his own affairs in order.

Gaertner and Bickman (1968) have extended the bystander studies to an examination of help across ethnic lines. They arranged for blacks and whites, with clearly identifiable accents, to call strangers through an apparent error in telephone dialing. The caller indicates that he is attempting to contact a garage and that he is stranded on an outlying highway. He has just used his last dime attempting to reach a garage but received the present number instead by mistake. The caller then requests that the subject assist him in his predicament by calling the garage; he provides a telephone number and locational information to pass on to the service station.

The experimenters compared the number of persons who called the garage in response to white as opposed to Negro solicitation. White-accented callers had a significantly better chance of obtaining assistance than black callers. The findings of Gaertner and Bickman suggest that ethnic allegiance may well be another vehicle for coping with overload: The white, city inhabitant can reduce excessive demands and screen out urban heterogeneity by responding along ethnic lines; overload is made more manageable by limiting the "span of sympathy."

Favor Doing Based on Trust

We may now move away from crisis situations to less urgent examples of social responsibility; for it is not only in situations of dramatic need, but in the ordinary, everyday willingness to lend a hand, that the city dweller is said to be deficient relative to his small-town cousin. The comparative method must be employed in any empirical examination of this question. A commonplace social situation is staged both in an urban setting and a small town, a situation to which a subject can respond either by extending help or withholding it. The responses in town and city are then compared.

One factor in the purported unwillingness of urbanites to extend themselves to strangers may well be their heightened sense of physical and emotional vulnerability—a feeling that is supported by urban crime statistics. A key test for distinguishing between city and town behavior, therefore, is how city dwellers compare with town dwellers in offering aid that increases their personal vulnerability and requires some trust of strangers. Altman, Levine, Nadien, and Villena (1969) devised a study to compare city and town dwellers in this respect. The criterion used in their study was the willingness of householders to allow strangers to enter their homes to use the telephone. Individually the investigators rang doorbells, explained that they had misplaced the address of a friend nearby, and asked to use the phone. The investigators (two males and two females) completed a total of 100 requests for entry in the city and 60 in the small towns. The results gleaned from middle-income housing developments in Manhattan were compared with data gathered in several small towns in Rockland County, outside of New York City (Stony Point,

TABLE 1. Percentage of entries by investigators for city and town homes.

Investigator	% entries	
	City (n = 100)	Small town (n = 60)
Male		
1	16	40
2	12	60
Female		
1	40	87
2	40	100

Spring Valley, Ramapo, Nyack, New City, and West Clarkstown).

As Table 1 shows, in all cases there was a sharp increase in the proportion of entries gained by an investigator when he moved from the city to a small town. In the most extreme case the investigator was five times more likely to gain admission to a home in a small town than in Manhattan. Although the female investigators had noticeably higher levels of entry in both cities and towns than the male investigators, all four students did at least twice as well in gaining access to small-town homes than they did to city homes, suggesting that the city-town distinction overrides even the predictably greater fear of male strangers than of female ones.

The lower level of helpfulness by city dwellers seems due in part to recognition of the *dangers* of Manhattan living, rather than to mere indifference or coldness. It is significant that 75% of all city respondents received and answered messages either by shouting through closed doors or by peering through peepholes; in the towns, by contrast, about 75% of the respondents opened the doors, with no barriers between themselves and the investigator.

Supporting the investigators' quantitative results was their general observation that the town dwellers were noticeably more friendly and less suspicious than the city dwellers. Even city dwellers who allowed the investigators to use the phone appeared more ill at ease than their town counterparts; city dwellers often refused to answer the doorbell even when they were at home;

and in a few cases city residents called the security police of the housing development. In seeking to explain the sense of psychological vulnerability city dwellers feel, above and beyond differences in actual crime statistics, Altman et al. (1969) point out that for a village resident, if a crime is committed in a neighboring village, he may not perceive it as personally relevant, though the geographic distance may be small. But a criminal act committed anywhere in the city, though miles from the city-dweller's home, is still verbally located within the city, "therefore . . . the inhabitant of the city possesses a larger vulnerable space."

Civilities

Even at the most superficial level of involvement, the exercise of everyday civilities, urbanites are reputedly deficient. Persons bump into each other and frequently do not apologize. They knock over another person's packages, and, as often as not, proceed on their way with a grump, rather than taking the time to help the victim. Such behavior, which many visitors to great cities find distasteful, is less common, we are told, in smaller communities where traditional courtesies are more likely to be maintained.

In some instances it is not simply that in the city traditional courtesies are violated; rather, the cities develop *new norms of noninvolvement*. They are so well defined and so deeply a part of city life that *they* constitute the norms people are reluctant to violate. Men are actually embarrassed to give up a seat on the subway for an old woman; they will mumble, "I was getting off anyway," instead of making the gesture in a straightforward and gracious way. These norms develop because everyone realizes that in situations of high-density people cannot implicate themselves in each other's affairs, for to do so would create conditions of continual distraction that would frustrate purposeful action.

The effects of overload do not imply that at every instant the city dweller is bombarded with an unmanageable number of inputs, and that his responses are determined by the input excess at any given instant. Rather, adaptation occurs in the form of the gradual evolution of norms of behavior. Norms are created in response to frequent discrete experiences of overload; they persist and become generalized modes of responding. They are part of the culture of the metropolis, and even newcomers may adapt to these manners in the course of time.

Overload on Cognitive Capacities: Anonymity

It is a truism that we respond differently toward those whom we know and those who are strangers to us. An eager patron aggressively cuts in front of someone in a long movie line to save time only to confront a friend; he then behaves sheepishly. A man gets into an automobile accident caused by another driver, emerges from his car shouting in rage, then moderates his behavior on discovering a friend driving the other car. The city dweller, when moving through the midtown streets, is in a state of continual anonymity vis à vis the other pedestrians. His ability to know everyone he passes is restricted by inherent limitations of human cognitive capacity. A continual succession of faces briefly appears before him then disappears. Minimal scanning for recognition occurs, but storage in long-term memory is avoided. (No one has yet calculated the number of faces scanned in a day by the typical midtown worker.)

The concept of "anonymity" is a shibboleth of social psychology, but few have defined it precisely or attempted to measure it quantitatively in order to compare cities and towns. Anonymity is part of a continuous spectrum ranging from total anonymity at one end to full acquaintance at the other, and it may well be that measurement of the precise degrees of anonymity in cities and towns would help to explain important distinctions between the quality of life in each. Conditions of full acquaintance, for example, offer security and familiarity, but they may also be stifling because the inhabitant is under continuous scrutiny by people who know him. Conditions of complete anonymity, by contrast, provide freedom from routine social ties, but they may also create feelings of alienation and detachment.

One could investigate empirically the proportion of activities in which the city dweller and town dweller are known by others at given times in their daily lives, and, if known, with what proportion of those the urbanite and town dweller interact. At his job, for instance, the city dweller may know fully as many people as his rural counterpart. While not fulfilling his occupational or family role, however—say, in traveling about the city—the urbanite is doubtlessly more anonymous than his rural counterpart. (One way to measure the difference in degrees of anonymity would be to display the picture of a New York inhabitant at a busy midtown intersection. One could offer a significant reward to any passerby who could identify the person pictured. Calculation of the total number of passersby during a given period, coupled with the proportion who could identify the picture, provides one measure of urban anonymity. Results could then be compared with those gleaned by displaying the picture of a town dweller on the main street in his town. This test could also be used to define a person's "neighborhood boundary," that area within which a high proportion of people could identify the inhabitant's picture.)

Limited laboratory work on anonymity has begun. Zimbardo (1968) has conducted pilot studies testing whether groups asked to perform certain aggressive acts while wearing masks administer more shock than control groups without masks. The results were inconclusive, though Zimbardo's findings suggest that if we could create laboratory conditions of true anonymity, more aggressive behavior would result.

A related experiment by Zimbardo tested whether the social anonymity and impersonality of the big city encourage greater vandalism than found in small towns. Zimbardo arranged for one car to be left for 64 hours near the New York University campus in the Bronx and a counterpart to be left near Stanford University in Palo Alto. The license plates on both cars were removed and the hoods opened, to provide "releaser cues" for potential vandals. The results were as expected: The New York car was stripped of all moveable parts within the first 24 hours, and was left a hunk of metal rubble by the end of three days. Unexpectedly, however, most destruction occurred during daylight hours usually under scrutiny by observers, and was led by well-dressed, white adults. The Palo Alto car was left untouched (Zimbardo notes that when it started to rain, one bystander even lowered the car's hood to protect the motor).

Zimbardo attributes the difference in the treatment accorded the two cars to the "acquired feelings of social anonymity provided by life in a city like New York," and he supports his study with several other anecdotes illustrating casual, wanton vandalism in the city. Any study comparing the effects of anonymity in city and town, however, must satisfactorily control for other confounding factors: the large number of drug addicts in New York, the higher proportion of slum dwellers in the city, etc.

Another direction for empirical study is the investigation of the beneficial effects of anonymity. Impersonality of city life breeds its own tolerance for the private lives of inhabitants. Individuality and even eccentricity, we may assume, can flourish more readily in the metropolis than in the small town. Stigmatized persons may find it easier to lead comfortable lives without the constant scrutiny of neighbors. To what degree can this assumed difference between city and town be shown empirically? Waters (1969) hypothesized that avowed homosexuals would be more likely to be accepted as tenants in a large city than in small towns. She dispatched letters from homosexuals and normals to real estate agents in cities and towns across the country. The results of her study were inconclusive, but the general idea of examining the protective benefits of city life to the stigmatized ought to be pursued.

Role Behavior in Cities and Towns

Another product of urban "overload" is the adjustment in roles made by urbanites in daily interactions. As Wirth has said: "Urbanites meet one another in highly segmental roles. . . . They are less dependent upon particular persons, and their dependence upon others is confined to a highly fractionalized aspect of the other's round of activity." This tendency is particularly noticeable in transactions between customers and those offering professional or sales services: The owner of a country store has time to become well acquainted with his dozen-or-so daily customers; but the girl at the checkout counter of a busy A & P, handling hundreds of customers a day, barely has time to toss the green stamps into one customer's shopping bag before the next customer has confronted her with his pile of groceries.

In his stimulating analysis of the city *A Communications Theory of Urban Growth,* Meier (1962) discusses several adaptations a system may make when confronted by inputs that exceed its capacity to process them. Specifically, Meier states that according to the principle of competition for scarce resources the scope and time of the transaction shrinks as customer volume and daily turnover rise (see Figure 1). This, in fact, is what is meant by the brusque quality of city life. New standards have developed in cities about what levels of services are appropriate in business transactions.

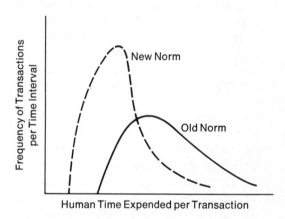

FIGURE 1.   Changes in the demand for time for a given task when overall transaction frequency increases in a social system. (Reprinted with permission from R. L. Meier, *A Communications Theory of Urban Growth,* 1962. Copyrighted by MIT Press, 1962.)

McKenna and Morgenthau (1969), in a seminar at the City University of New York, devised a study *(a)* to compare the willingness of city dwellers and small towners to do favors for strangers that entailed a small amount of time and inconvenience but no personal vulnerability, and *(b)* to determine whether the more compartmentalized, transitory relationships of the city would make urban salesgirls less likely than small-town salesgirls to carry out tasks for strangers not related to their customary roles.

To test for differences between city dwellers and small towners, a simple experiment was devised in which persons from both settings were asked to perform increasingly onerous favors for anonymous strangers. It was not possible for the investigators to travel around the country extensively, but by making use of a telephone they were able to reach persons in major cities (Chicago, New York, and Philadelphia) and 37 small towns in the same states in which the cities were located. The average population of the towns was 2,727 people, based on the 1960 census. Typical small towns used in the study were Coxsackie, Ravena, and Wappingers Falls (New York); Chenoa, St. Anne, and Fairbury (Illinois); and Doylestown, Sellersville, and McAdoo (Pennsylvania).

Within the cities, half the calls went to housewives, and the other half to salesgirls in women's apparel shops; the same division was made for the small towns. Each investigator represented herself as a long-distance caller who had mistakenly been connected with the respondent by the operator. The investigator began by asking for simple information about the weather for travel purposes. Next the investigator excused herself on a pretext stating "please hold on," put the phone down for almost a full minute, and then picked it up again and asked the respondent to provide the phone number of a hotel or motel in her vicinity at which the investigator might stay during a forthcoming visit. Scores were assigned to the subjects depending on how helpful they had been. Scores ranged from 1 (meaning that the respondent hung up without giving weather information and without an excuse) to 16 (meaning that the respondent remained on the phone during the delay and carried out all the requests).

McKenna summarizes her results in this manner: "People in the city, whether they are engaged in a specific job or not, are less helpful and informative than people in small towns. . . . People at home, regardless of where they live, are less helpful and informative than people working in shops [p. 8]." Representative quantitative results are

TABLE 2. People in each category with scores above overall median.

Category	City	Town
Home	13(11)	17(12.5)
Shop	16(11)	24(14)

Note.—Figures in parentheses indicate the median for that group. $n = 34$ for each cell.

shown in Table 2. It is important to note that the relatively high median for urban housewives and salesgirls alike does not jibe with the stereotype of the urbanite as aloof, self-centered, and unwilling to help strangers, and that the quantitative differences obtained by McKenna and Morgenthau are less great than one might have expected. This again points up the need for extensive empirical research on rural-urban differences, research that goes far beyond that provided in the few illustrative pilot studies presented in this paper. At this point we have very limited objective evidence on differences in the quality of social encounters in the city and small town.

The research on this subject needs to be guided by unifying theoretical concepts. As this section of the paper has tried to demonstrate, the concept of overload helps to explain a wide variety of contrasts between city and town behavior: *(a)* the differences in *role enactment* (the urban dwellers' tendency to deal with one another in highly segmented, functional terms; the constricted time and services offered customers by sales personnel); *(b)* the evolution of *urban norms* quite different from traditional town values (such as the acceptance of noninvolvement, impersonality, and aloofness in urban life); *(c)* consequences for the urban dweller's *cognitive processes* (his inability to identify most of the people seen daily; his screening of sensory stimuli; his development of blasé attitudes toward deviant or bizarre behavior; and his selectivity in responding to human demands); and *(d)* the far greater competition for scarce *facilities* in the city (the subway rush, the fight for taxis, traffic jams, standing in line to await services). I would suggest that contrasts between city and rural behavior probably reflect the responses of similar people to very different situations, rather than intrinsic differences between rural personalities and city personalities. The city is a situation to which individuals respond adaptively.

REFERENCES

Altman, D., Levine, M., Nadien, M., & Villena, J. Trust of the stranger in the city and the small town. Unpublished research, Graduate Center, City University of New York, 1969.

Gaertner, S., & Bickman, L. The ethnic bystander. Unpublished research, Graduate Center, City University of New York, 1968.

Latané, B., & Darley, J. Bystander apathy. *American Scientist,* 1969, **57**, 244–268.

McKenna, W., & Morgenthau, S. Urban-rural differences in social interaction: A study of helping behavior. Unpublished research, Graduate Center, City University of New York, 1969.

Meier, R. L. *A communications theory of urban growth.* Cambridge, Mass.: MIT Press, 1962.

Milgram, S., & Hollander, P. Paralyzed witness: The murder they heard. *The Nation,* 1964, **25**, 602–604.

Regional Plan Association (1969). The second regional plan. *The New York Times,* June 15, 1969, 119, Section 12.

Simmel, G. The metropolis and mental life. In K. H. Wolff (Ed.), *The sociology of George Simmel.* New York: The Free Press, 1950. (Originally published: *Die Grossstadte und das Geistesleben die Grossstadt.* Dresden: v. Zahn & Jaensch, 1903.)

Waters, J. The relative acceptance accorded a discreditable person in rural and metropolitan areas. Unpublished research, Graduate Center, City University of New York, 1969.

Wirth, L. Urbanism as a way of life. *American Journal of Sociology,* 1938, **44**, 1–24.

Zimbardo, P. G. The human choice: Individuation, reason and order vs. deindividuation, impulse and chaos. *Nebraska symposium on motivation,* 1969, **17**, 237–307.

SECTION SUMMARY

The laboratory research reported by Latané and Darley in the first article provides strong evidence that two variables—social influence and factors in the immediate social environment—can be of crucial importance in determining whether a person or persons will intervene in an emergency situation. To evaluate the effect of these social-influence factors, it may be pertinent to look at the model of the emergency-intervention *process* that Latané and Darley (1969, 1970a) have propounded.

They propose that, when a person is confronted with an emergency situation (defined in terms of the unique characteristics outlined in the section Introduction), there is a series of decision points through which he must pass if he is going to intervene. Only one particular set of choices will lead the person to take action in the situation. First, the bystander must *notice* the situation. The external event has to break into his thinking and intrude into his conscious mind. If the bystander is so lost in his own thoughts that the event does not "get through" to him and is not noticed, obviously he is not going to intervene.

If the person does notice the event, he must then *interpret* it. Is the man slumped on the street (or in the subway car) suffering a heart attack, or is he simply drunk or asleep? Is the man perched on the ledge of a building trying to decide whether to jump, or is he just a window washer going about his business? In other words, is the situation an emergency or not? The third step involves deciding whether one has a *responsibility* to act in the emergency situation. Perhaps help is already on the way, or perhaps someone else may be better qualified to help. Or perhaps the bystander will decide that the emergency is simply none of his business.

According to the model, if the bystander has made the "intervention" choice at each of the three points discussed thus far, he will have noticed the event, interpreted it as an emergency, and decided that it is his responsibility to take action. The fourth and fifth steps in this sequence, then, involve more practical questions: *what* to do and *how* to do it. The bystander may take either of two courses of action at this point. The first is the set of behaviors that Latané and Darley (1970a, pp. 34–35) call "direct intervention": swimming out to someone who is drowning, grabbing an extinguisher to put out a fire, and so on. The second set of acts is labeled "detour interventions," which involve attempts to report the emergency to the relevant authority (for example, lifeguard or the fire department) rather than to try to cope with it directly. Obviously, the amount of danger facing the bystander and the degree of skill that he has in such situations may be major determinants of which course of action he takes. As the first article in this section points out, witnesses to the Kitty Genovese murder took *neither* course of action.

Latané and Darley have proposed that the intervention process is most likely to break down at the second or third step: interpreting the situation as an emergency and deciding whether one is responsible for intervention. One of the social processes that they identify is that of *pluralistic ignorance.* Each member of a group of bystanders may be simultaneously trying to decide how to interpret an ambiguous situation by taking cues from the reactions of others. At the same time, each group member is trying to appear calm himself. Therefore, until or unless someone acts, each bystander sees only "calm," nonresponding bystanders around him. He is thus likely to decide that the ambiguous situation must not really be an emergency.

The crucial importance of the variable of situation ambiguity has been further demonstrated by Clark and Word (in press) and by Yakimovich and Saltz (1971). Clark and Word set up a situation similar to the Latané-Darley "fallen woman" experiment described in the first article. Whereas the "emergency" was transmitted via tape recorder in the Latané-Darley experiment, Clark and Word had their (male) confederate actually act out the emergency for each subject or pair of subjects. The confederate would climb a metal ladder in an adjoining room (door closed), fall from the top of the ladder to the floor, and pull the ladder over on top of him. He then moaned and groaned in pain. In this situation, presumably much less ambiguous than the Latané-Darley scenario, Clark and Word found 100% helping—*every* subject went to the confederate's aid. Clark and Word carried out a second experiment in which either one, two, or five naive persons overheard the same fall without any verbal signs of injury (high ambiguity). In this situation, the alone subject or at least one member of the

two- and five-man groups responded to the needs of the victim in only about 30% of the cases. Persons in the two- and five-man groups were less likely to help and intervened more slowly than would have been expected on the basis of the alone subjects' performances.

In another study wherein an unseen confederate fell from a ladder, Yakimovich and Saltz (1971) found that 81% of their subjects helped when the victim called for help, but only 29% helped when the victim moaned and cursed but did not call for help.

But what of situations that are nonambiguous and are clearly emergencies? Can the presence of other persons decrease the likelihood that any given bystander will react in this situation too? Latané and Darley suggest that it can, through the process of *diffusion of responsibility.* In the first article in this section they propose that the presence of other people can reduce the "cost" of not acting by reducing the guilt or blame that can be directed to any one individual for inaction. In addition, if others are known to be present, a bystander may assume that someone else has already initiated action to help in the emergency. (This process is illustrated in cases of serious automobile accidents in which an ambulance is not called for some time, apparently because all the bystanders are assuming that someone else has already done so.)

Bickman (1971) has demonstrated that the perceived *ability* of the other bystanders to help may have a significant effect on the diffusion of responsibility. He found that when one of two bystanders was represented as being unable to help, the other bystander helped as frequently and as quickly as did bystanders who were alone. Staub (1970) has presented evidence that the presence of others may have varying effects on intervention for children of different ages. He found that for older children (sixth grade) the presence of others seemed to inhibit intervention, whereas for younger children it seemed to facilitate it.

In the second article, Piliavin, Rodin, and Piliavin raise further questions about the diffusion of responsibility hypothesis. They found that there was *no* strong relationship between number of bystanders and the speed of helping, contrary to what the hypothesis would predict. The reader is encouraged to apply the model that Piliavin et al. develop, in which the costs and the rewards of helping are weighed against each other, to the results of the three studies discussed in the first article.

One hypothesis that could be drawn from a comparison of the first two articles is that the Latané-Darley model is applicable to laboratory situations but not to the "real world." Things are not this simple, however. Elsewhere, Latané and Darley (1969, pp. 258–259) have reported a study conducted in the "real world" that does support their model. They staged a series of 96 "robberies" of a discount liquor store over a two-week period. The robberies (of a case of beer) took place when there was either one or two customers (bystanders) in the store and when the cashier was out of sight in the rear of the store. None of the bystanders attempted to intervene in the robbery directly; about one-fifth of the customers spontaneously reported the robbery to the cashier when he returned. After prompting by the cashier ("Hey, what happened to that man who was in here? Did you see him leave?"), about half the remaining subjects (those who had not reported the robbery spontaneously) told the cashier about the theft. The number of robbers (one or two) had no major effect on the pattern of responses.

A total of 65% of the lone customers reported the theft; from this, probability theory would predict that 87% of the two-person groups would include at least one "reporter." However, in only 56% of the two-person groups did *even one* person report the theft. Latané and Darley interpret these results as indicative of the operation of diffusion of responsibility in the two-person groups. In a related vein, Milgram, in the third article, discusses the role that the norms of noninvolvement and ethnic allegiances may play in real-world emergency situations in urban environments.

The discussion of bystander intervention in emergency situations has thus far focused largely on situational variables. The reader may already have wondered about the influence of attitudinal or personality factors on behavior in emergency situations. It seems very probable that certain kinds of people will be more likely to intervene in emergency situations than others. To investigate this possibility, Latané and Darley gave a series of personality measures to the subjects who had participated in the "fit to be tried" experiment described in the first article. The subjects filled out the F Scale, a measure of authoritarianism; a scale of Anomia, alienation from social norms and institutions; a scale of Machiavellianism, the tendency to take a tough-minded, cynical, and opportunistic attitude toward others; a scale of Need for Approval, the tendency to try to present a socially desirable picture of oneself; and a Social Responsibility Scale, a measure of the extent to which subjects accept the social-responsibility norm.

Perhaps surprisingly, scores on *none* of these instruments were significantly related to speed of helping in the "fit" experiment. Other researchers (Yakimovich & Saltz, 1971) have reported a similar lack of relationship between responses to personality or attitude questionnaires and helping behavior. In addition, Latané and Darley looked at demographic characteristics of the subjects (social class, family size, length of stay in New York City, and so on). Out of 11 such variables, only one showed a significant relationship to speed of helping. The smaller the size of the community in which the subject grew up, the more likely she was to help the victim having the "fit" (see Latané & Darley, 1970a, pp. 113–120). As the experimenters comment, "This finding may provide comfort for those small town residents who claim 'It couldn't happen here'" (p. 117). Subsequent research will undoubtedly continue to look for personality characteristics that may be related to helping behavior, but it seems likely that in the case of these emergency-related behaviors, situational factors far outweigh personality factors in determining one's response.

In nonemergency situations, however, personality traits and temporary states of the individual may be significant determinants of behavior. For example, there is some evidence that if a "benefactor" (potential helper) is experiencing a positive state (such as a feeling of success or competence), he may be more likely to engage in altruistic behavior than if he is in a "neutral" state. There is also evidence, however, that an individual experiencing certain *negative* states may be more likely to participate in altruistic behavior than someone in a "neutral" state. As the article by Freedman, Wallington, and Bless in Section 6 demonstrates, the arousal of guilt—conceived of here as a negative state—can be a very effective way of inducing compliance in the absence of overt social-influence attempts. In some cases the increased tendency to comply may produce behavior that fits the definition of altruism quoted earlier.

A third type of relevant state in the benefactor could be that induced by the observation of altruistic models. Several studies have found that when subjects have observed a helpful and charitable model, they may be more likely to engage in such altruistic behavior themselves. Bryan and Test (1967), for example, found that motorists were more likely to stop and help a woman fix a flat tire if they had recently driven past another motorist who was helping someone fix a flat. They also found that shoppers were more likely to contribute money to a Salvation Army kettle if they had seen another person contribute than if they had not. Other research has suggested that the presence of *non*helping models may significantly *inhibit* altruistic behavior (Wagner & Wheeler, 1969). Krebs (1970) points out that such modeling effects may stem from the increased salience of behavioral alternatives and social norms, from new information about the appropriateness of behavioral alternatives, or from new information about the consequences of the model's altruistic behavior. Research on altruistic behavior in children has demonstrated that, although the model's role is important in eliciting altruistic behavior, the *processes* by which the behavior is elicited have still not been fully explicated (see Bryan & London, 1970; Severy & Davis, 1971).

The state of the potential recipient may also be an important determinant of altruistic behavior. One state that seems to elicit such behavior is dependency. If the potential recipient is seen as dependent, either specifically upon the potential benefactor or in a more general overall sense, such perceived dependency tends to increase altruism. Another factor that would seem likely to

affect altruism is the interpersonal attractiveness of the recipient. However, Krebs (1970) comments that "Although there are suggestive indications that attractiveness mediates altruism, the relationship is surprisingly weak" (p. 281). The reader is encouraged to recall these findings when "favor-doing," liking, and compliance are discussed in the Introduction to Section 6.

In terms of a general overview, Goranson and Berkowitz (1966) have suggested that two different, though perhaps related, normative expectations may account for helping behavior. These are the responsibility norm, proscribing that a dependent individual should be helped, and the reciprocity norm, a social standard calling for the repayment of benefits received from others. Subsequent research (Greenglass, 1969) has indicated that the reciprocity norm will be most salient to the potential helper if he has received prior help from the other, whereas the norm of responsibility is most salient when the individual has not received prior help. (On the other hand, Latané and Darley [1970b, p. 99] have argued that norms may not have the degree of importance that these authors have suggested. They argue that ". . . a person's helping behavior is too complexly determined by situational factors to be accounted for by norms.")

Investigations attempting to identify personality *traits* that may accompany or predict the likelihood of altruistic behavior have yielded some fairly consistent findings. For example, altruistic children seem to be better adjusted socially than others, although they do not differ in intelligence or achievement from others (Krebs, 1970). However, much additional research is needed in this area.

The study of altruism, in both emergency and nonemergency situations, is still in its infancy, and researchers are currently investigating the effects of many variables beyond those mentioned here. (For more extensive coverage of such studies, the interested reader may want to consult Krebs, 1970, or Macaulay and Berkowitz, 1970.) The research results reported in the articles in this section have attempted to make sense out of seemingly inexplicable social situations in which bystanders have not gone to the aid of persons who are apparently desperately in need of their help. Although many questions remain to be answered, such laboratory and field research, coupled with investigations of the more general concepts of altruism and helping behavior, may lead to findings that can be translated into social policies to reduce the likelihood that such tragic occurrences will take place in the future.

REFERENCES

Bickman, L. The effect of another bystander's ability to help on bystander intervention in an emergency. *Journal of Experimental Social Psychology,* 1971, 7, 367–379.

Bryan, J. H., & London, P. Altruistic behavior by children. *Psychological Bulletin,* 1970, 73, 200–211.

Bryan, J. H., & Test, M. A. Models and helping behavior: Naturalistic studies in aiding behavior. *Journal of Personality and Social Psychology,* 1967, 6, 400–407.

Clark, R. D. III, & Word, L. E. Why don't bystanders help? Because of ambiguity? *Journal of Personality and Social Psychology,* in press.

Goranson, R. E., & Berkowitz, L. Reciprocity and responsibility reactions to prior help. *Journal of Personality and Social Psychology,* 1966, 3, 227–232.

Greenglass, E. R. Effects of prior help and hindrance on willingness to help another: Reciprocity or social responsibility. *Journal of Personality and Social Psychology,* 1969, 11, 224–231.

Krebs, D. L. Altruism—An examination of the concept and a review of the literature. *Psychological Bulletin,* 1970, 73, 258–302.

Latané, B., & Darley, J. M. Bystander "apathy." *American Scientist,* 1969, 57, 244–268.

Latané, B., & Darley, J. M. *The unresponsive bystander: Why doesn't he help?* New York: Appleton-Century-Crofts, 1970. (a)

Latané, B., & Darley, J. M. Norms and normative behavior: Field studies of social interdependence. In J. R. Macaulay and L. Berkowitz (Eds.), *Altruism and helping behavior.* New York: Academic Press, 1970. Pp. 83–101. (b)

Macaulay, J. R., & Berkowitz, L. (Eds.) *Altruism and helping behavior.* New York: Academic Press, 1970.

Severy, L. J., & Davis, K. E. Helping behavior among normal and retarded children. *Child Development,* 1971, 42, 1017–1031.

Staub, E. A child in distress: The influence of age and number of witnesses on children's attempts to help. *Journal of Personality and Social Psychology,* 1970, 14, 130–140.

Wagner, C., & Wheeler, L. Model, need, and cost effects in helping behavior. *Journal of Personality and Social Psychology,* 1969, 12, 111–116.

Yakimovich, D., & Saltz, E. Helping behavior: The cry for help. *Psychonomic Science,* 1971, 23, 427–428.

SUGGESTED READINGS FOR FURTHER STUDY

Bickman, L., & Henchy, T. (Eds.) *Beyond the laboratory: Field research in social psychology.* New York: McGraw-Hill, 1972.

Bryan, J. H., & London, P. Altruistic behavior by children. *Psychological Bulletin,* 1970, 73, 200–211.

Bryan, J. H., & Test, M. A. Models and helping behavior: Naturalistic studies in aiding behavior. *Journal of Personality and Social Psychology,* 1967, 6, 400–407.

Kaufmann, H. *Aggression and altruism.* New York: Holt, Rinehart & Winston, 1970.

Krebs, D. L. Altruism—An examination of the concept and a review of the literature. *Psychological Bulletin,* 1970, 73, 258–302.

Latané, B., & Darley, J. M. Bystander "apathy." *American Scientist,* 1969, 57, 244–268.

Latané, B., & Darley, J. M. *The unresponsive bystander: Why doesn't he help?* New York: Appleton-Century-Crofts, 1970.

Macaulay, J. R., & Berkowitz, L. (Eds.) *Altruism and helping behavior.* New York: Academic Press, 1970.

Midlarsky, E. Aiding responses: An analysis and review. *Merrill-Palmer Quarterly,* 1968, 14, 229–260.

Staub, E. A child in distress: The influence of age and number of witnesses on children's attempts to help. *Journal of Personality and Social Psychology,* 1970, 14, 130–140.

SECTION 5

The Risky Shift

Suppose that you, a person in a position of leadership, are confronted with a problem for which some kind of decision is necessary. Suppose also that the decision can be either bold, daring, and risky or conservative and nonrisky. Finally, suppose that you are unable or unwilling to make that decision by yourself. What can you do? In many areas of American society the answer often chosen is quite simple: appoint a committee.

What kind of a decision will that committee make? Based on observations and on assumptions about people in the role of committee members, most people would probably answer: the committee is likely to make the most stodgy, unimaginative, conservative, cautious, nonrisky decision possible.

For example, in his well-known book *The Organization Man,* Whyte (1956) argued that the "team approach" in business enterprises inexorably leads to a reduction of boldness, of daring, and of risk-taking. He proposed that, in such situations, if a choice must be made between more and less risky courses of action, there will be a definite preference for the more conservative course. Along the same lines, Roger Brown (1965, p. 657) has drily observed that "The academic committees on which one has served . . . do not leave one breathless with their daring."

Thus our prediction seems reasonable enough. But, on the basis of a rapidly accumulating mass of psychological data pertaining to this question, it appears that the prediction is *not* likely to be correct. The committee is likely to recommend a course of action that is actually quite risky. In fact, the riskiness of the decision recommended by the group may be considerably greater than that which would have been recommended by the individual committee members if they had been working on the problem separately.

It is relatively rare that research interest in an area of social psychology can be pinpointed as originating in a single piece of work. But for the phenomenon outlined here, this is the case. This unexpected finding about the behavior of individuals in groups was first noted by Stoner in an unpublished master's thesis done at the Massachusetts Institute of Technology in 1961. Stoner was interested in individual differences in risk-taking behavior. To assess such differences, he used descriptions of a number of situations that a person might face; each situation required that the participant, acting as an adviser, choose between two courses of action. In each situation one possible action was "risky"—the potential rewards for the decision were high, but the stake was also high. By making the risky decision, the person had a chance to gain a considerable amount, but he also stood the chance of losing a lot (a less certain but more attractive alternative). A conservative choice was also possible—one in which the person would not risk much of a loss but also would not stand to gain much (a more certain but less attractive alternative).

An example of one such situation that has been used in this research is as follows:

Mr. A, an electrical engineer who is married and has one child, has been working for a large electronics corporation since graduating from college five years ago. He is assured of a lifetime job with a modest though adequate salary and liberal pension benefits upon retirement. On the other hand, it is very unlikely that his salary will increase much before he retires. While attending a convention, Mr. A is offered a job with a small, newly founded company which has a highly uncertain future. The new job would pay more to start and would offer the possibility of a share in the ownership if the company survives the competition of the larger firms.

Imagine that you are advising Mr. A. Listed below are several probabilities or odds of the new company's proving financially sound.

Please check the lowest probability that you would consider acceptable to make it worthwhile for Mr. A to take the new job.
——The chances are 1 in 10 that the company will prove financially sound.
——The chances are 3 in 10 that the company will prove financially sound.
——The chances are 5 in 10 that the company will prove financially sound.
——The chances are 7 in 10 that the company will prove financially sound.
——The chances are 9 in 10 that the company will prove financially sound.
——Place a check here if you think Mr. A should not take the new job no matter what the probabilities.

Stoner's subjects were first asked to make indi-

vidual decisions on each of 12 such problems. The subjects were then combined into groups and asked to come up with unanimous *group* decisions as to what course of action should be taken. Stoner found that, for 12 of 13 groups, the group decision was riskier than the average of the subjects' previous individual judgments had been. Many of the subjects apparently shifted their judgments to a more risky decision when they were in the group situation. It is this phenomenon that has been called the "shift to risk" or the "risky shift."

In the first article in this section, Wallach (who was one of Stoner's advisers at MIT), Kogan, and Bem describe their attempt to replicate and extend Stoner's findings in a study of male and female undergraduates in a liberal arts curriculum at a large state university. And, as they point out, they were able to obtain the same type of effect as had Stoner. Thus, although Wallach et al. report that Stoner's previous results "took us by surprise," their subsequent study provides evidence that the phenomenon of the risky shift was not limited to male MIT students or to only a short time period. Subsequent research has provided further evidence that the effect is quite consistent over different types of subjects and even different cultures.

Soon after these results were made known, psychologists began to address themselves to the next logical question: *why* does the risky shift take place? In the years since these findings were published, a number of hypotheses have been put forth to attempt to explain the phenomenon. Among the more well known are the familiarization hypothesis, the diffusion of responsibility hypothesis, the leadership hypothesis, and the risk-as-value hypothesis. (See Clark, 1971, and Vinokur, 1971, for more detailed analyses of these and additional hypotheses.) In brief, the familiarization hypothesis suggests that the risky shift is not a *true* group effect but a "pseudogroup effect"—that is, an effect that occurs in a group but does not actually result from group processes. According to this hypothesis, any procedure that increases familiarity with an issue involving risk (such as a problem utilized in this research) will cause individuals to become more risky with regard to that issue. So, viewed in this light, the risky shift is seen not as a product of group discussion per se but as a result of the increased boldness and riskiness that occur when someone becomes more familiar with an issue (see Bateson, 1966; Flanders & Thistlethwaite, 1967).

The diffusion of responsibility hypothesis, on the other hand, suggests that group discussion may produce emotional bonds between members and may lead the individual to feel less responsibility for the risky decision because it has been at least partially shaped by the group (see Kogan & Wallach, 1967). Therefore, if the suggested risky course of action should lead to failure, the individual alone is not responsible—the responsibility is diffused through the members of the group.

The leadership hypothesis (see Marquis, 1962) focuses on the attributes of those group members perceived by the other members as group leaders. It could be argued that people who are initially more inclined to advise a risky course of action also tend to be more dominant and influential in the group discussion. Thus the resulting risky group decision could result from the influence of "risky" group leaders.

Finally, the risk-as-value hypothesis, originally formulated by Brown (1965), focuses on the possibility that willingness to take (or to advise) at least a moderate degree of risk is a cultural value in American society. As one nonempirical argument in support of such a hypothesis, Brown suggested that "... riskiness is a concomitant of youth and since Americans like to appear youthful perhaps they also like to appear risky" (p. 700). This hypothesis would predict, then, that most individuals will see themselves as at least as willing as their peers to take risks. In the context of a group discussion, a process could be expected to take place in which the relatively cautious group members would be made to recognize their relative cautiousness and would therefore be motivated to change their judgments toward a more risky course of action in order to restore their perceptions of themselves as relatively risky. The risk-as-value hypothesis has been the most persistent and popular interpretation of the risky shift (Clark, 1971).

The risk-as-value hypothesis is tested and refined by Clark, Crockett, and Archer in the second article in this section. They describe two experiments designed to investigate more specific processes that may occur *within* the general interpretation in terms of the risk-as-value hypothesis. Their results favor a "knowledge of others' arguments" interpretation, rather than an "information-exchange per se" interpretation.

Most of the studies of the risky shift, including the first two included in this section, have utilized artificial research settings. A crucial question that may already have occurred to the reader is: are the conclusions derived from such laboratory studies applicable to the way things happen in the real world? Or, couched in more scientific terms, how great is the generalizability of the pattern of empirical results obtained? Cartwright, in the third article, addresses himself to this problem. In contrasting experimentally induced groups with "natural" groups in the real world, whose decisions may have real and important consequences for the group members themselves, Cartwright takes a rather skeptical stance. The reader is encouraged to decide for himself whether Cartwright's pessimism is warranted and, if so, to try to visualize ways in which future research might overcome some of the shortcomings of past research.

REFERENCES

Bateson, N. Familiarization, group discussion, and risk taking. *Journal of Experimental Social Psychology,* 1966, **2**, 119–129.

Brown, R. *Social psychology.* New York: Free Press, 1965.

Clark, R. D. III. Group-induced shift toward risk: A critical appraisal. *Psychological Bulletin,* 1971, **76**, 251–270.

Flanders, J. P. & Thistlethwaite, D. L. Effects of familiarization and group discussion upon risk taking. *Journal of Personality and Social Psychology,* 1967, **5**, 91–97.

Kogan, N., & Wallach, M. A. Group risk taking as a function of members' anxiety and defensive levels. *Journal of Personality,* 1967, **35**, 50–63.

Marquis, D. C. Individual responsibility and group decisions involving risk. *Industrial Management Review,* 1962, **3**, 8–23.

Stoner, J.A.F. A comparison of individual and group decisions involving risk. Unpublished master's thesis, School of Industrial Management, Massachusetts Institute of Technology, 1961.

Vinokur, A. Review and theoretical analysis of the effects of group processes upon individual and group decisions involving risk. *Psychological Bulletin,* 1971, **76,** 231–250.

Whyte, W. H., Jr. *The organization man.* New York: Simon & Schuster, 1956.

ARTICLE 13

Group Influence on Individual Risk Taking[1]

Michael A. Wallach, Nathan Kogan, and Daryl J. Bem

What are the effects of group interaction on risk and conservatism in decision making? By risk and conservatism we mean the extent to which the decision maker is willing to expose himself to possible failure in the pursuit of a desirable goal. Consider the situation in which several individuals working separately arrive at a series of decisions, and then are brought together to arrive at a group consensus regarding those decisions. What relationship should one expect to find between the individual decisions and the group consensus?

On the basis of prior experimental studies of individual and group judgment (e.g., Schachter, 1951; see also the section on group pressures and group standards in Cartwright & Zander, 1960, pp. 165–341), we should predict an averaging effect, i.e., group decisions randomly distributed around the average of the prediscussion individual decisions. Such an effect would seem to imply a process of minimizing individual losses, or minimizing the maximum individual concession. The cited studies report that inducements toward compromise and concession seem to be exerted most strongly toward group members whose initial individual views are most deviant from the central tendency.

An equally, if not more, compelling alternative hypothesis is that the group discussion will lead to increased conservatism, relative to the average of the prior individual decisions. . . . How are such effects to be explained? First, it may be that the very nature of the group process or atmosphere encourages such a trend: there may be a fear, for example, of appearing foolhardy to others. Alternatively, or in addition, it is possible that the mechanism underlying an increase in conservatism is one of greater influence being exerted within the group by members whose individual conservatism tendencies are stronger. These two interpretations are not incompatible, of course, since the group process, if encouraging of conservatism, will enhance the influence of the initially more conservative members.

Finally, consideration should be given to the remaining and least likely possibility—that group interaction will eventuate in increased risk taking relative to the average of the prior decisions of the group members working separately. In this regard, Osborn (1957) has reported that group interaction may lead to quite radical, bold, problem solutions. While Osborn claims that special conditions must exist if such effects are to be observed, attempts to produce such conditions experimentally (Taylor, Berry, & Block, 1958) have yielded no evidence whatever for the so-called "brainstorming" phenomenon. Thibaut and Kelley (1959, pp. 267–268) discuss the conflicting evidence on this issue. We might, in passing, also mention mass or crowd phenomena, in which extreme actions taken by groups are well

Abridged from *Journal of Abnormal and Social Psychology*, **65**, 1962, 75–86. Copyright 1962 by the American Psychological Association, and reproduced by permission of the authors and the publisher.

[1]This research was supported by a grant (G–17818) from the National Science Foundation. A master's thesis by J. A. F. Stoner at MIT's School of Industrial Management, with D. G. Marquis and M. A. Wallach as faculty advisers, was instrumental in inspiring the present investigation. We are greatly indebted to J. A. F. Stoner and D. G. Marquis for their aid and advice, and to V. Raimy and M. Wertheimer for facilities at the University of Colorado in Boulder. Thanks also are due S. Messick and A. Myers for comments.

beyond the capacities of the members of such groups considered individually (Brown, 1954; Turner & Killian, 1957). The relevance of such mass phenomena to group decision making in a laboratory context, however, is probably quite remote. In sum, increased risk taking as a consequence of group interaction appeared to us to be the least feasible of the three possibilities discussed above.

An examination of the literature reveals little experimental research which addresses itself explicitly to the problem of the present investigation. Lonergan and McClintock (1961) report that membership in an interdependent group led to no significant move toward greater conservatism or risk taking in a betting situation involving monetary gain or loss. Since the group situation was so structured that a consensus was not required, however, this experiment is not directly relevant to the aims of the present study. Hunt and Rowe (1960) report no difference between three-person groups and individuals in riskiness of investment decisions. However, the brevity of the group interaction (15 minutes) and the disruptive influence of having the various groups meet within sight of each other in a large room render their results inconclusive. Atthowe (1961), comparing individual and dyadic decisions in the choice of the better of two alternative wagers, found greater conservatism in the dyadic decisions. But the relevance of this result to the problem at hand is called into question when we learn that the alternative wagers were presented to the subjects as "problems taken from the mathematical reasoning section of an advanced intelligence test and arranged as wagers" (p. 115). This could well contribute to a conservative strategy.

We turn, finally, to a study by Stoner (1961), which provides the starting point for the research to be reported. Using male graduate students of industrial management as subjects, Stoner observed that a group consensus regarding degree of risk to be taken in resolving a "life dilemma" situation deviated from the average of prediscussion decisions in the direction of greater risk taking. These results took us by surprise. We wondered whether the finding could be generalized to other subject populations, whether it was

an enduring effect, and whether it might have anything to do with relationships between risk taking and perceived group influence.

One issue that arises in interpreting Stoner's (1961) study concerns the effect that expectations about one's role might have on the results. Thus, a group of male graduate students of industrial management might make more risky decisions qua group than would each such student individually—the result obtained by Stoner—because the presence of their peers reminds each that one of the positively sanctioned attributes of the business manager role which they occupy or aspire to occupy is a willingness to take risks in their decision making. Stoner's use of a male business school sample, therefore, leaves open the possibility that his results may be a function of this particular group's self-assigned professional role alone. It also is possible that a group of males, regardless of their professional role, might make more risky decisions when gathered together because the presence of other males serves as a reminder that one of the expected indications of manliness in our society is a willingness to be bold and daring in decision making. Conversely, a group of females might make more conservative decisions when gathered together, or at least might fail to shift in a risky direction, since risk taking tendencies are not likely to be mutually reinforced in groups for whom risk is not a positive social value (see, e.g., Komarovsky, 1950; Milner, 1949; Wallach & Caron, 1959).

In the present experiment, we shall employ samples of male and female undergraduates enrolled in a liberal arts curriculum at a large state university. If the effects observed by Stoner (1961) are found to hold for both of the above samples, this would constitute strong evidence for the generality of the phenomenon and its independence of occupational and sex role considerations. Furthermore, the use of previously unacquainted subjects whose ascribed status is initially equal will insure that whatever effects are obtained cannot be attributed to an association between initially high or low status, on the one hand, and risk or conservatism, on the other. If initial status levels were unequal, low status individuals might simply adopt the standards of those whose status is high—an outcome which would tell us nothing about the effect of group interactional processes as such on individual risk taking.

One should distinguish initially ascribed status from status indices (e.g., perceived influence and popularity) derived from the group experience. Since such indices may bear some relation to initial risk taking level, the necessary sociometric-type judgments will be obtained.

Finally, evidence will be presented with regard to the following two questions: Is the group induced effect on risk taking limited only to the group member's overt compliance in the group setting or does it also extend to his covert acceptance when he makes post-group decisions as an individual (see Festinger, 1953; Kelley & Thibaut, 1954)? To what extent are group effects on individual decision making relatively enduring or short-lived?

METHOD

Assessment of Level of Conservatism or Risk Taking

The instrument used for assessing level of conservatism or risk taking, as developed in some of our prior research (Kogan & Wallach, 1961; Wallach & Kogan, 1959, 1961), is called an "opinion questionnaire" and contains descriptions of 12 hypothetical situations. The central person in each situation must choose between two courses of action, one of which is more risky than the other but also more rewarding if successful. For each situation the subject must indicate the lowest probability of success he would accept before recommending that the potentially more rewarding alternative be chosen. The probabilities listed are 1, 3, 5, 7, and 9 chances of success in 10, plus a final category (scored as 10) in which the subject can refuse to recommend the risky alternative no matter how high its likelihood of success.

The response categories are arrayed from chances of 1 in 10 upward for the odd items and in the reverse order for the even items, thus counterbalancing for any possible order preference effect in choice of probability levels. An overall conservatism-risk taking score is derived by adding the scores for the separate items. The

larger this score, the greater the subject's conservatism.

Our prior research, cited above, yielded split-half Spearman-Brown reliability coefficients ranging from .53 to .80 for various age and sex samples, suggesting that the instrument possesses satisfactory internal consistency. The results of the present experiment will provide evidence, furthermore, of high test-retest reliability.

Regarding the instrument's construct validity as a risk taking measure, our earlier studies, cited above, have yielded findings consistent with a risk taking interpretation. For example, degree of conservatism as measured with the present instrument increases with age from young adulthood to old age for both males and females, and increases with degree of subjective probability of personal failure in a motor skill game and with actual motor skill controlled.

Experimental Condition

Subjects.   The subjects were invited to participate in an experiment which would take no longer than 2 hours and for which remuneration would be provided. Six subjects were scheduled for any one time, with every effort being made to insure that previously acquainted persons were not signed up for the same session. A total of 167 subjects participated in the experimental condition—14 all-male groups and 14 all-female groups.[2] The subjects were liberal arts students enrolled in summer session courses at the University of Colorado in Boulder.

Prediscussion Individual Decisions.   The experiment was run in a seminar room around a very long table. For the initial administration of the questionnaire, subjects took alternate seats with the experimenter at one end. The six subjects were requested to read the instructions to the

[2] Of the 14 male groups, 13 contained six subjects each, and one contained five subjects. A subject in one of the six-person male groups misunderstood instructions for the prediscussion individual decisions, so that his decision scores were removed prior to analysis. All 14 of the female groups contained six subjects each. A subject in each of 2 female groups misunderstood instructions for the prediscussion individual decisions, so that the decision scores of these two females were removed prior to analysis.

questionnaire and to look over the first item. The experimenter then emphasized two points in further standard instructions: that the more risky alternative is always assumed to be more desirable than the safer course, if the former should prove successful; that the odds which the subject marks indicate the lowest odds the subject would be willing to take and still advise the central figure to give the risky alternative a try. The subjects were told there was no time limit, that they should consider each of the 12 situations carefully, and that they could return to an earlier question if they wished to. The conservatism-risk instrument then was filled out individually by each of the six subjects in a group administration session that took about 20 minutes. To avoid giving any of the subjects the feeling that they were being rushed, the questionnaires were not collected until all had finished.

Group Discussion and Consensual Group Decisions. Without having had any prior expectation that they would be requested to discuss their decisions, the six subjects were then asked to move together into a discussion group at one end of the table. They now each were given another copy of the questionnaire, and a stand-up cardboard placard with the identification letter K, L, M, N, O, or P on it was placed before each subject. The experimenter then told them that the questionnaire now before them was the same one they just finished taking. They had taken it, he continued, to familiarize them with all the situations and to give them some idea where they might stand on each. Now he wanted the group to discuss each question in turn and arrive at a unanimous decision on each. This time they could not return to a question but rather had to discuss each one until the group decision was reached before going on to the next. When the group reached its decision on a question, all subjects were to mark it on their questionnaires in order to have a record. The group would be completely on its own, the experimenter not participating in the discussion at all.

The experimenter then retired to the other end of the table in order to be as far from the group as possible. A question that often arose before discussion had started was what to do if a deadlock occurs. The experimenter's standard reply was:

Most groups are able to come to some decision if those who disagree will restate their reasons and if the problem is reread carefully.

Most groups succeeded in reaching a unanimous decision on most items, although an occasional deadlock did occur on one or another item. The group discussions were of such a nature as to indicate that the participants were highly involved in the decision tasks.

Postdiscussion Individual Decisions. After the discussion was over, the experimenter proceeded to ask the group members to spread apart for some further individual work and to take their questionnaires and identification placards with them. In standard instructions, he requested them to go back over the situations and indicate their own present personal decisions with a "P." He noted that while in some cases the subjects may have agreed with the group decision, in other cases they may have disagreed with it. In the former case the P would be placed on the same line as the check mark; in the latter cases, on a different line.

While the consensual decisions by the group would indicate the public effect of the discussion process, the private postdiscussion decisions made once again on an individual basis would indicate whether the discussion process had influenced covert acceptance as well as public compliance.

Rankings for Influence and Popularity. After the postdiscussion individual decisions had been made, a ranking sheet was passed out to each subject requesting that he rank everyone in the group (identified by their letter placards), including himself, in terms of how much each influenced the final group decision. Then each subject was requested to rank everyone in the group (except, of course, himself) in terms of how much he would like to become better acquainted with each.

The rankings for influence provided the information needed for examining possible relationships between strength of individual risk taking or conservatism tendencies, on the one hand, and degree of influence in the group, on the other. If such relationships existed, it seemed to be of interest to determine whether they were specific to perceived influence or would prove to be dependent upon the subject's popularity; hence the second set of rankings.

Secrecy Instructions. After the ranking sheets were collected, the experimenter told the group that the research would be carried out in coming weeks, and that they could now appreciate why it would be important for the content of the experiment to be kept secret, since a person who even knew that the group would be discussing the same questions which he had filled out individually would have a tendency to mark logically defensible answers instead of his true opinion, etc. The subjects therefore all were sworn to secrecy. Various indications suggest that this pledge was faithfully kept.

Post-Postdiscussion Individual Decisions. A further session of individual decision making took place approximately 2–6 weeks later for some subjects. These subjects individually were given the conservatism-risk questionnaire a third time and were asked to reconsider the situations. The standard instructions emphasized that the experimenter was not interested in testing the subject's memory, but rather wanted the subject truly to *reconsider* each situation. The instructions thus oriented the subjects away from simply trying to recall their prior decisions. Each subject was paid for this further work.

Control Condition

Subjects. Control subjects were obtained in the same way as the experimental subjects, and likewise received remuneration for their work. The controls were signed up to participate in two sessions: the first to last about 20 minutes; the second, exactly 1 week later, to last about 15 minutes. A total of 51 subjects participated in the control condition—24 males and 27 females. Like the experimental subjects, the controls were liberal arts students enrolled in summer session courses at the University of Colorado in Boulder.

First Individual Decision Session. The first

session was identical to the prediscussion individual decision part of the experimental condition. From six to eight subjects of the same sex, scheduled for the same time, filled out the conservatism-risk instrument while sitting together in physical conditions identical to those of the experimental subjects and at approximately the same time of day as the experimental subjects had worked. Exactly the same instructions were provided as had been given the experimental subjects.

After the first session, the control subjects were sworn to secrecy. They also were told that they would be taking a similar questionnaire the next week, and that it was extremely important that they not discuss it with one another nor with anyone else, since such discussion might affect the way they filled out next week's questionnaire.

Second Individual Decision Session. The same control subjects who had participated in a particular first individual decision session came back exactly 1 week later. After checking that no discussion had taken place in the intervening week among the controls, the experimenter handed out new copies of the questionnaire and explained that this questionnaire was identical to the one taken last week. Each subject was requested to go back over the situations and reconsider them, the experimenter emphasizing that he was not interested in testing the subject's memory but rather wanted the subject truly to *reconsider* each situation. The instructions were so designed, therefore, as to dissuade the subject from assuming that the most socially acceptable thing to do would be to try to make the same decisions that he had made a week ago. Change was encouraged rather than discouraged. Control subjects were sworn to secrecy again at the end of the second session.

RESULTS

*Consensual Group Decisions
Compared with
Prediscussion Individual Decisions*

Tables 1 and 2 examine, for male and female groups, respectively, the significance of the conservatism difference between the mean of the pre-

TABLE 1. Significance of conservatism difference between mean of prediscussion individual decisions for a group's members and group's consensual decision: males.

Item	Mean difference[a]	Number of groups[b]	t
All combined	−9.4	14	6.46****
1	−1.0	14	4.34****
2	−0.2	14	< 1.00
3	−1.1	13	2.19*
4	−1.8	13	6.18****
5	+0.1	13	< 1.00
6	−1.2	13	3.35**
7	−2.0	14	9.64****
8	−1.1	14	1.97
9	−1.0	10	3.67**
10	−0.4	13	< 1.00
11	−1.1	12	4.37***
12	+0.8	11	2.34*

[a]In Tables 1 and 2, a negative difference signifies a risky shift, a positive difference signifies a conservative shift.

[b]In Tables 1 and 2, number of groups for an item is less than 14 when one or more groups deadlocked on that item. Any deadlocked item is, of course, not included when calculating scores for all items combined.

*p<.05.
**p<.01.
***p<.005.
****p<.001.

discussion individual decisions made by the members of each group and that group's consensual decisions. The basic test is carried out using the total conservatism score, which consists of all 12 item scores combined. Tests also are carried out for each item separately.

In the case of the total score, a group's difference score is the sum of the 12 unanimous group decision scores minus the average of the prediscussion total individual decision scores for the six members.[3] Since larger scores indicate greater conservatism, a negative difference (or score decrease) indicates a shift in the risky direction. A t test is used to determine whether the 14 difference scores for the groups of each sex are significantly different from zero (McNemar, 1955, pp. 108–109).[4] These total score data indicate a move in the risky direction significant beyond the .001 level for the 14 male groups, and a move in

[3]Any deadlocked item is, of course, not included in either term for the group in question.

[4]All significance levels cited in this study are based on two-tailed tests.

the risky direction significant beyond the .005 level for the 14 female groups. Furthermore, the degree of shift is not significantly different for the two sexes.

In the case of the scores for a single item, a group's difference score consists of the unanimous group decision on that item minus the average of the prediscussion individual decision scores on that item for the six members. Once again a negative difference or score decrease indicates a shift in the risky direction, and a t test is applied to determine whether the difference scores for all groups that reached a unanimous decision on the item in question are significantly different from zero. For both the male and female groups, we find that 10 of the 12 items show shifts in the risky direction, 7 of them significant in each case. Five of those 7 are the same for both sexes. Only 2 items show any indication for either sex of not sharing in the general shift toward greater risk taking: Items 5 and 12. It should be noted that these two items exhibited, in our previous research, the lowest correlations with the overall risk-conservatism score, suggesting that they are relatively impure measures of the psychological dimension being tapped by the other 10 items.

In sum, the evidence from Tables 1 and 2 indicates a strong move toward greater risk taking

TABLE 2. Significance of conservatism difference between mean of prediscussion individual decisions for a group's members and group's consensual decision: females.

Item	Mean difference	Number of groups	t
All combined	−9.4	14	3.91***
1	−1.0	13	4.17***
2	−0.6	14	1.65
3	−0.4	14	1.12
4	−1.4	14	2.60****
5	+0.7	14	1.90
6	−0.8	13	2.63****
7	−2.0	12	3.21**
8	−1.7	14	5.26*****
9	−0.8	12	1.19
10	−1.5	13	3.18**
11	−0.9	13	2.28*
12	+0.6	6	2.00

*p<.05.
**p<.01.
***p<.005.
****p<.025.
*****p<.001.

when groups arrive at unanimous decisions, compared with the risk levels ventured by the same persons in prediscussion individual decisions. Furthermore, this move toward greater risk taking obtains for females as well as for males.

A further question concerns the extent to which the risky shift is consistent from one group to another. Consider one example of several consistency tests that have been conducted, all of which yield highly similar results. Suppose we define a group as showing a risky shift from prediscussion individual decisions to consensual group decisions if the difference score for its total score, as defined above, is a negative one. Fourteen out of 14 male groups and 12 out of 14 female groups are found to move in the risky direction, both results being very significant by a sign test. Such a finding demonstrates, therefore, that the risky shift phenomenon is quite consistent across groups.

*Postdiscussion Individual Decisions
Compared with
Prediscussion Individual Decisions*

For the total score, a group's difference score consists of the average of the postdiscussion total individual decision scores for the members minus the average of the prediscussion total individual decision scores for the same members. Negative difference scores again indicate risky shifts, and a *t* test is applied to determine whether the 14 difference scores for the groups of each sex are significantly different from zero. We find, once again, a shift in the risky direction significant beyond the .001 level for the 14 male groups, and a risky shift significant beyond the .005 level for the 14 female groups. As before, the degree of shift is not significantly different for the two sexes.

Turning to the scores for each separate item, a group's difference score consists of the average of the postdiscussion individual decision scores on that item minus the average of the prediscussion individual decision scores on that item. With a negative difference score indicating a risky shift and a *t* test applied to indicate whether the 14 difference scores for each sex on an item are significantly different from zero, we find that 9 of the

12 items show separate significant shifts in the risky direction for the male groups (with one additional item shifting nonsignificantly in the same direction), and that 8 of the 12 items show separate significant shifts toward greater risk taking for the female groups (with two additional items shifting nonsignificantly in that direction). The 8 items showing significant risky shifts for the females are among the 9 showing significant risky shifts for the males. Items 5 and 12 once again are the only ones for either sex showing any indication of not sharing in the general shift toward greater risk taking found in both sexes.

There is clear evidence, therefore, that postdiscussion individual decisions exhibit a strong move toward greater risk taking when compared with prediscussion individual decisions arrived at by the same persons, and do so for both sexes. The group discussion process, in other words, seems to have an effect on private attitudes (postdiscussion individual decisions) that is just as significant as its effect on publicly expressed views (unanimous group decisions).

Once again we may inquire about the extent to which the risky shift is consistent from group to group. Several consistency tests have been carried out, all yielding highly similar results. As an example, suppose we define a group as exhibiting a shift in the risky direction from prediscussion to postdiscussion individual decisions if the difference score for its total score, as defined in this section, is a negative one. Fourteen out of 14 male groups and 12 out of 14 female groups are found to shift in the risky direction, both results being quite significant by a sign test. Such a finding demonstrates, therefore, that the risky shift phenomenon is quite consistent across groups in regard to covert acceptance as well as overt compliance.

Control Subjects

To insure that the move toward greater risk taking just described actually is a result of the group discussion process, we must turn to the findings for the control subjects. We note that, in the case both of males and females, the experimental and control subjects have approximately the same initial total conservatism scores, and also are approximately the same in age.[5] Item-by-item comparisons of experimental and control subjects of each sex on initial conservatism scores also were carried out and show that controls and experimentals within sex obtain highly similar scores.

It will be recalled that one week intervened between the two sessions, and that instructions for the second session requested the subjects not to try simply to remember what they had marked before, but to reconsider their decisions. It is evident that the total conservatism score shows no shift from first to second session for either sex. Turning to the separate tests carried out on each item, we find that none of the 12 items shows a significant shift for the males, and only 1 of the 12 items shows a significant shift for the females. When no group discussion and achievement of group consensus intervenes, then, there is no systematic shift toward greater risk taking or greater conservatism and this despite instructions that encourage shifts by emphasizing that we are not interested in the subjects' memories.

The data for the control subjects also provide us with an opportunity for determining the test-retest reliability of the conservatism-risk instrument, with one week intervening and under instructions that encourage change rather than constancy. For the 24 male subjects, the product-moment correlation coefficient between total conservatism scores in the first and second sessions is .78. For the 27 female subjects, the same correlation coefficient is .82. Test-retest reliability of the instrument, therefore, is quite high.

Prediscussion Risk Taking and Influence in the Group

Our data concerning perceived influence within the group consisted in each individual's ranking of all group members including himself, in terms of how much each influenced the group's decisions. A first question to ask of these influ-

ence rankings is: How consistent are they from member to member within a group? To determine the degree of agreement among a group's members in their rankings of one another for influence, Kendall's coefficient of concordance (Siegel, 1956, pp. 229–238) was applied to each group's influence rankings. If the members of a group agree regarding who among themselves are more influential and who less so, then W will be significantly large. Table 3 presents the results of these tests for all 28 groups. It is evident that agreement in influence rankings is quite high: the degree of agreement is significant for all 14 of the male groups and for 11 of the 14 female groups.

Given this high agreement among group members in their rankings of one another for influence, an approximate overall estimate of degree of influence for a given group member was obtained by averaging the influence ranks that had been assigned to that person by all members of the group (including that person). The lower the average, the greater that subject's perceived influence (i.e., the higher the assigned influence ranks for that person). These average influence scores for the subjects of each sex were correlated with the initial total conservatism scores obtained by the same subjects. The resulting product-moment

TABLE 3. Degree of agreement among group members in rankings of one another for influence[a].

Group	Males		Group	Females	
	N	W		N	W
1	6	.64**	1	6	.85**
2	6	.55**	2	6	.61**
3	6	.74**	3	6	.31
4	6	.72**	4	6	.79**
5	6	.70**	5	6	.47**
6	6	.50**	6	6	.67**
7	5	.56*	7	6	.13
8	6	.50**	8	6	.59**
9	6	.62**	9	6	.59**
10	6	.66**	10	6	.69**
11	6	.66**	11	6	.83**
12	6	.55**	12	6	.80**
13	6	.54**	13	6	.70**
14	6	.73**	14	6	.30

[a]Kendall's coefficient of concordance.
*$p < .05$.
**$p < .01$.

---

[5]It might also be mentioned that, in confirmation of earlier findings (Wallach & Kogan, 1959, 1961), there is no sex difference in initial total conservatism scores for either the experimental or the control subjects.

TABLE 4. Product-moment correlations among initial conservatism, influence, and popularity[a].

	Males (N = 82)[b]	Females (N = 82)[b]
	r	r
Initial overall risk taking and influence	.32****	.22*
Initial overall risk taking and popularity	.15	−.04
Influence and popularity	.72*****	.54*****
Initial overall risk taking and influence, popularity held constant[c]	.30***	.28**

[a]Small score values signify greater risk taking, greater influence, and greater popularity.

[b]While all influence and popularity scores are based on the 167 subjects in the experimental condition, the correlations are based on the 164 of those subjects for whom initial overall risk taking scores were available.

[c]Partial correlation coefficients.

*$p<.05$.
**$p<.02$.
***$p<.01$.
****$p<.005$.
*****$p<.001$.

correlation coefficients are shown in Table 4. They are significant beyond the .005 and the .05 levels for the 82 males and the 82 females respectively: persons higher in initial risk taking are rated as having more influence on the group decisions.

Average popularity scores for each group member were constructed by averaging the popularity rankings assigned by all the other members of the group. We note in Table 4 that there emerges a very strong relationship between this average popularity score and the average influence score for both the male and the female group members: persons rated high in influence also tend to be rated high in popularity. This general relationship has, of course, been known for some time (see, e.g., Back, 1951; Horowitz, Lyons, & Perlmutter, 1951; Tagiuri & Kogan, 1960), so that our obtaining it here increases our confidence in the respective measures being used to assess influence and popularity. It is further evident in Table 4, however, that degree of initial risk taking is *not* related to degree of popularity within the group for either sex.

Finally, we also find from Table 4 that risk taking and influence are significantly related for each sex when popularity ratings are held constant. The partial correlation coefficients are significant beyond the .01 and .02 levels for the males and females, respectively. It is evident, therefore, that the relationships obtained for both sexes between degree of initial risk taking and degree of influence on group decisions are not dependent upon members' popularity.

Maintenance of the Risky Shift over a Subsequent Period of Time

An interesting further question concerns the extent to which the shift toward greater risk taking, which we have found to result from group discussion, is maintained over a subsequent period of time. We were able to gather evidence on this point for males but not for females. In the case of the former, but not in the case of the latter, a random sample of subjects from the original groups could be obtained for further study. The 22 males who were available for further work were approximately evenly distributed among the 14 original male groups. After a time interval of roughly 2–6 weeks had elapsed since the group session, these subjects individually were given the conservatism-risk questionnaire a third time, as described in the section on procedure.

The comparability of the random male subsample of 22 to the original male experimental condition sample of 82 is evident from the following data on total conservatism scores. The mean prediscussion total conservatism score was 66.9 for the sample of 82, and also was 66.9 for the subsample of 22. The mean postdiscussion total conservatism score, in turn, was 56.6 for the whole sample and 56.2 for the subsample. The t test of the difference scores had yielded a t significant beyond the .001 level ($t = 9.12$) for the whole sample, and it also yielded a t significant beyond the .001 level ($t = 4.70$) for the subsample.

Turning now to the total conservatism scores obtained by this subsample when they took the questionnaire again 2–6 weeks after the group discussion (call these scores the "post-postdiscussion" individual decisions), the mean score is

54.6. The mean of the difference scores obtained by subtracting each subject's prediscussion total conservatism score from his post-postdiscussion total conservatism score is −12.3, with a t test of these difference scores yielding a t value of 4.92 (p < .001), hence indicating a risky shift from the prediscussion individual decisions to the post-postdiscussion individual decisions. The mean of the difference scores obtained, in turn, by subtracting each subject's postdiscussion total conservatism score from his post-postdiscussion total conservatism score is only −1.6, and a t test of these difference scores is not significant, hence indicating no further change from the postdiscussion individual decisions to the post-postdiscussion individual decisions. Item-by-item analyses tell the same story: the only significant item shifts are risky ones, and they are as strong from prediscussion to post-postdiscussion sessions as they are from prediscussion to postdiscussion sessions.

In sum, the data available on the point indicate that the shift in the risky direction found to occur as a result of the group discussion process is maintained over a subsequent period of time.

DISCUSSION AND CONCLUSIONS

The following conclusions may be drawn from the preceding evidence:

1. Unanimous group decisions concerning matters of risk show a shift toward greater risk taking when compared with prediscussion individual decisions made by the same persons and concerning the same matters. This holds for both sexes.

2. Postdiscussion individual decisions that follow unanimous group decisions exhibit the same kind of shift toward greater risk taking as appears in the group decisions. This is the case for both sexes. Covert acceptance as well as overt compliance, thus, are affected in the same manner by the discussion process.

3. This shift toward greater risk taking as a result of the discussion process is still maintained when 2–6 weeks have elapsed since the discussion occurred. Evidence on this point was available only for males.

4. No shift in risk taking level of individual decisions occurs over time in the absence of the discussion process. This holds for both sexes.

5. There is a positive relationship between degree of risk taking in prediscussion individual decisions and the extent to which group members are perceived by one another as influencing group decisions. This relationship is specific to judgments of influence, in that it obtains when judgments of popularity are held constant, and also no relationship is found between prediscussion individual risk taking and the extent to which group members are judged to be popular. These statements all hold for both sexes.

The present study indicates, then, that group interaction and achievement of consensus concerning decisions on matters of risk eventuate in a willingness to make decisions that are more risky than those that would be made in the absence of such interaction. Furthermore, although initial ascribed status levels of the group members are equal, it is found that persons with stronger individual risk taking proclivities tend to become more influential in the group than persons who are more conservative. Two alternative interpretations of these findings can be suggested; one more group centered, the other more person centered: It is possible that there is at work in these groups a process of diffusion or spreading of responsibility as a result of knowing that one's decisions are being made jointly with others rather than alone. Increased willingness to take risk would eventuate from this decreased feeling of personal responsibility. That initial risk taking and judged influence within the group are positively related could well occur as a consequence of this process, since one of its effects would be for the views of high risk takers to be given more weight by the rest of the group. Alternatively, the fact that high risk takers exert more influence may be a cause of the group's movement toward greater risk taking. It is possible that high risk takers are also more likely to take the initiative in social situations. Of course, these two interpretations are not necessarily mutually exclusive. Both of them may contribute to the group effect.

That females as well as males show the same change toward greater risk taking as a result of the group interaction condition, and that the samples of both sexes were liberal arts university students, renders it unlikely that the results can be explained on the basis of reinforcement by others of one's expectation as to whether one's appropriate role is to be more or less of a risk taker. We noted earlier that Stoner (1961) found a move toward greater risk taking in group as compared to individual decision making by male graduate students of industrial management, and we pointed out that this result might be accounted for in terms of the professional role that they had assigned themselves by becoming graduate students in a business school. Presence of peers might be expected to increase the salience of their business manager role, and a greater willingness to take risks in decision making might well be perceived as one of the attributes of that role. Such a role expectation interpretation is ruled out for the present study, however, through our use of liberal arts students as subjects. In addition, the possibility of explaining the results in terms of males' perceiving their appropriate role as one of willingness to be bold and daring, and being reinforced in this view by interaction with other like-minded males, is ruled out by the present study's obtaining the same results for females as for males. This outcome would not be expected if the findings depended on sex linked role expectations as to whether one should be more risky or more conservative. This outcome also, of course, rules out interpretation in terms of any possible sex linked differences in major fields of study.

That the group induced move toward greater risk taking in individual decisions is still maintained 2–6 weeks after the discussion, provides evidence, incidentally, which supports Lewin's (1947) view that "group carried" attitudinal changes maintain themselves (see also Pelz, 1958).

REFERENCES

Atthowe, J. M., Jr. Interpersonal decision making: The resolution of a dyadic conflict. *J. abnorm. soc. Psychol.,* 1961, **62**, 114–119.

Back, K. W. Influence through social communication. *J. abnorm. soc. Psychol.,* 1951, **46**, 9–23.

Brown, R. W. Mass phenomena. In G. Lindzey (Ed.), *Handbook of social psychology.* Vol. 2. *Special fields and applications.* Cambridge, Mass.: Addison-Wesley, 1954. Pp. 833–876.

Cartwright, D., & Zander, A. (Eds.) *Group dynamics.* (2nd ed.) Evanston, Ill.: Row, Peterson, 1960.

Festinger, L. An analysis of compliant behavior. In M. Sherif & M. O. Wilson (Eds.) *Group relations at the crossroads.* New York: Harper, 1953. Pp. 232–255.

Horowitz, M. W., Lyons, J., & Perlmutter, H. V. Induction of forces in discussion groups. *Hum. Relat.,* 1951, **4**, 57–76.

Hunt, E. B., & Rowe, R. R. Group and individual economic decision making in risk conditions. In D. W. Taylor (Ed.), *Experiments on decision making and other studies.* Arlington, Va.: Armed Services Technical Information Agency, 1960. Pp. 21–25. (Technical Report No. 6, AD 253952)

Kelley, H. H., & Thibaut, J. W. Experimental studies of group problem solving and process. In G. Lindzey (Ed.), *Handbook of social psychology.* Vol. 2. *Special fields and applications.* Cambridge, Mass.: Addison-Wesley, 1954. Pp. 735–785.

Kogan, N., & Wallach, M. A. The effect of anxiety on relations between subjective age and caution in an older sample. In P. H. Hoch & J. Zubin (Eds.), *Psychopathology of aging.* New York: Grune & Stratton, 1961. Pp. 123–135.

Komarovsky, Mirra. Functional analysis of sex roles. *Amer. sociol. Rev.,* 1950, **15**, 508–516.

Lewin, K. Frontiers in group dynamics. *Hum. Relat.,* 1947, **1**, 2–38.

Lonergan, B. G., & McClintock, C. G. Effects of group membership on risk-taking behavior. *Psychol. Rep.,* 1961, **8**, 447–455.

McNemar, Q. *Psychological statistics.* (Rev. ed.) New York: Wiley, 1955.

Milner, Esther. Effects of sex role and social status on the early adolescent personality. *Genet. psychol. Monogr.,* 1949, **40**, 231–325.

Osborn, A. F. *Applied imagination.* New York: Scribner, 1957.

Pelz, Edith B. Some factors in "group decision." In Eleanor E. Maccoby, T. M. Newcomb, & E. L. Hartley (Eds.), *Readings in social psychology.* (3rd ed.) New York: Holt, 1958. Pp. 212–219.

Schachter, S. Deviation, rejection, and communication. *J. abnorm. soc. Psychol.,* 1951, **46**, 190–207.

Siegel, S. *Nonparametric statistics for the behavioral sciences.* New York: McGraw-Hill, 1956.

Stoner, J. A. F. A comparison of individual and group decisions involving risk. Unpublished master's thesis, Massachusetts Institute of Technology, School of Industrial Management, 1961.

Tagiuri, R., & Kogan, N. Personal preference and the attribution of influence in small groups. *J. Pers.,* 1960, **28**, 257–265.

Taylor, D. W., Berry, P. C., & Block, C. H. Does group

participation when using brainstorming facilitate or inhibit creative thinking? *Admin. sci. Quart.,* 1958, **3**, 23–47.

Thibaut, J. W., & Kelley, H. H. *The social psychology of groups.* New York: Wiley, 1959.

Turner, R. H., & Killian, L. M. (Eds.), *Collective behavior.* Englewood Cliffs, N.J.: Prentice-Hall, 1957.

Wallach, M. A., & Caron, A. J. Attribute criteriality and sex-linked conservatism as determinants of psychological similarity. *J. abnorm. soc. Psychol.,* 1959, **59,** 43–50.

Wallach, M. A., & Kogan, N. Sex differences and judgment processes. *J. Pers.,* 1959, **27,** 555–564.

Wallach, M. A., & Kogan, N. Aspects of judgment and decision making: Interrelationships and changes with age. *Behav. Sci.,* 1961, **6,** 23–36.

ARTICLE 14

Risk-as-Value Hypothesis: The Relationship between Perception of Self, Others, and the Risky Shift[1]

Russell D. Clark III, Walter H. Crockett, and Richard L. Archer

The most common explanation advanced to account for the risky-shift phenomenon is the "risk-as-value" hypothesis. As formulated by Brown (1965), this interpretation makes the key assumption that moderate risk is a strong cultural value, so that most individuals come to view themselves as being at least as willing as their peers to take risks. When a group of such persons meets and discusses matters of risk taking, those whose initial private positions were actually less risky than the other group members are made to recognize their relative cautiousness; subsequently, they recommend greater risk than earlier, presumably to restore their perception of themselves as relatively risky. On this view, the principal function of the group discussion is to allow group members to compare their positions on the issue to those of other people.

There is considerable evidence that most people do, in fact, perceive themselves to be at least as willing as their peers to take risks. Hinds (1962) found that male graduate students in industrial management consistently guessed that

others would choose more cautiously than had the subjects themselves. Brown (1965) found in an undergraduate class of 30 and in a graduate seminar of 16 students that not 1 subject guessed that others would answer a choice-dilemmas problem more risky than himself. Wallach and Wing (1968), Levinger and Schneider (1969), and Willems (1969) have found similar results. Thus, the data unequivocally reveal a strong and pervasive tendency by persons of both sexes to view themselves as being at least as risky as their peers.

From this risk-as-value hypothesis, a prediction may be made concerning individual differences in susceptibility to the risky shift: Subjects who perceive themselves to be more cautious than their peers should not change toward risk; those who perceive themselves as relatively risky should show strong and consistent shifts. This follows from the assumption that the former subjects do not value risk, while the latter subjects do value it. Experiment I was designed to test this hypothesis.

From *Journal of Personality and Social Psychology*, **20**, 1971, 425–429. Copyright 1971 by the American Psychological Association, and reproduced by permission of the authors and the publisher.

[1]This investigation was supported in part by Training Grant BTTBT 217 from the National Institute of Mental Health to the Graduate Training Program in Social Psychology, University of Kansas. A shorter version of this paper was presented to a meeting of the Eastern Psychological Association in Atlantic City, New Jersey, in April of 1970. The authors are indebted to Daniel Lordahl for his statistical advice.

EXPERIMENT I

Method

Subjects. A total of 67 male undergraduates at the University of Kansas participated in the experiment. All were volunteers and received research credit for their participation.

Procedure. Risk taking was measured by the

149

choice-dilemmas instrument developed by Kogan and Wallach (1964), which was described to subjects as an opinion questionnaire. In order to maximize the risky-shift effect, only the six items that had produced the greatest amount of shift in other studies were used (Items 1, 3, 4, 6, 7, and 11).

Subjects participated in groups of four, sitting in chairs arranged in a circle. In an initial session, subjects gave only their private responses to the choice dilemmas and then recorded the recommendations they felt the majority of other people like themselves would make. Subjects were then dismissed and were rescheduled for a subsequent experiment approximately 8 days later. Three conditions were established.

Discussion, Risky Subjects. Twenty-four subjects were selected at random from those who, on at least four of the six items, had previously perceived themselves to be at least as risky as their peers. They were divided at random into six groups of four subjects each. Instructions for this condition were identical to those given by Clark and Willems (1969). Subjects were told that their first responses had constituted a practice session to familiarize them with the items; they were then asked to discuss each item for approximately 5 minutes. After the groups had discussed all six items, subjects once more responded privately to the Choice Dilemmas Questionnaire.

Discussion, Cautious Subjects. This condition consisted of those 16 subjects who, on at least four of the six items, had initially perceived themselves to be more cautious than their peers. They were divided at random into four groups of 4 subjects each. All other experimental manipulations were identical to the preceding conditions.

Control Subjects. These 27 subjects consisted principally of those who did not meet the criterion for the other two conditions; that is, those who were neither riskier nor more cautious on four of six items. Subjects in a large assemblage were told that their first recommendations had been for practice to familiarize them with the items, and that by reconsidering each item they might be more confident about their

TABLE 1. Pretest and posttest mean scores, summed across the six items, for the three conditions in Experiment I.

Test	Risky Ss	Cautious Ss	Control Ss
Pretest	32.58	43.00	35.04
Posttest	26.67	41.63	33.48

judgments. They then responded once more to the Choice Dilemmas Questionnaire.

Results

A 2 × 2 factorial design with repeated measures on the second factor was employed to analyze the data. Since the number of subjects in the two levels differed, an unweighted-means solution was used (Winer, 1962, pp. 374–378). Table 1 summarizes the pretest and posttest mean scores for each of the conditions. As may be seen in Table 2, there was a significant main effect for experimental conditions, confirming that risky subjects were significantly riskier overall than cautious subjects. Clearly, then, subjects who perceived themselves to be relatively cautious were actually more cautious than their peers, and those who perceived themselves to be relatively risky were so, in fact.

The main effect for pretest-posttest responses verified that subject's posttest responses were riskier than their pretest scores, indicating significant risky shifts. More interesting, however, is the interaction between conditions and pretest-posttest responses. The Newman-Keuls test showed that this interaction occurred because

TABLE 2. Summary of analysis of variance for Experiment I.

Source	SS	df	MS	F
Between Ss				
Conditions (A)	766.55	1	766.55	25.84**
Error between	237.38	8	29.66	
Within Ss				
Pretest-posttest (B)	63.12	1	63.12	15.32**
A X B	24.51	1	24.51	5.95*
Error within	32.95	8	4.12	

*$p < .05$.
**$p < .01$.

risky subjects shifted significantly toward risk, whereas cautious subjects did not.

The result of a *t* test, which tested the average change scores within the control group, yielded insignificant results ($t = 1.94$, $df = 26$).

Discussion

It is evident, then, that the results support the risk-as-value hypothesis, for greater shift toward risk occurred among subjects who perceived themselves to be at least as willing as their peers to take risks. A question remains as to the processes by which these differences between groups were mediated. According to the risk-as-value hypothesis, the principal function of the group discussion is informational: the subject discovers that he is not as risky on some items as are others in his reference group, and he changes his judgment in order to return the relationship between his own position and the perceived group norm to its optimal level. According to this strict interpretation of the hypothesis, a mere exchange of information with others, without any discussion of the reasons for their judgments, should be as effective an inducement to shift toward risk as is the personal involvement in group discussion.

In experiments which have tested the effects of exchanging judgments without verbal justification for them, a significant risky shift has occurred, but one which is likely to be smaller in magnitude than is the typical discussion conditions. Thus, Kogan and Wallach (1967) found significantly greater shifts among subjects who discussed the choice dilemmas than among subjects who listened to tape-recorded discussions of other groups. Similarly, Teger and Pruitt (1967) observed greater risky shift in the typical discussion condition than in the information-exchange condition without discussion.

Teger and Pruitt (1967) interpreted this outcome by arguing that the usual discussion procedure not only provides information about other subjects' positions on these items, but also increases the saliency of the norm of riskiness. That is, in the arguments that are given in discussions of the choice dilemmas, those who are objectively less risky become increasingly aware of the value that others place on risk and, therefore, are more susceptible to the effects of information about the group's judgments.

Experiment II was undertaken in an attempt to sort out these influences, knowledge of others' risk preferences and knowledge of arguments only, by comparing the typical information-plus-discussion condition with two other conditions: one where subjects exchanged judgments without discussion, a second where they discussed the alternatives without expressing their own preferences. If the risky shift is solely mediated by the knowledge of others' risk preferences, the information-exchange and regular-discussion conditions should yield shifts of the same magnitude. From Teger and Pruitt's interpretation we would expect larger shifts toward risk in the information-plus-discussion condition than in the information-exchange condition. If, as Madaras and Bem (1968) postulated, the risky shift is solely mediated by the preponderance of arguments in the favor of the risky alternatives, we would expect no risky shift in the information-exchange condition and a risky shift of the same magnitude in the two discussion conditions.

EXPERIMENT II

Method

Subjects.   A total of 120 male undergraduates participated in randomly assigned groups of 5, with 8 such groups (or 40 subjects) in each of the three experimental conditions.

Procedure.   The procedure was very similar to the one used in the preceding experiment. Subjects first made their own recommendations on the Choice Dilemmas Questionnaire and then recorded the recommendations they felt most people like themselves would make. Only those subjects who perceived themselves to be at least as risky as their peers on four of the six items were asked to return for a second meeting, held approximately 8 days after the first administration of the questionnaire.

Three experimental conditions were established:

Information Exchange.   Subjects were told

that their first recommendations had been for practice. Instructions similar to those given by Teger and Pruitt (1967) were employed, and subjects in each group shared their recommendations by holding up cards for each item so that other group members could see them. To assure full exchange of information, the responses to each item were presented three times, each time without verbal discussion (cf. also Clark & Willems, 1969).

Group-Discussion Condition. The procedure was identical to the discussion, risky-subjects condition in Experiment I.

Arguments-Only Condition. The procedure was identical to the group-discussion conditions, except that subjects were not allowed to reveal their preferred risk level probabilities on any item during the discussion. The subjects were instructed to discuss the positive and negative aspects of the various alternatives to each item, without indicating the odds they had selected. Observation of the group discussions confirmed subject's adherence to the instructions not to mention numerical probabilities.

Results

A 3 X 2 factorial design with repeated measures on the second factor was used to analyze the data. Pretest and posttest mean scores are presented in Table 3. As can be seen in Table 4, there was a significant main effect for the difference between pretest and posttest scores, indicating significant risky shifts. However, there was also a significant interaction, indicating that the magnitude of shift differed among conditions. The Newman-Keuls test showed that both the group-discussion and arguments-only groups shifted

TABLE 4.   Summary of analysis of variance for Experiment II.

Source	SS	df	MS	F
Between Ss	569.59	23		
Conditions (A)	30.59	2	15.30	< 1
Error between	539.00	21	25.67	
Within Ss	509.12	24		
Pretest-posttest (B)	235.85	1	235.85	24.29**
A X B	69.42	2	34.71	3.57*
Error within	203.85	21	9.71	

*$p<.05$.
**$p<.01$.

significantly toward risk, and there was a nonsignificant tendency for information-exchange groups to shift toward risk. The final means of both of the group-discussion and the arguments-only conditions were significantly riskier than that of the information-exchange condition.

Discussion

The results of Experiment II appear to be inconsistent with Brown's information-exchange *per se* interpretation of the risk-as-value hypothesis, for if risk is a value, and subjects perceive themselves to be at least as willing to take risks as their peers, they should need to reevaluate their own positions only when discovering that others had chosen riskier alternatives than they. Thus, a significant risky shift should not have occurred in the arguments-only condition. The hypothesis can be rescued, however, by assuming that listening to and participating in a discussion of arguments in favor of risk, even without clear commitment from each subject to an alternative, provides subtle but unequivocal information about each participant's choices. In this way, each discussant can learn that his peers are riskier than he had thought. There is evidence that such inferences about others' judgments were actually drawn. Subjects indicated before and after discussion of the choice dilemmas what they thought the majority of people like themselves would mark for each item. In both the group-discussion and the arguments-only conditions, subjects changed their estimates to represent other people as riskier than they had initially been ($p < .01$); in each case estimates in the two conditions did

TABLE 3.   Pretest and posttest mean scores, summed across the six items, for the three experimental conditions in Experiment II.

Test	Discussion	Arguments only	Information exchange
Pretest	31.35	30.30	30.45
Posttest	25.50	24.80	28.55

not differ significantly from each other either before or after discussion. Thus, the data do suggest that the mediation of the cultural value of risk through the specification of probabilities is still tenable. Nevertheless, a more adequate test is needed to substantiate this view.

Even if subjects can infer reliably the risk positions of others from listening to their arguments, the failure to find significant shifts in the information-exchange condition is embarrassing for the information-exchange per se interpretation of the risk-as-value hypothesis. The exchange of information should have been enough to show the more conservative persons that they were not as risky as most others in the group; those subjects should then have shifted toward risk. Yet, this was not what happened. Since Teger and Pruitt (1967), Clark and Willems (1969), and Willems and Clark (1969) have found significant risky shifts in information-exchange conditions, knowledge of others' risk preferences can not be completely ruled out as a mediator of the risky shift. The present results, however, favor the "knowledge of others' arguments" interpretation of the risk-as-value hypothesis. It remains to be seen whether this process is independent of or operates concurrently with the exchange of specific risk levels.

The results of these two experiments indicate that the shift occurred principally, as the risk-as-value hypothesis predicts, among subjects who perceived themselves to be relatively risky. However, the shift occurred even when subjects heard no direct statements about others' preferences, and was greater in each discussion condition than in the information-exchange without-discussion condition. For the information-exchange per se interpretation of the risk-as-value hypothesis to remain a plausible explanation of these results, it must be demonstrated that subjects can infer reliably from the group discussion alone the preferred positions of the others. Meanwhile, the

interpretation of Madaras and Bem (1968) and of Teger and Pruitt (1967), that the group discussion engages the value of risk, in addition to providing information about reference-group judgments, is strongly supported. It may turn out, in fact, that the engagement of this value alone, without information concerning others' preferences, would be sufficient to produce the shift toward risk.

REFERENCES

Brown, R. *Social psychology.* New York: Free Press of Glencoe, 1965.

Clark, R. D., III, & Willems, E. P. Where is the risky shift? Dependence on instructions. *Journal of Personality and Social Psychology,* 1969, **13**, 215–221.

Hinds, W. C., Jr. Individual and group decisions in gambling situations. Unpublished master's thesis, Massachusetts Institute of Technology, School of Industrial Management, 1962.

Kogan, N., & Wallach, M. A. *Risk taking: A study in cognition and personality.* New York: Holt, Rinehart & Winston, 1964.

Kogan, N., & Wallach, M. A. The risky-shift phenomenon in small decision making groups: A test of the information-exchange hypothesis. *Journal of Experimental Social Psychology,* 1967, **3**, 75–84.

Levinger, G., & Schneider, D. J. A test of the "risk is a value" hypothesis. *Journal of Personality and Social Psychology,* 1969, **11**, 165–169.

Madaras, G. R., & Bem, D. J. Risk and conservatism in group decision making. *Journal of Experimental Social Psychology,* 1968, **4**, 350–365.

Teger, A. I., & Pruitt, D. G. Components of group risk taking. *Journal of Experimental Social Psychology,* 1967, **3**, 189–205.

Wallach, M. A., & Wing, C. W., Jr. Is risk a value? *Journal of Personality and Social Psychology,* 1968, **9**, 101–106.

Willems, E. P. Risk is a value. *Psychological Reports,* 1969, **24**, 81–82.

Willems, E. P., & Clark, R. D., III. Dependency of risky-shift on instructions: A replication. *Psychological Reports,* 1969, **25**, 811–814.

Winer, B. J. *Statistical principles in experimental design.* New York: McGraw-Hill, 1962.

ARTICLE 15

Risk Taking by Individuals and Groups: An Assessment of Research Employing Choice Dilemmas[1]

Dorwin Cartwright

PROBLEMS IN GENERALIZING FINDINGS

One basic question remains to be considered: What do the findings for choice dilemmas tell us about the relative riskiness of individuals and groups in the "real world"? Clearly, they do not justify the proposition that groups are invariably riskier than individuals, for the effects of group discussion depend upon the content of the dilemmas and probably upon the distribution of initial choices within groups. A proper statement of the findings will have to recognize these and possibly other dependencies. But even if these influences are taken into account, the implications of the research for natural groups are not immediately obvious. The question of generalization requires careful consideration of the conditions under which the results have been obtained.

It is important, first of all, to recall that nearly all research on choice dilemmas has used a repeated-measures design. Strictly speaking, the results refer to *shifts* in choices and not to

Abridged from *Journal of Personality and Social Psychology,* **20,** 1971, 361–378. Copyright 1971 by the American Psychological Association, and reproduced by permission of the author and the publisher.

[1]The preparation of this paper was supported by Contract HSM-42-69-55 with the National Institute of Mental Health. It is based on a review of the literature on group decision making and on interviews and correspondence with a number of investigators who have contributed to this area of research. The author is greatly indebted to many people for the ideas contained in the paper, but he is solely responsible for its content.

differences between the choices of individuals and groups who are considering the dilemmas for the first time. It is possible, therefore, that individuals and groups who make choices *de novo* on the same dilemma would not differ in their choices. Data presented by McCauley, Teger, & Kogan (1971) suggest that this may actually be the case. If this finding were to be confirmed, the results of research on choice dilemmas could be generalized only to natural settings in which group members formulate personal preferences prior to group discussion.

The problem is further complicated by the fact that the groups studied have certain "unnatural" properties. They are created for experimental purposes and consequently have no history, future, established structure, or significant enduring relationships with a surrounding social system. Results derived from such groups can be extended to "groups in general" only if it is assumed that they are not dependent upon these unusual properties. Unfortunately, almost nothing is known about the effects of group properties on the basic findings. One might expect that, in a group with a status hierarchy, higher status members would have more influence on group decisions, but Mackenzie (1970) and Siegel & Zajonc (1967) found little support for this assumption. On the other hand, Dion, Miller, & Magnan (1971) have obtained data indicating that shifts in CDQ scores may be quite different in groups with different levels of cohesiveness.

Further investigation of the effects of these and other group properties is clearly needed.

The question as to whether results can be generalized from *ad hoc* experimental groups to natural groups with an extended history is especially interesting. If, as is maintained by one version of value theory, the critical feature of group discussion is to inform subjects of the risk-taking dispositions of others, then groups with a history of decisions involving risk would not be expected to show shifts. The confirmation of this hypothesis would seriously limit the applicability of findings to the "real world."

The properties of choice dilemmas also pose problems of generalization. Each dilemma refers to a hypothetical situation and calls for a recommendation to be given to an imaginary person who is not a member of the group. The assigned task is to select the minimum odds of success that would justify undertaking the uncertain alternative rather than to recommend simply whether it should be undertaken. And the consequences of abiding by the recommendation do not directly affect the members of the group. Few groups, if any, have ever faced a decision with this combination of properties.

Since it can no longer be assumed that choice dilemmas measure a general disposition to take risks, an understanding of the effects of these "unnatural" properties of choices becomes critical. A few investigators have rewritten the choice dilemmas so as to alter the relationship between the subject and the hypothetical person described in the dilemma. Results reported by Dion, Miller, & Magnan (1971), Fraser, Gouge, & Billig (1971), Graham & Harris (1969), and Rabow, *et al.* (1966) suggest that this relationship may affect shifts in scores, but the findings are not entirely consistent. Several investigators have also attempted to assess the importance of the hypothetical nature of outcomes by comparing individual and group decisions in situations where the outcome of the decision has direct and tangible consequences for the participants. But the experiments reported by Bem, Wallach, & Kogan (1965), Kogan & Zaleska (1969), Marquis & Reitz (1969), Pruitt & Teger (1969), Zajonc, *et al.* (1968), and Zajonc, *et al.* (1969) produce quite heterogeneous results. Sometimes groups are riskier than individuals, sometimes more cautious, and sometimes there is no difference. A great deal more research is required before we can confidently generalize from choice dilemmas to the kinds of decisions faced by natural groups.

The experimental conditions employed in research on choice dilemmas certainly cannot be conceived as simulating any typical natural setting. Nor can they be considered a representative sample of any known universe of such situations. How, then, can the findings from this research be generalized to the "real world"? The only feasible way would seem to be through the use of theory. If the findings can be given theoretical meaning, then they can be applied to any empirical situation that satisfies the requirements specified by the theory. Thus, for example, if there were a clearly defined theoretical concept of "risk," it could then be applied to both "artificial" and "natural" settings despite any phenotypic differences between them. A major reason for hesitation in generalizing findings from CDQ scores is the ambiguity concerning the theoretical meaning of these scores.

The problem of generalization, then, cannot be solved until the theoretical significance of the experimental findings is clearly understood. There would appear to be no short cut to relevance.

CONCLUSIONS

The research of the past decade has produced a number of firm findings and several ingenious "explanations." One is left, however, with the uncomfortable feeling that theoretical thinking has not kept pace with the discovery of facts. Most publications still refer to "the risky shift" as if it were a well established phenomenon. And until quite recently most theoretical efforts have been directed to the task of accounting for the "fact" that groups make riskier decisions than individuals. But the facts are not so simple. The assumption that CDQ scores measure a unitary disposition to take risks is no longer tenable, and it is now clear that shifts in means of these scores poorly reflect the concrete changes in specific choices brought about by group discussion. Explanations of "the risky shift" which postulate some mechanism that uniformly moves choices toward greater risk are unable to account for the total body of findings.

As so often happens in science, a paradigm has served to stimulate the discovery of facts which reveal the inadequacy of the paradigm itself. Research employing the risky-shift paradigm has cast serious doubt on the existence of "the risky shift" itself and on the usefulness of CDQ scores in the analysis of risk taking. The findings even suggest the possibility that the basic phenomena may have been mislabeled and that they have nothing specifically to do with risk at all. It would be unfortunate, however, if dissatisfaction with the original paradigm were to diminish interest in the findings that have been established. The critical problem is to find a conceptual framework capable of dealing with phenomena that have proved to be more complex than first anticipated.

A curious feature of the history of research on choice dilemmas is the early rejection of theories of conformity and social influence as explanatory orientations. "The risky shift" was interpreted from the beginning as being inconsistent with previous findings from research on conformity. The argument against conformity theory has relied mainly on the assertion that it implies a convergence of post-discussion choices toward the *mean* of initial choices. Actually, however, conformity theory provides no clear basis for making any predictions about the location, or content, of an emergent norm from the beliefs or preferences of group members, since it has concentrated primarily on processes arising after group norms have been established. To the extent that it makes use of theories of social influence, it would predict that an emergent norm will coincide with the mean of initial choices only under rather special circumstances, as for example when all members have equal "weight" in the influence process. The model developed by Miller (1970) assumes convergence but predicts shifts in means as a consequence of differential weights among group members. This model, together with those of French (1956) and Harary (1959), might well provide a way to relate the findings on choice

dilemmas to theories of conformity and social influence.

Since it is not yet clear how risk enters into the choices made by subjects, it is possible that shifts would best be conceived as instances of the effects of group discussion on attitudes. Such a view has been advocated by Moscovici & Zavalloni (1969), and its plausibility has been enhanced by results reported by Fraser, Gouge, & Billig (1971). These investigators asked subjects to respond to each dilemma by means of a Likert scale on which they were to indicate how strongly they favored one or the other of the two alternative courses of action. When these responses were compared with the usual probability choices, there was a remarkable similarity between the two kinds of responses both before and after group discussion. If responses to choice dilemmas are in fact indicators of attitudes, then theories of attitude change should help to improve our understanding of the processes that bring about changes in these responses.

There is a real possibility, however, that the attitudes related to choice dilemmas have certain special characteristics which influence the way in which group discussion affects them. The findings concerning subjects' expectations about the choices of others, the choices they most admire, and their evaluations of people who make various choices suggest that the dilemmas generate a conflict between ideals and reality. Several interesting suggestions have been advanced by Higbee (1971), Jellison & Riskind (1970), Levinger & Schneider (1969), and Pruitt (1969) concerning the nature of this conflict and the role of group discussion in resolving it. It may turn out that such a conflict is critical for the occurrence of shifts and that group discussion does not affect all attitudes alike. Since so little is known about the effects of group discussion on attitudes of any sort, the findings for choice dilemmas may contribute valuable information about this form of attitude change.

Perhaps the greatest uncertainty of all surrounds the question of how best to conceptualize the processes of group discussion and group decision. Should group discussion be conceived as providing persuasive arguments concerning the correct answer to a problem or as a mechanism for combining individual preferences into a single group decision? Despite the demonstrated importance of group discussion for the occurrence of shifts, almost nothing is known about its nature. It is clear that discussion serves in some way to reconcile differences in initial choices and brings about a reduction in their variance, but it is not clear how this is accomplished. A direct examination of the content of group discussion is needed to identify the immediate determinants of shifts in choices.

The search for a suitable theoretical home for the findings established by the research on choice dilemmas will require careful attention to the concrete processes that determine both initial choices and changes in these choices. Unless these processes are clearly identified and placed in an appropriate theoretical context, the work on "the risky shift" may well become nothing more than an interesting episode in the history of social psychology.

REFERENCES

Bem, D. J., Wallach, M. A., & Kogan, N. Group decision making under risk of aversive consequences. *Journal of Personality and Social Psychology,* 1965, **1**, 453–460.

Dion, K. L., Miller, N., & Magnan, M. A. Cohesiveness and social responsibility as determinants of group risk-taking. *Journal of Personality and Social Psychology,* 1971, **20**, 400–406.

Fraser, C., Gouge, C., & Billig, M. Risky shifts, cautious shifts, and group polarization. *European Journal of Social Psychology,* 1971, **1**, 7–29.

French, J. R. P., Jr. A formal theory of social power. *Psychological Review,* 1956, **63**, 181–194.

Graham, W. K., & Harris, S. G. Effects of group discussion on accepting risk and on advising others to be risky. Paper presented at the meeting of the Western Psychological Association, Vancouver, 1969.

Harary, F. A criterion for unanimity in French's theory of social power. In D. Cartwright (Ed.), *Studies in social power.* Ann Arbor, Mich.: Institute for Social Research, 1959.

Higbee, K. L. The expression of "Walter Mitty-ness" in actual behavior. *Journal of Personality and Social Psychology,* 1971, **20**, 416–422.

Jellison, J. M., & Riskind, J. A social comparison of abilities interpretation of risk taking behavior. *Journal of Personality and Social Psychology,* 1970, **15**, 375–390.

Kogan, N., & Zaleska, M. Level of risk selected by individuals and groups when deciding for self and others. *Proceedings, 77th Annual Convention, APA,* 1969, **4**, 423–424. (Summary)

Levinger, G., & Schneider, D. J. A test of the "risk as a value" hypothesis. *Journal of Personality and Social Psychology,* 1969, **11**, 165–169.

Mackenzie, K. D. The effects of status upon group risk taking. *Organizational Behavior and Human Performance,* 1970, **5**, 517–541.

Marquis, D. G., & Reitz, H. J. Effect of uncertainty on risk taking in individual and group decisions. *Behavioral Science,* 1969, **14**, 281–288.

McCauley, C. R., Teger, A. I., & Kogan, N. Effect of the pretest in the risky shift paradigm. *Journal of Personality and Social Psychology,* 1971, **20**, 379–381.

Miller, H. Is the risky shift the result of a rational group decision? *Proceedings, 78th Annual Convention, APA,* 1970, **5**, 333–334. (Summary)

Moscovici, S., & Zavalloni, M. The group as a polarizer of attitudes. *Journal of Personality and Social Psychology,* 1969, **12**, 125–135.

Pruitt, D. G. The "Walter Mitty" effect in individual and group risk taking. *Proceedings, 77th Annual Convention, APA,* 1969, **4**, 425–426. (Summary)

Pruitt, D. G., & Teger, A. I. The risky shift in group betting. *Journal of Experimental Social Psychology,* 1969, **5**, 115–126.

Rabow, J., Fowler, F. J., Bradford, D. L., Hofeller, M. A., & Shibuya, Y. The role of social norms and leadership in risk taking. *Sociometry,* 1966, **29**, 16–27.

Siegel, S., & Zajonc, R. B. Group risk taking in professional decisions. *Sociometry,* 1967, **30**, 339–349.

Zajonc, R. B., Wolosin, R. J., Wolosin, M. A., & Sherman, S. J. Individual and group risk-taking in a two-choice situation. *Journal of Experimental Social Psychology,* 1968, **4**, 89–106.

Zajonc, R. B., Wolosin, R. J., Wolosin, M. A., & Sherman, S. J. Group risk-taking in a two-choice situation: Replication, extension, and a model. *Journal of Experimental Social Psychology,* 1969, **5**, 127–140.

SECTION SUMMARY

Will the work on the risky shift become "nothing more than an interesting episode in the history of social psychology," as Cartwright suggests it might? Certainly there are scores of dedicated researchers now working in their laboratories who presumably do not believe that their work will come to naught. As more and better research has been done on the risky-shift phenomenon, the problem has appeared increasingly complex. As Cartwright points out, it now appears that ". . . the facts are not so simple." Perhaps we should take such complexity for granted when we are dealing with the behavior of humans.

In spite of the increasing complexity of research findings, however, it still appears to be the case that the risky-shift phenomenon does take place under some conditions. To return to the question raised in the section Introduction and in the Clark, Crockett, and Archer article: why does the risky shift occur? Of the four hypotheses outlined in the Introduction, three have not received much empirical support. If the familiarization hypothesis is viable, then subjects who familiarize themselves with an issue while alone should show the same degree of risky shift as subjects whose familiarization took place in a group discussion. Although earlier research (for example, Bateson, 1966; Flanders & Thistlethwaite, 1967) seemed to indicate that this might be the case, more recent researchers have been unable to replicate these results (for example, see Teger, Pruitt, St. Jean, & Haaland, 1970). These inconsistencies in research results question the viability of the familiarization hypothesis as an explanation for the risky-shift effect.

The leadership hypothesis proposes that the more risky persons will emerge as group leaders and will influence the group toward a risky decision. Research has demonstrated that high risk-takers may indeed be perceived to be more persuasive and influential; *however,* the risky shift has also been found in situations in which high risk-takers do *not* exert greater persuasiveness than low risk-takers and in groups in which no high risk-takers are present (see Vidmar, 1970). These latter two findings suggest that processes other than leadership are responsible for the phenomenon (Clark, 1971).

The existence of a diffusion of responsibility effect when a group of people observe an emergency situation has been well documented in the

research literature, as discussed in Section 4. The applicability of this effect as an explanation for the risky-shift phenomenon has not received a great deal of support, however. As mentioned in the Introduction, this hypothesis proposes that the emotional bonds formed between group members may free the individual from accepting full responsibility for his later decision. But recent research (Willems & Clark, 1971) indicates that the production of emotional bonds between group members does not by itself account for the risky shift. Another study (Pruitt & Teger, 1969) found that, even when emotional bonds were produced and the other group members were implicated in the group decision, such conditions were not sufficient to produce the risky-shift effect. With regard to the diffusion of responsibility hypothesis, Clark (1971) has also pointed out that ". . . most damaging of all, it appears to be the exchange of relevant information, not the development of emotional bonds, that is necessary for the risky shift to occur" (p. 260).

As Clark, Crockett, and Archer have suggested in the second article in this section, the risk-as-value hypothesis has received the most research support as an explanation for why the risky shift occurs. They review the conclusions of several studies that indicate that most people tend to view themselves as at least as risky as their peers. The Clark et al. study demonstrated that discussion groups composed of people who considered themselves at least as risky as their peers showed the risky shift; groups composed of people who perceived themselves as more cautious than their peers did not show the effect.

The risk-as-value hypothesis conceptualizes the main function of the group discussion as information-sharing: the level of risk that others in the group are willing to assume is made clear to each participant. Research evidence supporting such a function has been provided by studies that have compared heterogeneous groups (groups wherein the participants differ considerably on level of risk proposed) with homogeneous groups (groups that included members whose initial levels of risk were similar to each other's). Comparison of such groups has indicated that the risky shift does occur in the heterogeneous groups, but it occurs to a lesser extent or not at all in the homogeneous groups (Vidmar, 1970; Willems & Clark, 1971). These and additional data seem to provide strong support for the risk-as-value hypothesis.

But there is another aspect of the situation that may have already occurred to the reader. Is being risky *always* a value? Or could there be specific situations in which a *cautious* course of action might be the most valued? Probably so. It appears that the crucial factor may be the degree of potential *cost* involved in taking the risky course of action. That is, if the person takes the risky action and it fails (in the example given in the Introduction, if the new company does not prove financially sound), how drastic will the consequences of this failure be? Research seems to indicate that if the consequences are particularly great, a "cautious shift" may occur, wherein the group decision is actually less risky than individual decisions (Clark & Willems, 1969). Madaras and Bem (1968) have suggested that raising the "moral costs" of failure (for example, stating that the man's wife and children will suffer greatly if he fails at the risky course of action) is a particularly effective means of eliciting the cautious shift.

It would seem appropriate to return to the questions posed at the beginning of the Introduction and discussed by Cartwright: how widespread is the risky-shift phenomenon? Is the process equally likely to occur during meetings of the Army Joint Chiefs of Staff, during meetings in the corporate board room of General Motors, and during meetings of the local Board of Education?

As Cartwright points out, groups are not *invariably* riskier than individuals. As we have suggested, the effects of group discussion depend on the content of the dilemmas (especially, the magnitude of the consequences and moral costs of failure) and on the distribution of initial choices within groups (that is, homogeneous or heterogeneous). Other relevant variables may include status hierarchies within the group, the history of the group in previous decisions involving risk, and the general value placed on risky behavior in the subculture from which the group is formed (Army officers, college students, or corporate vice-presidents). It may be that, as Madaras and Bem (1968) suggest, in the context of real-life decision making the salience of moral costs may be much greater than in questionnaire situations. Until the systematic effects of these and other relevant variables can be specified within a theoretical framework, the extent to which research results can be generalized will remain ambiguous. As Cartwright states, "There would appear to be no short cut to relevance."

REFERENCES

Bateson, N. Familiarization, group discussion, and risk taking. *Journal of Experimental Social Psychology,* 1966, **2,** 119–129.

Clark, R. D. III. Group-induced shift toward risk: A critical appraisal. *Psychological Bulletin,* 1971, **76,** 251–270.

Clark, R. D. III, & Willems, E. P. Risk preferences as related to judged consequences of failure. *Psychological Reports,* 1969, **25,** 827–830.

Flanders, J. P., & Thistlethwaite, D. L. Effects of familiarization and group discussion upon risk taking. *Journal of Personality and Social Psychology,* 1967, **5,** 91–97.

Madaras, G. R., & Bem, D. J. Risk and conservatism in group decision-making. *Journal of Experimental Social Psychology,* 1968, **4,** 350–365.

Pruitt, D. G., & Teger, A. I. The risky shift in group betting. *Journal of Experimental Social Psychology,* 1969, **5,** 115–126.

Teger, A. I., Pruitt, D. G., St. Jean, R., & Haaland, G. A. A reexamination of the familiarization hypothesis in group risk taking. *Journal of Experimental Social Psychology,* 1970, **6,** 346–350.

Vidmar, N. Group composition and the risky shift. *Journal of Experimental Social Psychology,* 1970, **6,** 153–166.

Willems, E. P., & Clark, R. D. III. Shift toward risk and heterogeneity of groups. *Journal of Experimental Social Psychology,* 1971, **7,** 304–312.

SUGGESTED READINGS FOR FURTHER STUDY

Brown, R. *Social psychology.* New York: Free Press, 1965. Pp. 678–708.

Clark, R. D. III. Group-induced shift toward risk: A critical appraisal. *Psychological Bulletin,* 1971, **76,** 251–270.

Dion, K. L., Baron, R. S., & Miller, N. Why do groups make riskier decisions than individuals? In L. Berkowitz (Ed.), *Advances in experimental social psychology,* Vol. 5. New York: Academic Press, 1970. Pp. 305–377.

Pruitt, D. G. (Ed.) Special issue on the risky shift. *Journal of Personality and Social Psychology,* 1971, **20,** 339–510.

Vinokur, A. Review and theoretical analysis of the effects of group processes upon individual and group decisions involving risk. *Psychological Bulletin,* 1971, **76,** 231–250.

Obedience and Compliance

INTRODUCTION

Throughout our lives we are subjected to external pressures to comply with many different, and sometimes conflicting, norms and standards. In a similar vein, there are countless cases in which we are urged to obey the wishes or commands of another person. This person may be one's boss, parent, spouse, college professor, commanding officer in the Army, experimenter in a psychological study, and so forth. In the past two decades social psychologists have become increasingly interested in the conditions under which such compliance with, or obedience to, standards or requests is likely to be greatest. This interest can be seen as incorporating two general problem areas: how does one get people to comply, and what happens to relevant attitudes and values after compliance takes place? We shall address the first of these problem areas in this section; the second area will be discussed in Section 11.

In this section, then, we are concerned with the *conditions* under which compliance and obedience may be induced. Under what conditions will someone be most likely to comply with a request? Are there conditions under which some people will obey an order even when it appears cruel and inhumane? If so, is such obedience limited to people who already have such inhumane tendencies, or are "normal, everyday people" likely to obey also? The research endeavors described in this section examine such questions.

One method of getting someone to comply with a large request is to get him or her to comply first with a smaller request. This "foot-in-the-door technique" has probably been known to salespeople for a long time, but social psychology has recently provided empirical validation of its effectiveness. As an example, Freedman and Fraser (1966) had experimenters go from door to door asking housewives to sign a petition, sponsored by the Committee for Safe Driving, asking their senators to work for legislation to encourage safe driving. Almost all of the housewives signed the petition. Several weeks later, different experimenters went from door to door in the same neighborhood asking housewives to agree to put a large, unattractive sign saying "Drive Carefully" in their front yards. More than half of the women who had previously agreed to sign the petition (the small request) agreed to post the sign (the larger request). In contrast, only 17% of the women who had not been approached before (with the petition) agreed to post the sign.

This general technique was used in a destructive fashion in the Chinese Communist brainwashing attempts during the Korean War. Schein (1956) has described their technique as the "pacing of demands." In his words: "In the various kinds of responses that were demanded of the prisoners, the Chinese always started with trivial, innocuous ones and, as the habit of responding became established, gradually worked up to more important ones. Thus, after a prisoner had been 'trained' to speak or write out trivia, statements on more important issues were demanded of him. This was particularly effective in eliciting confessions, self-criticism, and information during interrogation" (Schein, 1956, p. 163).

Another way in which compliance may be increased is through the operation of norms concerning social justice and reparation. For instance, if someone does you a favor, you will probably be more likely to help him in return than if he had not helped you. If he asks you to do something, therefore, you will be more likely to comply with his request. Several studies have shown that this common-sense notion has validity—people will tend to "restore equity" by returning the favor and complying with a request (for example, Berkowitz & Daniels, 1964; Regan, 1971). The tendency to comply is particularly strong if the original favor is perceived as being entirely voluntary, rather than suggested or made compulsory by someone else (Goranson & Berkowitz, 1966). Interestingly, although people are more likely to comply with a request from a "favor-doer," it is apparently not because of any increase in liking for him (Lerner & Lichtman, 1968; Schopler & Thompson, 1968; Regan, 1971).

Still another method by which compliance might be increased is through the arousal of *guilt* in an individual. When one feels guilty because he has done something he considers wrong, he generally will try to do something to reduce that guilt. He may perform a good act to "balance" the bad (guilt-inducing) act, he may subject himself to some kind of unpleasantness and thereby punish himself for his misbehavior, or he may attempt to minimize the negative aspects of the guilt-arousing situation. The first two of these techniques might make the (guilty) person more likely to comply with an appropriate request. In the first article in this section, Jonathan Freedman, Sue Ann Wallington, and Evelyn Bless, all then at Stanford University, describe a series of three experiments designed to assess the effectiveness of guilt in increasing compliance.

The research and theory described thus far refer to methods by which the tendency to comply with a specific request can be increased. But what of cases in which the entire situation is structured toward obedience—in which compliance with *any* request by those in charge is expected. There are certain situations such as the military chain of command that seem to *demand* obedience. (The situation of the psychological experiment itself is one that seems to be perceived by many subjects as demanding their cooperation or obedience. The effect that such "demand characteristics" can have on research results was discussed in Section 1.) A relevant research question, then, is: how powerful are the pressures toward obedience in such situations? Are they so powerful that even "normal, everyday people" will obey inhumane or cruel demands?

In the second article in this section Stanley Milgram, then at Yale University, describes a study that addressed these questions directly. The results of this study, and subsequent modifications of it, have proved shocking and disturbing to most persons who have read them. (We shall describe Milgram's subsequent studies in the Section Summary.) Their relevance in adding to our understanding of how societal "atrocities" can occur has been, and still is, hotly debated.

The last article in this section is a response to Milgram's experiment by Diana Baumrind, of the Institute of Human Development, University of California at Berkeley. Her article is primarily concerned with (1) the ethical considerations involved in experiments such as Milgram's and (2) the generality of his findings on the blind pervasiveness of obedience. Her basic concern with the responsibilities of scientists is a broader one than our current topic. Yet that concern is an extremely important and contemporary issue. The American Psychological Association is presently reviewing its ethical standards and has published a first draft of a revised code of ethics. Although some may view the inclusion of Baumrind's article here as washing the profession's dirty linen in public, we believe that the issues it raises deal with the place of science in society. Such concerns should not be kept within the walls of the profession.

REFERENCES

Berkowitz, L., & Daniels, L. R. Responsibility and dependency. *Journal of Abnormal and Social Psychology,* 1964, **66**, 427–436.

Freedman, J. L. & Fraser, S. C. Compliance without pressure: The foot-in-the-door technique. *Journal of Personality and Social Psychology,* 1966, **4**, 195–202.

Goranson, R. E. & Berkowitz, L. Reciprocity and responsibility reactions to prior help. *Journal of Personality and Social Psychology,* 1966, **3**, 227–232.

Lerner, M. J. & Lichtman, R. R. Effects of perceived norms on attitudes and altruistic behavior toward a dependent other. *Journal of Personality and Social Psychology,* 1968, **9**, 226–232.

Regan, D. T. Effects of a favor and liking on compliance. *Journal of Experimental Social Psychology,* 1971, **7**, 627–639.

Schein, E. H. The Chinese indoctrination program for prisoners of war. *Psychiatry,* 1956, **19**, 149–172.

Schopler, J., & Thompson, V. D. Role of attribution processes in mediating amount of reciprocity for a favor. *Journal of Personality and Social Psychology,* 1968, **10**, 243–250.

ARTICLE 16

Compliance without Pressure: The Effect of Guilt

Jonathan L. Freedman, Sue Ann Wallington, and Evelyn Bless[1]

How can someone be induced to do something which he would rather not do? One kind of answer to this question involves increasing the pressure on the individual until he is forced to comply. If a person is subjected to enough social pressure, offered enough reward, threatened with enough pain, or given enough convincing reasons, he will, under most circumstances, eventually yield and perform the required act. Inducement through pressure of this kind is one very effective means of producing compliance. There are, however, occasions when it is impossible or inappropriate to apply sufficient pressure, or when the amount of available pressure produces less compliance than is desired. Under these circumstances the problem is to maximize the amount of compliance produced by a given amount of pressure, and the question becomes what other factors affect degree of compliance.

In a previous study (Freedman & Fraser, 1966) it was found that subjects who had been asked a small favor subsequently complied more with a large request than did subjects who were asked only the large request. This "foot-in-the-door" technique appears to be one way of increasing compliance without manipulating external pressure of the usual kind. The present study investigates an entirely different technique which is the arousal of guilt prior to the attempt at inducing compliance.

From *Journal of Personality and Social Psychology*, **7**, 1967, 117–124. Copyright 1967 by the American Psychological Association, and reproduced by permission.

[1] This study was supported in part by grants from the National Science Foundation.

The notion that guilt will lead to pressures toward expiation probably goes as far back as the concept of guilt itself. Presumably when someone feels that he has done something wrong there will be a tendency for him to make up for his wrongful deed. He can do this by subjecting himself to punishment or by doing something good to balance the bad. Either of these processes might lead to increased compliance if the request is appropriate. Given the opportunity to engage in some extremely unpleasant behavior, the guilty person should be more likely to agree than the nonguilty since the former can use this as a form of self-punishment. Similarly, if he is asked to do someone a favor, pleasant or otherwise, the guilty person should be more likely to agree than the nonguilty because the former can view it as his good deed for the day which will make up for the bad deed about which he feels guilty. This line of reasoning leads to the hypothesis that guilt will lead to greater compliance in a wide variety of situations.

There are a few studies in the literature that are directly relevant to this hypothesis. Wallace and Sadalla (1966) attempted to induce subjects to break an expensive machine and then asked them to volunteer for a psychology experiment. Other subjects did not break the machine, but were also asked to volunteer. There was a significant tendency for those who broke the machine to comply more than those who did not. Unfortunately, 30% of the subjects in the break condition did not break the machine, and the authors discarded these subjects from the analysis. Because of this self-selection problem, it is difficult to assess the effect of the manipulation, although the data suggest that guilt will increase compliance.

In a similar study, Brock and Becker (1966) reported that subjects who did a small amount of damage to a machine (i.e., a small puff of smoke emerged when they manipulated a dial) conformed less to a subsequent request than subjects who did a great deal of damage (i.e., the machine emitted a fantastic amount of smoke and noise). One peculiar aspect of this finding was that the low-damage subjects never complied; no subject in that condition ever agreed to the request. Since under any circumstances some subjects will agree to virtually anything, it is extremely surprising that there was this consistent zero compliance. A very serious problem was that the person who made the request knew which condition the subject was in. Since the manner of making a request can obviously have an enormous effect on how much compliance it elicits, it is even more critical in compliance studies than in other kinds of research that the experimenter be blind to the subject's experimental condition. Thus, although these two machine-breaking studies are clearly relevant to the present problem, neither provides unequivocal evidence on the effect of guilt on compliance.

A study recently conducted at Stanford does. Carlsmith and Gross[2] had subjects deliver either shocks or loud buzzes to another subject (actually a confederate) in a learning situation similar to that used by Milgram (1963). When the learning trials were completed, the confederate who had been shocked contrived to ask the subject to do him a favor (calling people to enlist support for a campaign to "Save the Redwoods in California"). Those who had delivered shocks complied significantly more than those who had delivered only buzzes. A second study showed that this was not due simply to sympathy for the shocked confederate, since subjects who watched him get shocked but did not deliver the shocks themselves complied significantly less than subjects who actually administered the shocks. One strong point

[2] J. M. Carlsmith and A. Gross, "The Effect of Guilt on Compliance with a Simple Request." Unpublished manuscript.

of this work which distinguishes it, for example, from Brock's, is that the person making the request did not know what condition the subject was in. Carlsmith and Gross argued that the increased compliance they found was due to the guilt felt by the subjects giving the shock, and the present authors are inclined to believe this interpretation.

The present paper reports three experiments which also deal with the effect of guilt on compliance. The major concern of the first study was to provide an additional demonstration that guilt increases compliance. It was designed to provide this evidence in such a way that it would be possible to have some confidence in the interpretation that it is guilt which is the mediating variable. Although we feel that Carlsmith and Gross were probably manipulating guilt by their procedure, this interpretation would be considerably more convincing if the same increase in compliance could be produced when guilt is manipulated in an entirely different way from the one they used.

EXPERIMENT I

Method

The basic method was to induce some subjects to tell a deliberate lie, while others did not tell a lie. Then all subjects were asked to volunteer for a future experiment. In order to assess the effect, if any, of the unpleasantness of the request and also to provide somewhat more generality to the findings, the future experiment was described to approximately half of the subjects in extremely unpleasant terms, while to the other subjects it was described in quite neutral terms. The major interest is in the amount of overall compliance shown by the lie and nonlie subjects. A secondary question is whether the difference between these two groups varies as a function of the unpleasantness of the request.

Procedure

Subjects. Sixty-six high school males were recruited through a newspaper advertisement. Each was paid $1.50 for the 1-hour experiment. Three of these subjects were never run through the study because they were suspicious or already knew about it. One subject in the lie group was omitted because, before he was questioned about it, he spontaneously volunteered the information that he already knew about the procedure. The remaining 62 subjects were divided equally between the lie and nonlie conditions.

When the subject arrived, he was seated in a waiting room and told that the previous subject had not yet completed his test. The experimenter left the room, and a few minutes later returned with a confederate who posed as the previous subject. The experimenter thanked the confederate for participating in the study, paid him, and asked him to sign a receipt for the money. While the experimenter rummaged through the desk for a receipt, the confederate mentioned that he had signed up for another experiment and was supposed to wait for the other experimenter to arrive. The confederate then signed the receipt (which finally turned up). The experimenter left the room to "prepare the test," and the subject and confederate were alone together for 5 minutes.

Guilt Manipulation

During this 5-minute period, the confederate introduced the manipulation which separated the subjects into lie and nonlie conditions. Which condition each subject was put in was determined by a random-number table, and in all cases the experimenter was unaware of the condition of the subject.

The manipulation itself was extremely simple. The confederate entered into a brief informal discussion with each subject. Although several topics were selected beforehand, the content of this discussion depended to some extent upon the responses of the subject. In the lie condition, at some time during the conversation the confederate described the test which the subject was going to take. He gave an example of the items used and some of his ideas about the theory of the test and how to do well on it. In other words, he told the subject all about the test except the answers. In the nonlie condition, the confederate gave no details of the test.

The experimenter returned to the room after 5

minutes and took the subject to the experimental room. Before giving instructions for the test, the experimenter said to all subjects:

This is a Remote Associates Test developed by Professor Mednick at the University of Michigan. Since we are testing a slightly different hypothesis, we must make sure that you have not taken this test before or heard about it from friends.

She then paused for an answer, and in all cases except one the subject said that he had not heard about it. One subject in the lie condition said that he had heard about it. The experimenter said that it probably did not matter very much if he had not heard too much, and he was run through the experiment in the standard way. His data are included in the lie condition although presumably he should have felt no guilt, and in fact he did not comply with the subsequent request. In two other instances, subjects in the guilt condition said they had heard only the name of the test. They are also included in the analysis, less reluctantly because it is assumed that this lie will produce approximately as much guilt as a flat "no."

Thus, the guilt manipulation consists of eliciting a direct lie from the subjects. All subjects say that they have not heard about the test, but those in the lie condition actually have just been given a complete description of it. They are lying, and we assume that they are experiencing guilt about this lie.

The experiment proceeded with the subject working on the Remote Associates Test for 40 minutes. At the end of this time, the experimenter returned to the room, thanked the subject for participating, paid him, and had him sign a receipt for the money.

Compliance Measure

As the subject opened the door to leave the experimental room, the experimenter said, in an offhand, unconcerned way, something approximating the following:

Oh, one more thing. There is a fellow in the department who is doing a study on [either] sensory judgments of light and sound or something like that [low unpleasantness] [or] judgments of pain with shock or something like that [high unpleasantness]. He doesn't have a grant to pay subjects so he asked all of us who are working here to mention this experiment to our subjects in case anyone was particularly interested. Do you think you would be willing to take part in this study?

The subject said "yes" or "no," and that terminated the experiment.

Summary of Method

Some subjects were induced to lie to the experimenter, while others did not lie. All subjects were subsequently asked to volunteer for an experiment which was described as either quite unpleasant or slightly unpleasant. The measure of compliance is simply whether or not they volunteered.

Results

The major hypothesis was that there would be more compliance in the lie than in the nonlie condition. Of the 31 subjects in each group, 20 complied in the guilt condition and only 11 in the nonguilt condition (see Table 1). This difference is in the predicted direction and is significant ($x^2=4.13$, $p<.05$). In other words, subjects who are induced to tell a lie to the experimenter subsequently are more likely to comply with a request she makes than are subjects who do not tell the lie.

TABLE 1. Number of subjects complying in each condition.

	Experimental (Lie)	Control (Nonlie)
Comply	20	11
Not comply	11	20

The degree of unpleasantness of the experiment for which they were volunteering had no effect on amount of compliance. The absolute amount of compliance and the difference between lie and nonlie conditions were almost identical for both requests. This lack of effect of the unpleasantness manipulation is somewhat surprising. It would seem that it should have, at least, affected the overall level of compliance across the two guilt conditions. Since we did not get even this, it must be assumed that the two experiments were seen by the subjects as about equally unpleasant, or that the lack of difference is due to a ceiling effect of some sort.

The method used for arousing guilt in this study involved telling a lie. This is quite different from delivering electric shocks, which was the method employed by Carlsmith and Gross. In both experiments a plausible alternative explanation is that the subject did not feel guilty, but rather felt sorry for the requester because he had been hurt (either by the shocks or because the test was not valid). Yet this explanation was ruled out in the previous study, and it is probably not applicable to the present one either because the request involved doing a favor not for the experimenter but for someone else entirely. Therefore, it would appear that the interpretation in terms of guilt is considerably more reasonable, and that these results taken together provide very strong evidence that the arousal of guilt can produce an increase in compliance.

This finding raises the interesting question of how specifically the guilt operates. If the person feels guilty because he has done something to a particular person, how relevant to that person does the request have to be in order for the guilt to increase compliance? In Experiment I the increase in compliance appears even though the request apparently in no way benefits the person toward whom the subject should feel guilty, but in this case she did make the request and thus was very intimately involved with it. If the guilt is alleviated only by restitution to the victim, the increase in compliance should occur only when it helps him or at least involves him. If, however, atonement may be accomplished by doing something good for anyone, the increase should occur even when the request is neither made by nor benefits the victim. The next experiment investigated this problem by explicitly varying the degree of relevance of the request to the victim.

A second purpose of the study was to demonstrate the effect of guilt on compliance when guilt was manipulated in still a different way from those used previously.

EXPERIMENT II

Method

Some subjects (guilt condition) were induced to upset a pile of supposedly carefully arranged index cards. In one control condition the cards were instead upset by a confederate; in a second control condition the cards were not upset. Subsequently an experimenter who knew nothing about the "accident" and who did not know what condition the subject was in asked the subject to volunteer for an experiment being run by a graduate student. For approximately half of the subjects in each condition this graduate student was the one whose office they had been using and whose cards had been knocked over (when they had been upset); for the other half, he had nothing to do with the office or cards. In other words, the request was to help either someone who had previously been hurt or to help someone who was irrelevant to the guilt manipulation.

Subjects

Sixty-seven college freshman girls at Stanford University served as subjects. They were each paid $1.50 for participating in the approximately 40-minute experiment. Two confederates were employed, each of whom took part in about half of the sessions.

Procedure

Subjects were met in the hall and taken down a corridor to the experimental room. As they walked down the corridor, the experimenter explained that she was so anxious to finish her thesis that she had scheduled two subjects for that hour. She said that she would give them the instructions at the same time and then put them in two separate rooms to work on the test. She also explained, and this was the important point, that a graduate student had let her use his office for her study.

The experimental room was a tiny, triangularly shaped room that was originally designed to be an observation room. It contained a large table completely covered with books and other materials, and a small table which was partially covered with books and papers. In particular, at the edge of the small table was a pile of approximately 1,000 index cards containing notes about psychology experiments such as one might make in preparing a dissertation. The cards were divided into subjects with orange index cards.

When the subject and experimenter entered the room, the other subject (actually the confederate) was seated at one end of the table. Directly across from her and next to the table was the only other chair in the room. The experimenter indicated that the subject should take the chair and excused herself, saying that she had to go to the psychology office and get the tests. The subject and confederate were left alone for 5 minutes.

The table at which they were seated was designed to make it very unstable. The leg which was next to and hidden by the confederate's chair was 2 inches shorter than the other leg, but a 2-inch block was available to stabilize the table. Before the subject entered the room, the confederate decided on the basis of a random-number table which condition was to be run. In two conditions she removed the block before the subject appeared; in the other, the block was left under the short leg.

Guilt Manipulation

With the block removed, the table was extremely unsteady. In the guilt condition, the subject eventually and inevitably brushed against the table or put her books on it, thus upsetting it. When this happened, the table pitched over enough to scatter the pile of index cards. The confederate immediately began picking up the cards and commented that they looked as if they had been in order for someone's thesis. The subject generally discovered that she had knocked the block out from under the table, replaced it, and straightened the cards on the now steady table. The cards were, of course, now mixed up, but the scene looked normal. If the subject did not discover the block, the confederate pointed it out and replaced it.

In one control condition (Control I) everything proceeded exactly as above except that the confederate knocked the table over herself and was careful to assume full responsibility for the disaster. In Control II the cards were not knocked over, but the confederate did call attention to the "cards for someone's thesis."

The experimenter returned after 5 minutes, administered the Remote Associates Test to the subject in the same room, and indicated that the confederate would take it in another room.

After 20 minutes the experimenter returned once more, collected the test, paid the subject, had her sign a receipt, and thanked her. As the subject was leaving, and with the confederate not present, the experimenter made the request, which was:

Oh, one more thing. [either] The graduate student who let me use this room [or] A graduate student in the department [indicating down the hall to make it quite clear that it was not the one whose office they were in] doesn't have a grant to pay subjects for an experiment he wants to do so he asked me to mention it to my subjects in case someone might like to volunteer. I'm just mentioning it because I said I would.

The experimenter was very vague about the experiment, but said that it would take about an hour. She attempted to seem quite uninterested in whether or not the subject volunteered. Once again, the measure of compliance is simply the number of subjects who agreed to take part in the experiment.

Summary of Design

There were six experimental conditions: subject knocking over the cards, confederate knocking them over, and cards not knocked over, within each of these some of the subjects were asked to volunteer for an experiment run by the graduate student whose office they were using (and whose cards had been upset), half for a different graduate student. There were 10 subjects in each of these conditions, except for the two control conditions involving the injured graduate student which had 11 subjects each. An

additional 5 subjects in the guilt condition with injured graduate student confessed their accident and are treated separately.

Results

The major concern is with the amount of compliance to the relevant and irrelevant requests shown by subjects in the guilt condition compared with those in the nonguilt conditions. Since the two control conditions complied almost the identical amount, they are combined in the analysis.

The first question is how guilt affected the overall amount of compliance. Knocking over the cards increased the tendency to comply. Whereas 75% of the subjects who knocked the cards over complied, less than 39% of those who did not upset the cards themselves complied. This difference is statistically significant ($x^2=5.98$, $p<.02$). If the confessing subjects are included, the results are quite similar (72% versus 39%, $x^2=5.91$, $p<.02$).

The second question is how the relevance of the request to the source of guilt affected the level of compliance. The figures are shown in Table 2. It may be seen that there is no overall effect of relevance. What does appear, however, is that the difference in compliance between guilty and nonguilty subjects shows up only when the request does *not* involve the person toward whom the guilt is felt. When the request is to assist a graduate student who had nothing to do with their present experience, the guilty subjects comply significantly more than do the nonguilty ($p<.01$ by Fisher exact test). When the request is to help the graduate student whose office it is and whose cards were upset, there is no difference between the groups. The interaction between guilt-nonguilt and relevant-irrelevant request is not signifi-

TABLE 2. Number of subjects complying in each experimental condition.

| | Relevant Request | | Irrelevant Request | |
	Guilt	Nonguilt	Guilt	Nonguilt
Comply	6	11	9	5
Not comply	4	11	1	15

cant, and this trend should accordingly be viewed as only that, not a clear finding. If the confessing subjects are added, the results do not change appreciably, but are, if anything, somewhat stronger.

What can be concluded from these findings? In the first place, it is very encouraging that the card-upsetting manipulation produced greater compliance than did the control conditions. The interpretation of this effect and of the previous ones in terms of guilt would seem to be considerably strengthened by the fact that three entirely different manipulations, all of which were presumed to arouse guilt, did increase compliance. Shocking someone, lying to someone, and upsetting someone's index cards all produce a subsequent increase in compliance with a direct request. The explanation in terms of guilt fits these separate findings very nicely and parsimoniously, and any alternative interpretation has the difficult task of providing a plausible and parsimonious explanation for all three effects.

The results on the relevance of the request are less strong and more difficult to explain. At first glance it would seem that the guilty person should comply more when he could help his victim than when he was helping someone else. Perhaps expiation need not be specific to the person injured, but one would think that the closer the better. Yet, the results are apparently in the opposite direction; the guilty person complies somewhat more when the victim is not involved.

This seemingly implausible finding suggested that some additional consideration was motivating the guilty subject. Perhaps the guilty person wants to avoid contact with the person he injured. Since confrontation might increase his guilt or conceivably even lead to discovery, it is reasonable that he should avoid this. Thus, he is under two pressures: to make up for his "crime," but at the same time to avoid contact with the victim. This might lead to the pattern of results found. The guilty person would want to comply more than would the nonguilty, but the guilty would also want to avoid meeting the victim. This is quite a speculative notion which fits the data, but is hardly supported by them. A third study was conducted to test this idea directly and

incidentally to provide still one more demonstration of the effect of guilt on compliance.

EXPERIMENT III

Method

The procedure was quite similar to that of Experiment II with one important difference: for all subjects the request was to help the student whose cards had been upset, but for half of the subjects it involved working with him (association condition), while for the others it was likely that they would not even meet him (nonassociation condition). The expectation was that the guilty subjects would comply more than the nonguilty in the nonassociation condition, but that there would be no difference in the association condition.

Subjects

Seventy-four freshman and sophomore girls at Stanford University served as subjects. Of these, 5 were suspicious, and 3 confessed that they had upset the table. These 8 were omitted from the analysis of the data, although none of the results would change appreciably if they had been included. The remaining 66 subjects were randomly assigned to conditions, with 17 in all of the cells except the nonassociation-guilt condition which had 15.

Procedure

The procedure was very similar to that used in Experiment II. The same room, same unstable table, same cards, etc., were employed. One difference was that the other person in the room, instead of being described as another subject, was supposed to be there to answer any questions the real subject might have. Also, only the control condition in which the cards are not spilled was run. Since the two control conditions in Experiment II did not differ in compliance, it seemed unnecessary to have both.

As in Experiment II, the confederate was not present when the request was made. The request itself was somewhat different from that previously used. The experimenter asked if the subject would volunteer to help a graduate student run a public opinion survey. It was made very clear that it was the student whose office they were using (and therefore whose cards had been spilled in the guilt conditions). The subject would have to go out to the shopping center and distribute questionnaires, and this would take about 2-3 hours. In the association condition she asked: "He would give you a ride in his car, and you'd work in a team with him the whole time." In the nonassociation condition she said instead: "He isn't going out to collect data himself, but you'd be given a ride with one of the other volunteers, and you'd work with him the whole time." Thus, the subject was either certain of interacting closely with the injured party or fairly certain of not having to meet him at all.

Once again the measure of compliance is how many in each condition agreed to help.

Results

To begin with it should be noted that once again the guilt manipulation produced significantly greater overall compliance than did the control procedure. Over 55% of the subjects in the guilt condition agreed to the request, compared to just over 28% in the control condition. This difference is significant ($x^2=4.88$, $p<.05$).

The other concern is the effect of the type of request on compliance by the two groups. The amount of compliance shown in the four experimental conditions is presented in Table 3. We had expected that the guilty subjects would comply more than the nonguilty to the nonassociation request, but that differences would be smaller or nonexistent with the association request. The results are in line with these predictions. When the subjects expect to interact with the victim, there is no difference in amount of compliance between

guilt and nonguilt groups. In contrast, when they are not going to meet the victim, the guilty subjects comply significantly more than do the nonguilty ($x^2=7.91$, $p<.01$). Neither the interaction between guilt-nonguilt and type of request nor the difference between the two guilt conditions is significant. Thus, although the results are in the expected direction, they must be considered only partial support for the hypothesis.

DISCUSSION

The original idea behind this research was that making people feel guilty will increase the likelihood of their complying with a request. Presumably there is a tendency to expiate the guilt by doing something good to balance it or by punishing oneself for the action which caused the guilt in the first place. Both of these mechanisms would make the guilty person more likely to comply with an appropriate request.

Although there is some experimental evidence supporting this notion, it seemed desirable to demonstrate the effect using a different manipulation of guilt than that used previously. Guilt was manipulated in two different ways in three experiments, and in all cases it was shown to increase compliance. The most likely alternative explanation of the results is that the subject feels sorry for the victim. Experiment II eliminates this possibility by having both the requester and the request irrelevant to the victim. The data from these three experiments, added to those of Carlsmith and Gross (see Footnote 2), provide convincing evidence that guilt does increase compliance.

Experiments II and III both produce evidence suggesting that guilty subjects are torn by two considerations: they want to expiate their guilt, and they also want to avoid confronting the person they have harmed. In both studies guilty subjects complied more than nonguilty subjects when the request did not involve meeting the victim, whereas the two groups did not differ when complying meant having contact with the victim. The implication of this dual motivation is that guilt will be effective in increasing compliance only or at least primarily when the subject need not interact with the victim.

TABLE 3. Number of subjects complying in each condition.

| | Association | | Nonassociation | |
	Guilt	Nonguilt	Guilt	Nonguilt
Comply	7	6	11	3
Not comply	10	11	4	14

REFERENCES

Brock, T. C., & Becker, L. A. Debriefing and suscepti-bility to subsequent experimental manipulations. *Journal of Experimental Social Psychology,* 1966, **2,** 314–323.

Freedman, J. L., & Fraser, S. C. Compliance without pressure: The foot-in-the-door technique. *Journal of Personality and Social Psychology,* 1966, **4,** 195–202.

Milgram, S. Behavioral study of obedience. *Journal of Abnormal and Social Psychology,* 1963, **67,** 371–378.

Wallace, J., & Sadalla, E. Behavioral consequences of transgression: I. The effects of social recognition. *Journal of Experimental Research in Personality,* 1966, **1,** 187–194.

ARTICLE 17

Behavioral Study of Obedience

Obedience is as basic an element in the structure of social life as one can point to. Some system of authority is a requirement of all communal living, and it is only the man dwelling in isolation who is not forced to respond, through defiance or submission, to the commands of others. Obedience, as a determinant of behavior, is of particular relevance to our time. It has been reliably established that from 1933–45 millions of innocent persons were systematically slaughtered on command. Gas chambers were built, death camps were guarded, daily quotas of corpses were produced with the same efficiency as the manufacture of appliances. These inhumane policies may have originated in the mind of a single person, but they could only be carried out on a massive scale if a very large number of persons obeyed orders.

Obedience is the psychological mechanism that links individual action to political purpose. It is the dispositional cement that binds men to systems of authority. Facts of recent history and observation in daily life suggest that for many persons obedience may be a deeply ingrained behavior tendency, indeed, a prepotent impulse overriding training in ethics, sympathy, and moral conduct. C. P. Snow (1961) points to its importance when he writes:

When you think of the long and gloomy history of man, you will find more hideous crimes have been committed in the name of obedience than have ever

From *Journal of Abnormal and Social Psychology*, **67**, 1963, 371–378. Copyright 1963 by the American Psychological Association, and reproduced by permission of the author and the publisher.

been committed in the name of rebellion. If you doubt that, read William Shirer's "Rise and Fall of the Third Reich." The German Officer Corps were brought up in the most rigorous code of obedience . . . in the name of obedience they were party to, and assisted in, the most wicked large scale actions in the history of the world [p. 24].

While the particular form of obedience dealt with in the present study has its antecedents in these episodes, it must not be thought all obedience entails acts of aggression against others. Obedience serves numerous productive functions. Indeed, the very life of society is predicated on its existence. Obedience may be ennobling and educative and refer to acts of charity and kindness, as well as to destruction.

General Procedure

A procedure was devised which seems useful as a tool for studying obedience (Milgram, 1961). It consists of ordering a naive subject to administer electric shock to a victim. A simulated shock generator is used, with 30 clearly marked voltage levels that range from 15 to 450 volts. The instrument bears verbal designations that range from Slight Shock to Danger: Severe Shock. The responses of the victim, who is a trained confederate of the experimenter, are standardized. The orders to administer shocks are given to the naive subject in the context of a "learning experiment" ostensibly set up to study the effects of punishment on memory. As the experiment proceeds the naive subject is commanded to administer increasingly more intense shocks to the victim, even to the point of reaching the level marked Danger: Severe Shock. Internal resistances become stronger, and at a certain point the subject refuses to go on with the experiment. Behavior prior to this rupture is considered "obedience," in that the subject complies with the commands of the experimenter. The point of rupture is the act of disobedience. A quantitative value is assigned to the subject's performance based on the maximum intensity shock he is willing to administer before he refuses to participate further. Thus for any particular subject and for any particular experimental condition the degree of obedience may be specified with a numerical value. The crux of the study is to systematically vary the factors believed to alter the degree of obedience to the experimental commands.

The technique allows important variables to be manipulated at several points in the experiment. One may vary aspects of the source of command, content and form of command, instrumentalities for its execution, target object, general social setting, etc. The problem, therefore, is not one of designing increasingly more numerous experimental conditions, but of selecting those that best illuminate the *process* of obedience from the socio-psychological standpoint.

Related Studies

The inquiry bears an important relation to philosophic analyses of obedience and authority (Arendt, 1958; Friedrich, 1958; Weber, 1947), an early experimental study of obedience by Frank (1944), studies in "authoritarianism" (Adorno, Frenkel-Brunswik, Levinson, & Sanford, 1950; Rokeach, 1961), and a recent series of analytic and empirical studies in social power (Cartwright, 1959). It owes much to the long concern with *suggestion* in social psychology, both in its normal forms (e.g., Binet, 1900) and in its clinical manifestations (Charcot, 1881). But it derives, in the first instance, from direct observation of a social fact; the individual who is commanded by a legitimate authority ordinarily obeys. Obedience comes easily and often. It is a ubiquitous and indispensable feature of social life.

METHOD

Subjects

The subjects were 40 males between the ages of 20 and 50, drawn from New Haven and the surrounding communities. Subjects were obtained by a newspaper advertisement and direct mail solicitation. Those who responded to the appeal believed they were to participate in a study of memory and learning at Yale University. A wide range of occupations is represented in the sample. Typical subjects were postal clerks, high school teachers, salesmen, engineers, and laborers. Subjects ranged in educational level from one who had not finished elementary school, to those who had doctorate and other professional degrees. They were paid $4.50 for their participation in the experiment. However, subjects were told that payment was simply for coming to the laboratory, and that the money was theirs no matter what happened after they arrived. Table 1 shows the proportion of age and occupational types assigned to the experimental condition.

Personnel and Locale

The experiment was conducted on the grounds of Yale University in the elegant interaction laboratory. (This detail is relevant to the perceived legitimacy of the experiment. In a further variation, the experiment was dissociated from the university, with consequences for performance.) The role of experimenter was played by a 31-year-

TABLE 1. Distribution of age and occupational types in the experiment.

Occupations	20-29 years n	30-39 years n	40-50 years n	Percentage of total (occupations)
Workers, skilled and unskilled	4	5	6	37.5
Sales, business, and white-collar	3	6	7	40.0
Professional	1	5	3	22.5
Percentage of total (age)	20	40	40	

Note—Total N = 40.

old high school teacher of biology. His manner was impassive, and his appearance somewhat stern throughout the experiment. He was dressed in a gray technician's coat. The victim was played by a 47-year-old accountant, trained for the role; he was of Irish-American stock, whom most observers found mild-mannered and likable.

Procedure

One naive subject and one victim (an accomplice) performed in each experiment. A pretext had to be devised that would justify the administration of electric shock by the naive subject. This was effectively accomplished by the cover story. After a general introduction on the presumed relation between punishment and learning, subjects were told:

But actually, we know *very little* about the effect of punishment on learning, because almost no truly scientific studies have been made of it in human beings.

For instance, we don't know how *much* punishment is best for learning—and we don't know how much difference it makes as to who is giving the punishment, whether an adult learns best from a youngster or an older person than himself—or many things of that sort.

So in this study we are bringing together a number of adults of different occupations and ages. And we're asking some of them to be teachers and some of them to be learners.

We want to find out just what effect different people have on each other as teachers and learners, and also what effect *punishment* will have on learning in this situation.

Therefore, I'm going to ask one of you to be the teacher here tonight and the other one to be the learner.

Does either of you have a preference?

Subjects then drew slips of paper from a hat to determine who would be the teacher and who would be the learner in the experiment. The drawing was rigged so that the naive subject was always the teacher and the accomplice was always the learner. (Both slips contained the word "Teacher.") Immediately after the drawing, the teacher and learner were taken to an adjacent room and the learner was strapped into an "electric chair" apparatus.

The experimenter explained that the straps were to prevent excessive movement while the learner was being shocked. The effect was to make it impossible for him to escape from the situation. An electrode was attached to the learner's wrist, and electrode paste was applied "to avoid blisters and burns." Subjects were told that the electrode was attached to the shock generator in the adjoining room.

In order to improve credibility the experimenter declared, in response to a question by the learner: "Although the shocks can be extremely painful, they cause no permanent tissue damage."

Learning Task.   The lesson administered by the subject was a paired-associate learning task. The subject read a series of word pairs to the learner, and then read the first word of the pair along with four terms. The learner was to indicate which of the four terms had originally been paired with the first word. He communicated his answer by pressing one of four switches in front of him, which in turn lit up one of four numbered quadrants in an answer-box located atop the shock generator.

Shock Generator.   The instrument panel consists of 30 lever switches set in a horizontal line. Each switch is clearly labeled with a voltage designation that ranges from 15 to 450 volts. There is a 15-volt increment from one switch to the next going from left to right. In addition, the following verbal designations are clearly indicated for groups of four switches going from left to right: Slight Shock, Moderate Shock, Strong Shock, Very Strong Shock, Intense Shock, Extreme Intensity Shock, Danger: Severe Shock. (Two switches after this last designation are simply marked XXX.)

Upon depressing a switch: A pilot light corresponding to each switch is illuminated in bright red; an electric buzzing is heard; an electric blue light, labeled "voltage energizer," flashes; the dial on the voltage meter swings to the right; various delay clicks are sounded.

The upper left-hand corner of the generator is labeled Shock Generator, Type ZLB, Dyson Instrument Company, Waltham, Mass. Output 15 volts–450 volts.

Details of the instrument were carefully handled to insure an appearance of authenticity. The panel was engraved by precision industrial engravers, and all components were of high quality. No subject in the experiment suspected that the instrument was merely a simulated shock generator.[1]

Sample Shock.   Each naive subject is given a sample shock on the shock generator, prior to beginning his run as teacher. This shock is always 45 volts, and is applied by pressing the third switch of the generator. The shock is applied to the wrist of the naive subject, and has its source in a 45-volt battery wired into the generator. This further convinces the subject of the authenticity of the generator.

Shock Instructions.   The subject is told to administer a shock to the learner each time he gives a wrong response. Moreover—and this is the key command—the subject is instructed to "move one level higher on the shock generator each time the learner flashes a wrong answer." He is also instructed to announce the voltage level before administering a shock. This serves to continually remind subjects of the increasing intensity of shocks administered to the learner.

Preliminary and Regular Run.   Pretests revealed that the procedure of reading words and administering shocks requires some practice before it can be handled smoothly. Therefore, immediately preceding the regular run, the teacher is given a preliminary series of 10 words to read to the learner. There are 3 neutral words in the practice series (i.e., words that the learner answers correctly), so that shocks are administered for 7 of the words, with the maximum shock at

[1] A related technique, making use of a shock generator, was reported by Buss (1961) for the study of aggression in the laboratory. Despite the considerable similarity of technical detail in the experimental procedures, both investigators proceeded in ignorance of the other's work. Milgram provided plans and photographs of his shock generator, experimental procedure, and first results in a report to the National Science Foundation in January 1961. This report received only limited circulation. Buss reported his procedure 6 months later, but to a wider audience. Subsequently, technical information and reports were exchanged. The present article was first received in the Editor's office on December 27, 1961; it was resubmitted with deletions on July 27, 1962.

105 volts (moderate shock). Almost all subjects master the procedure by the time the preliminary run is over.

Subjects are then presented with a second list, and are told that the procedure is the same as for the first list; the experimenter adds, however:

When you get to the bottom of the list, repeat it over again, and continue giving shocks, until the learner has learned all the pairs correctly.

The experimenter instructs the subject to

start from 15 volts and increase the shock level one step each time the learner gives a wrong answer.

Feedback from the Victim.   In all conditions the learner gives a predetermined set of responses to the word pair test, based on a schedule of approximately three wrong answers to one correct answer. In the present experimental condition no vocal response or other sign of protest is heard from the learner until Shock Level 300 is reached. When the 300-volt shock is administered, the learner pounds on the wall of the room in which he is bound to the electric chair. The pounding can be heard by the subject. From this point on, the learner's answers no longer appear on the four-way panel.

At this juncture, subjects ordinarily turn to the experimenter for guidance. The experimenter instructs the subject to treat the absence of a response as a wrong answer, and to shock the subject according to the usual schedule. He advises the subjects to allow 5–10 seconds before considering no response as a wrong answer, and to increase the shock level one step each time the learner fails to respond correctly. The learner's pounding is repeated after the 315-volt shock is administered; afterwards he is not heard from, nor do his answers reappear on the four-way signal box.

Experimenter Feedback.   At various points in the experiment the subject may turn to the experimenter for advice on whether he should continue to administer shocks. Or he may indicate that he does not wish to go on. It was important to standardize the experimenter's responses to these inquiries and reactions.

If the subject indicated his unwillingness to go on, the experimenter responded with a sequence of "prods," using as many as necessary to bring the subject into line.

Prod 1: Please continue. *or* Please go on.
Prod 2: The experiment requires that you continue.
Prod 3: It is absolutely essential that you continue.
Prod 4: You have no other choice, you *must* go on.

The prods were always made in sequence: Only if Prod 1 had been unsuccessful, could Prod 2 be used. If the subject refused to obey the experimenter after Prod 4, the experiment was terminated. The experimenter's tone of voice was at all times firm, but not impolite. The sequence was begun anew on each occasion that the subject balked or showed reluctance to follow orders.

Special prods. If the subject asked if the learner was liable to suffer permanent physical injury, the experimenter said:

Although the shocks may be painful, there is no permanent tissue damage, so please go on. [Followed by Prods 2, 3, and 4 if necessary.]

If the subject said that the learner did not want to go on, the experimenter replied:

Whether the learner likes it or not, you must go on until he has learned all the word pairs correctly. So please go on. [Followed by Prods 2, 3, and 4 if necessary.]

Dependent Measures

The primary dependent measure for any subject is the maximum shock he administers before he refuses to go any further. In principle this may vary from 0 (for a subject who refuses to administer even the first shock) to 30 (for a subject who administers the highest shock on the generator). A subject who breaks off the experiment at any point prior to administering the thirtieth shock level is termed a *defiant* subject. One who complies with experimental commands fully, and proceeds to administer all shock levels commanded, is termed an *obedient* subject.

Further Records. With few exceptions, experimental sessions were recorded on magnetic tape. Occasional photographs were taken through one-way mirrors. Notes were kept on any unusual behavior occurring during the course of the experiments. On occasion, additional observers were directed to write objective descriptions of the subjects' behavior. The latency and duration of shocks were measured by accurate timing devices.

Interview and Dehoax. Following the experiment, subjects were interviewed; open-ended questions, projective measures, and attitude scales were employed. After the interview, procedures were undertaken to assure that the subject would leave the laboratory in a state of well being. A friendly reconciliation was arranged between the subject and the victim, and an effort was made to reduce any tensions that arose as a result of the experiment.

RESULTS

Preliminary Notions

Before giving an account of the experimental results, it is instructive to consider how persons predict others will perform when commanded to administer powerful shocks to another person. Fourteen Yale seniors, all psychology majors, were provided with a detailed description of the experimental situation. They were asked to reflect carefully on it, and to predict the behavior of 100 hypothetical subjects. More specifically, they were instructed to plot the distribution of obedience of "100 Americans of diverse occupations, and ranging in age from 20 to 50 years," who were placed in the experimental situation.

There was considerable agreement among the respondents on the expected behavior of hypothetical subjects. All respondents predicted that only an insignificant minority would go through to the end of the shock series. (The estimates ranged from 0 to 3%; i.e., the most "pessimistic" members of the class predicted that of 100 persons, 3 would continue through to the most potent shock available on the shock generator—450 volts.) The class mean was 1.2%. The question was also posed informally to colleagues of the author, and the most general feeling was that few if any subjects would go beyond the designation Very Strong Shock.

Result of Experiment I

Subjects Accept Situation. With few exceptions subjects were convinced of the reality of the experimental situation, that they were administering shocks to another person, and the most potent shocks were extremely painful. In the post-experimental interview subjects were asked: "How painful to the learner were the last few shocks that you administered to him?" Subjects were instructed to indicate their answers on a printed 14-point scale ranging from "Not at all painful" to "Extremely painful." The modal response was 14 (Extremely painful) with the mean at 13.42.

Signs of Extreme Tension. Many subjects showed signs of nervousness in the experimental situation, and especially upon administering the more powerful shocks. In a large number of cases the degree of tension reached extremes that are rarely seen in sociopsychological laboratory studies. Subjects were observed to sweat, tremble, stutter, bite their lips, groan, and dig their fingernails into their flesh. These were characteristic rather than exceptional responses to the experiment.

One sign of tension was the regular occurrence of nervous laughing fits. Fourteen of the 40 subjects showed definite signs of nervous laughter and smiling. The laughter seemed entirely out of place, even bizarre. Full-blown, uncontrollable seizures were observed for 3 subjects. On one occasion we observed a seizure so violently convulsive that it was necessary to call a halt to the experiment. The subject, a 46-year-old encyclopedia salesman, was seriously embarrassed by his untoward and uncontrollable behavior. In the post-experimental interviews subjects took pains to point out that they were not sadistic types, and that the laughter did not mean they enjoyed shocking the victim.

Distribution of Scores. It had been conjectured that persons would not, in general, agree to administer shocks beyond the level designated as Very Strong Shock. The distribution of maximum shocks for this experiment is shown in Table 2. The obtained distribution of scores deviates radically from the prediction.

Upon command of the experimenter, each of the 40 subjects went beyond the expected breakoff point. No subject stopped prior to administering Shock Level 20. (At this level—300 volts—the victim kicks on the wall and no longer provides answers to the teacher's multiple-choice questions.)

Of the 40 subjects, 5 refused to obey the experimental commands beyond the 300-volt level. Four more subjects administered one further shock, and then refused to go on. Two broke off at the 330-volt level, and 1 each at 345, 360, and

TABLE 2.   Distribution of breakoff points.

Verbal designation and voltage indication	Number of subjects for whom this was maximum shock
Slight shock	
15	0
30	0
45	0
60	0
Moderate shock	
75	0
90	0
105	0
120	0
Strong shock	
135	0
150	0
165	0
180	0
Very strong shock	
195	0
210	0
225	0
240	0
Intense shock	
255	0
270	0
285	0
300	5
Extreme intensity shock	
315	4
330	2
345	1
360	1
Danger: severe shock	
375	1
390	0
405	0
420	0
XXX	
435	0
450	26

375 volts. Thus a total of 14 subjects defied the experimenter. It is instructive to reprint their remarks at the point of defiance, as transcribed from the tape recordings:

[0124] I think he's trying to communicate, he's knocking. . . . Well it's not fair to shock the guy . . . these are terrific volts. I don't think this is very humane. . . . Oh, I can't go on with this; no, this isn't right. It's a hell of an experiment. The guy is suffering in there. No. I don't want to go on. This is crazy. [Subject refused to administer more shocks.]
[0123] He's banging in there. I'm gonna chicken out. I'd like to continue, but I can't do that to a man. . . . I'm sorry I can't do that to a man. I'll hurt his heart. You take your check. . . . No really, I couldn't do it.

These subjects were frequently in a highly agitated and even angered state. Sometimes, verbal protest was at a minimum, and the subject simply got up from his chair in front of the shock generator, and indicated that he wished to leave the laboratory.

Of the 40 subjects, 26 obeyed the orders of the experimenter to the end, proceeding to punish the victim until they reached the most potent shock available on the shock generator. At that point, the experimenter called a halt to the session. (The maximum shock is labeled 450 volts, and is two steps beyond the designation: Danger: Severe Shock.) Although obedient subjects continued to administer shocks, they often did so under extreme stress. Some expressed reluctance to administer shocks beyond the 300-volt level, and displayed fears similar to those who defied the experimenter; yet they obeyed.

After the maximum shocks had been delivered, and the experimenter called a halt to the proceedings, many obedient subjects heaved sighs of relief, mopped their brows, rubbed their fingers over their eyes, or nervously fumbled cigarettes. Some shook their heads, apparently in regret. Some subjects had remained calm throughout the experiment, and displayed only minimal signs of tension from beginning to end.

DISCUSSION

The experiment yielded two findings that were surprising. The first finding concerns the sheer strength of obedient tendencies manifested in this situation. Subjects have learned from childhood that it is a fundamental breach of moral conduct to hurt another person against his will. Yet, 26 subjects abandon this tenet in following the instruction of an authority who has no special powers to enforce his commands. To disobey would bring no material loss to the subject; no punishment would ensue. It is clear from the remarks and outward behavior of many participants that in punishing the victim they are often acting against their own values. Subjects often expressed deep disapproval of shocking a man in the face of his objections, and others denounced it as stupid and senseless. Yet the majority complied with the experimental commands. This outcome was surprising from two perspectives: first, from the standpoint of predictions made in the questionnaire described earlier. (Here, however, it is possible that the remoteness of the respondents from the actual situation, and the difficulty of conveying to them the concrete details of the experiment, could account for the serious underestimation of obedience.)

But the results were also unexpected to persons who observed the experiment in progress, through one-way mirrors. Observers often uttered expressions of disbelief upon seeing a subject administer more powerful shocks to the victim. These persons had a full acquaintance with the details of the situation, and yet systematically underestimated the amount of obedience that subjects would display.

The second unanticipated effect was the extraordinary tension generated by the procedures. One might suppose that a subject would simply break off or continue as his conscience dictated. Yet, this is very far from what happened. There were striking reactions of tension and emotional strain. One observer related:

I observed a mature and initially poised businessman enter the laboratory smiling and confident. Within 20 minutes he was reduced to a twitching, stuttering wreck, who was rapidly approaching a point of nervous collapse. He constantly pulled on his earlobe, and twisted his hands. At one point he pushed his fist into his forehead and muttered: "Oh God, let's stop it." And yet he continued to respond to every word of the experimenter, and obeyed to the end.

Any understanding of the phenomenon of obedience must rest on an analysis of the particular conditions in which it occurs. The following features of the experiment go some distance in explaining the high amount of obedience observed in the situation.

1. The experiment is sponsored by and takes place on the grounds of an institution of unimpeachable reputation, Yale University. It may be reasonably presumed that the personnel are competent and reputable. The importance of this background authority is now being studied by conducting a series of experiments outside of New Haven, and without any visible ties to the university.

2. The experiment is, on the face of it, designed to attain a worthy purpose—advancement of knowledge about learning and memory. Obedience occurs not as an end in itself, but as an instrumental element in a situation that the subject construes as significant, and meaningful. He may not be able to see its full significance, but he may properly assume that the experimenter does.

3. The subject perceives that the victim has voluntarily submitted to the authority system of the experimenter. He is not (at first) an unwilling captive impressed for involuntary service. He has taken the trouble to come to the laboratory presumably to aid the experimental research. That he later becomes an involuntary subject does not alter the fact that, initially, he consented to participate without qualification. Thus he has in some degree incurred an obligation toward the experimenter.

4. The subject, too, has entered the experiment voluntarily, and perceives himself under obligation to aid the experimenter. He has made a commitment, and to disrupt the experiment is a repudiation of this initial promise of aid.

5. Certain features of the procedure strengthen the subject's sense of obligation to the experimenter. For one, he has been paid for coming to the laboratory. In part this is canceled out by the experimenter's statement that:

Of course, as in all experiments, the money is yours simply for coming to the laboratory. From this point on, no matter what happens, the money is yours.[2]

[2] Forty-three subjects, undergraduates, at Yale University, were run in the experiment without payment. The results are very similar to those obtained with paid subjects.

6. From the subject's standpoint, the fact that he is the teacher and the other man the learner is purely a chance consequence (it is determined by drawing lots) and he, the subject, ran the same risk as the other man in being assigned the role of learner. Since the assignment of positions in the experiment was achieved by fair means, the learner is deprived of any basis of complaint on this count. (A similar situation obtains in Army units, in which—in the absence of volunteers—a particularly dangerous mission may be assigned by drawing lots, and the unlucky soldier is expected to bear his misfortune with sportsmanship.)

7. There is, at best, ambiguity with regard to the prerogatives of a psychologist and the corresponding rights of his subject. There is a vagueness of expectation concerning what a psychologist may require of his subject, and when he is overstepping acceptable limits. Moreover, the experiment occurs in a closed setting, and thus provides no opportunity for the subject to remove these ambiguities by discussion with others. There are few standards that seem directly applicable to the situation, which is a novel one for most subjects.

8. The subjects are assured that the shocks administered to the subject are "painful but not dangerous." Thus they assume that the discomfort caused the victim is momentary, while the scientific gains resulting from the experiment are enduring.

9. Through Shock Level 20 the victim continues to provide answers on the signal box. The subject may construe this as a sign that the victim is still willing to "play the game." It is only after Shock Level 20 that the victim repudiates the rules completely, refusing to answer further.

These features help to explain the high amount of obedience obtained in this experiment. Many of the arguments raised need not remain matters of speculation, but can be reduced to testable propositions to be confirmed or disproved by further experiments.[3]

The following features of the experiment con-

[3] A series of recently completed experiments employing the obedience paradigm is reported in Milgram (1965).

cern the nature of the conflict which the subject faces.

10. The subject is placed in a position in which he must respond to the competing demands of two persons: the experimenter and the victim. The conflict must be resolved by meeting the demands of one or the other; satisfaction of the victim and the experimenter are mutually exclusive. Moreover, the resolution must take the form of a highly visible action, that of continuing to shock the victim or breaking off the experiment. Thus the subject is forced into a public conflict that does not permit any completely satisfactory solution.

11. While the demands of the experimenter carry the weight of scientific authority, the demands of the victim spring from his personal experience of pain and suffering. The two claims need not be regarded as equally pressing and legitimate. The experimenter seeks an abstract scientific datum; the victim cries out for relief from physical suffering caused by the subject's actions.

12. The experiment gives the subject little time for reflection. The conflict comes on rapidly. It is only minutes after the subject has been seated before the shock generator that the victim begins his protests. Moreover, the subject perceives that he has gone through but two-thirds of the shock levels at the time the subject's first protests are heard. Thus he understands that the conflict will have a persistent aspect to it, and may well become more intense as increasingly more powerful shocks are required. The rapidity with which the conflict descends on the subject, and his realization that it is predictably recurrent may well be sources of tension to him.

13. At a more general level, the conflict stems from the opposition of two deeply ingrained behavior dispositions: first, the disposition not to harm other people, and second, the tendency to obey those whom we perceive to be legitimate authorities.

REFERENCES

Adorno, T., Frenkel-Brunswik, E., Levinson, D. J., & Sanford, R. N. *The authoritarian personality.* New York: Harper, 1950.

Arendt, H. What was authority? In C. J. Friedrich (Ed.), *Authority.* Cambridge: Harvard University Press, 1958. Pp. 81–112.

Binet, A. *La suggestibilité.* Paris: Schleicher, 1900.

Buss, A. H. *The psychology of aggression.* New York: Wiley, 1961.

Cartwright, S. (Ed.) *Studies in social power.* Ann Arbor: University of Michigan, Institute for Social Research, 1959.

Charcot, J. M. *Oeuvres complètes.* Paris: Bureaux du Progrès Médical, 1881.

Frank, J. D. Experimental studies of personal pressure and resistance. *Journal of General Psychology,* 1944, **30,** 23–64.

Friedrich, C. J. (Ed.) *Authority.* Cambridge: Harvard University Press, 1958.

Milgram, S. Dynamics of obedience. Washington, D. C.: National Science Foundation, January 25, 1961. (Mimeo.)

Milgram, S. Some conditions of obedience and disobedience to authority. *Human Relations,* 1965, **18,** 57–76.

Rokeach, M. Authority, authoritarianism, and conformity. In I. A. Berg and B. M. Bass (Eds.), *Conformity and deviation.* New York: Harper, 1961. Pp. 230–257.

Snow, C. P. Either-or. *Progressive,* Feb. 1961, 24.

Weber, M. *The theory of social and economic organization.* Oxford: Oxford University Press, 1947.

ARTICLE 18

Reactions to Milgram's "Behavioral Study of Obedience"

Diana Baumrind

... Most experimental conditions do not cause the subjects pain or indignity, and are sufficiently interesting or challenging to present no problem of an ethical nature to the experimenter. But where the experimental conditions expose the subject to loss of dignity, or offer him nothing of value, then the experimenter is obliged to consider the reasons why the subject volunteered and to reward him accordingly.

The subject's public motives for volunteering include having an enjoyable or stimulating experience, acquiring knowledge, doing the experimenter a favor which may some day be reciprocated, and making a contribution to science. These motives can be taken into account rather easily by the experimenter who is willing to spend a few minutes with the subject afterwards to thank him for his participation, answer his questions, reassure him that he did well, and chat with him a bit. Most volunteers also have less manifest, but equally legitimate, motives. A subject may be seeking an opportunity to have contact with, be noticed by, and perhaps confide in a person with psychological training. The dependent attitude of most subjects toward the experimenter is an artifact of the experimental situation as well as an expression of some subjects' personal and need systems at the time they volunteer.

Excerpted from "Some thoughts on ethics of research: After reading Milgram's 'Behavioral study of obedience,'" *American Psychologist,* 1964, **19,** 421–423. Copyright 1964 by the American Psychological Association, and reproduced by permission of the author and the publisher.

The dependent, obedient attitude assumed by most subjects in the experimental setting is appropriate to that situation. The "game" is defined by the experimenter and he makes the rules. By volunteering, the subject agrees implicitly to assume a posture of trust and obedience. While the experimental conditions leave him exposed, the subject has the right to assume that his security and self-esteem will be protected.

There are other professional situations in which one member—the patient or client—expects help and protection from the other—the physician or psychologist. But the interpersonal relationship between experimenter and subject additionally has unique features which are likely to provoke initial anxiety in the subject. The laboratory is unfamiliar as a setting and the rules of behavior ambiguous compared to a clinician's office. Because of the anxiety and passivity generated by the setting, the subject is more prone to behave in an obedient, suggestible manner in the laboratory than elsewhere. Therefore, the laboratory is not the place to study degree of obedience or suggestibility, as a function of a particular experimental condition, since the base line for these phenomena as found in the laboratory is probably much higher than in most other settings. Thus experiments in which the relationship to the experimenter as an authority is used as an independent condition are imperfectly designed for the same reason that they are prone to injure the subjects involved. They disregard the special quality of trust and obedience with which the subject appropriately regards the experimenter.

Other phenomena which present ethical decisions, unlike those mentioned above, *can* be reproduced successfully in the laboratory. Failure experience, conformity to peer judgment, and isolation are among such phenomena. In these cases we can expect the experimenter to take whatever measures are necessary to prevent the subject from leaving the laboratory more humiliated, insecure, alienated, or hostile than when he arrived. To guarantee that an especially sensitive subject leaves a stressful experimental experience in the proper state sometimes requires special clinical training. But usually an attitude of compassion, respect, gratitude, and common sense will suffice, and no amount of clinical training will substitute. The subject has the right to expect that the psychologist with whom he is interacting has some concern for his welfare and the personal attributes and professional skill to express his good will effectively.

Unfortunately, the subject is not always treated with the respect he deserves. It has become more commonplace in sociopsychological laboratory studies to manipulate, embarrass, and discomfort subjects. At times the insult to the subject's sensibilities extends to the journal reader when the results are reported. Milgram's (1963) study is a case in point. The following is Milgram's abstract of his experiment:

This article describes a procedure for the study of destructive obedience in the laboratory. It consists of ordering a naive *S* to administer increasingly more severe punishment to a victim in the context of a learning experiment. Punishment is administered by means of a shock generator with 30 graded switches ranging from Slight Shock to Danger: Severe Shock. The victim is a confederate of *E*. The primary dependent variable is the maximum shock the *S* is willing to administer before he refuses to continue further. 26 *S*s obeyed the experimental commands fully, and administered the highest shock on the generator. 14 *S*s broke off the experiment at some point after the victim protested and refused to provide further answers. The procedure created extreme levels of nervous tension in some *S*s. Profuse sweating, trembling, and stuttering were typical expressions of this emotional disturbance. One unexpected sign of tension—yet to be explained—was the regular occurrence of nervous laughter, which in some *S*s developed into uncontrollable seizures. The variety of interesting behavioral dynamics observed in the experiment, the reality of the situation for the *S*,

and the possibility of parametric variation within the framework of the procedure, point to the fruitfulness of further study (p. 371).

The detached, objective manner in which Milgram reports the emotional disturbance suffered by his subject contrasts sharply with his graphic account of that disturbance. Following are two other quotes describing the effects on his subjects of the experimental conditions:

I observed a mature and initially poised businessman enter the laboratory smiling and confident. Within 20 minutes he was reduced to a twitching, stuttering wreck, who was rapidly approaching a point of nervous collapse. He constantly pulled on his earlobe, and twisted his hands. At one point he pushed his fist into his forehead and muttered: "Oh, God, let's stop it." And yet he continued to respond to every word of the experimenter, and obeyed to the end (p. 377).

In a larger number of cases the degree of tension reached extremes that are rarely seen in sociopsychological laboratory studies. Subjects were observed to sweat, tremble, stutter, bite their lips, groan, and dig their fingernails into their flesh. These were characteristic rather than exceptional responses to the experiment.

One sign of tension was the regular occurrence of nervous laughing fits. Fourteen of the 40 subjects showed signs of nervous laughter and smiling. The laughter seemed entirely out of place, even bizarre. Full-blown, uncontrollable seizures were observed for 3 subjects. On one occasion we observed a seizure so violently convulsive that it was necessary to call a halt to the experiment . . . (p. 375).

Milgram does state that,

After the interview, procedures were undertaken to assure that the subject would leave the laboratory in a state of well being. A friendly reconciliation was arranged between the subject and the victim, and an effort was made to reduce any tensions that arose as a result of the experiment (p. 374).

It would be interesting to know what sort of procedures could dissipate the type of emotional disturbance just described. In view of the effects on subjects, traumatic to a degree which Milgram himself considers nearly unprecedented in sociopsychological experiments, his casual assurance that these tensions were dissipated before the subject left the laboratory is unconvincing.

What could be the rational basis for such a posture of indifference? Perhaps Milgram supplies the answer himself when he partially explains the subject's destructive obedience as follows: "Thus they assume that the discomfort caused the victim is momentary, while the scientific gains resulting from the experiment are enduring (p. 378)." Indeed such a rationale might suffice to justify the means used to achieve his end if that end were of inestimable value to humanity or were not itself transformed by the means by which it was attained.

The behavioral psychologist is not in as good a position to objectify his faith in the significance of his work as medical colleagues at points of breakthrough. His experimental situations are not sufficiently accurate models of real-life experience; his sampling techniques are seldom of a scope which would justify the meaning with which he would like to endow his results; and these results are hard to reproduce by colleagues with opposing theoretical views. Unlike the Sabin vaccine, for example, the concrete benefit to humanity of his particular piece of work, no matter how competently handled, cannot justify the risk that real harm will be done to the subject. I am not speaking of physical discomfort, inconvenience, or experimental deception per se, but of permanent harm, however slight. I do regard the emotional disturbance described by Milgram as potentially harmful because it could easily affect an alteration in the subject's self-image or ability to trust adult authorities in the future. It is potentially harmful to a subject to commit, in the course of an experiment, acts which he himself considers unworthy, particularly when he has been entrapped into committing such acts by an individual he has reason to trust. The subject's personal responsibility for his actions is not erased because the experimenter reveals to him the means which he used to stimulate these actions. The subject realizes that he would have hurt the victim if the current were on. The realization that he also made a fool of himself by accepting the experimental set results in additional loss of self-esteem. Moreover, the subject

finds it difficult to express his anger outwardly after the experimenter in a self-acceptant but friendly manner reveals the hoax.

A fairly intense corrective interpersonal experience is indicated wherein the subject admits and accepts his responsibility for his own actions, and at the same time gives vent to his hurt and anger at being fooled. Perhaps an experience as distressing as the one described by Milgram can be integrated by the subject, provided that careful thought is given to the matter. The propriety of such experimentation is still in question even if such a reparational experience were forthcoming. Without it I would expect a naive, sensitive subject to remain deeply hurt and anxious for some time, and a sophisticated, cynical subject to become even more alienated and distrustful.

In addition the experimental procedure used by Milgram does not appear suited to the objectives of the study because it does not take into account the special quality of the set which the subject has in the experimental situation. Milgram is concerned with a very important problem, namely, the social consequences of destructive obedience. He says,

Gas chambers were built, death camps were guarded, daily quotas of corpses were produced with the same efficiency as the manufacture of appliances. These inhumane policies may have originated in the mind of a single person, but they could only be carried out on a massive scale if a very large number of persons obeyed orders (p. 371).

But the parallel between authority-subordinate relationships in Hitler's Germany and in Milgram's laboratory is unclear. In the former situation the SS man or member of the German Officer Corps, when obeying orders to slaughter, had no reason to think of his superior officer as benignly disposed towards himself or their victims. The victims were perceived as subhuman and not worthy of consideration. The subordinate officer was an agent in a great cause. He did not need to feel guilt or conflict because within his frame of reference he was acting rightly.

It is obvious from Milgram's own descriptions that most of his subjects were concerned about their victims and did trust the experimenter, and that their distressful conflict was generated in part by the consequences of these two disparate but appropriate attitudes. Their distress may have resulted from shock at what the experimenter was doing to them as well as from what they thought they were doing to their victims. In any case there is not a convincing parallel between the phenomena studied by Milgram and destructive obedience as that concept would apply to the subordinate-authority relationship demonstrated in Hitler Germany. If the experiments were conducted "outside of New Haven and without any visible ties to the university," I would still question their validity on similar although not identical grounds. In addition, I would question the representativeness of a sample of subjects who would voluntarily participate within a non-institutional setting.

In summary, the experimental objectives of the psychologist are seldom incompatible with the subject's ongoing state of well being, provided that the experimenter is willing to take the subject's motives and interests into consideration when planning his methods and correctives. Section 4b in *Ethical Standards of Psychologists* (APA, undated) reads in part:

> Only when a problem is significant and can be investigated in no other way, is the psychologist justified in exposing human subjects to emotional stress or other possible harm. In conducting such research, the psychologist must seriously consider the possibility of harmful aftereffects, and should be prepared to remove them as soon as permitted by the design of the experiment. Where the danger of serious aftereffects exists, research should be conducted only when the subjects or their responsible agents are fully informed on this possibility and volunteer nevertheless (p. 12).

From the subject's point of view procedures which involve loss of dignity, self-esteem, and trust in national authority are probably most harmful in the long run and require the most thoughtfully planned reparations, if engaged in at all. The public image of psychology as a profession is highly related to our own actions, and some of these actions are changeworthy. It is important that as research psychologists we protect our ethical sensibilities rather than adapt our personal standards to include as appropriate the kind of indignities to which Milgram's subjects were exposed. I would not like to see experiments such as Milgram's proceed unless the subjects were fully informed of the dangers of serious aftereffects and his correctives were clearly shown to be effective in restoring their state of well being.

REFERENCES

American Psychological Association. Ethical standards of psychologists: A summary of ethical principles. Washington, D. C.: APA, undated.

Milgram S. Behavioral study of obedience. *Journal of Abnormal and Social Psychology*, 1963, **67**, 371–378.

SECTION SUMMARY

The article by Freedman, Wallington, and Bless demonstrates that the arousal of guilt can be a very effective means of inducing compliance in the absence of direct, overt social influence. Freedman et al. point out that there is an important qualification to the guilt-compliance relationship, however. They suggest that the guilty person is torn between two considerations: (1) expiation of guilt and (2) desire to avoid confronting the person whom he thinks he has harmed. The greatest amount of compliance, therefore, will be obtained when adherence to the request does *not* require further interaction with the victim (see also Carlsmith & Gross, 1969).

Another important variable is the opportunity to confess one's transgression. If one is allowed to confess, perhaps some of the guilt pressure will be relieved and subsequent compliance will not be so great. Carlsmith, Ellsworth, and Whiteside (1968) found this to be the case; subjects who were allowed the opportunity to confess what they had done were less likely than other subjects to comply with a request that they volunteer to take part in further experiments. There is also evidence that apparently undiscovered private transgressions may not lead to compliance as much as public transgressions do (Wallace & Sadalla, 1966; Silverman, 1967).

Finally, another important factor is the ease with which one is able to make reparations to one's victim. If the guilty person cannot pay back the victim fully or if the available payment is too great, he may react in other ways. Research has suggested that, in such a situation, the subject may *devalue* the victim and minimize his perception of the amount of harm done (Berscheid & Walster, 1967; Lerner & Matthews, 1967). Or, he may justify his behavior by deciding that he caused the harm for good reason, such as for the sake of science or because he was ordered to and had no choice.

Milgram's study provides a chilling example of the extent to which human behavior can be dictated when a person is in a situation in which he feels he should or must obey. Would you have predicted that more than 60% of the subjects would have gone "all the way" and delivered the highest shock intensity? If you are like most people, you probably would not have. Milgram described his procedure in detail to 40 psychiatrists at a leading medical school; they predicted that less than 1% of the subjects would deliver the highest shock on the board! A sample of college undergraduates made similar predictions (Milgram, 1965b).

In a later series of experiments, Milgram (1965a, 1965b) varied the following four aspects of the experimental situation to see how they would affect the degree of obedience: (1) immediacy of the victim, (2) immediacy of the authority figure, (3) prestige of the sponsoring institution, and (4) effects of group pressure.

1. *Immediacy of the Victim.* In this study Milgram employed four conditions:

   a. *Remote-Feedback condition:* The victim was in another room and could not be heard or seen by the subject until, when the 300-volt level was reached, the victim pounded on the wall. After 300 volts he no longer answered or made any noise.
   b. *Voice-Feedback condition:* It is identical to the first condition except that the victim did make vocal protests that could be heard through the wall and through the slightly open doorway between the rooms.
   c. *Proximity condition:* The victim was placed in the same room as the subject and 1 1/2 feet from him. Thus both visual and audible clues to the victim's pain were available to the subject.
   d. *Touch-Proximity condition:* This condition is identical to the third, except that, beyond the 150-volt level, the victim momentarily refused to put his hand on the shockplate. Thus, on every subsequent trial, the experimenter ordered the subject to force the victim's hand on the shockplate.

A different set of 40 adult males participated in each one of the four conditions. The percentages of men who obeyed the experimenter (administered the highest shock) are as follows: Remote-Feedback, 65%; Voice-Feedback, 62.5%; Proximity, 40%; and Touch-Proximity, 30%. Thus, as you might have expected, when the victim is less distant, more subjects refuse to obey.

2. *Immediacy of the Authority Figure.* Milgram completed three more studies in which he varied the closeness of the authority figure to the subject. In one condition (like the procedure in Article 17) the experimenter sat only a few feet away from the subject. In a second condition the experimenter was present at the beginning to give initial instructions but then left the room, using the telephone for further instructions. In the third condition the experimenter was never present; instructions were given by means of a tape recording.

Obedience was almost three times more frequent when the experimenter remained physically present. Moreover, when the experimenter was absent, several subjects administered shocks of a lower voltage than was required. As Milgram indicates, the response clearly violated the avowed purpose of the experiment, but perhaps it was easier for the subject to handle his conflict in this way than to defy authority openly.

3. *Prestige of the Sponsoring Institution.* As Milgram mentions in his article in this section, a large part of the obedience might be accounted for by the fact that the research took place on the grounds of Yale University, in Milgram's words,

"an institution of unimpeachable reputation." To check this factor, Milgram conducted the experiment again, this time in downtown Bridgeport, Connecticut. The sponsor of the study was supposedly Research Associates of Bridgeport, and the three-room office suite was in a "somewhat run-down commercial building located in the downtown shopping area" (Milgram, 1965b, p. 70). Subjects were again paid $4.50 for their participation. Even under these conditions, almost half (48%) of the subjects delivered the maximum shock possible! Therefore the prestige of the sponsoring institution does not appear to be of crucial importance.

4. *Effects of Group Pressure.* To assess the effects of group pressure, Milgram ran two additional studies that employed three confederates instead of one. The experimenter explained that three teachers and one learner would be required. The (real) subject became teacher 3; two of the confederates became teachers 1 and 2 and the other became the learner. In one study both confederate-teachers were *obedient*—they followed the experimenter's commands and neither showed sympathy for the victim nor commented on his apparent discomfort. Did such obedient models increase the number of real subjects willing to deliver the maximum shock? Not much. In this experiment 29 of the 40 subjects went all the way; this proportion is not significantly greater than the 26 of 40 found in Milgram's original study.

In the second variation of this paradigm, the two teacher-confederates were *defiant.* One confederate refused to continue after the shocks reached the 150-volt level, and the other refused to continue past the 210-volt level. In contrast to the findings in the "obedient" condition, the defiance of the confederates apparently had a major effect on the real subjects. In this study only 10% (4/40) of the real subjects delivered the maximum shock. Yet interestingly enough, three-fourths of the 36 subjects who refused to go all the way claimed that they would have stopped even without the other teachers' (confederates') example. The results of Milgram's other studies strongly suggest that this is not so.

Diana Baumrind is not alone in her criticisms of the ethics involved in Milgram's research and other research that might be detrimental to the unsuspecting subject. As we write this, a debate is currently raging within psychology concerning a draft of a revised Code of Ethics created by the ad hoc Committee on Ethical Standards in Psychological Research of the American Psychological Association (Cook, Kimble, Hicks, McGuire, Schoggen, & Smith, 1971). The committee's first published draft adopted a "risk/benefit" approach, wherein it is clearly stated that potential risks to the subject should be very carefully weighed against the benefits that the research may have in advancing psychological knowledge. The overall approach of the committee is illustrated in the following passage:

... we adopt as a guiding principle that where risks or gains are in doubt, priority must be given to the subject's welfare. As near as we come to an immutable "thou shalt" or "thou shalt not" is the insistence that the human subject emerge from his research experience unharmed—or at least that he is exposed only to such risks as he himself knowingly and freely consents to—and, if possible, with an identifiable benefit [Cook et al., 1971, p. 10].

In a response to this code, Baumrind (1971) has expressed the fear that the risk/benefit approach may have the undesirable effect of allowing researchers to justify violations of the rights of the subjects by appealing to the anticipated "benefits" to society of the proposed research. On the other hand, there are many researchers who feel that the proposed code is too *restrictive.* They feel that, although the rights of the subjects should certainly be protected, the use of over-restrictive guidelines may seriously hamper research and reduce the amount of societal benefit that could result from such research, if carried out.

In this light we should point out that Milgram carried out an extensive follow-up study to try to assess whether participation in his experiments had had any long-lasting effects on the subjects involved. Of the subjects contacted, 84% indicated that they were glad to have taken part in the research, 15% reported neutral feelings, and 1% reported that they regretted having participated. Four-fifths of the subjects felt that more experiments of this sort should be carried out. Some caution should be employed in interpreting these figures, however. Persons who have administered shocks to others may be motivated later to justify their behavior to themselves regardless of what they initially thought of the experiment. A university psychiatrist also interviewed a sample of experimental subjects; he was unable to uncover possible injurious effects resulting from participation in the studies (Milgram, 1964, 1965b).

The potential importance of Milgram's results and the apparent concern for the welfare of his subjects have led some social scientists to propose that this research is among the most powerful and important programs carried out in social psychology. For example, Etzioni (1968, p. 279) has commented: ". . . Milgram's experiment seems to be one of the best carried out in this generation. It shows that the often-stated opposition between meaningful, interesting, humanistic study and accurate, empirical, quantitative research is a false one: The two perspectives can be combined to the benefit of both."

The question that remains is: how far can the results of Milgram's studies be generalized? Has he identified the "latent Eichmann" that resides in most of us, as Etzioni (1968) proposes? Or can much of the variance in his results be attributed to the "demand characteristics" of an unusual research situation? It could be cogently argued that "obedience" is an expected behavior in research subjects, who, in other circumstances, such as complying with traffic laws, might not so readily obey. To many persons "science" has become a sacred cow; we take seriously our responsibilities as participants in a research enterprise. Furthermore, in this particular situation— contrary to real life—the subject's behavior was closely monitored by an authority figure. (Obedience to traffic regulations would be much greater if we always had a policeman sitting in the car with us.) Do laboratory results mean that we can or cannot generalize Milgram's findings to real-life situations in which we are forced to violate our values under the close supervision of an authority figure? Social scientists are not in agree-

ment with one another; the interested reader should see Orne and Holland (1968) and Milgram (1972) for two opposing positions on this issue.

Baumrind believes that there may be no relationship between the phenomenon demonstrated in Milgram's laboratory subjects and the behavior of Adolf Eichmann and other Nazi German officers. Milgram (1964), in a reply to Baumrind, disagrees. He states that a soldier's obedience is "no less meaningful" just because it occurs in a military context. The shocking atrocities apparently committed by "ordinary" American soldiers in Vietnam in the late 1960s provide compelling evidence of the possible relevance of Milgram's findings. For example, columnist Stanley Karnow (1971) has suggested that Milgram's original experiment was "remarkably prescient. He demonstrated in the laboratory what Lt. William Calley and his unit would later dramatize at My Lai—that man's behavior is almost invariably dominated by authority rather than by his own sense of morality." Karnow quotes Milgram as commenting: "If we now recoil at our own conduct, it is because we are just as capable as the Nazis of committing crimes in the name of obedience." The reader is encouraged to think about whether or not man's behavior is "almost always" dominated by authority and whether the persons he knows would be "just as capable as the Nazis" of committing such crimes.

The extent to which Milgram's findings can be generalized is still open to debate. But, in any case, he has provided a new and sobering frame of reference for the evaluation of human behavior under conditions of extreme authority pressure.

REFERENCES

Baumrind, D. Principles of ethical conduct in the treatment of subjects: Reaction to the draft report of the Committee on Ethical Standards in Psychological Research. *American Psychologist,* 1971, **26,** 887–896.

Berscheid, E., & Walster, E. When does a harm-doer compensate a victim? *Journal of Personality and Social Psychology,* 1967, **6,** 435–441.

Carlsmith, J. M., Ellsworth, P., & Whiteside, J. Guilt, confession, and compliance. Unpublished manuscript, Stanford University, 1968.

Carlsmith, J. M., & Gross, A. E. Some effects of guilt on compliance. *Journal of Personality and Social Psychology,* 1969, **11,** 232–239.

Cook, S. W., Kimble, G. A., Hicks, L. H., McGuire, W. J., Schoggen, P. H., & Smith, M. B. Ethical Standards for Psychological Research: Proposed ethical principles submitted to the APA membership for criticism and modification (by the) ad hoc Committee on Ethical Standards in Psychological Research. *APA Monitor,* July 1971, **2**(7), 9–28.

Etzioni, A. A model of significant research. *International Journal of Psychiatry,* 1968, **6,** 279–280.

Karnow, S. Calley, Eichmann both obedient. *St. Petersburg Times,* March 30, 1971.

Lerner, M. J., & Matthews, G. Reactions to the suffering of others under conditions of indirect responsibility. *Journal of Personality and Social Psychology,* 1967, **5,** 319–325.

Milgram, S. Issues in the study of obedience: A reply to Baumrind. *American Psychologist,* 1964, **19,** 848–852.

Milgram, S. Liberating effects of group pressure. *Journal of Personality and Social Psychology,* 1965, **1,** 127–134. (a)

Milgram, S. Some conditions of obedience and disobedience to authority. *Human Relations,* 1965, **18,** 57–76. (b)

Milgram, S. Interpreting obedience: Error and evidence. In A. G. Miller (Ed.), *The social psychology of psychological research.* New York: Free Press, 1972. Pp. 138–154.

Orne, M. T., & Holland, C. H. On the ecological validity of laboratory deceptions. *International Journal of Psychiatry,* 1968, **6,** 282–293.

Silverman, T. W. Incidence of guilt reactions in children. *Journal of Personality and Social Psychology,* 1967, **7,** 338–340.

Wallace, J., & Sadalla, E. Behavioral consequences of transgression: The effects of social recognition. *Journal of Experimental Research in Personality,* 1966, **1,** 187–194.

SUGGESTED READINGS FOR FURTHER STUDY

Adorno, T., Frenkel-Brunswik, E., Levinson, D., & Sanford, R. N. *The authoritarian personality.* New York: Harper & Row, 1950.

Christie, R., & Jahoda, M. (Eds.) *Studies in the scope and method of "The authoritarian personality."* New York: Free Press, 1954.

Kelman, H. C. Compliance, identification, and internalization: Three processes of attitude change. *Journal of Conflict Resolution,* 1958, **2,** 51–60.

Kiesler, C. A., & Kiesler, S. B. *Conformity.* Reading, Mass.: Addison-Wesley, 1969.

Milgram, S. Some conditions of obedience and disobedience to authority. *Human Relations,* 1965, **18,** 57–76.

Rokeach, M. *The open and closed mind.* New York: Basic Books, 1960.

Schein, E. H. The Chinese indoctrination program for prisoners of war. *Psychiatry,* 1956, **19,** 149–172.

Wheeler, L. *Interpersonal influence.* Boston: Allyn and Bacon, 1970.

Aggression and Violence

INTRODUCTION

The decade of the 1960s witnessed a sharp increase in levels of aggression and violence in American society. Rates of violent crimes such as murder, forcible rape, and aggravated assault increased dramatically; the nation was shaken by assassinations of a President, a Nobel Peace Prize winner, and a popular U.S. Senator; mass violence wracked many of our large urban centers; college campuses were often the sites of violent outbursts and tense group confrontations. Governmental recognition of, and reaction to, this problem was indicated in 1968 by the appointment of a Presidential Commission on the Causes and Prevention of Violence. The United States also found itself embroiled in an undeclared war halfway across the world—a war that cost well over 40,000 American lives and many times this many casualties among the populations of North and South Vietnam. This war also brought to the nation's consciousness the fact that ordinary "American boys" could be involved in brutal massacres of civilian populations, as was discussed in Section 6.

The scientific study of the causes of aggression and violence, and of ways through which their prevalence can be reduced, is obviously of crucial importance. This is true from the perspective that significant human events and behaviors should be subjected to scientific scrutiny; it is also true from the broader perspective that we had better do all that we can to develop techniques and expertise applicable to the survival of mankind in a world seemingly characterized by increasing aggression, both interpersonal and international.

Perhaps the most basic question about human aggression concerns its origin. Are aggressive impulses in humans biologically determined, instinctive, and innate, or are they socially determined, the result of learning experiences? The answer to this question has large-scale implications for social policies designed to reduce the level of aggression in society.

This question is directly relevant to a study of the effects derived from observing aggressive behavior in others. If aggressive tendencies are innate, and if each of us carries around a "pool" of aggressive impulses, then the viewing of aggressive behavior by others may serve a very valuable function—it may allow us to release or drain off our pent-up aggressive impulses while watching (and perhaps identifying with) the aggressive action. This release may prevent a future *direct* release of the aggressive energy in socially undesirable activities. This idea stems all the way back to Aristotle, who wrote in *The Art of Poetry* that drama is concerned with ". . . incidents arousing pity and fear in such a way as to accomplish a purgation of such emotions" (Berkowitz, 1964, p. 35). The term *catharsis,* derived from the Greek word for purgation, has been used to describe this process of releasing aggressive tendencies through viewing the aggressive behavior of others. Freud (1959) used the term in a somewhat related sense. He proposed that expressing a particular impulse will reduce its strength. Thus, if you are angry, then acting angrily or aggressively should make you less angry. Even if direct expression is not possible, Freud noted, indirect expression of a feeling should reduce its strength somewhat. Thus, if you feel angry and aggressive, watching someone else behave aggressively may allow you to indirectly express your anger and hence feel less angry as a result.

The catharsis position is often applied today as an explanation for the popularity of (and perhaps the social value of) professional football. In essence, the argument holds that the typical football fan builds up a pool of aggressive potential over the week, having been frustrated and mistreated by his boss, his family, and so on. This potentially harmful aggressiveness is then released every Sunday afternoon when he is able to watch and identify with the institutionalized aggression of pro football. He then walks away from the stadium or TV set a less aggressive man, ready to face the next week. Alfred Hitchcock has puckishly defended violent TV programs in the following manner: "One of television's great contributions is that it brought murder back into the home where it belongs. Seeing a murder on television can be good therapy. It can help work off one's antagonisms. If you haven't any antagonisms, the commercials will give you some" (from Schellenberg, 1970, p. 31).

But what if aggressive urges are not innate or instinctually determined? What if they are the result of socialization and learning experiences? Many social scientists feel that this latter position is true. They point out that humans are constantly learning from their environment. When a person witnesses an act of aggression, this provides him or her with a model of one way to behave. If the aggression is successful—that is, if the aggressive model obtains what he or she wanted by the use of aggression—is it not possible that the viewer will be *more* likely to become aggressive when he finds himself in a similar situation? If children are constantly exposed to violence on television, will they come to believe that it is commonplace, acceptable, or even desirable? Social psychology has accumulated a wealth of evidence that children learn from and imitate many behaviors that they see other people perform. Will this imitation take place in regard to the aggression viewed on television? Proponents of this viewpoint, which is often called the *modeling* position, argue that it will. In support of such a position, Berkowitz has commented that "For me at least, it is quite interesting that nobody has ever maintained that sexual desires can readily be satisfied through watching a couple make love. If aggressive urges are drained through seeing aggression, why aren't sexual urges lessened by watching sexual activity?" (in Larsen, 1968, p. 279).

The National Commission on the Causes and Prevention of Violence issued an official statement in September 1969 saying, in part:

> Children begin to absorb the lessons of television before they can read or write. . . . In a fundamental way, television helps to create what children expect of themselves and of others, and what constitutes the standards of civilized society. . . . Yet we daily permit our children during their formative years to enter a world of police interrogation, of gangsters beating enemies, of spies performing fatal brain surgery, of routine demonstrations of killing and maiming [from Siegel, 1970, p. 197].

This basic nature-nurture controversy, concerned with whether human aggression is largely innate or learned, is examined in the first article in this section, by Leonard Berkowitz of the University of Wisconsin. In discussing this issue, Berkowitz responds to the authors of several recent popular books on human aggression. These authors, Konrad Lorenz, Robert Ardrey, Desmond Morris, and Anthony Storr, all take the general position that human aggressive tendencies *are* largely innate and are parallel to aggressive tendencies in other animal species. Berkowitz, on the other hand, chides these authors for their "conceptual simplicity" and advocates the learning, or modeling, position.

The two remaining articles focus on the specific problem of the effects on children of observing aggression and violence. James Bryan and Tanis Schwartz, of Northwestern University, review the experimental research literature concerning the effects of film material on aggressive behavior in children. The reader is encouraged to decide whether the studies they review justify their conclusion (in a portion of the article not reprinted here) that "The catharsis principle has received scant support in the experimental literature, while a number of studies have suggested the facilitating effect of models upon aggressive behavior" (Bryan & Schwartz, 1971, p. 57).

Although our first two articles seem to suggest that the catharsis position is of dubious value at best, in the third article Seymour Feshbach and Robert D. Singer, of UCLA and the University of California at Riverside, respectively, describe the results of a longitudinal study on the relationship between the viewing of violent and nonviolent television programs and subsequent aggression. Since the excerpt from their book included in this section does not describe the methods and scope of the study, we will summarize their design. They studied boys in institutional settings (private boarding schools and boys' homes) in which the type of television program watched could be controlled. The boys were required to watch a minimum of six hours of television a week for six weeks. Feshbach and Singer's sample was large: 625 boys aged 8 to 18 participated in the study; complete data were available on 395 of them. Approximately half of the boys watched an "aggressive diet" of TV programs; the other half were allowed to watch only nonaggressive programs. A number of personality tests and attitude scales were administered at the beginning and end of the six-week experimental period. In addition, daily behavior-rating forms were completed for each boy for the experimental period and, in most instances, during the week before and the week after the six-week TV-viewing period. The majority of items on the behavior-rating forms related to aggressive acts.

The reader should keep in mind that the Feshbach and Singer study includes two important methodological characteristics that have *not* been utilized in most earlier studies of the effects of viewing aggression: the use of directly observed aggression (via the behavior-rating scales) and the use of regular TV watching over a reasonable period of time. We will discuss the impact and importance of such experimental studies in more detail in the Summary.

REFERENCES

Berkowitz, L. The effects of observing violence. *Scientific American,* 1964, **210** (February), 35–41.

Bryan, J. H. & Schwartz, T. Effects of film material upon children's behavior. *Psychological Bulletin,* 1971, **75**, 50–59.

Freud, S. *Beyond the pleasure principle.* New York: Bantam Books, 1959.

Larsen, O. N. (Ed.) *Violence and the mass media.* New York: Harper & Row, 1968.

Schellenberg, J. A. *An introduction to social psychology.* New York: Random House, 1970.

Siegel, A. E. Violence and aggression are not inevitable. In M. Wertheimer (Ed.), *Confrontation: Psychology and the problems of today.* Glenview, Ill.: Scott, Foresman, 1970. Pp. 196–199.

ARTICLE 19

Simple Views of Aggression:
An Essay Review

Leonard Berkowitz

The theme of this essay will be drawn from a dust jacket. On the back of the book *Human Aggression* by the British psychiatrist Anthony Storr, we find the following comment by Konrad Lorenz, widely renowned as the "father of ethology": "An ancient proverb says that simplicity is the sign of truth—and of fallacy . . . However, if the simple explanation is in full agreement with a wealth of data, and quite particularly, if it dovetails with data collected in altogether different fields of knowledge, simplicity certainly is indicative of truth." Four of the books reviewed here offer essentially simplistic messages. With the writers represented in the fifth work, I shall argue that the conceptual simplicity advocated by these volumes is definitely *not* "indicative of the truth." All of the books deal with man's capacity for violence, a problem deserving —no, demanding—careful and sophisticated consideration. The four volumes I shall concentrate on, those by Lorenz, Ardrey, Storr, and Morris—and especially the first three—provide only easy formulas readily grasped by a wide audience rather than the necessary close analysis. Being easily understood, their explanation of human aggression helps relieve the anxiety born of the public's concern with war, social unrest, race riots, and student protests, but is an inadequate, and perhaps even dangerous, basis for social policy.

All four voice essentially the same message:

Reprinted from *American Scientist,* 1969, **57**(3), 372–383, with the permission of the author and the Society of the Sigma Xi.

Much of human behavior generally, and human aggression in particular, must be traced in large part to man's animal nature. Aggression often arises for innately determined reasons, they say. The authors differ somewhat, however, in how they believe this nature leads to aggression. For Lorenz, Ardrey, and Storr (whom I shall refer to as the Lorenzians), a spontaneously engendered drive impels us to aggression, even to the destruction of other persons. Morris, on the other hand, views many of our aggressive acts as genetically governed responses to certain environmental conditions and to signals sent to us by other people. Nonetheless, over and above their similarities and differences, all four volumes present a highly simplified conception of the causes of and possible remedies for human aggression, and I think it would be well for us to look at a number of these misleading oversimplifications.

THE ROLE OF LEARNING IN HUMAN AGGRESSION

Facing the writers at their own level, one misconception I shall not deal with here is their relative neglect of the role of learning in human aggression. Our behavior is influenced by our experiences *and* our inherited biological characteristics. I have argued elsewhere that innate determinants do enter into man's attacks on others, primarily in connection with impulsive reactions to noxious events and frustrations. These constitutionally governed impulsive responses can be modified by learning, however. The Lorenzians do not appear to recognize this kind of modification in these volumes. They draw a very sharp distinction between learned and innately determined responses, thus ignoring what is now known of the complex interplay between nature and nurture. Lorenz has admitted this on occasion, and the journalist, Joseph Alsop, has recently reported him as saying, "We ethologists were mistaken in the past when we made a sharp distinction between 'innate' and 'learned.' " Of course, there is also an experience-is-all imperialism at the opposite extreme. In sharp contrast to many ethologists and zoologists, social scientists typically have long ignored and even denied the role of built-in, biological determinants. Ashley Montagu's critical discussion of Lorenz in his introduction to *Man and Aggression* is illustrative. "The notable thing about human behavior," he says, "is that it is learned. Everything a human being does as such he has had to learn from other human beings."

Some book reviewers for the popular press, aware of these opposing stances, have approached the present volumes in terms of this kind of polarization. *If* human aggressiveness is learned, Lorenz, *et al.,* are obviously incorrect, but on the other hand, innate determinants to aggression presumably must operate as described by Ardrey, Lorenz, Morris, and Storr. Ardrey, Lorenz, and Storr pose the issue in these simple terms. Critics dispute their views, they maintain, primarily because of a misguided "American optimism"; American social scientists, psychologists and psychiatrists, having a liberal belief in the perfectibility of man, want to attribute social ills—including violence—to environmental flaws which might be remedied rather than to intractable human nature. The critics certainly would recognize the existence of man's innate aggressive drive if they could only shed their honorable but mistaken vision of Utopia.

There are other alternatives, however. Some of human aggressiveness might derive from man's biological properties, characteristics which he shares to some degree with the other animals. He might even be innately "programmed" to respond violently to particular kinds of stimulation, much as other animals do. But his animal charac-

teristics do not have to function the way Lorenz and his associates say they do. The Lorenzian analysis of aggression can be criticized on a logical and empirical basis independently of any general assumptions about the nature of man.

The volume *Man and Aggression,* edited by Montagu, serves as a counterpoise to the Lorenzian books. A number of journalist-reviewers have assumed that Lorenz' views are shared by virtually all students of animal behavior. The Montagu volume clearly shows that there is not the unanimity of support that the laymen believe exists. Many eminent zoologists, as well as comparative psychologists, have taken Lorenz's analysis of aggression seriously to task. *Man and Aggression* is a compilation of generally damning criticisms of the Lorenz and Ardrey books by such authorities as S. A. Barnett, J. H. Crook, T. C. Schneirla, and Sir Solly Zuckerman, as well as Lorenz' old opponent, J. P. Scott. For those people who have read only the Lorenzian analyses, Lorenz may speak for all ethologists; Lorenz is equated with all of ethology in the Storr book, *Human Aggression.* Yet he is not all of the science of animal behavior, and there are many good reasons in the animal as well as human research literature to question the over-all thrust of Dr. Lorenz' argument on grounds besides the "overbold and loose" nature of the Lorenzian contentions generally recognized by many readers.

We need not here review the many objections to the Lorenz and Ardrey volumes that are summarized by the critics included in *Man and Aggression.* However, some of the oversimplifications and errors of reasoning and fact that are characteristic of these two books are also prevalent in the Storr and Morris works, and I think it is important to point out several of these common weaknesses in the extension of popular biology to human aggression.

THE USE OF ANALOGIES

As nearly every critic of these Lorenzian books has pointed out, the writers are excessively freewheeling in their use of analogies. They frequently attempt to explain various human actions by drawing gross analogies between these behaviors and supposedly similar response patterns exhibited by other animal species. Attaching the same label to these human and animal behaviors, the writers then maintain that they have explained the actions. For Lorenz, man is remarkably similar to the Greylag Goose. The resemblances (that occur to Lorenz but not necessarily to other observers) are supposedly far from superficial ones, and he believes that they can only be explained by the operation of the same mechanisms in man and goose. " . . . highly complex norms of behavior such as falling in love, strife for ranking order, jealousy, grieving, etc. are not only similar but down to the most absurd details the same . . . " and therefore, all of these actions must be governed by instincts.

The analogy emphasized by Ardrey, of course, is based on animal territoriality. Man's genetic endowment supposedly drives him to gain and defend property, much as other animals do, presumably because this territorial behavior provides identity, stimulation, and security. Basing part of his argument on a study of the lemurs of Madagascar, Ardrey contends that there are two types of societies, noyaux (societies said to be held together by the inward antagonism of the members) and nations (societies in which joint defense of territory has given rise to ingroup leadership and cooperation). The examples of noyaux listed by Ardrey include, in addition to the Madagascar lemurs, herring gull colonies, certain groups of gibbons, and Italy and France.

Morris' analogy, needless to say, is between humans and apes. His theme is that "*Homo sapiens* has remained a naked ape . . . in acquiring lofty new motives, he has lost none of the earthy old ones." We cannot understand the nature of our aggressive urges, he says along with Ardrey, Lorenz, and Storr, unless we consider "the background of our animal origins." Unlike the Lorenzians, however, he doubts the existence of an innate, spontaneous aggressive drive, and emphasizes, to the exclusion of such a drive, the genetically determined signals he believes both apes and people send to their fellows. All four authors make much of the control of aggression by supposedly innate appeasement gestures, although

Morris seems to have greater confidence in their efficacy than do the others. He even tells us how we should respond to an angry traffic policeman on the basis of this analogy between human and animal behaviors: The policeman's aggression can (theoretically) be turned off automatically by showing abject submission in our words, body postures, and facial expressions. Moreover, it is essential to "get quickly out of the car and move away from it towards the policeman." This prevents the policeman from invading our territory (our car) and weakens feelings of territorial rivalry. The looks people give each other are very important signals, Morris maintains in accord with a rapidly growing body of experimental-social psychological research, but, in contrast to these investigators, he oversimplifies greatly. Morris contends that prolonged looking at another is an aggressive act. In reality, persistent eye-contact can also be a very intimate, even sexual, encounter, or may arise from a search for information or social support.

This type of crude analogizing is *at best* an incomplete analysis of the behavior the writers seek to explain. Important data are neglected and vital differences are denied. J. H. Crook's excellent paper in *Man and Aggression* (which should be read by every person who has written a favorable review of the Lorenz and Ardrey books) notes the many important considerations omitted by the Lorenzians in general and Ardrey's treatment of territoriality in particular. Where Ardrey, following Lorenz, maintains that territorial behavior is a highly fixed, species-specific action pattern produced by energy accumulating in certain centers in the nervous system, the truth cannot be packaged as easily as this. Many different conditions enter into animal territoriality. The outcome is a complex interaction of ecological and social conditions with internal states so that territorial behavior is far from inevitable as a species characteristic. Territorial maintenance, furthermore, involves different components, such as attack and escape. These components are probably governed by somewhat different, although often interrelated, mechanisms, and appear to be susceptible to different environmental and internal conditions. Given these complexities and the multiplicity of factors involved in the territoriality displayed by birds, we cannot make simple statements about the functions and causes of territoriality even in these species, and it is highly unlikely that human concern with property is controlled by the same processes. Crook's conclusion is certainly reasonable: "The likelihood that the motivation control of territorial behavior is at a different level from that of fishes and birds suggests that human resemblances to the lower animals might be largely through analogy rather than homology." Sixteen years ago, Daniel Lehrman remarked, in an outstanding critique of Lorenzian theory, "it is not very judicious, and actually is rash ... to assume that the mechanisms underlying two similar response characteristics are in any way identical, homologous, or even similar," merely because the actions of different species or entities seem to resemble each other (in the eyes of the writer, we might add).

THE NOTION OF RITUALIZATION

The same comment can be made about the analogizing involved in Lorenz' and Storr's use of the notion of ritualization. Theorizing that there are evolutionary changes in behavior as well as structure, and that particular action patterns, such as appeasement gestures, have evolved from other behaviors, Lorenz argues that responses originally serving one function can undergo alteration in the course of evolution so that they come to have a different function as well. The drive or energy motivating the original action presumably still powers this altered behavior. According to Lorenz, the appeasement or greetings ceremonies performed by humans and animals alike have become ritualized in this manner through evolutionary developments but still make use of transformed aggressive motivation. Lorenz thinks that the smile of greeting, as an example, might have "evolved by ritualization of redirected threatening." Storr, adopting Lorenz' reasoning, also speaks of "ritualizing the aggressive drive in such a way that it serves the function of uniting" people. For both of these writers, diverted aggressive energy powers the social bonds which tie individuals together in affection and even love. Now, we must ask, is there really good reason to contend, as Lorenz does so authoritatively, that the human smile, the appeasement gesture of the macaques (baring the teeth), and the triumph ceremony of the geese must have evolved in the same way from some original aggressive display? The supposed similarity between the human, monkey, and goose behavior does not mean, as Lehrman pointed out, that the processes underlying these actions are "identical, homologous, or even similar." Elaborating further, in his essay in *Man and Aggression,* Barnett says there is no justification for the "confident, dogmatic assertions Lorenz and his followers have made about the hypothetical process, 'ritualization.' " Harlow's observations regarding monkey development are also troublesome for the Lorenzian analysis of the genesis of social bonds. Affectional patterns generally emerge *before* aggressive ones in these animals, making it unlikely that the earlier, affectional-social acts are "driven" by aggressive motivation.

The dangers of unwarranted analogizing can also be illustrated by referring to another example of "ritualization" mentioned by Storr. It appears that the Kurelu, a primitive people in the heart of New Guinea, engage in frequent intertribal warfare. But instead of killing one another, the warriors shoot arrows at each other from a distance just beyond arrow range and rarely hit each other. Although this type of warfare seems to resemble the threat ceremonies exhibited by a number of animal species, we certainly cannot argue that the Kurelu behavior and animal threats have evolved in exactly the same manner or are based on similar biological mechanisms. Furthermore, both action patterns may ultimately lead to a cessation of attacks—but probably for very different reasons. It is also improper to insist, as the Lorenzians do, that competitive sports are the same type of ritual as the Kurelu warfare and animal threats merely because some writers have applied the same label to all three sets of phenomena; the surface resemblances do not guarantee that all have the same evolutionary causes and that all operate in the same or even in a similar way.

When we come right down to it, there seems to be a kind of "word magic" in this analogizing. The writers appear to believe that they have provided an adequate explanation of the phenomenon at issue by attaching a label to it: a person's smile is an *appeasement gesture;* athletic events are *rituals* comparable to certain animal displays, etc. Storr shows just this kind of thinking in the "proof" he offers for the notion of a general aggressive drive. Aggression is not all bad, Storr insists (in agreement with Lorenz); aggression is necessary to the optimal development of man. It is "the basis of intellectual achievement, of the attainment of independence, and even of that proper pride which enables a man to hold his head high amongst his fellows." The evidence he cites for this statement is word usage: " . . . the words we use to describe intellectual effort are aggressive words. We *attack* problems, or *get our teeth* into them. We *master* a subject when we have *struggled with* and *overcome* its difficulties. We *sharpen* our wits . . . " (Italics in the original.) Waving his words over the particular behavior (in this case, striving for independence and achievement), he has thus supposedly accounted for these actions—and has also swept aside the many studies of achievement motivation by McClelland and his associates suggesting that there is very little similarity between the instigation to aggression and achievement motivation.

Popular discussions of the role of evolution in behavior can also be criticized on this basis. Even if it can be shown that a given behavior pattern has "evolved," such a demonstration does not explain the performance of that action by a particular individual in a specific setting. The application of the word "evolution" does not really help us to understand what mechanisms govern the behavior in this individual or what stimulus conditions affect these mechanisms.

INSTINCTIVE HUMAN ACTIONS

The Lorenzians (and Morris as well) also display this same word magic in the ease with which they refer to human actions as instinctive. Without taking the trouble to specify the criteria they employ in making their designations, they go scattering the label "instinct" around with great relish. As an illustration, in his book *On Aggression,* Lorenz talks about people having an "instinctive need to be a member of a closely knit group fighting for common ideals," and insists that "there cannot be the slightest doubt that militant enthusiasm is instinctive and evolved out of a communal defense response." Doubts must exist, however. The Lorenzians offer neither a precise definition of what they mean by "instinct" nor any substantial evidence that the behavior in question, whether human aggression or militant enthusiasm, is innate even in their vague usage of this term. Several of the writers in *Man and Aggression* (e.g., Barnett and Schneirla), as well as other scientists such as Lehrman, criticize Lorenz severely for his excessively casual employment of the instinct concept. Lorenz elsewhere has acknowledged this imprecision in his popular utterances (see, for example, the previously mentioned article by Alsop), saying that he has used the word only in a shorthand sense.

Nevertheless, the over-simplification regarding "instincts" so prevalent in the Lorenz-Ardrey-Storr writings is difficult to excuse as only shorthand. To say this is not to deny the role of innate processes in human behavior; such determinants apparently exist. Psychologists, together with other students of behavior, have shown, as an example, that human babies have a built-in preference for certain visual stimuli, and do not start with blank neural pages, so to speak, in learning to see and organize complex visual stimulation. The difficulty is that ideas such as Lorenz' "instinctive need to be a member of a closely knit group fighting for common ideals" are, in actuality, extremely drastic departures from the more precise instinct concept found in technical ethological discussions. When they write for an audience of their peers, ethologists generally describe instincts, or better still, instinctive movements, as behavioral sequences culminating in "fixed action patterns." These patterns, which are at the core of the instinct concept, are thought of as rigid and stereotyped species-specific *consummatory* responses generally serving to end a chain of ongoing behavior. Can this definition be applied to "militant enthusiasm"? What is the rigid and stereotyped action that unerringly unfolds to consummate the hypothetical enthusiasm pattern?

SPORTS AS OUTLETS FOR AGGRESSION

We now come to the most important part of the Lorenzian instinct conception, and the feature that has the gravest social implications: the supposed spontaneity of the behavior. The stereotyped instinctive action is said to be impelled by a specific energy that has accumulated in that part of the central nervous system responsible for the coordination of the behavior. The energy presumably builds up spontaneously and is discharged when the response is performed. If the instinctive activity is not carried out for a considerable period of time, the accumulated energy may cause the response to "pop off" *in vacuo.* Aggression, according to Lorenz, Ardrey, and Storr—but not Morris—follows this formula. "It is the spontaneity of the (aggressive) instinct," Lorenz tells us, "that makes it so dangerous." The behavior "can 'explode' without demonstrable external stimulation" merely because the internal accumulating energy has not been discharged by aggressive actions or has not been diverted into other response channels as, for example, in the case of such "ritualized" activities as sports. If violence is to be lessened, suitable outlets must be provided. Lorenz believes that "present-day civilized man suffers from insufficient discharge of his aggressive drive," and together with Ardrey and Storr, calls for more athletic competitions—bigger and better Olympic games. (Denying the Lorenzian formulation, Morris maintains that we do not have an inborn urge to destroy our opponents—only to dominate them—and argues that the only solution is "massive de-population" rather than "boisterous international football.")

This conception can be discussed at various levels. Neurologically, for one thing, Lorenz bases his assertions on observations regarding cardiac and respiratory activities and simple motor coordinations. With such critics as Lehrman and Moltz we must question whether or not these

findings can be extended to more complex neural organizations, to say nothing of human aggression. (The Lorenzian interpretation of these observations can also be disputed, as Moltz has shown in the 1965 *Psychological Review.*)

There are empirical difficulties as well as this problem of the long inductive leap. Basing their arguments on a number of studies, Hinde and Ziegler (the latter in an important 1964 *Psychological Bulletin* paper) have proposed that many apparent demonstrations of internally-driven spontaneity can be traced to external stimuli and the operation of associative factors. The responses evidently are evoked by environmental stimuli rather than being driven out by spontaneously accumulating internal excitation. Moltz has also summarized evidence disputing the Lorenzian notion that response performance is necessary if there is to be a reduction in the elicitability of the instinctive action pattern. As Hinde has suggested in several papers, stimulus satiation rather than a response-produced discharge of instinctive action-specific energy may cause a lessening in response elicitability.

COMPLEX ASPECTS OF ANIMAL AND HUMAN AGGRESSION

Going from the simple motor coordinations of the lower animals to the more complex aspects of animal and human aggression, the available data are even less kind to the Lorenzian formulation. Of course Lorenz maintains that his ideas are supported by a substantial body of observations. They are upheld, he says, by the failures of "an American method of education" to produce less aggressive children, even though the youngsters have been supposedly "spared all disappointments and indulged in every way." However, as I have pointed out elsewhere in discussing this argument, excessively indulged children probably expect to be gratified most of the time, so that the inevitable occasional frustrations they encounter are actually relatively strong thwartings for them. There is little doubt that these frustrations can produce aggressive reactions, and Lorenz' criticism of the frustration-aggression hypothesis is a very weak one. Belief in this hypothesis, by the way, does not necessarily mean advocating a completely frustration-free environment for children. Child specialists increasingly recognize that youngsters must learn to cope with and adapt to life's inescapable thwartings, and thus must experience at least some frustrations in the course of growing up. Nor do most contemporary psychologists believe that frustration is the only source of aggression. Violence can have its roots in pain as well as in obstacles to goal attainment, and can also be learned as other actions are learned.

Aggression, in other words, has a number of different causes, although the Lorenzians seem to recognize (or at least discuss) only one source. Here is yet another erroneous oversimplification: their notion of a unitary drive that is supposedly capable of powering a wide variety of behaviors from ritualized smiling to strivings for independence or dominance. This general drive conception is very similar to the motivational thinking in classical psychoanalysis, but is running into more and more difficulty under the careful scrutiny of biologists and psychologists. Indeed, contrary to Storr's previously cited argument, there is no single instigation to aggression even in the lower animals. Moyer recently has suggested (in the 1968 *Communications in Behavioral Biology*), on the basis of many findings, that there are several kinds of aggression, each of which has a particular neural and endocrine basis.

THE FLOW OF AGGRESSIVE ENERGY

Also like the traditional psychoanalysts, the Lorenzians speak loosely of aggressive energy flowing from one channel of behavior to another. This hypothetical process, mentioned earlier in conjunction with "ritualization," must be differentiated from the more precisely defined response-generalization concept developed by experimental psychologists. Reinforcements provided to one kind of reaction may strengthen other, similar responses. Rewarding a child for making aggressive remarks can increase the likelihood of other kinds of aggressive reactions as well. The reinforcement influence generalizes from one kind of response to another because the actions have something in common. (The actor might regard both types of responses as *hurting* someone.) It is theoretically unparsimonious and even inadvisable to interpret this effect as an energy transfer from one response channel to another. The Lorenz-Storr discussion of ritualization, and the related psychoanalytic concept of sublimation as well, employs just this kind of energy-diversion idea. We cannot here go into the conceptual pitfalls of this analytical model. (The interested reader might wish to read Hinde's article on energy models of motivation in the 1960 *Symposia of the Society for Experimental Biology*.) But there is a fairly obvious flaw in the Lorenzian statement that pent-up aggressive energy can be discharged in competitive sports. Rather than lessening violence, athletic events have sometimes excited supporters of one or both of the competing teams into attacking other persons. This has happened in many countries: in England, as Crook points out and as Storr should have recognized, in this country at times when white and Negro high school basketball teams have competed against each other, and most dramatically, this past March in Czechoslovakia when the Czechs defeated the Russians in hockey. In these cases, the team supporters were so aroused, even when their team won, that they were extremely responsive to aggressive stimuli in the environment.

Experimental tests of the hostility catharsis hypothesis also argue against the energy-diversion idea inherent in both Lorenzian and psychoanalytic theorizing. This well-worn notion maintains, of course, that the display of aggressive behavior in fantasy, play, or real life, will reduce the aggressive urge. Although there is no explicit reference to a catharsis process in Storr's book, his belief that aggressive energy can be sublimated certainly is consistent with the catharsis doctrine. Lorenz comes much closer to a frank acceptance of this idea in his contention that "civilized man suffers from insufficient discharge of his aggressive drive," and in a bit of advice he offers to people on expeditions to the remote corners of the world. Members of socially isolated groups, he says in *On Aggression,* must inevitably experience a build-up of aggressive drive; outsiders aren't available to be attacked and thus provide an outlet for the accumulating aggressive energy. If a person in such an isolated group wishes to prevent the intra-group conflict that otherwise must develop (Lorenz insists), he should smash a vase with as loud and resounding a crash as possible. We do not have to attack other people in order to experience a cathartic reduction in our aggressive urge; it's enough merely to destroy inanimate objects.

SUMMARY

Summarizing (and simplifying) a great many studies, research results suggest that angry people often do (a) feel better, and (b) perhaps even experience a temporarily reduced inclination to attack their tormentors, upon learning that these persons have been hurt. This phenomenon seems to be quite specific, however; the provoked individual is gratified when he finds that the intended target of his aggression has been injured, and does not appear to get the same satisfaction from attacks on innocent bystanders. Besides this, the apparent reduction in the instigation to aggression following an attack is probably often due to guilt- or anxiety-induced restraints evoked by the attack and/or the arousal of other, nonaggressive motives, and is not really the result of an energy discharge. Standard experimental-psychological analysis can do a far better job than the energy-discharge model in explaining the available data. Recent experiments indicate, for example, that the lessening of physiological tension produced by injuring the anger instigator comes about when the aggressor has learned that aggression is frequently rewarded. This tension reduction, or gratification, is evidently akin to a reinforcement effect, and is not indicative of any long-lasting decline in the likelihood of aggression; people who find aggression rewarding are more, not less, likely to attack someone again in the future. The reinforcement process can also account for the appetitive behavior Lorenz and Storr seem to regard as prime evidence for the existence of a spontaneous aggressive drive. Provoked animals will go out of their way to obtain suitable targets to attack, while youngsters who are frequently aggressive toward their peers generally prefer violent TV programs to more peaceful ones. But this search for an appropriate target or for aggressive scenes probably arises from the reinforcing nature of these stimuli rather than from some spontaneous drive, and again, does not mean that there has been an energy discharge when these stimuli are encountered. Quite the contrary. There is some reason to believe that the presence of such aggression-reinforcing stimuli as other people fighting can evoke aggressive responses from those who are ready to act aggressively— much as the sight of food (which is a reinforcement for eating) can elicit eating responses from those who are set to make such responses.

In the end, the Lorenzian analyses must be questioned because of their policy implications as well as because of their scientific inadequacies. Their reliance on casual anecdotes instead of carefully controlled, systematic data, their use of ill-defined terms and gross analogies, and their disregard of hundreds of relevant studies in the interest of an over-simplified theory warrant the disapproval generally accorded them by technical journals. But more than this, the Lorenz-Ardrey-Storr books can also have unfortunate social as well as scientific consequences by impeding recognition of the important roles played by environmental stimuli and learning in aggressive behavior, and by blocking awareness of an important social principle: Aggression is all too likely to lead to still more aggression.

REFERENCES

Ardrey, R. *The territorial imperative.* New York: Atheneum, 1966.

Lorenz, K. *On aggression.* New York: Harcourt Brace Jovanovich, 1966.

Montagu, M. F. A. (Ed.) *Man and aggression.* New York: Oxford University Press, 1968.

Morris, D. *The naked ape.* New York: McGraw-Hill, 1968.

Storr, A. *Human aggression.* New York: Atheneum, 1968.

ARTICLE 20

Effects of Film Material upon Children's Behavior[1]

James H. Bryan and Tanis Schwartz

This paper reviews recent studies concerning the influence of film material (television and movies) upon human behavior. Considerable data now exist relevant to these effects, much of which is recent and worthy of review. The present effort is limited to those investigations directly addressed to the role of films in affecting socially sanctioned behaviors such as aggression and altruism. Those studies pertaining to the content of film and television entertainment or those addressed to the demographic or personality characteristics associated with viewing habits are not included. The focus is upon experimental studies conducted within laboratory settings.

AGGRESSION

Most experimental studies have given attention to the effects of film upon aggressive behaviors. This focus seems particularly relevant not only because of its social significance, but because of the frequency of such themes within film presentations (Berkowitz, 1962).

Discussion of the impact of aggressive film content upon behavior has been dominated by the now-old controversy concerning the notion of catharsis. The evidence suggests, however, that the

Abridged from *Psychological Bulletin*, **75**, 1971, 50–59. Copyright 1971 by the American Psychological Association, and reproduced by permission of the authors and the publisher.

[1]Parts of this effort were supported by the National Institute of Child Health and Human Development, under Research Grant 1R01HD03234.

witnessing of symbolic aggression (e.g., films) will increase aggressive propensities, both for children and adults, as predicted from social learning theory (Bandura, 1969). Walters, Llewellyn-Thomas, and Acker (1962) found that male hospital attendants who had seen an aggressive fight scene would give stronger electric shocks for longer durations to the experimenter's accomplice than attendants who had viewed a film of innocuous teenage activities. Berkowitz and Geen (1966) exposed 88 male college undergraduates to one of two films. One group viewed a film of a prize fight scene from the movie *The Champion,* the other an exciting movie of a track meet. Using the same measure of effects as Walters et al. (administering electric shocks), subjects, previously insulted by the experimenter, who had viewed the fight scene and whose target was similar by name to that of the film's victim, gave more electric shocks than control subjects. They thus suggest those particular characteristics of person and film which may trigger aggressive acts by the viewer. These conditions are reviewed subsequently.

The impact of television models upon behavior has not been limited to the responses of adults. Bandura, Ross, and Ross (1963a) compared the effectiveness of real-life aggressive models, filmed models, or a filmed model dressed as a cat (presumably analogous to a cartoon figure) upon the aggressive behavior of nursery school children. A control group witnessed no film, but was frustrated in the same manner as experimental subjects. Observations of the children's imitation of highly novel forms of aggressive behavior as well as nonimitative aggression were made by two judges while the child was in a setting other than that in which he viewed the films. The authors reported that any exposure to an aggressive model—be it a live, filmed, or cartoon figure—increased the viewer's total aggressive behavior toward inanimate objects. All models had a significant effect in evoking imitation of novel forms of aggression, the most influential being the live model. The film model was not more effective than the cartoon figure in altering imitative aggression. The three types of models did not differ in their impact upon total aggression or more specific types of specific imitative aggressive performance.

Since the measures of aggression were striking a toy doll, shooting a toy pistol, verbal imitation of aggressive themes, and shooting darts, Aronfreed (1968) has suggested that such behavior reflected play, not anger. While this may be true, Bandura et al. (1963a) speculated that most aggressive behavior may be learned for "prosocial" purposes, and they suggested that high arousal produced, for example, by frustration, may elicit overlearned responses, and thus may be employed in the service of aggressive goals. If they are right, Aronfreed's criticism becomes irrelevant.

While Bandura et al. (1963a) have demonstrated the generalization of imitative aggression across situations, Mussen and Rutherford (1961) found that the objects of aggression need not be those originally presented as the filmed model's target. They found that verbal statements by first-grade boys and girls suggesting their desire to destroy a balloon were increased after exposure to a cartoon film showing aggressive behavior by animated animals and flowers. However, one can reasonably challenge the degree to which verbalizations of "pop" reflect behavioral dispositions towards aggressive actions. Unfortunately, their experimental design did not allow for a motoric expression of such a disposition.

Two experiments have been conducted concerning the role of film models in affecting children's aggressive behavior directed toward other persons. While evidence exists concerning the role of symbolic models in affecting assaults upon a variety of inanimate objects and verbal expressions of such intents, few experiments have employed another human as the object of children's aggression. Siegel (1956) exposed children between the ages of 3.9 and 5.1 years to two cartoons, one emphasizing aggression (Woody Woodpecker), the other lacking such a theme (Little Red Hen). The order of film presentation was counterbalanced with a week's separation between the occasion of exposure and testing. Each child was rated as to his aggressive behavior toward a peer by a judge who was unfamiliar with the treatment conditions after each film showing. No film effects were found. In a later experiment, Hanratty, Liebert, Morris, and Fernandez[2] found that children are more likely to emit assaultive behavior toward a person dressed as a Bobo doll after having viewed a filmed model aggress against an actual Bobo. Thus, it appears that aggressive responses of children that are provoked by a filmed model can be directed toward living as well as inanimate objects.

There is reason to believe that preferences concerning the viewing of aggressive activity can be altered through films. Lovaas (1961) found that 4- to 6-year-olds, from low-income families, preferred witnessing one doll striking another doll to a nonaggressive scene after viewing a film demonstrating aggressive acts.

While it does appear likely that aggressive themes can elicit aggression or dissipate inhibitions concerning such acts, it is important to determine those conditions within the film which heighten its effects. Berkowitz and Rawlings (1963) exposed male and female undergraduate students to either an anger-provoking or a neutral experience and then to a film of a prize fight in which the aggression was either "justified" or not on the basis of instructions concerning the victim's character. Anger toward the experimenter, as indexed by one of two questionnaire items, was increased if the subject was made angry toward

[2]Hanratty, M. A., Liebert, R. M., Morris, L. W., & Fernandez, L. E. Imitation of film-mediated aggression against live and inanimate victims. Paper presented at the meeting of The American Psychological Association, Washington, D. C., September 1969.

the experimenter prior to the film and had witnessed a "justified" aggression. As the authors pointed out, the "just desserts" rationale for aggression may be a powerful disinhibitor of such behavior by the viewer.

Consequences of the aggressive action of the filmed model will also affect the children's imitation of that model. Bandura, Ross, and Ross (1963b) exposed nursery school children to one of the several types of films depicting a controversy among two children concerning one child's toys. One film showed a boy hitting and kicking the owner, and, as a result, subsequently possessing the toy and receiving other rewards (cookies, toys, and a coke). The film terminated with the announcer indicating that the boy was the "victor." A second group viewed a film demonstrating a repulsed attack with the aggressing child losing his bid for possession of the rewards. Another group of children witnessed a third film showing the two television models playing vigorously but not aggressively, while a fourth group of subjects did not view any film presentations. Imitation of aggression, as measured by observation of the child's unsupervised play behavior in a setting other than the original experimental setting, was significantly altered by the films. Children who saw the model engage in a successful theft displayed significantly more aggression than children in the other three groups. Unfortunately, the experimental design was such as to allow a confounding of obtained resources with differential-affect arousal and perhaps experimenter approval. The rewarded aggression scene showed the victor as quite happy, while the successful defender was portrayed as being affectively neutral. While this arrangement is perhaps more analogous to real life than that which would show an affectively neutral aggressor obtaining the new resources, it does confuse the effects of obtained rewards with those produced by empathic responses. Given the importance of empathy in guiding children's behavior (Aronfreed, 1968; Midlarsky & Bryan, 1967), such a confound would seem a serious one. It is perhaps because of this differential affect arousal that children did not imitate the successful defender while

imitating the successful thief. Additionally, though details are lacking, the experimenter appeared to praise the successful aggressor but not the unsuccessful one. Interestingly, children indicated in a postexperimental interview that they esteemed the aggressive model and disparaged the victim under those conditions where rewards were given for the aggression. Apparently, some children reasoned that the victim deserved such treatment because of his selfishness and his lack of ability to control the aggressor. According to the viewer, the defeated victim was culpable for having lost. On the other hand, children morally condemned the unsuccessful thief. Whether such judgments of the models were the result of dissonance reduction, as the authors suggested, or conformity to the judgments expressed by the film announcer, or due to differential affect arousal, cannot be determined.

A relationship between success and emulation was also reported by Albert (1957). He exposed 8- to 10-year-old children to one of three conditions. In one film, Hopalong Cassidy behaved aggressively and successfully against the villain. A second film depicted the same sequence with the exception that Cassidy lost the fight by being shot by the villain, while the third film demonstrated the fight scene without a resolution. Using the Rosenzweig Picture-Frustration Test to measure the child's extrapunitiveness, aggression scores increased from the pretest measure only under those conditions in which Cassidy was successful. The outcome of aggression was again demonstrated to alter aggressive verbal behavior.

The importance of obtained resources in affecting children's judgments of the attraction of the model is demonstrated in a study by Zajonc (1954), using a different medium, the comic book. In that experiment, 10- to 14-year-old children esteemed the hero on the basis of the hero's success in meeting a crisis rather than his assumption of either an affiliative and cooperative interaction or a power-oriented position vis-à-vis his subordinates. One might reasonably challenge Zajonc's assumption concerning the degree to which power orientations of an adult in a crisis significantly depart from commonly accepted social norms held by children. No independent measures of children's reactions to these orientations were obtained.

In a recent experiment (Bryan[3]), 7-year-old children viewed one of three filmed scenes. In one, a 9-year-old girl forcibly confiscated candy from a 7-year-old girl; in another, the oldest model unsuccessfully attempted to take the younger child's goods, while a third film depicted a cooperative interaction with no transgressions. Viewers were asked to make judgments concerning the oldest model and her desirability on such dimensions as niceness, naughtiness, likableness, as a playmate, sibling, and object of emulation. Children rejected both the unsuccessful and successful transgressor, but were significantly more critical of the latter. The results thus contrast with those reported by Bandura et al. (1963b) and perhaps those reported by Zajonc (1954). These conflicting results may be attributable to a number of methodological differences, including the gender of the transgressing models, age of viewers, the opportunity to imitate socially inappropriate behaviors, experimenter reaction to the transgression, the magnitude of the "sin" involved, and victim responses.

Another dimension of film which may bear an important role in affecting aggressive behavior is the similarity of the filmed scene or characters with those of the viewer (Feshbach, 1961). Berkowitz and Geen (1966) showed that frustrated subjects would administer stronger and longer electric shocks to another person than control subjects after observing a film in which the victim of the aggression bore the same name as the subject's frustrator. Hicks (1965) exposed 3- to 6-year-old children to a film depicting an adult male or female, or a peer male or female, assaulting an inflated plastic doll. In the same manner as the experimental groups, a group of children were frustrated prior to test trials, but saw no film. Two judges observed the viewer's imitative aggressive responses to the plastic doll. Both the main effects of film and viewer gender were sig-

nificant. However, no significant interaction of sex of subject and sex of model was found. The imitative aggression of subjects witnessing the peer male aggressor was significantly greater than of those who viewed the adult male or the peer female model conditions. When compared to the control subjects, all varieties of models significantly increased imitative performance. Not surprisingly, a 6-month follow-up found no lasting effects of the film models upon these responses.

Recently, studies have been conducted to establish those viewer traits which interact with aggressive film themes to facilitate subsequent aggressive action by the observer. Of the viewer characteristics related to aggressive behavior, the most important appears to be frustration and its correlate, aggression. Feshbach (1961) has added new complexity to the catharsis concept by suggesting that the subject's experience of vicarious aggression will reduce subsequent aggressive action only if he is angered at the time of the film presentation. He found that previously angered college students exposed to a fight film were less likely to emit aggressive words on a word-association test administered by the insulting experimenter than subjects not so angered, or than those exposed to the aggressive film scenes without being frustrated. Berkowitz and Rawlings (1963) have suggested that subjects in the insult group exposed to the aggressive film may not have felt that the filmed aggression was justified and thus became more inhibited about such behavior than the noninsulted group. The description of the scene did not include sufficient details to evaluate this possibility. Virtually all other investigations of the interaction of anger with film-instigated aggression suggest that frustrated subjects may be particularly likely to show an increase in such responses following a film depicting violence.

While frustration may not be a necessary condition for eliciting aggression (see Walters et al., 1962), it certainly does serve as an instigator to it. As reported earlier, Berkowitz and Geen (1966) found that angered males gave longer and stronger electric shocks to another if they had been negatively evaluated (as indexed by seven

[3]Bryan, J. H. Children's judgments of successful and unsuccessful televised social transgressors. Unpublished manuscript, Northwestern University, 1969.

electric shocks) rather than positively evaluated (as indexed by a single shock) by him, at least under those conditions where the eventual target of aggression had the same name as the victim in the film. Moreover, Berkowitz and Rawlings (1963) found that subjects, insulted by the experimenter prior to exposure to the aggressive film, indicated greater personal rejection of that experimenter than subjects insulted but not exposed to a violent film scene, or those exposed to the scene without being previously demeaned.

Maccoby, Levin, and Selya (1955) have demonstrated that frustration affects the subjects' recall of aggressive behaviors. Fifth- and sixth-grade children, matched on sex and intelligence, were frustrated or not frustrated by means of a rigged spelling bee, and then were exposed to filmed aggression. A week later the children who had been frustrated were found to recall better than nonfrustrated children the film's central aggressive themes, such as the identity of the aggressor. Interestingly, however, the nonfrustrated children had better recall than their frustrated counterparts, for both the incidental details of the aggression (such as the position of incidental characters) and nonaggressive content. In a follow-up investigation employing children from a semirural region, these results were not replicated.

While some studies have failed to find sex differences in film-mediated aggression (Berkowitz & Rawlings, 1963; Mussen & Rutherford, 1961), several experiments have reported that boys are more likely than girls to both demonstrate film-produced aggression (Bandura et al., 1963a; Hicks, 1965) and to better recall aggressive content (Maccoby & Wilson, 1957). Since children of both sexes were exposed to both aggressive boy and girl models in studies by Bandura et al. (1963a) and Hicks (1965), and sex differences in imitative aggression were found, but not a model by sex of subject interaction, it seems reasonable to assume that gender role rather than identificatory objects (model-subject similarity) within the film inhibited the female's aggressive behavior.

While such other personal characteristics of respondents as intelligence (Himmelweit, Oppenheim, & Vince, 1958; Schramm, Lyle, & Parker, 1961), social class (Maccoby, 1954), age (Hale, Miller, & Stevenson, 1968), and personal adjustment (Bailyn, 1959; Maccoby, 1954) have been correlated with various aspects of television viewing, it is yet to be determined that any are important influences upon imitative aggression of film models. Thus, while gender roles and frustration appear to play an important role in imitation of aggressive models, such typically powerful variables as intelligence and social class generally have been ignored in laboratory studies.

REFERENCES

Albert, R. S. The role of mass media and the effect of aggressive film content upon children's aggressive responses and identification choices. *Genetic Psychology Monographs,* 1957, **55,** 221–285.

Aronfreed, J. *Conduct and conscience.* New York: Academic Press, 1968.

Bailyn, L. Mass media and children: A study of exposure habits and cognitive effects. *Psychology Monographs,* 1959, **73**(1, Whole No. 471).

Bandura, A. Social learning theory of identificatory processes. In D. A. Goslin & D. C. Glass (Eds.), *Handbook of socialization theory and research.* Chicago: Rand-McNally, 1969.

Bandura, A., Ross, D., & Ross, S. Imitation of film-mediated models. *Journal of Abnormal and Social Psychology,* 1963, **66,** 3–11. (a)

Bandura, A., Ross, D., & Ross, S. Vicarious reinforcement and imitative learning. *Journal of Abnormal and Social Psychology,* 1963, **67,** 601–608. (b)

Berkowitz, L. *Aggression.* New York: McGraw-Hill, 1962.

Berkowitz, L., & Geen, R. Film violence and the cue properties of available targets. *Journal of Personality and Social Psychology,* 1966, **3,** 525–530.

Berkowitz, L., & Rawlings, E. Effect of film violence on inhibitions against subsequent aggression. *Journal of Abnormal and Social Psychology,* 1963, **66,** 405–412.

Feshbach, S. The stimulating versus cathartic effects of a vicarious aggressive activity. *Journal of Abnormal and Social Psychology,* 1961, **63,** 381–385.

Hale, G., Miller, L., & Stevenson, H. Incidental learning of film content: A developmental study. *Child Development,* 1968, **39,** 69–79.

Hicks, D. Imitation and retention of film-mediated aggressive peer and adult models. *Journal of Personality and Social Psychology,* 1965, **2,** 97–100.

Himmelweit, H., Oppenheim, A. N., & Vince, P. *Television and the child.* London: Oxford University Press, 1958.

Lovaas, O. I. Effect of exposure to symbolic aggression of aggressive behavior. *Child Development,* 1961, **32,** 37–44.

Maccoby, E. Why do children watch television? *Public Opinion Quarterly,* 1954, **18,** 239–244.

Maccoby, E., Levin, H., & Selya, B. Effects of emotional arousal on retention of aggressive and non-aggressive movie content. *American Psychologist,* 1955, **10,** 359. (Abstract)

Maccoby, E., & Wilson, W. C. Identification and observational learning from film. *Journal of Abnormal and Social Psychology,* 1957, **55,** 76–87.

Midlarsky, E., & Bryan, J. H. Training charity in children. *Journal of Personality and Social Psychology,* 1967, **5,** 408–415.

Mussen, P. H., & Rutherford, E. Effects of aggressive cartoons on children's aggressive play. *Journal of Abnormal and Social Psychology,* 1961, **62,** 461–464.

Schramm, W., Lyle, J., & Parker, E. *Television in the lives of our children.* Stanford, Calif.: Stanford University Press, 1961.

Siegel, A. Film-mediated fantasy aggression and strength of aggressive drive. *Child Development,* 1956, **27,** 365–378.

Walters, R. H., Llewellyn-Thomas, E., & Acker, C. W. Enhancement of punitive behavior by audiovisual displays. *Science,* 1962, **135,** 872–873.

Zajonc, R. Some effects of the "space" serials. *Public Opinion Quarterly,* 1954, **18,** 367–374.

ARTICLE 21

Television and Aggression: An Experimental Field Study

Seymour Feshbach and Robert D. Singer

CONCLUSIONS

The experimental results are, on the whole, consistent, and some of the findings, particularly those bearing on the acting out of aggression, are striking. The most modest conclusion we can make from the data is that exposure to aggressive content in television over a six-week period does not produce an increment in aggressive behavior. The only measure on which the controls decreased relative to the aggressive TV group was fantasy aggression. About all one can state regarding this latter finding is that boys who witness mostly nonaggressive content in television make up fewer stories in which fighting takes place than boys who watch a great deal of fighting on television. The results, in fact, indicate that witnessing aggressive TV programs reduces rather than stimulates the acting out of aggressive tendencies in certain types of boys. This generalization requires qualification, particularly in regard to the populations to which it applies. The effect is pronounced in children with certain personality and social characteristics and is weak or absent in other personality constellations. We need also to examine the conditions of the experiment and consider possible alternate explanations of the findings. Nevertheless, what is most compelling about the data is the regularity with which

Excerpted from S. Feshbach and R. D. Singer, *Television and Aggression: An Experimental Field Study.* San Francisco: Jossey-Bass, Inc., 1971. Pp. 140–146. Reprinted with the permission of the authors and Jossey-Bass, Inc.

the obtained differences in aggressive behaviors and changes in aggressive attitudes and values point to a reducing or controlling rather than to a stimulating or disinhibiting effect of exposure to aggressive interaction in television programs.

Since a fairly detailed analysis of the data was undertaken and since there are exceptions to the overall generalization, a brief review of the specific findings may be helpful: Boys exposed to aggressive TV content manifested significantly less behavioral aggression toward peers and authority than boys exposed to nonaggressive TV content. For convenience, this finding will be referred to as the experimental effect. The experimental effect holds only for residents of the boys' homes, there being little difference in aggression toward peers and toward authority between control and aggressive TV groups in the private schools. Among the boys' home residents, the aggressive TV group manifested less physical and verbal aggression toward peers than did the controls. There were also highly reliable differences between the controls and the aggressive TV groups in physical and verbal aggression toward authority. The trend analysis revealed a significant decline in authority aggression in boys' home residents exposed to the aggressive diet, the difference in linear trend between the aggressive TV and control groups being highly reliable for the verbal aggression toward authority factor. There was a large initial difference on the verbal aggression toward peers factor between the aggressive TV and control groups. Although the difference is not statistically reliable (at the .05 level) and may in part reflect the influence of the experimental treatment, it could have affected the findings for this factor. However, when the population was divided into three groups on the basis of their initial peer aggression scores, the experimental effect was still obtained on at least one behavior dimension for each of the three levels of aggression.

Age does not appear to be an important variable, although the most reliable experimental effects for the boys' home sample were obtained for high school students and the next most reliable for elementary school students. The differences between the aggressive TV and control groups for the junior high sample are in the same direction as the other comparisons but are not statistically reliable. Of particular interest is the suggested reversal of the experimental effect in the private school sample for junior high school boys on the physical aggression toward authority factor. In view of the overwhelming number of nonsignificant findings obtained for the private school sample, it is reasonable to attribute to chance such occasional evidence of a significant difference. Nevertheless, because of the social implications of these results, special attention should be given to deviant findings. Within the boys' home population, the experimental effect is strongest for boys high in overt and covert hostility, high in peer nomination for aggression, high in neurotic undercontrol, and low in aggression anxiety. That is, exposure to aggressive content in television produces a decrement in aggression relative to exposure to nonaggressive television in boys who have strong aggressive tendencies coupled with weak inhibitory and ego controls. The one exception to this pattern is fantasy aggression, boys below the median in fantasy aggression being most reliably and strongly affected by exposure to the aggressive or the control diet. In both boys' home and private school samples, the controls manifested a significantly greater increase in aggressive values than did the aggressive TV groups for boys high in overt hostility and high in peer aggression nominations. When personality factors are not taken into ac-

count, the differences between the aggressive TV and control groups are insignificant.

In both boys' home and private school samples, the controls manifested a significantly greater increase in aggressive options on the situation test than did the aggressive TV group. These data suggest that at least some boys in the private schools displayed a response to the experimental treatment similar to that of the boys' home residents. Again, the experimental effect measure is strongest for subjects high in peer nominations of aggression. Also, the increment in the control group is significantly greater than the increment in the aggressive TV group in boys high in aggression anxiety and in boys low in fantasy aggression. No significant differences between the aggressive TV and control groups were found on the aggressive activity preference measure. Differences in changes in severity of sentence advocated for a delinquent were small but in a direction consistent with the other experimental findings. When personality variables are taken into account, the control mean increment tends to be greater than the aggressive TV mean increment for boys high in neurotic undercontrol, low in overt hostility, high in covert hostility, and low in fantasy aggression. Significant differences between aggressive TV and control groups on the peer nomination of aggression measure were obtained only for some personality groups. Reliably greater increments in peer nominations for aggression in the controls than in the aggressive TV group were manifested in the low aggression anxiety, high fantasy aggression subsample in the boys' homes. A similar effect was obtained for low overt hostility boys for the combined boys' homes and private school population.

In contrast to the changes shown on the other dependent measures, the controls manifested a significantly greater decrement in fantasy aggression than did the aggressive TV group. The trends were similar for both boys' homes and private schools, the differences being most pronounced in boys above the median for several of the initial measures of aggressive disposition. Responses to the viewing habits measure, administered at the beginning and conclusion of the experiment, on which participants expressed their degree of liking for six TV shows with aggressive content and six programs with primarily nonaggressive content, indicated preference for aggressive programs, although nonaggressive programs were also liked. In addition, the boys' home controls showed an increase in liking of this selected sample of nonaggressive shows following their experimental experience. This effect is strongest for boys who were initially above the median on the peer nomination measure of aggression. The experimental variation in TV diet had little effect on the behavior rating scores of children in boys' homes who were initially high in fantasy aggression and low in overt hostility, but tended to produce strong differences in boys low in fantasy aggression and high in overt hostility. The findings were very similar when the peer aggression nomination index instead of the overt hostility questionnaire was used as the measure of manifest aggressive tendencies. However, private school boys who were initially high in fantasy aggression and high in peer aggression nominations displayed significantly more verbal aggression toward authority figures when exposed to aggressive content in television than when exposed to nonaggressive content. Significant differences were not obtained on other behavior comparisons for this personality subgroup. In addition opposite effects were obtained on some of the before-after change score measures, suggesting again that the occasional finding of a significant effect in the private schools is a chance effect.

Using responses to the list of six aggressive and six nonaggressive TV shows to establish initial frequency of TV viewing, we found that the experimental differences in the behavior rating scores were at least as strong for those boys in the boys' homes who had watched relatively little television as for those boys who were average or high in the frequency with which they had viewed TV before initiation of the experiment. Ratings submitted for the programs viewed indicated that both the control and aggressive TV subjects liked a substantial majority of the programs they observed.

The interpretation of these findings is constrained by the particular methodological approach which was taken in investigating the effects of violence in television and by cultural variables which characterize the population from which the experimental samples were drawn. In the design of this study, it was decided to use as experimental materials standard television fare rather than specially constructed or selected programs. In so doing, we sacrificed control of the structure, format, and precise content of the experimental stimuli but gained in representativeness and the extent to which the findings can be generalized to the kinds of programs that are presented on television. This generalization also implies a restriction. The aggressive content which the boys witnessed by no means encompassed the full range of violence and brutality that it is possible to depict on film or videotape. It may be that programs in which particular forms of aggression and brutality are rampant and are reinforced would have different effects than the programs observed by the aggressive TV group. These data apply only to the aggressive material that is portrayed on television in this country, or, to be more specific, in southern California and greater New York.

Generalization about the effects of these programs is further limited by the six-week duration of the experiment. A longer period could conceivably have resulted in the elimination of differences between the experimental and control groups and perhaps even in a reversal of trends. This latter possibility seems most unlikely. There are no indications of a trend which if extrapolated would result in the aggressive TV group manifesting more aggression than the control group did. A longer duration might exaggerate the differences between the experimental and control groups and would very likely produce boredom and indifference in both. The question of the effects of the length of duration of the experimental period is a different question from that of the length of time to which children in this culture are exposed to violence on television. Our experimental sample was drawn from a population that has had a history of exposure to television and to other mass media. We began with boys who had already been conditioned by their society and then considered the behavioral consequences of systematic variation of their subsequent experiences. How this experimental variation would influence children from a different culture or children who have never been previously exposed to television or films or preschool and primary grade children are questions to which the present study was not addressed.

Within the restrictions of sample characteristics, range of stimuli utilized, and duration of the experiment, two major conclusions are indicated by the experimental findings: First, exposure to aggressive content in television does not lead to an increase in aggressive behavior. Second, exposure to aggressive content in television seems to reduce or control the expression of aggression in aggressive boys from relatively low socioeconomic backgrounds.

The first conclusion is a weaker inference than the second. Although a negative assertion or statement of no difference tends to have little theoretical import, its applied or social implications may have considerable significance. The major question that arises in evaluating any such assertion is methodological, particularly in regard to the reliability of the measures, their sensitivity to changes, and the degree in which the laboratory procedure relates to the real life phenomena of interest. The measures employed were in fact sufficiently reliable and sensitive to record significant effects of the experimental treatment. As for the degree to which the experiment reflects normal phenomena, a salient feature of the experimental design was the degree of representativeness achieved by incorporating experimental control into a field setting. The manipulation of aggressive content was accomplished by controlling exposure to regular television programs. The effectiveness of this controlled variation is reflected by the fact that the great majority of programs which each group watched were in accord with their experimental assignment. The import of the observed changes in aggression can be questioned in view of the gap between aggressive action and the measures of aggressive value and

aggressive fantasy, although the latter are still of great interest. However, the ratings of peer and authority aggression were addressed to precisely the kinds of behaviors which are of social concern.

SECTION SUMMARY

The results of the study carried out by Feshbach and Singer seem to run counter to the general trends outlined by Bryan and Schwartz in the second article. Feshbach and Singer describe two major findings: (1) exposure to aggressive content in television did *not* lead to an increase in aggressive behavior in the boys they studied, and (2) exposure to aggressive content in television seemed to reduce or control the expression of aggression in aggressive boys from relatively low socioeconomic backgrounds. These trends would seem to lend support to the notion of innate aggressive tendencies and to the concept of catharsis. Yet the articles by Bryan and Schwartz and by Berkowitz strongly suggest that there is much more evidence to support the modeling position than to support the catharsis position. Where does the real answer lie?

Jerome L. Singer (1971, p. 37) has summarized the results of studies on children's imitation of live or film-mediated models as follows: (1) The evidence seems clear that nursery-school-aged children do imitate the aggressive behavior of adults or cartoon-type figures observed live or on film. (2) This imitation often takes the form of rather direct imitation but also may involve the expression of more general aggressive patterns. (3) The observation of film-mediated aggression leads to imitation, especially if: (a) the model is not punished, (b) the model is of the same sex as the child, (c) the child is moderately frustrated, and (d) no disapproval of the model's behavior is provided by adults in the child's presence.

There are a number of limitations on such generalizations, however. These limitations stem from the nature of the research studies carried out and may shed some light on the apparent discrepancy between the findings described by Bryan and Schwartz and those described by Feshbach and R. Singer. First of all, most studies of children have involved nursery-school children of predominantly middle-class backgrounds. Such children may be particularly compliant imitators of adult models. Second, the measures of aggression employed have usually involved play situations and attacks on inanimate objects. It is an open question whether aggressive play is at all the same as direct assault on another child.

Further, a "one-shot" viewing of a film of an aggressive model in the laboratory is simply not the same thing as television viewing over an extended period of time. Not only is the time factor much different, but the complexity of the television stimulus is considerably greater. Many "messages" come from television viewing; not all are violent, and some may even be antiviolent (see J. Singer, 1971, for extended discussions of these points).

The Feshbach-R. Singer study differed from the nursery-school studies on all these points. Their subjects were older, were of varying socioeconomic status, and were observed for an entire six-week period. In addition, measures of subjects' direct interpersonal aggression in the real world were obtained. Finally, the artificiality of their field study (see Section 1 of this book) was presumably considerably less than in many of the laboratory studies involving either nursery-school children or college students.

It should also be noted, however, that methodological difficulties and shortcomings are more likely to occur in large-scale field studies than in carefully controlled laboratory investigations. For example, is it possible that youths watching "nonviolent" television programs might become more aggressive because of their frustration at being deprived of their favorite (violent) programs? Feshbach and Singer do not think that this was the case in their study. But it is interesting to note that the investigators were forced to include *Batman* (certainly a violent program) among the TV programs seen by *both* groups because the youths on the "nonviolent diet" protested so loudly when it was initially omitted

from their programming.* Another factor that makes interpretations difficult is the fact that only six hours a week of TV viewing time was controlled by the experimenters. What type of TV were the youths watching on their own time? Although the amount of time they were allowed to watch TV varied from institution to institution, the youths had unlimited viewing privileges in some institutions. Were youths in the nonviolent group more likely to watch violent programs on their own time, to "make up" for the violent programming that they had been "deprived" of?

The issue of the effect of witnessed aggression on future behavior is obviously of great complexity. Difficulties in determining a clear-cut answer are perhaps increased by the fact that sociopolitical values and vested interests are of such importance in this area. Television and movie executives are naturally very much concerned with any research and theorizing that may threaten their livelihood. At the other pole, abhorrence of violence in any form is an article of faith to many people of particular sociopolitical persuasions. Neither of these orientations is conducive to the operation of solid, objective scientific research, since each suggests the likelihood of making prejudgments before the facts are in or of interpreting existing findings in a nonobjective manner.

A vivid example of the way in which vested interests and values can hamper scientific research is provided by the case of the Surgeon General's Scientific Advisory Committee on Television and Social Behavior. In 1969 the chairman of the Senate Subcommittee on Communications asked the Department of Health, Education, and Welfare (HEW) to appoint a blue-ribbon committee "to devise techniques and to conduct a study . . . which will establish scientifically insofar as possible what harmful effects, if any, these (violent) programs have on children" (Boffey & Walsh, 1970, p. 949).

In selecting this committee, a list of names of 40 knowledgeable persons was drawn up. The list

---

*This experiment is unique, then, in that the control group was able to agitate successfully to receive a portion of the experimental treatment!

was then sent to the three major television networks—CBS, NBC, and ABC—and to the National Association of Broadcasters for "comment." The result of this procedure was that the broadcasting industry was allowed to veto the appointment of potentially hostile critics (that is those who might support the modeling position) while the industry was given prominent representation on the panel. For example, among the seven rejected candidates were Leonard Berkowitz, Albert Bandura (see the Bryan and Schwartz article), and Otto Larsen, editor of *Violence and the mass media* (1968). Included on the final panel were an NBC vice-president and Joseph Klapper, director of social research for CBS (see Klapper, 1960). Three of the remaining ten committee members were either serving as consultants to industry or had previously been employed by or consulted for industry (Boffey & Walsh, 1970). James Jenkins, chairman of the board of scientific affairs of the American Psychological Association, commented that "It looks like an exemplar of the old story of the 'regulatees' running the 'regulators' or the fox passing on the adequacy of the eyesight of the man assigned to guard the chicken coop" (Boffey & Walsh, 1970, pp. 951–952).

As one might predict, the committee's 279-page report, released in early 1972, also stimulated a great deal of controversy. The report's summary suggested that violence in television programming does not have an adverse effect on the majority of the nation's youth but may influence small groups of youngsters already predisposed by many factors to aggressive behavior. Criticisms of the committee and the report centered on four factors: (1) that the selection procedures were biased, (2) that the report softened the findings (of a link between viewed aggression and violence) contained in the five volumes of original research on which it was based, (3) that the summary of the report was made even more equivocal than the report itself, and (4) that, in reporting the outcome, the mass media inadvertently misread the summary in such a way as to largely absolve television violence of any significant effect on children (*Newsweek*, March 6, 1972, p. 55).

The upshot of this controversy is that the Senate Subcommittee on Communications, which had requested the report in the first place, scheduled hearings to investigate the investigation (Shaffer, 1972). The television networks themselves have also initiated their own studies of the effects of violent TV programming. Such research programs have come under attack from academicians for their possible bias, lack of objectivity, and potential use as a delaying tactic (see Goldsen, 1971).

On the other side of the coin, Berkowitz (1971) has given his view of how the values of "liberal intellectuals" may bias their interpretations of research results. He states that the President's Commission on the Causes and Prevention of Violence concluded that media violence *can* induce persons to act aggressively (see Lange, Baker, & Ball, 1969). On the other hand, the majority of the President's Commission on Obscenity and Pornography concluded that exposure to pornography might have a temporary stimulating effect but that it has no long-term harmful effect. Berkowitz argues that the research results obtained by the two commissions were actually "strikingly similar"—that is, both observed aggression and observed (media) sex have a temporary stimulating effect, and it is largely unknown whether they have long-term consequences independently of other environmental supports.

Yet the policy recommendations of the two commissions were quite different. The Violence Commission urged television to do away with children's cartoons containing "serious, non-comic violence" and to lessen the amount and duration of violent episodes in all programs. The Pornography Commission, on the other hand, recommended the repeal of all legislation prohibiting the sale, exhibition, or distribution of sexual materials to consenting adults. Berkowitz suggests that the sociopolitical values of the committee members are the causes of these contrasting policy recommendations. It is difficult to evaluate the actual degree of similarity in the tasks of the committees and of the research results they reviewed. Nevertheless, Berkowitz' analysis is an intriguing one.

It should be painfully obvious to the reader that there is little clear-cut, definitive evidence on the effects of viewing violence and aggression on television. Laboratory studies suggest that such viewing may have the deleterious result of increasing aggressive tendencies in young children. One relatively large-sized field study (Feshbach & Singer) suggests that this may not be the case, at least for boys aged 8 to 18. And vested interests and sociopolitical values may lead one to question the objectivity and validity of many of the studies presently being carried out and the policy recommendations derived from them. Any conclusions as to the effect of televised aggression and violence on violent behavior must await the results of thoughtful, in-depth research programs carried out by objective social scientists. The larger issue of whether aggressive tendencies are chiefly innate or learned also must await further research.

REFERENCES

Berkowitz, L. Sex and violence: We can't have it both ways. *Psychology Today,* 1971, **5** (December), 14ff.

Boffey, P. M., & Walsh, J. Study of TV violence: Seven top researchers blackballed from panel. *Science,* 1970, **168,** 949–952.

Goldsen, R. K. NBC's make-believe research on TV violence. *Trans-Action,* 1971, **8** (October), 28–35.

Klapper, J. T. *The effects of mass communication.* New York: Free Press, 1960.

Lange, D. L., Baker, R. K., & Ball, S. J. *Mass media and violence.* Washington, D. C.: U. S. Government Printing Office, 1969.

Larsen, O. N. (Ed.) *Violence and the mass media.* New York: Harper & Row, 1968.

Shaffer, H. B. Violence study pulls punch. *St. Petersburg Times,* March 20, 1972, p. 1–D.

Singer, J. L. The influence of violence portrayed in television or motion pictures upon overt aggressive behavior. In J. L. Singer (Ed.), *The control of aggression and violence.* New York: Academic Press, 1971. Pp. 19–60.

Violence revisited. *Newsweek,* March 6, 1972, pp. 55–56.

SUGGESTED READINGS FOR FURTHER STUDY

Ardrey, R. *The territorial imperative.* New York: Atheneum, 1966.

Berkowitz, L. (Ed.) *Roots of aggression.* New York: Atherton Press, 1969.

Berkowitz, L. The contagion of violence: An S-R mediational analysis of some effects of observed aggression. In W. J. Arnold and M. M. Page (Eds.), *Nebraska symposium on motivation, 1970.* Lincoln: University of Nebraska Press, 1971. Pp. 95–136.

Buss, A. H. *The psychology of aggression.* New York: Wiley, 1961.

Goranson, R. E. Media violence and aggressive behavior: A review of experimental research. In L. Berkowitz (Ed.), *Advances in experimental social psychology,* Vol. 5. New York: Academic Press, 1970. Pp. 2–33.

Grimshaw, A. D. *Racial violence in the United States.* Chicago: Aldine, 1969.

Lange, D. L., Baker, R. K., & Ball, S. J. *Mass media and violence.* Washington, D. C.: U. S. Government Printing Office, 1969.

Larsen, O. N. (Ed.) *Violence and the mass media.* New York: Harper & Row, 1968.

Lorenz, K. *On aggression.* New York: Harcourt, Brace & World, 1966.

Megargee, E. I., & Hokanson, J. E. (Eds.) *The dynamics of aggression.* New York: Harper & Row, 1970.

Montagu, M. F. A. (Ed.) *Man and aggression.* New York: Oxford University Press, 1968.

Singer, J. L. (Ed.) *The control of aggression and violence.* New York: Academic Press, 1971.

Racial Differences in Intelligence

INTRODUCTION

Are different races equal in their innate mental abilities? Do the different racial groups that the American population comprises—Caucasians, Negroes, American Indians, Orientals, and others—possess the same intellectual potential? Is heredity or environment a more important determinant of mental ability? These questions are some of the most complex and controversial ones in social science today. They deal with theoretical concepts central to a variety of the social sciences, including anthropology and genetics as well as social psychology, sociology, and psychology. In addition, the answers to these questions have ramifications for solving one of the United States' most urgent domestic problems, the integration of minority groups into American life in such a way as to make available all the opportunities and benefits offered to members of the majority group.

Before reformulating these questions in more researchable terms, we need to look at the meanings of the terms used and the cautions we should follow in interpreting them. When we speak of intelligence, we are referring to an abstract unobservable quality. One's level of intelligence is usually inferred by his score on an IQ test, but intelligence and IQ-test performance *are not the same thing.* Many factors beyond intelligence per se are possible causes for racial differences in *test performance.* Levels of performance are influenced by myriad environmental factors such as quality and length of schooling, type of home life, opportunities to travel, and so on, as well as by possible genetic factors. The fact that most members of minority groups in the United States have suffered environmental handicaps must be kept in mind when we interpret the racial differences in mean IQ score. The score obtained by a particular person at a particular time also reflects his or her motivations and apprehensions in taking the test. These factors can cause racial groups to differ in IQ score, even though these groups may not differ much—or at all—in abstract intelligence.ʼ

When we consider the term *race,* we note that it has been used throughout history as a way of distinguishing among groups of people who are different. But different in what way? Early definitions of race were based on variations in skin color alone. This approach proved unsatisfactory because, among other reasons, it was apparent that there was great variety in skin shades even among members of a group that had completely inbred for many generations. A more recent approach, still using surface characteristics, or *phenotypes,* utilized a variety of features—body physique, skin color, hair quality and texture, and facial characteristics—to classify races. This approach is still used by many sociologists and social anthropologists, even though such approaches have led to proposals of as few as 2 races or as many as 63 in the world.

Such a physical approach rejects the use of cultural, or nonbiological, attributes in the differentiation of races. (In fact, every type of technical definition of *race* does so.) If two groups differ in customs, language, and location but are similar in physical characteristics, we do not say that they are members of different races but rather of different *ethnic groups.* Therefore there is no Jewish *race,* no Chinese *race,* no Italian *race.*

Most recently, geneticists and physical anthropologists have used genetic similarities and differences between people as a way of differentiating races. This genetic approach defines races as "populations which differ in the frequencies of some gene or genes" (Dunn & Dobzhansky, 1952, p. 118). For example, one's blood type is determined by genes inherited from his or her ancestors. The blood of each person throughout the world is one of four general types: O, A, B, or AB. Groups in different parts of the world can be differentiated on the basis of percentages that possess each type. For example, almost no American Indians have type B or AB, whereas about 45% of Chinese are of one of these types. This genetic approach, although offering the benefits of greater objectivity and a *genotypic* approach (focusing on underlying characteristics), still does not permit us to assign a specific individual to a particular race with confidence.

Such technical definitions of race often have little in common with the definitions of race used by the man on the street. In everyday life, why is one person categorized as black, another as white? Such labels are often self-determined or determined by society, although influenced by one's physical characteristics, his family traditions, customs, and the law. As we consider "racial" differences in intelligence, we must realize that studies of these differences have used a *popular* definition of race, rather than the technical definition. The category system used by the man on the street permits little consideration of the fact that most of us are not pure in our racial ancestry; his system is literally a black-or-white classification. Yet it has been estimated that 70% of those Americans classified as "Negroes" according to the popular definition possess some Caucasian background (Roberts, 1955). Some American "Negroes" have almost complete Caucasian ancestry but are classified as Negro because of state laws that label as Negro any person with *some* Negro ancestry. (In such a context it is ironic to consider the case of Plessy, the Louisiana "Negro" whose refusal to sit in a segregated train coach brought about the 1896 U.S. Supreme Court decision accepting "separate but equal" accommodations. Plessy was seven-eighths Caucasian and one-eighth Negro in ancestry.)

Similarly, it is estimated that approximately 20% of those Americans classified as Caucasians according to the popular definition possess some genetic background of Negro origin, as a result of intermarriage or other interbreeding. Truly, when we attempt to compare black and white groups in the United States and Canada, we are comparing groups that are partly different and partly alike in genetic background, in culture, and in environment. Nevertheless, numerous comparisons (in fact, more than 250 published ones) have been done. The following articles will indicate that the studies have been generally consistent in finding that the average intelligence-test *performance* of blacks in the United States is below that of the average performance of whites. Does this finding mean that blacks are innately different from whites? Some psychologists consider this a possibility. For example, Arthur Jensen of the University of California at Berkeley has suggested that genetic differences in ability between races may exist. Jensen's 1969 article in the *Harvard Educational Review* was highly publicized, although in reality he was not saying anything new. Jensen's position is that of a hereditarian; he interprets the data on family resemblances in IQ to conclude that about 80% of the variation in IQ scores between persons is hereditary in origin. If this were the case, it would mean that one's environment contributes relatively little. (It should be noted that Jensen has always granted that environmental differences do have some influence in determining each individual's IQ.)

Jensen's *Harvard Educational Review* article was 123 pages in length. Rather than selecting an appropriate excerpt, we have included a long selection from a more recent article of his, which gives the reader an understanding of Jensen's theoretical viewpoint as well as an exposure to his reactions to criticisms of his earlier analysis.

We have in this section followed the pattern of presenting first a theoretical article—representing only one possible viewpoint—then a research report that tests a relevant hypothesis, and then a critique or evaluative review of the field. The second article in this section, by Steven R. Tulkin, of the State University of New York at Buffalo, is a research report that compares intelligence and achievement-test performance of black and white children. As does Jensen in the first article, Tulkin puts racial differences within the context of the heredity-environment controversy. The reader may wish to compare Tulkin's conclusions with Jensen's hypotheses.

Tulkin's article is a modern version of a long tradition in studying the causes of racial differences. In seeking to separate the effects of heredity from those of the environment, psychologists have endeavored to select for study two racial groups whose environments were as nearly identical as possible. In the "equated-environment" strategy, if blacks and whites still differ in average measured IQ when their environments are the same, the conclusion is offered that an innate

difference exists. This strategy was originally used in the 1930s and 1940s, when studies by Tanser (1939), Bruce (1940), and others attempted to "equate" blacks and whites by using subjects from the same socioeconomic level. These studies found that average differences of 10 –15 points still occurred between lower-class whites and lower-class blacks. We should question whether such procedures were adequate, as Tulkin has. Note that Tulkin seeks a more sophisticated and thorough equating of environments, by studying the effects of participation in cultural activities, size of family, number of rooms per family member, and other variables. This is clearly an advancement over the earlier "equated environment" studies.

But can we, *at present,* identify in the United States or Canada a condition in which the environment of a black is "equal to" that of a white? Such a provision is not possible, concludes the third article in this section, by Philip S. Gallo, Jr., of San Diego State College, and Donald D. Dorfman, of the State University of Iowa. This article also summarizes the findings of the Tulkin article preceding it.

REFERENCES

Bruce, M. Factors affecting intelligence test performance of whites and Negroes in the rural South. *Archives of Psychology,* New York, 1940 (No. 252).

Dunn, L. C., & Dobzhansky, T. *Heredity, race and society.* (Rev. ed.) New York: New American Library, 1952.

Jensen, A. R. How much can we boost IQ and scholastic achievement? *Harvard Educational Review,* 1969, **39,** 1–123.

Roberts, D. F. The dynamics of racial intermixture in the American Negro: Some anthropological considerations. *American Journal of Human Genetics,* 1955, **7,** 361–367.

Tanser, H. A. *The settlement of Negroes in Kent County, Ontario, and a study of the mental capacity of their descendants.* Chatham, Ont.: Shepherd, 1939.

ARTICLE 22

Can We and Should We Study Race Differences?

Arthur R. Jensen

ARE THERE RACIAL DIFFERENCES IN IQ?

. . . In the United States persons classed as Negro by the common social criteria obtain scores on the average about one standard deviation (i.e., 15 IQ points on most standard intelligence tests) below the average for the white population. One standard deviation is an *average* difference, and it is known that the magnitude of Negro-white differences varies according to the ages of the groups compared, their socioeconomic status, and especially their geographical location in the United States. Various tests differ, on the average, relatively little. In general, Negroes do slightly better on verbal tests than on nonverbal tests. They do most poorly on tests of spatial ability, abstract reasoning and problem solving (Shuey, 1966; Tyler, 1965). Tests of scholastic achievement also show about one standard deviation difference, and this difference appears to be fairly constant from first grade through twelfth grade, judging from the massive data of the Coleman study (1966). The IQ difference of 1 SD, also, is fairly stable over the age range from about 5 years to adulthood, although some studies have shown a tendency for a slight increase in the difference between 5 and 18 years of age. Another point that has been suggested, but which requires much more systematic investigation before any firm

Adapted from an article by A. R. Jensen in J. Hellmuth (Ed.), *Compensatory education: A national debate.* (Vol. III, *Disadvantaged child.*) New York: Brunner-Mazel, 1970. Pp. 140–156. Copyright 1970, A. R. Jensen. Reprinted by permission of the author.

conclusions can be reached, is that there is a larger sex difference in IQ's for Negroes than for whites (Bronfenbrenner, 1967). The presumed difference favors the females. The point is especially worthy of research because, if true, it would have considerable social and educational consequences, which would be especially evident in the upper tail of the IQ distribution. For example, if girls are a few IQ points higher than boys, on the average, one should expect a greatly disproportionate number of Negro girls to qualify, as compared with boys, in any selection based on cut-off scores well above the mean, such as selection for college. Assuming a general mean of 85, an SD of 15, and a normal distribution, a 5 point IQ difference between Negro boys and girls and a college selection cut-off score of 115, for example, we would expect the number of qualified girls to boys to be approximately in the ratio of 2 to 1. . . .

A point that should be stressed is the fact that neither the white nor the Negro population, by common social classification, is genetically homogenous. It has already been noted that the American Negro is not of pure African ancestry but has, on the average, an admixture of 20% to 30% Caucasian genes, varying from less than 5% in some regions of the country to 40% or 50% in others (Reed, 1969). The white population contains many different subgroups which most probably differ genetically in potential for intellectual development. To point to one particular subgroup of one socially defined racial population as being higher or lower in IQ than some subgroup in another racial population proves nothing other than the fact that there exists an overlap between the racial groups. The fact that relatively large mean IQ differences are found between certain subgroups within the same race does not mean that these differences must be entirely of environmental origin and that therefore racial differences of similar magnitude must also be entirely attributable to environment.

Finally, it should be noted that IQ tests are taken by individuals. There is no such thing as measuring the IQ of a group as a group. Individuals' IQ's are obtained as individuals. The basis on which individuals may be grouped is a separate issue, depending upon the purposes of the investigator. When test scores are grouped according to some criteria of racial classification, we find mean differences between the groups. If we group test scores by some criteria of socioeconomic status, we find mean differences between the groups. Conversely, if we group persons by levels of IQ, we find the groups differ in their proportions of persons of different races and social classes.

ARE RACE DIFFERENCES IMPORTANT?

There is, of course, nothing *inherently* important about anything. Race differences in intelligence are important only if people think these differences, or their consequences, are important. It so happens that in our society great importance is given to these differences and their importance is acknowledged in many official public policies. Racial inequality in educational and occupational performance, and in the social and economic rewards correlated therewith, is today clearly one of the uppermost concerns of our nation.

Most persons are not concerned with those racial characteristics that are patently irrelevant to performance. The real concern results from the observed correlation between racial classification and educational and occupational performance. Persons who feel concerned about these observed differences demand an explanation for the differences. It is apparently a strongly ingrained human characteristic to need to understand what one perceives as a problem, and to ask for answers. People inevitably demand explanations about things that concern them. There is no getting around that. We have no choice in the matter. Explanations there will be.

But we do have a choice of essentially two paths in seeking explanations of intelligence differences among racial groups. On the one hand, we can simply *decree* an explanation based on prejudice, or popular beliefs, or moral convictions, or one or another social or political ideology, or on what we might think it is best for society to believe. This is the path of propaganda. Or, on the other hand, we can follow the path of science and investigate the problem in the same way that any other phenomenon would be subjected to scientific study. There is nothing to compel us to one path or the other. This is a matter of personal preference and values. And since persons differ markedly in their preferences and values, we will inevitably see both of these paths being followed for quite some time. My own preference is for a scientific approach to the study of these phenomena. It is certainly the more interesting and challenging intellectually. And our experience tells us that the scientific approach, by and large, leads to more reliable knowledge of natural phenomena than any other method that man has yet devised. If solutions to educational problems depend upon recognizing certain psychological realities in the same sense that, say, building a workable spaceship depends upon recognizing certain physical realities, then surely we will stand a better chance of improving education for all children by choosing the path of scientific investigation. In facing the issue of race differences in abilities we should heed the statement of John Stuart Mill:

If there are some subjects on which the results obtained have finally received the unanimous assent of all who have attended to the proof, and others on which mankind have not yet been equally successful; on which the most sagacious minds have occupied themselves from the earliest date, and have never succeeded in establishing any considerable body of truths, so as to be beyond denial or doubt; it is by generalizing the methods successfully followed in the former enquiries, and adapting them to the latter, that we may hope to remove this blot on the face of science.

Once we subscribe to a scientific approach, we are obligated to act accordingly. This means, for one thing, that we entertain alternative hypotheses. To entertain a hypothesis means not just to pay lip service to it or to acknowledge its possible merit and let it go at that. It means to put it into a testable form, to perform the test, and report the results with information as to the degree of statistical confidence with which the hypothesis in question can be accepted or rejected. If we can practice what is called "strong inference," so much the better. Strong inference consists of formulating opposing hypotheses and pitting them against one another by actually testing the contradictory predictions that follow from them. This is the way of science. How much of our educational research, we may ask, has taken this form? How much of the research . . . on the causes of the educational handicaps of children called culturally disadvantaged has followed this path? The only sensible conclusion one can draw from a perusal of this evidence is that the key question in everyone's mind about racial differences in ability—are they genetic?—has, in effect, been ruled out as a serious alternative hypothesis in the search for the causal factors involved in inequalities of educational performance. Sundry environmental hypotheses are considered, but rarely, if ever, are alternative genetic hypotheses suggested. If a genetic hypothesis is mentioned, it is usually for the sake of dismissing it out of hand or to point out why it would be impossible to test the hypothesis in any case. Often, more intellectual ingenuity is expended in trying to find reasons why a particular genetic hypothesis could not be tested than in trying to discover a way of formulating the hypothesis so that it can be put to a test. The emotional need to believe that genetic factors are unimportant in individual or group differences in ability can be seen in many statements by dedicated workers in those fields of psychology and education most allied to the problems of children called disadvantaged. For example, Dr. Bettye Caldwell, a prominent worker in compensatory and early childhood education, has noted:

Most of us in enrichment . . . efforts—no matter how much lip service we pay to the genetic potential of the child—are passionate believers in the plasticity of the human organism. We need desperately to believe that we are all born equalizable. With any failure to demonstrate the effectiveness of compensatory experiences offered to children of any given age, one is entitled to conclude parsimoniously that perhaps the enrichment was not offered at the proper time [Caldwell, 1968, p. 81].

But genetic factors in rate of development are never considered as a possible part of the explanation.

It is important not to evaluate persons in terms of group membership if we are to ensure equality of opportunity and social justice. All persons should be treated as individuals in terms of their own merits, if our aim is to maximize opportunities for every person to develop his abilities to their fullest capacity in accord with his own interests and drives. But the result of *individual* selection (for higher education, better jobs, etc.) makes it inevitable that there will be unequal representation of the parent populations in any subgroup that might be selected whenever there are average differences between parent populations.

Many questions about the means of guaranteeing equality of educational opportunity are still moral and political issues at present. When there is no compelling body of scientific evidence on which policy decisions can be based, such decisions must be avowedly made in terms of one's personal social philosophy and concepts of morality. Many goals of public policy must be decided in terms of values. The results of research are of greatest use to the technology of achieving the value-directed goals of society. The decision to put a man on the moon was not a scientific decision, but once the decision was made the application of scientific knowledge was necessary to achieve this goal. A similar analogy holds for the attainment of educational goals.

CAN RACE DIFFERENCES BE RESEARCHED?

It is sometimes argued that even though it is not unreasonable to hypothesize genetic racial differences in mental ability, we cannot know the direction or magnitude of such genetic differences and the problem is much too difficult and complex to yield to scientific investigation. Therefore, the argument often continues, we should go on pretending as though there is no question of genetic differences, as was officially stated by the U. S. Office of Education in 1966: "It is a demonstrable fact that the talent pool in any one ethnic group is substantially the same as that in any other ethnic group."

First, we will never know to what extent research can yield answers on a subject unless we at least try our best to do the research. It is doubtful that any major scientific advances could have been made in any field if it were decided beforehand that the problems could not be researched. I cannot agree that a scientific approach should be restricted to only the easy problems. If all the necessary methodology for studying the genetics of race differences in psychological characteristics is not yet sufficiently developed, this should not be surprising, since so little effort has been made thus far. The methodology of a field of inquiry does not grow in a vacuum. Scientists do not *first* develop a complete methodology for the investigation of a complex area and then apply it all at once to get the final answers. An appropriate methodology evolves as a result of grappling with difficult problems in the spirit of scientific research.

What are some of the thinking blocks in this area? One is the frequent failure to distinguish between raw facts, on the one hand, and inference from the facts in terms of some hypothesis, on the other. The Society for the Psychological Study of Social Issues (SPSSI), for example, in a press release (May 2, 1969) criticizing my article in the *Harvard Educational Review* (Jensen, 1969), stated, "There is no *direct* (italics mine) evidence that supports the view that there is an innate difference between members of different racial groups." Of course there is not *direct* evidence, nor can there be direct evidence if by "direct" we mean evidence that is immediately palpable to our physical senses. The gradual disappearance of ships over the horizon is not *direct* evidence of anything, but it can be interpreted in terms of the hypothesis that the earth is round. It would be harder to explain if we hypothesized that the earth is flat. So even as relatively simple an hypothesis as that the world is round cannot be

proved by direct evidence, but depends upon logical inference from diverse lines of evidence. If all that was needed was direct evidence, even a monkey would know that the world is round, in the same sense that it knows that a lemon is sour. The substantiation of an hypothesis in science depends upon *objective* evidence but does not necessarily depend upon direct evidence alone.

Another inhibition to thought on this topic is the notion that before research can yield any answers, the environment must be absolutely equal for all groups involved in comparisons. The SPSSI statement went so far as to say that ". . . a more accurate understanding of the contribution of heredity to intelligence will be possible only when social conditions for all races are equal and when this situation has existed for several generations." Since no operationally testable meaning is given to "equal" social conditions, such a statement, if taken seriously, would completely preclude the possibility of researching this important question, not just for several generations, but indefinitely. Actually, large environmental differences between racial groups can be revealing when the environmental ratings are positively correlated with IQ or scholastic performance *within* the groups but show a negative correlation *between* the groups. If group A on the average has a poor environment in terms of variables claimed to be important to intellectual development and group B has a good environment, and if group A performs better than group B on intelligence tests which are appropriate to the experience of both groups, this is evidence that some factors other than the measured environmental variables are involved in the relatively higher intellectual performance of group A as compared with group B. If environmental factors cannot be found that will account for the difference, it is presumptive evidence in favor of the genetic hypothesis. Genetical tests of the hypothesis are preferable, of course. (These are discussed in a later section.) But what one also looks for are consistencies among various lines of evidence, especially lines of evidence that lead to opposite predictions from different hypotheses.

Many investigators now would question the view that the lack of early stimulation in the preschool years can be counted among the chief causes of the poorer IQ performance of Negro children, since when children are grouped in several categories according to the parents' socioeconomic status, the Negro children in the highest SES category still score two to three IQ points below white children in the lowest SES level (Shuey, 1966). Thus, what we generally think of as a reasonably good environment is apparently not sufficient to equalize the performance of Negro and white groups.

Such findings lead to hypothesizing increasingly subtle and hard to measure environmental effects. But it should be recognized that at present most of the environmentally "damaging" effects that are assumed to be accountable for performance differences are hypothetical and not factual. Poor self-concept and alienation are among the currently prevailing explanations, but what has not yet been satisfactorily explained is why such general motivational dispositions should affect some cognitive abilities so much more than others. Performance is not uniformly low on all tasks, by any means. There are distinct high and low points in the profile of various abilities in different ethnic groups (Stodolsky & Lesser, 1967), and no one has yet attempted to explain how such profile differences, which are invariant across social classes, could come about as a result of differences in generalized attitudes and motivation in the test situation.

Finally, unnecessary difficulties arise when we allow the scientific question to become mixed up with its possible educational, social, and political implications. The scientific question and its solution should *not* be allowed to get mixed up with the social-political aspects of the problem, for when it does we are less able to think clearly about either set of questions. The question of whether there are or are not genetic racial differences in intelligence is independent of any questions of its implications, whatever they may be. But I would say that the scientific question should have priority and the answer should be sought through scientific means. For although the answer might have educational and social implications, and there are indeed grave educational

and social problems that need to be solved, we must first understand the causes of problems if we are to do anything effectively toward solving them. Gaining this knowledge is a scientific task. As it is accomplished, we are then in a better position to consider alternative courses of action and evaluate their feasibility and desirability in terms of society's values and goals. . . .

GENETIC RESEARCH TO REDUCE THE HEREDITY-ENVIRONMENT UNCERTAINTY

. . . The term "heredity-environment uncertainty" refers mainly to the question of race differences in intelligence. The answer to this question is still in the realm of uncertainty in terms of the normal scientific meaning of this word. *Absolute* certainty is never attained in an empirical science. . . . Empirical science deals in probability statements, and "certainty" refers to a high degree of probability that a proposition is "true," meaning that certain objective consequences can be predicted from the proposition with a stated probability. A decisive increase in this probability with respect to any given scientific proposition rarely results from a single experiment or discovery. I take exception to the impression that might be given by some writers that unless a scientific study can be perfect and 100% certain, we cannot know anything. This is not how scientific knowledge advances. We do not devise perfect methods or obtain complete answers on the first try. Certainty, in the sense of probability, is generally increased very incrementally in science. Research aims to add reliable increments to statements of probability.

This we must continue to do with respect to the question of genetic race differences in intelligence. It is still an open question by all reasonable scientific standards. The existing evidence is in all cases sufficiently ambiguous, due largely to the confounding of racial and environmental factors, as not to permit statements with a sufficiently high probability such that all reasonable and qualified persons attending the evidence will agree that it is conclusive. The issue of genetic race differences may be likened to theories of the moon's craters—whether they were caused by volcanic eruptions or by the impact of meteors. All the evidence obtainable by astronomers could support either interpretation, and different scientists could argue for one theory or another. A substantial increment could be subtracted from this uncertainty only by obtaining new evidence not obtainable through telescopic study—namely, directly obtaining and analyzing material from the surface of the moon.

I believe that, similarly, the heredity-environment uncertainty about race differences in IQ will be substantially reduced only by obtaining new evidence—new *kinds* of evidence. Exclusive reliance on anthropological, sociological, and psychological evidence would probably not substantially advance our knowledge. I believe that application of the methods of biometrical genetics (also called population genetics or quantitative genetics) to the question of race differences will substantially reduce our uncertainty.

Someone suggested that the only way one could prove race differences in intelligence would be to dye one member of a pair of white identical twins black and adopt it out to a Negro family while the co-twin is reared by a white family. How much difference would it make in their IQ's? Better yet is the suggestion of Professor Arthur Stinchcombe (1969): find pairs of identical twins in which one [parent] of each pair is Negro and one is white, separate them at birth and rear them in Negro and white families, and see how their IQ differences compare with those found for twins where both are of the same race! These suggestions sound ridiculous; one is infeasible and the other is impossible. Yet as conceptual experiments they are good, because they suggest the necessary ingredients of the information we must obtain to reduce the heredity-environment uncertainty. Both examples rightly recognize skin color (and, by implication, other visible racial features) as a part of the individual's environment. They are based on comparing genetically equivalent persons reared in different environments. Another possibility consists of

rearing genetically and racially different persons in essentially similar environments—including the factor of skin color, etc. Is such a study possible? Yes.

Geneticists already know the frequencies of a large number of genetically independent blood groups in European and African populations. On the basis of such data, it is entirely possible to determine the proportion of Caucasian genes in a population sample of Negroes, socially defined. Furthermore, it should be possible by the same means to classify individuals on a probabilistic basis in terms of their relative proportions of African and Caucasian genes. Since the *average* admixture of Caucasian genes for American Negroes is between 20 and 30 percent, there should be enough variance to make it possible to assign large numbers of individuals to at least several categories according to their amount of admixture, and the probable error in classification could be quite definitely specified. A sufficient number of blood groups or other genetic polymorphisms with known frequency distributions in African and Caucasian populations would have to be employed to ensure a high degree of statistical certainty that the categories represented different degrees of genetic racial admixture. A wide range of admixtures probably exists among Negroes living in highly similar environments, so that it should be quite possible in such a study to obtain samples which do not differ across the admixture categories in a number of socioeconomic or other environmental indices. What about skin color? It is polygenetic and is very imperfectly correlated with the amount of Caucasian admixture. Individuals, for example, whose genes are derived in equal (50–50) proportions from African and Caucasian ancestors evince the full range of skin colors from white to black, including all the shades between. This makes it possible statistically to control the effect of skin color; that is, one can compare a number of persons all of whom have the same skin color but different degrees of African/Caucasian admixture, or conversely, the same degree of admixture but different skin colors. (Skin color can be quantified precisely and objectively by means of a photoelectric device which measures reflectance.) The question, then, would be: do the mean IQ's (or any other mental ability tests) of the several categories of racial admixture differ significantly and systematically? The genetic equality hypothesis would predict no difference; the genetic inequality hypothesis would predict a difference between the groups.

A further refinement, in order to ensure greater equality of environmental conditions across the admixture categories, *including* prenatal environment, would be to include in the study a large number of half-siblings all related through the mother and reared together. Some half-siblings will inevitably fall into different admixture categories. Do they differ significantly on mental tests when skin color is controlled? Birth order, maternal age, and other factors would have to be noted, but in large samples these factors would probably tend to be random with respect to racial admixture. One would also want a white control group with no African admixture in order to rule out the remote possibility that the blood groups themselves are causally related to IQ, since they are intended in this study only as genetic markers or indices of racial admixture. Such a study would go further toward answering the question of Negro-white genetic differences in intelligence than the sum total of all the other studies that we now have.

The possibility has been suggested of using genetic linkages for studying the inheritance of intelligence and race differences, but evaluation of its potential merits will have to be decided by geneticists. If the genes for some clearly identifiable physical trait are located on the same chromosome as the genes for some measurable mental ability, we should expect to find a marked correlation in the population between the appearance of the physical characteristics and the mental attribute whose genes share the same chromosome. The physical characteristics would thus serve as an objective genetic marker for the mental trait.

The major difficulty with this approach may be that what we call intelligence is so polygenetic that the relevant genes are carried on most or all of the chromosomes, so that specific linkages could never be established. If intelligence consists of a large number of subabilities, each of which is conditioned independently by a very limited number of genes which are carried on a single chromosome, then it may be possible to study linkages, provided we can reliably measure the subabilities. I have described elsewhere how psychologists might make their measurements of abilities of greater interest and value to researchers in genetics (Jensen, 1968). Briefly, it would consist of the fractionation of mental abilities to the most extreme limits that reliability of measurement will permit, and then seeing if these subabilities show any signs of relatively simple genetic inheritance (such as showing Mendelian ratios) or genetic linkages.

Are there any known linkages between physical and mental characteristics in the normal distribution of intelligence? I do not know of any established examples. We should begin looking for such possible mental linkages with blood groups, biochemical variations, and other physical traits. One set of interesting findings concerns the association between uric acid level in the blood and intellectual achievement. Whether this is an instance of genetic linkage or whether there is a causal connection between uric acid and brain functions is not yet established. Stetten and Hearon (1958) reported a correlation between serum uric acid concentration and scores on the Army intelligence test of 817 inductees. A study of serum urate levels of 51 University of Michigan professors found a positive correlation with drive, achievement, and leadership (Brooks & Mueller, 1966), and high school students have been found to show a similar relationship (Kasl, Brooks, & Cobb, 1966). It would be interesting to know if these correlations are found within other racial groups and also if there are differences between groups in serum uric acid levels. Every bit of such various kinds of information, if it points consistently in the same direction, reduces to some extent the heredity-environment uncertainty.

There are other promising approaches to this problem through biometrical genetics, but explication of the technical aspects of these methods is clearly beyond the possible scope of the present discussion.

IMPLICATIONS FOR EDUCATION

Since educators have at least officially assumed that race and social class differences in scholastic performance are not associated with any genetic differences in growth rates or patterns of mental abilities but are due entirely to discrimination, prejudice, inequality of educational opportunity, and factors in the child's home environment and peer culture, we have collectively given little if any serious thought to whether we would do anything differently if we knew in fact that all educational differences were not due solely to these environmental factors.

There have been and still are obvious environmental inequities and injustices which have disfavored certain minorities, particularly Negroes, Mexican-Americans, and American Indians. Progress has been made and is continuing to be made to improve these conditions. But there is no doubt still a long way to go, and the drive toward further progress in this direction should be given top priority in our national effort. Education is one of the chief instruments for approaching this goal. Every child should receive the best education that our current knowledge and technology can provide. This should not imply that we advocate the same methods or the same expectations for all children. There are large individual differences in rates of mental development, in patterns of ability, in drives and interests. These differences exist even among children of the same family. The good parent does his best to make the most of each child's strong points and to help him on his weak points but not make these the crux of success or failure. The school must regard each child, and the differences among children, in much the same way as a good parent should do.

I believe we need to find out the extent to which individual differences, social class differences, and race difference in rates of cognitive development and differential patterns of relative strength and weakness in various types of ability are attributable to genetically conditioned biological growth factors. The answer to this question might imply differences in our approach to improving the education of all children, particularly those we call the disadvantaged, for many of whom school is now a frustrating and unrewarding experience.

Individuals should be treated in terms of their individual characteristics and not in terms of their group membership. This is the way of a democratic society, and educationally it is the only procedure that makes any sense. Individual variations within any large socially defined group are always much greater than the average differences between groups. There is overlap between groups in the distributions of all psychological characteristics that we know anything about. But dealing with children as individuals is not the greatest problem. It is in our concern about the fact that when we do so, we have a differentiated educational program, and children of different socially identifiable groups may not be proportionately represented in different programs. This is the "hang-up" of many persons today and this is where our conceptions of equal opportunity are most likely to go awry and become misconceptions.

Group racial and social class differences are first of all individual differences, but the causes of the *group* differences may not be the same as those of the *individual* differences. This is what we must find out, because the prescription of remedies for our educational ills could depend on the answer.

Let me give one quite hypothetical example. We know that among middle-class white children, learning to read by ordinary classroom instruction is related to certain psychological developmental characteristics. Educators call it "readiness." These characteristics of readiness appear at different ages for different kinds of learning, and at any given age there are considerable individual differences among children, even among siblings reared within the same family. These developmental differences, in middle-class white children, are largely conditioned by genetic factors. If we try to begin a child too early in reading instruction, he will experience much greater difficulty than if we waited until we saw more signs of "readiness." Lacking readiness, he may even become so frustrated as to "turn off" reading, so that he will then have an emotional block toward reading later on when he should have the optimal readiness. The readiness can then not be fully tapped. The child would have been better off had we postponed reading instruction for six months or a year and occupied him during this time with other interesting activities for which he was ready. Chances are he would be a better reader at, say, 10 or 11 years of age, for having started a year later, when he could catch on to reading with relative ease and avoid the unnecessary frustration. It is very doubtful in this case that some added "enrichment" to his preschool environment would have made him learn to read much more easily a year earlier. If this is largely a matter of biological maturation, then the time at which a child is taught in terms of his own schedule of development becomes important. If, on the other hand, it is largely a matter of preschool environmental enrichment, then the thing to do is to go to work on the preschool environment so as to make all children equally ready for reading in the first grade. If a child's difficulty is the result of both factors, then a combination of both enrichment and optimal developmental sequencing should be recommended.

There is a danger that some educators' fear of being accused of racial discrimination could become so misguided as to work to the disadvantage of many minority children. Should we deny differential educational treatments to children when such treatment will maximize the benefits they receive from schooling, just because differential treatment might result in disproportionate representation of different racial groups in various programs? I have seen instances where Negro children were denied special educational facilities commonly given to white children with learning difficulties, simply because school authorities were reluctant to single out *any* Negro children, despite their obvious individual needs, to be treated any differently from the majority of youngsters in the school. There was no hesitation

about singling out white children who needed special attention. Many Negro children of normal and superior scholastic potential are consigned to classes in which one-fourth to one-third of their classmates have IQ's below 75, which is the usual borderline of educational mental retardation. The majority of these educationally retarded children benefit little or not at all from instruction in the normal classroom, but require special attention in smaller classes that permit a high degree of individualized and small group instruction. Their presence in regular classes creates unusual difficulties for the conscientious teacher and detracts from the optimal educational environment for children of normal ability. Yet there is reluctance to provide special classes for these educationally retarded children if they are Negro or Mexican-American. The classrooms of predominantly minority schools often have 20 to 30 percent of such children, which handicaps the teacher's efforts on behalf of her other pupils in the normal range of IQ. The more able minority children are thereby disadvantaged in the classroom in ways that are rarely imposed on white children for whom there are more diverse facilities. Differences in rates of mental development and in potentials for various types of learning will not disappear by being ignored. It is up to biologists and psychologists to discover their causes, and it is up to educators to create a diversity of instructional arrangements best suited to the full range of educational differences that we find in our population. Many environmentally caused differences can be minimized or eliminated, given the resources and the will of society. The differences that remain are a challenge for public education. The challenge will be met by making available more ways and means for children to benefit from schooling. This, I am convinced, can come about only through a greater recognition and understanding of the nature of human differences.

REFERENCES

Bronfenbrenner, U. The psychological costs of quality and equality in education. *Child Development,* 1967, **38,** 909–925.

Brooks, G. W., & Mueller, E. Serum urate concentrations among university professors. *Journal of the American Medical Association,* 1966, **195,** 415–418.

Caldwell, B. The fourth dimension in early childhood education. In R. Hess and R. Bear (Eds.), *Early education: Current theory, research and action.* Chicago: Aldine, 1968.

Coleman, J. S. et al. *Equality of educational opportunity.* Washington, D. C.: U. S. Department of Health, Education, and Welfare, 1966.

Jensen, A. R. Another look at culture-fair testing. In *Western Regional Conference on Testing Problems, Proceedings for 1968,* "Measurement for Educational Planning." Berkeley, Calif.: Educational Testing Service, Western Office, 1968. Pp. 50–104.

Jensen, A. R. How much can we boost IQ and scholastic achievement? *Harvard Educational Review,* 1969, **39,** 1–123.

Kasl, S. V., Brooks, G. W., & Cobb, S. Serum urate concentrations in male high school students. *Journal of the American Medical Association,* 1966, **198,** 713–716.

Kennedy, W. A., Van de Riet, V., & White, J. C. A normative sample of intelligence and achievement of Negro elementary school children in the Southeastern United States. *Monographs of the Society for Research in Child Development,* 1963, **28** (6).

Reed, T. E. Caucasian genes in American Negroes. *Science,* 1969, **165,** 762–768.

Shuey, A. M. *The testing of Negro intelligence.* (2nd ed.) New York: Social Science Press, 1966.

Stetten, D., Jr., & Hearon, J. Z. Intellectual level measured by Army classification battery and serum acid concentration. *Science,* 1958, **129,** 1737.

Stinchcombe, A. L. A critique of Arthur R. Jensen's "How much can we boost IQ and scholastic achievement?" *Harvard Educational Review,* 1969, **39** (3).

Stodolsky, S. S., & Lesser, G. Learning patterns in the disadvantaged. *Harvard Educational Review,* 1967, **37,** 546–593.

Tyler, L. E. *The psychology of human differences.* (3rd ed.) New York: Appleton-Century-Crofts, 1965.

ARTICLE 23

Race, Class, Family, and School Achievement[1]

Steven R. Tulkin

The debate surrounding heredity versus environmental influences on the development of intelligence is one of the oldest in the social sciences. The effects of characteristics such as social class have been acknowledged since Binet's work with intelligence testing (Binet & Simon, 1916). Although many social scientists interpret racial differences in tested intelligence and school achievement as resulting from social class differences, so-called "caste" differences, and various other environmental influences (Pettigrew, 1964, pp. 132–135), the advocates of the heredity view can still be heard (Burt, 1958; McGurk, 1959; Shuey, 1958, 1966). Still others have argued that the question has not been answered and insist that genetic differences be further investigated rather than assumed not to exist (Ingle, 1964).

The problem is a complex one, involving the

From *Journal of Personality and Social Psychology,* **9,** 1968, 31–37. Copyright 1968 by the American Psychological Association, and reproduced by permission of the author and the publisher.

[1]This report summarizes and expands certain aspects of an investigation conducted while the author was at the Department of Psychology, University of Maryland. Marvin G. Cline was very helpful in both planning the investigation and interpreting the results. The research was carried out as part of the Reading Ability and Outcome Study of the Mental Health Study Center (National Institute of Mental Health). J. R. Newbrough and Dee Norman Lloyd were especially helpful throughout the investigation. Grateful appreciation is also extended to Victor Rice, supervisor of testing and research of the Prince George's County (Maryland) Board of Education; Leo Walder, University of Maryland, and John Muller, Harvard University, for their help in obtaining and analyzing the present data; and to Thomas F. Pettigrew, J. R. Newbrough, and Jerome Kagan for their thoughtful comments on the present paper. Computer analyses were supported by the Computer Science Center of the University of Maryland and by a Field Foundation Grant to the Laboratory of Social Relations of Harvard University.

interaction of race (caste), social class, family environments, and sex differences, as well as methodological questions such as random sampling and use of "culturally biased" tests. All of these problems must be considered when attempting to examine this complex question.

There have been many hypotheses about how these various factors influence intelligence. Some have related differential environmental experiences of Negroes and whites to differential academic performance. Deutsch (1960), for example, related racial differences on intelligence and achievement tests to the fact that the Negro student, not being a part of the majority culture, finds that identification with a set of majority culture symbols is not personally relevant. This "racial" difference is seen as existing all along the social class continuum, and, in fact, Deutsch and Brown (1964) reported that racial differences are greatest in the upper socioeconomic status (SES) groups. Similarly, Roen (1960) hypothesized that the psychological experiences of socioeconomic exclusion and generally more erratic family ties negatively influence the emerging personalities or self-perceptions of Negroes, especially as these relate to their intellectual potentials.

These authors, then, have suggested that Negro students—because of special environmental experiences associated with being Negro Americans—tend to be alienated from the majority culture, to have family backgrounds which are less conducive to the development of intellectual skills, and to have personality traits which themselves limit intellectual performance.

In contrast to the view that racial differences are found in each social class, Bloom, Whiteman, and Deutsch (1963) found that the relationships between social class and various family and environmental conditions are very similar in white and Negro samples. In fact, they reported that the association of environmental conditions with social class tends to be stronger than with race, and they tentatively concluded that "social class may be a more potent variable than race in predicting to environmental and attitudinal factors [p. 10]" which have been shown to be related to test scores on intelligence and achievement tests.

Sex has also been found to relate to measures of intelligence and school achievement. Kennedy, Van de Riet, and White (1963) reported that although in the first grade there are no differences in the achievement scores of 1,800 Negro students, with each higher grade sex differences become greater. By Grade 6, achievement scores of the females are more than three-fourths of a grade level higher than the scores of the males. This is consistent with a report by Minigione (1965) that among Negroes the girls have a greater need for achievement than the boys, as would be expected, according to Veroff, Atkinson, Feld, and Gurin (1960), as a natural result of matriarchal Negro families.

This brief review serves to illustrate the complex interactions of race, social class, and sex, all of which may influence scores on tests of intelligence and school achievement. The majority of studies which have attempted to control these three factors have still found significant differences between racial groups, as is reported in both of Shuey's (1958, 1966) reviews of the literature. However, rather than conclude, as Shuey did, that the differences are caused by a genetic factor, one must ask whether, in fact, the groups studied were really equated. It has been shown that the more closely white and Negro groups are equated, the smaller are the differences that are found. McCord and Demerath (1958), for example, controlled for social class, father's occupation, nationality, generation of entry into America, and the "personality and emotional climate of the home." They found no significant differences among racial groups. However, in addition to the fact that this study has been criticized for its methodology (Shuey, 1966), the data

were mostly on lower-middle- and lower-class subjects. The relationships among these factors in the middle and upper classes remain unstudied.

The present research is a study of a group of upper and lower SES Negroes and whites in which differences on intelligence and achievement tests are examined from the points of view of race, social class, family environments, and sex. Of particular interest is the extent to which environmental variables relate to differences between Negroes and whites on measures of intelligence and school achievement, and whether test-score differences are reduced as more of these environmental factors are controlled.

METHOD

The subjects were 389 fifth- and sixth-grade students from a suburban Maryland school system. They were divided into two SES groups (upper and lower), two racial groups (Negro and white), and two sexes, yielding eight groups (see Table 1). Background information was obtained from the students' permanent record cards. SES was determined by a modification of the Hollingshead (1957) Two-Factor Index of Social Position (occupation and education), with Levels 1 and 2 being used as upper SES and Level 5 as lower SES. Students from SES Levels 3 and 4 were not included in the sample. The Lorge-Thorndike Intelligence Test (Level Three) and the Iowa Tests of Basic Skills were administered by the local school system as a part of its regular testing program, and scores were obtained from the records.

A specially developed questionnaire consisting of items related to cultural participation, family participation, and family structure was also administered. The Cultural Participation Scale consists of four 1-point items (visit library, visit museum, attend concert, and read newspaper) and five items on which 1 point was given for each time an activity was performed (books read in previous 2 months, culturally related trips, etc.). The Family Participation Scale has two parts: time spent with parents (I), and verbal interaction between children and parents (II). In Section I, 1 point is given for each activity of the child in which one or both parents participate (Sunday activities, trips, visits to museums, libraries, etc.). In Section II, the student uses a scale from 0 to 3 to indicate how often he talks with parents about homework, personal problems, what to do on a rainy day, what he reads in the newspapers, and what is going on in school. These scores are summed and added to the total from Section I. Family-structure items include a crowdedness ratio (number of people living in the house divided by the number of rooms), data on maternal employment, marital status of parents, and number of siblings.

The questionnaire was developed in three stages: (a) testing of construct validity, (b) pretesting the instructions and vocabulary to improve clarity, and (c) obtaining sample distributions from pretest subjects on the Cultural Participation Scale, the Family Participation Scale, and the family-structure indexes. Construct validity is based on a set of judgments by 10 members of the professional staff of the Mental Health Study Center (National Institute of Mental Health). Each of the judges rated all

TABLE 1. Race, class, and sex distribution of sample population.

SES	White		Negro		Total
	Male	Female	Male	Female	
Upper	70	67	29	23	189
Lower	48	37	57	58	200
Total	118	104	86	81	389

questions on the amount of relationship to the desired construct. Following this, the questionnaire was pretested with students from one white and one Negro classroom and administered by individual interview to two students representing each of the eight cells shown in Table 1. Questions which were ambiguous to the subjects or were not discriminating in the same direction as the total scale were modified or eliminated.

Analysis of the data consisted of two major phases. First, the data were analyzed on the basis of race and class only. Significance tests were computed on all variables, and an attempt was made to control further for environmental differ-

TABLE 2. Means, standard deviations, and significance levels for standard tests and family scales.

	Upper SES white		Upper SES Negro		Lower SES white		Lower SES Negro	
	M	SD	M	SD	M	SD	M	SD
Verbal IQ	114.48	14.56	109.15[**]	12.88	92.67	12.84	90.04	12.08
Nonverbal IQ	112.10	12.20	107.81[*]	11.79	95.41	13.57	91.01[**]	12.38
Vocabulary achievement[a]	6.22	1.38	5.88	1.18	4.40	.78	4.51	.65
Reading achievement	5.92	1.50	5.44[*]	1.38	4.12	.88	4.11	.92
Language achievement	6.42	1.44	6.16	1.38	4.48	.98	4.44	1.04
Work study achievement	5.80	1.00	5.42[***]	.74	4.48	.64	4.26[*]	.66
Arithmetic achievement	5.75	.83	5.33[***]	.76	4.74	.68	4.36[****]	.67
Total achievement	6.06	1.13	5.64[***]	.93	4.48	.72	4.36	.84
Crowdedness	.72	.25	.92[***]	.43	1.28	.54	1.73[****]	1.12
Cultural participation scale	13.89	3.98	13.60	3.83	7.82	3.79	8.44	4.27
Family participation scale	15.58	4.54	16.87	4.48	11.27	4.48	13.24[***]	5.46
Number of siblings	2.47	1.60	2.08	1.36	3.34	2.00	4.97[***]	2.56

Note.—Significance levels represent difference between white and Negro means within each SES group.
[a]Achievement test scores are reported as "grade equivalents."
[*]$p = .05.$
[**]$p = .02.$
[***]$p = .01.$
[****]$p = .001.$

Ed. note.—Statistical significance refers to the question of whether a difference in the mean scores between two groups could have occurred by chance or not. For example, notice in Table 2 that the mean verbal IQ for the upper SES white sample is 114.48, whereas for the upper SES Negro sample it is 109.15. The [**] by the latter indicates that this difference in means is "statistically significant," with a p value of .02." This means that there is a probability of only .02 (p = probability) that the difference as large as the one between these two means would have occurred by chance. Therefore, since this likelihood is so small, it is concluded that it represents a real difference—a difference that has some cause other than coincidence. In the table, starred differences indicate statistically significant ones.

ences by use of a multivariate analysis of variance in which the environmental differences were statistically controlled through the use of covariate adjustors.[2]   Correlations were also examined within each race-class group. In Phase 2, the data were examined to determine the importance of sex differences.

RESULTS

Table 2 presents race within class comparisons of the means, standard deviations, and significance levels of the test scores and home and family scales. Three-fourths of the tests yield significant differences in the upper SES group, while half of the differences are significant in the lower SES group. In the upper SES group, there are differences on both verbal and nonverbal tests, while differences in the lower SES group are found only on nonverbal measures. On the family variables, there are racial differences on the crowdedness ratio in both SES groups, a difference in the number of siblings, and a difference on the Family Participation Scale in the lower SES group only.[3]   (Univariate analyses of variance were done on each test separately and yielded identical significance levels.)

SES group differences were also tested within each race (upper white versus lower white and

[2]The program used was the Multivariate Analysis of Variance, General Linear Hypothesis Model, Biometric Laboratory, George Washington University.

[3]Since large racial differences were also found on "social desirability" questions that were asked in the questionnaire, and since "faking" was much easier on the Family Participation Scale, this latter difference may be largely attributable to social desirability.

TABLE 3. Intact and broken homes by race and class.

SES	White		Negro	
	Intact	Broken	Intact	Broken
Upper	126	11	42	10
Lower	66	19	91	24

Note.—Difference between upper and lower SES groups is significant for the white sample by chi-square analysis at $p < .01$. Difference between white and Negro upper SES groups is significant by chi-square analysis at $p < .05$.

upper Negro versus lower Negro). On *every measure* presented in Table 2, social class differences are significant beyond the .001 level of confidence. Thus the breakdown into SES groups yields a greater number and larger differences than does the breakdown into racial groups.

In order to determine if other home and family differences existed among racial groups of similar SES background, comparisons were made on two other variables, broken homes and maternal employment. Tables 3 and 4 present these data. Again it appears that controlling for SES does not equate white and Negro samples. Broken homes are more common, proportionately, in the upper SES Negro group than in the upper SES white group. In fact, there is no significant difference between upper and lower SES Negro groups. Similarly, maternal employment seems to vary more along racial than SES lines.

In an attempt to further equate the groups in light of the environmental differences reported above, a multivariate analysis of variance was

TABLE 4. Maternal employment by race and class.

SES	White			Negro		
	Employed full time	Employed part time	Not employed	Employed full time	Employed part time	Not employed
Upper	33	17	87	31	8	12
Lower	32	4	49	59	27	29

Note.—Difference between upper and lower SES groups is significant for the white sample by chi-square analysis at $p < .05$. Differences between white and Negro upper and lower SES groups are both significant by chi-square analysis at $p < .001$.

performed in which the environmental measures were used as covariate controls.[4] Table 5 presents this analysis both with and without the covariate controls. It can be seen that while the covariate controls reduce the size of the F for race in the upper SES group, they do not change the race effect in the lower SES group. Univariate analyses of variance on the individual tests also showed that individual F ratios in the upper SES group were all reduced by the introduction of the covariates, while none of the ratios were reduced in the lower SES group. The present measures, then, were unable to account for the test-score differences between the racial groups at the lower SES level.

More information about the above relationships can be seen in the correlations between total achievement and the other variables in each race-class group (Table 6). Two important relationships are evident. Significant SES differences are seen within each racial group in the correlations of verbal intelligence to total achievement. Verbal intelligence accounts for a much larger portion of the variance of total achievement in the upper SES groups. Since racial differences on these correlations are minimal, it appears that the extent to which a student achieves at a level which is correlated with his verbal intelligence tends to be more strongly related to SES than to race. Second, Table 6 shows that none of the home and

[4]Since there are no reliable racial differences on the Cultural Participation Scale or the Family Participation Scale, these scales are not used as covariate controls.

TABLE 5.   Multivariate analysis of variance on intelligence and achievement tests with and without covariate controls[a].

Effect	F			
	Upper SES		Lower SES	
	Without	With	Without	With
Race	2.34[*]	1.52	5.55[**]	5.57[**]
Sex	3.91[**]	3.55[**]	7.05[**]	7.88[**]
Race X Sex	0.86	0.98	1.12	1.12

[a]Covariate controls are intact home, maternal employment, and crowdedness ratio.
[*]$p = .05$.
[**]$p = .01$.

family scores are significantly correlated with total achievement in the lower SES Negro group. This corroborates the previous assertion that factors other than those controlled in the present study are affecting the scores of the lower SES Negroes.

Since Table 5 has shown that the sex effect is highly significant in both SES groups, the data were also examined to determine if the racial differences discussed above are found in both males and females. Reanalysis of the racial differences controlling for sex showed that in the upper SES group all of the significant differences were attributable to racial differences between the male groups, while none of the differences between the female groups reached an acceptable level of significance. At the lower SES level, for the most part, the pattern was reversed, and differences

TABLE 6.   Correlations between total achievement and other major variables.

Variable	Upper SES white	Lower SES white	Upper SES Negro	Lower SES Negro
Verbal IQ	.81[**]	.64[**]	.81[**]	.62[**]
Nonverbal IQ	.63[**]	.54[**]	.57[**]	.43[**]
Cultural Participation Scale	.36[**]	.34[**]	.40[**]	.12
Family Participation Scale	.00	.26[*]	.21	−.01
Crowdedness	−.11	−.08	−.31[*]	−.10

Note.−For Verbal IQ, correlations in upper SES groups are significantly higher than correlations in lower SES groups.
[*]$p = .05$.
[**]$p = .01$.

were more often significant in the female group. Some sex differences in correlations were also obtained when the data presented in Table 6 were analyzed separately by sex groups.[5]

DISCUSSION

Shuey (1966) contended that racial differences in tested intelligence cannot be explained on the basis of environmental differences, and that research evidence points to the presence of some "native differences" in intelligence between white and Negro samples. One cannot deny that most studies previously reported have found racial differences, regardless of the controls that have been employed. It is possible from the present findings, however, to question whether all of these previous studies have adequately equated the racial groups. Equating experimental groups is difficult even when one draws samples from a relatively homogeneous population. Attempting to equate the environments and psychological experiences of individuals from different racial groups is a considerably more complex problem. It would seem that Shuey's argument is based largely on the weight of poorly controlled research. The present study demonstrates that controlling for SES (social class) alone does not equate white and Negro students on their home environments. When these family influences are controlled, the racial groups are certainly more similar, although still not "equated." Differences between these groups in the present study are minimal. No differences are found, in fact, between upper SES whites and Negroes when broken homes, maternal employment, and crowdedness of the home are controlled, and no differences are found between upper SES white and Negro females—even without the additional covariate controls. These results are contrary to the previous finding that racial differences are more pronounced in the upper SES groups (Deutsch & Brown, 1964), although quite possibly this difference could be accounted for by the different measures of social class employed by the

two investigations, or other uncontrolled characteristics of the populations studied.

The fact that the present analysis failed to eliminate racial differences among the lower SES students merits further discussion. First, it should be pointed out that at the time of the study over 90% of the Negro students in the present sample attended all-Negro schools. Research has shown that this factor by itself is significant as a determinant of the level of school performance (United States Commission on Civil Rights, 1967). In addition, the present correlational analysis (Table 6) has shown that in the lower SES Negro group (compared with the lower SES whites), a larger amount of the variance of total achievement is not accounted for either by intelligence or by the home and family variables that were employed in the present investigation. This is perhaps where the "caste" analogy (Dreger & Miller, 1960) is most useful. Many lower SES Negroes seem to be at a distinct social class level, and, therefore, equating lower class groups appears to be particularly difficult, at least with the type of procedures used in the present study. Even on so-called "culture-fair" tests, significant differences are found. With the present subjects, for example, Tulkin and Newbrough (1968) found no significant differences on Raven's Progressive Matrices between upper SES groups, but did find a significant difference between the lower SES groups.

How can one explain a racial difference that is found among lower SES students and not among upper SES students? Pettigrew (1964) noted that the economic floor for lower class Negroes is "distinctively below" the floor of the whites. A recent review of economic trends among Negroes in the United States based on the 1960 census (Brimmer, 1966) supports this argument and further demonstrates that economic differences between the races are greatest at the lower income level. Furthermore, the difference between whites and nonwhites with incomes in the upper fifth group decreased since 1947, while the gap between white and nonwhite incomes in the bottom fifth group actually increased during that 13-year period. Brimmer (1966) concluded that within the Negro community "the middle and upper income groups are getting richer, while the

[5]A more detailed presentation of the data on sex differences is available from the author.

lowest income group is getting poorer [p. 267]."
The psychological feelings of hopelessness and
helplessness resulting from this economic situation would be quite difficult to control statistically.

Another variable not usually considered when
studying racial differences in academic performance is prematurity. Prematurity is related to
intelligence (Kagan & Henker, 1966) and is more
frequent in Negroes than in whites (Abramowicz
& Kass, 1966). Here also, however, differences
are greatest at the lower SES levels. Block, Lippsett, Redner, and Hirschl (1952), for example,
found that the racial difference in the prematurity
rates for the lower SES group is more than 2½
times larger than the difference in the upper SES
group.

These findings point to the need for multidisci-
plinary studies to determine how the environment influences intellectual growth and behavior
in general, and to determine the extent to which
these environmental influences interact with "genetic predispositions." Poorly controlled research only adds confusion to the attempt to
define the relationships between environmental
backgrounds of students and their performance
on tests of intelligence and achievement. Specifically, controls for race, class, sex, and home and
family variables—including income—are prereq-
uisites for meaningful results. The present study
suggests that with adequate control measures it is
possible to demonstrate that racial groups are not
significantly different on measures of intelligence
and school achievement. Although results are
still inconclusive concerning the measures necessary to equate racial groups at the lower social
class level, they do suggest that intellectual differences are not to be found between different racial
groups with similar social class status and experiences.

REFERENCES

Abramowicz, M., & Kass, E. H. Pathogenesis and
prognosis of prematurity. *New England Journal of
Medicine,* 1966, **275**, 878.

Binet, A., & Simon, T. *The development of intelligence
in children.* (Trans. by E. S. Kite) Baltimore: Williams & Wilkins, 1916.

Block, H., Lippsett, H., Redner, B., & Hirschl, D.
Reduction of mortality in the premature nursery: II.
Incidence and causes of prematurity: Ethnic, socioeconomic and obstetric factors. *Journal of Pedia-
trics,* 1952, **41**, 300–304.

Bloom, R., Whiteman, M., & Deutsch, M. Race and
social class as separate factors related to social environment. Paper presented at the meeting of the
American Psychological Association, Philadelphia,
September, 1963.

Brimmer, A. F. The Negro in the national economy.
In J. P. Davis (Ed.), *The American Negro reference
book.* Englewood Cliffs, N.J.: Prentice-Hall, 1966.

Burt, C. The inheritance of mental ability. *American
Psychologist,* 1958, **13**, 1–15.

Deutsch, M. Minority group and class status as related
to social and personality factors in scholastic
achievement. *Monographs of the Society for Applied Anthropology,* 1960, No. 2.

Deutsch, M., & Brown, B. Some data on social influences in Negro-white intelligence differences. *Journal of Social Issues,* 1964, **20**, 24–35.

Dreger, R. M. & Miller, K. S. Comparative studies of
Negroes and whites in the United States. *Psychological Bulletin,* 1960, **57**, 361–402.

Hollingshead, A. *The Two-Factor Index of Social Position.* New Haven, Conn.: Author, 1957.

Ingle, D. J. Racial differences and the future. *Science,*
1964, **146**, 375–379.

Kagan, J., & Henker, B. A. Developmental psychology. *Annual Review of Psychology,* 1966, **17**,
1–50.

Kennedy, W. A., Van de Riet, V. & White, J. C. Normative sample of intelligence and achievement of
Negro elementary school children in the southeastern United States. *Monographs of the Society for
Research in Child Development,* 1963, **28**(6).

McCord, W. M., & Demerath, N. J., III. Negro versus
white intelligence: A continuing controversy. *Harvard Educational Review,* 1958, **28**, 120–135.

McGurk, F. Negro versus white intelligence: An answer. *Harvard Educational Review,* 1959, **29**, 54–
62.

Minigione, A. D. Need for achievement in Negro and
white children. *Journal of Consulting Psychology,*
1965, **29**, 108–111.

Pettigrew, T. F. *A profile of the Negro American.*
Princeton, N.J.: Van Nostrand, 1964.

Roen, S. R. Personality and Negro-white intelligence.
Journal of Abnormal and Social Psychology, 1960,
61, 148–150.

Shuey, A. M. *The testing of Negro intelligence.* Lynchburg, Va.: Randolph-Macon Women's College,
1958.

Shuey, A. M. *The testing of Negro intelligence.* (2nd
ed.) New York: Social Science Press, 1966.

Tulkin, S. R., & Newbrough, J. R. Social class, race,
and sex differences on the Raven (1956) Standard

Progressive Matrices. *Journal of Consulting and Clinical Psychology,* 1968, **32.**

United States Commission on Civil Rights. *Racial isolation in the public schools.* Washington, D.C.: Unites States Government Printing Office, 1967.

Veroff, J., Atkinson, J. W., Feld, S., & Gurin, G. The use of thematic apperception to assess motivation in a nationwide interview study. *Psychological Monographs,* 1960, **74**(12, Whole Number 499).

ARTICLE 24

Racial Differences in Intelligence: Comment on Tulkin

Philip S. Gallo, Jr., and Donald D. Dorfman

The question of whether or not genetic differences in intelligence exist between races clearly has great import for both science and society. It is not amiss, therefore, to demand that scientific research in this area *actually* demonstrate what it purports to demonstrate. One of the more recent studies dealing with this problem has been reported by Tulkin in the May 1968 issue of the *Journal of Personality and Social Psychology*. [The Tulkin article immediately precedes this one in this book—Eds.] A number of I.Q. and achievement tests were administered to 389 Negro and white fifth- and sixth-grade students in the Maryland area. Holding constant the factors of socioeconomic status and family differences, no significant racial differences were found in the upper SES group. Significant racial differences in favor of whites were found in the lowest SES group. Tulkin cites a number of environmental factors that could account for differences in the lower SES group. With race held constant, there were very large differences between the higher and lower SES groups. The general thrust of the article is that there are no genetic differences between the races if relevant environmental factors are statistically controlled.

The purpose of this reply is two-fold. First, with regard to Tulkin's study, we shall attempt to demonstrate that the results are inconclusive and that it is impossible to obtain results that would be germane to the question of genetic differences.

Reprinted with permission of the authors and the publisher. From *Representative Research in Social Psychology*, 1970, **1**, 24–28.

Second, and of greater importance, we shall attempt to demonstrate that at the present level of scientific technology and societal organization, there is no conceivable study that can be designed to answer this question.

Investigators in this area have long been aware of the importance of environmental factors in determining intelligence test performance. Even Garrett and Schneck (1933), proponents of the genetic differences theory, have written that comparisons are permissible only when environmental differences are absent or negligible. Tulkin cites Bloom, Whiteman, and Deutsch (1963), who found that social class may be the most important variable in predicting performance. Thus, Tulkin's decision to separate his subjects on the basis of SES seems to be unavoidable.

The Hollingshead Two Factor Index of Social Position (1957) was used as the criterion for selection. Students whose parents occupied levels 1 and 2 were considered upper class, those whose parents occupied level 5 were considered lower class. Students from levels 3 and 4 were not included in the study. The methodology takes into account the fact that I.Q. is a function of SES. It does not take into account the very real possibility that SES is at least in part a function of I.Q. Although high I.Q. is certainly not a sufficient cause for advancement into high SES, it is no doubt a necessary cause. Except in cases where high SES is inherited, it is unlikely that people deficient either in innate ability or experience will obtain the education or employment that would qualify them for high SES. Thus, people of either race who attain high SES tend to have reasonably high levels of intellectual achievement. The correlation of $+.49$ between parents' and children's I.Q. obtained by Burt and Howard (1956) suggests that parents' level of intellectual attainment is transmitted to their children through both hereditary and environmental mechanisms.

The very nature of social mobility suggests that SES and I.Q. are inextricably confounded. Tulkin's data indicate there are no differences in performance, when family differences are statistically controlled, between white and Negro children whose parents have attained high SES. These results are in no way germane to the question of how genetic potential is distributed in unselected racial groups.

Although Tulkin's study found no differences in the high SES group, consider whether the question of genetic differences could have been answered had his results been different. We shall assume the hypothetical case of a 15-point I.Q. difference found in favor of the Negro children. This result could be interpreted as an indication of genetic superiority on the part of the Negro children. However, an equally compelling argument could be made that discrimination in our society is so widespread that a Negro must be considerably superior to a white before he is given the same educational and employment opportunities as a less intelligent white citizen.

If the results had indicated a 15-point superiority for the white children, it could be argued that the white children are genetically superior. This genetic interpretation could be countered by the same environmental arguments that Klineberg (1963) has put forth so persuasively. In either case, the data do not permit us to choose between the genetic and the environmental arguments. The only conclusion to be drawn from Tulkin's study is that people of high SES tend to perform about the same on I.Q. tests, regardless of race. In view of the selection process involved in attaining high SES, these are precisely the results one would expect whether or not genetic differences exist between the races.

The most important remaining question is to determine if there is any conceivable cross-sectional study of this type that can provide a definitive resolution to the issue of genetic differences. Because of the impact of SES on I.Q. performance, any study that does not control for this variable can be discarded as methodologically unsound. Any study that does control for it is immediately subject to the criticism that people who have been selected for inclusion in the independent variable categories have in fact been preselected on the dependent variable. The problem of independent and dependent variable confounding renders all such cross-sectional studies meaningless in terms of the genetic question.

The probability that longitudinal studies can provide answers to this problem is equally poor. Proving genetic differences from a behavioral viewpoint requires a demonstration that environments for the two groups have been equal. Certainly, environmental experiences of American Negroes and whites today are not equal. Even if, during the next few years, radical changes occur providing Negroes with greatly enhanced educational, employment, and housing opportunities, it will still be virtually impossible to "prove" that their experiences are the same as those of whites. Dreger and Miller (1960) have argued that even when social class and economic variables are equated between ethnic groups, there are still important differences in life style and experience.

The one remaining behavioral possibility is that children be taken at birth and randomly assigned to families who have been carefully equated on all possible relevant variables. Although this technique is theoretically possible, it obviously is socially impossible. One cannot envision a time when parents, randomly selected, will willingly give up their children to further the cause of science. Although such a program might be feasible if done in conjunction with orphanages, the problem of random sampling diminishes the usefulness of such a study. Children who are given for adoption do not represent a random sample of all children, and there may very well be systematic racial biases determining which children from which parents are placed with adoption agencies.

In short, it is time that social scientists face the fact that this question cannot be answered now—and perhaps it can never be answered—at least behaviorally. It is not unreasonable to hope that the science of genetics can someday provide a direct answer. All that is really known at this point is that there are differences in performance between randomly selected groups of whites and Negroes and that deficient I.Q. performance can be improved by enriching cultural, social, and educational opportunities. It is to this latter problem that social scientists should be addressing their energies.

REFERENCES

Bloom, R., Whiteman, M., & Deutsch, M. Race and social class as separate factors related to social environment. Paper presented at the meeting of the American Psychological Association, Philadelphia, September 1963.

Burt, C., & Howard, M. The multiple factorial theory of inheritance and its application to intelligence. *British Journal of Statistical Psychology,* 1956, **9,** 95–131.

Dreger, R. M., & Miller, K. S. Comparative psychological studies of Negroes and whites in the United States. *Psychological Bulletin,* 1960, **57,** 361–402.

Garrett, H. E., & Schneck, M. R. *Psychological tests, methods and results.* New York: Harper, 1933.

Hollingshead, A. *The Two Factor Index of Social Position.* New Haven, Conn.: Author, 1957.

Klineberg, O. Negro-white differences in intelligence test performance: A new look at an old problem. *American Psychologist,* 1963, **18,** 198–203.

Tulkin, S. R. Race, class, family, and school achievement. *Journal of Personality and Social Psychology,* 1968, **9,** 31–37.

SECTION SUMMARY

In considering the position expressed by Arthur Jensen in the first article in this section, we need to review some chronology. For many years *some* social scientists have claimed that innate racial differences in intelligence exist. In the last 20 years, such conclusions (see, for example, Garrett, 1962, 1964, 1969) have been based primarily on studies that find that racial differences in IQ still exist, even after purportedly having "equated" the environments of blacks and whites. But articles such as those by Klineberg

(1963) and Gallo and Dorfman (in this section) effectively question whether such equated environments really exist.

Yet Jensen's argument, first widely publicized in his *Harvard Educational Review* (1969a) article, approached the issue in a different way, by questioning the degree to which *any one person's* heredity determines his level of mental development. From that position, Jensen speculated about the existence of many types of group differences, including social-class differences and sex differences in intelligence, as well as racial ones.

Jensen's basic viewpoint on the origin of individual differences may be expressed through the following statements:

1. Individual differences in intelligence are *predominantly* attributable to heredity, although environmental factors can play some role.

2. There are socioeconomic-status differences in measured IQ (as Tulkin's article also shows), the upper-middle-class children having higher tested IQs than lower-class children. Jensen proposes that part of this difference may be attributed to hereditary factors.

3. The *causes* of tested IQ differences between racial or ethnic groups are "scientifically still an open question" (1969b, p. 6). Jensen here speculates that an innate difference may exist, for he goes on to say that:

The fact that different racial groups in this country have widely separated geographic origins and have quite different histories which have subjected them to different selective social and economic pressures makes it highly likely that their gene pools differ from some genetically conditioned behavioral characteristics, including intelligence . . . [1969b, p. 6].

Jensen's article led to an enormous number of reactions, some of which were emotional and some of which responded to the issues. Most of the published reactions have been generally critical, although some have supported and even extended Jensen's conclusions. (See, for example, Herrnstein's article in the September 1971 issue of the *Atlantic* magazine.) The selection by Jensen reprinted in this book takes into account many of these criticisms. (The Spring 1969 and

Summer 1969 issues of the *Harvard Educational Review* contain many of these comments, as well as an article by Jensen responding to them.)

We believe that the primary limitation in Jensen's statement is the implicit assumption that one's tested IQ score and one's level of intelligence are the *same thing*. Recall the *social* nature of test taking (reviewed in Section 1). There is ample evidence that characteristics of the testing situation cause certain persons' tested scores to differ from their true level of intelligence (Katz, 1964, 1967; Forrester & Klaus, 1964; Sattler, 1970). An examiner may have expectations about the performance level of a subject; these expectations often have effects. A black child, tested by a white examiner, may be so apprehensive that he or she does not perform up to his or her level of ability. A Puerto Rican or a French Canadian may be hampered by language difficulties. An American Indian child may be constrained by the expectations of his or her tribe that no individual seek to stand out from the crowd. As do many other psychologists, Jensen seems to assume that we can take tested IQ differences and use them as 100%-pure indications of intellectual differences.

Beyond this limitation, is the available evidence adequate to support Jensen's conclusions? We think not. For example, Jensen reports that hereditary differences account for 80% of the difference in IQ scores among middle-class whites, the only type of subject population from whom heritability estimates were available at that time. Jensen assumed that these heritability estimates would be equally high in black and lower-class populations—that is, that in these latter populations individual differences in IQ arise much more from hereditary than environmental differences. More recent research by Scarr-Salapatek (1971a, 1971b) has provided us with heritability estimates for these latter groups. She found that in lower-class white and black populations, the heritability values were lower (from 50% to 60%) than they were for her middle-class samples or those reported by Jensen. In other words, differences in environment have more of an effect on differences in IQ between two lower-class children or two black children than they do

on two white middle-class children. Her results cause us to question the applicability of Jensen's conclusions when they are applied to lower-class or black children. Beyond this, Scarr-Salapatek's findings imply that the tested IQ differences between social classes (or between races) "may be considerably larger than the genotypic differences" (1971b, p. 1225). Improvement in the quality of the environment will have the effect of increasing the heritability of intelligence in black and lower-class groups, but it will increase their average IQs, also.

Thus environmental deprivation most assuredly accounts for much of the difference in average tested IQ between Negroes and Caucasians. Included under the rubric of "environmental deprivation" are such phenomena as unstable family life, crowded homes, lower family income, poorer health care, attendance at older schools with less experienced teachers and fewer teaching aids, fewer opportunities for travel, and many others. Discrimination and environmental deprivation may lead members of minority groups in the United States to believe that they *are* less capable, which influences their motivation to perform well on intelligence tests. Such self-fulfilling prophecies may even serve as a source of support when one has not succeeded in life.

We know that an enriched environment can raise the tested IQ of black children. Those children whose families moved from the South to the North in the 1930s and 1940s showed year-by-year increases in IQ the longer they spent in the better Northern schools (Lee, 1951; Klineberg, 1935). The Coleman report (Coleman, Campbell, Hobson, McPartland, Mood, Weinfield, & York, 1966) shows that achievement-test performance and IQ scores of black children improve if the children are placed in racially mixed classes. Attempts to provide a stimulating kindergarten experience for lower-class black children (Gray & Klaus, 1965, 1970) have increased IQs on the average of 6–9 points.

So we know that environmental deprivation plays a role. What about heredity? We agree with Gallo and Dorfman that this is an unanswerable question at this time, for it is impossible to control the relevant variables. What kind of study would be necessary to do this? Gallo and Dorfman suggest one in which black and white children are taken at birth and are randomly assigned to families who have been equated on all possible variables. Jensen's article makes similar proposals. But even these procedures would not suffice. First, there would still be the differences in prenatal environments of the children stemming from differences in the nutrition and health care of the mother. And second, the parents would probably respond differently to the child if the child were of a different race from them. The environment can exact its cost in subtle ways.

In a reply to Gallo and Dorfman, Tulkin (1970) has noted that one purpose of his study was to demonstrate that the earlier research on racial differences often ignored major environmental factors by assuming that a gross measurement of socioeconomic status was enough. Tulkin grants that hereditary differences in intellectual development may exist between individuals, but he also points out that "a great deal of the variance that has been attributed to social class and race might be traced, more specifically, to differences in experiences from as early as the first year of life" (Tulkin, 1970, p. 29). The recent comprehensive research project on children in Philadelphia (Scarr-Salapatek, 1971a, 1971b) also indicates that we need a refinement of what is *race* and *social class*.

If hereditary racial differences do exist, they are probably meaningless in any practical sense. Even when two groups differ in *average* score by 10–15 points, many members of the "inferior" group score higher than the average of the other group. If we consider that 50% of whites are above 100 in measured IQ, we need to recognize that in most studies anywhere from 15% to 50% of blacks are also above the average white in measured IQ.

Any classification of persons into mental-ability groups on the basis of race should be discouraged. Hicks and Pellegrini (1966) have reviewed 27 studies of racial comparisons and have concluded that knowing a person's race reduces by only 6% the uncertainty in estimating his IQ score. Even if racial segregation were not in conflict with our country's democratic value system,

such segregation would not be an efficient way to place children into homogeneous mental-ability groups. But more importantly, the enforcement of segregation places respect for the IQ above respect for the individual. As Dreger writes, ". . . the brutalizing effects of a system of segregation on both segregated and segregators are not worth keeping any race 'pure' " (1967, p. 50).

One further issue of great importance should be noted on this topic. What is the ethical responsibility of a scientist when he is aware that his data and findings may be used to achieve outcomes that he or society considers undesirable? For example, Jensen (1969a; also in the article reprinted in this book) has explicitly stated that any possible innate racial differences should *not* be used to segregate schoolchildren by race. But a scant five days after Jensen's *Harvard Educational Review* article appeared, it was being quoted by lawyers in a court case attempting to delay the desegregation of Virginia public schools (Brazziel, 1969). Hunt (1969, p. 149) has reminded scientific practitioners that they "must learn to think of political and social consequences of how and what they write and say." In reply to such charges, Jensen (1969c) has stated:

I would plead for more faith in the wisdom of the First Amendment. To refrain from publishing discussions on socially important issues because possibly there will be some readers with whose interpretations or use of the material we may disagree is, in effect, to give these persons the power of censorship over the publication of our own questions, findings, and interpretations [pp. 239–240].

By reprinting Jensen's writings, we affirm our belief that scientific speculations need to be aired, even if their implications may run counter to accepted values of our society. (The publication of Milgram's research on obedience, in Section 6, also reflects this view.) Our goal is to give interpretation to such speculations as Jensen's so that wise decisions can be made from them.

REFERENCES

Brazziel, W. F. A letter from the South. *Harvard Educational Review*, 1969, **39**, 200–208.

Coleman, J., Campbell, E., Hobson, C., McPartland, J., Mood, A., Weinfield, F., & York, R. *Equality of educational opportunity.* Washington, D. C.: U. S. Government Printing Office, 1966.

Dreger, R. M. Hard-hitting hereditarianism. *Contemporary Psychology,* 1967, **12,** 49–51.

Forrester, B. J., & Klaus, R. A. The effect of race of the examiner on intelligence test scores of Negro kindergarten children. *Peabody Papers in Human Development,* 1964, **2**(7), 1–7.

Garrett, H. E. The SPSSI and racial differences ("Comment" section). *American Psychologist,* 1962, **17,** 260–263.

Garrett, H. E. McGraw's need for denial ("Comment" section). *American Psychologist,* 1964, **19,** 815.

Garrett, H. E. Reply to Psychology Class 338 (Honors Section). *American Psychologist,* 1969, **24,** 390–391.

Gray, S. W., & Klaus, R. A. An experimental preschool program for culturally deprived children. *Child Development,* 1965, **36,** 887–898.

Gray, S. W., & Klaus, R. A. The Early Training Project: A seventh year report. *Child Development,* 1970, **41,** 909–924.

Herrnstein, R. I.Q. *Atlantic,* 1971, **228**(3), 44–64.

Hicks, R. A., & Pellegrini, R. J. The meaningfulness of Negro-white differences in intelligence test performance. *Psychological Record,* 1966, **16,** 43–46.

Hunt, J. McV. Has compensatory education failed? Has it been attempted? *Harvard Educational Review,* 1969, **39,** 130–152.

Jensen, A. R. How much can we boost IQ and scholastic achievement? *Harvard Educational Review,* 1969, **39,** 1–123. (a)

Jensen, A. R. Input: Arthur Jensen replies. *Psychology Today,* 1969, **3**(5), 4–6. (b)

Jensen, A. R. Reducing the heredity-environment uncertainty: A reply. *Harvard Educational Review,* 1969, **39,** 449–483. (c)

Katz, I. Review of evidence relating to effects of desegregation in the intellectual performance of Negroes. *American Psychologist,* 1964, **19,** 381–399.

Katz, I. Some motivational determinants of racial differences in intellectual achievement. *International Journal of Psychology,* 1967, **2,** 1–12.

Klineberg, O. *Negro intelligence and selective migration.* New York: Columbia University Press, 1935.

Klineberg, O. Negro-white differences in intelligence test performance: A new look at an old problem. *American Psychologist,* 1963, **18,** 198–203.

Lee, E. S. Negro intelligence and selective migration: A Philadelphia test of the Kleinberg hypothesis. *American Sociological Review,* 1951, **16,** 227–233.

Sattler, J. M. Racial "experimenter effects" in experimentation, testing, interviewing, and psychotherapy. *Psychological Bulletin,* 1970, **73,** 137–160.

Scarr-Salapatek, S. Race, social class, and IQ. *Science,* 1971, **174,** 1285–1295. (a)

Scarr-Salapatek, S. Unknowns in the IQ equation. *Science,* 1971, **174,** 1223–1228. (b)

Tulkin, S. Environmental influences on intellectual achievement: A reply to Gallo and Dorfman. *Representative Research in Social Psychology,* 1970, **1,** 29–32.

SUGGESTED READINGS FOR FURTHER STUDY

Baughman, E. E. *Black Americans.* New York: Academic Press, 1971.

Bodmer, W. F., & Cavalli-Sforza, L. L. Intelligence and race. *Scientific American,* 1970, **223,** 19–29.

Coon, C. S. *The origin of races.* New York: Knopf, 1962.

Deutsch, M. Organizational and conceptual barriers to social change. *Journal of Social Issues,* 1969, **25,** 5–18.

Dreger, R. M., & Miller, K. S. Comparative studies of Negroes and whites in the United States: 1959–1965. *Psychological Bulletin,* 1968, **70,** 1–58. (Monograph Supplement)

Gottesman, I. I. Biogenetics of race and class. In M. Deutsch, I. Katz, and A. R. Jensen (Eds.), *Social class, race, and psychological development.* New York: Holt, Rinehart & Winston, 1968. Pp. 11–51.

Jensen, A. R. IQ's of identical twins reared apart. *Behavior Genetics,* 1970, **1**(2), 133–148. 209–243.

Rosenthal, R., & Jacobson, L. *Pygmalion in the classroom.* New York: Holt, Rinehart & Winston, 1968.

Simpson, G. E., & Yinger, J. M. *Racial and cultural minorities.* (3rd ed.) New York: Harper & Row, 1965.

SPSSI Council statement on race and intelligence. *Journal of Social Issues,* 1969, **25,** 1–3.

SECTION 9

Prejudice and Racism

We all know people whose reactions to another person are highly influenced by the racial, ethnic, or religious background of the other person. Such people may even misjudge the qualities of the other person if they know that he or she belongs to a certain group. Why do some people have these "prejudiced" reactions? Does the fault reside in the racial, ethnic, or religious group that is stigmatized? Or does the person reject certain groups because of defects in his own emotional adjustment? Or is his reaction simply a reflection of the environment to which he has been exposed?

In this section we will discuss some of the factors that contribute to the existence of hostile racial attitudes and, on a broader scope, to the existence of a societal structure that may permit or even encourage mistreatment of minority-group members. We will look at the effects that such mistreatment may have on the minority-group members themselves and at ways in which changes in this situation may be set in motion.

To begin, we should clarify what is usually meant by the terms *prejudice* and *racism.* The traditional social psychological definition of prejudice has been well stated by Gordon Allport (1954, p. 9), who defined ethnic prejudice as:

> . . . an antipathy based upon a faulty and inflexible generalization. It may be felt or expressed. It may be directed toward the group as a whole, or toward an individual because he is a member of that group. The net effect of prejudice, thus defined, is to place the object of prejudice at some disadvantage not merited by his own conduct.

We propose one extension to Allport's definition. That is, prejudice is not only a negative or hostile attitude, as Allport implies, but it is also an attitude that has something *wrong* about it. All of us have negative attitudes toward many objects, but it is doubtful that we would treat all these negative attitudes as cases of prejudice. As the term *prejudice* is generally used, it is reserved for undesirable or unjustified negative attitudes.

With specific reference to attitudes toward minority ethnic groups, some of the factors that

243

might cause a negative attitude to be regarded as prejudiced are as follows: the attitude may serve as the basis for unjust discriminatory social practices (as Allport mentions); the beliefs associated with the attitude may be factually incorrect; the attitude may be the product of a "faulty" or illogical thought process; it may be derived from an unacceptable source, such as hearsay or distorted perceptions; it may be characterized by inordinate rigidity; the fact that the attitude is widespread within the majority culture may imply a lack of individual thought in adopting it; and the attitude may ascribe to ethnic inheritance characteristics that are actually cultural acquisitions. The reader can probably think of additional factors that are relevant.

It is obvious that a prejudicial attitude may lead to discriminatory behavior. But, although prejudice and discrimination often go hand in hand, this is not always the case. A person may have prejudiced attitudes and yet not be discriminatory in his behavior (a white may dislike blacks intensely yet not move when one sits next to him on the bus). Or, he may appear unprejudiced in his attitudes and yet be discriminatory in his behavior (a cab driver may avoid picking up black passengers because he feels that the possibility of being robbed is greater in the ghetto areas in which many blacks are forced to live). In such cases in which a discrepancy exists, there is a tendency to conclude that the attitudes are unimportant and the behavior is crucial. This resolution implies that behavior is the only criterion, and a pure one at that. Unfortunately, life is not that simple. Each instance of behavior is determined by a variety of factors; attitudes are a part. We should not neglect the study of attitudes and prejudice just because they do not always forecast a specific action. The study of attitudes is still useful in that an attitude alone, or in combination with other attitudes, may be predictive of certain actions. We shall discuss this point further in Section 11.

Not all cases of discrimination can be attributed to the hostile attitudes of individuals. Recently a great deal of attention has been paid to the concept of *institutional racism,* as originally identified by Carmichael and Hamilton

(1967). The hostile ethnic attitudes of individuals may be described as cases of prejudice or of individual racism. But when some or all of the major societal institutions are structured so that they permit or encourage the subjugation and mistreatment of large groups of people, this is institutional racism. It has been convincingly argued that present-day American society is so structured. A vivid example of institutional racism is provided by Carmichael and Hamilton (1967, p. 4): "When white terrorists bombed a black church and killed five black children, that was an act of individual racism, widely deplored by most segments of the society. But when in that same city — Birmingham, Alabama—five hundred black babies die each year because of the lack of proper food, shelter, and medical facilities, and thousands more are destroyed and maimed physically, emotionally, and intellectually because of conditions of poverty and discrimination in the black community, that is the operation of institutional racism." We will discuss some of the most salient instances of institutional racism in the Summary.

The articles in this section focus on the effects of prejudice and institutional racism on minority-group members and on the conditions that are crucial for changing this situation. In the first reading, Thomas F. Pettigrew, of the Department of Social Relations at Harvard University, discusses the question of paramount importance in this complex area of prejudice, discrimination, and institutional racism: shall Americans of the future live racially separate or together? He focuses on five key assumptions often proposed by white and black separatists. Pettigrew then devotes his attention to the best "route" to the societal state of "true integration," wherein true personal and group autonomy can be retained in a situation of racial togetherness. The reader is encouraged to apply his own analytical talents within the frame of reference provided by Pettigrew.

The effects of prejudice and institutional racism on minority-group members can obviously be awesome. On the one hand, the objective standard of living of minority ethnic groups in the United States (blacks, Mexican-Americans,

Asian Americans, Indians, Puerto Ricans) is dismal when compared with that enjoyed by majority-group Americans. Numerous studies and surveys have shown that minority-group members have much lower levels of housing, education, and income and much higher levels of unemployment, infant mortality, and so forth.

The cumulative *psychological* effects of racism for the minority-group member can also be vast. Not only must he deal with everyday rebuffs and personal unpleasantries, but he must also be aware of the structure of society. As has been noted repeatedly, the pressures of such a society may set up a "self-fulfilling prophecy" whereby the minority-group member actually adopts those negative traits ascribed to him, perhaps as a conscious means of adapting and "getting along," perhaps as a "to-hell-with-it" reaction to repeated frustrations, or perhaps simply due to eventual acceptance of the majority-group and institutional orientation.

In the second article in this section, Stephen Asher and Vernon Allen, of the University of Wisconsin, utilized a research paradigm originally developed by Clark and Clark (1947). The Clarks asked a large sample of black children to respond to a number of questions by choosing one of two dolls. One of the dolls had "white" skin and the other dark-brown skin. Included in the questions were such queries as: "Which is the good doll? Which is the bad doll? Which doll would you rather play with? Which doll looks like you? Which is the white doll? Which is the colored doll?"

The Clarks found that their sample of black children preferred the white doll to play with and perceived the white doll as good and the brown doll as bad. When asked to identify the white and "colored" doll, more than 90% of the children were able to do so correctly. The Clarks were disturbed, however, to find that one-third of their sample of black children, when asked to pick "the doll that looks like you," chose the white doll. This latter finding led the investigators to conclude that many black children had a confused sense of self-identity. In fact, these findings were used in legal arguments in the momentous 1954 *Brown vs. Board of Education* Supreme Court

decision that struck down school segregation laws.

The Clark and Clark study was carried out more than 30 years ago. Asher and Allen are concerned with the intervening social processes that might affect more recent patterns of preference by black children. If widespread attempts to enhance feelings of black identity, pride, black power, and black competence have been successful, they propose, then black children should have much less reason to prefer the white doll. On the other hand, recent economic progress in the black community may have led blacks to compare themselves more frequently with whites. And although the economic status of blacks has improved in recent years, the economic status of whites has improved at least as fast. If this is the case, social comparison theory (Pettigrew, 1968) would predict that blacks, since they are still no better off *relative to whites,* would suffer from even greater feelings of inferiority. Such feelings of inferiority could be expected to lead to greater preference for the white doll. Their data support the latter position. In three of four cases, black children (ages 3 to 8) showed a greater preference for the white doll than had black children in the Clark and Clark study.

The final selection describes still another replication of the Clark and Clark design. Unlike previous studies, however, Joseph Hraba of Iowa State University and Geoffrey Grant of the University of Nebraska found that black children in 1969 showed a much greater preference for the black dolls, even though their sample was taken from integrated schools. Although Asher and Allen suggested that increased exposure to whites would make black children prefer white even more (social comparison theory), the Hraba and Grant results do not support such a hypothesis. In fact, those children who presumably have had the most exposure to whites (the oldest children in the sample) preferred the black dolls most. If the results found by Hraba and Grant represent a lasting trend in American society, then we should expect the "white preference" findings of the Clarks, Asher and Allen, and other researchers in the 1950s and 1960s to be granted the status of historical findings—findings that adequately described the state of affairs in American society at one period in time but that are no longer applicable to contemporary American society.

REFERENCES

Allport, G. W. *The nature of prejudice.* Reading, Mass.: Addison-Wesley, 1954.

Carmichael, S., & Hamilton, C. V. *Black power: The politics of liberation in America.* New York: Random House, 1967.

Clark, K. B., & Clark, M. P. Racial identification and preference in Negro children. In T. M. Newcomb and E. L. Hartley (Eds.), *Readings in social psychology.* New York: Holt, 1947. Pp. 169–178.

Pettigrew, T. F. Social evaluation theory: Convergences and applications. In D. Levine (Ed.), *Nebraska symposium on motivation, 1967.* Lincoln: University of Nebraska Press, 1968.

ARTICLE 25

Racially Separate or Together?[1]

Thomas F. Pettigrew

The United States has had an almost perpetual racial crisis for a generation. But the last third of the twentieth century has begun on a new note, a change of rhetoric and a confusion over goals. Widespread rioting is just one expression of this. The nation hesitates: it seems to have lost its confidence that the problem can be solved; it seems unsure as to even the direction in which a solution lies. In too simple terms, yet in the style of the fashionable rhetoric, the question has become: Shall Americans of the future live racially separate or together?

This new mood is best understood when viewed as part of the eventful sweep of recent years. Ever since World War I, when war orders combined with the curtailment of immigration to encourage massive migration to industrial centers, Negro Americans have been undergoing rapid change as a people. The latest products of this dramatic transformation from Southern peasant to Northern urbanite are the second and third generations of young people born in the North. The most significant fact about this "newest new Negro" is that he is relatively released from the principal social controls recognized by his parents and grandparents, from the restraints of an extended kinship system, a conservative religion, and an acceptance of the inevitability of white supremacy.

Consider the experience of the 20-year-old Negro in 1971. He was born in 1951; he was only 3 years old when the Supreme Court ruled against *de jure* public school segregation; he was only 6 years old at the time of disorders over desegregation in Little Rock, Arkansas; he was 9 years old when the student-organized sit-ins began at segregated lunch counters throughout the South; he was 12 when the dramatic march on Washington took place and 15 when the climactic Selma march occurred. He has witnessed during his short life the initial dismantling of the formal structure of white supremacy. Conventional wisdom holds that such an experience should lead to a highly satisfied generation of young black Americans; but newspaper headlines and social-psychological theory tell us that precisely the opposite is closer to the truth.

The young black surveys the current scene and observes correctly that the benefits of recent racial advances have disproportionately accrued to the expanding middle class, leaving the urban lower class ever further behind. While the middle-class segment of Negro America has expanded from roughly 5 to 25 percent of the Negroes since 1940,[2] the vast majority of blacks remain poor. The young Negro has been raised on the proposition that racial integration is the basic solution to racial injustice, but his doubts

[1] An earlier draft of this paper was the author's presidential address to the Society for the Psychological Study of Social Issues, delivered at the annual convention of the American Psychological Association in San Francisco, California, on September 1, 1968.

[2] These figures derive from three gross estimates of "middle class" status: annual family income of $6,000 or more, high school graduation, or white-collar occupation. Thus, in 1961 roughly one-fifth of Negro families received in excess of $6,000 (a percentage that now must approach one-fourth, even in constant dollars); in 1960, 22 percent of Negroes over 24 years of age had completed high school; and in 1966, 21 percent of employed Negroes held white-collar occupations.

grow as opportunities open for the skilled while the daily lives of the unskilled go largely un-affected. Accustomed to a rapid pace of events, many Negro young people wonder if integration will ever be possible in an America where the depth of white resistance to racial change becomes painfully more evident: in 1964, the equivocation of the Democratic Party Conven-tion when faced with the challenge of the Missis-sippi Freedom Democratic Party; in 1965, the brutality at the bridge in Selma; in 1966, the sum-mary rejection by Congress of anti-discrimina-tion legislation for housing; in 1968, the wanton assassinations within ten weeks of two leading symbols of the integration movement; and, finally, the retrogression in Federal action for civil rights under the Nixon administration. These events create understandable doubts as to whether Dr. Martin Luther King's dream of equality can ever be achieved.

It is tempting to project this process further, as many analyses in the mass media unhesitantly have done, and suggest that all of black America has undergone this vast disillusionment, that blacks now overwhelmingly reject racial integra-tion and are instead turning to separatist goals. As we shall note shortly when reviewing evidence from surveys, this is not the case. Strictly separat-ist solutions for the black ghettos of urban Amer-ica have been most elaborately and en-thusiastically advanced not by Negro writers but by such popular white writers as the newspa-per columnist Joseph Alsop and William H. Ferry, formerly of the Center for the Study of Democratic Institutions (Alsop, 1967a, 1967b; Ferry, 1968).[3] These white analysts, like many white spokesmen for three centuries before them, are prepared to abandon the American dream of equality as it should apply to blacks, in the name of "hard realities" and under a conveniently mis-taken notion that separatism is what blacks want anyway.

[3]For answers to these articles see: Schwartz, Pettigrew, and Smith (1967, 1968). Ferry even proposes that "black colo-nies" be formally established in American central cities, com-plete with treaties enacted with the Federal government. The position of black militants is in sharp contrast to this; they complain of having a colonial status now and do not consider it a desirable state of affairs.

Yet the militant stance and rhetoric have shifted in recent years. In a real sense, integration has not failed in America, for it still remains to be tried as a national policy. Many Negroes of all ages sense this; they feel that the nation has failed integration rather than that integration has failed the nation. Influential black opinion turned in the late 1960s from integration as the primary goal to other goals—group power, culture, iden-tity, integrity, and pride. Only a relatively small segment of blacks see these new goals as conflict-ing with integration; but this segment and their assumptions are one focus of this chapter, for they play a disproportionately critical role for the two chief concerns of this volume—racial inte-gration and white racism. The principal conten-tion throughout this book has been that *integration is a necessary condition for the eradi-cation of white racism at both the individual and institutional levels.* But no treatment of this the-sis in America of the 1970s would be complete unless it included a brief discussion of this new black mood and its apparently separatist fringe.

Even much of this fringe of young ideological blacks should be described as "apparently" sepa-ratist, for the labels that make sense for white Americans necessarily must shift meaning when applied to black Americans. Given the national events that have occurred in their short lives, it is not surprising that this fringe regard racial inte-gration less as an evil than as irrelevant to their preoccupations. They often call for *selective* sep-aratism of one or more aspects of their lives while also demanding their rights of entry into the soci-ety's principal institutions. It is no accident that the most outspoken members of this faction are college students in prestigious and predominantly white universities.

Through the eyes of some whites, this behavior seems highly inconsistent; it looks as though they talk separation and act integration. But actually the inconsistency is often, though not always, more apparent than real. Consistent with the new emphasis upon power and pride, these young blacks are attempting to define their situation for themselves with particular attention to group au-tonomy. They are generally as opposed to forced separatism as were Negroes of past generations, and they reject other imposed doctrines as well. And for many of them, integration appears to be imposed by white liberals. "Why is it that you white liberals only insist on *racial* integration," they often ask, "when separation by class and ethnicity is a widespread fact of American life? Why is it no one gets upset by Italian separatism or Jewish separatism, only black separatism?" That the imposed separation of Negroes in America is qualitatively different and more vast than that practiced against or by any other sizable American minority, that integration as a doctrine was a creation not of white liberals but of their own fathers and grandfathers—these answers to the young blacks' insistent question are intellectually sound. But such responses do not relate to the feelings underlying the question, for they ignore the positive functions of the new emphasis which excite many young black Americans today.

The positive functions of the new militancy and ideology are exciting precisely because they go to the heart of many young blacks' personal feelings. If the new ideology's analysis of power at the societal level is incomplete, its analysis of racial self-hate at the individual level is right on the mark. Its attention to positive identity and "black is beautiful" is needed and important. Indeed, the abrupt shift from "Negro" to "black" is an integral part of this movement. Many members of older generations would have taken offense at being called "black"; it was considered a slur. But in facing the issue squarely, young blacks want to be called by the previously forbidden term in order to externalize the matter and convert it into a positive label. The fact that the historical justification sometimes cited for the shift is thin at best is not the point.[4] The important consideration is psychological, and on this

[4] It is sometimes held that "Negro" was the term for slaves; but actually both "Negro" and "black" were frequently used in documents concerning slaves. Some critics argue that the true skin color of Negro Americans is basically brown, not black, and that the term "black" is therefore inappropriate. But of course "white" Americans are seldom white either; besides, "Negro" is simply the Spanish word for "black." The importance of the term "black" is in fact basically psychological. I have used both terms interchangeably because surveys indicate each is preferred by different segments of the Negro community.

ground there is every reason to believe that the change is healthy.

Racial integration has shifted, then, in much black thought from the status of a principal goal to that of one among other mechanisms for achieving "liberation." "Liberation," in its broadest meaning for American race relations, means the total elimination of racial oppression. Similar to the older usage of "freedom," "liberation" means the eradication of the burden of racism that black Americans have borne individually and collectively since 1621. From this particular black perspective, "racially separate or together" is not the issue so much as what mix of strategies and efforts can actually achieve liberation.

There are, then, positive functions internal to black communities and individuals which this new stance and line of thought appear to have. Much of the present writing in race relations is devoted to these positive functions. But what do these trends spell out for the possibility of effectively combating white racism? While accepting the conclusion of the Kerner Commission that this is the basic problem, some recent black thought takes the position that wholly *black* concerns must take such precedence that the fight against white racism is, if not irrelevant, at least of secondary importance. Worse, some elements of the separatist fringe actively contribute to the growth and legitimacy of white racism. Hence, when Roy Innis, the national chairman of the Congress of Racial Equality (CORE), goes on a publicized tour to meet governors of the Deep South in order to advocate his program of separate-but-equal public schools, it hardly helps the effort to eliminate white racism.

This truly separatist fringe, then, is neither necessary to nor typical of the new black thrust. It gains its importance from, and becomes potentially dangerous because of, the way it nourishes white racism at both the individual and institutional levels. And it is for this reason that we need to compare it with white segregationist thought. Obviously, the two groups of separatists have sharply different sources of motivation: the blacks to withdraw, the whites to maintain racial supremacy. Nor are their assumptions on a par for destructive potential. But the danger is that black and white separatism could congeal as movements in the 1970s and help perpetuate a racially separate and racist nation. Because of this danger, it is well to examine the basic assumptions of both groups.

SEPARATIST ASSUMPTIONS

White segregationists, both in the North and in the South, base their position upon three bedrock assumptions. *Assumption 1* is that separation benefits both races because each feels awkward and uncomfortable with the other: *Whites and Negroes are happiest and most relaxed when in the company of "their own kind"* (Armstrong & Gregor, 1964).

Assumption 2 is blatantly racist: *Negroes are inherently inferior to whites, and this is the underlying reality of all racial problems.* The findings of both social and biological science place in serious jeopardy every argument put forward for this assumption, and a decreasing minority of white Americans subscribe to it (Pettigrew, 1964). Yet it remains the essential substratum of the thinking of white segregationists; racial contact must be avoided, according to this reasoning, if standards of whites are not to be lowered. Thus, attendance at a desegregated school may benefit black children, but is deemed by segregationists to be inevitably harmful to white children.[5]

Assumption 3 is derived from this assumption of white superiority: *Since contact can never be mutually beneficial, it will inevitably lead to racial conflict.* The White Citizens' Councils in the Deep South, for example, insist that they are opposed to violence and favor racial separation as the primary means of maintaining racial harmony. As long as Negroes "know their place," as long as white supremacy remains unchallenged, strife will be at a minimum.

Black separatists base their position upon three

[5]Analysis specifically directed on this point shows that this contention is not true for predominantly white classrooms as contrasted with comparable all-white classrooms (United States Commission on Civil Rights, 1967, Vol. 1, p. 160).

somewhat parallel assumptions. They agree with Assumption 1, that both whites and Negroes are more at ease when separated from each other. It is a harsh fact that blacks have borne the heavier burden of desegregation and have entered previously all-white institutions where open hostility is sometimes practiced by segregationist whites in order to discourage the process, and this is a partial explanation of agreement among blacks with Assumption 1. Yet some of this agreement stems from more subtle situations: the demands by some black student organizations on interracial campuses for all-black facilities have been predicated on this same assumption.

A second assumption of black separatists focuses directly upon white racism. Supported by the chief conclusion of the National Advisory Commission on Civil Disorders, black separatists consider that white racism is the central problem, and that "white liberals" should confine their energies to eradicating it (National Advisory Commission on Civil Disorders, 1968). Let us call this *Assumption 4: White liberals must eradicate white racism.* This assumption underlies two further contentions: namely, that "white liberals" should stay out of the ghetto except as their money and expertise are explicitly requested, and that it is no longer the job of black militants to confront and absorb the abuse of white racists.

The third assumption of black separatists is the most basic of all, and is in tacit agreement with the segregationist notion that interracial contact as it now occurs makes only for conflict. Interaction between black and white Americans, it is held, can never be truly equal and mutually beneficial until blacks first gain personal and group autonomy, self-respect, and power. This makes *Assumption 5: Autonomy is necessary before contact.* It often underlies a two-step theory of how to achieve meaningful integration: the first step requires separation so that Negroes can regroup, unify, and gain a positive self-image and identity; only when this is achieved can the second step, real integration, take place. Ron Karenga, a black leader in Los Angeles, states the idea forcefully: "We're not for isolation, but interdependence. But we can't become interdependent unless we have something to offer. We can live with whites interdependently once we have black power" (Calame, 1968).[6]

Each of these ideological assumptions deserves examination in the light of social-psychological theory and findings.

SOCIAL-PSYCHOLOGICAL CONSIDERATIONS OF SEPARATIST ASSUMPTIONS

Assumption 1: Whites and Negroes are more comfortable apart than together.

There can be no denying that many black and white Americans initially feel uncomfortable and ill at ease when they encounter each other in new situations. This reality is so vivid and so generally recognized that both black and white separatists use it widely in their thinking, though they do not analyze the nature and origins of the situation.

The literature of social science is replete with examples of the phenomenon. Irwin Katz has described the initial awkwardness in biracial task groups in the laboratory: white partners usually assumed an aggressive, imperious role, black partners a passive role. Similarly, Yarrow found initial tension and keen sensitivity among many Negro children in an interracial summer camp, much of which centered on fears that they would be rejected by white campers (Katz, 1964; Yarrow, 1958). But, more important, such tension does not continue to pervade a truly integrated situation. Katz noted that once blacks were cast in assertive roles, behavior in his small groups became more equalitarian and this improvement generalized to new situations. Yarrow, too, observed a sharp decline in anxiety and sensitivity among the black children after two weeks of successful integration at the summer camp.

This is not to say that new interracial situations invariably lead to acceptance. The *conditions* of the interracial contact are crucial; and even under optimal conditions, the cross-racial acceptance generated by contact is typically limited to the

particular situation which created it. A segregated society restricts the generalization effects of even truly integrated situations; and at times like the present, when race assumes such overwhelming salience, the racial tension of the larger society may even poison previously successful interracial settings.

Acquaintance and similarity theory helps to clarify the underlying process. Newcomb (Newcomb, Turner, & Converse, 1965) states the fundamental tenet as follows:

Insofar as persons have similar attitudes toward things of importance to both or all of them, and discover that this is so, they have shared attitudes; under most conditions the experience of sharing such attitudes is rewarding, and thus provides a basis for mutual attraction.

Rokeach has applied these notions to race relations in the United States with some surprising results. He maintains that rejection of black Americans by white Americans is motivated less by racism than by assumed differences in beliefs and values. In other words, whites generally perceive Negroes as holding beliefs contrasting with their own, and it is this perception—not race *per se*—that leads to rejection. Indeed, a variety of subjects have supported Rokeach's ideas by typically accepting in a social situation a Negro with beliefs similar to their own over a white with different beliefs (Rokeach, Smith, & Evans, 1960; Rokeach & Mezei, 1966; Smith, Williams, & Willis, 1967; Stein, 1966; Stein, Hardyck, & Smith, 1965).[7]

Seen in the light of this work, racial isolation has two negative effects, both of which operate to make optimal interracial contact difficult to achieve and initially tense. First, isolation prevents each group from learning of the beliefs and

---

[6]Karenga's contention that blacks presently have nothing "to offer" a racially interdependent America strangely echoes similar contentions of white racists.

[7]The resolution (Triandis & Davis, 1965) of the earlier controversy between Triandis and Rokeach takes on added weight when the data from studies favorable to Rokeach's position are examined carefully (Triandis, 1961; Rokeach, 1961). That interpersonal realms lead to varying belief-race weightings is borne out by Table 4 in Stein et al. (1965); that intensely prejudiced subjects, particularly in environments where racist norms even extend into less intimate realms, will act on race primarily is shown by one sample of whites in the Deep South in Smith et al. (1967).

values they do in fact share. Consequently, Negroes and whites kept apart come to view each other as very different; this belief, combined with racial considerations, causes each race to reject contact with the other. Second, isolation leads in time to the evolution of genuine differences in beliefs and values, making interracial contact in the future even less likely.[8]

A number of findings of social-psychological research support this extrapolation of interpersonal-attraction theory. Stein et al. (1965) noted that relatively racially isolated white ninth-graders in California assumed an undescribed Negro teen-ager to be similar to a Negro teen-ager who was described as being quite different from themselves. Smith et al. (1967) found that similarity of beliefs was more critical than racial similarity in desegregated settings, less critical in segregated settings. And the U. S. Commission on Civil Rights, in its study of *Racial Isolation in the Public Schools,* found that both black and white adults who as children had attended interracial schools were more likely as adults to live in an interracial neighborhood and hold more positive racial attitudes than comparable adults who had known only segregated schools (U. S. Commission on Civil Rights, 1967). Or, to put it negatively, Americans of both races who experienced only segregated education are more likely to reflect separatist behavior and attitudes as adults.

Racial separatism, then, is a cumulative process. It feeds upon itself and leads its victims to prefer continued separation. In an open-choice situation in Louisville, Kentucky, black children were far more likely to select predominantly white high schools if they were currently attending predominantly white junior high schools.[9] From these data, the U. S. Commission on Civil Rights concluded: "The inference is strong that

[8]Both black and white observers tend to exaggerate racial differences in basic values. Rokeach and Parker note from data from national surveys that, while there appear to be real value differences between the rich and the poor, once socioeconomic factors are controlled there are no sharp value differences between black and white Americans (Rokeach & Parker, 1970).

[9]For twelve junior highs, the Spearman-Brown rank-order correlation between the white junior high percentage and the percentage of Negroes choosing predominantly white high schools is +.82 (corrected for ties)—significant at better than the 1 percent level of confidence.

Negro high school students prefer biracial education only if they have experienced it before. If a Negro student has not received his formative education in biracial schools, the chances are he will not choose to enter one in his more mature school years" (U. S. Commission on Civil Rights, 1963). Similarly, Negroes who attended segregated schools, the Civil Rights Commission finds, are more likely to believe as adults that interracial schools "create hardships for Negro children" and are less likely to send their children to desegregated schools than are Negroes who attended biracial schools (U. S. Commission on Civil Rights, 1963). Note that those who most fear discomfort in biracial settings are precisely those who have experienced such situations *least.* If desegregation actually resulted in perpetual and debilitating tension, as separatists are so quick to assume, it seems unlikely that children already in the situation would willingly opt for more, or that adults who have had considerable interracial contact as children would willingly submit themselves to biracial neighborhoods and their children to biracial schools.

Moreover, in dealing with the fact that some tension does exist, a social-cost analysis is needed. The question becomes: What price comfort? Racially homogeneous settings are often more comfortable for members of both races, though, as we have just noted, this seems to be most true at the start of the contact and does not seem to be so debilitating that those in the situation typically wish to return to segregated living. But those who remain in racial isolation, both black and white, find themselves increasingly less equipped to compete in an interracial world. Lobotomized patients are more comfortable, too, but they are impaired for life.

Moreover, there is nothing inevitable about the tension that characterizes many initial interracial encounters in the United States. Rather, tension is the direct result of the racial separation that has traditionally characterized our society. In short, separation is the cause of awkwardness in interracial contacts, not the remedy for it.

Assumption 2: Negroes are inferior; and Assumption 4: White liberals must eradicate white racism.

These two assumptions, though of vastly different significance, raise related issues; and both also are classic cases of self-fulfilling prophecies. Treat a people as inferior, force them to play subservient roles,[10] keep them essentially separate, and eventually the people produced by this must come to support the initial racist notions. Likewise, assume that whites are unalterably racist, curtail efforts by Negroes to confront racism directly, separate Negroes from whites even further, and the result will surely be a continuation, if not a heightening, of racism.

The core of racist attitudes, the assumption of innate racial inferiority, has been under sharp attack from social science for over three decades.[11] Partly because of this work, attitudes of white Americans have undergone massive change over these years. Yet a sizable minority of white Americans, perhaps still as large as a fifth of the adult population, persist in harboring racist attitudes in their most vulgar and naive form. This is an important fact in a time of polarization, such as the present, for this minority becomes the vocal right anchor in the nation's process of social judgment. Racist assumptions not only are nourished by separatism but in turn rationalize separatism. Equal-status contact is avoided because of the racist stigma placed on black Americans by three centuries of slavery and segregation. But changes are evident both here and in social-distance attitudes. Between 1942 and 1963 the percentage of white Americans who favored racially desegregated schools rose from 30 to 63; the percentage of those with no objections to a Negro neighbor rose from 35 to 63 (Hyman & Sheatsley, 1964; Sheatsley, 1966). This trend did not abate during the mid-1960s of increasing white polarization mistakenly labeled "white backlash." This trend slowed, however, at the very close of the 1960s and in the early 1970s —possibly as a result of less insistence for integration.

The slow but steady erosion of racist and separatist attitudes among white Americans occurred during years of confrontation and change, although the process has been too slow to keep pace with the Negro's rising aspirations for full justice and complete eradication of racism. In a period of confrontation, dramatic events can stimulate surprisingly sharp changes in a short period of time.

The most solid social-psychological evidence about changes in racial attitudes comes from the studies of contact. Repeated research in a variety of newly desegregated situations showed that the attitudes of whites and blacks toward each other markedly improved: in department stores, public housing (Deutsch & Collins, 1951; Jahoda & West, 1951; Wilner, Walkley, & Cook, 1955; Works, 1961), the armed services (Stouffer, et al., 1949; MacKenzie, 1948), and the Merchant Marine (Brophy, 1946), and among government workers (MacKenzie, 1948), the police (Kephart, 1957), students (MacKenzie, 1948), and general small-town populations (Williams, 1964). Some of these findings can be interpreted not as results of contact, but as an indication that more tolerant white Americans seek contact with Negro Americans. A number of the investigations, however, restrict this self-selection factor, making the effects of the new contact itself the only explanation of the significant alterations in attitudes and behavior.

Surveys bear out these findings on a national scale. Hyman and Sheatsley found that among whites the most extensive changes in racial attitudes have occurred where extensive desegregation of public facilities had already taken place (Hyman & Sheatsley, 1964).[12] Recall, too, that data from the Coleman Report indicate that white students who attend public schools with blacks are the least likely to prefer all-white classrooms and all-white "close friends"; and this effect is strongest among those who began their interracial schooling in the early grades (Cole-

---

[10]For a role-analysis interpretation of racial interactions in the United States, see Pettigrew (1964).

[11]One of the first significant efforts in this direction was the classic intelligence study by O. Klineberg (1935). For a summary of current scientific work relevant to racist claims regarding health, intelligence, and crime, see Pettigrew (1964).

[12]This is, of course, a two-way causal relationship. Not only does desegregation erode racist attitudes, but desegregation tends to come first to areas where white attitudes are least racist to begin with. Hyman and Sheatsley's finding, however, specifically highlights the former phenomenon: "In those parts of the South where some measure of school integration has taken place official action has preceded public sentiment, and public sentiment has then attempted to accommodate itself to the new situation."

man et al., 1966). This fits neatly with the findings of the U. S. Commission on Civil Rights (1967) for both black and white adults who had attended biracial schools as children.

Not all intergroup contact, of course, leads to increased acceptance; sometimes it only makes matters worse. Keep in mind Allport's criteria: prejudice is lessened when the two groups (1) possess equal status in the situation, (2) seek common goals, (3) are cooperatively dependent upon each other, and (4) interact with the positive support of authorities, laws, or customs (Allport, 1954). These criteria are actually an application of the broader theory of interpersonal attraction. All four conditions maximize the likelihood that shared values and beliefs will be evinced and mutually perceived. Rokeach's belief-similarity factor is, then, apparently important in the effects of optimal contact. Following Triandis and Davis's (1965) findings, we would anticipate that alterations in attitudes achieved by intergroup contact, at least initially, will be greatest in formal areas and least in intimate areas.

From this social-psychological perspective, the assumption of black separatists that "white liberals" should eliminate white racism seems to be an impossible and quixotic hope. One can readily appreciate the militants' desire to avoid further abuse from white racists; but their model for change is woefully inadequate. White liberals can attack racist attitudes publicly, conduct research on racist assertions, set the stage for confrontation. But with all the will in the world they cannot accomplish by themselves the needed push, the dramatic events, the actual interracial contact which have gnawed away at racist beliefs for a generation. A century ago the fiery and perceptive Frederick Douglass phrased the issue pointedly (Douglass, 1962, pp. 366–367):

I have found in my experience that the way to break down an unreasonable custom is to contradict it in practice. To be sure in pursuing this course I have had to contend not merely with the white race but with the black. The one has condemned me for my presumption in daring to associate with it and the other for pushing myself where it takes it for granted I am not wanted.

Assumption 3: Contact must lead to conflict; *and Assumption 5: Autonomy is needed before contact.*

History reveals that white separatists are correct when they contend that racial change creates conflict, that if only the traditions of white supremacy were to go unchallenged racial harmony might be restored. One of the quietest periods in American racial history, 1895–1915, witnessed the construction of the massive system of institutional racism as it is known today—the "nadir of Negro American history," as Rayford Logan (1957) calls it. The price of those two decades of relative peace is still being paid by the nation. Even if it were possible now to gain racial calm by inaction, the United States could not afford the enormous cost.

But if inaction is clearly impossible, the types of action necessary are not so clear. Black separatists believe that efforts to further interracial contact should be abandoned or at least delayed until greater personal and group autonomy is achieved by Negroes. This view and the attitudes of white separatists just mentioned are two sides of the same coin. Both leave the struggle against racism in attitudes completely in the hands of "white liberals." And the two assumptions run a similar danger. Racism is reflected not only in attitudes but, more importantly, in institutionalized arrangements that operate to restrict the choices open to blacks. Both forms of racism are fostered by segregation, and both have to be confronted directly by Negroes. To withdraw into the ghetto, psychologically tempting as this may be for many, is essentially to give up the fight to alter the racially discriminatory operations of the nation's chief institutions. The Rev. Jesse L. Jackson, the Chicago black leader of Operation Breadbasket, makes the same point in forceful terms (Jackson & Poussaint, 1970):

Let's use this analogy. Assuming that racism is a hot fire. If we're gonna take over things and run them and destroy racism, we got to get to the core of the fire. You can't destroy it by running away from it. The fact is, at this point in American history, racism is in trouble in terms of the government, economy, political order and even the psychological order.

The issues involved are shown schematically in Figure 1. By varying contact-separation and an

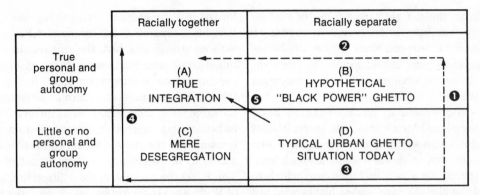

FIGURE 1. Schematic diagram of autonomy and contact-separation. Dotted lines denote hypothetical paths; solid lines, actual paths. The author is indebted to Professor Karl Deutsch of Harvard University for several stimulating conversations out of which came this diagram.

ideologically vague concept of "autonomy," four cells may be set up that represent the various possibilities under discussion. Cell A, true integration, refers to institutionalized biracial situations where there is cross-racial friendship, racial interdependence, and a strong measure of personal and group autonomy. Such situations do exist in America today, but they are rare islands in a sea of conflict. Cell B represents the autonomous ghetto postulated by advocates of black separatism, relatively independent of the larger society and far more viable than is commonly the case now. This is an ideologically derived hypothetical situation, for no such urban ghettos exist today. Cell C stands for merely desegregated situations. These are often mistakenly called "integrated." They are institutionalized biracial settings which involve little cross-racial acceptance and, often, patronizing legacies of white supremacy. Cell D represents today's typical highly separate urban ghetto with little or no personal or group autonomy.

Definitional confusions may obscure the meaning of Figure 1, especially the definition of "integration." This term became almost a hallowed symbol of the civil rights movement of previous decades, and its present disparagement in newer black thought may be traced in part to this fact. But most disparagement of "integration" is due to definitional confusion between it and "assimilation" and between it and desegregation as diagrammed in Figure 1. As Lerone Bennett (1970, pp. 37–38) rightly points out, these confusions

among both whites and blacks stem from employing exclusively a white standard of reference:

... One of the greatest enemies of integration in America today is the word integration. Contrary to the hopes of some and the fears of others, integration does not mean black elimination. Integration may or may not lead to assimilation, but assimilation does not necessarily mean the disappearance of a minority. ... Differences can be eliminated in favor of a creative minority. Both "integrationists" and "separatists" forget that there is a blackening process as well as a whitening process. Liberationists, who recognize this dialectic, say blacks must assimilate and not be assimilated. ... Integration is not disappearance; nor is it simple contiguity ... since men have given the word integration a bad name, we shall use the word transformation to refer to the real thing.

Cell A refers to "the real thing," to the integration of *whites* as well as blacks, to the end product of Lerone Bennett's "transformation."

Except for white separatists, observers of diverse persuasions agree that the achievement of true integration (cell A) should be the ultimate goal. But there are, crudely speaking, three contrasting ways of getting there from the typical current situation (cell D). The black separatist assumes that only one route is possible: from the depressed ghetto of today to the hypothetical ghetto of tomorrow and then, perhaps, on to true integration (lines 1 and 2 in Figure 1). The desegregationist assumes precisely the opposite route: from the present-day ghetto to mere desegregation and then, hopefully, on to true integration (lines 3 and 4 in Figure 1). But there is a third, more direct route, right across from the current ghetto to true integration (line 5 in Figure 1). Experience to date combines with a number of social-psychological considerations to favor the last of these possibilities with some important qualifications.

The route favored by black separatists has a surprising appeal for an untested theory; besides those whites who welcome any alternative to integration, it seems to appeal to militant black leaders searching for a new direction into which to channel the ghetto's rage, and to blacks who just wish to withdraw as far away from whites as possible. Yet, on reflection, it can be seen that the argument involves the perverse notion that the way to bring two groups together is to separate them further. One is reminded of the detrimental consequences of isolation in economics, through "closed markets," and in genetics, through "genetic drift." In social psychology, isolation between two contiguous groups generally leads to: (1) the development of diverse values, (2) reduced intergroup communication, (3) uncorrected perceptual distortions of each other, and (4) the growth of vested interests within both groups for continued separation. Race relations in the United States already suffer from each of these conditions; and the proposal for further separation, even if a gilded ghetto were possible, can only exacerbate them.

In fairness, it should be emphasized again that the criticisms here are directed against the concept of the insulated ghetto, not the shrewder and more subtle notions of power and regrouping combined with challenges to the restriction of choice imposed by the nation's leading institutions. As was mentioned at the beginning of this chapter, a much larger segment of militant blacks, judging from their actions, adheres to the latter program. The fascinations of the more romantic notions of a totally self-sufficient black community and even occasional expressions of black chauvinism are apparently diminished by many of the unromantic facts of the situation.

We will not pursue the many economic and political difficulties inherent in the concept of the insulated ghetto, but it should be mentioned that the resources immediately available in the ghetto

for the task are meager. Recognizing this limitation, black separatists call for massive Federal aid with no strings attached. But this requires a national consensus. Some separatists consider that the direct path to integration (line 5 in Figure 1) is idealistic dreaming, then turn and assume that the same racist society that resists integration will unhesitatingly pour a significant portion of its treasure into the ghetto. "Local control" without access to the necessary tax base is not control. This raises the question of the political limitations of this route. Irish-Americans entered the mainstream through the political system, and this method is often cited as appropriate to black separatism—but is it really? Faster than any other immigrant group except Jewish Americans, the Irish have assimilated on the direct route of Figure 1. Forced to remain in ghettos at first, the Irish did not settle for "local control" but strove to win city hall itself. Boston's legendary James Michael Curley won "Irish power" not by becoming mayor of the South Boston ghetto, but by becoming mayor of the entire city. Analogies between immigrants and blacks contain serious inaccuracies, however, since immigrants never suffered from slavery and legalized separation. But to the extent an analogy is appropriate, Mayor Carl Stokes of Cleveland, Mayor Richard Hatcher of Gary, and Mayor Kenneth Gibson of Newark are far closer to the Irish-American model than are black separatists.

A critical part of the thinking of black separatists centers on the psychological concept of "fate control"—more familiar to psychologists as Rotter's (1966) internal control of reinforcement variable. "Until we control our own destinies, our own schools and areas," goes the argument, "blacks cannot possibly achieve the vital sense of fate control." Data from the Coleman Report are cited to show that fate control is a critical correlate of achievement in school for black children (Coleman et al., 1966). But no mention is made of the additional fact that levels of fate control among black children were found by Coleman to be significantly higher in interracial schools than in all-Negro schools. Black separatists brush this important finding aside because all-Negro schools today are not what they envision for the future. Yet the fact remains that interracial schools appear to be facilitating the growth of fate control among Negro students now; the ideological contention that fate control can be developed as well or better in uniracial schools remains an untested and hypothetical assertion.

Despite the problems, black separatists feel that their route (lines 1 and 2 in Figure 1) is the only way to true integration, in part because they regard the indirect route of desegregation (lines 3 and 4) as an affront to their dignity. Anyone familiar with the blatantly hostile and subtly rejecting acts that typify some interracial situations will understand this repudiation of nonautonomous desegregation (cell C).[13] Merely desegregated schools, defined as biracial institutions typified by racial tension and little cross-racial friendship, have scant benefits over segregated schools (U. S. Commission on Civil Rights, 1967).[14]

This finding reflects Allport's conditions for optimal contact. Truly integrated institutions afford the type of contact that maximizes cross-racial acceptance and the similarity of beliefs described by Rokeach.[15] They apparently also maximize the positive and minimize the negative factors which Katz (1964, 1967) has isolated as important for performance of Negroes in biracial task groups. And they also seem to increase the opportunity for beneficial cross-racial evaluations, which may well be critical mediators of the effects of biracial schools (Pettigrew, 1967). Experimental research following up these leads is now called for to detail the precise social-psycho-

logical processes operating in the truly integrated situation (Pettigrew, 1968).

The desegregation route (lines 3 and 4 in Figure 1) has been successfully navigated, though the contention of black separatists that Negroes bear the principal burden for this effort is undoubtedly true. Southern institutions that have attained integration, for example, have typically traveled this indirect path. This route, then, is not as hypothetical as the route advocated by black separatists, but it is hardly to be preferred over the route of direct integration (line 5).

Why not the direct route, then? The standard answer is that it is impossible, that demographic trends and resistance from whites make it out of the question in our time. One is reminded of the defenders of slavery in the 1850s, who attacked the Abolitionists as unrealistic dreamers and insisted that slavery was so deeply entrenched that efforts should be limited to making it into a benign institution. If the nation acts on such speculations, of course, they will probably be proven correct. What better way is there to prevent racial change than to act on the assumption that it is impossible?

The belief that integration is impossible, however, is based on some harsh facts of urban racial demography. Between 1950 and 1960, the average annual increment of Negro population in the central cities of the United States was 320,000; from 1960 to 1966 the estimated annual growth climbed to 400,000, though reduced in-migration from the rural South has lowered this annual growth rate considerably since 1966. In the suburbs, however, the average annual growth of the Negro population declined from 60,000 between 1950 and 1960 to an estimated 33,000 between 1960 and 1966, though it has sharply increased since 1966 (U. S. Departments of Labor and Commerce, 1970). In other words, it would require several times the present trend in growth of Negro populations in the suburbs just to maintain the sprawling central-city ghettos at their present size. In the nation's largest metropolitan areas, then, the trend is still pushing in the direction of ever increasing separatism.

But these bleak data are not the whole picture. In the first place, they refer especially to the very

[13]For extreme examples of this phenomenon in public schools in the Deep South, see Chessler (1967).

[14]More recent evidence for this distinction is provided in Koslin, Koslin, Pargament, and Waxman (1970).

[15]Another white observer enthusiastic about black separatism even denies that the conclusions of the contact studies are applicable to the classroom and other institutions which do not produce "continual and extensive equal-status contact under more or less enforced conditions of intimacy." Stember selectively cites the investigations of contact in public housing and the armed forces to support his point (Stember, 1968); but he has to omit the many studies from less intimate realms which reached the same conclusions—such as those conducted in schools (Pettigrew, 1968), and employment situations (Harding & Hogrefe, 1952; Kephart, 1957; MacKenzie, 1948; Williams, 1964), and even one involving brief contact between clerks and customers (Saenger & Gilbert, 1950).

largest of the metropolitan areas—to New York City, Chicago, Los Angeles, Philadelphia, Detroit, Washington, D. C., and Baltimore. Most Negro Americans do not live in these places, but rather in areas where racial integration is in fact possible in the short run if attempts in good faith are made. There are more Berkeleys—small enough for school integration to be effectively achieved—than there are New York Cities. In the second place, the presumed impossibility of reversing racial trends in the central city is based on anti-metropolitan assumptions. Without metropolitan cooperation central cities—and many suburbs, too—will find their racial and other basic problems continuing. Do we need to assume such cooperation impossible? We previously proposed effective state and Federal incentives to further this cooperation. Moreover, some large black ghettos are already extending into the suburbs (e.g., east of Pittsburgh and west of Chicago); the first tentative metropolitan schemes to aid racial integration are emerging in a variety of cities (e.g., Boston, Hartford, Rochester, and Portland, Oregon); and several major metropolitan areas have even consolidated (e.g., Miami-Dade County and Nashville-Davidson County). Once the issue is looked at in metropolitan terms, its dimensions become more manageable. Black Americans are found in America's metropolitan areas in almost the same ratio as white Americans: about two-thirds of each group reside in these 212 regions. On a metropolitan basis, therefore, Negroes are not disproportionately metropolitan.

Yet it must be admitted that many young blacks, separatist and otherwise, are simply not convinced by such arguments. Such large-scale proposals as metropolitan educational parks strike them as faraway pipe dreams of no significance to their immediate problems. Contact theory holds little appeal. They rightfully argue that Allport's four conditions do not typify the American national scene. How often, they ask, do blacks actually possess equal status in situations with whites? And in struggles for racial power, as they view it, can there be a cooperative seeking of common goals? And as for the possibility that true integration of cell A will be sanctioned by

those in authority, they say ruefully, consider the public images on racial matters of Nixon, Mitchell, Agnew, Carswell. Maybe the demographic arguments against the possibility of integration are overdrawn, they concede, but can one realistically expect Allport's conditions of positive contact to become the rule in the foreseeable future of the United States?

Underlying this criticism is less a theoretical and ideological difference than a sharply contrasting assessment of the probabilities and possibilities of America's race relations. These black spokesmen may well be right. The United States may indeed be so racist both as to individuals and structure that the type of institutional changes advocated throughout this volume will never be achieved. No footnoting of references or social-psychological theory can refute this possibility, but I hope it is wrong. The entire analysis of this book is predicated on the more optimistic view that somehow American society will muddle through. To assume otherwise, once again, is to risk contributing to the problem by engaging in a self-fulfilling prophecy.

Moreover, the attack on contact theory is based in part on a misreading of it. *Situations* meeting Allport's four conditions do exist in the United States, and we have seen that they are becoming more numerous in such realms as employment. True, as noted, these truly integrated situations are still isolated islands and together do not constitute a critical mass nationally. Yet the status of Negroes is rising in the United States. Indeed, the personal lives of the black critics themselves typically attest to this social mobility, for roughly 90 percent of middle-class blacks today derive from families which were lower class in 1940. But these very gains create rapidly rising expectations and a keen sense of relative deprivation, some of which gets channeled among some blacks into the separatist ideology under discussion.

Nor are power struggles as completely racial and competitive as critics claim. For one thing, power conflicts almost invariably involve class as well as racial interests, and to the extent that class is involved there are at least potential white allies. White Americans, after all, are an even more diverse assortment than black Americans. But actually the theory requires only that blacks and some whites share common goals to the point where coalitions become important to both; one of the coalitions is called the Democratic Party, which since Franklin Roosevelt has consisted of a precarious combination of minorities which together total a registration far larger than that of the rival party.

Finally, concerning Allport's fourth condition on the sanction of laws and authorities, there is solid evidence in civil rights legislation and other institutional changes that we are moving toward the sanctioning of true integration. By and large, of course, America's institutions still do not play this role; they are racist, in the Kerner Commission's plain language, in that their normal operations still act typically to restrict choice for blacks. But positive change is evident from the appearance of Negroes on television to their participation in former bastions of white privilege. True, as far as race is concerned the Nixon Administration is a throwback to the naivete of early twentieth-century administrations; it offers no "authority sanction," nor does it promise to in its remaining years. Yet there are other political alternatives which would willingly offer the racial leadership the nation so desperately needs. To opt out of the opposition, to assume that the Mitchells and Agnews are inevitable and typical products of the American political system, is to ensure that such men will in fact remain in power.

To argue for route 5 in Figure 1 is not to assume that it will be easy to achieve, or that Allport's optimal conditions for intergroup contact apply generally throughout America at present. The direct path does stress that *simultaneous* attention must be given to both integration and individual and collective autonomy, for today's cell D has neither and tomorrow's cell A must have both. And neither the desegregation (paths 3 and 4 of Figure 1) nor the separatist (paths 1 and 2) route gives this simultaneous attention. Once again, Bennett (1970, p. 38) phrases the argument cogently:

It is impossible, Simon de Beauvoir said, to draw a straight line in a curved space. Both "integrationists" and "separatists" are trying to create right angles in a situation which only permits curves. The only option is Transformation of a situation which does not permit a clear-cut choice in either direction. This means that we must face the fact that it is impossible to move 30 million African-Americans anywhere.

IMPLICATIONS FOR POLICY

Much of the confusion over policy seems to derive from the assumption that since *complete* integration in the biggest cities will not be possible in the near future, present efforts toward opening opportunities for integration for both Negro and white Americans are premature. This thinking obscures two fundamental issues. First, the democratic objective is not total racial integration and the elimination of black neighborhoods; the idea is simply to provide an honest choice between separation and integration. Today only separation is available; integration is closed to blacks who would choose it. The long-term goal is not a complete obliteration of cultural pluralism, of distinctive Negro areas, but rather the transformation of these ghettos from racial prisons to ethnic areas freely chosen or not chosen. Life within ghettos can never be fully satisfactory as long as there are Negroes who reside within them only because discrimination requires them to.

Second, the integrationist alternative will not become a reality as long as we disparage it or abandon it to future generations. *Exclusive* attention to programs for enriching life in the ghetto is almost certain, to use Kenneth Clark's pointed word, to "embalm" the ghetto, to seal it in even further from the rest of the nation (making line 2 in Figure 1 even less likely). This danger explains the recent interest of conservative whites in enrichment programs for the ghetto. The bribe is straightforward: "Stop rioting and stop demanding integration, and we'll minimally support separatist programs within the ghetto." Even black separatists are understandably ambivalent about such offers, as they come from sources long identified with opposition to all racial change. Should the bargain be struck, however, race relations in the United States will be dealt still another serious blow.

Yet a policy concentrating *exclusively* on integration, like one concentrating exclusively on enrichment, runs its own danger of worsening the situation. As many black spokesmen correctly point out, a single-minded pursuit of integration is likely to blind us to the urgent requirements of today's black ghettos. Either policy followed mechanically and exclusively, then, has serious limitations which the rival strategy is designed to correct. This fact strongly suggests that a national transformation from a racist society to an open society will require a judicious mix of both the strategies.

The outlines of the situation, then, are these: (1) Widespread integration is possible everywhere in the United States except in the largest central cities. (2) It will not come unless present trends are reversed and considerable resources are provided for the process. (3) Big central cities will continue to have significant concentrations of Negroes even with successful metropolitan dispersal. (4) Large Negro ghettos are presently in need of intensive enrichment. (5) Some enrichment programs for the ghetto run the clear and present danger of embalming the ghetto further.

Given this situation and the social-psychological considerations we have been discussing, the overall strategy needed must contain the following elements:

1. A major effort toward racial integration must be mounted in order to provide genuine choice to all Negro Americans in all realms of life. This effort should envisage complete attainment of the goal in smaller communities and cities by the late 1970s and a halting of separatist trends in major central cities, with a movement toward metropolitan cooperation.

2. A simultaneous effort is required to enrich the vast central-city ghettos of the nation, to change them structurally, and to improve life in them. In order to avoid "embalming" them, however, strict criteria must be applied to proposed enrichment programs to ensure that they will not hinder later dispersal and integration. Restructuring the economics of the ghetto, especially by developing urban cooperatives, is a classic example of productive enrichment. Effective job training programs offer another example of productive

enrichment. The building of enormous public housing developments within the ghetto presents a good illustration of counterproductive enrichment. Some programs, such as the decentralization of huge public school systems or the encouragement of business ownership by Negroes, can be either productive or counterproductive depending upon how they are focused. A decentralization plan of many small homogeneous school districts for New York City is clearly counterproductive for later integration; a plan involving a relatively small number of heterogeneous school districts for New York City could well be productive. Likewise, black entrepreneurs who are encouraged to open small shops and are expected to prosper with an all-black clientele are not only part of a counterproductive plan, but are probably committing economic suicide. Negro businessmen who are encouraged to pool their resources to establish somewhat larger operations and to appeal to white as well as black customers on major traffic arteries in and out of the ghetto could be an important part of a productive plan.

In short, a mixed strategy is called for—both integration and enrichment—and it must contain safeguards that the two aspects will not impede each other. Results of recent surveys strongly suggest that such a mixed strategy would meet with widespread approval among black Americans.

Young men prove to be the most forthright separatists, but even here the percentages of men aged 16 to 19 who were separatists ranged only from 11 to 28 (Campbell & Schuman, 1968). An interesting interaction between type of separatism and educational level of the respondent appears in Campbell and Schuman's data. Among the 20- to 39-year-olds, college graduates tended to be more separatist in those realms where their training gives them a vested interest in positions free of competition—black-owned stores for black neighborhoods, black teachers in mostly black schools. The poorly educated were most likely to believe that whites should be discouraged from taking part in civil rights organizations and to agree that "Negroes should have nothing to do with whites if they can help it" and that "there should be a separate black nation here" (Campbell & Schuman, 1968).

But if separatism draws little favorable response even in the most politicized ghettos, positive aspects of cultural pluralism attract wide interest. For example, 42 percent endorse the statement that "Negro school children should study an African language." And this interest seems rather general across age, sex, and education categories. Campbell and Schuman regard this as evidence of a broadly supported attempt ". . . to emphasize black consciousness *without* rejection of whites. . . . A substantial number of Negroes want *both* integration and black identity." Or in the terms of this paper, they prefer cell A in Figure 1—"true integration."

When viewed historically, this preferred combination of black consciousness without separation is not a new position for black Americans. It was, for example, their dominant response to the large-scale movement of Marcus Garvey in the 1920s. Garvey, a West Indian, stressed pride in Africa and black beauty and successfully mounted a mass movement throughout the urban ghettos of the day, but his famous "back to Africa" separatist appeals were largely ignored as irrelevant.

A FINAL WORD

Racially separate or together? Our social-psychological examination of separatist assumptions leads to the assertion of one imperative: the attainment of a viable, democratic nation, free from personal and institutional racism, requires extensive racial integration in all realms of life as well as vast programs of ghetto enrichment. To prescribe more separation because of discomfort, racism, conflict, or the need for autonomy is like getting drunk again to cure a hangover. The nation's binge of *apartheid* must not be exacerbated but alleviated.

REFERENCES

Allport, G. W. *The nature of prejudice.* Reading, Mass: Addison-Wesley, 1954.

Alsop, J. No more nonsense about ghetto education! *New Republic,* July 22, 1967, **157,** 18–23. (a)

Alsop, J. Ghetto schools. *New Republic,* Nov. 18, 1967, **157,** 16–19. (b)

Armstrong, C. P., & Gregor, A. J. Integrated schools and Negro character development: Some considerations of the possible effects. *Psychiatry,* 1964, **27,** 69–72.

Bennett, L., Jr. Liberation. *Ebony,* August, 1970, Vol. 25, pp. 36–43.

Brophy, I. N. The luxury of anti-Negro prejudice. *Public Opinion Quarterly,* 1946, **9,** 456–466.

Calame, B. E. A west coast militant talks tough but helps avert racial trouble. *The Wall Street Journal,* July 26, 1968, Vol. 172, No. 1, p. 15.

Campbell, A., & Schuman, H. Racial attitudes in fifteen American cities. In The National Advisory Commission on Civil Disorders, *Supplemental Studies.* Washington, D. C.: U. S. Government Printing Office, 1968. P. 5.

Chessler, M. *In their own words.* Atlanta: Southern Regional Council, 1967.

Coleman, J. S., Campbell, E. Q., Hobson, C. J., McPartland, M., Mood, A. M., Weinfield, F. D., & York, R. L. *Equality of educational opportunity.* Washington, D. C.: U. S. Government Printing Office, 1966.

Deutsch, M., & Collins, M. *Interracial housing: A psychological evaluation of a social experiment.* Minneapolis: University of Minnesota Press, 1951.

Douglass, F. *Life and times of Frederick Douglass: The complete autobiography.* New York: Collier Books, 1962. (original edition in 1892).

Ferry, W. H. Black colonies: A modest proposal. *The Center Magazine,* January 1968, Vol. 1, pp. 74–76.

Harding, J., & Hogrefe, R. Attitudes of white department store employees toward Negro co-workers. *Journal of Social Issues,* 1952, **8,** 18–28.

Hyman, H. H., & Sheatsley, P. B. Attitudes toward desegregation. *Scientific American,* July 1964, **211,** 16–23.

Jackson, J. L., & Poussaint, A. F. A dialogue on separatism. *Ebony,* August 1970, Vol. 25, pp. 62–68.

Jahoda, M., & West, P. Race relations in public housing. *Journal of Social Issues,* 1951, **7,** 132–139.

Katz, I. Review of evidence relating to effects of desegregation on the performance of Negroes. *American Psychologist,* 1964, **19,** 381–399.

Katz, I. The socialization of competence motivation in minority group children. In D. Levine (Ed.), *Nebraska symposium on motivation.* Lincoln: University of Nebraska Press, 1967.

Kephart, W. M. *Racial factors and urban law enforcement.* Philadelphia: University of Pennsylvania Press, 1957.

Klineberg, O. *Negro intelligence and selective migration.* New York: Columbia University Press, 1935.

Koslin, S., Koslin, B., Pargament, R., & Waxman, H.

Classroom racial balance and students' interracial attitudes. Unpublished paper, Riverside Research Institute, New York City, 1970.

Logan, R. W. *The Negro in the United States: A brief history.* Princeton, N. J.: Van Nostrand, 1957.

MacKenzie, B. The importance of contact in determining attitudes toward Negroes. *Journal of Abnormal and Social Psychology,* 1948, **43,** 417–441.

National Advisory Commission on Civil Disorders, *U. S. riot commission report.* Washington, D. C.: U. S. Government Printing Office, 1968.

Newcomb, T. M., Turner, R. H., & Converse, P. E. *Social psychology: The study of human interaction.* New York: Holt, Rinehart and Winston, 1965.

Pettigrew, T. F. *A profile of the Negro American.* Princeton, N. J.: Van Nostrand, 1964.

Pettigrew, T. F. Social evaluation theory: Convergences and applications. In D. Levine (Ed.), *Nebraska symposium on motivation.* Lincoln: University of Nebraska Press, 1967.

Pettigrew, T. F. Race and equal education opportunity. *Harvard Educational Review,* 1968, **38,** 66–76.

Riley, R. T., & Pettigrew, T. F. Dramatic events and racial attitude change. Unpublished paper, Harvard University, August 1970.

Rokeach, M. Belief versus race as determinants of social distance: Comment on Triandis' paper. *Journal of Abnormal and Social Psychology.* 1961, **62,** 184–186.

Rokeach, M., & Mezei, L. Race and shared belief as factors in social choice. *Science,* 1966, **151,** 167–172.

Rokeach, M., & Parker, S. Values as social indicators of poverty and race relations in America. *Annals of the American Academy of Political and Social Science,* 1970, **388,** 97–111.

Rokeach, M., Smith, P., & Evans, R. Two kinds of prejudice or one? In M. Rokeach (Ed.), *The open and closed mind.* New York: Basic Books, 1960.

Rotter, J. B. Internal versus external control of reinforcement. *Psychological Monographs,* 1966, **80** (609).

Saenger, G., & Gilbert, E. Customer reactions to the integration of Negro sales personnel. *International Journal of Opinion and Attitude Research,* 1950, **4,** 57–76.

Schwartz, R., Pettigrew, T., & Smith, M. Fake panaceas for ghetto education. *New Republic,* Sept, 23, 1967, **157,** 16–19.

Schwartz, R., Pettigrew, T., & Smith, M. Is desegregation impractical? *New Republic,* Jan. 6, 1968, **1,** 74–76.

Sheatsley, P. B. White attitudes toward the Negro. In T. Parsons and K. B. Clark (Eds.), *The Negro American.* Boston: Houghton Mifflin, 1966.

Smith, C. R., Williams, L., & Willis, R. H. Race, sex and belief as determinants of friendship acceptance. *Journal of Personality and Social Psychology,* 1967, **5,** 127–137.

Stein, D. D. The influence of belief systems on interpersonal preference. *Psychological Monographs,* 1966, **80**(616).

Stein, D. D., Hardyck, J. A., & Smith, M. B. Race and belief: An open and shut case. *Journal of Personality and Social Psychology,* 1965, **1,** 281–290.

Stember, C. H. Evaluating effects of the integrated classroom. *The Urban Review,* June 1968, **2,** 30–31.

Stouffer, S. A., Suchman, E. A., DeVinney, L. C., Star, S. A., & Williams, R. M., Jr. Studies in social psychology in World War II. Vol. 1, *The American soldier: Adjustment during army life.* Princeton, N. J.: Princeton University Press, 1949.

Triandis, H. C. A note on Rokeach's theory of prejudice. *Journal of Abnormal and Social Psychology,* 1961, **62,** 184–186.

Triandis, H. C., & Davis, E. E. Race and belief as determinants of behavioral intentions. *Journal of Personality and Social Psychology,* 1965, **2,** 715–725.

United States Commission on Civil Rights. *Civil rights USA: Public schools, southern states, 1962.* Washington, D. C.: U. S. Government Printing Office, 1963.

United States Commission on Civil Rights. *Racial isolation in the public schools.* Washington, D. C.: U. S. Government Printing Office, 1967.

U. S. Departments of Labor and Commerce. *The social and economic status of Negroes in the United States, 1969.* Washington, D. C.: U. S. Government Printing Office, 1970.

Williams, R. M., Jr. *Strangers next door; Ethnic relations in American communities.* Englewood Cliffs, N. J.: Prentice-Hall, 1964.

Wilner, D. M., Walkley, R., & Cook, S. W. *Human relations in interracial housing: A study in the contact hypothesis.* Minneapolis: University of Minnesota Press, 1955.

Works, E. The prejudice-interaction hypothesis from the point of view of the Negro minority group. *American Journal of Sociology,* 1961, **67,** 47–52.

Yarrow, M. R. (Ed.) Interpersonal dynamics in a desegregation process. *Journal of Social Issues,* 1958, **14**(1), 3–63.

ARTICLE 26

Racial Preference and Social Comparison Processes

Steven R. Asher and Vernon L. Allen

A number of studies have demonstrated that children negatively evaluate Negroes and positively evaluate whites. The original work by Clark and Clark (1947) found that Negro children preferred a white doll and rejected a black doll when asked to choose which was nice, which looked bad, which they would like to play with and which was the nice color.

This basic result has been found repeatedly in studies using a variety of testing materials, and within various geographical and social settings. The findings hold for Northern Negro children (Clark and Clark, 1947; Goodman, 1952; Greenwald and Oppenheim, 1968; Helgerson, 1943; Radke *et al.,* 1950; Radke and Trager, 1950) as well as for Southern (Clark and Clark, 1947; Morland, 1962; Stevenson and Stewart, 1958), and for integrated as well as segregated children (Goodman, 1952; Stevenson and Stewart, 1958).

Studies of white children have with similar consistency demonstrated the same pattern of white preference and black rejection (Greenwald and Oppenheim, 1968; Horowitz, 1936; Helgerson, 1943; Morland, 1962; Stevenson and Stewart, 1958). As with Negro children, the same basic finding of white preference has been repeatedly noted over a range of materials, locations and settings.

Despite this rather sizable literature on racial preference, important variables have been neglected, and unfortunately no well-controlled direct comparisons have been made with the original Clark and Clark (1947) data. The present study was a partial replication and extension of the Clarks' work. Previously neglected social class and sex variables as well as age were investigated. Both white and Negro children were studied to assess the relative amount of preference and to determine whether variables influenced both groups in a similar fashion. Present data on Negro children's responses were compared with Clark and Clark's data to determine whether the past three decades of change in status have resulted in a change in skin color preference.[1]

In addition, past studies have given little attention to theoretical issues. Rather than making direct predictions the present study tests two competing theoretical models. One model posits that social and economic progress, as success experiences and extensions of control over the environment, create enhanced feelings of competence and racial pride. This view follows from the thinking of White (1959), Erikson (1950), and others. It can be seen as a fundamental assumption of the poverty program. Coleman, *et al.* (1966) have recently articulated a similar view regarding the effects of integration. Specifically, this model predicts that Negro children today will show more black color preference than children tested earlier by the Clarks, and furthermore, that middle-class Negroes will respond more favorably to their own race than lower-class Negroes.

Reprinted from *Journal of Social Issues,* 1969, **25**(1), 157–166, with the permission of the authors and the Society for the Psychological Study of Social Issues.

This research was supported in part by a grant from the Institute for Research on Poverty. The authors wish to thank Marvin Phinazee and Bess Norman for their assistance.

[1]The Clark and Clark (1947) data were collected in 1939–40.

Social comparison theory (Festinger, 1954) offers opposite predictions. Economic progress and social mobility should lead to more frequent comparison with whites (Pettigrew, 1967). The result of such comparisons would be greater feelings of inferiority, since whites still are generally more advantaged. This model predicts, then, that white preference will be greater among Negro children today. It also predicts that lower-class Negro children will respond more favorably to their own race than middle-class Negro children.

Social class differences in white children's preferences are not predicted, since the extent to which whites of different classes engage in social comparison with Negroes is unknown. Intuitively, it seems reasonable to believe that both middle- and lower-class whites use middle-class whites as a comparison group. It could be argued, however, that the lower-class whites' closer social position and more frequent contact with Negro people will make for greater comparison with them. Given this ambiguity, straightforward predictions about white children's responses do not follow. Thus the two competing models discussed above are relevant only to data of Negro children.

METHOD USED

Subjects

A total of 341 white and Negro children from Newark, New Jersey and surrounding areas were tested. Of this number 186 were Negro and 155 were white. Children ranged in age from three to eight and were divided into middle and lower class according to parents' occupation (Strodtbeck, 1958). Falling into the middle-class category were 167 children; lower-class children totaled 174. Children were grouped into age categories of 3–4, 5–6, 7–8 to maximize number of Ss per cell.

Materials

Three pairs of puppets, manufactured by Creative Play Things, were used to match as closely as possible the sex and age of the subject. Within each pair, puppets were identical except for skin and hair color. The "Negro" puppet had medium brown facial color and black hair; the "white" puppet had light skin and light hair. Puppets were chosen rather than dolls so that the testing situation would be appropriate to both girls and boys.

Procedure

Children were tested in fifteen different settings which included private nursery schools, neighborhood centers, pre-school programs, play streets run by the city, and nurseries receiving support through the poverty program. The majority of settings were de facto segregated by virtue of neighborhood, costs of the program or social class criteria for selection. Only one setting was completely segregated, and only two were fairly well-integrated. Most settings, then, had an overwhelming number of children from either one race or the other.

Two puppets, one brown and one white, were placed in a prone position before each child. Younger children (ages three, four, and five) were shown the baby puppets (two boys of about two years old). Older children (ages six, seven, and eight) were shown puppets which were the same sex as the subject (these puppets appear to be about eleven years old). Each child was tested individually in a room apart from the other children.

Two experimenters, one Negro and one white, were employed to control for race. Each experimenter tested children of his own race. Both were male and within one year of age of each other. In this way response bias due to effects of the experimenter's race, age and sex were minimized.

After asking the child his name and generally helping the child to feel comfortable, the experimenter asked the following questions adapted from Clark and Clark (1947):

(a) Which puppet is the nice puppet?
(b) Which puppet would you like to play with?
(c) Which puppet looks bad?
(d) Which puppet is the nice color?

Questions were asked randomly to prevent any possible order effect. Children responded by pointing to one of the two puppets. Following the child's response, he and the experimenter briefly played with the puppets and the child was returned to the general play area.

TABLE 1.   Racial preferences of Negro and white children (per cent).

| Item | Negro children (N = 186) | | | |
	White puppet	Brown puppet	χ^2	p
Nice Puppet	76	23	26.0	<.001
Plays With	69	30	14.5	<.001
Looks Bad	24	73	22.8	<.001
Nice Color	69	29	15.5	<.001

| Item | White children (N = 155) | | | |
	White puppet	Brown puppet	χ^2	p
Nice Puppet	76	20	24.9	<.001
Plays With	75	22	22.4	<.001
Looks Bad	18	77	28.1	<.001
Nice Color	74	20	24.1	<.001

OVERALL PREFERENCES

Presented in Table 1 are overall preferences of Negro and white children. Included in the table are the response categories "brown puppet" and "white puppet."[2] It is clear from Table 1 that the large majority of both Negro and white children preferred the white puppet and rejected the brown puppet. All of these percentages were significant at the .001 level by chi-square tests. Furthermore, Negro and white children did not significantly differ in their preference for the white puppet and rejection of the brown puppet. Only on "nice color" was there a large Negro-white discrepancy in response ($X^2 = 2.72$, $p <$ .10). In general, then, there was remarkable consistency between Negro and white children in their preference for the white puppet and rejection of the brown puppet.

SOCIAL CLASS DIFFERENCES

Social class did not produce a substantial difference on any item for Negro children; however, on all four questions middle-class children responded with a slightly higher proportion of white puppet preference. This tendency was strongest on the item "nice puppet," with 82 per cent of the middle-class Negro children choosing the white puppet and 71 per cent of the lower-

[2]The small number of "no preference" responses were excluded from the analysis, which accounts for the failure of some percentages to sum to 100%.

class Negro children giving this response. Class difference on the items "play with," "looks bad," and "nice color" was less sharp, but on each there was somewhat greater white preference by the middle class (average of about 8 per cent).

For white children, there was little meaningful social class difference in racial preference. On three of the items lower-class whites more frequently chose the white puppet, while on one of the items ("play with") direction of results were reversed. All of the differences were small and did not approach significance.

Social class data were analyzed another way. Children were categorized according to whether they consistently preferred the white puppet across the four items, consistently favored the brown puppet, or were inconsistent in their preference. Results showed a strong tendency for middle-class Negro children consistently to prefer the white puppet, while lower-class children showed inconsistent responses ($X^2 = 6.30$, $p <$ .05). White children showed no difference in consistency of response across items as a function of social class.

SEX DIFFERENCES

Table 2 presents male-female differences in racial preference among Negro children. On all four items boys favored the white puppet more than girls. The sex difference reached significance on the items "nice puppet," "looks bad," and "nice color." Smallest sex difference was found

TABLE 2.   Sex comparisons for Negro children.

Item	Males %	Females %	χ^2	p
Nice Puppet				
White Puppet	83	68		
Brown Puppet	16	31	5.41	<.05
Play With				
White Puppet	73	64		
Brown Puppet	27	33	1.25	ns
Looks Bad				
White Puppet	19	30		
Brown Puppet	79	67	2.81	<.10
Nice Color				
White Puppet	74	63		
Brown Puppet	24	34	2.80	<.10

Note.—Male N = 96; Female N = 85.

on the item "play with," though here also there was greater white preference among boys.

The same direction on sex difference was found for white children, as shown in Table 3. Again, on all items males showed greater white preference than females. The items "nice puppet" and "looks bad" reached significance at the .10 level.

AGE TRENDS

Age trends were quite complex, and less consistent across items than social class and sex findings. Among Negro children only the item "play with" yielded a significant change with age, as white preference increased from 73 per cent at age 3–4 to 80 per cent at age 5–6, and then decreased to 51 per cent at 7–8 ($X^2 = 12.25$, $p <$ .01). Among whites, only one item ("nice color")

TABLE 3.   Sex comparisons for white children.

Item	Males %	Females %	χ^2	p
Nice Puppet				
White Puppet	80	72		
Brown Puppet	15	26	3.08	<.10
Play With				
White Puppet	78	72		
Brown Puppet	17	27	2.06	ns
Looks Bad				
White Puppet	12	25		
Brown Puppet	81	73	3.54	<.10
Nice Color				
White Puppet	77	72		
Brown Puppet	16	25	1.40	ns

Note.—Male N = 77; Female N = 71.

approached significance: from 77% at age 3–4 there was an increase to 84% at 5–6, then a decrease to 59% at 7–8 ($X^2 = 5.37$, $p <$ .10).

No significant interactions emerged from the Sex by Age analyses. However, among Negro children there was a tendency for male-female differences in racial preference to widen with age, as males increased somewhat in white puppet preference while females decreased. Results for white children disclosed a general tendency for both males and females to follow a curvilinear relationship between age and racial preference.

HISTORICAL COMPARISON

Table 4 compares present findings with those of Clark and Clark (1947). (Data are presented under the year in which the study was conducted, 1939.) The Clarks' Northern data are used to maximize comparability with the present sample.[3]

TABLE 4.   Comparison of present results with Clark and Clark's data.

Item	1939 %	1967 %	χ^2	p
Nice Puppet				
White Puppet	68	76	2.02	ns
Brown Puppet	30	23		
Play With				
White Puppet	72	69		
Brown Puppet	28	27	0.19	ns
Looks Bad				
White Puppet	17	24		
Brown Puppet	71	73	1.19	ns
Nice Color				
White Puppet	63	69		
Brown Puppet	37	29	1.94	ns

While degree of consistency between the 1939 and 1967 data is perhaps most striking, there is some evidence of an increase in white color preference among Negro children. On three of the four items there was greater white preference today than 28 years ago: only one item ("play

[3]The Clarks' Northern sample was an integrated one while the present sample was largely segregated. From a social comparison viewpoint integration would lead to greater white preference among Negroes; thus it is possible that the comparison presented in Table 4 underestimates the amount of change from 1939 to 1967.

with") showed decreased white preference. On none of the items did differences reach statistical significance.

SOCIAL COMPARISON MODEL FINDS SOME SUPPORT

Results of the present study are more consistent with a social comparison model than an individual competence model. Social class data for Negro children and the historical comparison with the Clarks' results suggest that enhanced status will not necessarily lead to greater racial pride, but may instead contribute, through more frequent comparison with whites, to increased feelings of inferiority.

Caution is advisable in appraising the social class data and historical differences in view of the lack of statistical support; however, these data are consistent with other findings. Clark and Clark (1947) found significant differences on two items between their Northern integrated and Southern segregated samples. The Northern sample showed greater white preference, a finding congruent with the social comparison model. Similarly, the "Coleman report" noted lower "academic self-concept" for Negro children in integrated schools despite the fact that they showed higher achievement than Negro children attending segregated schools. Integration is probably an important variable leading to increased comparison with whites. Finally, the relatively high proportion of seven and eight year old Negro children in the present study who chose the brown puppet to "play with," is a finding consistent with social comparison theory. Festinger (1954) has postulated a tendency to avoid the presence of those who remind one of a large discrepancy in attitude and ability. Perhaps Negro children, as they grow older, chose increasingly to play with members of their own race to avoid threatening social comparisons.[4]

The greater white preference of males is one of the most interesting results of the present study.

[4]These children are, of course, avoiding more than threatening social comparisons. They are avoiding, as well, the insults and disparagement likely to be given by white children. Coles (1967) notes that Negro mothers are likely to caution their children at an early age against playing with whites.

That both races yielded a sex difference suggests that the greater white preference of males is not the result of personal attacks on one's competence but of a general awareness of the relatively inferior position of Negroes, an awareness made more salient for those enacting the male role. It is the male who suffers the greatest consequences of prejudice and oppression.

The hypothesis of differential sensitivity to Negro-white status differences as a function of the child's own sex role must be offered cautiously. Nonetheless, there is evidence of considerable awareness of social reality in young children. A majority of three year olds showed a strong preference for white skin color. Small children have also been found to assign poorer houses and stereotyped social roles to brown dolls (Radke and Trager, 1950; Stevenson and Stewart, 1958).

SOME OF THE MANY QUESTIONS

Results of the present study suggest questions for future research. First there is a need to determine the relationship between racial preference and behavior. Are black people who express white preference less assertive, more likely to do well in school, less likely to participate in a civil rights demonstration? Racial preference can be conceptualized as an attitude; unfortunately we know little about the relationship between attitudes and behavior (Deutscher, 1966; Festinger, 1964).

Second, present results suggest that the variables usually believed to be crucial in effecting a positive change in black peoples' identity may be less important than previously thought. As long as a large discrepancy exists between the living conditions and skills of blacks and whites a small closing of the gap may only psychologically magnify the difference. If integration and small socioeconomic gains are insufficient to the development of racial pride, then other potential sources of change should be investigated. The relationship between involvement in social and political movements and change in self and race evaluation is worthy of scrutiny.

Possibly such movements contribute to increased feelings of competence not only through victories in social struggles but also by encouraging participants to select new social comparison groups. For example, black people are urged by militant leaders to develop their own values and goals and to cease striving toward middle-class ideals (Carmichael and Hamilton, 1967). Rejection of social comparison with whites may result in a more positive racial and self conception. It is interesting, though only suggestive, that in the present study two children from Black Muslim homes chose the brown puppet. Hopefully, the examination of the effect on self of black peoples' participation in a wide range of social and political movements will allow for more optimism than can be generated from the present study.

REFERENCES

Carmichael, S. F. and Hamilton, C. V. *Black power: politics of liberation in America.* New York: Random House, 1967.

Clark, K. B. and Clark, M. P. Racial identification and racial preference in Negro children. In T. M. Newcomb and E. L. Hartley (Eds.), *Readings in social psychology.* New York: Holt, 1947. Pp. 169–178.

Coleman, J. S., Campbell, E. Q., Hobson, C. J., McPartland, M., Mood, A. M., Weinfeld, F. D. and York, R. L. *Equality of opportunity.* Washington, D.C.: United States Government Printing Office, 1966.

Coles, R. *Children of crisis: a study of courage and fear.* Boston: Little, Brown and Co., 1967.

Deutscher, I. Words and deeds: social science and social policy. *Social Problems,* 1966, **13,** 235–254.

Erikson, E. H. *Childhood and society.* New York: Norton, 1950.

Festinger, L. A theory of social comparison processes. *Human Relations,* 1954, **7,** 117–140.

Festinger, L. Behavioral support for opinion change. *Public Opinion Quarterly,* 1964, **28,** 404–417.

Greenwald, H. J. and Oppenheim, D. B. Reported magnitude of self-misidentification among Negro children—artifact? *Journal of Personality and Social Psychology,* 1968, **8,** 49–52.

Goodman, M. E. *Race awareness in young children.* Cambridge, Mass.: Addison-Wesley, 1952.

Helgerson, E. The relative significance of race, sex and facial expression in choice of playmate by the preschool child. *Journal of Negro Education,* 1943, **12,** 617–622.

Horowitz, E. L. The development of attitude toward the Negro. *Archives of Psychology,* N. Y., 1936, (194).

Morland, J. K. Racial acceptance and preference of nursery school children in a southern city. *Merrill-Palmer Quarterly,* 1962, **8,** 217–280.

Pettigrew, T. F. Social evaluation theory: convergences and application. *The Nebraska Symposium on Motivation,* 1967, **15,** 241–311.

Radke, M., Sutherland, J. and Rosenberg, P. Racial attitudes of children. *Sociometry,* 1950, **13,** 154–171.

Radke, M. J. and Trager, H. G. Children's perceptions of the social roles of Negroes and whites. *Journal of Psychology,* 1950, **29,** 3–33.

Stevenson, H. W. and Stewart, E. C. A developmental study of race awareness in young children. *Child Development,* 1958, **29,** 399–410.

Strodtbeck, F. L. Family interaction values and achievement. In D. C. McClelland, A. L. Baldwin, U. Bronfenbrenner and F. L. Strodtbeck (Eds.), *Talent and society: new perspectives in the identification of talent.* New York: Van Nostrand, 1958.

White, R. W. Motivation reconsidered: the concept of competence. *Psychological Review,* 1959, **66,** 297–333.

ARTICLE 27

Black Is Beautiful: A Reexamination of Racial Preference and Identification

Joseph Hraba and Geoffrey Grant

Clark and Clark (1947) found that black children preferred white dolls and rejected black dolls when asked to choose which were nice, which looked bad, which they would like to play with, and which were a nice color. This implies that black is not beautiful.

This observation has been repeated, using a variety of methods and in a variety of settings (Asher & Allen, 1969; Frenkel-Brunswik, 1948; Goodman, 1952; Greenwald & Oppenheim, 1968; Landreth & Johnson, 1953; Morland, 1958, 1966; Radke, Sutherland, & Rosenberg, 1950; Radke, Trager, & Davis, 1949; Trager & Yarrow, 1952).

However, Gregor and McPherson (1966) found that Southern, urban black children, 6 and 7 years old, generally preferred a black doll. Their procedures were identical to Clark and Clark's, except only two dolls were presented. They proposed that black children's preference for white stems from their contact with whites; ". . . Negro children tend to be more outgroup oriented the more systematically they are exposed to white contact [p. 103]." Clark and Clark did find that black children in interracial nursery schools were more pronounced in their preference for white dolls than those in segregated nursery schools. However, Morland (1966), using a picture technique, found just the opposite.

Still, Clark and Clark and Goodman (1952), when using similar techniques, found that black

Reprinted from *Journal of Personality and Social Psychology,* 1970, **16,** 398–402, with the permission of the authors and the American Psychological Association.

children in interracial settings preferred objects representing whites. However, Johnson (1966) found 18 black youths (mean age of 12) in a Harlem freedom school rated black equal to white. He concluded that his "study presents evidence that not all Negroes have negative self-attitudes . . . [p. 273]." Perhaps, but the techniques used by Johnson and Clark and Clark differ. Johnson had groups of respondents rate black and white on four semantic differential scales. Furthermore, the samples are not comparable on age and social setting. Possibly techniques, sampling, and attitudes are confounded in a comparison of these two studies.

The thesis that for black children interracial contact engenders preference for white cannot be overlooked in this literature. Some have advocated this interpretation (Gregor, 1963; Armstrong & Gregor, 1964; Gregor & McPherson, 1966). Unfortunately, any comparison of the evidence confounds time, techniques, sampling, and setting with the dependent variable. The present study will test this thesis in an interracial setting by duplicating the Clark and Clark doll study.

METHOD

Procedure

The procedures used by Clark and Clark were followed as closely as possible. The respondents were interviewed individually using a set of four dolls, two black and two white, identical in all other respects. The same questions used by the Clarks were asked. They were as follows:

269

TABLE 1.   A comparison of the present results with the Clark and Clark (1939) data.

Item	Clark & Clark[a] (1939) blacks	Lincoln sample (1969) blacks	χ^2 (1939-1969) blacks	Lincoln sample (1969) whites
1. (Play with)				
White doll	67 (169)	30 (27)	36.2**	83 (59)
Black doll	32 (83)	70 (62)		16 (11)
Don't know or no response				1 (1)
2. (Nice doll)				
White doll	59 (150)	46 (41)	5.7*	70 (50)
Black doll	38 (97)	54 (48)		30 (21)
3. (Looks bad)				
White doll	17 (42)	61 (54)	43.5**	34 (24)
Black doll	59 (149)	36 (32)		63 (45)
Don't know or no response		3 (3)		3 (2)
4. (Nice color)				
White doll	60 (151)	31 (28)	23.1**	48 (34)
Black doll	38 (96)	69 (61)		49 (35)
Don't know or no response				3 (2)

Note.–Data in percentages. Ns in parentheses.
[a]Individuals failing to make either choice not included, hence some percentages add to less than 100.
*$p<.02$.
**$p<.001$.

1. Give me the doll that you want to play with.
2. Give me the doll that is a nice doll.
3. Give me the doll that looks bad.
4. Give me the doll that is a nice color.
5. Give me the doll that looks like a white child.
6. Give me the doll that looks like a colored child.
7. Give me the doll that looks like a Negro child.
8. Give me the doll that looks like you.

Clark and Clark contended that Items 1–4 measure racial preference, Items 5–7 measure racial awareness or knowledge, and Item 8 measures racial self-identification.

In an attempt to identify the behavioral consequences of racial preference and identification, we asked the children to name and indicate the race of their best friends. We also asked the teachers for the same information.

Sample

For our sample, respondents had to be 4–8 years of age. Five public schools provided a sampling frame containing 73% of the correct age black children in the public school system of Lincoln, Nebraska. The total sample consisted of 160 children, 89 blacks, or 60% of the eligible blacks attending Lincoln public schools. The 71 white children were drawn at random from the class-rooms containing black respondents. The interviews were completed at the five schools during May 1969.

The respondents were assigned to both black and white interviewers. Previous research has controlled for race of interviewer (Asher & Allen, 1969; Morland, 1966). Morland reported that race of interviewer does not significantly affect respondents' choices. Nevertheless, we controlled for race of interviewer.

Setting

Blacks comprise approximately 1.4% of the total population of Lincoln. The five public schools reflected this fact. Blacks accounted for 3% of the enrollment of three schools, and 7% and 18% of the other two schools. Furthermore, 70% of the black sample reported they had white friends.

RESULTS

Racial Preference

The Clarks' finding that the majority of the black children preferred a white doll has been interpreted that they would rather be white. This was one of the Clarks' important findings and is the focus of this paper.

Table 1 provides two comparisons. First, the differences in racial preference of the Clark and Clark (1939) sample and the Lincoln sample of 1969 are striking. On all the items the difference reaches statistical significance using chi-square.

Secondly, the sample of white children was collected to provide a bench mark against which to compare the racial preferences of black children. Gregor and McPherson (1966) and Morland (1966) have found that white children are more likely to prefer their own race than are black children. Table 1 shows that black and white children preferred the doll of their own race. The white children were significantly more ethnocentric on Items 1 and 2, there was no significant difference on Item 3, and the black children were significantly more ethnocentric on Item 4 using chi-square.

Age. The Clarks found that black children preferred white dolls at all ages (3–7), although this decreased with age. We found that a majority of the black children at all ages (3–8) preferred a black doll, and this preference increased with age. With white children there was a similar age trend except on Item 4.

Skin Color. The Clarks classified their subjects by skin color into three categories: light (practically white), medium (light brown to dark brown), and dark (dark brown to black). The interviewers in our study used the same criteria. The Clarks found that the children of light skin color showed the greatest preference for the white doll and the dark children the least. We did not find this trend. The children of light skin color were at least as strong in their preference for a black doll as the others.

Racial Identification

Items 5, 6, and 7 were to measure knowledge of racial differences, while Item 8 was to measure racial self-identification. On Items 5 and 6 the Clarks found that a majority of their respondents correctly identified white and "colored" dolls

(94% and 93%, respectively). Our black sample was comparable. Ninety percent correctly identified a white doll and 94% correctly identified a colored doll. In regard to Item 7 (doll that looks like a Negro child), we found that more of our respondents made the correct identification (86% as compared to 72%).

Age. Like the Clarks, we found an inverse relationship between misidentification (Items 5–8) and age. This relationship held for whites as well.

Skin Color. Like the Clarks, we found insignificant differences in misidentification (Items 5–7) among black children by skin color. However, on Item 8 the Clarks had found that more black children with light skin color misidentified themselves (80%). Adding a mulatto doll, Greenwald and Oppenheim (1968) reduced the misidentification for these respondents to 11%. Fifteen percent of our black respondents with light skin color misidentified themselves. However, there was no significant difference in misidentification on Item 8 by skin color.

Race of Interviewer. Race of interviewer was not related to choice of doll on any of the items for both black and white children.

Race of Respondents' Friends. For both black and white children there was no apparent relationship between doll preference and race of friends. The sociometric information agreed and were combined. If a relationship were to be found, it would be most pronounced for those who preferred dolls of their own race without exception. Furthermore, only these respondents demonstrated reliability in their doll preferences. Twenty-three black and 20 white children made the choices favorable to their own race on all four items measuring racial preference.

Even for these children there appears to be no relationship between doll preference and race of friends. Twenty, or 87%, of the 23 black children had white friends. Twelve, or 60%, of the 20 white children had all white friends. However, 41% of all white children had all white friends.

DISCUSSION

Doll Preference

These results indicate that black children in interracial settings are not necessarily white oriented. We will offer possible interpretations. First, times may be changing. That is, Negroes are becoming Blacks proud of their race. If change is occurring, previous research indicates that it is not at a universal rate across the country (Asher & Allen, 1969; Gregor & McPherson, 1966).

A second interpretation is that even 30 years ago black children in Lincoln, unlike those in other cities, would have chosen black dolls. This interpretation cannot be examined. A third and more reasonable interpretation is that conditions indigenous to Lincoln have mediated the impact of the "Black Movement." Johnson (1966) suggested that local organizations in the black communities disseminate black pride. We note that during the past 2 years a black pride campaign, sponsored by organizations which are black conscious, has been directed at adolescents and young adults in Lincoln. Black children through interaction with kin and friends may be modeling these attitudes.

The fourth interpretation is that interracial contact may engender black pride. Pettigrew (1967) proposed that interracial acceptance mediated the effect of interracial contact on the academic performance of blacks. Perhaps it influences black pride. The fact that 70% of the black sample had white friends and 59% of the white sample had black friends, given the racial composition of the schools, suggests this interpretation.

Doll Preference and Friendship

The above interpretations have assumed that doll choice corresponds with interpersonal behavior. Our findings suggest that such correspondence cannot be presumed. Three explanations of the lack of relationship between doll choice and friendship will be offered. These explanations are predicated on two assumptions, one about the

doll technique and the other about the meaning of "Black is beautiful."

The first explanation assumes that children will use the same criteria in friendship and doll choice. "Black is beautiful" is assumed to mean a rejection of whites. Combining these two assumptions, we expected those black children who without exception preferred black dolls to have all black friends. This expectation was not realized. However, being pupils of predominately white schools, these respondents may have found it impractical to have all black friends in spite of their preferences.[1]

The second explanation makes the same assumption about the doll technique. But it assumes that "Black is beautiful" translates into an acceptance of and by whites. Combining these we expected black children who without exception preferred black dolls to have both black and white friends. The expectation was nearly realized. More black children who had friends of both races preferred black dolls (except on Item 4) than those who had all black friends. This relationship approaches statistical confirmation.

The third explanation does not assume doll choice corresponds with interpersonal behavior. First, in the experimental setting, four dolls, which were identical except for race, were presented to the respondents. Although black children may prefer a doll of their own race when race is the only cue that differentiates it from other dolls, they may consider other criteria more important in friendship. Perhaps race is not salient in friendship at this age (Criswell, 1937; Moreno, 1934). Secondly, Piaget has observed that children before 11 or 12 years of age cannot detect conceptual self-contradictions (Hunt, 1961; Maier, 1969). The fact that a majority of the respondents who were consistent in answering the four preference questions did not clearly reflect the bases for their doll preferences in their friendships suggests this possibility. Furthermore, the fact that a majority (73%) of respondents were inconsistent in answering the four preference questions supports this suggestion.

[1]The restricted racial composition previously noted and sample size prevented a test of this possibility.

REFERENCES

Armstrong, C. P., & Gregor, A. J. Integrated schools and Negro character development. *Psychiatry,* 1964, **27,** 69–72.

Asher, S. R., & Allen, V. L. Racial preference and social comparison processes. *Journal of Social Issues,* 1969, **25,** 157–165.

Clark, K. B., & Clark, M. K. The development of consciousness of self in the emergence of racial identification in Negro pre-school children. *Journal of Social Psychology,* 1939, **10,** 591–597.

Clark, K. B., & Clark, M. K. Racial identification and preference in Negro children. In T. Newcomb & E. Hartley (Eds.), *Readings in social psychology.* New York: Holt, 1947.

Criswell, J. H. Racial cleavage in Negro-white groups. *Sociometry,* 1937, **1,** 81–89.

Frenkel-Brunswik, E. A study of prejudice in children. *Human Relations,* 1948, **1,** 295–306.

Goodman, M. E. *Racial awareness in young children.* Cambridge, Mass.: Addison-Wesley, 1952.

Greenwald, H. J., & Oppenheim, D. B. Reported magnitude of self-misidentification among Negro children—artifact? *Journal of Personality and Social Psychology,* 1968, **8,** 49–52.

Gregor, A. J. Science and social change: A review of K. B. Clark's "Prejudice and your child." *Mankind Quarterly,* 1963, **3,** 229–237.

Gregor, A. J., & McPherson, D. A. Racial attitudes among white and Negro children in a deep south standard metropolitan area. *Journal of Social Psychology,* 1966, **68,** 95–106.

Hunt, J. McV. *Intelligence and experience.* New York: Ronald Press, 1961.

Johnson, D. W. Racial attitudes of Negro freedom school participants and Negro and white civil rights participants. *Social Forces,* 1966, **45,** 266–272.

Landreth, C., & Johnson, B. C. Young children's responses to a picture and inset test designed to reveal reactions to persons of different skin color. *Child Development,* 1953, **24,** 63–80.

Maier, H. W. *Three theories of child development.* New York: Harper & Row, 1969.

Moreno, J. L. *Who shall survive?* (Monograph No. 58) Washington, D. C.: Nervous and Mental Disease, 1934.

Morland, K. J. Racial recognition by nursery school children in Lynchburg, Virginia. *Social Forces,* 1958, **37,** 132–137.

Morland, K. J. A comparison of race awareness in northern and southern children. *American Journal of Orthopsychiatry,* 1966, **36,** 22–31.

Pettigrew, T. F. Social evaluation theory: Convergences and applications. *Nebraska Symposium on Motivation,* 1967, **15,** 241–319.

Radke, M. J., Sutherland, J., & Rosenberg, P. Racial attitudes of children. *Sociometry,* 1950, **13,** 151–171.

Radke, M. J., Trager, H., & Davis, H. Social perception and attitudes of children. *Genetic Psychology Monographs,* 1949, **10,** 327–447.

Trager, H., & Yarrow, M. *They live what they learn.* New York: Harper & Row, 1952.

SECTION SUMMARY

The findings reported by Hraba and Grant in the third article indicate that the doll preferences of black children in interracial settings may no longer be "white-oriented." This suggests that racial preferences on other topics may also be less white-oriented than previously. As Hraba and Grant note, their results do not provide direct evidence on the causes of this apparent change in preferences. Intuitively it would seem probable that programs stressing black pride and identity could lead to such a change. There is increasing evidence that such programs may be effective in this regard.

Bunton and Weissbach (1971) have presented evidence that black children exposed to 12 weeks of "pro-black" education in an all-black community-controlled school were significantly more likely to give pro-black responses in a Clark-and-Clark-type study than were similar black children who had not been exposed to such a program. In the same vein, Brigham (1971) found that, contrary to what the results of the earlier doll studies would predict, black children (grades 4-12) in 1970 were significantly *more* likely than white children to attribute positive traits to their own race and negative traits to the other. Despite the tendency of both races to attribute positive traits to one's own race, there was still a significant degree of interracial agreement in trait attributions in grades 8 through 11. Banks (1970) found that black college students in 1967 were more antiwhite and less anti-Negro than black college students in 1957 had been. Paige (1970) found that antiwhite attitudes were positively related to feelings of black pride and identity.

Taken together, these results suggest that the

change noted by Hraba and Grant is not an isolated finding but the identification of a powerful
new trend in the self-attitudes of black Americans. There is apparently less self-hatred (anti-
Negro attitudes) and more overt hostility toward
whites than in the recent past. White-oriented
color preferences are also apparently less pervasive among black children.

But what of the prejudicial attitudes of whites
and the spectre of institutional racism? Ashmore
(1970) has identified two general classes of causal
factors regarding prejudice: individual-level and
sociocultural-level factors. Individual-level factors are aspects of an individual's *personality
structure* that may lead him to adopt prejudicial
attitudes. Volumes of research attempts have
been carried out to identify personality factors
that tend to accompany, and perhaps help cause,
prejudicial attitudes in whites. Although enumer-
ation of all such factors is beyond the scope of this
summary, some of those factors most often identified are: an authoritarian personality structure
(Adorno, Frenkel-Brunswik, Levinson, & Sanford, 1950), excessive cognitive category width
(Allport & Ross, 1967), fear of loss of status
(status-dread), frustration and the aggression
that this may produce, concreteness (as opposed
to abstractness) in cognitive functioning (Severy
& Brigham, 1971), and the use of attitudes to
perform an ego-defensive function (Katz, 1960).

To change attitudes that are products of personality structures such as those just listed, it may
be necessary to induce changes in the personality
itself. Techniques of this sort that have been attempted are psychotherapy and self-insight training (see Ashmore, 1970). At a more general level,
changes in child-rearing practices so that these
practices are not conducive to the development of
prejudice-prone personalities might be an important factor. Since the racial attitudes of whites *are*
apparently becoming less prejudiced (Brigham &
Weissbach, 1972; Greeley & Sheatsley, 1971), the
changes in general child-rearing techniques that
have taken place in recent years may be one of the
factors in this change. Finally, if general conflict-
causing aspects of the environment are reduced,
individuals' feelings of deprivation and frustration and the accompanying prejudice may also be
reduced.

As we mentioned in the Introduction, the concept of institutional racism has received increasing attention in the past decade. A very brief
outline of some of the causes and manifestations
of institutional racism follows (for more detailed
discussion of these phenomena, see Knowles &
Prewitt, 1969; Daniels & Kitano, 1970; Brigham
& Weissbach, 1972).

One of the institutions in the United States
thought by many to have played a decisive role in
the formulation of institutional racism is organized religion. The historical emphasis on "civi-
lizing" the ignorant "heathen" through
missionary work, along with the general international policy of manfully shouldering the "white
man's burden," of helping our "little brown
brothers," certainly connotes a paternalistic assumption of the superiority of the majority
American culture.

Another major force has been Social Darwinism. Arising soon after the acceptance of
Charles Darwin's theory of biological evolution,
this doctrine holds that "survival of the fittest" is
as applicable to cultures and groups and races of
people as it is to species of animals. Therefore, the
implication is that those cultures or races who
have "survived best" and gained control (the majority group) must be the "fittest." Ignoring all
the mammoth practical barriers that may exist
for minority groups, it is naively assumed that the
cream (of the culture) will inevitably rise to the
top.

American immigration policies provide another illustration of the nonequalitarian nature of
societal institutions. Traditionally, "quotas" have
been set up so that large numbers of "desirable"
ethnic groups (that is, northern Europeans) are
allowed to emigrate to the United States, but the
immigration of other peoples is drastically limited. In 1962, for example, less than 5% of the
immigrants permitted by the quotas to emigrate
were non-European; about 70% of those allowed
were from Great Britain, Germany, and Ireland
alone (Berry, 1965).

A conceptual stance similar to the Social Dar-
winist approach is apparent in the application of
the "immigrant analogy" by whites to the problems faced by blacks. Basically, the often-heard
statement is of the type: "My (immigrant) grand-

parents made it OK in America! Why can't the blacks?" The U.S. Riot Commission (Kerner Commission) has enumerated several reasons why this anology is utterly inappropriate. The conditions that blacks have faced and still face in the United States simply are not parallel to those faced by European immigrants of several generations past. The crucial differences involve the following factors: (1) the maturing economy— unlike the situation several generations ago, today's economy has little use for the unskilled labor that an undereducated group may have to offer; (2) the disability of race—the structure of discrimination faced by blacks is more pervasive than that ever faced by European immigrants; (3) entry into the political system—such entry, via ward politics or political machines, is much more difficult today than in the past; (4) cultural factors —the segregation and lack of job opportunities faced by blacks, and the increasing gap between opportunities and aspirations, have placed great stresses on the black culture (Kerner et al., 1968, pp. 278–282).

The role of the public schools in contributing to this legacy has also been described by many analysts. It has been pointed out that the content of traditional textbooks subtly adds to the flow of racism. In many cases, as the reader is undoubtedly aware, minority-group members have been presented in a stereotyped, derogatory manner. Although recent attention to these inequities has brought forth a flood of "ethnically balanced" books, the problem remains. A related problem concerns the appropriateness of the content of schoolbooks for minority children. Educators are realizing that stories about trips to Grandmother's farm have no relevance to ghetto black children who have never even seen a farm. The use of such materials, which may be of no relevance to minority children, necessarily dampens their enthusiasm for education and contributes to an ongoing pattern of poor academic performance. Such inadequate educational materials, coupled with the use of "ability groupings" in schools, may lead to essential segregation by socioeconomic status and hence often by ethnicity. And so the cycle is repeated. Traditional "histories" of American society also have utterly ignored the crucial contributions made by minority-group members and by minority cultures to the establishment of present-day American culture. Only during the 1960s did many educators begin to become aware of this glaring omission.

Finally, the influence of the general media (books, radio, TV, movies, and so on) is another factor in this pattern. Examples from *Little Black Sambo* and *Amos 'n Andy* to "Frito Bandito" and "skin-colored" (that is, pink) Band-Aids make it painfully clear how such portrayals can provide fodder for further stereotyping and derogation by majority-group members. Even the language of the American majority is studded with phrases that can reinforce racism, such as "That's white of you."

The forces of institutional racism also continue to affect the perceptions, attitudes, and behaviors of majority-group members. In Section 11 we present an example of how "forced" nonprejudicial behaviors may lead to nonprejudicial attitudes on the part of majority-group members. The same effect in the opposite direction can also be postulated. That is, if "forced" to act in a discriminatory manner (by the institutionalized racist pressures), the majority-group member may develop attitudes to justify such behavior to himself. The more susceptible to societal conformity pressure he is, the more his behaviors may correspond to the institutional sanctions (Pettigrew, 1961). In a related sense, a majority child may develop negative attitudes through the affectively neutral process of making inferences from available evidence or "putting two and two together" (Ashmore, 1970). If the child becomes aware that the societal institutions encourage racism, he or she is likely to assume that there must be a good reason for this—that is, that the minority group must deserve such treatment. Furthermore, if the minority-group members with whom he or she comes into contact can be perceived (or misperceived) as having some of the expected "bad" traits, perhaps due to the self-fulfilling prophecy, then the child's negative orientation will be strengthened.

Legacies of institutional racism may operate in more subtle ways yet. Although many majority Americans do not express acceptance of negative ethnic stereotypes, they nevertheless are aware of their existence. When asked to list the most common societal stereotypes of five ethnic groups, for instance, white college students in 1970 were able to do so with remarkable intersubject agreement (Brigham, 1972). Therefore, even if a majority-group member does not consciously *believe in* such negative trait attributions, they are "psychologically available" for use. And the person may draw upon them if he is in an uncomfortable situation, seeking to project or displace hostility, or if he sees a minority-group member who manifests such a trait.

Given this network of prejudice and racism, then, what general steps could be taken to reduce the level of hostility and mistreatment? One situation that has been investigated by a number of social scientists (Allport, 1954; Cook, 1970) is interracial contact. There is a growing body of evidence that interracial contact, when it is of a particular sort, may lead to a significant reduction in prejudice for the participants. Stuart Cook (1970) has specified those conditions of the contact situation that must be met if maximal attitude change is to occur. These conditions are: (1) The participants in the contact situation must be of *equal status* within the situation. (2) The situation should be structured so that mutual interdependence and cooperation are encouraged. Moreover, such cooperation should lead to a successful outcome. (3) The social norms applicable to the situation should encourage interracial association. (4) The situation should be one that promotes personal, intimate relationships and friendship formation. (5) The attributes of the participants should contradict the prevailing negative ethnic stereotypes. (6) The situation should be one that encourages the participants to generalize their (changed) attitudes to other situations and other ethnic-group members.

Cook (1970) created an experimental situation in which all these situational criteria were met. The situation involved three college students—a black girl, a nonprejudiced white girl, and a prejudiced white girl—and two experimenters, one black and one white. The first two girls were actually experimental confederates, and the prejudiced girl was the real subject. The experiment itself consisted of a complex "game" that contin-

ued for two hours a day for four weeks. The results of this long-term study are encouraging. About 40% of the subjects had changed their racial attitudes to a large degree (more than one standard deviation on three separate attitude measures) when they were measured in a completely different setting a month or more after the "game" had ended.

Cook also attempted to see if personality factors could account for the fact that some girls drastically changed their attitudes in this situation although other girls did not. It was found that a group of measures assessing positive attitudes toward people (low cynicism and low anomie) effectively differentiated the "changers" from the "nonchangers" (Wrightsman & Cook, 1967). The girls who became significantly less prejudiced were those who had the most positive attitudes toward people. In addition, the changers also tended to have a higher need for social approval and lower self-esteem than nonchangers. These last two measures probably serve as indices of general "persuasibility."

An imaginative suggestion for a way in which attitude change might result from contact on a massive scale has been made by Pierce (1969). He has proposed that a Children's Domestic Exchange (CDE) program be initiated. Under this program, children of *all* socioeconomic and ethnic persuasions between the ages of 10 and 18 would be given travel grants. Ideally, each child would travel at least once a year, always to a situation distinctive from his own cultural background. The length of his stay in the new situation could vary from days to months. For example, a majority-group child from Wilson, North Carolina, might stay with a Navajo family in Arizona; a Mexican-American from Los Angeles might go to a farm in Ohio.

Pierce proposed that, given our present technological expertise and computer-aided communications systems, such a program is feasible. It would require a staff cadre modeled after VISTA or the Peace Corps. Pierce suggests, and the present writers concur, that for such volunteer participants, the "transcultural, transethnic experiences . . . would broaden each of them and facilitate meaningful attitude changes" (Pierce,

1969, p. 565). This should hold true for both the children and the volunteer adults at whose homes the children would stay.

But such far-reaching attitude change, even if accomplished, might be inadequate to significantly reduce the degree of oppression of minority groups if major societal institutions continue to support discriminatory behaviors. Therefore many analysts have suggested that the most efficient way to reduce oppression is to attempt to eliminate institutional racism.

A thorny problem exists with respect to the eradication of institutional racism, however. The persons who are in the most advantageous positions to modify our major societal institutions are those who hold positions of power within the institutions. But it is precisely these people who might be expected to be *least* aware of the ethnic bias in "their" institution. Having worked within the institution for so long, any biases of the institution might go completely unrecognized (or, perhaps, be effectively rationalized). In short, such power figures might be "unable to see the forest for the trees." Such a suggestion has even been made about the institution of psychology itself (see Baratz & Baratz, 1970; Thomas, 1970). It is apparent that if far-reaching progress is to be made toward a truly egalitarian society, massive changes must take place on at least two fronts. The ethnic attitudes, beliefs, and behavioral inclinations (particularly, but not solely) of the American majority must undergo major changes, perhaps partially through contact and massive reeducation programs. At the same time, the ways in which society and its institutions contribute to oppression of minority-group members must be fully recognized, and drastic measures must be taken to eliminate these societal barriers. Only then will it be possible for the condition of "true integration" described by Pettigrew to become a reality in American society.

REFERENCES

Adorno, T. W., Frenkel-Brunswik, E., Levinson, D. J., & Sanford, R. N. *The authoritarian personality.* New York: Harper, 1950.

Allport, G. W. *The nature of prejudice.* Reading, Mass.: Addison-Wesley, 1954.

Allport, G. W., & Ross, J. M. Personal religious orientation and prejudice. *Journal of Personality and Social Psychology,* 1967, **5**, 432–443.

Ashmore, R. D. Prejudice: Causes and cures. In B. E. Collins, *Social psychology.* Reading, Mass.: Addison-Wesley, 1970. Pp. 247–339.

Banks, W. M. The changing attitudes of black students. *Personnel and Guidance Journal,* 1970, **48**, 739–745.

Baratz, S. S., & Baratz, J. C. Early childhood intervention: The social science base of institutional racism. *Harvard Educational Review,* 1970, **40**, 29–50.

Berry, B. *Race and ethnic relations.* (3rd ed.) Boston: Houghton Mifflin, 1965.

Brigham, J. C. Beliefs of white and black schoolchildren concerning racial personality differences. Paper presented at Midwestern Psychological Association Meeting, Detroit, May 1971.

Brigham, J. C. Racial stereotypes: Measurement variables and the stereotype-attitude relationship. *Journal of Applied Social Psychology,* 1972, **2**, 63–76.

Brigham, J. C., & Weissbach, T. A. (Eds.) *Racial attitudes in America: Analyses and findings of social psychology.* New York: Harper & Row, 1972.

Bunton, P. L., & Weissbach, T. A. Social comparison processes and racial misidentification. Paper presented at the California State Psychological Association Meeting, San Diego, January 1971.

Cook, S. W. Motives in a conceptual analysis of attitude-related behavior. In W. J. Arnold and D. Levine (Eds.), *Nebraska symposium on motivation 1969.* Lincoln: University of Nebraska Press, 1970. Pp. 179–231.

Daniels, R., & Kitano, H. H. L. *American racism: Exploration of the nature of prejudice.* Englewood Cliffs, N.J.: Prentice-Hall, 1970.

Greeley, A. M., & Sheatsley, P. B. Attitudes toward racial integration. *Scientific American,* 1971, **225** (6), 13–19.

Katz, D. The functional approach to the study of attitudes. *Public Opinion Quarterly,* 1960, **24**, 163–204.

Kerner, O. et al. *Report of the national advisory commission on civil disorders.* New York: Bantam Books, 1968.

Knowles, L. L., & Prewitt, K. *Institutional racism in America.* Englewood Cliffs, N. J.: Prentice-Hall, 1969.

Paige, J. M. Changing patterns of anti-white attitudes among blacks. *Journal of Social Issues,* 1970, **26**, 67–86.

Pettigrew, T. F. Social psychology and desegregation research. *American Psychologist,* 1961, **16**, 105–112.

Pierce, C. M. Violence and counterviolence: The need for a Children's Domestic Exchange. *American Journal of Orthopsychiatry,* 1969, **39**, 553–568.

Severy, L. J., & Brigham, J. C. Personality, prejudice,

and voting behavior under conditions of high involvement. Paper presented at Rocky Mountain Psychological Association, Denver, 1971.

Thomas, C. W. Psychologists, psychology, and the black community. In F. F. Korten, S. W. Cook, and J. I. Lacey (Eds.), *Psychology and the problems of society.* Washington, D.C.: American Psychological Association, 1970. Pp. 259–267.

Wrightsman, L. S., Jr., & Cook, S. W. The factorial structure of "positive attitudes toward people." Paper presented at the Southeastern Psychological Association Meetings, Atlanta, 1967.

SUGGESTED READINGS FOR FURTHER STUDY

Allen, V. L. (Ed.) Ghetto riots. *Journal of Social Issues,* 1970, **26** (1).

Allport, G. W. *The nature of prejudice.* Reading, Mass.: Addison-Wesley, 1954.

Ashmore, R. D. Prejudice: Causes and cures. In B. E. Collins, *Social psychology.* Reading, Mass.: Addison-Wesley, 1970. Pp. 247–339.

Baughman, E. E. *Black Americans.* New York: Academic Press, 1971.

Brigham, J. C. Ethnic stereotypes. *Psychological Bulletin,* 1971, **76,** 15–38.

Brigham, J. C., & Weissbach, T. A. (Eds.) *Racial attitudes in America: Analyses and findings of social psychology.* New York: Harper & Row, 1972.

Carmichael, S., & Hamilton, C. V. *Black power: The politics of liberation in America.* New York: Random House, 1967.

Cleaver, E. *Soul on ice.* New York: McGraw-Hill, 1968.

Cook, S. W. Motives in a conceptual analysis of attitude-related behavior. In W. J. Arnold and D. Levine (Eds.), *Nebraska symposium on motivation 1969.* Lincoln: University of Nebraska Press, 1970. Pp. 179–231.

Daniels, R., & Kitano, H. H. L. *American racism: Exploration of the nature of prejudice.* Englewood Cliffs, N. J.: Prentice-Hall, 1970.

Goldschmid, M. L. (Ed.) *Black Americans and white racism.* New York: Holt, Rinehart & Winston, 1970.

Harding, J., Proshansky, H., Kutner, B., & Chein, I. Prejudice and ethnic relations. In G. Lindzey and E. Aronson (Eds.), *The handbook of social psychology,* Vol. 5. Reading, Mass.: Addison-Wesley, 1969. Pp. 1–76.

Jones, J. M. *Prejudice and racism.* Reading, Mass.: Addison-Wesley, 1972.

Kerner, O. et al. *Report of the national advisory commission on civil disorders.* New York: Bantam Books, 1968.

Knowles, L. L., & Prewitt, K. *Institutional racism in America.* Englewood Cliffs, N. J.: Prentice-Hall, 1969.

Malcolm X, with the assistance of Alex Haley. *The autobiography of Malcolm X.* New York: Grove Press, 1965.

Marx, G. T. *Protest and prejudice.* (Rev. ed.) New York: Harper & Row, 1969.

Pettigrew, T. F. *Racially separate or together?* New York: McGraw-Hill, 1971.

Simpson, G. E., & Yinger, J. M. *Racial and cultural minorities.* (3rd ed.) New York: Harper & Row, 1965.

Young, R. P. (Ed.) *Roots of rebellion: The evolution of black politics and protest since World War II.* New York: Harper & Row, 1970.

SECTION 10

Sexism

INTRODUCTION

Consider the following situation:

A man and his teenage son are driving in an automobile when they are involved in a very serious accident. The man is killed and the boy is critically injured. He is rushed by ambulance to the local hospital and is wheeled into the emergency room. The staff surgeon in charge looks at the boy, shudders, and says "I can't operate on this boy. This boy is my son."

How can this statement be explained?

If your answer did not indicate that the staff surgeon is a woman and is the boy's mother, you may be reflecting sexism. (Incidentally, it is unlikely that Russian students would have difficulty with this question, since three-fourths of the physicians in the U.S.S.R. are women.)

Sexism can be defined as any attitude, action, or institutional structure that subordinates a person because of his or her sex. In this sense sexism is similar to racism, which was analyzed in Section 9, and the causes and outcomes of racism and sexism are in many ways similar. Although in the abstract, either men or women can be subordinated because of their sex, the vast majority of sexist attitudes and acts are directed against women. This type of sexism will be reviewed in this section.

The examples of sexism are numerous. Some are blatant, such as paying women less than men for identical work or denying women access to certain occupations. (Some specifics are given in the third article in this section.) Sexism permeates our religious heritage and our language, as exemplified by the assumption that God is male and by the use of such words as *chairman,* or *mankind,* as well as reliance on the pronoun *he* when referring to a nonspecific person who could be of either sex.

Sexism is learned at an early age. Although some recent books for children are trying to modify the pattern, most literature for infants and young children depicts girls playing with dolls or sewing and boys playing with toys and mechanical objects. Portrayals of adults in such materials are equally stereotyped. At day's end, Father is pictured as returning from the office or the factory while Mother has stayed home and acted as a domestic worker all day.

In line with the situation posed at the beginning of this Introduction, one of us (J.C.B.) asked his daughter, aged 4½, what she wanted to be when she grew up. She said "a nurse" because she wants "to doctor people." When it was suggested to her that, in that case, she might want to be a doctor, she was utterly appalled. "But I'm not a little boy. I can't be a doctor." She was astounded to hear that women, too, could be doctors and that men could even be nurses.

Sexism can have either subtle or obvious manifestations. Adherents of the Women's Liberation Movement have recently referred to some men as "male chauvinist pigs," implying that they manifest extremely discriminatory behaviors against females. ("Chauvinist" derives from Nicolas Chauvin, a soldier-follower of Napoleon I who attained much notoriety for his grotesque displays of attachment for the fallen Napoleon. "Male chauvinism" is an unreasoning, wildly extravagant devotion to the viewpoint that men are superior to women.) But sexism can be manifested unintentionally by both men and women in ways not readily apparent to them. As the Women's Liberationists tell us, we need to have our "consciousness raised" about the subtle ways that women are "put down" in contemporary American and Canadian life. The third article in this section, by Sandra L. Bem and Daryl J. Bem of Stanford University, gives examples of the ways that sexism operates as an insidious, nonconscious ideology in our society.

To some social psychologists a particularly aggravating manifestation of sexism is found in the theorizing of male psychologists about the nature of feminine personality and behavior. Male theorists have not been reluctant to speculate about the nature of the female psyche and female sexuality, and often their speculations are condescending and paternalistic. Sigmund Freud is an example, and we have chosen an article of Freud's as the theory-oriented article for the topic of sexism because it (1) advances a theory of the development of mature female sexuality and (2) manifests some rampant examples of sexism itself.

You may recall from Section 2 that Freud proposed that a child passes through several psychosexual stages of development on the way to adulthood. In his male chauvinistic way Freud always used male terms and examples, and he referred to the third of these stages as the "phallic" (the first two were the "oral" and "anal"), even though the vast majority of his patients were women.

According to Freud, each stage is associated with the investment of psychic energy, or *libido*, in a different part of the body. The infant, at the oral stage, is concerned with his or her mouth because it is the organ by which the child takes in food and expresses distress. The anal stage occurs as the child learns to be toilet-trained; at least some of the child's psychic energy becomes shifted toward the development of this activity. And toilet training is the precursor of many behaviors in which the child must learn to modify or subordinate selfish impulses in light of the rules of society.

During the phallic stage the child "discovers" his or her sexual organs. Desires to stimulate the sexual organs are likely to be punished by parents. But this does not dampen the motivation. During this period a boy, according to Freud, "rather naively wishes to use his new-found source of pleasure, the penis, to please his oldest source of pleasure, the mother" (Schaeffer, 1971, p. 12). He envies his father, who is occupying the position he craves and is doing the thing he wishes to do. Thus emerges the Oedipus conflict, which Freudian theory sees as being resolved by the boy's gradual identification with his father. The boy, in effect, says "I will get *vicarious satisfaction* by identifying with my father. What *he* does will bring *me* some sense of pleasure and satisfaction." In this way Freud handles the important question of how masculine identification develops in boys. Of course, the scenario we have described is an idealized one; many boys will not achieve the identification. Their fathers may be absent or, even if present, may be weak or otherwise not worthy of identification or emulation.

So much for boys. As Schaeffer (1971) indicates, Freudian theory has difficulty with the process of identification in females. The cornerstone of Freud's psychoanalytic theory is the physiological structure and development of humans.

Males and females differ in sexual anatomy, and this difference would have to be recognized in a theory, like Freud's, built on biological considerations. Additionally, the problem of identification by females is different from that of males because girls have from infancy invested their libidinal energy in their mother, the source of gratification when the girl was hungry or distressed. Does this mean that the process of identification with the parent of the same sex is easier for girls? Not necessarily so, according to the first article in this section.

In this article Freud discusses what he sees as the consequences of the anatomical and physiological differences between the sexes. From this article we can derive five testable hypotheses about general differences in attitude, personality, and behavior between the sexes. We will review the evidence for support or rejection of these hypotheses in the Summary to this section.

One of Freud's hypotheses in the article is that females, as well as males, perceive females as inferior. Here again sexism, like racism, may lead to a self-fulfilling prophecy. Just as blacks may come to internalize whites' negative stereotypes about them, so may females come to believe that they cannot achieve the levels of success that males

can. Later in this section Bem and Bem review two empirical studies of this phenomenon. In one (Horner, 1969, 1970) a "fear of failure" was shown by females in situations in which achievement was under scrutiny. Females who succeed in achievement-oriented situations were seen as unhappy misfits. The other study, by Goldberg (1968), serves as a stimulus for the second article in this section. The reprinted study by Pheterson, Kiesler, and Goldberg replicates and amplifies the earlier demonstration that females devaluate the quality of an artistic product when they believe it has been done by another female.

REFERENCES

Goldberg, P. Are women prejudiced against women? *Trans-action,* 1968, **5**(4), 28–30.

Horner, M. S. Fail: Bright women. *Psychology Today,* 1969, **3**(6), 36–38f.

Horner, M. S. Femininity and successful achievement: A basic inconsistency. In J. M. Bardwick, E. Douvan, M. S. Horner, & D. Gutmann, *Feminine personality and conflict.* Monterey, Calif.: Brooks/Cole, 1970. Pp. 45–74.

Schaeffer, D. L. (Ed.) *Sex differences in personality: Readings.* Monterey, Calif.: Brooks/Cole, 1971.

ARTICLE 28

Some Psychological Consequences of the Anatomical Distinction between the Sexes

Sigmund Freud

In my own writings and in those of my followers more and more stress is laid upon the necessity for carrying the analyses of neurotics back into the remotest period of their childhood, the time of the early efflorescence of sexual life. It is only by examining the first manifestations of the patient's innate instinctual constitution and the effects of his earliest experiences that we can accurately gauge the motive forces that have led to his neurosis and can be secure against the errors into which we might be tempted by the degree to which they have become remodelled and overlaid in adult life. This requirement is not only of theoretical but also of practical importance, for it distinguishes our efforts from the work of those physicians whose interests are focussed exclusively upon therapeutic results and who employ analytic methods, but only up to a certain point. An analysis of early childhood such as we are considering is tedious and laborious and makes demands both upon the physician and upon the patient which cannot always be met. Moreover it leads us into dark regions where there are as yet no sign-posts. Indeed, analysts may feel reassured, I think, that there is no risk of their work becoming mechanical, and so of losing its interest, during the next few decades.

In the following pages I bring forward some findings of analytical research which would be of great importance if they could be proved to apply universally. Why do I not postpone publication of them until further experience has given me the necessary proof, if such proof is obtainable? Because the conditions under which I work have undergone a change, with implications which I cannot disguise. Formerly, I was never one of those who are unable to hold back what seems to be a new discovery until it has been either confirmed or corrected. My *Interpretation of Dreams* (1900) and my "Fragment of an Analysis of a Case of Hysteria" (1905b) (the case of Dora) were suppressed by me—if not for the nine years enjoined by Horace—at all events for four or five years before I allowed them to be published. But in those days I had unlimited time before me and material poured in upon me in such quantities that fresh experiences were hardly to be escaped. Moreover, I was the only worker in a new field, so that my reticence involved no danger to myself and no risk of loss to others.

But now everything has changed. The time before me is limited. The whole of it is no longer spent in working, so that my opportunities for making fresh observations are not so numerous. If I think I see something new, I am uncertain whether I can wait for it to be confirmed. And further, everything that is to be seen upon the surface has already been exhausted; what remains has to be slowly and laboriously dragged up from the depths. Finally, I am no longer alone. An eager crowd of fellow-workers is ready to make use of what is unfinished or doubtful, and I can leave to them that part of the work which I

From Chapter XVII of Volume 5 of *The Collected Papers of Sigmund Freud,* edited by Ernest Jones, M. D. Reprinted with permission of the publisher, Basic Books, Inc. Copyright, 1959.

should otherwise have done myself. On this occasion, therefore, I feel justified in publishing something which stands in urgent need of confirmation before its value or lack of value can be decided.

In examining the earliest mental shapes assumed by the sexual life of children we have been in the habit of taking as the subject of our investigations the male child, the little boy. With little girls, so we have supposed, things must be similar, though in some way or other they must nevertheless be different. The point in development at which this difference lay could not clearly be determined.

In boys the situation of the Oedipus complex is the first stage that can be recognized with certainty. It is easy to understand, because at that stage a child retains the same object which he previously cathected with his pregenital libido during the preceding period while he was being suckled and nursed. The further fact that in this situation he regards his father as a disturbing rival and would like to get rid of him and take his place is a straightforward consequence of the actual state of affairs. I have shown elsewhere how the Oedipus attitude in little boys belongs to the phallic phase, and how it succumbs to the fear of castration, that is, to narcissistic interest in their own genitals. The matter is made more difficult to grasp by the complicating circumstance that even in boys the Oedipus complex has a double orientation, active and passive, in accordance with their bisexual constitution; a boy also wants to take his *mother's* place as the love-object of his *father*—a fact which we describe as the feminine attitude.

As regards the prehistory of the Oedipus complex in boys we are far from complete clarity. We know that that period includes an identification of an affectionate sort with the boy's father, an identification which is still free from any sense of rivalry in regard to his mother. Another element of that stage is invariably, I believe, a masturbatory stimulation of the genitals, the masturbation of early childhood, the more or less violent suppression of which by the persons in charge of the child sets the castration complex in action. It is to be assumed that this masturbation is attached to the Oedipus complex and serves as a discharge

for the sexual excitation belonging to it. It is, however, uncertain whether the masturbation has this character from the first, or whether on the contrary it makes its first appearance spontaneously as an activity of a bodily organ and is only brought into relation with the Oedipus complex at some later date; this second possibility is by far the more probable. Another doubtful question is the part played by bed-wetting and by the breaking of that habit through the intervention of training measures. We are inclined to adopt the simple generalization that continued bed-wetting is a result of masturbation and that its suppression is regarded by boys as an inhibition of their genital activity, that is, as having the meaning of a threat of castration; but whether we are always right in supposing this remains to be seen. Finally, analysis shows us in a shadowy way how the fact of a child at a very early age listening to his parents copulating may set up his first sexual excitation, and how that event may, owing to its after-effects, act as a starting-point for the child's whole sexual development. Masturbation, as well as the two attitudes in the Oedipus complex, later on become attached to this early experience, the child having subsequently interpreted its meaning. It is impossible, however, to suppose that these observations of coitus are of universal occurrence, so that at this point we are faced with the problem of "primal phantasies." Thus the prehistory of the Oedipus complex, even in boys, raises all of these questions for sifting and explanation; and there is the further problem of whether we are to suppose that the process invariably follows the same course, or whether a great variety of different preliminary stages may not converge upon the same terminal situation.

In little girls the Oedipus complex raises one problem more than in boys. In both cases the mother is the original object; and there is no cause for surprise that boys retain that object in the Oedipus complex. But how does it happen that girls abandon it and instead take their father as an object? In pursuing this question I have been able to reach some conclusions which may throw light upon the prehistory of the Oedipus relation in girls.

Every analyst has come across certain women

who cling with especial intensity and tenacity to the bond with their father and to the wish in which it culminates of having a child by him. We have good reason to suppose that the same wishful phantasy was also the motive force of their infantile masturbation, and it is easy to form an impression that at this point we have been brought up against an elementary and unanalysable fact of infantile sexual life. But a thorough analysis of these very cases brings something different to light, namely, that here the Oedipus complex has a long prehistory and is in some respects a secondary formation.

The old paediatrician Lindner once remarked that a child discovers the genital zones (the penis or the clitoris) as a source of pleasure while indulging in sensual sucking (thumb-sucking)[1]: I shall leave it an open question whether it is really true that the child takes the newly found source of pleasure in exchange for the recent loss of the mother's nipple—a possibility to which later phantasies (fellatio) seem to point. Be that as it may, the genital zone is discovered at some time or other, and there seems no justification for attributing any psychical content to its first stimulations. But the first step in the phallic phase which begins in this way is not the linking-up of the masturbation with the object-cathexes of the Oedipus situation, but a momentous discovery which little girls are destined to make. They notice the penis of a brother or playmate, strikingly visible and of large proportions, at once recognize it as the superior counterpart of their own small and inconspicuous organ, and from that time forward fall a victim to envy for the penis.

There is an interesting contrast between the behaviour of the two sexes. In the analogous situation, when a little boy first catches sight of a girl's genital region, he begins by showing irresolution and lack of interest; he sees nothing or disowns what he has seen, he softens it down or looks about for expedients for bringing it into line with his expectations. It is not until later, when some threat of castration has obtained a hold upon him, that the observation becomes important to him; if he then recollects or repeats it, it arouses a terrible storm of emotion in him and

[1]Cf. *Three Essays on the Theory of Sexuality* (1905a).

forces him to believe in the reality of the threat which he has hitherto laughed at. This combination of circumstances leads to two reactions, which may become fixed and will in that case, whether separately or together or in conjunction with other factors, permanently determine the boy's relations to women: horror of the mutilated creature or triumphant contempt for her. These developments, however, belong to the future, though not to a very remote one.

A little girl behaves differently. She makes her judgment and her decision in a flash. She has seen it and knows that she is without it and wants to have it.[2]

From this point there branches off what has been named the masculinity complex of women, which may put great difficulties in the way of their regular development toward femininity, and it cannot be got over soon enough. The hope of some day obtaining a penis in spite of everything and so of becoming like a man may persist to an incredibly late age and may become a motive for the strangest and otherwise unaccountable actions. Or again, a process may set in which might be described as a "denial," a process which in the mental life of children seems neither uncommon nor very dangerous but which in an adult would mean the beginning of a psychosis. Thus a girl may refuse to accept the fact of being castrated, may harden herself in the conviction that she *does* possess a penis and may subsequently be compelled to behave as though she were a man.

The physical consequences of penis-envy, in so far as it does not become absorbed in the reaction-formation of the masculinity complex, are various and far-reaching. After a woman has become aware of the wound to her narcissism, she develops, like a scar, a sense of inferiority. When she has passed beyond her first attempt at explaining her lack of a penis as being a punishment personal to herself and has realized that that sexual char-

[2]This is an opportunity for correcting a statement which I made many years ago (Freud, 1905a). I believed that the sexual interest of children, unlike that of pubescents, was aroused, not by the differences between the sexes, but by the problem of where babies come from. We now see that, at all events with girls, this is certainly not the case. With boys it may no doubt happen sometimes one way and sometimes the other; or with both sexes chance experiences may determine the event.

acter is a universal one, she begins to share the contempt felt by men for a sex which is the lesser in so important a respect, and, at least in the holding of that opinion, insists upon being like a man.[3]

Even after penis-envy has abandoned its true object, it continues to exist: by an easy displacement it persists in the character-trait of *jealousy*. Of course, jealousy is not limited to one sex and has a wider foundation than this, but I am of the opinion that it plays a far larger part in the mental life of women than of men and that that is because it is enormously reinforced from the direction of displaced penis-envy. While I was still unaware of this source of jealousy and was considering the phantasy "A Child Is Being Beaten" (1919), which occurs so commonly in girls, I constructed a first phase for it in which its meaning was that another child, a rival of whom the subject was jealous, was to be beaten. This phantasy seems to be a relic of the phallic period in girls. The peculiar rigidity which struck me so much in the monotonous formula "a child is being beaten" can probably be interpreted in a special way. The child which is being beaten (or caressed) may at bottom be nothing more nor less than the clitoris itself, so that at its very lowest level the statement will contain a confession of masturbation, which has remained attached to the content of the formula from its beginning in the phallic phase up to the present time.

A third consequence of penis-envy seems to be a loosening of the girl's relation with her mother as a love-object. The situation as a whole is not

[3]In my first critical account of the "History of the Psychoanalytic Movement," written in 1914 (1914b), I recognized that this fact represents the core of truth contained in Adler's theory. That theory has no hesitation in explaining the whole world by this single point ("organ inferiority," "the masculine protest," breaking away from "the feminine line") and prides itself upon having in this way robbed sexuality of its importance and puts the desire for power in its place. Thus the only organ which could claim to be called "inferior" without any ambiguity would be the clitoris. On the other hand, one hears of analysts who boast that, although they have worked for dozens of years, they have never found a sign of the existence of a castration complex. We must bow our heads in recognition of the greatness of this achievement, even though it is only a negative one, a piece of virtuosity in the art of overlooking and mistaking. The two theories form an interesting pair of opposites: in one of them not a trace of a castration complex, in the other nothing at all but its effects.

very clear, but it can be seen that in the end the girl's mother, who sent her into the world so insufficiently equipped, is almost always held responsible for her lack of a penis. The way in which this comes about historically is often that soon after the girl has discovered that her genitals are unsatisfactory she begins to show jealousy of another child on the grounds that her mother is fonder of it than of her, which serves as a reason for her giving up her affectionate relation to her mother. It will fit in with this if the child which has been preferred by her mother is made into the first object of the beating-phantasy which ends in masturbation.

There is yet another surprising effect of penis-envy, or of the discovery of the inferiority of the clitoris, which is undoubtedly the most important of all. In the past I had often formed an impression that in general women tolerate masturbation worse than men, that they more frequently fight against it and that they are unable to make use of it in circumstances in which a man would seize upon it as a way of escape without any hesitation. Experience would no doubt elicit innumerable exceptions to this statement, if we attempted to turn it into a rule. The reactions of human individuals of both sexes are of course made up of masculine and feminine traits. But it appeared to me nevertheless as though masturbation, at all events of the clitoris, is a masculine activity and that the elimination of clitoral sexuality is a necessary pre-condition for the development of femininity. Analyses of the remote phallic period have now taught me that in girls, soon after the first signs of penis-envy, an intense current of feeling against masturbation makes its appearance, which cannot be attributed exclusively to the educational influence of those in charge of the child. This impulse is clearly a forerunner of the wave of repression which at puberty will do away with a large amount of the girl's masculine sexuality in order to make room for the development of her femininity. It may happen that this first opposition to auto-erotic stimulation fails to attain its end. And this was in fact the case in the instances which I analyzed. The conflict continued, and both then and later the girl did everything she could to free herself from the compulsion to masturbate. Many of the later manifestations of sexual life in women remain unintelligible unless this powerful motive is recognized.

I cannot explain the opposition which is raised in this way by little girls to phallic masturbation except by supposing that there is some concurrent factor which turns her violently against that pleasurable activity. Such a factor lies close at hand in the narcissistic sense of humiliation which is bound up with penis-envy, the girl's reflection that after all this is a point on which she cannot compete with boys and that it would therefore be best for her to give up the idea of doing so. Thus the little girl's recognition of the anatomical distinction between the sexes forces her away from masculinity and masculine masturbation on to new lines which lead to the development of femininity.

So far there has been no question of the Oedipus complex, nor has it up to this point played any part. But now the girl's libido slips into a new position by means—there is no other way of putting it—of the equation "penis = child." She gives up her wish for a penis and puts in place of it a wish for a child: and *with this purpose in view* she takes her father as a love-object. Her mother becomes the object of her jealousy. The girl has turned into a little woman. If I am to credit a single exaggerated analytic instance, this new situation can give rise to physical sensations which would have to be regarded as a premature awakening of the female genital apparatus. If the girl's attachment to her father comes to grief later on and has to be abandoned, it may give place to an identification with him and the girl may thus return to her masculinity complex and perhaps remain fixated in it.

I have now said the essence of what I had to say: I will stop, therefore, and cast an eye over our findings. We have gained some insight into the prehistory of the Oedipus complex in girls. The corresponding period in boys is more or less unknown. In girls the Oedipus complex is a secondary formation. The operations of the castration complex precede it and prepare for it. As regards the relation between the Oedipus and castration complexes there is a fundamental contrast between the two sexes. *Whereas in boys the Oedipus complex succumbs to the castration complex,*[4] *in girls it is made possible and led up to by the castration complex.* This contradiction is cleared up if we reflect that the castration complex always operates in the sense dictated by its subject matter: it inhibits and limits masculinity and encourages femininity. The difference between the sexual development of males and females at the stage we have been considering is an intelligible consequence of the anatomical distinction between their genitals and of the physical situation involved in it; it corresponds to the difference between a castration that has been carried out and one that has merely been threatened. In their essentials, therefore, our findings are self-evident and it should have been possible to foresee them.

The Oedipus complex, however, is such an important thing that the manner in which one enters and leaves it cannot be without its effects. In boys (as I have shown at length in the paper to which I have just referred and to which all of my present remarks are closely related) the complex is not simply repressed, it is literally smashed to pieces by the shock of threatened castration. Its libidinal cathexes are abandoned, desexualized and in part sublimated; its objects are incorporated into the ego, where they form the nucleus of the super-ego and give that new structure its characteristic qualities. In normal, or rather in ideal, cases, the Oedipus complex exists no longer, even in the unconscious; the super-ego has become its heir. Since the penis (to follow Ferenczi) owes its extraordinarily high narcissistic cathexis to its organic significance for the propagation of the species, the catastrophe of the Oedipus complex (the abandonment of incest and the institution of conscience and morality) may be regarded as a victory of the race over the individual. This is an interesting point of view when one considers that neurosis is based upon a struggle of the ego against the demands of the sexual function. But to leave the standpoint of individual psychology is not likely to be of any immediate help in clarifying this complicated situation.

[4]Cf. "The Passing of the Oedipus-Complex" (1924).

In girls the motive for the destruction of the Oedipus complex is lacking. Castration has already had its effect, which was to force the child into the situation of the Oedipus complex. Thus the Oedipus complex escapes the fate which it meets with in boys; it may either be slowly abandoned or got rid of by repression, or its effects may persist far into women's normal mental life. I cannot escape the notion (though I hesitate to give it expression) that for women the level of what is ethically normal is different from what it is in men. Their super-ego is never so inexorable, so impersonal, so independent of its emotional origins as we require it to be in men. Character traits which critics of every epoch have brought up against women—that they show less sense of justice than men, that they are less ready to submit to the great necessities of life, that they are more often influenced in their judgements by feelings of affection or hostility—all these would be amply accounted for by the modification in the formation of their super-ego which we have already inferred. We must not allow ourselves to be deflected from such conclusions by the denials of the feminists, who are anxious to force us to regard the two sexes as completely equal in position and worth; but we shall, of course, willingly agree that the majority of men are also far behind the masculine ideal and that all human individuals, as a result of their bisexual disposition and of cross inheritance, combine in themselves both masculine and feminine characteristics, so that pure masculinity and femininity remain theoretical constructions of uncertain content.

I am inclined to set some value on the considerations I have brought forward upon the psychological consequences of the anatomical distinction between the sexes. I am aware, however, that this opinion can only be maintained if my findings, which are based on a handful of cases, turn out to have general validity and to be typical. If not, they would remain no more than a contribution to our knowledge of the different paths along which sexual life develops.

In the valuable and comprehensive studies upon the masculinity and castration complex in women by Abraham (1921), Horney (1923), and Helene Deutsch (1925) there is much that touches closely upon what I have written but nothing that coincides with it completely, so that here again I feel justified in publishing this paper.[5]

REFERENCES

Abraham, K. Manifestations of the female castration complex (1921). *Selected papers.* London: Hogarth, 1927.

Deutsch, H. *Zur Psychologie der weiblichen Sexualfunktionen* (On female sexuality). Vienna: Internationaler Psychoanalytischer Verlag, 1925.

Freud, S. *Interpretation of dreams* (1900), Standard Edition, Vols. 4–5. London: Hogarth, 1924.

Freud, S. *Three essays on the theory of sexuality* (1905a), Standard Edition, Vol. 7. London: Hogarth, 1924.

Freud, S. Fragment of an analysis of a case of hysteria (1905b). *Collected papers,* Vol. 3. London: Hogarth, 1925.

Freud, S. On the sexual theories of children (1908). *Collected papers,* Vol. 2. London: Hogarth, 1924.

Freud, S. On narcissism (1914a). *Collected papers,* Vol. 4. London: Hogarth, 1924.

Freud, S. On the history of the psychoanalytic movement (1914b). *Collected papers,* Vol. 1. London: Hogarth, 1924.

Freud, S. The passing of the Oedipus complex (1924). *Collected papers,* Vol. 2. London: Hogarth, 1924.

Freud, S. Female sexuality (1931). *Collected papers,* Vol. 5. London: Hogarth, 1952.

Horney, K. On the genesis of the castration complex in women. *International Journal of Psychoanalysis,* 1923, **5,** 50–65.

[5]Freud returned to this subject in a later work, "Female Sexuality" (1931).

ARTICLE 29

Evaluation of the Performance of Women as a Function of their Sex, Achievement, and Personal History[1]

Gail I. Pheterson, Sara B. Kiesler, and Philip A. Goldberg

One explanation for the apparent failure of women to achieve as much success as men is prejudicial evaluations of their work by men (cf. Klein, 1950; Scheinfeld, 1944). If men undervalue the accomplishments of women, women also may do so. Women's misjudgment of themselves should contribute to an actual lack of achievement. If women devalue their own and each other's work, they should be less willing to try to achieve and less supportive of their fellow women's efforts. The present study investigates the conditions under which women devalue female performance.

Goldberg (1968) designed a study to investigate prejudice among women toward women in the areas of intellectual and professional competence. College women were asked to evaluate supposedly published journal articles on linguistics, law, art history, dietetics, education, and city planning; for each article, half of the subjects saw a male author's name and half saw a female author's name. The results confirmed the hypothesis that college women value the professional work of men more highly than the identical work of women. Women devalued female work for no other reason than the female name associated with the article. Sensitivity to the sex of the au-

thor served to distort judgment and thereby prejudice women against the work of other women.

Using the identical procedure, Pheterson (1969) explored prejudice against women among middle-aged, uneducated women. The professional articles were on marriage, child discipline, and special education. The results did not support the findings of Goldberg. Women judged female work to be equal to male work; in fact, evaluations were almost significantly more favorable for female work than for male work.

The differing results of Goldberg and Pheterson were perhaps due to the different subjects used, to the different articles, or to some combination of the two. One plausible explanation might be that the printed articles had different significance for the two sets of subjects. College women see the printed word frequently, are taught to be critical, and may take the publication of a paper relatively lightly. They might have viewed the articles simply as vehicles for presenting ideas or proposals. Uneducated women, on the other hand, might regard the publication or, even, writing of an article as a big accomplishment in itself, regardless of the specific ideas presented. Perhaps all women judge women less favorably than men when evaluating their proposals or unfinished work because men are more likely to succeed. That is, given a piece of work which has uncertain status, the man's, rather than woman's, is more likely in our society to eventually be successful. On the other hand, women may judge the recognized accomplish-

Reprinted from *Journal of Personality and Social Psychology,* 1971, **19,** 114–118. Reprinted with permission of the authors and the publisher; copyright 1971, American Psychological Association.

[1]This study was supported, in part, by funds from National Science Foundation Grant GS 27292 to the second author.

ments or already successful work of women to be equal or even better than the same work of men. Success is less common for women. A contrast effect may cause people to overvalue achievement when they expect none. Also, women may overvalue female accomplishment because they assume that women face greater obstacles to success and therefore must exert more energy, display more competence, or make more sacrifices than men.

The present study was designed to investigate the divergent results of Goldberg (1968) and Pheterson (1969) and, further, to test the previously presented arguments. Women were asked to judge paintings created by men and women. Some paintings represented attempts to accomplish—that is, were entries in art competitions. Other paintings represented actual accomplishments—they had already won prizes. The first hypothesis was that women will evaluate male attempts to accomplish more highly than female attempts. The second hypothesis was that women will evaluate female accomplishments as equal to or better than male accomplishments.

The above hypotheses suggest that people judge successful persons more highly when they have more odds against them (as women presumably do). Thus, a woman's accomplishment might be praised more than a man's accomplishment because women face greater obstacles. Our culture shows great admiration for the achievements of the handicapped or underprivileged (Allport, 1958). A third hypothesis was formulated to explore this admiration and its influence on female judgments. It stated that women will evaluate the accomplishments of people with personal odds against them more favorably than the accomplishments of people without such odds.

METHOD

Subjects

The subjects were 120 freshmen and sophomore women students at Connecticut College. College women were used to permit a replication of the Goldberg (1968) study within the experimental design. They volunteered in student

dormitories for immediate participation in the 15-minute task.

Experimental Design

There were three experimental manipulations constituting a 2 X 2 X 2 design. Eight paintings were presented to small groups of subjects for evaluation. The sex of the artist, the status of the paintings, and the personal odds faced by the artist were manipulated, such that for each painting half of the subjects thought that it had been created by a male artist, and half thought that it had been created by a female artist; half thought it was a prize-winning painting, and half thought it was just an entry in a show; half thought the artist had faced unusually severe obstacles, and half thought the artist had faced no unusual obstacles. Each subject participated in each experimental condition, evaluating all eight paintings sequentially. The identity of each painting was counterbalanced among subjects, so that all conditions were represented for each painting.

Procedure

Subjects were seated in a room equipped with a slide projector and screen. Each subject was given a booklet and was told to read the directions:

Slides of eight paintings will be shown in conjunction with brief biographical sketches of the artists. After viewing the slide, turn the page and answer five evaluative questions about the painting. No personal information about your identity, talents, or tastes is required. This is a study of the artistic judgments of college students.

The subjects were then instructed to read the first artist sketch, inspect the projected painting, turn the page and answer the appropriate questions, and then proceed in the same manner for each of the eight slides.

Eight slides of unfamiliar modern art painting were used. To accompany them, fictitious artist profiles were composed to include the eight experimental conditions. These profiles appeared in the booklets in different orders for the different subjects. Half of the profiles described a female artist, and half described a male. Their age, residence, and occupations were briefly described (identical for male and female). For example, "Bob (Barbara) Soulman, born in 1941 in Cleveland, Ohio, teaches English in a progressive program of adult education. Painting is his (her) hobby and most creative pastime." Cross-cutting the sex manipulation, half of the profiles described the painting as a contest entry (e.g., "She has entered this painting in a museum-sponsored young artists' contest"), and half described it as a recognized winner (e.g., "This painting is the winner of the Annual Cleveland Color Competition").In a third manipulation, half of the profiles described the painter as having had obstacles to success (e.g., "An arm amputee since 1967, he has been amazingly productive as an artist").

After each slide, the subjects turned a booklet page. Five questions asked the subjects to evaluate the paintings on a scale of 1-5, with higher ratings representing more favorable evaluations. After every slide, the following questions were posed: (a) Judging from this painting, how technically competent would you judge Mr. (or Miss)____to be? (b) How creative would you judge Mr. (or Miss)____to be? (c) What rating would you give to Mr. (or Miss)____for the overall quality and content of his (her) painting? (d) What emotional impact has Mr. (or Miss)____instilled in his (her) painting? (e) Judging from this painting, what prediction would you make for the artistic future of Mr. (or Miss)____?

After all eight slides were shown, the study was explained, and the subjects were asked not to discuss it.

RESULTS

The questionnaire data were analyzed using four-way analyses of variance, with three experimental conditions and subjects as the fourth factor. Three questions asked the subjects to evaluate the artists; these were assumed to be directly relevant to the hypotheses.

The first question, technical competence, revealed an overall rating of the male artists as significantly superior to the female artists (F

=3.99, df=1/119, $p<.05$).* There was a significant Sex X Painting Status interaction (F=5.42, df=1/119, $p<.05$). Inspection of the mean ratings of males and females under winner and entry conditions indicates that the main effect of male superiority was attributable to the entry condition and showed no differences in the winner condition. Means in the entry condition differed significantly in favor of men (t=1.99, $p<.05$);** means in the winner condition were identical (see Table 1). All other main effects and interactions were not significant.

TABLE 1. Mean competence ratings of male and female artists with winning or entry paintings.

Status of painting	Sex of artist	
	Male	Female
Winner	3.483	3.483
Entry	3.562	3.354

The question concerning the artistic future of the artist produced results paralleling the competence data (see Table 2). There was a significant Sex X Painting Status interaction (F=4.52, df=1/119, $p<.05$). Males were evaluated significantly more favorably than females for their entry paintings (t=1.92, $p<.06$). Evaluations did not differ significantly for the winning paintings, although evaluations tended to favor the female winners.

A third question, asking about the artist's creativity, yielded no significant differences. (Intuitively, these data are not surprising, given the

TABLE 2. Mean ratings of artistic future of male ahd female artists with winning and entry paintings.

Status of painting	Sex of artist	
	Male	Female
Winner	2.970	2.987
Entry	3.062	2.812

*For a definition of the F test, see footnote on page 17.

**For a definition of the t test, see footnote on page 23 or Glossary.

ambiguity of the term "creative." Also, "creativity" has some feminine connotations which judges may not wish to attribute to men, even when they believe the men are better artists.) In addition, the subjects evaluated the paintings themselves, equally among conditions (their quality and their emotional impact). Bias apparently was directed toward the performer, rather than toward his or her work.

The data presented above support our first and second hypotheses. Women value male work more highly than female work when it is only an attempt or entry; however, this bias dissipates when the work advances from entry to winner. The third hypothesis concerning the odds condition was not confirmed; there were no significant differences among the odds conditions.

DISCUSSION

Some professional women have claimed that their work is evaluated by men less well than it would be if they were men (e.g., Klein, 1950). The recent data of Goldberg (1968) and Pheterson (1969) have added a new dimension to the attitudinal factors inhibiting female success. Under certain conditions, even women are prejudiced against the performance of other women. The present study investigated one aspect of this prejudice. Women evaluated female entries in a contest less favorably than identical male entries, but female winners equally to identical male winners.

The implications of this finding are far-reaching. The work of women in competition is devalued by other women. Even work that is equivalent to the work of a man will be judged inferior until it receives special distinction, and that distinction is difficult to achieve when judgment is biased against the work in competition. According to the present data and those of Goldberg, women cannot expect unbiased evaluations until they prove themselves by award, trophy, or other obvious success. Obvious success is perceived differently by some groups than by others. The present research was based on the speculation that uneducated, middle-aged women perceived published articles as signs of obvious success, whereas college women perceived such work simply as a presentation of ideas. Women were prejudiced against female ideas but not against female success. The manipulation of entry and winner in this study permitted controlled examination and confirmation of that speculation.

A question might be raised regarding the strength of the present findings. Of five questionnaire items, only two supported our hypothesis. These were the first question (technical competence of the artist) and the fifth (the artist's future). However, a priori reasoning would suggest that these were the very questions where one would expect bias against women to occur. As mentioned earlier, creativity is ambiguous and may have feminine connotations. The paintings themselves were abstract, unknown, and also difficult to judge on the dimensions covered (quality and emotional impact). If people are expecting men to perform better than women, they should have the strongest expectations about tasks on which society has already labeled men as superior. In everyday life, many professional men are regarded as technically competent and are successful; we see fewer women in these positions (girls are not raised to be engineers or business executives). Thus, the subjects might simply be described as reflecting attitudes in society at large. They assume the men to be more competent and predicted a more successful future for men *unless* there was evidence to the contrary— that is, that the women had, in fact, succeeded. The subjects probably did not have very strong convictions about whether men are more creative than women (husbands usually leave such creative tasks as home decorating and sewing to their wives). The quality and emotional impact of an abstract painting are also unlikely to have aroused strong attitudes favoring men. We argue, then, that our questionnaire data reflected the differing expectations which women (or men) have about men and women. That is, a woman will probably be less competent and her accomplishments fewer than a man's, although she may be as creative (but probably not in science or business) and certainly as "emotional." Such an analysis implies that the subjects were not really judging the artists or paintings at all, but were simply expressing attitudes they held prior to the study. This, of course, was our purpose.

The third hypothesis, which predicted evaluations of paintings by people with odds against them to be more favorable in the winner condition than evaluations of identical paintings by people without odds, was not supported by the data. It is possible that the odds manipulation was too obvious. Perhaps some subjects were immediately aware of their special admiration for achievers with odds and therefore controlled their responses or underrated them, thus masking any positive bias the odds may have instilled. Informal subjects' feedback after the task supports this explanation. No subject suspected the importance of artist sex differences; however, many subjects reported the suspicion that they were expected to overvalue paintings of the handicapped or underprivileged. This suspicion may have caused a reaction which obscured prejudicial responses. Remaining to be demonstrated, then, is the hypothesis that obstacles make successes seem greater.

Why do women devalue each others' performance? If one accepts women as a group which has important similarities to minority groups in our society, the answer is obvious. The members of minority groups, and women, have less power and fewer opportunities than do the dominant group, white Anglo-Saxon males. Self-defeating as it is, groups feeling themselves to be the target of prejudice nevertheless tend to accept the attitudes of the dominant majority. This process has also been called identification with the aggressor (Allport, 1958). Women, then, when confronted with another woman who is trying to succeed in some endeavor, will assume that she is less motivated, less expert, or simply less favored by others than a man would be (all these assumptions may be perfectly true).

Our data suggest that women do not devalue another woman when she has attained success. Without evidence, we think men do not either. In fact, a woman who has succeeded may be overevaluated. The present study apparently did not afford a proper test of this hypothesis. Perhaps if the artists had been identified as famous and really superior, women would have been rated more highly than men.

REFERENCES

Allport, G. W. *The nature of prejudice.* New York: Addison-Wesley, 1958.

Goldberg, P. A. Are women prejudiced against women? *Trans-action,* April 1968, 28–30.

Klein, X. V. The stereotype of femininity. *Journal of Social Issues,* 1950, **6,** 3–12.

Pheterson, G. I. Female prejudice against men. Unpublished manuscript, Connecticut College, 1969.

Scheinfeld, A. *Women and men.* New York: Harcourt, Brace, 1944.

ARTICLE 30

Training the Woman to Know Her Place:
The Power of a Nonconscious Ideology

Sandra L. Bem and Daryl J. Bem*

In the beginning God created the heaven and the earth. ... And God said, Let us make man in our image, after our likeness; and let them have dominion over the fish of the sea, and over the fowl of the air, and over the cattle, and over all the earth. ... And the rib, which the Lord God had taken from man, made he a woman and brought her unto the man. ... And the Lord God said unto the woman, What is this that thou has done? And the woman said, The serpent beguiled me, and I did eat. ... Unto the woman He said, I will greatly multiply thy sorrow and thy conception; in sorrow thou shalt bring forth children; and thy desire shall be to thy husband, and he shall rule over thee (Gen. 1, 2, 3).

And lest anyone fail to grasp the moral of this story, Saint Paul provides further clarification:

For a man ... is the image and glory of God; but the woman is the glory of the man. For the man is not of the woman, but the woman of the man. Neither was the man created for the woman, but the woman for the man (1 Cor. 11).

Let the woman learn in silence with all subjection. But I suffer not a woman to teach, nor to usurp authority over the man, but to be in silence. For Adam was first formed, then Eve. And Adam was not deceived, but the woman, being deceived, was in the transgression. Notwithstanding, she shall be saved in childbearing, if they continue in faith and charity and holiness with sobriety (1 Tim. 2).

And lest it be thought that only Christians have this rich heritage of ideology about women,

From Bem, S. L., & Bem, D. J. Case study of a nonconscious ideology: Training the woman to know her place. In D. J. Bem, *Beliefs, attitudes, and human affairs*. Monterey, Calif.: Brooks/Cole, 1970. (Revised: March 1971) Reprinted with permission of the authors and the publishers.

*Order of authorship determined by the flip of a coin.

consider the morning prayer of the Orthodox Jew:

Blessed art Thou, oh Lord our God, King of the Universe, that I was not born a gentile.
Blessed art Thou, oh Lord our God, King of the Universe, that I was not born a slave.
Blessed art Thou, oh Lord our God, King of the Universe, that I was not born a woman.

Or the Koran, the sacred text of Islam:

Men are superior to women on account of the qualities in which God has given them pre-eminence.

Because they think they sense a decline in feminine "faith, charity, and holiness with sobriety," many people today jump to the conclusion that the ideology expressed in these passages is a relic of the past. Not so. It has simply been obscured by an equalitarian veneer, and the ideology has now become nonconscious. That is, we remain unaware of it because alternative beliefs and attitudes about women go unimagined. We are like the fish who is unaware that his environment is wet. After all, what else could it be? Such is the nature of all nonconscious ideologies. Such is the nature of America's ideology about women. For even those Americans who agree that a black skin should not uniquely qualify its owner for janitorial or domestic service continue to act as if the possession of a uterus uniquely qualifies *its* owner for precisely that.

Consider, for example, the 1968 student rebellion at Columbia University. Students from the radical left took over some administration buildings in the name of equalitarian principles which they accused the university of flouting. Here were the most militant spokesmen one could hope to find in the cause of equalitarian ideals. But no sooner had they occupied the buildings than the male militants blandly turned to their sisters-in-arms and assigned them the task of preparing the food, while they—the menfolk—would presumably plan further strategy. The reply these males received was the reply they deserved, and the fact that domestic tasks behind the barricades were desegregated across the sex line that day is an everlasting tribute to the class consciousness of the ladies of the left.

But these conscious coeds are not typical, for the nonconscious assumptions about a woman's "natural" talents (or lack of them) are at least as prevalent among women as they are among men. A psychologist named Philip Goldberg (1968) demonstrated this by asking female college students to rate a number of professional articles from each of six fields. The articles were collated into two equal sets of booklets, and the names of the authors were changed so that the identical article was attributed to a male author (e.g., John T. McKay) in one set of booklets and to a female author (e.g., Joan T. McKay) in the other set. Each student was asked to read the articles in her booklet and to rate them for value, competence, persuasiveness, writing style, and so forth.

As he had anticipated, Goldberg found that the identical article received significantly lower ratings when it was attributed to a female author than when it was attributed to a male author. He had predicted this result for articles from professional fields generally considered the province for men, like law and city planning, but to his surprise, these coeds also downgraded articles from the fields of dietetics and elementary school education when they were attributed to female authors. In other words, these students rated the male authors as better at everything, agreeing with Aristotle that "we should regard the female nature as afflicted with a natural defectiveness." We repeated this experiment informally in our own classrooms and discovered that male students show the same implicit prejudice against female authors that Goldberg's female students showed. Such is the nature of a nonconscious ideology!

It is significant that examples like these can be drawn from the college world, for today's students have challenged the established ways of looking at almost every other issue, and they have been quick to reject those practices of our society which conflict explicitly with their major values. But as the above examples suggest, they will find it far more difficult to shed the more subtle aspects of a sex-role ideology which—as we shall now attempt to demonstrate—conflicts just as surely with their existential values as any of the other societal practices to which they have so effectively raised objection. And as we shall see, there is no better way to appreciate the power of a society's nonconscious ideology than to examine it within the framework of values held by that society's avant-garde.

INDIVIDUALITY AND SELF-FULFILLMENT

The dominant values of today's students concern personal growth on the one hand, and interpersonal relationships on the other. The first of these emphasizes individuality and self-fulfillment; the second stresses openness, honesty, and equality in all human relationships.

The values of individuality and self-fulfillment imply that each human being, male or female, is to be encouraged to "do his own thing." Men and women are no longer to be stereotyped by society's definitions. If sensitivity, emotionality, and warmth are desirable human characteristics, then they are desirable for men as well as for women. (John Wayne is no longer an idol of the young, but their pop-art satire.) If independence, assertiveness, and serious intellectual commitment are desirable human characteristics, then they are desirable for women as well as for men. The major prescription of this college generation is that each individual should be encouraged to discover and fulfill his own unique potential and identity, unfettered by society's presumptions.

But society's presumptions enter the scene much earlier than most people suspect, for parents begin to raise their children in accord with the popular stereotypes from the very first. Boys are encouraged to be aggressive, competitive, and independent, whereas girls are rewarded for being passive and dependent (Barry, Bacon, & Child, 1957; Sears, Maccoby, & Levin, 1957). In one study, six-month-old infant girls were already being touched and spoken to more by their mothers while they were playing than were infant boys. . . .

As children grow older, more explicit sex-role training is introduced. Boys are encouraged to take more of an interest in mathematics and science. Boys, not girls, are given chemistry sets and microscopes for Christmas. Moreover, all children quickly learn that mommy is proud to be a moron when it comes to mathematics and science, whereas daddy knows all about these things. When a young boy returns from school all excited about biology, he is almost certain to be encouraged to think of becoming a physician. A girl with similar enthusiasm is told that she might want to consider nurse's training later so she can have "an interesting job to fall back upon in case —God forbid—she ever needs to support herself." A very different kind of encouragement. And any girl who doggedly persists in her enthusiasm for science is likely to find her parents as horrified by the prospect of a permanent love affair with physics as they would be by the prospect of an interracial marriage.

These socialization practices quickly take their toll. By nursery school age, for example, boys are already asking more questions about how and why things work (Smith, 1933). In first and second grade, when asked to suggest ways of improving various toys, boys do better on the fire truck and girls do better on the nurse's kit, but by the third grade, boys do better regardless of the toy presented (Torrance, 1962). By the ninth grade, 25% of the boys, but only 3% of the girls, are considering careers in science or engineering (Flanagan, unpublished; cited by Kagan, 1964). When they apply for college, boys and girls are about equal on verbal aptitude tests, but boys score significantly higher on mathematical aptitude tests—about 60 points higher on the College Board examinations, for example (Brown, 1965, p. 162). Moreover, girls improve their mathemat-

ical performance if problems are reworded so that they deal with cooking and gardening, even though the abstract reasoning required for their solutions remains the same (Milton, 1958). Clearly, not just ability, but the motivation and confidence to tackle a mathematical problem have been undermined.

But these effects in mathematics and science are only part of the story. A girl's long training in passivity and dependence appears to exact an even higher toll from her overall motivation to achieve, to search for new and independent ways of doing things, and to welcome the challenge of new and unsolved problems. In one study, for example, elementary school girls were more likely to try solving a puzzle by imitating an adult, whereas the boys were more likely to search for a novel solution not provided by the adult (McDavid, 1959). In another puzzle-solving study, young girls asked for help and approval from adults more frequently than the boys; and, when given the opportunity to return to the puzzles a second time, the girls were more likely to rework those they had already solved, whereas the boys were more likely to try puzzles they had been unable to solve previously (Crandall & Rabson, 1960). A girl's sigh of relief is almost audible when she marries and retires from the outside world of novel and unsolved problems.

This, of course, is the most conspicuous outcome of all: the majority of American women become full-time homemakers. And of those who work, 78% end up in dead-end jobs as clerical workers, service workers, factory workers, and sales clerks. Only 15% of all women workers are classified by the Labor Department as professional or technical workers, and even this figure is misleading. For the poorly paid occupation of non-college teacher absorbs nearly half of these women, and an additional 25% are nurses. Fewer than 5% of all professional women—fewer than 1% of all women workers—fill those positions which, to most Americans, connote "professional": physician, lawyer, engineer, scientist, college professor, journalist, and the like. Such are the consequences of a nonconscious ideology.

But why does this process violate the values of

individuality and self-fulfillment? It is *not* because some people may regard the role of homemaker as inferior to other roles. That is not the point. Rather, the point is that our society is managing to consign a large segment of its population to the role of homemaker—either by itself or in conjunction with typing, teaching, nursing, or unskilled labor—just as inexorably as it has in the past consigned the individual with a black skin to the role of janitor or domestic. It is not the quality of the role which is at issue here, but the fact that in spite of their unique identities, the majority of America's women end up in the *same* role.

Even an I.Q. in the genius range does not guarantee that a woman's unique potential will find expression. In a famous study of over 1300 men and women whose I.Q.'s averaged 151 (Terman & Oden, 1959), 86% of the men have achieved prominence in professional and managerial occupations. In contrast, only a minority of the women are even employed. Of those who are, 37% are nurses, librarians, social workers, and non-college teachers. An additional 26% are secretaries, stenographers, bookkeepers, and office workers! Only 11% are in the higher professions of law, medicine, college teaching, engineering, science, economics, and the like. And even at age 44, well after their children have gone to school, 61% of these highly gifted women are full-time homemakers. This homogenization of America's women is the major consequence of our society's sex-role ideology.

Even so, however, several arguments are typically advanced to counter the claim that America's homogenization of its women subverts individuality and self-fulfillment. The three most common arguments invoke, respectively, (1) free will, (2) biology, and (3) complementarity.

1. The free will argument proposes that a 21-year-old woman is perfectly free to choose some other role if she cares to do so; no one is standing in her way. But that is hardly the case. Even the woman who has managed to finesse society's attempt to rob her of her career motivations is likely to find herself blocked by society's trump card: the feeling that one cannot have a career and be a successful woman simultaneously. A

competent and motivated woman is thus caught in a double-bind which few men have ever faced. She must worry not only about failure, but also about success. If she fails in her achievement needs, she must live with the knowledge that she is not living up to her potential. But if she succeeds, she must live with the knowledge that she is not living up to her own—and society's—conception of a feminine woman. Thus, even the woman who is lucky enough to have retained some career motivation is likely to find herself in serious conflict: she has a motive to achieve as well as a motive to avoid success.

This conflict was strikingly revealed in a study which required college women to complete the following story: "After first-term finals, Anne finds herself at the top of her medical-school class" (Horner, 1969). The stories were then examined for unconscious, internal conflict about success and failure. The women in this study all had high intellectual ability and histories of academic success. They were the very women who could have successful careers. And yet, over two-thirds of their stories revealed a clear-cut inability to cope with the concept of a feminine, yet career-oriented woman.

The most common "fear-of-success" stories showed strong fears of social rejection as a result of success. The women in this group showed anxiety about becoming unpopular, unmarriageable, and lonely:

Anne starts proclaiming her surprise and joy. Her fellow classmates are so disgusted with her behavior that they jump on her in a body and beat her. She is maimed for life.

Anne is an acne-faced bookworm. . . . She studies twelve hours a day, and lives at home to save money. "Well, it certainly paid off. All the Friday and Saturday nights without dates, fun—I'll be the best woman doctor alive." And yet a twinge of sadness comes through—she wonders what she really has. . . .

Although Anne is happy with her success, she fears what will happen to her social life. The male med students don't seem to think very highly of a female who has beaten them in their field. . . . She will be a proud and successful but alas a very lonely doctor.

Anne is pretty darn proud of herself, but everyone hates and envies her.

Anne doesn't want to be number one in her class. . . . She feels she shouldn't rank so high because of social reasons. She drops to ninth and then marries the boy who graduates number one.

In the second "fear-of-success" category were stories in which the women seemed concerned about definitions of womanhood. These stories expressed guilt and despair over success and doubts about their femininity and normality:

Unfortunately Anne no longer feels so certain that she really wants to be a doctor. She is worried about herself and wonders if perhaps she is not normal. . . . Anne decides not to continue with her medical work but to take courses that have a deeper personal meaning for her.

Anne feels guilty. . . . She will finally have a nervous breakdown and quit medical school and marry a successful young doctor.

A third group of stories could not even face up to the conflict between having a career and being a woman. These stories simply denied the possibility that any woman could be so successful:

Anne is a code name for a nonexistent person created by a group of med students. They take turns writing for Anne.

Anne is really happy she's on top, though Tom is higher than she—though that's as it should be. Anne doesn't mind Tom winning.

Anne is talking to her counselor. Counselor says she will make a fine nurse.

It was luck that Anne came out on top because she didn't want to go to medical school anyway.

By way of contrast, here is a typical story written not about Anne, but about John:

John has worked very hard and his long hours of study have paid off. . . . He is thinking about his girl, Cheri, whom he will marry at the end of med school. He realizes he can give her all the things she desires after he becomes established. He will go on in med school and be successful in the long run.

Nevertheless, there were a few women in the study who welcomed the prospect of success.

Anne is quite a lady—not only is she top academically, but she is liked and admired by her fellow students—quite a trick in a man-dominated field. She is brilliant—but she is also a woman. She will continue to be at or near the top. And . . . always a lady.

Hopefully the day is approaching when as many "Anne" stories as "John" stories will have happy endings.

It should be clear that the "free-will" argument conveniently overlooks the fact that the society which has spent twenty long years carefully marking the woman's ballot for her has nothing to lose in that twenty-first year by pretending to let her cast it for the alternative of her choice. Society has controlled not her alternatives, but her motivation to choose any but one of those alternatives. The so-called "freedom-to-choose" is illusory, and it cannot be invoked to justify the society which controls the motivation to choose.

2. The biological argument suggests that there may really be inborn differences between men and women in, say, independence or mathematical ability. Or that there may be biological factors beyond the fact that women can become pregnant and nurse children which uniquely dictate that they, but not men, should stay home all day and shun serious outside commitment. Maybe female hormones really are responsible somehow. One difficulty with this argument, of course, is that female hormones would have to be different in the Soviet Union, where one-third of the engineers and 75% of the physicians are women. In America, women constitute less than 1% of the engineers and only 7% of the physicians (Dodge, 1966). Female physiology *is* different, and it may account for some of the psychological differences between the sexes, but America's sex-role ideology still seems primarily responsible for the fact that so few women emerge from childhood with the motivation to seek out any role beyond the one that our society dictates.

But even if there really were biological differences between the sexes along these lines, the biological argument would still be irrelevant. The reason can best be illustrated with an analogy. Suppose that every black American boy were to be socialized to become a jazz musician on the assumption that he has a "natural" talent in that direction, or suppose that his parents should subtly discourage him from other pursuits because it is considered "inappropriate" for black men to become physicians or physicists. Most liberal Americans, we submit, would disapprove. But suppose that it *could* be demonstrated that black Americans, *on the average,* did possess an inborn better sense of rhythm than white Americans.

Would *that* justify ignoring the unique character-istics of a *particular* black youngster from the beginning and specifically socializing him to become a musician? We don't think so. Similarly, as long as a woman's socialization does not nur-ture her uniqueness, but treats her only as a mem-ber of a group on the basis of some assumed *average* characteristic, she will not be prepared to realize her own potential in the way that the val-ues of individuality and self-fulfillment imply she should.

The irony of the biological argument is that it does not take biological differences seriously enough. That is, it fails to recognize the range of biological differences between individuals within the same sex. Thus, recent research has revealed that biological factors help determine many per-sonality traits. Dominance and submissiveness, for example, have been found to have large inher-itable components; in other words, biological fac-tors *do* have the potential for partially determining how dominant or submissive an indi-vidual, male or female, will turn out to be. But the effects of this biological potential could be de-tected only in males (Gottesman, 1963). This im-plies that only the males in our culture are raised with sufficient flexibility, with sufficient latitude given to their biological differences, for their "natural" or biologically determined potential to shine through. Females, on the other hand, are subjected to a socialization which so ignores their unique attributes that even the effects of biology seems to be swamped. In sum, the biological ar-gument for continuing America's homogeniza-tion of its women gets hoist with its own petard.

3. Many people recognize that most women do end up as full-time homemakers because of their socialization and that these women do exemplify the failure of our society to raise girls as unique individuals. But, they point out, the role of the homemaker is not inferior to the role of the pro-fessional man: it is complementary but equal.

This argument is usually bolstered by pointing to the joys and importance of taking care of small children. Indeed, mothers *and* fathers find child rearing rewarding, and it is certainly important. But this argument becomes insufficient when one considers that the average American woman now lives to age 74 and has her *last* child at about age

26; thus, by the time the woman is 33 or so, her children all have more important things to do with their day-time hours than to spend them entertaining an adult woman who has nothing to do during the second half of her life span. As for the other "joys" of homemaking, many writers (e.g., Friedan, 1963) have persuasively argued that the role of the homemaker has been glam-orized far beyond its intrinsic worth. This charge becomes plausible when one considers that the average American homemaker spends the equiv-alent of a man's working day, 7.1 hours, in pre-paring meals, cleaning house, laundering, mending, shopping, and doing other household tasks. In other words, 43% of her waking time is spent in activity that would command an hourly wage on the open market well below the federally set minimum for menial industrial work.

The point is not how little she would earn if she did these things in someone else's home, but that this use of time is virtually the same for home-makers with college degrees and for those with less than a grade school education, for women married to professional men and for women mar-ried to blue-collar workers. Talent, education, ability, interests, motivations: all are irrelevant. In our society, being female uniquely qualifies an individual for domestic work.

It is true, of course, that the American home-maker has, on the average, 5.1 hours of leisure time per day, and it is here, we are told, that each woman can express her unique identity. Thus, politically interested women can join the League of Women Voters; women with humane interests can become part-time Gray Ladies; women who love music can raise money for the symphony. Protestant women can play Canasta; Jewish women play Mah-Jongg; brighter women of all denominations and faculty wives play bridge; and so forth.

But politically interested *men* serve in legisla-tures; *men* with humane interests become physi-cians or clinical psychologists; *men* who love music play in the symphony; and so forth. In other words, why should a woman's unique iden-tity determine only the periphery of her life rather than its central core?

Again, the important point is not that the role of homemaker is necessarily inferior, but that the woman's unique identity has been rendered irrelevant. Consider the following "predictability test." When a boy is born, it is difficult to predict what he will be doing 25 years later. We cannot say whether he will be an artist, a doctor, or a college professor because he will be permitted to develop and to fulfill his own unique potential, particularly if he is white and middle-class. But if the newborn child is a girl, we can usually predict with confidence how she will be spending her time 25 years later. Her individuality doesn't have to be considered; it is irrelevant.

The socialization of the American male has closed off certain options for him too. Men are discouraged from developing certain desirable traits such as tenderness and sensitivity just as surely as women are discouraged from being assertive and, alas, "too bright." Young boys are encouraged to be incompetent at cooking and child care just as surely as young girls are urged to be incompetent at mathematics and science.

Indeed, one of the errors of the early feminist movement in this country was that it assumed that men had all the goodies and that women could attain self-fulfillment merely by being like men. But that is hardly the utopia implied by the values of individuality and self-fulfillment. Rather, these values would require society to raise its children so flexibly and with sufficient respect for the integrity of individual uniqueness that some men might emerge with the motivation, the ability, and the opportunity to stay home and raise children without bearing the stigma of being peculiar. If homemaking is as glamorous as the women's magazines and television commercials portray it, then men, too, should have that option. Even if homemaking isn't all that glamorous, it would probably still be more fulfilling for some men than the jobs in which they now find themselves.

And if biological differences really do exist between men and women in "nurturance," in their inborn motivations to care for children, then this will show up automatically in the final distribution of men and women across the various roles: relatively fewer men will choose to stay at home. The values of individuality and self-fulfillment do not imply that there must be equality of outcome, an equal number of men and women in each role,

but that there should be the widest possible variation in outcome consistent with the range of individual differences among people, regardless of sex. At the very least, these values imply that society should raise its males so that they could freely engage in activities that might pay less than those being pursued by their wives without feeling that they were "living off their wives." One rarely hears it said of a woman that she is "living off her husband."

Thus, it is true that a man's options are limited by our society's sex-role ideology, but as the "predictability test" reveals, it is still the woman in our society whose identity is rendered irrelevant by America's socialization practices. In 1954, the United States Supreme Court declared that a fraud and hoax lay behind the slogan "separate but equal." It is unlikely that any court will ever do the same for the more subtle motto that successfully keeps the woman in her place: "complementary but equal."

INTERPERSONAL EQUALITY

Wives, submit yourselves unto your own husbands, as unto the Lord. For the husband is the head of the wife, even as Christ is the head of the church; and he is the savior of the body. Therefore, as the church is subject unto Christ, so let the wives be to their own husbands in everything (Eph. 5).

As this passage reveals, the ideological rationalization that men and women hold complementary but equal positions is a recent invention of our modern "liberal" society, part of the equalitarian veneer which helps to keep today's version of the ideology nonconscious. Certainly those Americans who value open, honest, and equalitarian relationships generally are quick to reject this traditional view of the male-female relationship; and, an increasing number of young people even plan to enter "utopian" marriages very much like the following hypothetical example:

Both my wife and I earned Ph.D. degrees in our respective disciplines. I turned down a superior academic post in Oregon and accepted a slightly less desirable position in New York where my wife could obtain a part-time teaching job and do research at one of the several other colleges in the area. Although I would have preferred to live in a suburb, we purchased a home near my wife's college so that she could have an office at home where she would be when the children returned from school. Because my wife earns a good salary, she can easily afford to pay a maid to do her major household chores. My wife and I share all other tasks around the house equally. For example, she cooks the meals, but I do the laundry for her and help her with many of her other household tasks.

Without questioning the basic happiness of such a marriage or its appropriateness for many couples, we can legitimately ask if such a marriage is, in fact, an instance of interpersonal equality. Have all the hidden assumptions about the woman's "natural" role really been eliminated? Has the traditional ideology really been exorcised? There is a very simple test. If the marriage is truly equalitarian, then its description should retain the same flavor and tone even if the roles of the husband and wife were to be reversed:

Both my husband and I earned Ph.D. degrees in our respective disciplines. I turned down a superior academic post in Oregon and accepted a slightly less desirable position in New York where my husband could obtain a part-time teaching job and do research at one of the several other colleges in the area. Although I would have preferred to live in a suburb, we purchased a home near my husband's college so that he could have an office at home where he would be when the children returned from school. Because my husband earns a good salary, he can easily afford to pay a maid to do his major household chores. My husband and I share all other tasks around the house equally. For example, he cooks the meals, but I do the laundry for him and help him with many of his other household tasks.

It seems unlikely that many men or women in our society would mistake the marriage *just* described as either equalitarian or desirable, and thus it becomes apparent that the ideology about the woman's "natural" role nonconsciously permeates the entire fabric of such "utopian" marriages. It is true that the wife gains some measure of equality when her career can influence the final place of residence, but why is it the unquestioned assumption that the husband's career solely determines the initial set of alternatives that are to

be considered? Why is it the wife who automatically seeks the part-time position? Why is it *her* maid instead of *their* maid? Why *her* laundry? Why *her* household tasks? And so forth throughout the entire relationship.

The important point here is not that such marriages are bad or that their basic assumptions of inequality produce unhappy, frustrated women. Quite the contrary. It is the very happiness of the wives in such marriages that reveals society's smashing success in socializing its women. It is a measure of the distance our society must yet traverse toward the goals of self-fulfillment and interpersonal equality that such marriages are widely characterized as utopian and fully equalitarian. It is a mark of how well the woman has been kept in her place that the husband in such a marriage is often idolized by women, including his wife, for "permitting" her to squeeze a career into the interstices of their marriage as long as his own career is not unduly inconvenienced. Thus is the white man blessed for exercising his power benignly while his "natural" right to that power forever remains unquestioned.

Such is the subtlety of a nonconscious ideology!

A truly equalitarian marriage would permit both partners to pursue careers or outside commitments which carry equal weight when all important decisions are to be made. It is here, of course, that the "problem" of children arises. People often assume that the woman who seeks a role beyond home and family would not care to have children. They assume that if she wants a career or serious outside commitment, then children must be unimportant to her. But of course no one makes this assumption about her husband. No one assumes that a father's interest in his career necessarily precludes a deep and abiding affection for his children or a vital interest in their development. Once again America applies a double standard of judgment. Suppose that a father of small children suddenly lost his wife. No matter how much he loved his children, no one would expect him to sacrifice his career in order to stay home with them on a full-time basis—*even if he had an independent source of income.* No one would charge him with selfishness or lack of parental feeling if he sought professional care for his children during the day. An equalitarian marriage simply abolishes this double standard and extends the same freedom to the mother, while also providing the framework for the father to enter more fully into the pleasures and responsibilities of child rearing. In fact, it is the equalitarian marriage which has the most potential for giving children the love and concern of two parents rather than one.

But few women are prepared to make use of this freedom. Even those women who have managed to finesse society's attempt to rob them of their career motivations are likely to find themselves blocked by society's trump card: the feeling that the raising of the children is their unique responsibility and—in time of crisis—ultimately theirs alone. Such is the emotional power of a nonconscious ideology.

In addition to providing this potential for equalized child care, a truly equalitarian marriage embraces a more general division of labor which satisfies what might be called "the roommate test." That is, the labor is divided just as it is when two men or two women room together in college or set up a bachelor apartment together. Errands and domestic chores are assigned by preference, agreement, flipping a coin, giving to hired help, or—as is sometimes the case—left undone.

It is significant that today's young people, many of whom live this way prior to marriage, find this kind of arrangement within marriage so foreign to their thinking. Consider an analogy. Suppose that a white male college student decided to room or set up a bachelor apartment with a black male friend. Surely the typical white student would not blithely assume that his black roommate was to handle all the domestic chores. Nor would his conscience allow him to do so even in the unlikely event that his roommate would say: "No, that's okay. I like doing housework. I'd be happy to do it." We suspect that the typical white student would still not be comfortable if he took advantage of this offer, if he took advantage of the fact that his roommate had been socialized

to be "happy" with such an arrangement. But change this hypothetical black roommate to a female marriage partner, and somehow the student's conscience goes to sleep. At most it is quickly tranquilized by the thought that "she is happiest when she is ironing for her loved one." Such is the power of a nonconscious ideology.

Of course, it may well be that she *is* happiest when she is ironing for her loved one.

Such, indeed, is the power of a nonconscious ideology!

REFERENCES

Barry, H., III, Bacon, M. K., & Child, I. L. A cross-cultural survey of some sex differences in socialization. *Journal of Abnormal and Social Psychology,* 1957, **55**, 327–332.

Brown, R. *Social psychology.* New York: Free Press, 1965.

Crandall, V. J., & Rabson, A. Children's repetition choices in an intellectual achievement situation following success and failure. *Journal of Genetic Psychology,* 1960, **97**, 161–168.

Dodge, N. D. *Women in the Soviet economy.* Baltimore: Johns Hopkins Press, 1966.

Flanagan, J. C. Project talent. Unpublished manuscript.

Friedan, B. *The feminine mystique.* New York: Norton, 1963.

Goldberg, P. Are women prejudiced against women? *Trans-Action,* 1968, **5**, 28–30.

Goldberg, S., & Lewis, M. Play behavior in the year-old infant: Early sex differences. *Child Development,* 1969, **40**, 21–31.

Gottesman, I. I. Heritability of personality: A demonstration. *Psychological Monographs,* 1963, **77** (Whole No. 572).

Horner, M. Woman's will to fail. *Psychology Today,* 1969, **3** (6), 36–38f.

Kagan, J. Acquisition and significance of sex typing and sex role identity. In M. L. Hoffman and L. W. Hoffman (Eds.), *Review of child development research,* Vol. 1. New York: Russell Sage Foundation, 1964. Pp. 137–167.

McDavid, J. W. Imitative behavior in preschool children. *Psychological Monographs,* 1959, **73** (Whole No. 486).

Milton, G. A. Five studies of the relation between sex role identification and achievement in problem solving. Technical Report No. 3, Department of Industrial Administration, Department of Psychology, Yale University, December 1958.

Sears, R. R., Maccoby, E. E., & Levin, H. *Patterns of*

child rearing. Evanston, Ill.: Row-Peterson, 1957.

Smith, M. E. The influence of age, sex, and situation on the frequency of form and functions of questions asked by preschool children. *Child Development,* 1933, **3,** 201–213.

Torrance, E. P. *Guiding creative talent.* Englewood Cliffs, N.J.: Prentice-Hall, 1962.

Terman, L. M., & Oden, M. H. *Genetic studies of genius, V. The gifted group at mid-life: Thirty-five years' follow-up of the superior child.* Stanford, Calif.: Stanford University Press, 1959.

SECTION SUMMARY

In a useful book of readings on sex differences in personality, Dirk Schaeffer (1971) has evaluated Freud's theory of sex differences. Schaeffer extracts five hypotheses from Freud's article reprinted in this section:

1. Males and females both perceive females as inferior.

2. Females have a weaker superego than males.

3. Females identify with the mother less than males identify with the father.

4. Females are more jealous than males.

5. Masturbation, particularly during puberty, is much less common in girls than in boys.

The second article in this section offers some clarification of the first hypothesis. Previous studies (Goldberg, 1968; MacBrayer, 1960) had indeed supported Freud's hypothesis that females view themselves as inferior. But the more recent work of Pheterson, Kiesler, and Goldberg indicates that there are limits to this reaction; for example, if an artistic product has been recognized as exemplary, such a designation outweighs the "fact" that it has been done by a woman. Women do not devalue the *successful* products of another woman.

Freud's hypothesis that men have stronger superegos than women proposed that women do not possess as *internalized* a superego; they do not incorporate the superego in their personality to the degree that men do (Hall, 1964). The less internalized superego is more dependent on the outside world (parents, peers, authority figures, society in general) for sources of "correct" behav-

ior. The more internalized superego is more independent of such sources—more self-reliant. Using the content of dreams as material by which to judge strength of superego, Hall (1964) finds confirmation for Freud's hypothesis. However, there are several assumptions of a debatable nature in Hall's use of dream content. For example, it is assumed that dreams in which the dreamer is a *victim of aggression* reflect an externalized superego, whereas dreams in which the dreamer is a *victim of misfortune* show an internalized superego, the latter supposedly reflecting a greater acceptance of guilt and self-blame. The reasoning is certainly tenuous.

Other research (Sears, Maccoby, & Levin, 1957; Rempel & Signori, 1964) finds the opposite, when the variable under study is the child's conscience. Sears et al. report that 29% of the girls observed had strong consciences, compared to 20% of the boys. Freud's hypothesis of retarded moral development in females lacks consistent support at this time.

Do females identify with their mother less than males identify with their father, as Freud's third hypothesis proposes? Blum (1949), using data from a projective test, concludes that Freud's hypothesis was correct, but Blum's study has been severely criticized (Seward, 1950). More recent research (Lynn, 1966) questions the accuracy of this hypothesis.

Freud also hypothesized that females are more jealous than males. The operational definition of jealousy was not specified, and the topic has apparently not been investigated by psychologists.

Freud's fifth hypothesis—dealing with sex differences in extent of masturbation—receives confirmation in the famous Kinsey studies of sexual behavior (Kinsey, Pomeroy, & Martin, 1948; Kinsey, Pomeroy, Martin, & Gebhard, 1953). Less than two-thirds (62%) of Kinsey's adult female sample reported that they had ever masturbated, whereas 93% of adult males reported having done so. Even more pronounced are sex differences in first masturbatory experience; 61% of the boys but only 8% of the girls reported having had their first such experience during puberty. But Kinsey's data are self-reports, are subject to faking, and come from all-volunteer samples, the weaknesses of which we discussed in Section 1.

However, more recent self-report studies of female college students confirm the differential rates reported by Kinsey (Davis, 1971; Kaats & Davis, 1970). Only 34% of the female subjects in a University of Colorado study (most of whom were age 20 or younger) reported that they had ever masturbated.*

So the majority of Freud's hypotheses regarding female sexuality receive little clear-cut confirmation. And even the generality of the initial hypothesis—that both males and females perceive females as inferior—has its limits, as the second article shows.

Yet a belief in some "different status" to female sexuality dies hard, as do many other assumptions about female dependence and weakness. For example, Erik Erikson, a highly regarded contemporary neo-Freudian, has beneficially extended Freud's thinking in many areas. (For example, he is not content to see the stages of psychological development ending at puberty but instead theorizes that they continue through adolescence, maturity, and even old age.) But although Erikson is quite critical of Freud's theory of sexual identification in women, he maintains a view of women as relatively passive and masochistic. And Erikson, like Freud, bases his conclusion primarily on anatomical and physiological differences; he states that "there are aspects of the body ... in which women are basically so different from men that the feminine ego has a very specific task to perform in integrating body, role, and individuality" (quoted in Evans, 1969, p. 47).

It is Erikson's view rather than Freud's that is most often invoked today by those who emphasize innate differences between the sexes. But Erikson himself, despite his condescending neosexist orientation, advocates some of the same changes that the Women's Liberationists do; he argues that women must be given positions of

*Judith Bardwick (1970) attributes the low rates of masturbation to the physiology of the female reproductive system. "The (pre-adolescent) girl has an insensitive vagina, no breasts, and a small and relatively inaccessible clitoris" (1970, p. 6).

power in our society. But, paradoxically, he does so precisely because of what he calls their "feminine qualities" and the possible new directions he believes they have to offer (Erikson, 1965). So Erikson is right for the wrong reasons, and the nonconscious ideology of sexism remains alive and intransigent in contemporary psychoanalytic thinking.

Traditional views of women's nature and role may be found elsewhere in contemporary literature. *The Prisoner of Sex* (1971), by Norman Mailer, contains a highly articulate exploration of this novelist's attitudes toward sex. Mailer is aware that he has been the recipient of violent attacks by many Women's Liberationists because of the ways he has portrayed women and sexual relationships in his writings; hence he struggles in this book to understand his feelings toward women—their nature, their role in society, and their relationship to him.

And yet the outcome is not a step toward liberation for anyone. Mailer ends his analysis with the question he posed at the beginning: when a man and a woman live together, who finally does the dishes? Should the household banalities be equally divided? He reprints a "Marriage Agreement" (Schulman, 1970) offered by the Women's Liberation Movement, which included the following preamble:

We reject the notion that the work which brings in more money is more valuable. The ability to earn more money is already a privilege which must not be compounded by enabling the larger earner to buy out his/her duties and put the burden on the one who earns less, or on someone hired from outside. . . .

As parents we believe we must share all responsibilities for taking care of our children and home—not only the work, but the responsibility [Schulman, 1970, p. 6].

Then follow a set of detailed procedures that operationalize the agreement. Mailer finds the following ones the most bothersome:

10. Cleaning: Husband does all the house-cleaning, in exchange for wife's extra childcare (3:00 to 6:30 daily) and sick care.
11. Laundry: Wife does most home laundry. Husband does all dry cleaning delivery and pick up. Wife strips beds, husband remakes them [Schulman, 1970, p. 6].

Mailer refuses to buy such an agreement. No, he would not be married to such a woman. He would not be happy about helping her "if his work should suffer, no, not unless her work was as valuable as his own" (Mailer, 1971, p. 165). But it is sadly clear that for Mailer *women's work could never be as valuable as his own.* He is a man, and man's work is "meaningful." After three months of self-analysis and 165 pages of print, the nonconscious ideology remains—women's work is inferior. Truly this does reflect male chauvinism—it affirms that "my" work, just because it is more creative or more financially remunerative, is more "valuable" than hers.

One reason for the pervasiveness of the nonconscious ideology is that sex-role stereotyping begins at such an early age. Boys learn early that they are more important than girls. As Bem and Bem indicate, parents differentially respond to male and female infants, and different kinds of clothing and toys are given to boys and girls. Girls are taught early to serve in menial roles. Parents assume that girls are more dependent and tied to the home.

Despite these parental behaviors, the evidence that male infants are less dependent than female infants is not that clear. Maccoby and Jacklin (1971), in reviewing the research, conclude that *ratings* (by observers) attribute more dependency to females, but actual recording of behaviors does not show any heightened level of dependent behavior in females. It is the *expectation* of observers that is different for each sex. Maccoby and Jacklin conclude:

It is our opinion that the bulk of evidence indicates that dependency and attachment behavior are characteristic of all human children, and that there is little or no differentiation by sex in this behavior from infancy through the preschool period. There may be some situations that elicit more of the behavior from one sex than the other, but so far we do not have a clear picture as to what the important situational factors are. Meanwhile, we cannot accept the generalization that girls are more passive-dependent than boys in early childhood [Maccoby & Jacklin, 1971, p. 7].

At present we cannot say whether any significant sex differences in dependency exist during infancy. If female infants *are* no more dependent than male infants, despite efforts of parents to make them so, an implication is that as adults they need not manifest a heightened degree of such behavior. The heightened dependency in adult females is a product of their learning of certain expectations and roles.

We are not advocating a position that there are no irrevocable sex differences in personality or temperament. The structural and physiological differences between the sexes are not to be denied, and they may influence one's response. For example, Maccoby and Jacklin conclude that the male sex is more aggressive than the female sex and speculate that this difference has biochemical, if not instinctual, causes.

The menstrual cycle in the female has a potential effect on changes in her temperament. Judith Bardwick (1970), after reviewing the relevant research, suggests that "there are regular and predictable changes in the personality of sexually mature women that correlate with changes in the menstrual cycle. These personality changes are extreme, they occur in spite of individual personality differences, and they are the result of the endocrine or other physical changes that occur during the cycle" (1970, p. 21).

In line with this evaluation, self-reports of irritability, depression, and anxiety quite consistently occur in women just before the onset of menstruation. Are these physiological in determination, or the result of learning a stereotype about the expected behavior of females? A large proportion of the suicides and criminal acts of violence committed by women occur during the premenstrual and menstrual phases of the cycle (Dalton, 1964), which indicates that the physiological changes may be at least part of the cause.

But we need to recognize that men, too, may undergo changes in mood that are influenced by physiological changes. Men do not experience menstrual changes, but the fluctuations in their energy level, mood, and well-being from day to day and month to month may still be heavily influenced by physiological shifts (Luce, 1971). More body-based mood changes exist than most of us realize. To base explanations of female temperament changes on menstrual cycles, while avoiding any understanding of the causes of mood changes in men, reflects scientific male chauvinism!

Also, we need to recognize that the mood shift resulting from menstrual changes is not so great in some women as in others. We must reject a conclusion that the menstrual cycle strongly determines temperamental changes in *all* females. As Bem and Bem remind us, the most important difference is not the difference between the sexes but the difference *within* each sex.

Even if males as a group are more aggressive, there are large variations in degree of aggressiveness within that group. Although males as a group are physically stronger than females, there are some women who are physically stronger than some men. And even though it is the female sex that is capable of childbearing, not all females are able to do so. Our goal is a society in which these *individual* variations in personality and behavior are recognized and allowed to develop as they see fit.

For that to occur, we must shift our focus away from "the nature of women" to an understanding of the socialization of sex roles in our society. We must consider not only how women learn their "proper place," but also how men learn theirs. We need to consider the changing conceptions of "feminine" and "masculine." What do these terms mean now? What should they mean in the future? What reforms are necessary to liberalize women—and men?

REFERENCES

Bardwick, J. M. Psychological conflict and the reproductive system. In J. M. Bardwick, E. Douvan, M. S. Horner, and D. Gutmann, *Feminine personality and conflict.* Monterey, Calif.: Brooks/Cole, 1970.

Blum, G. S. A study of psychoanalytic theory of psychosexual development. *Genetic Psychology Monographs,* 1949, **33**, 3–99.

Dalton, K. *The premenstrual syndrome.* Springfield, Ill.: Charles C Thomas, 1964.

Davis, K. E. Sex on campus: Is there a revolution? *Medical Aspects of Human Sexuality,* 1971, **5**, 128–142.

Erikson, E. Reflections of womanhood. In R. J. Lifton (Ed.), *The woman in America.* Boston: Houghton Mifflin, 1965. Pp. 1–26.

Evans, R. I. *Dialogue with Erik Erikson.* New York: Dutton, 1969.

Goldberg, P. Are women prejudiced against women? *Trans-action,* 1968, **5**(4), 28–30.

Hall, C. A modest confirmation of Freud's theory of a distinction between the superego of men and women. *Journal of Abnormal and Social Psychology,* 1964, **69**, 440–442.

Kaats, G. R., & Davis, K. E. The dynamics of sexual behavior of college students. *Journal of Marriage and the Family,* 1970, **32**, 390–399.

Kinsey, A. C., Pomeroy, W. B., & Martin, C. E. *Sexual behavior in the human male.* Philadelphia: Saunders, 1948.

Kinsey, A. C., Pomeroy, W. B., Martin, C. E., & Gebhard, P. H. *Sexual behavior in the human female.* Philadelphia: Saunders, 1953.

Luce, G. G. *Body time.* New York: Pantheon, 1971.

Lynn, D. B. The process of learning parental and sex-role identification. *Journal of Marriage and the Family,* 1966, **28**, 466–470.

Maccoby, E. E., & Jacklin, C. N. Sex differences and their implications for sex roles. Paper presented at the meeting of the American Psychological Association, Washington, D. C., September 1971.

MacBrayer, C. T. Differences in the perception of the opposite sex by males and females. *Journal of Social Psychology,* 1960, **52**, 309–314.

Mailer, N. *The prisoner of sex.* New York: New American Library, 1971.

Rempel, H., & Signori, E. I. Sex differences in self-rating of conscience as a determinant of behavior. *Psychological Reports,* 1964, **15**, 277–278.

Schaeffer, D. L. (Ed.) *Sex differences in personality: Readings.* Monterey, Calif.: Brooks/Cole, 1971.

Schulman, A. Marriage agreement. *Off Our Backs,* Nov. 8, 1970, p. 6.

Sears, R. R., Maccoby, E., & Levin, H. *Patterns in child rearing.* Evanston, Ill.: Row-Peterson, 1957.

Seward, J. P. Psychoanalysis, deductive methods, and the Blacky test. *Journal of Abnormal and Social Psychology,* 1950, **45**, 529–535.

SUGGESTED READINGS FOR FURTHER STUDY

Bardwick, J. M. *The psychology of women.* New York: Harper & Row, 1971.

Bardwick, J. M., Douvan, E., Horner, M. S., & Gutmann, D. *Feminine personality and conflict.* Monterey, Calif.: Brooks/Cole, 1970.

Bird, C. *Born female: The high cost of keeping women down.* New York: David McKay, 1968.

Friedan, B. *The feminine mystique.* New York: Norton, 1963.

Garskof, M. H. (Ed.) *Roles women play: Readings toward women's liberation.* Monterey, Calif.: Brooks/Cole, 1971.

Howe, F. Sexual stereotypes start early. *Saturday Review,* October 16, 1971, pp. 76–82 *ff.*

Maccoby, E. E. The meaning of being female. (A review of Bardwick's *Psychology of women.*) *Contemporary Psychology,* 1972, **17,** 369–372.

Mednick, M., & Tangri, S. (Eds.) New perspectives on women. Special issue of *Journal of Social Issues,* 1972, **28.**

Morgan, R. (Ed.) *Sisterhood is powerful: An anthology of writings from the Women's Liberation Movement.* New York: Random House, 1970.

Schaeffer, D. L. (Ed.) *Sex differences in personality: Readings.* Monterey, Calif.: Brooks/Cole, 1971.

Scheinfeld, A. *Women and men.* New York: Harcourt, Brace, 1944.

Weisstein, N. Woman as nigger. *Psychology Today,* 1969, **3,** 20–28 *f.*

SECTION 11

Theories of Attitude Change: Focus on Cognitive Consistency

Why do people change their attitudes? Are there principles by which we can predict and explain attitude change? More specifically, what happens when a person is required to take a public position that is contrary to his private opinion? Does this situation force his private opinion to change in order to be consistent? A concern with attitude change has great implications for everyday life. Everyone, from the door-to-door encyclopedia salesman to the Chinese Communist "brainwasher," is concerned with the processes that form and change attitudes. McGuire (1966a) has noted that the concept of "attitude" receives more space in current social psychology textbooks than does any other topic. Social psychologists have been concerned with the development and organization of attitudes, with the measurement of attitudes and the sampling of opinions, and with the reasons why attitudes do or do not change.

Perhaps the most effective way of approaching the question of why attitudes change is to begin by considering a related point: why do people hold their present attitudes? That is, what *reason* do you have for holding *any* attitude? The key factor here may be the *function* that the attitude serves for you. Daniel Katz (1960) and Smith, Bruner, and White (1956) have attempted to identify the major types of functions that an attitude can serve for its holder. They have described four general functions, which we will briefly discuss.

One function that an attitude can serve is to give a person a frame of reference or standard for evaluating attitude-relevant objects, or a way of structuring the world as he knows it. This function of an attitude can be labeled the *knowledge* function. A rational, information-based appeal to change one's attitude might be effective if the attitude were serving this function.

Attitudes can also allow one to identify with, or gain the approval of, important reference groups. In addition, the expression of appropriate attitudes may be directly rewarded by important persons in one's environment—parents, teachers, friends, and so forth. Attitudes that allow a person to achieve such rewards can be seen as serv-

307

ing the *social adjustment* function. In such a case, an appeal to one's reference-group consciousness or a change in the pattern of rewards and punishments might be an effective attitude-change technique.

A third function is the *value-expressive* function, wherein attitudes can be used to give expression to an individual's central values and to his self-concept. If the individual can be convinced that a new or different attitude would reflect his or her central values more accurately than the existing attitude, then attitude change may take place.

The fourth general function is the *ego-defensive* function. In this case the attitude is a reflection (or externalization) of the holder's unresolved inner personal problems. As defense mechanisms, such attitudes may allow the individual to protect himself from acknowledging uncomplimentary basic truths about himself. Prejudicial attitudes toward minority-group members may serve such a function; the hostility may have little or no relationship to the actual characteristics of the minority-group members but may instead stem from the holder's unresolved personality problems, such as unexpressed aggression, fear of losing status, and so forth.

Recognition of these functions can provide an important frame of reference for evaluating procedures and techniques concerned with attitude change. In brief, they suggest two major types of *reasons* why an attitude may change. The first general reason is to become able to *function better* in one's environment. By means of a persuasive communication, someone may be able to convince you that the attitude he or she advocates (attitude B) more accurately reflects the facts relevant to the attitude object than does your present attitude (attitude A). Or, that person may demonstrate how attitude B can allow you more easily to make sense out of the world (knowledge function). Focusing on the social adjustment function, he might attempt to convince you that attitude B is likely to lead to more interpersonal rewards and will make it less likely that you will violate social norms. In a related vein, he might simply reward you over a long period of time

(with money, praise, and so on) for expressing attitude B. Finally, if your personality structure undergoes major changes over time—say in the direction of a strengthened self-concept—then an attitude that was serving an ego-defensive function may no longer be "needed" for defense of the self-concept. The attitude may now be "excess baggage" and thus susceptible to change.

The second type of general reason for changing one's attitude can be to obtain some kind of *internal satisfaction*. For example, if someone can show you that attitude B is more representative than attitude A of the values that are important to you, it should be more "satisfying" to you, all other things being equal, to hold attitude B than attitude A (value-expressive function). If he can show you that attitude A is inconsistent with your other related attitudes, a parallel process can be expected to occur. If he can convince you that attitude B is more ethically or morally "right," the internal satisfaction associated with holding the "right" attitude might form a strong basis for attitude change. Finally, if he can force you to take an action that goes counter to your attitude (that is, an action supporting attitude B), the inconsistency that you now perceive between your attitude and your action may motivate you to change your attitude to make it less discrepant with your behavior.

Taking these reasons for changing an attitude into account, four general *ways* through which attitude change may take place can be identified: (1) through the receipt of *new information,* from persuasive communications or from actual contact with the attitude object; (2) through *behavioral coercion,* via direct rewards and punishments or via induced counterattitudinal behavior; (3) through *a change in norms* relevant to the attitude; and (4) through *change in the attitude holder himself* (for example, changes in self-concept or in underlying values). Any of these processes may induce attitude change (see also McGuire, 1966b, for a somewhat similar analysis).

The articles in this section focus on one theory of attitude change—cognitive dissonance theory. This theory, originally formulated by Leon Festinger (1957), has stimulated an avalanche of research, criticisms, and countercriticisms in social psychology. The theory itself is basically quite straightforward. Festinger proposed that any two "cognitive elements" (any knowledge, opinion, or belief about the environment, about oneself, or about one's behavior) that a person holds can exist in one of three general forms: irrelevant (no relationship to each other), consonant (consistent with each other), or dissonant (wherein the opposite of one element would follow from the other). If two cognitive elements have a dissonant relationship to each other, the existence of dissonance creates psychological tension or discomfort that will *motivate* the person to reduce dissonance and achieve consonance. The more important the two elements are, the greater the magnitude of the dissonance created.

In terms of the reasons for changing one's attitude, cognitive dissonance theory deals directly with the internal satisfaction factor; the existence of dissonance describes a state of internal *dis*satisfaction. To reduce or eliminate this dissatisfaction, the person may change one of his attitudes, he may change his behavior, or he may expose himself to new information (add new cognitive elements) to strengthen or bolster one of the cognitive elements.

As Elliot Aronson of the University of Texas states in the first article, this basically simple theory has generated a good bit of hostility within social psychology. Aronson describes the problems inherent in the theoretical imprecision and "conceptual fuzziness" of cognitive dissonance theory and makes his own propositions about modes of analysis that may reduce this fuzziness. The reader is encouraged to keep these modifica-

tions in mind while reading the remaining articles in this section.

One of the "nonobvious" predictions of dissonance theory involves the role of counterattitudinal behavior in attitude change. As we have mentioned, the behaver may be expected to modify his attitude in the direction of the counterattitudinal behavior. But what are the effects of the magnitude of incentive offered and the perceived freedom *not* to take part in the behavior? How do they interact with the amount of attitude change produced? The second article in this section, by Darwyn Linder, Joel Cooper, and Edward E. Jones, all then at Duke University, provides clear-cut data on these points.

In the third article, Daryl Bem of Stanford University sounds a cautionary note to the abstruse theorizing that cognitive dissonance theory has engendered. His reservations about the "fastidious pool of cognitive clarity" that dissonance theory may imply should be carefully considered.

REFERENCES

Festinger, L. *A theory of cognitive dissonance.* Stanford, Calif.: Stanford University Press, 1957.

Katz, D. The functional approach to the study of attitudes. *Public Opinion Quarterly,* 1960, **24,** 163–204.

McGuire, W. J. Attitudes and opinions. In P. R. Farnsworth, O. McNemar, and Q. McNemar (Eds.), *Annual review of psychology,* Vol. XVII. Palo Alto, Calif. Annual Reviews, 1966. Pp. 475–514. (a)

McGuire, W. J. The current status of cognitive consistency theories. In S. Feldman (Ed.), *Cognitive consistency.* New York: Academic Press, 1966. Pp. 1–46. (b)

Smith, M. B., Bruner, J. S., & White, R. W. *Opinions and personality.* New York: Wiley, 1956.

ARTICLE 31

Dissonance Theory: Progress and Problems

Elliot Aronson

As a formal statement, Festinger's theory of cognitive dissonance (1957) is quite primitive; it lacks the elegance and precision commonly associated with scientific theorizing. Yet its impact has been great. As McGuire has observed in his recent survey in the *Annual Review of Psychology* (1966, p. 492), "Over the past three years, dissonance theory continued to generate more research and more hostility than any other one approach." I will allude to the "hostility" part of this statement from time to time throughout this chapter; but first let us discuss the research.

The research has been as diverse as it has been plentiful; its range extends from maze running in rats (Lawrence & Festinger, 1962), to the development of values in children (Aronson & Carlsmith, 1963); from the hunger of college sophomores (Brehm, Back, & Bogdonoff, 1964), to the proselytizing behavior of religious zealots (Festinger, Riecken, & Schachter, 1956). For descriptive summaries of dissonance experiments, the reader is referred to Festinger, 1957; Festinger and Aronson, 1960; Brehm and Cohen, 1962; Festinger and Bramel, 1962; Festinger and Freedman, 1964.

The proliferation of research testing and extending dissonance theory is due for the most part to the generality and simplicity of the theory.

Excerpted with abridgment from R. P. Abelson, E. Aronson, W. J. McGuire, T. M. Newcomb, M. J. Rosenberg, and P. H. Tannenbaum (Eds.), *Theories of cognitive consistency: A sourcebook,* Rand-McNally, 1968, pp. 5–27, with the permission of the author and Rand-McNally, Inc.

This chapter was prepared while the author's research was being supported by grants from the National Science Foundation (NSF GS 750) and the National Institute of Mental Health (MH 12357), which he gratefully acknowledges.

Although it has been applied primarily in social psychological settings, it is not limited to social psychological phenomena such as interpersonal relations or feelings toward a communicator and his communication. Rather, its domain is in the widest of places: the skull of an individual organism.[1]

The core notion of the theory is extremely simple: Dissonance is a negative drive state which occurs whenever an individual simultaneously holds two cognitions (ideas, beliefs, opinions) which are psychologically inconsistent. Stated differently, two cognitions are dissonant if, considering these two cognitions alone, the opposite of one follows from the other. Since the occurrence of dissonance is presumed to be unpleasant, individuals strive to reduce it by adding "consonant" cognitions or by changing one or both cognitions to make them "fit together" better—i.e., so that they become more consonant with each other.[2] To use Festinger's time-worn (but still cogent) example, if a person believes that cigarette smoking causes cancer and simultaneously knows that he himself smokes cigarettes, he experiences dissonance. Assuming that the person would rather not have cancer, his cognition "I

[1] An additional reason for the great number of experiments on dissonance theory is completely *ad hominem:* Leon Festinger has an unmatched genius for translating interesting hypotheses into workable experimental operations and for inspiring others to do so. He has produced a great deal of research irrespective of any particular theoretical approach.

[2] Although dissonance theory is an incredibly simple statement, it is not quite as simple as a reading of this chapter will indicate. Many aspects of the theory (for example, the propositions relevant to the magnitude of dissonance) will not be discussed here because they are peripheral to the major focus of this chapter.

smoke cigarettes" is psychologically inconsistent with his cognition "cigarette smoking produces cancer." Perhaps the most efficient way to reduce dissonance in such a situation is to stop smoking. But, as many of us have discovered, this is by no means easy. Thus, a person will usually work on the other cognition. There are several ways in which a person can make cigarette smoking seem less absurd. He might belittle the evidence linking cigarette smoking to cancer ("Most of the data are clinical rather than experimental"); or he might associate with other cigarette smokers ("If Sam, Jack, and Harry smoke, then it can't be very dangerous"); or he might smoke filter-tipped cigarettes and delude himself that the filter traps the cancer-producing materials; or he might convince himself that smoking is an important and highly pleasurable activity ("I'd rather have a shorter but more enjoyable life than a longer, unenjoyable one"); or he might actually make a virtue out of smoking by developing a romantic, devil-may-care image of himself, flaunting danger by smoking. All of these behaviors reduce dissonance, in effect, by reducing the absurdity involved in going out of one's way to contract cancer. Thus, dissonance theory does not rest upon the assumption that man is a *rational* animal; rather, it suggests that man is a rational*izing* animal—that he attempts to appear rational, both to others and to himself. To clarify the theoretical statement and to illustrate the kind of research generated by the theory, I will briefly describe a few experiments.

Dissonance Following a Decision

One of the earliest experiments testing derivations from dissonance theory was performed by Brehm (1956). Brehm gave individuals their choice between two appliances which they had previously evaluated. He found that following the decision, when the subjects reevaluated the alternatives, they enhanced their liking for the chosen appliance and downgraded their evaluation of the unchosen one. The derivation is clear. After making a difficult choice, people experience dissonance; cognitions about any negative attributes of the preferred object are dissonant with having

chosen it; cognitions about positive attributes of the unchosen object are dissonant with *not* having chosen it. To reduce dissonance, people emphasize the positive aspects and deemphasize the negative aspects of the chosen object while emphasizing the negative and deemphasizing the positive aspects of the unchosen object (see also Festinger, 1964).

Dissonance Resulting from Effort

Aronson and Mills (1959) reasoned that, if people undergo a great deal of trouble in order to gain admission to a group which turns out to be dull and uninteresting, they will experience dissonance. The cognition that they worked hard in order to become members of the group is dissonant with cognitions concerning the negative aspects of the group. One does not work hard for nothing. To reduce dissonance, they will distort their perception of the group in a positive direction. In the Aronson-Mills experiment, college women underwent an initiation in order to become a member of a group discussion on the psychology of sex. For some of the girls the initiation was very embarrassing—it consisted of reciting a list of obscene words in the presence of the male experimenter. For others the initiation was a mild one. For still others there was no initiation at all. All of the subjects then listened to the same tape-recording of a discussion being held by the group they had just joined. As predicted, the girls in the Severe Initiation condition rated the discussion much more favorably than did those in the other two conditions (see also Aronson, 1961; Zimbardo, 1965; Lewis, 1964; Gerard & Mathewson, 1966).

Insufficient Justification

Aronson and Carlsmith (1963) predicted that if threats are used to prevent people from performing a desired activity, the *smaller* the threat, the greater will be the tendency for people to derogate the activity. If an individual refrains from performing a desired activity, he experiences dissonance: The cognition that he likes the activity is dissonant with the cognition that he is not performing it. One way to reduce dissonance is by derogating the activity—in that way he can justify the fact that he is not performing it. However, any threat provides cognitions that are consonant with not performing the activity; and the more severe the threat, the greater the consonance. In short, a severe threat provides ample justification for not performing the activity; a mild threat provides less justification, leading the individual to add justifications of his own in the form of convincing himself that he *doesn't like* to perform the activity. In their experiment, Aronson and Carlsmith found that children who were threatened with *mild* punishment for playing with a desired toy *decreased* their liking for the toy to a greater extent than did children who were severely threatened (see also Turner & Wright, 1965; Freedman, 1965).

WHAT IS PSYCHOLOGICAL INCONSISTENCY?

The very simplicity of the core of the theory is at once its greatest strength and its most serious weakness. We have already discussed the heuristic value of its simplicity. It should be emphasized that many of the hypotheses which are obvious derivations from the theory are *unique* to that theory—i.e., they could not be derived from any other theory. This increases our confidence in dissonance theory as an explanation of an important aspect of human behavior. The weakness occurs primarily in the difficulty involved with defining the limits of the theoretical statement. While at the "center" of the theory it is relatively easy to generate hypotheses that are clear and direct, at its "fringes" it is not always clear whether or not a prediction can be made from the theory and, if so, exactly what that prediction will be.[3] Although investigators who have had experience working with the theory seem to have little difficulty intuiting its boundary conditions, they have had considerable difficulty communicating this to other people; indeed, a situation has evolved which can best be described by the statement: "If you want to be sure, ask Leon." This

[3]Further along in this chapter some attempt will be made to specify exactly what we mean by "center" and "fringes."

has proved to be both a source of embarrassment for the proponents of the theory as well as a source of annoyance and exasperation to its critics.

Why is it so difficult to make a more precise theoretical statement? Perhaps the most basic reason has to do with the nature of the inconsistency involved in the core definition of dissonance theory. It would be easy to specify dissonant situations if the theory were limited to *logical* inconsistencies. There exist relatively unequivocal rules of logic which can be applied without ambiguity or fear of contradiction. But recall that the inconsistency that produces dissonance, although it can be logical inconsistency, is not necessarily logical. Rather, it is *psychological* inconsistency. While this aspect of the theory increases its power, range, and degree of interest, at the same time it also causes some serious problems. Thus, returning to our friend the cigarette smoker, the cognition regarding smoking cigarettes is not logically inconsistent with the cognition linking cigarette smoking to cancer; i.e., strictly speaking, having information that cigarette smoking causes cancer does not make it illogical to smoke cigarettes. But these cognitions do produce dissonance because, taken together, they do not make sense psychologically. Assuming that the smoker does not want cancer, the knowledge that cigarettes cause cancer should lead to *not* smoking cigarettes. Similarly, none of the research examples mentioned above deals with logical inconsistency; e.g., it is not illogical to go through hell and high water to gain admission to a dull discussion group; it is not illogical to choose to own an appliance that one considers slightly more attractive than the unchosen alternative; it is not illogical to refrain from playing with a toy at the request of an adult.

Festinger (1957) lists four kinds of situations in which dissonance can arise: (1) logical inconsistency, (2) inconsistency with cultural mores, (3) inconsistency between one cognition and a more general, more encompassing cognition, (4) past experience.

1. Logical inconsistency: Suppose a person believed that all men are mortal but also held the belief that he, as a man, would live forever. These

two cognitions are dissonant because they are logically inconsistent. The contrary of one follows from the other on strict logical grounds.

2. Cultural mores: If a college professor loses his patience with one of his students and shouts at him angrily, his knowledge of what he is doing is dissonant with his idea about what is the proper, acceptable behavior of a professor toward his students—in our culture. In some other cultures this might be appropriate behavior and, therefore, would not arouse dissonance.

3. Inconsistency between one cognition and a more encompassing cognition: In a given election, if a person who has always considered himself to be a Democrat votes for a Republican candidate, he should experience dissonance. The concept "I am a Democrat" encompasses the concept "I vote for Democratic candidates."

4. Past experience: If a person stepped on a tack while barefoot and felt no pain, he would experience dissonance because he knows from experience that pain follows from stepping on tacks. If he had never had experience with tacks or other sharp objects, he would *not* experience dissonance.

The illustrations presented above are clear examples of dissonance. Similarly, the situations investigated in the experiments I have described above are clearly dissonant. But there *are* situations where for all practical purposes it is not perfectly clear whether two cognitions are dissonant or merely irrelevant. Because dissonance is *not* limited to logical inconsistencies it is occasionally difficult to specify a priori whether or not a cultural more is being violated, whether or not an event is markedly different from past experience, or whether or not it is different from a more general cognition. Recall the basic theoretical statement: Two cognitions are dissonant if, considering these two cognitions alone, the opposite of one follows from the other. The major source of conceptual ambiguity rests upon the fact that Festinger has not clarified the meaning of the words "follows from."

For example, if I learn that my favorite novelist beats his wife, does this arouse dissonance? It is difficult to be certain. Strictly speaking, being a wife-beater is not incompatible with being a great novelist.[4] However, there may be a sense in which the term "great novelist" implies that such a person is wise, sensitive, empathic, and compassionate—and wise, sensitive, empathic, and compassionate people do not go around beating their wives. This is not a logical inconsistency; nor is it a clear violation of a cultural more; moreover, it may have nothing to do with past experience—and it is not *necessarily* imbedded in a more general cognition. Thus, a knowledge of the kinds of situations in which dissonance *can* occur is not always useful in determining whether dissonance *does* occur.

A rule of thumb which I have found useful is to state the situation in terms of the violation of an expectancy. For example, one might issue the following instructions: "Consider Thurgood Marshall. I'm going to tell you something about his beliefs about the native I.Q. of Negroes relative to that of Caucasians. What do you expect these beliefs to be?" I imagine that most people would have a firm expectancy that Justice Marshall would have said that there are no innate differences. Consequently, one could then conclude that if individuals were exposed to a statement by Justice Marshall to the effect that Negroes were innately stupider than Caucasians, most would experience dissonance. Let us try our difficult example: Suppose we confronted a large number of people with the following proposition: "Consider the great novelist X. I am about to tell you something about whether or not he beats his wife. What do you expect me to say?" My guess is that most people would shrug; i.e., they would not have a strong expectancy (but, again, this is an empirical question; I am not certain that it would come out this way). If this occurred, one could conclude that X's wife-beating behavior is irrelevant to his status as a novelist. An empirical rule of thumb may be of practical utility but is, of course, no substitute for a clearer, less ambiguous, more precise theoretical statement. Near the end of this chapter we will elaborate upon this

[4] If *I* had beaten my wife I might experience dissonance because of *my* violation of a cultural more. But since I know that many people beat their wives, discovering that a particular person beats his wife is not necessarily inconsistent with my cognition about the world and human nature. More will be said about this later.

rule of thumb and indicate how it might be used conceptually.

THE "NOTHING BUT" CRITIQUE

Scientists tend to be conservative, parsimonious creatures. This is generally a healthy attitude which most frequently manifests itself in a reluctance to accept a new theory or a novel explanation for a phenomenon if the phenomenon can be squeezed (even with great difficulty) into an existing approach. In this regard, dissonance theory has been referred to as nothing but a new name for an old phenomenon. This has been most persistently stated in regard to that aspect of the theory related to decision making. In this context dissonance theory has been referred to as nothing but another name for conflict theory.

In fact, there are several differences. Conflict occurs before a decision is made, dissonance occurs after the decision. During conflict it is assumed that an individual will devote his energies to a careful, dispassionate, and sensible evaluation and judgment of the alternatives. He will gather all of the information, pro and con, about all of the alternatives in order to make a reasonable decision. Following the decision, a person is in a state of dissonance—all negative aspects of X are dissonant with having chosen X; all positive aspects of Y are dissonant with *not* having chosen Y. Far from evaluating the alternatives impartially (as in conflict), the individual experiencing dissonance will seek biased information and evaluations designed to make his decision appear more reasonable. As in Brehm's (1956) experiment, he will seek to spread the alternatives apart. The more difficulty a person had making a decision, the greater the tendency toward this kind of behavior as a means of justifying his decision.

But how can we be certain that the spreading apart of the alternatives in Brehm's experiment occurred after the decision? Could it not have occurred during the conflict stage? That is, it is conceivable that, in order to make their decision easier, subjects in Brehm's experiment began to reevaluate the appliances in a biased manner *be-*

fore the decision. If this were the case, then there is no essential difference between predecisional and postdecisional processes; if so, this behavior can be considered part of conflict—and there is, indeed, no need to complicate matters by bringing in additional terminology.

Brehm's experiment does not allow us to determine whether the evaluation of chosen and unchosen alternatives was spread apart before or after the decision. Recent experiments by Davidson and Kiesler (1964) and by Jecker (1964) serve to clarify this issue. In Jecker's experiment, subjects were offered their choice between two phonograph records. In three conditions there was *low conflict*; i.e., subjects were told that there was a very good chance that they would receive *both* records no matter which they chose. In three other conditions, *high conflict* was produced by telling them that the probability was high that they would be given only the record that they chose. All of the subjects rated the records before the instructions; in each of the conflict conditions subjects rerated the records either (a) after they discovered that they received both records, (b) after they discovered that they received only the one record they chose, or (c) before they were certain whether they would get one or both. The results are quite clear: No spreading apart occurred when there was no dissonance; i.e., when the subject actually received both records or when he was not certain whether he would receive one or both he did *not* reevaluate the alternatives systematically. Where dissonance did occur there was a systematic reevaluation; i.e., subjects spread their evaluation of the alternatives when they received only one record—this occurred independently of the degree of conflict. This experiment provides clear evidence that conflict and dissonance are different processes; whatever else dissonance theory might be, it is *not* "nothing but conflict theory."

THE MULTIPLE MODE PROBLEM

As indicated earlier, several problems are central to the theoretical statement. One of the knottiest and most interesting conceptual problems in dissonance theory involves the fact that, in a given situation, there is usually more than one way for a person to reduce dissonance. For example, the cigarette smoker has several techniques at his disposal. He may use any one, or several simultaneously. Experimentally, this problem can be eliminated by the simple device of blocking alternative techniques of dissonance reduction. This is part of the definition of experimental control; any experimenter worth his salt will attempt to control the environment so that the behavior elicited by his independent variable will occur in a manner which is measurable and at a time and place where the measuring instruments have been set up. To illustrate: In a typical communication-persuasion experiment, if a highly credible communicator states a position which is discrepant from the position of the recipient, the recipient experiences dissonance. He can reduce dissonance in one of four ways: (1) he can change his opinion to make it coincide with the communicator's; (2) he can attempt to change the communicator's opinion; (3) he can seek social support from other members of the audience; (4) he can derogate the communicator. If one is interested in measuring opinion change (No. 1), one can eliminate No. 2 and No. 3 by making it impossible for the subject to interact either with the communicator or his fellow subjects. Furthermore, one can reduce the subject's ability to derogate the communicator by assigning the latter high enough prestige so that he becomes virtually nonderogatable. Thus, if these four techniques exhaust the universe, the only way that a subject can reduce dissonance is by changing his attitude on the issue. The prudent experimenter will have built his experiment to make it appear reasonable to measure the subject's attitudes after the communication and he will use the most sensitive measuring instrument he can construct.

Thus, if the question one asks is "Does dissonance occur in such a situation and does it get reduced?" the answer can be easily determined experimentally. But we may have a different question in mind: "In a given situation, how do people generally reduce dissonance?" And the answer to this question may be strikingly different from the mode found in the laboratory experi-

ment. Thus, in the above example, most people might prefer to argue with the communicator rather than change their opinion.

The above argument suggests that the results from carefully controlled laboratory experiments, on occasion, may be somewhat misleading. For example, suppose a young Ph.D. is being considered for a teaching position in a major department at a prestigious Ivy League university. What happens if the members of that department decide not to hire him? If he feels that he is a good and worthy scholar, he will experience cognitive dissonance: His cognition that he is a good scholar is dissonant with his cognition that he was rejected by members of a good department. As I see it, he can reduce dissonance in at least two ways: (a) he can convince himself that his rejectors are, in reality, stupid, defensive, unprofessional, and/or senile people who cannot or will not recognize a good man when they see one; (b) he can convince himself that if they can reject him (as good as he is), then their standards must be astronomically high and therefore they are a fine group of nonsenile professionals. Both of these techniques succeed in reducing dissonance; moreover, they both protect the individual's ego —he leaves for his job at East Podunk State Teacher's College with the conviction that he is a good scholar. But note that the results of his dissonance-reducing behavior can leave him with totally opposite opinions about the members of the staff at the Ivy League university. Thus, if one wanted to arouse dissonance in an individual for the specific purpose of enhancing his impressions of the people at Ivy University, one had better be careful. The same dissonance-producing situation can result in quite the opposite dissonance-reducing behavior.

This is a serious conceptual problem. One way that it can be solved is by coming up with a set of specific propositions that can lead one to state the conditions under which one mode or the other is more likely to occur. I have previously outlined a possible solution in a specific situation. The situation I was concerned with involved alternative modes of dissonance reduction following the unsuccessful expenditure of effort. If a person struggles to reach a goal and fails, he experiences dissonance. His cognition that he exerted effort to attain the goal is dissonant with his cognition that he did not reach it. He could reduce dissonance by convincing himself that the goal was not worth it anyway; recall that this was the way that Aesop's fox reduced dissonance in the fable of the sour grapes. There is another reasonable way to reduce dissonance: by the person's finding something else in the situation to which he can attach value in order to justify his expenditure of effort without achieving his avowed goal. Thus, the fox might convince himself that he got some much-needed exercise while leaping for the grapes—and that even though he failed to get those luscious, sweet grapes, it was worth the effort because of the muscles he developed while trying.

Under what conditions will an individual take one path rather than the other? In my paper (Aronson, 1961) I suggested that the first solution is probably easier—but only in a situation where the effort expended is of short duration. But if the situation consists of a long and repeated expenditure of effort, it becomes a less viable solution. To use our previous illustration, if the fox made a few leaps at the grapes and failed, he could convince himself that they were probably sour anyway; but if he spent the entire afternoon struggling to reach the grapes, it would not effectively reduce dissonance to maintain that the grapes were sour —for if that were the case, why in the world did he try to reach them over and over and over again? The data from my experiment indicate that, after the repeated expenditure of effort, people *do* attach value to an incidental stimulus; however, the definitive factorial experiment remains to be done.

It is encouraging to note that experimenters are beginning to focus their efforts on this kind of problem. A good example of this trend is described in a very recent article by Walster, Berscheid, and Barclay (1967), who hypothesize that individuals will choose that mode of dissonance reduction which is least likely to be challenged by future events. In their experiment, children were given their choice between two toys. In a situation like this, individuals can reduce dissonance in two ways: by cognitively increasing the attractiveness of the chosen alternative and/or by cognitively decreasing the attractiveness of the unchosen alternative. One-half of the children were led to expect that they would subsequently hear objective information about the toy they chose; one-half of the children were led to expect that they would hear objective information about the rejected toy. The investigators found, as predicted, that individuals reduced dissonance by distorting the attractiveness of that toy which they were not going to hear information about. That is, they opted to reduce dissonance in a manner which was less likely to run up against objective reality.

In order to be of maximum use, such specific solutions should be restated into more general propositions, where possible, and incorporated into the theory. An important step in this direction was taken by Brehm and Cohen (1962) in emphasizing the importance of commitment and volition in determining not only the strength of the dissonance involved, but, perhaps more important, the nature of the dissonance and, hence, the kind of mechanism needed to reduce dissonance. Whether or not a high degree of volition is present can often change the nature of the prediction. For example, as part of one study, Aronson, Turner, and Carlsmith (1963) reasoned that disagreement with a highly credible source produces more dissonance than disagreement with a source having low credibility. The cognition that a highly sentient person believes X is dissonant with the cognition that I believe *not*-X. The higher the credibility of the source, the greater the dissonance—because the less sense it makes to be in disagreement with him. This should lead to greater attitude change in the Highly Credible condition—to reduce dissonance. The results were consistent with this reasoning. On the other hand, Zimbardo (1960) and Brehm and Cohen (1962) reasoned that under certain conditions a source having low credibility would produce *greater* attitude change than one having high credibility. Specifically, if a person had chosen of his own volition to go to hear a speech by a low credibility source, he would experience dissonance. The cognition involving volition and commitment is dissonant with the cognition that the credibility of the communicator is low; after all, it is absurd to choose to go out of one's way to hear a low prestige source make a speech which is discrepant with one's own opinion. In order to reduce dissonance, one might convince oneself that there was no essential discrepancy—that one always held the position espoused by the low credibility source. Thus, both Zimbardo and Brehm and Cohen suggested that under conditions of high commitment one might get greater agreement with a low credibility source than with a high credibility source. This prediction made by Zimbardo and by Brehm and Cohen is consistent with other data involving choice and commitment. For example, Smith (1961) found that soldiers who volunteered to eat grasshoppers when induced by an unpleasant leader, came to like the grasshoppers better than did those who volunteered to eat them when induced by an affable leader. Similar results are reported by Zimbardo (1964).

It should be clear that the prediction made by Aronson, Turner, and Carlsmith and that made by Zimbardo and by Brehm and Cohen are not mutually exclusive; rather, they apply to a crucially different set of circumstances. Although both predictions are derived from dissonance theory, they involve different aspects of the theory; the crucial distinction is whether or not a high degree of volition is present. Nonetheless, to avoid confusion, these distinctions should be stated with even greater clarity.

To sum up this section, dissonance theory, as originally stated *does* have some areas of conceptual fuzziness. In my opinion, much of this fuzziness can be eliminated by empirical research. Again, this research should be focused on the conditions and variables which maximize and minimize the occurrence of dissonance and dissonance reduction as well as the conditions which lead to one or another mode of dissonance reduction. This position will be elaborated upon in a moment.

THE "UNDERLYING COGNITION" PROBLEM

The importance of commitment emerges most clearly when we scrutinize the phenomenon of the white lie more thoroughly. Clearly, every time we say something that we do not believe, we do *not* experience dissonance. Under certain conditions there are some underlying cognitions which serve to prevent the occurrence of dissonance. For example, if we stated a counter-attitudinal position in the context of a formal debate, we would not experience dissonance (see Scott, 1957, 1959; Aronson, 1966). It is clearly understood both by the speaker and the audience that a debator's own personal views have nothing to do with the opinions he expresses. The rules of the game of debating provide an underlying cognition which prevents the occurrence of dissonance. Similarly, as teachers we frequently are exposed to a great many stupid ideas from our students. I think that unless we know the student well—know that he is capable of better ideas and know that he is capable of "taking it"—most teachers refrain from tearing the idea to pieces. Instead, we tend to give the student our attention, nod and smile, and suggest that it is not such a bad idea. We do this because we have a general underlying cognition that we should not discourage students early in their careers and that it is wrong to be unkind to people who are relatively powerless to fight back. It would be ludicrous to suggest that teachers begin to believe that a student's poor idea is really a pretty good one simply because the teacher had said "pretty good idea" to the student. The underlying cognition prevents the occurrence of dissonance. But observe how commitment can make it a dissonant situation. If, on the basis of the teacher's statement, the student had decided to read his paper at the state psychological convention, the teacher might begin to convince himself that it was not such a bad idea—because the teacher has now been committed—he has misled the student into taking some action. This increases the teacher's commitment to the situation and is probably more powerful than the underlying consonant cognition "this is how we treat students." The teacher now seeks additional justification for having misled the student, perhaps by convincing himself that it was not such a bad idea after all.

The general point to be made here is an important one. Inconsistency is said to arise between two cognitive elements if, "considering these two alone, the [opposite] of one element follows from the other" (Festinger, 1957, pp. 260–261). But we know that in most situations two cognitions are almost never taken by themselves. Occasionally, two cognitions which in the abstract would appear to be dissonant fail to arouse dissonance because of the existence of a neutralizing underlying cognition. For example, suppose I know a brilliant fellow who is married to an incredibly stupid woman. These cognitions are inconsistent but I would contend that they do not necessarily produce dissonance. I can tolerate this inconsistency—it does not cause me pain, it does not necessarily lead me to change my opinion about the brilliant fellow or his wife, I do not conclude that he is dumber than I thought or that she is smarter. Why? Because I have a general, underlying, pervasive cognition that there are a multitude of factors which determine mate selection—similarities of intelligence being only one of them. Moreover, I know that it is extremely rare for all of these to be matched in a marital relationship. Therefore, although taken by themselves the above two cognitions are incompatible, I simply do not ever take them by themselves.

Festinger suggests that one way to reduce dissonance is to martial consonant cognitions—thus, he might say that the above reasoning is one way of reducing dissonance. But it is a moot and important point whether I martialed the above cognitions as a result of the inconsistency, or whether I walked around with these cognitions about mate selection before the fact. If the latter is the case, then it can hardly be said that I dredged up this overriding cognition as a means of reducing dissonance. For example, let us look at the finding (Aronson & Carlsmith, 1963; Turner & Wright, 1965; Freedman, 1965) that children threatened with mild punishment for playing with a toy tend to derogate that toy after refraining from playing with it. Suppose that many children entered the situation with the strong feeling that adults must be obeyed always, even when commands are arbitrary and threats are nonexistent ("My mother, right or wrong!"). Put another way (which will become important in a moment), suppose that part of the self concept of these children was "obedience to adult authority." If this were the case there would have been no dissonance—even though, *taken by itself,* the

cognition "I like that toy" is dissonant with the cognition "I'm not playing with it." If this were *not* already a part of the person's self concept, it might have become one as a function of the experiment—i.e., developing a belief in the importance of obedience is one way of reducing dissonance in the above situation. But if it were already there—there would have been no dissonance to begin with.

This added complexity should not lead us to throw our hands up in despair. Rather, it should lead us to a more careful analysis of the situations we are dealing with and perhaps even to a greater concern with individual differences.

THE IMPORTANCE OF THE SELF CONCEPT AND OTHER EXPECTANCIES

In discussing the difficulties in making precise predictions from dissonance theory in some situations, we have purposely tiptoed around the problem of individual differences. The fact that all people are not the same presents intriguing problems for dissonance theory as it does for all general motivational theories. Of course, one man's "problem" is another man's primary datum; i.e., psychologists who are interested in personality regard individual differences as being of great interest. For those who are primarily interested in establishing nomothetic laws, individual differences usually constitute nothing more than an annoying source of error variance. Nevertheless, whether or not we are interested in individual differences *per se,* an understanding of the way people differ in dissonant situations can be an important means to clarify and strengthen the theory. Basically, there are three ways that individuals differ which should be of concern to people investigating dissonance theory:

1. People differ in their ability to tolerate dissonance. It seems reasonable to assume that some people are simply better than others at shrugging off dissonance; i.e., it may take a greater *amount* of dissonance to bring about dissonance-reducing behavior in some people than in others.

2. People probably differ in their preferred mode of dissonance reduction. E.g., some people

may find it easier to derogate the source of a communication than to change their own opinion. Others may find the reverse resolution easier.

3. What is dissonant for one person may be consonant for someone else; i.e., people may be so different that certain events are regarded as dissonant for some but not for others.

I shall not dwell on the first two here save to say that, earlier in this chapter, I underscored the difficulty of ascertaining the proper conditions for establishing whether or not dissonance exists for *most people* and the conditions for determining which mode of dissonance reduction *most people* will use; the existence of individual differences complicates matters further by adding another important dimension which should eventually be specified. The third case will be discussed here because it is of great relevance for the general theory. Furthermore, I regard it as prior to the other two, for before one can determine (a) whether an individual is experiencing *enough* dissonance to reduce it or (b) *how* he will reduce it, we must first determine whether the events are indeed dissonant, consonant, or irrelevant to him.

Dissonant or consonant with what? Recall the earlier discussion wherein I described a rule of thumb based upon an expectancy (e.g., the Thurgood Marshall and wife-beating novelist illustrations). In my judgment, dissonance theory makes a clear prediction when a firm expectancy is involved as one of the cognitions in question. Thus, our cognition about Thurgood Marshall's *behavior* can be dissonant with our expectancy about how Justice Marshall *will* behave. Dissonance theory is clearer still when that firm expectancy involves the individual's self concept, for—almost by definition—our expectancies about our own behavior are firmer than our expectancies about the behavior of another person. Thus, at the very heart of dissonance theory, where it makes its clearest and neatest prediction, we are not dealing with just any two cognitions; rather, we are usually dealing with the self concept and cognitions about some behavior. If dissonance exists it is because the individual's behavior is inconsistent with his self concept.

As I pointed out several years ago (Aronson, 1960), this point has been elusive because most of the experiments testing dissonance theory have made predictions based upon the tacit assumption that people have a high self concept. Why do people who buy new cars selectively expose themselves to ads about their own make of car (Ehrlich, Guttman, Schönbach, & Mills, 1957) and try to convince themselves that they made the right choice? Because the knowledge that one has bought a junky car is dissonant with a high self concept. But suppose a person had a low self concept? Then, the cognition that he bought a junky car would *not* be dissonant. Indeed, if the theory holds, such a person should engage in all kinds of "bizarre" behavior like exposing himself to ads about other cars, hearing squeaks and rattles that are not even there, and saying, in effect, "Just my luck, I bought a lemon—these things are always happening to me." In short, if a person conceives of himself as a "schnook," he will expect to behave like a schnook; consequently, wise, reasonable, successful, un-schnooky behavior on his part should arouse dissonance. One of the advantages of this kind of statement is that it allows us to separate the effects of dissonance from other hedonic effects. That is, people with *high* self concepts who fail *do* experience dissonance; but they experience many other negative feelings as well—due simply to the fact that failure is unpleasant. No one can deny that success brings pleasant consequences for people with high and low self concepts alike. That is, regardless of a person's self concept, successful achievement is often accompanied by such pleasant things as acclaim, money, fame, admiration, popularity, etc. But dissonance theory allows us to predict that, for people with low self concepts, the "good feelings" aroused by the products of success will be tempered by the discomfort caused by dissonance—the dissonance between a low self concept and cognitions about high performance. Several experiments have demonstrated that people who expect failure are somewhat discomforted by success (Aronson & Carlsmith, 1962; Cottrell, 1965; Brock *et al.*, 1965), but the data are by no means unequivocal.

Thus, although we may not have been fully aware of it at the time, in the clearest experiments performed to test dissonance theory, the dissonance involved was between a self concept and cognitions about a behavior that violated this self concept. In the experiments on counterattitudinal advocacy, for example, I would suggest that it is incorrect to say that dissonance existed between the cognition "I believe the task is dull" and "I told someone that the task was interesting." This is not dissonant for a psychopathic liar —indeed, it is perfectly consonant. What is dissonant is the cognition "I am a decent, truthful human being" and the cognition "I have misled a person; I have conned him into believing something which just isn't true; he thinks that I really believe it and I cannot set him straight because I probably won't see him again." In the initiation experiments, I would maintain that dissonance does not exist between the cognition, "I worked hard to get into a group" and the cognition "The group is dull and stupid." Recall that for a "schnook" these cognitions are not at all dissonant. What is dissonant in this situation is the cognition "I am a reasonable and intelligent person" and the cognition "I have worked hard for nothing." Reasonable, intelligent people usually get a fair return for their investment—they usually do not buy a pig in a poke (unless there is some reasonably implicit guarantee, as in Freedman's [1963] experiment discussed above).

As an empirical refinement this self concept notion is probably trivial. The experimenters who made the tacit assumption that people have high self concepts achieved positive results—which indicates that this assumption is valid for most people in these situations. But it may constitute a valuable and interesting *theoretical* refinement. A theory becomes infinitely more meaningful when its domain is clearly demarcated; i.e., when it states clearly where it does not apply. If it is the case that dissonance theory makes unequivocal predictions only when the self concept or another strong expectancy is involved, then an important set of boundary conditions has been drawn. What I described earlier as a rule of thumb may actually be a conceptual clarification.

I stated early in this chapter that "at the 'center' of the theory" predictions are unequivocal, but at the "fringes" they are somewhat fuzzy. At this point, we can say that "at the center" means

situations in which the self concept or other firm expectancies are involved—and in which most people share the same self concepts or other firm expectancies. Thus, most people have self concepts about being truthful and honest so that we can make clear predictions intuitively, as in the Carlsmith, Collins, and Helmreich (1966) experiment. Most people have self concepts involving making reasonable and wise decisions so that we can intuit clear predictions, as in the Brehm (1956) or Jecker (1964) experiments. Also, most people have firm expectancies about what Thurgood Marshall would say about Negro intelligence, so that a dissonance theory prediction makes sense and can be made clearly, even though a self concept is not involved. The prediction about the great novelist who beats his wife gives the theory trouble precisely because people differ tremendously with regard to whether or not they expect a particular novelist to be a gentle and considerate man. In a specific instance, the knowledge of whether or not individual X has this expectancy would increase the accuracy of the prediction. I do not regard this of great importance. What I do regard as important is merely the recognition of the fact that dissonance theory may be best suited for making general predictions in situations where expectancies are firm and nearly universal.

Several years ago, Zajonc (1960) raised a very interesting and reasonable question: If dissonance is bothersome, why do we enjoy magicians? That is, magicians can be thought of as people who arouse dissonance. Should we not experience pain and discomfort when we see rabbits pulled from hats, women sawed in half, or dimes turned into quarters? Perhaps the reason why we are not upset by magicians is because the behavior of a magician is consonant with our expectancy regarding magicians. That is, since we know in advance that magicians use tricks and sleight-of-hand techniques to produce interesting illusions, why should we experience dissonance when we see him do these things? Is this not akin to the schnook who expects to purchase an inferior car?

Before the reader dismisses this as mere sophistry, let me hasten to say that this is an empirical question. What I am suggesting is that we enjoy magicians *only* when they are billed as magicians. If they were not billed as magicians, they would cause quite a bit of discomfort. If the fellow sitting next to us at the bar suddenly "became" a fat woman, this would be very upsetting—unless the bartender had forewarned us that we were sitting next to a professional quick-change artist known as "Slippery Sam, the man of a thousand faces." If he then "became" a fat woman, we would be thrilled and delighted. It is interesting to note that the bartender could have produced a similar result if he had forewarned us that he had placed some LSD in our drink. In short, either being told a man is a magician or being told we were fed a hallucinogen is consistent with seeing a man "become" a fat woman! Empirically, this can be tested by finding some young children or some people from a different culture who have never seen or heard of magicians. My guess is that without the expectancy regarding magicians that Zajonc and I share, these subjects would be quite upset by the goings on.

MAN CANNOT LIVE BY CONSONANCE ALONE

The implication of this essay is that dissonant situations are ubiquitous and that man expends a good deal of time and energy attempting to reduce dissonance. It should be obvious that man does many other things as well. Festinger never intended dissonance theory to be imperial or monolithic. In 1957, he clearly recognized the fact that dissonance reduction is only one of many motives and can be counteracted by more powerful drives. We have already discussed how dissonance effects and reward-incentive effects can both occur in the same experimental design. Even more basic is the confrontation that occurs when consonance needs meet utility needs head-on. An extremely high drive to reduce dissonance would lead man to weave a cocoon about himself, never admitting his mistakes and distorting reality to make it compatible with his behavior. But if a person is ever going to grow, improve, and avoid repeating the same errors, he must sooner or later learn to profit from past mistakes. One

cannot profit from one's mistakes without first admitting that one has *made* a mistake. And yet, the admission of error almost always arouses some dissonance. The fact is, people frequently *do* profit from their mistakes; thus, people occasionally do not avoid or reduce dissonance.

To illustrate, if a man spends $50,000 for a home, dissonance theory would suggest that he may be the last to notice that, during the rainy season, there is water in the basement. Noticing water would arouse dissonance by making his purchase appear to have been a mistake. But to notice the water has great utility—for he must notice it in order to repair it, prepare for the flood, or check the basement of the next house he buys. Thus, dissonance and utility are in constant tension by virtue of the fact that under certain conditions dissonant information may be extremely useful, and, conversely, useful information can arouse dissonance. Mills, Aronson, and Robinson (1959) suggested that one reason that people frequently do not avoid dissonant information is that it often has great utility. In their experiment, they found that many subjects who had recently committed themselves to taking essay exams as opposed to multiple-choice exams opted to read articles explaining why essay exams were more difficult, anxiety-provoking, etc. In this situation, apparently, the utility of the information was considered worth the price to be paid in dissonance. More recent experiments by Canon (1964) and Aronson and Ross (1966) have begun to indicate the requisite conditions for these effects: Basically, as utility increases and dissonance becomes weaker, individuals begin to show a preference for dissonance-arousing but useful information. But as dissonance increases (i.e., immediately after a decision or when commitment is high, etc.), individuals tend to manifest dissonance-reducing behavior in spite of the fact that the future consequences of such behavior tend to be unpleasant.

EPILOGUE

The theory of cognitive dissonance is much more complicated than it was thought to be ten years ago. A good deal of research has been done since 1957. Many of the problems which were specified early have been solved; many new problems have been unearthed, some of which remain to be solved. Hopefully, future research will lead to the emergence of still new problems, which will lead to still more research, which will continue to yield an increased understanding of human behavior. I guess that is what science is all about. In their critique of five years of dissonance theory, Chapanis and Chapanis concluded with the pronouncement "Not proven." Happily, after ten years, it is still not proven; all the theory ever does is generate research!

REFERENCES

Aronson, E. The cognitive and behavioral consequences of the confirmation and disconfirmation of expectancies. Unpublished manuscript, Harvard University, 1960.

Aronson, E. The effect of effort on the attractiveness of rewarded and unrewarded stimuli. *Journal of Abnormal and Social Psychology,* 1961, **63**, 375–380.

Aronson, E. The psychology of insufficient justification: An analysis of some conflicting data. In S. Feldman (Ed.), *Cognitive consistency: Motivational antecedents and behavioral consequences.* New York: Academic Press, 1966, Pp. 109–133.

Aronson, E., & Carlsmith, J. M. Performance expectancy as a determinant of actual performance. *Journal of Abnormal and Social Psychology,* 1962, **65**, 178–182.

Aronson, E., & Carlsmith, J. M. Effect of the severity of threat on the valuation of forbidden behavior. *Journal of Abnormal and Social Psychology,* 1963, **66**, 584–588.

Aronson E., & Mills, J. The effect of severity of initiation on liking for a group. *Journal of Abnormal and Social Psychology,* 1959, **59**, 177–181.

Aronson, E., & Ross, A. The effect of support and criticism on interpersonal attractiveness. Unpublished data, 1966.

Aronson, E., Turner, J., & Carlsmith, J. M. Communicator credibility and communication discrepancy as determinants of opinion change. *Journal of Abnormal and Social Psychology,* 1963, **67**, 31–36.

Brehm, J. W. Post-decision changes in the desirability of alternatives. *Journal of Abnormal and Social Psychology,* 1956, **52**, 384–389.

Brehm, J. W., & Cohen, A. R. *Explorations in cognitive dissonance.* New York: Wiley, 1962.

Brehm, M. L., Back, K. W., & Bogdonoff, M. D. A physiological effect of cognitive dissonance under stress and deprivation. *Journal of Abnormal and Social Psychology,* 1964, **69**, 303–310.

Brock, T. C., Eidelman, S. K., Edwards, D. C., &

Schuck, J. R. Seven studies of performance expectancy as a determinant of actual performance. *Journal of Experimental Social Psychology,* 1965, **1**, 295–310.

Canon, L. Self-confidence and selective exposure to information. In L. Festinger, *Conflict, decision, and dissonance.* Stanford, Calif.: Stanford University Press, 1964. Pp. 83–96.

Carlsmith, J. M., Collins, B. E., & Helmreich, R. L. Studies in forced compliance: I. The effect of pressure for compliance on attitude change produced by face-to-face role playing and anonymous essay writing. *Journal of Personality and Social Psychology,* 1966, **4**, 1–13.

Chapanis, N. P., & Chapanis, A. Cognitive dissonance: Five years later. *Psychological Bulletin,* 1964, **61**, 1–22.

Cottrell, N. B. The effect of expectancy-performance dissonance upon reaction time performance. Paper presented at a meeting of the Midwestern Psychological Association, April 1965.

Davidson, J. R., & Kiesler, S. Cognitive behavior before and after decisions. In L. Festinger, *Conflict, decision, and dissonance.* Stanford, Calif.: Stanford University Press, 1964. Pp. 10–21.

Ehrlich, D., Guttman, I., Schönbach, P., & Mills, J. Post-decision exposure to relevant information. *Journal of Abnormal and Social Psychology,* 1957, **54**, 98–102.

Festinger, L. *A theory of cognitive dissonance.* Evanston, Ill.: Row, Peterson, 1957.

Festinger, L. *Conflict, decision, and dissonance.* Stanford, Calif.: Stanford University Press, 1964.

Festinger, L., & Aronson, E. The arousal and reduction of dissonance in social contexts. In D. Cartwright & A. Zander (Eds.), *Group dynamics.* (2nd ed.) Evanston, Ill.: Row, Peterson, 1960. Pp. 214–231.

Festinger, L., & Bramel, D. The reactions of humans to cognitive dissonance. In A. Bachrach (Ed.), *The experimental foundations of clinical psychology.* New York: Basic Books, 1962. Pp. 254–279.

Festinger, L., & Freedman, J. L. Dissonance reduction and moral values. In P. Worchel & D. Byrne (Eds.), *Personality change.* New York: Wiley, 1964. Pp. 220–243.

Festinger, L., Riecken, H., & Schachter, S. *When prophecy fails.* Minneapolis: University of Minnesota Press, 1956.

Freedman, J. L. Attitudinal effects of inadequate justification. *Journal of Personality,* 1963, **31**, 371–385.

Freedman, J. L. Long-term behavioral effects of cognitive dissonance. *Journal of Experimental Social Psychology,* 1965, **1**, 145–155.

Gerard, H. B., & Mathewson, G. C. The effects of severity of initiation on liking for a group: A replication. *Journal of Experimental Social Psychology,* 1966, **2**, 278–287.

Jecker, J. D. The cognitive effects of conflict and dissonance. In L. Festinger, *Conflict, decision, and disso-*

nance. Stanford, Calif.: Stanford University Press, 1964. Pp. 21–32.

Lawrence, D. H., & Festinger, L. *Deterrents and reinforcement.* Stanford, Calif.: Stanford University Press, 1962.

Lewis, M. Some nondecremental effects of effort. *Journal of Comparative and Physiological Psychology,* 1964, **57,** 367–372.

McGuire, W. J. Attitudes and opinions. *Annual Review of Psychology,* 1966, **17,** 475–514.

Mills, J., Aronson, E., & Robinson, H. Selectivity in exposure to information. *Journal of Abnormal and Social Psychology,* 1959, **59,** 205–253.

Scott, W. A. Attitude change through reward of verbal behavior. *Journal of Abnormal and Social Psychology,* 1957, **55,** 72–75.

Scott, W. A. Attitude change by response reinforcement: Replication and extension. *Sociometry,* 1959, **22,** 328–335.

Smith, E. E. The power of dissonance techniques to change attitudes. *Public Opinion Quarterly,* 1961, **25,** 626–639.

Turner, E. A., & Wright, J. Effects of severity of threat and perceived availability on the attractiveness of objects. *Journal of Personality and Social Psychology,* 1965, **2,** 128–132.

Walster, E., Berscheid, E., & Barclay, A. M. A determinant of preference among modes of dissonance reduction. *Journal of Personality and Social Psychology,* 1967, **7,** 211–216.

Zajonc, R. B. Balance, congruity and dissonance. *Public Opinion Quarterly,* 1960, **24,** 280–296.

Zimbardo, P. G. Involvement and communication discrepancy as determinants of opinion conformity. *Journal of Abnormal and Social Psychology,* 1960, **60,** 86–94.

Zimbardo, P. G. A critical analysis of Smith's "grasshopper" experiment. Unpublished manuscript, New York University, 1964.

Zimbardo, P. G. The effect of effort and improvisation on self-persuasion produced by role-playing. *Journal of Experimental Social Psychology,* 1965, **1,** 103–120.

ARTICLE 32

Decision Freedom as a Determinant of the Role of Incentive Magnitude in Attitude Change[1]

Darwyn E. Linder, Joel Cooper, and Edward E. Jones

If a person can be induced to behave publicly in a manner that does not follow from his private attitudes, he will experience cognitive dissonance. The magnitude of dissonance will be greater when there are few reasons for complying than when there are many reasons (Festinger, 1957). This dissonance may be reduced by an accommodating change in private attitude if other ways of reducing dissonance are not available. Thus a person who has been induced to behave in a counterattitudinal fashion will change his private attitude more the less he has been rewarded for complying. Festinger and Carlsmith (1959) found support for this proposition in a study in which subjects were persuaded (for $1 or $20) to extol the attractiveness of a dull and tedious task for the benefit of the next subject. Also, Cohen (1962) found that Yale students who were induced to write essays in favor of the New Haven police later showed more positive attitudes the smaller the incentive they had been offered to write the essay.

Rosenberg (1965) has recently questioned the generality of this proposed relationship and has suggested that subjects in the Festinger and Carlsmith (1959) and the Cohen (1962) experiments

must have considered the incentive excessive and, because of the "evaluation apprehension" that subjects in psychology experiments commonly feel, those in the high-incentive conditions may have interpreted the experiment as one testing their honesty and autonomy. To resist influence in the face of a substantial bribe, therefore, would cause the experimenter to evaluate them favorably. Alternatively, Rosenberg suggests that the subjects may have suspected deception in the high-incentive condition and angrily resisted confirming the perceived hypothesis. Either reaction might conceivably account for the obtained inverse relationship between incentive amount and degree of ultimate congruence between attitude and behavior.

Rosenberg proceeded to conduct an experiment loosely replicating Cohen's (1962), the major difference being that one experimenter provided the incentive for essay writing and another measured the subsequent attitude. The two tasks were presented to the subjects as unrelated, and thus there was presumably no chance for evaluation apprehension to affect the results. Rosenberg found that attitude and behavior were most congruent when subjects were offered $5 for writing essays and least in line when they were offered $.50. Rosenberg's results are clearly at variance with the apparent dissonance prediction and with the findings obtained by Cohen and by Festinger and Carlsmith. Instead, the results seem to favor a reinforcement position or, as Ro-

Reprinted from *Journal of Personality and Social Psychology,* 1967, **6,** 245–254, with the permission of the authors and the American Psychological Association.

[1]This experiment was facilitated by National Science Foundation Grant 8857. We are indebted to H. B. Gerard for his valuable suggestions.

senberg would prefer, a theoretical position that considers the effects of reinforcement in the context of an affect-cognition consistency model. In Rosenberg's view, either the expectation or the receipt of reward strengthens and stabilizes the cognitions associated with the counterattitudinal statement—the greater the reward, the greater the stabilizing effect. There is then a change in attitudinal affect in the interests of cognitive-affective consistency.

Nuttin (1964) carefully replicated Rosenberg's experiment and found that—even with evaluation apprehension removed in the same manner —inferred attitude change varied inversely with the amount of incentive offered. While Nuttin's results were of only borderline significance, they clearly offered more support for the dissonance proposition than for the counterproposition reflecting reinforcement theory. Aronson (1966) has criticized Rosenberg's reasoning and his conclusions on many different grounds. Perhaps his most telling criticism was that Rosenberg should have tried to reproduce the inverse incentive effects previously attributed to dissonance theory by adding conditions to his design in which the same experimenter called for the essay and measured the subsequent attitude. Aronson argued that there were many differences between the Cohen experiment and the Rosenberg replication, and to assume that his results reversed the dissonance proposition solely because evaluation apprehension was removed is unwarranted.

The fact remains that Rosenberg (1965) was able to obtain a positive relationship between amount of incentive and inferred attitude change, and the intriguing empirical and theoretical problem is how to account for the fact that both dissonance and reinforcement effects have been found within the forced-compliance paradigm. Carlsmith, Collins, and Helmreich (1966) have predicted and successfully produced these opposing effects in a context approximating the original Festinger and Carlsmith (1959) study. When the subject was induced to describe the task as attractive to the next "unsuspecting subject," the former's subsequent task-attractiveness ratings were more positive in low- than in high-incentive con-

ditions. When the subject was instead asked to write an essay praising the task, portions of which might later be used by the experimenter, rated attractiveness varied directly with the amount of incentive offered. Carlsmith et al. argued that amount of incentive will relate directly to attitude change (a reinforcement effect) whenever the dissonance involved in a counterattitudinal act is minimal. The subject who complied in the essay-writing conditions of their experiment had a number of legitimate reasons for doing so, and the experimenter, the only person to read the essay, knew full well that the essay did not express the subject's private opinion. Dissonance should be much greater in the conditions requiring the subject to dupe another person like himself.

The Carlsmith et al. (1966) experiment is especially important because of the care with which it was conducted, the clear replication of the Festinger and Carlsmith (1959) results it provides, and the separate elicitation of both dissonance and reinforcement effects within the same general design. But while they may account for the Rosenberg reinforcement effect, Carlsmith et al. are left without any clear explanation for Cohen's (1962) results. After all, he required an essay rather than a deceitful confrontation with another subject and obtained dissonance rather than reinforcement effects. One could argue that attitudes toward the New Haven police are likely to be more central and important than attitudes toward a boring task, and thus a counterattitudinal essay is more inherently dissonant in the former case. Or, one could argue that the subjects in Cohen's experiment were not really assured anonymity (as in Carlsmith et al.'s). Nevertheless, the empirical discrepancies existing in the forced-compliance literature are not entirely reconciled by the Carlsmith et al. study.

The major focus of these studies has been the relationship between the amount of incentive offered and subsequent attitude change, but a clear prediction from dissonance theory cannot be made unless the subject makes his decision to comply *after* considering the incentive magnitude. The incentive must be one of the conditions potentially affecting the decision to comply rather than a reward for having already so decided.

Both Cohen (1962) and Rosenberg (1965) reported that they took care to assure subjects that the decision to write the essay was entirely their own. It may be argued, however, that Rosenberg's major alteration of Cohen's procedure, the separation of the compliant-behavior setting from the attitude-measurement setting to eliminate evaluation apprehension, reduced his subjects' freedom not to comply. When Rosenberg's subjects arrived for the experiment, they found him busily engaged and were given the option of waiting for "15 or 20 minutes" or, as an afterthought, participating in "another little experiment some graduate student in education is doing." Professing to know little about this other experiment except that it "has to do with attitudes" and "I gather they have some research funds," Rosenberg did not pressure the subject into a decision, but let him decide for himself whether he wanted to participate or wait. Having made the decision to participate, each subject further strengthened his commitment by walking to the location of the second experiment. The choice then offered by the second experimenter was considerably less than a free one. Being already effectively committed, the subject would be more likely to treat the subsequent monetary offering as a bonus for prior compliance than as one of the conditions to be considered in making a free choice.

If the preceding argument is correct, Rosenberg's findings cannot be compared with Cohen's because different conditions prevailed in the two experiments when the counterattitudinal essays were written. Rosenberg inadvertently made it difficult for subjects not to comply and found that degree of attitude change was positively related to incentive magnitude, in support of a reinforcement position or an affective-cognitive consistency model (Rosenberg, 1960). In contrast to this, Cohen's procedure presented the choice not to comply as a more viable alternative and found that attitude change was inversely related to incentive magnitude, in support of a derivation from dissonance theory. A meaningful resolution of these discrepant findings would be to show that

the effects of incentive magnitude on attitude change are either direct or inverse, depending on the presence or absence of freedom not to comply. The first experiment to follow was conducted as a direct test of the role of such freedom to choose not to engage in counterattitudinal behavior.

EXPERIMENT I

Method

Attitude Issue and Subjects.   At the time of the first experiment a rather heated controversy was raging in the state of North Carolina concerning the wisdom of a law that forbade Communists and Fifth Amendment pleaders from speaking at state-supported institutions. On the basis of informal opinion sampling, fortified by the plausible expectation that students deplore implied restrictions on their own freedom to listen, we assumed that college-student subjects would be strongly opposed to speaker-ban legislation. The issue thus seemed comparable to "the actions of the New Haven police" (Cohen, 1962) and to a ban on Ohio State's participation in the Rose Bowl (Rosenberg, 1965).

Fifty-five introductory psychology students at Duke University served as subjects in the experiment. Forty subjects (15 males and 25 females) were randomly assigned to four experimental conditions[2]; 13 were subsequently assigned to a control condition. All experimental subjects were asked to write a "forceful and convincing essay" in favor of the speaker-ban law. After writing the essay, each subject was asked to indicate his opinion about the speaker-ban law by checking a point on a 31-point scale comparable to Cohen's (1962) and Rosenberg's (1965) measure. The scale read, "In my opinion the Speaker Ban Law of North Carolina is . . . ," followed by 31 horizontal dots with seven labels ranging from "not justified at all" to "completely justified." Subjects

[2]Two more experimental subjects were actually run whose data were not analyzed. One of these was obviously in favor of the speaker-ban law at the outset, and the other was the victim of experimenter error in presenting instructions.

in the control condition merely filled out the scale without having previously written a pro-speaker-ban essay.

Procedure and Design

The basic procedure was closely modeled after that of Cohen (1962) except that the subjects were recruited from the introductory psychology course and came individually to the laboratory, rather than being approached in their dormitory rooms. The experimenter introduced himself as a graduate student in psychology. In the *free-decision condition* he immediately said, "I want to explain to you what this task is all about. I want to make it clear, though, that the decision to perform the task will be entirely your own." In the *no-choice condition* he merely said, "I want to explain to you what this task that you have volunteered for is all about." He then proceeded in both conditions to provide the following rationale for the essay-writing task:

The Association of Private Colleges of the Southeast, of which Duke is a member, is considering the adoption of a uniform speaker policy that would be binding on its member schools. Before they can decide what kind of policy to adopt, if indeed they decide to adopt one, they have undertaken a large scale research program in order to help them understand what the issues really are. This study is part of that program. The APCSE is working through the Department of Psychology here at Duke and through the departments of psychology at other private schools in the area because of the access which the department has to a wide cross-section of students such as yourself who must participate in psychological experiments and because of the number of graduate students that are available to conduct research. We have found, from past experience, that one of the best ways to get relevant arguments on both sides of the issue is to ask people to write essays favoring only one side. We think we know pretty much how you feel about the student's rights in this matter. [Here the experimenter paused and waited for a comment that would confirm the subject's initial opinion opposing the speaker-ban law. Only one subject expressed a favoring opinion at this point; see Footnote 2.] Nonetheless, what we need now are essays favoring the speaker ban.

At this point, the free-decision and no-choice conditions again diverged. In the free-decision

condition the subjects were told that the APCSE was paying $.50 (low incentive) or $2.50 (high incentive) in addition to the standard experimental credit given to all subjects. The experimenter again stressed that the decision to write the essay was entirely up to the subject and that he would receive experimental credit in any case. In the no-choice condition the experimenter acted as if, naturally, the subject in volunteering for the experiment had committed himself to its requirements. He simply pointed out that the experiment involved writing a strong and forceful essay favoring the speaker-ban law. After the subject was handed a pencil and some paper, but before he began to write, the experimenter broke in: "Oh yes, I almost forgot to tell you. . . . The APCSE is paying all participants $.50 [or $2.50] for their time."

In all conditions subjects were paid, *before* they wrote the essay, the amount of money promised them. The experimenter then left the room and allowed the subject 20 minutes to complete his essay. When he returned, the experimenter collected the essay, administered the brief attitude scale, and interviewed the subject concerning his perceptions of the experiment. No subject indicated any suspicion regarding the true purpose of the experiment. The purpose was then explained to each in detail, and all deceptions were revealed. None of the subjects recalled having any doubts about the existence of the fictitious APCSE. Each subject was ultimately allowed to keep $1.50. Because they were made to realize that they were assigned by chance to the high-inducement condition, those who had initially received $2.50 were quite agreeable when asked to return $1 of their money. Subjects in the low-inducement condition were delighted to learn of their good fortune—that they would receive $1 more than they had bargained for.

Results

Before the results bearing on the central hypothesis are presented, it is of interest to note the difference in decision time in the two free-decision conditions. After the experimenter began to notice that *free decision* subjects in the low-incentive condition took much longer to make up their minds about writing the essay than *free-decision* subjects in the high-incentive condition, he started to record decision times with a hidden stopwatch. The last seven subjects in the low-incentive condition took an average of 25.29 seconds to reach a decision; the comparable mean for the last seven subjects in the high-incentive condition was 11.00 seconds. In spite of the reduced n, this difference is significant ($p < .025$, U test). This evidence strongly suggests that there was greater predecisional conflict in the low-incentive condition, and thus the conditions are appropriate for testing the dissonance hypothesis: since predecisional conflict leads to postdecisional dissonance (Festinger, 1964), more dissonance and hence more attitude change should occur in the free-decision—low-incentive condition.

After establishing that the means for female and male subjects were nearly identical ($t = .18$), the posttreatment attitude scores were placed in a simple 2 (for Degree of Decision Freedom) x 2 (for Level of Incentive) factorial design. The means for each condition are presented in Table 1. Scale values could range from 1.0 (antispeaker ban) to 7.0 (prospeaker ban). Table 2 summarizes the analysis of variance and appropriate orthogo-

TABLE 2. Summary of analysis of variance: Experiment I.

Source of variation	MS	F
Choice (A)	0.90	< 1
Incentive (B)	1.02	< 1
A × B	10.00	8.70[****]
Error	1.15	
Low incentive vs. high incentive within free-decision conditions	8.71	7.57[****]
Low incentive vs. high incentive within no-choice conditions	2.31	2.01[*]

Note.—Two-way analysis of experimental conditions.
[*]$p < .20$, $df = 1/36$.
[****]$p < .01$, $df = 1/36$.

nal comparisons. The prediction that the amount of inferred attitude change would relate positively to inducement level in the no-choice conditions and negatively in the free-decision conditions is clearly confirmed ($F_{1, 36} = 8.70$; $p < .01$). The dissonance effect in the free-decision condition was itself significant; the reinforcement effect in the prior-commitment condition was not. The control subjects, who checked the scale without writing an essay, were about as much against the speaker ban as subjects in the conditions where little or no change was predicted.

In an effort to shed light on possible mechanisms underlying these findings, the essays themselves were examined. The average number of words per essay was 192.3, and there were no significant differences among the four conditions in essay length. The essays were evaluated in a manner similar to that described by Rosenberg (1965). Two independent raters, blind as to the subject's condition, rated the essays in terms of the degree of organization manifested and the degree of "intent to persuade." Each of these ratings were made in terms of a 5-point scale. The judges agreed or were 1 point discrepant in 72% of the organization ratings and 85% of the persuasiveness ratings. These percentages of agreement were comparable to those obtained by Rosenberg (1965), but two independent judges using 5-point rating scales should, by chance, be no more than 1 point discrepant on more than 50% of their ratings. When a more traditional estimate of the reliability of the ratings was calculated (Winer, 1962, pp. 124 *ff.*), it was found that

TABLE 1. Attitude-scale means obtained in the five conditions: Experiment I.

	Incentive	
	$.50	$2.50
No choice	1.66[a]	2.34
Free decision	2.96	1.64
Control[b]	1.71	

Note.—$n = 10$ under both incentives for free-choice and free-decision conditions. For the control condition, $n = 13$.
[a]The higher the number, the more the speaker-ban law was considered to be justified.
[b]Since subjects in the control conditions were all run after the main experiment was completed, the mean for this condition is presented only as an estimate of student opinion toward the issue in the absence of dissonance or incentive effects. The data from the control condition were not included in the statistical analysis.

the reliability coefficient for the ratings of degree of organization was .54, and the coefficient for the ratings of persuasiveness was .55. These coefficients estimate the reliability of the ratings that result from averaging over the two judges. When these ratings were submitted to an analysis of variance, there were no differences among conditions in either organization or persuasiveness.

Since the reliability of the ratings discussed above was quite low, an attempt was made to obtain ratings of acceptably high reliability. Two varsity debate partners agreed to rate the essays. General criteria to be used in determining the ratings were discussed, but the ratings were made independently. Each essay was rated for the persuasiveness of the presentation on a 7-point scale. Sixty percent of these ratings were no more than 1 point discrepant; the reliability coefficient was .48. (The chance percentage for agreements or 1-point discrepancies is 39% when a 7-point scale is used by two independent judges.) There were again no differences among the conditions in the rating received. Also, no between-condition differences appeared on the ratings made by any individual judge.

Discussion

The major purpose of the present experiment was achieved: to show that dissonance and reinforcement effects can be obtained within the same forced compliance paradigm by varying the degree to which the subject is committed to comply before learning about the monetary incentive. Subjects who commit themselves after weighing the unpleasantness of the essay-writing task against the amount of incentive offered show the effects predicted by dissonance theory. The decision-time data strongly suggest that the subjects do in fact consider the essay-writing task unpleasant. Subjects who are not free to decide against compliance and then learn about a financial "bonus" produce results in line with reinforcement theory (that which is associated with something of value itself takes on value) or in line with the more complex affective-cognitive consistency model espoused by Rosenberg.

The present study was stimulated by Rosenberg's (1965) experiment, but the relevance of the results to a critique of Rosenberg's conclusions rests on the claim that his way of removing evaluation apprehension precommitted the subject to an unpleasant task before he had a chance to weigh the incentive for compliance. If this criticism is valid, then it should be possible to reproduce Rosenberg's results by closely replicating his procedures, and to obtain the converse of these results (confirming the dissonance prediction) by insuring that the subject does not commit himself before being confronted with the incentive for compliance. A second experiment was planned in an attempt to do precisely this.

EXPERIMENT II

Method

Attitude Issue. As we prepared to run the second experiment, certain paternalistic policies of the Duke University administration were being challenged by the undergraduates, and there was a movement toward liberalization of *in loco parentis* social regulations. It was assumed, therefore, that undergraduates who were induced to write forceful and convincing essays in support of strict enforcement of *in loco parentis* policies would be performing a counterattitudinal task.

Subjects. Fifty-nine male introductory psychology students volunteered to participate for experimental credit in a study described as an "Attitude Survey." The data of 50 of these students, who were randomly assigned to the four experimental conditions and the control condition, were used in the reported analysis. Six subjects were eliminated because they did not complete the experimental procedure. Usually, they chose to read or study while waiting for the first experimenter rather than go to the second experimenter. Another subject was eliminated because he was initially in favor of strict *in loco parentis* policies, and writing the essay would not have been counterattitudinal for him.

Only two subjects who had completed the procedure were eliminated from the analysis. The first of these was excluded when it was discovered during the final interview that he had misinterpreted the attitude questionnaire. The second was eliminated because he accurately perceived the true purpose of the experiment. Both subjects had been assigned to the *free-decision—high-incentive condition*. The results of the study are not changed if these two subjects are included in the analysis.

Procedure and Design. The procedure was a close approximation to that used by Rosenberg (1965). All subjects reported to the office of the first experimenter (E_1) where they found E_1 engaged in conversation with another student and were told, "I'm sorry, but I'm running late on my schedule today, and I'll have to keep you waiting for about 15 or 20 minutes. Is that all right?" All subjects agreed to wait.

Each experimental subject was then told:

Oh, I've just thought of something; while you're waiting you could participate in another little experiment that some graduate student in education is doing. This fellow called me the other day and said he needed volunteers in a hurry for some sort of study he's doing —I don't know what it's about exactly except that it has to do with attitudes and that's why he called me, because my research is in a similar area as you'll see later. Of course, he can't give you any credit but I gather they have some research funds and they are paying people instead. So, if you care to do that, you can.

At this point, one-half of the experimental subjects (*prior-commitment condition*) were allowed to leave for the second experiment without further comment by E_1. Since it was believed that Rosenberg's procedure restricted subjects' freedom not to comply with the task of the "little experiment," it was decided to manipulate degree of choice by removing this restriction. Thus, for subjects in the *free-decision* condition, after the subject had agreed to participate in the second experiment, E_1 added:

All I told this fellow was that I would send him some subjects if it was convenient but that I couldn't obligate my subjects in any way. So, when you get up there, listen to what he has to say and feel free to decide from there.

All experimental subjects then reported to the second experimenter (E_2). To control for the effects of experimenter bias, E_2 was not informed whether the subject was in the prior-commitment condition or the free-decision condition. E_2 presented himself as a graduate student in the Department of Education and introduced the essay-writing task using a procedure that, as in Experiment I, very closely approximated Cohen's (1962).

Rather than the free-decision versus no-choice manipulation of Experiment I, E_2 began by saying to all subjects, "At the present time, Duke University is beginning to question the wisdom of assuming the role of 'substitute parent' to its students." From that point, the instructions paralleled those of Experiment I with the substitution of *in loco parentis* regulations for the speaker-ban law. After confirming that the subject held an opinion opposed to rigid *in loco parentis* regulations, E_2 concluded:

What we need now are essays favoring a strict enforcement of *in loco parentis*. So, what we would like you to do—if you are willing[3]—is to write the strongest, most forceful and most convincing essay that you can in favor of a strict enforcement of the substitute parent concept here at Duke.

It was then explained that the sponsoring agency was offering either $.50 (*low-incentive* conditions) or $2.50 (*high-incentive* conditions) for participation in the study. When the subject agreed to write the essay, he was paid the money promised to him and then began the task.

After completing the essay and being thanked and dismissed by E_2, all experimental subjects returned to E_1's office. To introduce the dependent measure, E_1 explained:

What I had wanted you to do was participate in a continuing study I carry on every semester as a sort of Gallup poll to keep a check on opinion patterns on different University issues. I'd like you to fill out this questionnaire as an objective indication of your opinions and when you've finished I'd like to chat for a while about various issues on campus. OK?

[3]This vague statement of choice was given to all subjects in order to keep the instructions constant across experimental groups and to enable E_2 to remain "blind" as to the condition of each subject. It was assumed that the crucial manipulation of free decision versus prior commitment had already been accomplished by E_1.

E_1 was not informed of the amount of money the subject had received, and in no case did he find out until after the subject had completed the dependent measure.

The dependent measure consisted of an eight-item questionnaire dealing with various university issues. The critical item read, "How justified is the University's policy of assuming parental responsibilities for its students?" and was accompanied by the familiar 31-point scale. When the subject had completed the questionnaire, E_1 put it aside (without looking at the responses) and began a structured interview that included probes for suspicion and checks on perceptions of the manipulations. When E_1 was satisfied that the subject had not perceived the true purpose of the experiment, he revealed the deceptions and explained the necessity for them. As in Experiment I, all experimental subjects agreed to accept $1.50 for their time.

Subjects assigned to the control condition also found E_1 engaged in conversation and were asked if they could return in 15 or 20 minutes. Upon their return they were treated exactly as experimental subjects.

These procedures resulted in five conditions: two levels of incentive magnitude under a condition of free decision, the same two levels under a condition of prior commitment, and the control condition.

Results

The mean attitude-scale scores on the critical item for each of the five conditions are presented in Table 3. It can be seen that the results are very similar to those of Experiment I. The data were submitted to a one-way analysis of variance, summarized in Table 4. The overall treatment effect was significant ($F_{4,45} = 4.02$; $p < .01$). The two comparisons reflecting the hypotheses of this study were also significant: Within the free-decision conditions a low incentive produced more inferred attitude change than a high incentive ($F_{1,45} = 6.82$; $p < .025$). Within the prior-commitment conditions this effect was reversed, and a high incentive produced more inferred attitude change than a low incentive ($F_{1,45} = 4.90$; $p <$

.05). The position of the control group indicates that differences between the experimental conditions resulted from positive attitude change rather than a combination of positive and negative changes.

TABLE 3.   Attitude-scale means obtained in the five conditions: Experiment II.

	Incentive	
	$.50	$2.50
Prior commitment	2.68[a]	3.46
Free decision	3.64	2.72
Control	2.56	

Note.—n = 10 in all conditions.
[a]The higher the number, the more strict application of *in loco parentis* regulations was considered justified.

TABLE 4.   Summary of analysis of variance: Experiment II.

Source of variation[a]	MS	F
Treatment	2.49	4.02[****]
Error	.62	
Low incentive vs. high incentive free-decision conditions	4.23	6.82[***]
Low incentive vs. high incentive prior-commitment conditions	3.04	4.90[**]

Note.—One-way analysis of five conditions.
[a]The control condition differs significantly from both the prior-commitment–high-incentive and the free-decision–low-incentive conditions.
[**]$p < .05$, df = 1/45.
[***]$p < .025$, df = 1/45.
[****]$p < .01$, df = 4/45.

Once again we attempted to investigate the possibility that these effects were mediated by some aspect of the counterattitudinal performance. Two raters, working independently and without knowledge of the experimental conditions, rated each essay on 7-point scales for the extremity of attitudinal position advocated, the persuasiveness of the essay, and its degree of organization. The two raters agreed or were within 1 point of each other for 65% of the essays when estimating the attitudinal position, 60% when rating them for persuasiveness, and 52.5% when rating them for organization. The reliability coefficient for the estimated attitudinal position

(Winer, 1962, pp. 124 *ff.*) was .67, the coefficient for the persuasiveness ratings was .51, and the coefficient for the organization ratings was .38. There were no differences among conditions on any of these ratings. The essays were then rated for the persuasiveness of the presentation on a 7-point scale by the same varsity debaters as had rated the essays from Experiment I. The debaters agreed or were within 1 point of each other for 65% of the essays, and the reliability coefficient was a somewhat more acceptable .71. Again, however, there were no differences among conditions on these ratings, whether the judges' ratings were averaged or each judge's ratings were examined separately. In a final attempt to find a performance difference among the conditions the number of words in each essay was counted; the conditions were compared on this measure of performance and were found not to differ from one another.

Discussion

The results of Experiment II support the argument that Rosenberg's (1965) procedure for the elimination of evaluation apprehension committed his subjects to perform the essay-writing task before they learned of the nature of the task and the amount of reward offered. The positive relationship between incentive magnitude and attitude change in the prior-commitment conditions of the present experiment replicates the no-choice results of Experiment I and the relationship found by Rosenberg (1965). It could be argued on this basis alone that such procedures as Rosenberg's have the same effect as allowing the subject no choice concerning performance of the counterattitudinal act. The argument becomes much more convincing, however, if it can be shown that appropriate alteration of Rosenberg's procedure, reducing the prior commitment of the subject, leads to an *inverse* relationship between incentive magnitude and attitude change. The free-decision conditions of Experiment II demonstrate precisely this point: when the subject does not feel that he has previously committed himself to performance of the counterattitudinal action requested by E_2, attitude change is an inverse function of incentive magnitude.

It should be noted here that a "balanced replication" (Aronson, 1966) of Rosenberg's (1965) study was required. Had Experiment II included only the free-decision conditions it would be possible to argue that our procedure was not successful in eliminating evaluation apprehension and that the results reflected once again the effect of this contaminant in research on forced compliance. The results of the prior-commitment conditions of Experiment II, however, counter this criticism. A persistent critic might still argue that the free-decision manipulation reintroduced evaluation apprehension. Perhaps the comment added to create the free-decision condition in some way increased the chances that subjects would see the experiments as related. However, the structured interview conducted by E_1 revealed no differential level of suspicion between the prior-commitment and free-decision conditions. In the absence of a reliable and valid measure of evaluation apprehension, we can do no more than contend that our interview was sensitive enough to detect suspicion and that we found no indication of differential suspicion among the conditions.

The results of the two studies reported above imply that the discrepancy between Cohen's (1962) findings and the results of Rosenberg's (1965) experiment may indeed be resolved in the manner indicated earlier in this paper. For Cohen's subjects the decision not to comply was a viable alternative at the time they were confronted with the essay-writing task and offered an incentive of certain value. Under such conditions dissonance will be induced whenever the incentive is not large enough to justify performance of the task, and incentive magnitude will be inversely related to subsequent attitude change. However, if a subject's freedom not to comply has been restricted before he is confronted with the task and with a clear description of the incentive, dissonance cannot be induced by an incentive of insufficient magnitude. Under these conditions, the reinforcing properties of the incentives will lead to a positive relationship between incentive magnitude and attitude change. Although Rosenberg (1965) demonstrated such a relationship, his assertion that it may be obscured by failure to remove evaluation apprehension seems no longer tenable. No attempt was made in the procedure of Experiment I to remove evaluation apprehension, and yet the results are very similar to the results of Experiment II.

Rosenberg (1966) has more recently advanced two additional hypotheses intended to resolve discrepancies in the forced-compliance literature. The first of these is that we must distinguish counterattitudinal actions that are simple and overt from those featuring the elaboration of a set of arguments. Supposedly a performance of the former kind (e.g., eating a disliked food) will lead to the inverse relationship between attitude change and incentive magnitude, while an act of the latter kind (e.g., writing a counterattitudinal essay) will result in a positive relationship. The second hypothesis is that we must distinguish between two kinds of counterattitudinal performances: (a) those carried out under instructions that lead the subject to believe his performance will be used to deceive others, and (b) those following from instructions to elaborate, for some reasonable and legitimate purpose, a set of arguments opposite to his private opinion. It is hypothesized that even if the actual task is the same, say essay writing, the first type of instruction will lead to an inverse relationship between incentive magnitude and attitude change, and the second type of instruction will lead to a positive relationship.

In the studies reported above the subject's task was presented with no hint that his performance would be used to deceive anyone, and the task in all cases was to elaborate a set of arguments opposite to his own opinion. It follows from the two hypotheses suggested by Rosenberg (1966) and presented above that we should not have been able to obtain the inverse relationship between incentive magnitude and attitude change using our procedures. However, in both experiments, we obtained the positive *and* the inverse relationship. We are forced to conclude that neither the "simple versus complex" hypothesis nor the "duplicity versus legitimate" hypothesis can account for the present results.

In place of these hypotheses we conclude that at least some of the discrepancies in the forced-

compliance literature may be resolved by closer attention to the role of decision freedom at the time the incentive is offered. A barely sufficient incentive for making counterattitudinal statements *does* result in dissonance and subsequent attitude change if the subject feels he is quite free not to comply. When the freedom not to comply is removed or markedly decreased, on the other hand, attitude change is greater the greater the incentive for compliance.

REFERENCES

Aronson, E. The psychology of insufficient justification. In S. Feldman (Ed.), *Cognitive consistency: Motivational antecedents and behavioral consequents.* New York: Academic Press, 1966. Pp. 115–133.

Carlsmith, J. M., Collins, B. E., & Helmreich, R. L. Studies in forced compliance: I. The effect of pressure for compliance on attitude change produced by face-to-face role playing and anonymous essay writing. *Journal of Personality and Social Psychology,* 1966, **4,** 1–13.

Cohen, A. R. An experiment on small rewards for discrepant compliance and attitude change. In J. W. Brehm & A. R. Cohen, *Explorations in cognitive dissonance.* New York: Wiley, 1962. Pp. 73–78.

Festinger, L. *A theory of cognitive dissonance.* Evanston, Ill.: Row, Peterson, 1957.

Festinger, L. *Conflict, decision, and dissonance.* Stanford: Stanford University Press, 1964.

Festinger, L., & Carlsmith, J. M. Cognitive consequences of forced compliance. *Journal of Abnormal and Social Psychology,* 1959, **58,** 203–210.

Nuttin, J. M., Jr. Dissonant evidence about dissonance theory. Paper read at 2nd conference of experimental social psychologists in Europe, Frascati, Italy, 1964. (Mimeo)

Rosenberg, M. J. An analysis of affective-cognitive consistency. In C. I. Hovland & M. J. Rosenberg (Eds.), *Attitude organization and change.* New Haven: Yale University Press, 1960. Pp. 15–64.

Rosenberg, M. J. When dissonance fails: On eliminating evaluation apprehension from attitude measurement. *Journal of Personality and Social Psychology,* 1965, **1,** 28–42.

Rosenberg, M. J. Some limits of dissonance: Toward a differentiated view of counter-attitudinal performance. In S. Feldman (Ed.), *Cognitive consistency: Motivational antecedents and behavioral consequents.* New York: Academic Press, 1966. Pp. 135–170.

Winer, B. J. *Statistical principles in experimental design.* New York: McGraw-Hill, 1962.

ARTICLE 33

The Case for Nonconsistency

Daryl J. Bem

Up to this point, I have tried to state the strongest possible case for the thesis that men do not merely subscribe to a random collection of beliefs and attitudes but rather possess coherent *systems* of beliefs and attitudes which are internally and psychologically consistent. I have even implied that whenever an individual's beliefs and attitudes appear to be inconsistent, if we would only look deeper into the basic premises of his belief system, consistency will be forthcoming.

We have seen that the consistency theorists themselves have taken the further step of postulating that men possess a drive toward cognitive consistency. As I have done, these theorists emphasize that this consistency is most often psychological rather than logical, and they are alert to the nonrationality of some of the strategies which individuals often employ to attain consistency. In addition, consistency theorists do not claim that individuals need to be aware of the inconsistencies in order to be motivated toward consistency. The consistency theorists are thus quite flexible, and collectively they have marshaled an impressive amount of evidence to document their main hypothesis that inconsistency motivates belief and attitude change. Indeed, a recently published book called *Theories of Cognitive Consistency: A Sourcebook* (known affectionately by the in-group as TOCCAS) contains 84 chapters, 830 pages of text, 41 pages of references (about 1000 references), and more about cognitive consistency than almost anyone would

care to know (Abelson, Aronson, McGuire, Newcomb, Rosenberg, & Tannenbaum, 1968). Inconsistency, they seem to be trying to tell us, motivates belief and attitude change.

But I don't believe it. At least not very much. In my view, a vision of inconsistency as a temporary turbulence in an otherwise fastidious pool of cognitive clarity is all too misleading. My own suspicion is that inconsistency is probably our most enduring cognitive commonplace. That is, I suspect that for most of the people most of the time and for all the people some of the time inconsistency just sits there. I think that we academic psychologists, including the consistency theorists, probably spend too much time with bright college students who are as eager to achieve a respectable overall unity in their cognitions as we, their instructors, are eager to impress them and ourselves with the same admirable coherence of thought. We have already seen that we psychologists are well represented in the population of liberal-intellectuals who are willing to spend restless nights agonizing over the apparent inconsistencies between integration and black power, and you will find us striving for cognitive quiescence on similar dilemmas at any meeting of the American Civil Liberties Union. I believe, in short, that there is more inconsistency on earth (and probably in heaven) than is dreamt of in our psychological theories.

Psychologists and political scientists who have analyzed the public mind outside the laboratory have arrived at similar conclusions. For example, Herbert McClosky, a man who has spent much time trying to understand the political attitudes of Americans, has said, "As intellectuals and students of politics we are disposed by training and sensibility to take political ideas seriously. . . . We are therefore prone to forget that most people take them less seriously than we do, that they pay little attention to issues, rarely worry about the consistency of their opinions, and spend little or no time thinking about the values, presuppositions and implications which distinguish one political orientation from another." (Quoted by Abelson, 1968.) Let me illustrate.

LIBERALS OR
CONSERVATIVES?

Lloyd Free, a pollster and political analyst, and Hadley Cantril, a social psychologist, have conducted a large-scale study of the political beliefs of Americans (1967). Using the resources of the Gallup polling organization, these two men in 1964 interviewed over 3,000 people representing a cross-section of the American public. One of their purposes was to study the nature of liberalism and conservatism, both at a practical, or operational, level and at a more ideological level. First they constructed a five-item questionnaire to identify what they called operational liberalism and conservatism. It covered most of the controversial "welfare" programs of the Democratic administration then in office, including federal aid to education, Medicare, federal low-rent housing programs, urban renewal programs, and federal attempts to reduce unemployment. An individual was then defined as completely or predominantly liberal if he favored all or all but one of the programs on which he had an opinion. To qualify as completely or predominantly conservative, an individual had to oppose all or all but one of the programs on which he had an opinion. Others, providing that they had an opinion on at least three of the programs, were labeled as "middle-of-the-road."

The American public distributed itself as follows:

Completely or predominantly liberal   65%
Middle-of-the-road   21%
Completely or predominantly conservative 14%

In other words, about two thirds of the American public qualified as "liberal" with respect to the favoring of specific government programs; and within the liberal category itself, over two thirds of the individuals were "completely liberal" in that they favored all the government programs about which they had an opinion. As the table shows, only 14% of the American public could be labeled conservative at the operational level.

These results are in line with previous polls which show that the American public has been "liberal" in this sense at least since the days of the New Deal three decades ago. Even though "conservative" shifts of other kinds have occasionally intervened (e.g., with respect to civil rights activity) and though the 1966 and 1968 elections were interpreted by some as a trend toward conservatism, the general liberal trend toward welfare programs has never changed. Thus, a poll in February, 1967, showed that 54% of the American public favored even the controversial Community Action programs to combat poverty. The Head Start schooling program for young children was favored by 67%, and federally financed job training was endorsed by 75% of the American public; majorities also opposed any reduction in current programs involving federal grants for low-income housing and for welfare and relief payments. When it comes right down to the specifics of the welfare state, Americans are, for the most part, "liberals."

But what about ideology? What about the conservatives who supported Barry Goldwater in 1964 or voted for the conservative candidates in 1966 and 1968? Surely more than 14% of the American people are "conservative." And surely they are, as Free and Cantril discovered on a second questionnaire designed to identify not operational, but ideological, liberals and conservatives by asking the following questions:

1.   The federal government is interfering too much in state and local matters.
2.   The government has gone too far in regulating business and interfering with the free enterprise system.
3.   Social problems here in this country could be solved more effectively if the government would only keep its hands off and let people in local com-

TABLE 1. Comparison of results on ideological and operational scales. (Adapted from Free & Cantril, 1967, p. 32.)

	Ideological Scale	Operational Scale
Completely or predominantly liberal	16%	65%
Middle-of-the-road	34%	21%
Completely or predominantly conservative	50%	14%

munities handle their own problems in their own ways.

4. Generally speaking, any able-bodied person who really wants to work in this country can find a job and earn a living.

5. We should rely more on individual initiative and ability and not so much on governmental welfare programs.

A person had to disagree with all or all but one of the statements on which he had an opinion to qualify as completely or predominantly liberal on this "ideological" scale. To be defined as completely or predominantly conservative, he had to agree with all or all but one of the items on which he had an opinion. Others were classified as middle-of-the-road if they had an opinion on at least three statements. Table 1 shows the results of the ideological part of the survey in comparison with the operational part.

As we see, a very different picture emerges. Half the American public is conservative in ideology, whereas only 14% of the American public would have the government pull out of any of its major welfare activities. Conversely, whereas 65% of Americans are liberal at the operational level, only 16% were either completely or predominantly liberal ideologically. Somebody here has cognitive schizophrenia.

We can identify that "somebody" by combining the results of the survey into a single table which shows how each group on the ideological scale stood on the operational scale.

Table 2 shows that 90% of the ideological liberals also qualified as liberals on the operational scale, but among ideological conservatives almost half (46%) proved to be operational liberals! Another way of stating this result is to say that nearly one out of every four Americans (23%, that is, 46% of 50%) is an ideological conservative and at the same time an operational liberal. Barry Goldwater might have fared much better in 1964 if he could have attacked government programs in general while avoiding mention of any program in particular. The Republicans had apparently learned this lesson well by 1968, when Richard Nixon continued to make many ideologically conservative statements, just like those on the questionnaire, while at the same time proposing such things as increased Social Security benefits.

There is one flaw in the Free-Cantril study. Perhaps you noticed that the way all the questions were worded, anyone who agreed or approved of statements on the operational scale would be classified as "liberal" whereas anyone who agreed with statements on the ideological

TABLE 2. Operational scale and ideological scale combined. (Adapted from Free & Cantril, 1967; p. 37.)

	Ideological Scale		
	Liberal	Middle-of-the-road	Conservative
Operational Scale			
Liberal	90%	78%	46%
Middle-of-the-road	9%	18%	28%
Conservative	1%	4%	26%

scale would be classified as "conservative." Consequently, a person who tends to agree with any plausible-sounding statement without examining it critically would automatically end up being inconsistent in this study. Indeed, research shows that such individuals do exist; they are called "yea-sayers" (Couch & Keniston, 1960). I think it is quite likely that many of the individuals in the Free-Cantril study who ended up being classified as both ideological conservatives and operational liberals were simply pleasant people who tended to agree with anything the nice man said that seemed reasonable; they were yea-sayers. Perhaps it is more accurate to say that such people are nonconsistent or nonlogical rather than that they are inconsistent or illogical.

Of course, for purposes of my argument it doesn't matter why so many Americans ended up simultaneously as ideological conservatives and operational liberals. Whether they are truly inconsistent or simply nonconsistent (yea-sayers), the fact remains that at least 23% of the American people, unlike the intellectuals who make up consistency theories, "pay little attention to issues, rarely worry about the consistency of their opinions, and spend little or no time thinking about the values, presuppositions and implications which distinguish one political orientation from another."

Thus, I would suggest that consistency theories are all right in their place, but what we need is a good theory of nonconsistency. And when such needs arise, I consult Robert Abelson, the psychologist with theories for all occasions.[1]

OPINION MOLECULES: TOWARD A THEORY OF NONCONSISTENCY

Abelson (1968) suggests that an individual's beliefs and attitudes are often composed of encapsulated, isolated "opinion molecules." Each

[1] Abelson has already been cited in this book as one of the men who coined the word psycho-logic, as the discoverer of alternative strategies for removing inconsistency, and as an editor of the cognitive consistency sourcebook. He is often considered to be a consistency theorist. Fortunately, he would rather be right than consistent.

molecule is made up of (1) a belief, (2) an attitude, and (3) a perception of social support for them. Or, as Abelson likes to put it, each opinion molecule contains a fact, a feeling and a following. For example: "It's a fact that when my Uncle Charlie had back trouble, he was cured by a chiropractor [*fact*]. You know, I feel that chiropractors have been sneered at too much [*feeling*], and I'm not ashamed to say so because I know a lot of people who feel the same way [*following*]." Or, "Nobody on this block wants to sell to Negroes [*following*], and neither do I [*feeling*]. The property values would decline [*fact*]."

Opinion molecules serve such a simple function that psychologists have usually ignored them. They are conversational units. They give us something coherent to say when a particular topic comes up in conversation. Accordingly, they do not need to have logical interconnections between them, and they are notoriously invulnerable to argument because of their isolated, molecular character. I suspect that the majority of our knowledge comes packed in little opinion molecules like these, just waiting for the topic to come up.

In conclusion: (1) It's a fact that there is more nonconsistency in heaven and earth than is dreamt of in our psychological theories; (2) I feel that the "opinion molecule" theory applies even to intellectuals—more often than they would like to think; and (3) I'm not ashamed to say so because I know Robert Abelson feels the same way.

REFERENCES

Abelson, R. P. Computers, polls, and public opinion—Some puzzles and paradoxes. *Trans-action,* September 1968, **5**, 20–27.

Abelson, R. P., Aronson, E., McGuire, W. J., Newcomb, T. M., Rosenberg, M. J., & Tannenbaum, P. H. (Eds.) *Theories of cognitive consistency: A sourcebook.* Chicago: Rand-McNally, 1968.

Couch, A., & Keniston, K. Yeasayers and naysayers: Agreeing response set as a personality variable. *Journal of Abnormal and Social Psychology,* 1960, **60**, 151–174.

Free, L. A., & Cantril, H. *The political beliefs of Americans.* New Brunswick, N.J.: Rutgers University Press, 1967.

SECTION SUMMARY

As Shaw and Constanzo (1970) have pointed out, cognitive dissonance theory has been "tested, questioned, applied, modified, villified, accepted, and rejected" (p. 215). It has been hailed as the most important theoretical advance in recent social psychology, and it has been criticized as a research area characterized by poor methodology, inadequate definitions, and oversimplification (see Chapanis & Chapanis, 1964; Silverman, 1964).

Although the research evidence is very complex and sometimes apparently contradictory, some of the major propositions of cognitive dissonance theory have received impressively solid support. As Aronson mentions in the first article, in "free-choice" situations in which the subject must choose between two alternatives of approximately equal desirability to him, his evaluation of the chosen alternative will tend to rise and his evaluation of the nonchosen (rejected) alternative will tend to drop after he has made his choice. Interestingly, there is some evidence that a "regret phase" may sometimes exist, wherein the evaluation of the nonchosen alternative may rise immediately after the decision is made (Walster, 1964). However, as dissonance reduction through devaluing the nonchosen alternative goes into motion, this phase ends and the evaluation of the nonchosen alternative drops.

Research results also indicate that, if people undergo a great deal of trouble to gain admission to a group that turns out to be worthless and dull, they will experience dissonance stemming from the *disconfirmed expectancy* that the group would be valuable and interesting. This dissonance may be reduced by deciding that the group really is more interesting than it initially appeared (see Aronson & Mills, 1959; Gerard & Mathewson, 1966).

Research results concerning counterattitudinal behaviors (forced compliance) are quite complex, as the Linder, Cooper, and Jones article suggests. In brief, their research, coupled with that of Carlsmith, Collins, and Helmreich (1966) and others, suggests that whether or not a person feels free to comply (volition) is a crucial mediating variable.

When the subject feels relatively free to exercise his volition and is committed to the outcome of his behavior, the maximum amount of dissonance will be produced by counterattitudinal behavior. It is in this situation that the greatest amount of attitude change is likely to occur (Triandis, 1971, p. 83). In practical terms it appears that, if you wanted to use this paradigm as a means to change someone's attitude toward a given issue, the most effective technique would be to use as little incentive as is necessary to get him to undertake the counterattitudinal behavior, in a situation in which he still feels free to reject your request. The behavior itself should be of a type that encourages commitment (for example, making a public speech rather than writing an anonymous essay). (The importance of commitment was also discussed in Section 6 with reference to ways of inducing compliance with a request.)

In terms of the frame of reference proposed in the Section Introduction, cognitive dissonance theory and research have focused on situations involving "internal satisfaction"—more specifically, cognitive consistency. Despite the misgivings Bem expresses in his article, it appears that, for most people in most situations, consistency between cognitive elements is, in some sense, "satisfying." It is also clear that cognitive inconsistency *can* function as a strong motivation toward attitude change to reduce the inconsistency. It is also clear, however, that sometimes inconsistency "just sits there," in Bem's words. And it may "sit there" more frequently for some people than for others. We should note here that Bem (1967, 1972) has suggested an alternative way of interpreting the results of many cognitive dissonance experiments. Bem's *self-perception theory* proposes that the individual, in identifying his own internal states, partially relies on the same external cues that *others* use when they infer his internal states. Suppose a person finds himself in a situation like that described in the Linder, Cooper, and Jones article: he feels relatively free to refuse to undertake a counterattitudinal action, he is receiving only a small incentive for undertaking it, and yet he does choose to undertake it. Both Bem and Linder et al. would expect subsequent attitude change to take place. But this change occurs, Bem proposes, not because of the arousal of an aversive state of dissonance, but because of a more passive process of self-perception. The person observes his own behavior and may think "I did that for very little reward when I was free to refuse. I must be more favorable to that position than I thought." Therefore his attitude changes in the direction of the counterattitudinal behavior. This way of looking at things has precipitated a lively controversy between Bem and cognitive dissonance theorists.

In addition to the interpretive problems suggested by self-perception theory, dissonance theory has been faced with other theoretical problems. One such problem is that, at least at present, there is no way of measuring dissonance directly. The presence of dissonance must be *inferred* from knowledge of the situation in which a person finds himself, the strength and quality of his relevant cognitions, and his behavior. Suppose you set up a study to see if dissonance causes subjects to change their attitudes in the direction predicted by dissonance theory. You find, however, that the subjects do *not* change their attitudes in your experiment. Does this mean that the theoretical predictions are incorrect in this situation—that is, that dissonance did not cause attitude change? Or do your results indicate that your experimental situation simply failed to create the state of dissonance in your subjects that you thought it would? From the results of your study alone, you cannot tell. A few of the researchers in the early 1960s simply assumed that, when subjects failed to show the expected attitude change, this was evidence that dissonance had not been aroused. Therefore they omitted these subjects from their analysis. As several critics have vehemently pointed out (see Chapanis & Chapanis, 1964; Silverman, 1964), this is *not* methodologically permissible. (It is a nice way of making sure that your results support your predictions, though.)

As originally proposed, dissonance theory makes no provisions for individual differences (although Festinger was aware of the importance of this issue). It seems reasonable that the same situation can create different levels of dissonance in different people and, furthermore, that individuals will be able to tolerate different amounts of dissonance before feeling the need to reduce it.

Finally, as Aronson mentions, in any given situation there is usually more than one way for a person to reduce dissonance. What determines which *mode* of dissonance reduction any specific individual will choose? For further discussion of these points the interested reader should see the books by Kiesler, Collins, and Miller (1969, Chapters 4 and 5) and Insko (1967, Chapter 10).

One factor that may affect the mode of dissonance reduction chosen, as well as the amount of dissonance induced by any given situation, is the function or functions that the attitudes are serving, as outlined in the Section Introduction. For example, attitudes that are serving a function central to a person's self-concept (an ego-defensive or value-expressive function) may be particularly resistant to change, and a relatively high level of dissonance might need to be present before any change takes place. For attitudes serving a more "mundane" function (knowledge or social adjustment), a much smaller amount of dissonance may be sufficient to create meaningful attitude change.

At least some aspects of cognitive dissonance theory have received impressive research support. But are such notions relevant to everyday life and occurrences? We think so. An example could be in the area of racial attitudes and prejudice (see Section 9). It is a popular belief that "you can't legislate morality"—that is, that passage of new legislation such as civil rights laws will have no effect on the underlying attitudes of hostility and racial prejudice that make such laws necessary. This idea stems originally from William Graham Sumner (1906), one of the pioneers of sociology, who asserted around the turn of the twentieth century that mores and folkways were much stronger than formal laws: "stateways cannot change folkways."

Sumner's stand was clearly dominant in the legal position of the courts on racial matters for most of this country's history. In the 1896 decision of the Supreme Court (*Plessy vs. Ferguson*) that set the precedent for the separate-but-equal doctrine, the Court said: "Legislation is powerless to eradicate racial instincts or to abolish distinctions based upon physical differences, and the attempt to do so can only result in accentuating the difficulties of the present situation. . . . If one race is inferior to the other socially, the

Constitution of the United States cannot put them on the same plane." The argument has raged anew recently in debates about the efficacy of civil rights legislation.

The force of recent law (particularly, but not exclusively, since the 1954 *Brown vs. Board of Education* decision, which made *de jure* school segregation illegal) has been to ignore the problem of whether or not attitudes can be changed. Nevertheless, behavior and attitudes *have* changed, partially, at least, as a result of the statutes and court decisions. For example, in areas where parents have no choice about which public school their child attends, white parents whose children are attending integrated schools tend to be much more favorable toward integration than those whose children attend segregated schools, even in the same area of the country (Brigham & Weissbach, 1972, Chapter 7).

Changes in the law are one way in which attitudes toward minority groups may come to be changed. But what is it that legal change *does* that sometimes results in attitude change? As the reader may already have realized, both cognitive dissonance theory and self-perception theory suggest mechanisms by which such attitude change may occur. Suppose that parents believe in racial segregation and yet their child is legally "forced" (forced compliance) to attend an integrated school. Suppose also that, through a great deal of financial hardship, the parents *could* afford to scrape together enough money to send the child to a segregated private school, but that they have decided to use this hard-earned money for other things. Analyzed from a dissonance theory approach, the two cognitive elements (belief in segregation and knowledge that the child is attending an integrated school) are in conflict, and the parents are presumably in a state of dissonance. Since, in most cases, the parents cannot change the racial makeup of their child's school, the easiest route to dissonance reduction may be to change their beliefs (for example, "Well, maybe integration isn't so bad after all"). If this type of accommodation takes place on a widespread scale, then the attitudes of such parents when measured should show an appreciable change. And the public-opinion poll data suggest that this is indeed the case (see Brigham & Weiss-

back, 1972, Chapter 1). (The reader is encouraged to apply a self-perception theory analysis to the same situation.)

Cognitive dissonance theory will necessarily continue to undergo modifications such as those suggested by Aronson and by Linder et al. Research devoted to resolving the conflict with self-perception theory should also serve to clarify the area. As Deutsch and Krauss (1965, p. 76) have stated, "Undoubtedly Festinger would rather be stimulating than right. ... This attitude is entirely sensible. In the present stage of development of social psychology, no one is ever 'right' for very long." But by its simplicity and provocativeness, the theory of cognitive dissonance continues to stimulate new research that adds to our knowledge of how attitudes can be changed.

REFERENCES

Aronson, E., & Mills, J. The effect of severity of initiation on liking for a group. *Journal of Abnormal and Social Psychology,* 1959, **59,** 177–181.

Bem, D. J. Self-perception: An alternative interpretation of cognitive dissonance phenomena. *Psychological Review,* 1967, **74,** 183–200.

Bem, D. J. Self-perception theory. In L. Berkowitz (Ed.), *Advances in experimental social psychology,* Vol. 6. New York: Academic Press, 1972.

Brigham, J. C., & Weissbach, T. A. (Eds.) *Racial attitudes in America: Analyses and findings of social psychology.* New York: Harper & Row, 1972.

Carlsmith, J. M., Collins, B. E., & Helmreich, R. L. Studies in forced compliance: I. The effect of pressure for compliance on attitude change produced by face-to-face role-playing and anonymous essay writing. *Journal of Personality and Social Psychology,* 1966, **4,** 1–13.

Chapanis, N. P., & Chapanis, A. C. Cognitive dissonance: Five years later. *Psychological Bulletin,* 1964, **61,** 1–22.

Deutsch, M., & Krauss, R. M. *Theories in social psychology.* New York: Basic Books, 1965.

Gerard, H. B., & Mathewson, G. C. The effects of severity of initiation on liking for a group: A replication. *Journal of Experimental Social Psychology,* 1966, **2,** 278–287.

Insko, C. A. *Theories of attitude change.* New York: Appleton-Century-Crofts, 1967.

Kiesler, C. A., Collins, B. E., & Miller, N. *Attitude change: A critical analysis of theoretical approaches.* New York: Wiley, 1969.

Shaw, M. E., & Constanzo, P. R. *Theories of social psychology.* New York: McGraw-Hill, 1970.

Silverman, I. In defense of dissonance theory: Reply to

Chapanis and Chapanis. *Psychological Bulletin,* 1964, **62,** 205–209.

Sumner, W. G. *Folkways.* New York: Ginn, 1906.

Triandis, H. C. *Attitude and attitude change.* New York: Wiley, 1971.

Walster, E. The temporal sequence of post-decision processes. In L. Festinger (Ed.), *Conflict, decision and dissonance.* Stanford, Calif.: Stanford University Press, 1964. Pp. 112–128.

SUGGESTED READINGS FOR FURTHER STUDY

Abelson, R. P., Aronson, E., McGuire, W. J., Newcomb, T. M., Rosenberg, M. J., & Tannenbaum, P. H. *Theories of cognitive consistency: A sourcebook.* Chicago: Rand-McNally, 1968.

Bem, D. J. *Beliefs, attitudes, and human affairs.* Monterey, Calif.: Brooks/Cole, 1970.

Brehm, J. W., & Cohen, A. R. *Explorations in cognitive dissonance.* New York: Wiley, 1962.

Festinger, L. *Conflict, decision and dissonance.* Stanford, Calif.: Stanford University Press, 1964.

Insko, C. A. *Theories of attitude change.* New York: Appleton-Century-Croft, 1967.

Kiesler, C. A., Collins, B. E., & Miller, N. *Attitude change: A critical analysis of theoretical approaches.* New York: Wiley, 1969.

McGuire, W. J. The nature of attitudes and attitude change. In G. Lindzey and E. Aronson (Eds.), *The handbook of social psychology,* Vol. 3. Reading, Mass.: Addison-Wesley, 1969. Pp. 136–314.

Triandis, H. C. *Attitude and attitude change.* New York: Wiley, 1971.

Zimbardo, P., & Ebbesen, E. B. *Influencing attitudes and changing behavior.* Reading, Mass.: Addison-Wesley, 1969.

SECTION 12

The Attribution of Attitudes and Emotional States

In social situations each of us is constantly attempting to understand the behaviors of others and to infer from these behaviors the underlying characteristics of the other person. As Fritz Heider (1944, 1958) has pointed out, all of us would like to be able to structure our worlds so that interactions with others would be more likely to have favorable outcomes for us. The success of such structuring depends at least in part on our ability to infer other people's dispositions (for example, attitudes, personality traits) and hence predict their behavior. When a customer approaches a used-car salesman, the salesman may use the other's behavior to "size him up" and make judgments about his degree of gullibility or sophistication (as well as how much cash he has). On the basis of this inferring of dispositions, the salesman designs the specific "sales pitch" he will use with that customer.

Attribution theory has been developed by social psychologists to deal with this process of analyzing the actions of others. One of the purposes of this section is to investigate the ways in which social psychologists have studied the attribution of others' attitudes from their behavior.

But it is not just the behavior of others that people are always trying to understand. We also seek an explanation for *our own reactions.* Let us say that a male college student, as a part of a campus dramatic production, has to play a love scene with a young woman he does not particularly like. As he does so, his fiancee and many others in the audience watch. He finds that he is sweating, his face is flushed, his heart is beating fast. Clearly his behavior is emotional. But what emotion is he experiencing? Embarrassment? Guilt? Lust? Anxiety? Or a combination of several of these?

We could ask this young man to label the emotion. He doubtless could do so, and his labeling would represent another type of attribution: the attribution of one's *own* emotional state. In recent years there has been a large body of research, generated by the work of Stanley Schachter (1964; Schachter & Singer, 1962; Schachter & Wheeler, 1962), that seeks to understand how we determine the particular label we use for our own

343

behavior, particularly our emotional behavior. This section will explore this topic also. In many ways the attribution of causes to other's behavior and to our own emotional reactions reflects the same process.

To return to our earlier analysis of the actions of others, we conclude that people are disposed toward a *causal analysis.* According to Heider, most of us feel that we control and determine at least part of our actions, and we also perceive others to have similar powers of control. Thus we seek to understand the causes of events so that we are better prepared to predict future events. If the behavior of someone else (referred to as the "target person") can be seen as caused by a *disposition* that he or she has (such as a tendency to be shy or a way of always disagreeing with others) then knowledge of this disposition enables the observer to predict the target person's behavior in subsequent situations in which the particular disposition may be relevant.

But we must not neglect the realization that not only dispositions but also external, environmental conditions affect one's behavior. In Heider's model the resultant behavior is seen as a function of environmental forces plus personal forces. Environmental forces are those characteristics present in the situation that "press" for a specific type of behavior. Personal force is seen as the product of ability (or power) and of the effort that one exerts. As this relationship is hypothesized to be a multiplicative one (amount of ability X amount of effort = amount of personal force), if either ability or effort is nonexistent, the entire strength of personal force will be zero.

But the attribution of environmental forces and personal forces may depend on the observer. Some behaviors may cause us to attribute more influence to environmental forces and some less. Jones and Nisbett (1971) note that, when a freshman at the state university comes to discuss his poor grades with his faculty adviser, there may occur a fundamental difference in attribution by the two participants. The student may point to environmental forces (factors such as a noisy dormitory or a heavy course load) to account for his difficulties. Although the faculty member would like to agree, he is more likely not to, because he

will attribute the deficient behavior to personal forces. He will believe instead "that the failure is due to enduring qualities of the student—to lack of ability, to irremediable laziness, to neurotic ineptitude" (Jones & Nisbett, 1971, p. 1). In the first article in this section, Edward E. Jones and his colleagues at Duke University look at the ways in which environmental and personal forces are combined in the attribution process. They ask: what conclusions do subjects make about another person's attitude toward marijuana after they have read an essay that person has written for or against legalization of marijuana? Jones et al. vary four aspects to see how each affects the attribution process:

1. The subject is shown other attitude responses of the essay writer; on these other topics (including censorship, liquor-by-the-drink laws, and invasions of privacy) the essay writer either is in favor of social controls *or* favors individual freedom of choice.

2. The subject is told *either* that the essay writer has written the essay under conditions of free choice *or* that he has written it in line with a general position assigned him by the experimenter.

3. The essay that the subject reads takes *either* a pro-legalization position *or* a negative position toward legalizing marijuana.

4. Regardless of the *direction* of the essay, it takes either a very strong stand or a very mild one on the issue.

Thus in the experiment in the first article, there are 16 types of subjects, but each has read an essay regarding marijuana legalization purportedly written by another student. The subject's job is to decide what the essay writer's "true attitudes" regarding marijuana are. Through analysis of the results the authors look at the role of environmental forces (for example, whether the direction of the essay was assigned or not) and personal forces (the strength or mildness of the essay written).

As Jones et al. indicate, when a person is interpreting an interpersonal event, he may attribute the behavioral outcome to internal factors ("He wrote that because that's what he believes") or external ones ("The experimenter made him do it"). Behavior that is brought about by environmental forces is seen as externally caused, whereas internally caused behavior is seen as reflecting the person's abilities and efforts. To make an attribution of internal or external causality, the perceiver (or subject, in the Jones et al. study) must estimate the relative strengths of the environmental and personal forces. In reviewing the first article in this section, the reader should assess the relative impact of environmental and personal forces in the subject's attribution of the essay writer's true attitude.

Turning to the attribution of one's own emotional states, we find that much of the relevant research has dealt with situations in which one is aware that he is experiencing bodily changes but is unaware *why* he is. That is, he knows that physiological changes associated with emotion are occurring—he can feel them—but he has no appropriate label for them. He seeks an explanation, an attribution of a label. One way of resolving such a dilemma is illustrated in the second article in this section, by Stuart Valins, now at the State University of New York at Stony Brook. Valins' study of reactions to false information about the speed of one's heartbeat stems from Schachter's cognitive-physiological theory of emotion, which Valins reviews in the introduction to his article.

More recently, Schachter's own interest has moved from the attribution of emotional states to a related topic: the self-attribution of hunger and the determinants of eating behavior. Introductory psychology textbooks inform us that we are hungry when the hypothalamus, a small structure in the brain, tells us that we are, and that the hypothalamus bases its conclusion on its continuous analysis of the changing properties of the blood passing through the brain. Although this is so, there appear to be vast individual differences in reliance on this signal—or on stomach contractions, too—as a stimulus to eating. Schachter, now at Columbia University, proposes that obese people are much less sensitive to internal triggers to hunger than are people of normal weight. In the last article in this section he describes and reviews an ingenious set of experiments that illustrate this phenomenon.

REFERENCES

Heider, F. Social perception and phenomenal causality. *Psychological Review,* 1944, **51,** 358–374.

Heider, F. *The psychology of interpersonal relations.* New York: Wiley, 1958.

Jones, E. E., & Nisbett, R. E. *The actor and the observer: Divergent perceptions of the causes of behavior.* New York: General Learning Corporation, 1971.

Schachter, S. The interaction of cognitive and physiological determinants of emotional state. In L. Berkowitz (Ed.), *Advances in experimental social psychology,* Vol. 1. New York: Academic Press, 1964. Pp. 49–80.

Schachter, S., & Singer, J. E. Cognitive, social and physiological determinants of emotional state. *Psychological Review,* 1962, **69,** 379–399.

Schachter, S., & Wheeler, L. Epinephrine, chlorpromazine, and amusement. *Journal of Abnormal and Social Psychology,* 1962, **65,** 121–128.

ARTICLE 34

Prior Expectancy and Behavioral Extremity as Determinants of Attitude Attribution[1]

Edward E. Jones, Stephen Worchel, George R. Goethals, and Judy F. Grumet

Jones and Harris (1967) report the results of three studies converging on the basic conclusion that the attitudes of a target person will be directly inferred from relevant behavior (such as an opinion statement) to the extent that the target person is seen to have the freedom to express himself as he pleases. This difference in attribution as a function of the degree of behavioral choice was predicted, and found, to be greater when the opinions expressed departed from the expected norm. Thus it made a great deal of difference for the attribution of true attitude whether a target person taking a pro-Castro stand had freedom of choice. The variable of choice made little or no difference when he took the more normative, high probability, anti-Castro position: regardless of the context in which the stand was taken, subjects continued to assume that the target person was against Castro.

This pattern of results is quite consistent with correspondent inference theory (Jones & Davis, 1965), the essence of which is that both choice and prior probability are crucial determinants of attribution. If the attribute in question is underlying attitude and the behavior observed is in the form of an opinion statement, the more extraneous reasons a target person has for making the statement, the less perceived choice he will have, and the less the perceiver will learn about attitude from behavior. Prior probability enters as a further determinant of attribution in the absence of behavioral freedom: a statement that espouses the most probable attitude is not very informative regardless of the degree of perceived choice. When perceived choice is low, and the target person makes a high probability statement, the perceiver's best assumption is that the target person would have made the same statement under free choice conditions.

Although Jones and Harris (1967) demonstrated the importance of the choice and probability variables, they also found a strong tendency even under conditions of no choice to attribute attitudes in line with behavior. For example, in a context where a debating coach assigned sides to members of his team, a target person who was allegedly assigned, and thereafter delivered, a pro-Castro speech was seen as significantly more in favor of Castro than a team member who was assigned and delivered an anti-Castro speech. Jones and Harris saw this as evidence of over-attribution to the person at the expense of the situation, a tendency that Heider (1958) refers to as "behavior engulfing the field."

The implications of the Jones and Harris studies are clouded by two limitations in their design. First of all, in each study prior probability was varied only in the roughest way, and the success and precision of the variations depended in each case on certain hunches regarding the normative attitudinal position of the population from which

Excerpted from the *Journal of Experimental Social Psychology*, 1971, *7*, 59–80. Reprinted with permission of the authors and the publisher; copyright 1971, Academic Press, Inc.

[1]This research was supported by Grant NSF-G8857.

the target person allegedly came. A second limitation was that the strength of the speech was held constant in most of the previous studies, and no attempt was made to study the interactive effects of choice and behavioral extremity.

Assuming that prior probability (or perceiver expectancy) could be more precisely manipulated, how should variations along this dimension affect attribution? When behavior departs from expectation, how much weight should be assigned to each source of information? Should the resulting attitudinal attribution reflect primarily the prior expectation, should the behavior and expectation cancel each other out, or should there be a contrast effect such that the behavior is a stronger determinant of attribution than if it had been in line with prior expectation? Whether the expectancy or the behavior predominates should depend on the degree of choice under which the target person is perceived to be operating. The prediction under no choice conditions is straightforward. Consider a target person who is forcefully instructed to write an essay in favor of advocating the withdrawal of U. S. troops from Europe, and who complies. Readers of this essay might have had varying prior expectations about the most probable private attitude of the essay author. Since the behavioral evidence is presumably quite ambiguous, being elicited by constraining instructions, it seems highly likely that each reader faced with the task of inferring true attitude would fall back on his prior expectations and discount the behavior.

The role of prior expectancy is not as clear under choice conditions. Here, of course, the behavior itself is more informative relative to the expectancy. Where the behavior is unequivocal in its implications and the expectancy only vague or tentative, the former should clearly dominate the latter. But when the expectancy and the behavior are both quite unequivocal and in conflict, we predict a contrast effect: the expectancy should serve as an anchor for judging the magnitude of the behavioral stimulus. The more dramatically a clear expectancy is disconfirmed by clear behavior, the more will the attitude attribution reflect that behavior.

This prediction is not firmly grounded in prior data or theory, but it is consistent with Helson's (1964) concept of adaptation level and other models of attribute judgment and preference (Stevens, 1957; Campbell, Lewis, & Hunt, 1958). The conditions of contrast versus assimilation are not yet clearly understood, but contrast seems to require an early set of contextual stimuli that imply a level of expected value for the entire series, but do not compel judgmental commitment (cf. Thibaut & Ross, 1969), and a later set of stimuli that are quite discrepant in value from the early contextual set. A final condition is that the later stimuli cannot be discounted as reflecting extraneous influences (or more fundamentally, as evidence of a different "entity" than that characterized by the earlier contextual stimuli). Unexpected opinion statements under free choice conditions should fit these latter specifications well enough to predict an effect of contrast, resulting in highly correspondent inferences about underlying attitude.

This prediction gains credence from calling to mind relevant mundane examples. We meet someone with a reputation for being gruff and cold and are therefore especially charmed by his warm and gracious manner. The scientist who forgets a name may be considered absent-minded to the extent that he was previously considered brilliant. The prediction of judgmental contrast rests on an assumption that the behavioral violation of expectancy makes the behavior more perceptually salient and therefore its implications are accentuated in the mind of the perceiver.

In addition to a more precise manipulation of prior expectancy, the present study set out to manipulate systematically the extremity of the behavior (an opinion statement in the form of an essay). In one of the studies reported by Jones and Harris (1967), subjects were asked to judge the attitude towards Castro of a target person who made an ambivalent speech. The results showed that if the target person had been previously instructed to make a pro-Castro speech, he was seen as more anti-Castro than if he had been instructed to make an anti-Castro speech. This suggests what might be called a "foot dragging" or equivocation effect. A more precise manipulation of behavior intensity and degree of choice should reveal the following pattern of results: (1) under no choice conditions (where the target person is constrained to take a certain position), a weak statement consistent with instructions should lead to attribution of the opposite attitude; (2) under choice conditions, however, strength and direction of opinion statement should relate directly to the strength and direction of the attributed attitude.

Putting together these interests in clarifying and extending previous findings gives rise to a 2 X 2 X 2 X 2 design with the following factors: direction of behavior (pro, anti); strength of behavior (strong, weak); degree of constraint on behavior (choice, no choice); and prior expectation (expect pro, expect anti). The variables of choice, strength, and expectancy are each predicted to have an effect on correspondence or the degree to which the opinion statement is taken to reflect a similar underlying attitude. Clearly a statement given freely will yield greater correspondence than the same statement given in response to authoritative instructions. It also seems obvious that the more extreme such a statement is the greater will be the tendency to attribute a strong attitude. The effects of expectancy variations are more complex, and the factors of the design should combine to produce a number of interesting comparisons and contrasts.

More specifically the fate of attribution in the present experiment is predicted by the following set of five hypotheses. When a sample of attitudinally relevant behavior is clear-cut (i.e., the strong essay condition):

1. Attributed attitudes are more in line with behavior under choice than under no choice conditions.

2. Even in the no choice conditions, however, attitude is attributed in line with behavior that follows the constraining no choice instructions.

3. The difference between choice and no choice conditions is especially marked when the behavior tends to disconfirm the subject's prior expectations.

Regardless of essay strength:

4. Prior expectation directly influences attribution in the no choice conditions and leads to contrast in the choice conditions.

When an essay is relatively weak or equivocal:

5. The opposite attitude is attributed under no choice conditions, whereas under choice conditions, weak behavior is perceived to reflect moderate "true" attitudes in whichever direction the essay leans.

METHOD

Overview

The subjects were first given selected results of an attitude questionnaire supposedly filled out by the target person, a student at a neighboring university. His responses to the attitude items were contrived to create expectancies that he would be either for or against legalizing marijuana. The subject then read an essay that was either for or against legalization of marijuana. The target person had either written the essay under conditions of free choice or in line with the general position assigned by his experimenter. The essay either took a very strong stand or a rather weak one. After studying the essay, the subject was asked to predict the target person's "true" attitude with regard to the marijuana issue. Thus, the experiment was a 2 X 2 X 2 X 2 factorial design with expectancy, choice, essay direction, and essay strength being the four variables.

Subjects

The subjects were 224 male and female students enrolled in introductory psychology who volunteered for an experiment on "impression formation." Subjects were run in six different sessions, and though the subjects in each session varied in number from 18–62, experimental booklets were interleafed so that all conditions were run simultaneously in each session.

Procedure

When subjects arrived at the experimental room, the experimenter explained that the purpose of the experiment was to "study the accuracy with which people can form impressions about another person when they have very limited information about him." Subjects were told that there were actually 10 different target persons being rated and that there were 10 different combinations of information being passed out. They were informed that this information might be in the form of interview comments, statements about the target person from friends, projective test data, or statements of belief on a selected sample of opinion issues. Subjects were also led to believe that the target persons had been hired through the employment office of a nearby university and that the first 10 people who applied had been hired. The experimenter stated that these people had agreed to give the necessary information and he concluded by saying, "I want to emphasize that each of you has information about a target person who is a student like yourself and that the information has been checked and double checked for accuracy." Booklets were then given to each subject.

Manipulation of Expectancy. The cover sheet of the booklet contained innocuous information about the target person's hometown, father's occupation, and number of brothers and sisters. On the second page of the booklet were 10 opinion items with ratings supposedly given by the target person. Each of these items concerned potential interference with the individual's rights to live his own life and control his own destiny. The responses rather consistently favored individual autonomy or socially imposed restraints. The former pattern was designed to create an expectancy that the target person would favor the legalization of marijuana. The latter was designed to create an anti-marijuana expectancy. For example, the expect-pro target person strongly agreed with the statement, "It would be a great step forward if abortions were permitted by law." The expect-anti target person disagreed. Other issues on which the expect-pro and expect-anti target persons were made to disagree were liquor-by-the-drink laws, censorship, student control of universities, invasion of privacy, the meaning of beards and beads, and permissiveness in child rearing.

After subjects had read a target person's position on the attitude issues, they were asked to predict how he would stand on a number of other issues that also dealt in general with individual autonomy versus socially imposed restraints. The

other issues will be identified below when the results are described, but one—the crucial marijuana issue—was included at this point in the procedure to provide a check on the expectancy manipulation.

On the next page of the booklet were the instructions supposedly given to the target person by the experimenter. He was told that he would be asked to write an essay on a number of issues and under varying conditions. For subjects whose booklets placed them in the free choice condition, the experimenter asked the target person to write a persuasive statement, like the opening statement of a debate, expressing his views on legalizing marijuana. The target person was told that he had 45 minutes in which to prepare the statement and that he could use materials on the marijuana issue to be provided by the experimenter if he found them useful. The instructions emphasized that the target person was completely free to choose the side of the issue on which he wished to write.

In the no choice conditions the experimenter asked the target person to write a persuasive statement in favor of legalizing marijuana in half the booklets or against such legalization in the remaining half. Again, the target person was told that he would have 45 minutes in which to prepare the paper and that he could use any of the materials provided for him by the experimenter. Instructions emphasized that the target person was expected to support the assigned position.

Communications. The next two pages of the subjects' booklet contained the statements supposedly written by the target person. There were four different essays—strong pro-marijuana, weak pro-marijuana, strong anti-marijuana, and weak anti-marijuana—which were equated for length, style of writing, and number of arguments. The essays were approximately 400 words in length. The strong pro-marijuana essay contained four points for legalizing marijuana: legalization would reduce organized crime, marijuana was a safe and effective tension reducer, marijuana could increase creativeness, and marijuana was neither harmful nor addictive. The strong anti-marijuana essay argued that legalizing marijuana would lead to more crimes by its users, that marijuana would cause irrational and irresponsible behavior, that marijuana would invite the use of other addictive drugs, and that marijuana would be used as an escape from problems. In the closing statements of the strong speeches, the target person stated unequivocally that he was for (against) legalizing marijuana.

The weak essays contained two arguments favoring one side of the argument and two favoring the other. The arguments were taken directly from the strong speeches, and in fact the same arguments were used in each of the weak speeches. The difference was that pro arguments appeared first and fourth in the weak-pro and second and third in the weak-anti speech. The closing statements of the weak speeches were, "There are good points on both sides of the issue, but all things considered, I guess I'm somewhat for (against) legalizing marijuana."

The marijuana issue was chosen as the crucial one for this experiment because there were no clearly established norms in the student population and it was quite feasible, therefore, to manipulate attitudinal expectancies. The subjects had filled out a questionnaire earlier in the semester which included an item on the legalization of marijuana. The responses to this item were bimodal though there was slightly more spread on the pro-marijuana side. On a 31-point scale, 25% of the subjects scored between 1–6 (pro) and 25% scored between 27–31 (anti).

Response Measures

The last two pages of the experimental booklet contained the dependent measures. Subjects were again asked how they believed the target person would respond on the five attitude issues used to check on the expectancy manipulation. Each scale was in a 6-point Likert format, with the possible responses ranging from "agree very much" to "disagree very much." Also included were questions relating to the subjects' own beliefs about marijuana, the amount of choice the target person was perceived to have had in choosing a side to defend, the amount he used the materials which had been provided for him by the experimenter, and the extremity of the speech.

RESULTS

Subjects' Own Attitudes

The subjects' own attitudes, measured several months before the experiment, did not vary with experimental condition. There is thus no reason to question the assumption of random assignment of subjects to conditions. It is also of interest to note that the overall correlation ($n=224$) between own attitude and attributed attitude was .011 for the postexpectancy, preessay measure and .056 for the final postessay attribution. There is no apparent tendency across all conditions for subjects to make attributions in line with, or in opposition to, their own attitudes.

Validation of Experimental Manipulations

The design of the present experiment featured four cross-cutting dichotomous variables: expectancy, choice, direction, and strength of essay. Interpretation of the dependent variable attribution data depends on the success with which these

TABLE 1. Judged direction and extremity of essay.

Strongly favor legalization	$\overline{X}_1$			$\overline{X}_2$			$\overline{X}_3$			$\overline{X}_4$		Strongly oppose legalization
	1	2	3	4	5	6	7	8	9	10	

$\overline{X}_1$: Strong pro essay (1.96)
$\overline{X}_2$: Weak pro essay (4.16)
$\overline{X}_3$: Weak anti essay (6.10)
$\overline{X}_4$: Strong anti essay (8.80)

variations were induced. Validation evidence is considered for each manipulation in turn.

Expectancy. The attempt to vary expected attitude involved informing subjects about selected opinions of the target person. It was assumed that someone who favored strict abortion laws, prohibition of liquor-by-the-drink, movie censorship, and other institutionalized intrusions on individual freedom, would be expected to be against the legalization of marijuana. One who opposed such intrusions should be expected to be more in favor of marijuana legalization. In order to check on this assumption subjects were asked to predict the target person's attitude toward marijuana legalization immediately after learning about his other opinions on related issues. The results show quite clearly that the expectancy variable was successfully manipulated. Those in the expect-pro condition predicted that the target person would favor legalization more than those in the expect-anti condition prior to reading the target person's essay (F=1198.72, 1 and 208 df, p<.001). No differences were expected or obtained as a function of the subsequently manipulated variables of choice or speech direction and strength.

Choice. As one of a set of postexperimental questions, subjects were asked to indicate the extent to which the target person was free to choose the particular position he took on the essay. This question discriminated very effectively between subjects in the choice and no choice conditions (F=196.06, 1 and 204 df, p<.001).

Direction and Extremity of Behavior. On the same postexperimental questionnaire, subjects were asked to indicate where the attitude statement conveyed by the essay fell on a 10-point scale ranging from pro- to anti-legalization. As Table 1 shows, the essays were perceived as intended and placed, on the average, at nearly equal points on the anti-pro continuum. The combined effects of direction and extremity displayed in this table were highly significant (F=433.08, 3 and 204 df, p< .001) and each essay was reliably seen as different from its neighbor on the continuum. Clearly, and with more than a little bit of luck, we

TABLE 2. Attribution of attitude against marijuana legalization (means and variances for each condition)[a]

| | | Anti essays | | Pro essays | |
		Strong	Weak	Weak	Strong
Choice					
Exp	$\overline{X}$	5.43	4.36	2.14	1.21
Anti	s^2	.26	.40	.13	.18
Exp	$\overline{X}$	5.79	5.00	2.50	1.57
Pro	s^2	.18	.00	.27	.26
No choice					
Exp	$\overline{X}$	5.57	3.00	4.93	3.57
Anti	s^2	42	1.69	1.61	1.65
Exp	$\overline{X}$	4.29	2.21	3.93	1.21
Pro	s^2	2.84	1.57	1.92	.18

[a]N=14 in each condition, total n=224. The larger the mean, the greater the tendency to attribute an attitude opposed to marijuana legalization.

succeeded in constructing essays judged to be equally weak and strong in both the pro and anti directions.

Attribution of Attitudes toward Marijuana

After examining the particular essay included

TABLE 3. Analysis of variance summaries.

Source	df	F_1[a]	F_2[a]	F_3[a]
Choice (A)	1	--	--	--
Expectancy (B)	1	14.16***	17.66***	87.00***
Strength (C)	1	--	--[b]	--
Direction (D)	1	219.11***	375.24***	20.56***
A X B	1	52.62***	39.08***	4.44*
A X C	1	--	--[b]	6.51*
A X D	1	141.62***	23.19***	22.97***
B X C	1	4.67*	--[b]	--
B X D	1	--	--	--
C X D	1	159.54***	--[b]	4.11*
A X B X C	1	--	--[b]	--
A X B X D	1	--	27.32***[c]	--
A X C X D	1	22.26***	--[b]	--
B X C X D	1	--	--[b]	10.34**
A X B X C X D	1	--	--[b]	--
Error	208			

[a]F_1: Question 1; legalization of marijuana. F_2: Question 1; strong essay only. F_3: Questions 2 + 3 + 4 + 5; other area of legal intrusion.
[b]Not applicable.
[c]This interaction effect was computed by an orthogonal comparison reflecting the absolute difference between choice and no choice unexpected essays minus the absolute difference between choice and no choice expected essays.
*p<.05.
**p<.01.
***p<.001.

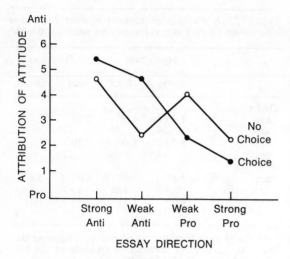

FIGURE 1. Attribution of attitude as function of essay direction and choice.

in his booklet, each subject made his "final prediction of attitude." Subjects were warned not to turn back to the previous pages and were instructed to record their estimates of the target person's "true opinions" about (1) legalization of marijuana, (2) the rights of every man to destroy himself, (3) depriving Chicago of convention business until a new mayor is elected, (4) banning cigarettes, and (5) making it as much of a crime to use as to sell drugs. Each item was presented in the form of a statement followed by six categories ranging from agree very much to disagree

very much. Confidence ratings on a 7-point scale were also requested for the subjects' attributions of true opinion on each item.

The first question was the critical one for testing the major hypotheses of the study. The means for each condition are presented in Table 2. The results of the analysis of variance on these data are presented in Table 3. Careful examination of each of these tables, along with some subsidiary analyses of predicted effects, shows that each hypothesis was strongly confirmed. *Hypothesis 1* predicted that the direction of behavior would make a greater difference under choice than under no choice conditions. *Hypothesis 2* predicted that there would be a significant effect of behavior direction even under no choice conditions. Each hypothesis was intended to refer only to those essay conditions in which the target person took a strong stand, and thus column F_2 in Table 3 presents the appropriate summary. The first hypothesis predicts the statistical interaction that is depicted by the extreme points of Fig. 1. The interaction is highly significant ($F=23.19$, 1 and 208 df, $p < .001$). The obvious main effect for direction of the strong essays ($F=375.24$, 1 and 208 df, $p < .001$) remains highly significant when only the no choice conditions are singled out ($F=105.89$, 1 and 208 df, $p < .001$). This latter result confirms hypothesis 2 and is in line with the results obtained by Jones and Harris (1967).

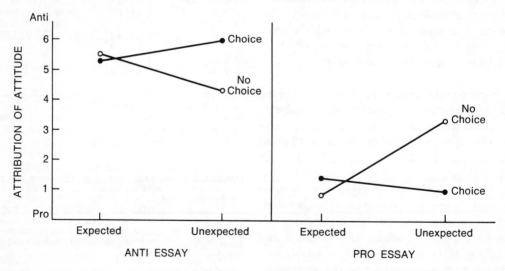

FIGURE 2. Attribution of attitude as a function of expectancy, choice, and essay direction (strong essays only).

Choice is clearly an important factor, but unequivocal behavior in a no choice setting still carries a powerful message to the subject.

Hypothesis 3 predicted that the interaction of choice and behavior direction would be pronounced only when the behavior tends to disconfirm the subject's prior expectations. It has already been noted that the subjects' own attitudes were bimodal. In answer to a postexperimental question, furthermore, the attitude attributed to the "typical student" had an overall mean of 3.56 on a 1–6 scale. We may assume that prior expectancy was almost entirely under the control of the specific information each subject received about the target person's opinions on related issues, and that there was no general bias to expect an anti- or pro-legalization attitude. The third hypothesis was tested by focusing on the strong essay conditions and examining the interaction between choice, expectation, and essay direction. The hypothesis was clearly confirmed by this test ($F=27.32$, 1 and 208 df, $p <$ .001). The form of the interaction is depicted in Figure 2, which shows that choice and no choice conditions are similar except when the behavior is unexpected. Alternatively, it might be said that no clear inference is made about a target person who behaves as instructed but who argues against what one would expect to be his private beliefs. When the target person writes in line with instruction *and* expectation, he is attributed the same private attitudes as the subjects who have freedom of choice.

Hypothesis 4 predicted that prior expectation would directly affect attribution in the no choice conditions and lead to contrast in the choice conditions. The appropriate test of this hypothesis is the interaction between choice and expectation in the overall factorial design (see Table 3: $F =56.62$, 1 and 208 df, $p < .001$). As Table 2 shows, the direct effect of expectancy in the no choice conditions is greater than the inverse or contrast effect in the choice conditions. For the no choice conditions, the expectancy effect is highly reliable ($F=60.67$, 1 and 208 df, $p <$ .001); the contrast effect in the choice conditions is also statistically reliable, but less so ($F=6.05$, 1 and 208 df, $p < .05$).

In setting the stage for the contrast hypothesis,

we at least implied that contrast would be especially evident in the strong essay, choice conditions. It is apparent in Table 2, however, that the contrast effect was quite general when the target person had choice and that the effect was at least as clear in the weak as in the strong essay conditions. This raises some uncertainty concerning the requirement that contrast requires collision between a strong expectancy and unequivocal behavior and suggests that the phenomenon may occur over a wider range of expectancy-behavior discrepancies.

Hypothesis 5 was the only one dealing specifically with weak or equivocal behavior. In line with the hypothesis, under no choice conditions an equivocal essay does lead to attributions of the opposite attitude. Under choice conditions, also as predicted, the weak essay is seen to reflect a moderate attitude in the direction espoused. Restricting the analysis to the weak essay conditions, there is a highly significant interaction between choice and direction ($F=143.79$, 1 and 208 df, $p < .001$). This interaction shows itself clearly in the middle (weak essay) points of Figure 1. . . .

DISCUSSION

The present experiment confirms a number of tentative conclusions proposed by Jones and Harris (1967) and adds new information about the effects of clearly established behavioral expectancies in the attribution process. The context from which this and the previous studies emerged is correspondent inference theory (Jones & Davis, 1965). This theory states that attitudes will be directly inferred from behavior only to the extent that the behavior is unexpected and the target person could just as well have behaved in some other way. The present study once again has demonstrated that unexpected and unequivocal behavior in a free-choice setting gives rise to highly correspondent inferences.

Correspondent inference theory essentially provides a rational model of the attribution process, since it describes in general terms those settings in which a perceiver should logically conclude that he has gained information. Thus information is gained when one observes behavior that was not forced by circumstances, but only to the extent that one would normally expect some *other* form of behavior in the absence of constraints. Under highly constraining (no choice) conditions, the most sensible thing to do is to stick with one's prior expectations and to discount the externally determined behavior. In relative terms this is what clearly happens, resulting in the interaction between choice and expectancy observed in the present study and the ones preceding it. What is not quite so sensible, however, is that subjects nevertheless do attribute different attitudes in line with behavior under no choice conditions. Their inferences under no choice conditions are, in other words, more "correspondent" than the theory would predict.

Jones and Harris (1967) discuss this tendency for behavior to "engulf the field" and suggest that it may vary with the range of expression remaining open to the target person. Jones and Harris remark: "If the target person had been merely handed a speech to read under very strong external constraints, his compliance would have conveyed little or no information to the subjects . . . Short of some extreme degree of specification, behavior does engulf the field and it is difficult for the perceiver to assign appropriate weight to the situational context" (p. 23). Although the present experimental instructions clearly stated that the target person had "materials on the issues of marijuana" to work with, and 45 minutes to prepare his essay, he was told only to write a "persuasive essay," thus leaving the quality and strength of the essay relatively unspecified.

The results show that behavior does not engulf the field when the behavior is sufficiently weak or ambivalent. On the contrary, the target person who writes a weak essay in the direction called for is seen as actually in favor of the opposing position. When the behavior is somewhat equivocal, then, it does not engulf the field but apparently is "confined to its proper position as a local stimulus whose interpretation requires the additional data of the surrounding field" (Heider, 1958, p. 54). The weak essay results suggest at least some rough boundary conditions for the effect of behavior engulfing the field. If we could vary essay

strength parametrically between the weak and the strong versions in the present experiment, presumably there would be some point of neutral attribution where the subject would in effect declare that he received zero information from the no choice essay. The strong essay apparently does convey information in the no choice conditions, and it would be very difficult if not impossible to determine whether this should be judged as attributional distortion. It seems reasonable that each subject himself would agree to express false opinions under comparable circumstances of authoritative assignment and that he would probably construct an essay at least as strong as those featured in the present experiment. Only if we make such assumptions, however, can we argue that there is indeed bias in the direction of assigning too much weight to behavior and not enough to the situation.

The most intriguing of the present set of results are those concerned with expectancy confirmation and expectancy violation. The attribution data show a direct effect of expectancy in the no choice conditions and apparent contrast in the choice conditions. The first effect of expectancy is readily understandable. In the no choice conditions there are two kinds of expectancies. The first is the expectancy that the target person will write an essay in the direction assigned to him. This expectancy is always confirmed, although the weak essay conditions indicate a certain amount of foot-dragging. Secondly, there is the expectancy that derives from prior knowledge about the target person's opinions on related issues. This expectancy is confirmed in some conditions and not in others, but the lack of confirmation is readily explained by the fact that the target person had no choice. It is hardly surprising, therefore, that the prior expectancy based on related opinions should pull substantial weight as a determinant of attribution. In effect, a strong prior expectancy tends to subvert the tendency to look at behavior out of its situational context and helps the subject keep the new "evidence" in its proper place.

In the choice conditions, however, the state of affairs is quite different. Here there are cases in which the behavior is unexpected and cannot readily be discounted or explained away. Although prior expectation is strong in all cases, the subject has no specific evidence concerning the target person's attitude toward marijuana until he sees the essay. The essay is informative, of course, because the instructions to the target person were quite permissive about the position to be defended. When the expectancy is in conflict with behavior, the attribution tendency should shift from what is predicted on the basis of circumstantial evidence to what is directly revealed in behavior. The question is how much of a shift will occur. It is apparent that the shift is striking indeed, as if the subject, having been earlier misled to form one impression of the target person, now swings too far in the other direction.

This result is somewhat reminiscent of Walster's overcompensation reaction (Walster, Walster, Abrahams, & Brown, 1966; Walster & Prestholdt, 1966) though her experiments deal specifically with attraction and evaluation rather than attribution per se. The basic overcompensation argument is that people who are drawn toward overly positive or negative early evaluations tend to overreact to fuller information that shows they were in error. It is of further interest that this effect of overcompensation apparently occurs only when the subject has not publicly committed himself to an impression or evaluation that he might feel obliged to defend. Subjects in the present experiment do make a minor commitment in their ratings after the expectancy manipulation, but the public nature of this was certainly not stressed and all subjects were quite aware that additional information was coming.

Whatever the eventual explanation for the contrast effect observed in the present experiment, the phenomenon itself is an interesting one. At some point on the continuum of environmental constraint, the tendency to discount new information in favor of a prior expectancy shifts into a tendency to reject the expectancy and to embrace completely the new information. This obviously has something to do with the strength of the new information relative to the strength of the expectancy. In the present experiment, however, the contrast effect was at least as strong in the weak as in the strong essay conditions. Holding

strength of expectancy constant, then, the degree to which there is disconfirmation (strong vs. weak essay) is less important than the absence of extenuating circumstances (as in the no choice condition) by which the disconfirmation may be readily explained.

We may conclude from the present results that the attribution of an attitude based on a relevant opinion statement is a predictable function of prior expectancy, the degree of freedom to make an alternative opinion statement, and the strength of the opinion statement. There is persuasive but not conclusive evidence for Heider's contention that behavior is overweighted in the attribution process. When there is conflicting information about the attributional significance of a particular opinion statement, measurable individual differences do play a role in the extent to which contextual factors are considered. Subjects who tend to feel that events are under their own control distinguish more clearly than externalizing subjects between choice and no choice conditions. Finally, there is an intriguing flipover in the relative weights attached to expectancy and behavior at some point along the continuum of external constraint or justification. When the subject cannot easily explain away behavior that disconfirms expectancy, the expectancy serves as an anchoring stimulus against which the behavior is contrasted. When the disconfirming behavior may be assigned to compelling external circumstances, attributions are made in terms of prior expectancies.

REFERENCES

Campbell, D. T., Lewis, N. A., & Hunt, W. A. Context effects with judgmental language that is absolute, extensive, and extra-experimentally anchored. *Journal of Experimental Psychology,* 1958, **55,** 220–228.

Heider, F. E. *The psychology of interpersonal relations.* New York: Wiley, 1958.

Helson, H. *Adaptation-level theory.* New York: Harper & Row, 1964.

Jones, E. E., & Davis, K. E. From acts to dispositions. In L. Berkowitz (Ed.), *Advances in experimental social psychology,* Vol. II. New York: Academic Press, 1965. Pp. 219–266.

Jones, E. E., & Harris, V. A. The attribution of attitudes. *Journal of Experimental Social Psychology,* 1967, **3,** 1–24.

Rotter, J. B. Generalized expectancies for internal versus external control of reinforcement. *Psychological Monographs,* 1966, **80** (Whole No. 609), 1–28.

Rotter, J. B., & Mulry, R. C. Internal versus external control of reinforcement and decision time. *Journal of Personality and Social Psychology,* 1965, **2,** 598–604.

Stevens, S. S. On the psychophysical law. *Psychological Review,* 1957, **63,** 153–181.

Thibaut, J., & Ross, M. Commitment and experience as determinants of assimilation and contrast. *Jour-nal of Personality and Social Psychology,* 1969, **13,** 322–329.

Walster, E., & Prestholdt, P. The effect of misjudging another: overcompensation or dissonance reduction? *Journal of Experimental Social Psychology,* 1966, **2,** 85–97.

Walster, E., Walster, G. W., Abrahams, D., & Brown, Z. The effect on liking of underrating or overrating another. *Journal of Experimental Social Psychology,* 1966, **2,** 70–84.

ARTICLE 35

Cognitive Effects of False Heart-Rate Feedback[1]

Stuart Valins

Reprinted from *Journal of Personality and Social Psychology,* 1966, **4,** 400–408, with permission of the author and the publisher; copyright 1966, American Psychological Association.

[1]This research was conducted at Duke University while the author was a National Institutes of Health Postdoctoral Fellow in the Research Training Program in Sciences Related to the Central Nervous System.

Although there is considerable evidence that emotional states are accompanied by physiological changes (Duffy, 1962; Woodworth & Schlosberg, 1962), until recently there was little indication that these internal events facilitate the development of emotional behavior. Several experiments have now shown that emotional behavior is affected by the experimental manipulation of sympathetic activity. Emotional behavior is more readily learned when the sympathetic nervous system is intact than when it is surgically enervated (Wynne & Solomon, 1955), and more readily manifested during epinephrine-induced states of sympathetic activation than during states of relative inactivation (Latané & Schachter, 1962; Schachter & Singer, 1962; Schachter & Wheeler, 1962; Singer, 1963).

In an attempt to account for the influence of autonomic arousal on emotional behavior, Schachter (1964) has emphasized the importance of the cognitive effects of internal events. Within his cognitive-physiological theory of emotion, physiological changes are considered to function as stimuli or cues and are represented cognitively as feelings or sensations. These feelings, in turn, arouse further cognitive activity in the form of attempts to identify the situation that precipi-

tated them. Emotional behavior results when the feeling state is attributed to an emotional stimulus or situation. The optimum conditions for the development of an emotion are thus present when an individual can say, "That stimulus (emotional) has affected me internally." In accord with these notions, it has been found that when subjects are pharmacologically aroused and exposed to stimuli designed to induce emotion, more emotional behavior is manifested when the arousal state is attributed to the emotional situation than when it is attributed to the injection (Schachter & Singer, 1962). Furthermore, the results of a recent experiment suggest that the effects of internal cues on emotional behavior may be mediated by an alteration in the perceived intensity of the emotional stimulus. Nisbett and Schachter (1966) found that when a series of electric shocks were administered to subjects who were in a mild state of fear, the shocks were judged to be more painful by those subjects who correctly attributed their internal symptoms to the shocks than by subjects who incorrectly attributed their symptoms to a pill.

Once it is granted that internal events can function as cues or stimuli then these events can now be considered as a source of cognitive information. They can, for example, result in cognitions such as, "My heart is pounding," or "My face is flushed." As potential cognitive information, however, these events are subject to the same mechanisms that process any stimulus before it is represented cognitively. Such mechanisms can result in their being denied, distorted, or simply

357

not perceived. It is thus plausible that the cognitive representation of an internal event can be nonveridical; a particular reaction can fail to register or can be misperceived, and a nonexistent reaction can be represented cognitively. Mandler (1962) also has questioned the veridicality of internal sensations and suggests that:

> ... someone may learn to make statements about his internal private events under the control of environmental stimuli or irrelevant internal stimuli. Thus, I could say, "I am blushing," in an embarrassing situation without showing any signs of peripheral vasodilation. Or I may have learned to talk about tenseness in my stomach in a stress situation without stomach events exerting any influence on such a remark [p. 317].

If cognitive representations of internal events are important for emotional behavior, then these nonveridical representations of physiological changes should have the same effects as veridical ones. They will be evaluated by reference to a precipitating situation and result in emotional behavior if the situation is an emotional one. Using Mandler's example, his "symbolic" blusher should be equally embarrassed with or without the presence of peripheral vasodilation. He should be less embarrassed, however, if he now has a mirror at his disposal and observes that he is not blushing. Embarrassment should be greatest only when he *thinks* that he has blushed in response to the situation.

The present experiment represents an attempt to determine the effects of nonveridical cognitive cues concerning internal reactions on the labeling of emotional stimuli. This will be accomplished by manipulating the extent to which a subject believes his heart has reacted to slides of seminude females and by observing the effects of his "liking" for the slides. The research of Schachter and his associates suggests that if a subject were covertly injected with epinephrine and shown a slide of a nude female, he would interpret his internal sensations as due to the nude stimulus and he would label the girl as more attractive than if he had been injected with placebo and he had experienced no internal sensations. If, however, it is the cognitive effect of internal events that influences emotional behavior, then this same influence should be observed when subjects think that they have reacted to a given stimulus, regardless of whether they have indeed reacted. As such, it is hypothesized that the cognition, "That girl has affected my heart rate," will induce subjects to consider the girl more attractive or appealing than the cognition, "That girl has not affected my heart rate."

These effects are predicted regardless of whether the heart-rate feedback matches the subjects' stereotyped expectations. Most of us would expect that, if anything, our heart rates would increase in response to photographs of nude females. How would we interpret our heart-rate changes, however, if the rate remained normal to some photographs but decreased substantially to others? If all of the photographs were of attractive females, we could not interpret a decrease as indicating that a girl is a "dog." If we felt it necessary to evaluate these reactions at all, it is likely that we would interpret any change in our heart rates as indicating greater attraction or appeal. Only if all of the photographs were relatively unattractive would we expect that a decrease in heart rate be interpreted as less attraction. Thus, under the appropriate cognitive conditions (highly attractive females), feedback indicating that heart rate has decreased should affect the labeling of emotional stimuli in a manner similar to that of feedback indicating that heart rate has increased.

PROCEDURE

Male introductory psychology students, whose course requirements included 6 hours of participation in experiments, volunteered for a psychophysiological experiment. When the subjects arrived at the laboratory, the experiment was described as a study of physiological reactions to sexually oriented stimuli. These reactions were allegedly being recorded while the subjects viewed 10 slides of seminude females. Two groups of subjects were led to believe that they were hearing an amplified version of their hearts beating while watching the slides and heard their "heart rate" change markedly to half of them. Two other groups of subjects heard the identical sounds, but did not associate them with their own heart beats. Several measures of the attractiveness of each slide were subsequently obtained from all subjects and used to evaluate the effects of the heart-rate feedback.

Bogus Heart-Rate Conditions

Subjects in these conditions were told that the experiment was concerned with heart-rate reactions to sexually oriented stimuli. It was explained that:

Most of our research is conducted over at the Bell Medical Research Building. We have all sorts of electronic wizardry and sound proof chambers over there. Right now there are several experiments being conducted and our facilities at Bell are too overcrowded. Because of this situation, we are doing this experiment here, and are forced to use a fairly crude but adequate measure of heart rate. In our other lab we record heart rate using electrodes which are taped to the chest. They pick up the electrical impulses from the heart which are then recorded on a polygraph. Here we are recording heart rate the way they used to do it 30 years ago. I will be taping this fairly sensitive microphone to your chest. It picks up each major heart sound which is amplified here, and initiates a signal on this signal tracer. This other microphone then picks up the signal and it is recorded on this tape recorder (the signal tracer, amplifier, and tape recorder were on a table next to the subject). By appropriately using a stop watch and this footage indicator, I can later determine exactly where each stimulus occurred and evaluate your heart rate reaction to it.

Unfortunately, this recording method makes it necessary to have audible sounds. They would be a serious problem if we were employing a task which required concentration. Since our procedure does not require concentration, it won't be too much of a problem and it is not likely to affect the results. All that you will be required to do is sit here and look at the slides. Just try to ignore the heart sounds. I will be showing the slides from the next room through this one-way screen. I'll tape this microphone to your chest and after recording your resting heart rate for a while, I will present 10 slides to you at regular intervals. Then I will record your resting heart rate again for several minutes and I will repeat the same slides again in the same order.

After taping the microphone to the subject's chest, the experimenter started the tape recorder and left the room. The sounds which these subjects were hearing were in reality prerecorded. A concealed wire from the tape recorder fed these sounds into the signal tracer speaker. Twenty subjects heard a tape recording which indicated that their heart rates had increased substantially to five slides, but had not changed to five others (heart-rate increase group); 20 other subjects heard a tape recording which indicated that their heart rates had decreased substantially to five of the slides, but had not changed to the other five (heart-rate decrease group).[2]

Extraneous Sound Conditions

Subjects in these conditions thought that the experiment was investigating vasomotor reactions to sexually oriented stimuli. They were told that:

Most of our research is conducted over at the Bell Medical Research Building. We have all sorts of electronic wizardry and sound proof chambers over there. I am doing this experiment now because of the conflicting results which we have obtained in two other identical experiments which we have done over at Bell. One experiment was done in a completely sound proof chamber. Another one was done in an office in which extraneous sounds could be heard, bells ringing in the hallway, people walking up and down, etc. Well, the results in these two experiments were not the same. We feel that it is possible that the results may have been different due to the extraneous sounds which were heard in the experiment where the subject was in an office. To determine whether extraneous sounds can affect finger temperature reactions to sexual stimuli, throughout this experiment you will hear sounds from

---

[2]It should be mentioned that Gerard and Rabbie (1961) and Bramel (1963) have used a similar technique in order to make subjects think that they were more or less frightened or homosexual. They accomplished this by allowing subjects to see dial readings which purportedly indicated internal reactions to experimental stimuli, but which were actually under the control of the experimenter. These investigators, however, were not primarily concerned with the evaluation and labeling of internal states. Their manipulations included detailed explanations of the "meaning" of the dial readings, so that subjects had no choice but to later indicate that they were or were not frightened or homosexual. In contrast, subjects in the present experiment were (a) specifically instructed to ignore the bogus heart sounds, (b) told nothing about the meaning of heart-rate changes, and (c) told that the experimenter could not hear the heart sounds and thus would not know for some time how the subject had reacted. It is the purpose of the present experiment to determine whether subjects will *spontaneously* label their feelings toward a stimulus by reference to their knowledge of how their hearts have reacted.

this tape recorder, sounds that are completely meaningless but are just our way of controlling and producing extraneous sound. Later I will compare your finger temperature reactions to sexual stimuli with those of subjects who do not hear any sounds. I can then assess the physiological effects of the extraneous sounds and determine whether they were the reason why we obtained directionally different results in the two other experiments.

These sounds have absolutely no meaning for you. Just try to ignore them. I will be showing the slides from the next room through this one-way screen. I'll tape this thermistor to your finger and after recording your resting finger temperature for a while, I will present 10 slides to you at regular intervals. Then I will record your resting finger temperature again for several minutes and I will repeat the same slides again in the same order.

A dummy thermistor was then taped to the subject's finger, the tape recorder started, and the experimenter left the room. Ten of these subjects (sound increase group) heard the same tape recording as the heart-rate increase group, and 10 (sound decrease group) heard the same recording as the heart-rate decrease group. The sounds emanated from the signal tracer as in the experimental conditions, but the subjects were now told that it was just an elaborate speaker.

Tape Recordings

The tape recordings were made by recording square wave pulses produced by a Hewlett-Packard low-frequency signal generator, a signal tracer used as a capacitance network, and an external speaker. Pulses of a given frequency per minute could be varied over a wide range.

Heart Beat and Sound Increase Recording. This recording began with the pulse rate varying every 5 seconds between 66 and 72 beats per minute (BPM). At the start of the third minute the rate increased in 5-second segments from 72 to 84 and then to 90 BPM. It then decreased to 84, 78, and to 72 BPM, and subsequently continued to vary between 66 and 72 BPM. The identical rate increase was recorded at minutes 5, 8, 10, 11, 15, 17, 20, 22, and 23. The rate continued to vary between 66 and 72 BPM at minutes 4, 6, 7, 9, 12, 13, 14, 16, 18, 19, 21, and 24.

Heart Beat and Sound Decrease Recording. This recording was the same as the previous one except for the minutes at which the rate increased. At the start of the third minute for this recording, the rate decreased from 66 to 54 and then to 48 BPM. It then increased to 54, 60, and to 66 BPM, and subsequently continued to vary between 66 and 72 BPM. This same decrease in rate was recorded whenever an increase had been recorded on the other tape.

Coordination of Slides with Tape Recordings

Ten color slides were made from photographs of seminude females which had been published by *Playboy* magazine. The slides were projected at 1-minute intervals, each for 15 seconds. The first slide was presented approximately 1 minute, 58 seconds after the tape-recorded sounds had begun so that a marked change in the rate of the sounds was evident 2 seconds afterward. Since the remaining nine slides were presented at 1-minute intervals, this same slide-sound change contingency was apparent for slides 3, 6, 8, and 9. Slides 2, 4, 5, 7, and 10 were presented at the minutes when no change in the rate of the sounds occurred. After the tenth slide (Minute 12 on the tape recording), there was a 3-minute break during which the rate of the sounds varied between 66 and 72 BPM. The slides were then repeated in the same manner starting at Minute 15. The slide order was also systematically rotated within conditions so that each slide was followed by a sound change as often as it was not.

To further clarify the procedure, consider the experimental situation as viewed by a subject who thought he was hearing his heart beating. For 2 minutes, he hears it beating at what appears to be a normal and reasonable rate. The first slide is then presented, and shortly afterward he notices a marked change in his heart rate. After 15 seconds of observing the slide, his heart rate gradually returns to what has been established as normal. The second slide is presented, but there is not any noticeable effect on his heart rate. It continues to vary between 66 and 72 BPM. After seeing all 10 slides, it is apparent that 5 of them have affected his heart rate, but the other 5 have not. This conclusion is reinforced when, after a 3-minute period of normal heart rate, the slides are shown again, and the same ones affect his heart rate, while the others have no effect.

Attractiveness Measures

The effects of heart-rate feedback were assessed by determining the extent to which it influenced the subject's opinions of how attractive the girls were. Three measures of these opinions were obtained: (a) attractiveness ratings which were made immediately after the bogus feedback, (b) choice of photographs as remuneration, (c) attractiveness rankings made several weeks after the experiment.

Slide Ratings.   After the second presentation of the slides, the experimenter disengaged the apparatus and briefly discussed the slides with the subject. The subject was then told that 12 slides were originally being used but that 2 were eliminated in order to shorten the procedure. It was explained that the experimenter was now considering reducing the number of slides to 7 or 8. He was asking a number of subjects to rate the slides so that only the 7 or 8 most attractive or appealing ones would be included. The slides were quickly shown again to the subject and, using a 100-point scale ranging from "Not at all" to "Extremely," he rated them as to: "How attractive or appealing each girl is to you."

Photograph Choices.   The subject then completed a short questionnaire which was followed by an intensive interview to determine whether he had accepted the experimental deceptions. The physiology of sexual arousal was also discussed, but no mention was ever made of the true purpose of the experiment or of the experimental deceptions. The experimenter apologized for being unable to pay the subject and offered to give him some photographs of the girls which had been donated by the publisher. The 10 photographs from which the slides had been made were casually spread on a table, and the subject was told to take 5. The experimenter left the room and thanked the subject before he made his choices. As the subject was leaving, he was intercepted

and the photographs taken back. It was explained that the photographs had been offered to the subject only to determine if there were differences in attractiveness estimates relating to slide versus photograph modes of presentation.

Delayed Photograph Rankings.   Three weeks after participating in the experiment, the subject received a letter from a fictitious "social scientist." The letter requested the subject's cooperation for an attitude survey and asked him to permit an interviewer to question him. Approximately 1 week later an interviewer arrived at the subject's dormitory room and described the survey as a study of undergraduate attitudes toward the psychological and physical characteristics of members of the opposite sex. The subjects first ranked three sets of photographs, each consisting of a model in 12 different dresses, according to how attractive the girl was in each photograph. He then ranked 12 photographs of seminude females on the same dimension. Ten of the photographs were those which he had seen in the experiment proper. After ranking these photographs, the interviewer questioned the subject as to whether he had previously seen them and determined whether he had associated the interview with the original experiment. It should be emphasized that throughout these interviews,[3] the subjects were totally unaware that the feedback in the original experiment was nonveridical.

RESULTS

Adequacy of the Experimental Manipulations

In order to be effective, the manipulation of differential heart-rate feedback must be accurately perceived by the subjects and adequately accepted as a reflection of their internal reactions. Although they were instructed to ignore the bogus heart sounds, the subjects' interest in their reactions and the amplification of the sounds resulted in all subjects being aware of the different slide-sound change contingencies. The bogus

[3]These interviews were skillfully conducted by Joseph Mancusi.

heart beats were also accepted as veridical. None of the 40 experimental subjects had substantial suspicions that the sounds might not be their heart beats. Several had what they described as momentary doubts when first hearing the sounds, but these were quickly forgotten or dispelled. The slightly varying sound rate during the first 2 minutes seemed quite reasonable and served, as intended, to convince the subjects of the veridicality of the bogus beats. The bogus heart-rate reactions to the different slides were also accepted as veridical. Although the heart-rate decrease subjects were overwhelmingly surprised by this feedback, they simply considered as wrong their previous expectations of how they react to these stimuli. Suspicions concerning the veridicality of the feedback were also not increased when the subjects were confronted with a marked discordance between their presumed heart-rate reactions and their initial "liking" for a slide. This discordance was apparently reconciled by many subjects in precisely the manner which was predicted. They changed their estimates of how attractive the girls were.

Heart-Rate Feedback and Attractiveness Measures

It was hypothesized that the cue function of internal events affects the labeling of emotional stimuli. A nonveridical cognitive cue which indicates that one has reacted markedly to a slide of a seminude female should, in this situation, be interpreted as indicating that the stimulus object is attractive or appealing.

Slide Ratings. The prerecorded sounds were played throughout the first two presentations of the slides. During the third presentation, the tape recorder was turned off, and the subjects rated the attractiveness or appeal of each girl. If heart-rate feedback has had the predicted effect, the experimental subjects, in comparison to the control subjects, should rate the slides followed by a change in the sound rate (reinforced) as more attractive than the slides not followed by a change (nonreinforced). Table 1 presents the mean ratings of the reinforced and nonreinforced slides for each of the experimental groups and for

the combined control groups.[4] When the sounds were not considered heart beats they had virtually no effect on the subjects' ratings. Since the control groups rated the reinforced and nonreinforced slides similarly, it is evident that the sounds alone did not have any differential excitatory effects.

It can be seen, however, that when subjects thought the sounds were their heart beats, there was a substantial effect of differential feedback on their ratings. Subjects in the heart-rate decrease condition rated the reinforced slides 6.69 points higher than the nonreinforced ones; subjects in the heart-rate increase condition rated the reinforced slides 18.31 points higher than the nonreinforced ones. Each of these differences is significantly greater than that of the combined control groups. The heart-rate increase feedback also had a greater effect than the decrease feedback. Subjects in the former condition apparently lowered their ratings of the nonreinforced slides as well as raising their ratings of the reinforced ones. The effects of the manipulations are more clearly portrayed in Table 2 which presents the number of subjects in each condition who rated the reinforced slides higher than the nonreinforced ones. This analysis shows that the bogus feedback affected the ratings of the majority of the subjects in the experimental conditions, whereas extraneous sounds had little effect in the control conditions.

Photograph Choices. Differential heart-rate feedback has obviously affected the subjects' ratings of the slides. It may be asked, however, to what extent these ratings are truly indicative of the way subjects feel about these stimuli. Will they now, for example, choose more photographs of the reinforced nudes than the nonreinforced ones as remuneration for participating in the experiment? It will be recalled that each subject selected five photographs. Table 3 tabulates the number of subjects in each condition who chose three or more of the previously reinforced nudes and the number choosing two or less. It can be

[4]The data of the control groups were combined to facilitate presentation. Their means did not differ significantly on any measure, and both were always in a direction opposite to that of the experimental groups.

TABLE 1. Mean slide attractiveness ratings.

Slides	Conditions		
	Heart-rate increase (N=20)	Heart-rate decrease (N=20)	Sound increase + sound decrease (N=10 + 10)
Reinforced	72.42	69.26	60.86
Nonreinforced	54.11	62.57	63.76
Difference	18.31	6.69	-2.90

Note.—All p values reported are 2-tailed. p value of difference score comparisons (t tests): heart-rate increase versus sound increase and decrease, $p<.001$; heart-rate decrease versus sound increase and decrease, $p<.05$; heart-rate increase versus heart-rate decrease, $p<.05$.

TABLE 2. Number of subjects rating reinforced slides higher and number rating them lower than nonreinforced slides.

Reinforced slides rated	Conditions			
	Heart-rate increase (N=20)	Heart-rate decrease (N=19)[a]	Heart-rate increase + decrease (N=20 + 19)[a]	Sound increase + sound decrease (N=10 + 10)
Higher	17	15	32	9
Lower	3	4	7	11
p value (sign test)	.002	.02	.001	ns

[a]One subject rated the reinforced and nonreinforced stimuli identically.

TABLE 3. Number of subjects choosing three or more reinforced photographs and number choosing two or less.

No. of reinforced photographs chosen	Conditions			
	Heart-rate increase (N=20)	Heart-rate decrease (N=20)	Heart-rate increase + decrease (N=20 + 20)	Sound increase + sound decrease (N=10 + 10)
3 or more	15	14	29	6
2 or less	5	6	11	14
p value (sign test)	.04	ns	.007	ns

TABLE 4. Number of subjects ranking reinforced photographs higher and number ranking them lower than nonreinforced photographs.

Reinforced photographs ranked	Conditions			
	Heart-rate increase (N=20)	Heart-rate decrease (N=20)	Heart-rate increase + decrease (N=20 + 20)	Sound increase + sound decrease (N=10 + 9)[a]
Higher	14	14	28	7
Lower	6	6	12	12
p value (sign test)	ns	ns	.02	ns

[a]One subject could not be contacted for the interview.

seen that a significant number of experimental subjects chose more of the photographs that had been reinforced than photographs that had not been reinforced. The data for the heart-rate decrease condition alone are not quite significant, whereas that of the control groups appear just as strong, but in the opposite direction. An analysis of the mean number of reinforced nudes chosen by each group, however, shows that the heart-rate decrease subjects chose significantly more than that expected on a chance basis, but the control groups did not choose significantly less. The control groups chose an average of 2.25 reinforced photographs ($t=1.55$, *ns*), whereas the heart-rate decrease subjects chose 3.10 reinforced photographs ($t=2.41$, $p<.05$), and the heart-rate increase subjects chose 3.20 reinforced photographs ($t=2.45$, $p<.05$). With the exception that on this measure the experimental groups did not differ from one another, the analysis of photograph choices clearly supports that of the ratings. A marked change in heart rate which is considered as effected by a nude female is interpreted as attraction and results in greater liking for the stimulus.

Delayed Photograph Rankings. It may also be asked whether the observed effects of the heart-rate feedback are temporary or whether they are sufficiently substantial to result in relatively long-lasting cognitive change. In order to answer this question, interviews were conducted with the subjects 4-5 weeks after the experiment proper. During the course of these interviews, the subjects were asked to rank, from most to least attractive, 12 photographs of seminude females. Since 10 of these photographs were used in the experiment proper, an analysis of these rankings permits an evaluation of the relative permanency of the feedback effects. It should be mentioned that the interviewer made every effort to avoid allowing the subjects to associate the interview procedure with the original experiment. Since the source of the photographs was identified as *Playboy* magazine, the subjects did not think it unusual that two experiments would be using similar stimuli. The subjects were, in fact, quite surprised when subsequently informed of the true purpose of the interview. In addition, most of the subjects appeared to rank the photographs on the basis of how they felt at the moment. They were not aware of, or at least did not verbalize, any tendency to rank them according to their previous attractiveness estimates.

It can be seen in Table 4 that the analysis of the delayed photograph rankings is generally consistent with the previous analyses. In comparison to the control subjects, more of the experimental subjects ranked the reinforced photographs as more attractive than the nonreinforced ones ($X^2=4.57$, $p<.05$). Thus, differential heart-rate feedback has had effects which are relatively long lasting (mean delay=31.25 days). Presumed internal reactions have served as cues and have resulted in distinctly different evaluations of emotional stimuli.

DISCUSSION

The major hypothesis of this study has received considerable experimental support. When a subject thought that his heart had reacted markedly to certain slides of seminude females, he rated these slides as more attractive and chose them more often than slides that he thought had not affected his heart rate. These results are exactly what one would have expected had heart-rate changes and veridical feelings of palpitation been pharmacologically induced to some slides but not to others. The mechanism operating to produce these effects is presumably the same regardless of the veridicality of the feedback. Internal events are a source of cognitive information and, as Schachter has proposed, individuals will want to evaluate and understand this kind of information. When an emotional explanation is prepotent, they will label their reactions accordingly. This process is apparently what has been observed in the present experiment. The subjects did attempt to evaluate their reactions, and, having done so, the conditions were such that it was most appropriate for them to explain their reactions by referring to the slides and to interpret them as indicating varying degrees of attraction.

A given heart-rate reaction, however, was not always evaluated as attraction. Post-experimental interviews revealed that, at times, a particular reaction was attributed to surprise, since the subject was daydreaming, and the presentation of the slide shook him out of his reverie, or to a sudden fit of coughing or sneezing, or to a slight resemblance to a former girl friend. It was often evident that these alternative explanations were sought when subjects could not convince themselves that they liked a particular slide. In such cases, it was apparently necessary for them to explain their reactions by referring to other causes. The subjects' attempts to label their reactions suggest that the attractiveness estimates reflected more than shallow verbal definitions of internal reactions. A number of subjects seemed to actively persuade themselves that a reinforced nude was attractive. They reported looking at the slide more closely, and it was evident that they attempted to justify the feedback by magnifying the girl's positive characteristics. Although these subjects realized that they were looking for an explanation for the feedback, they did not feel that they were distorting the slide. Closer inspection simply showed them what their "subconscious" knew all the time. The girl's breasts or buttocks were indeed nicer than they originally thought. Although there is no systematic evidence available, it would be difficult to explain how the feedback could still have effects after several weeks were it not for a process similar to this active self-persuasion.

It is of some interest to consider whether the heart-rate feedback had a direct physiological excitatory effect. If the bogus heart-rate changes resulted in actual physiological change, the differential attractiveness ratings might be attributed to veridical internal cues rather than nonveridical ones. Although physiological variables were not measured there is little reason to suspect that the bogus feedback had any direct effects other than cognitive ones. If these auditory stimuli had excitatory effects that were not due to their "meaning," then the extraneous-sound subjects should have manifested differential attractiveness ratings depending upon the slide-sound change contingencies. However, the differences observed for these subjects, between their ratings of the reinforced and nonreinforced stimuli, were slight and in a direction opposite to that which would be expected. Furthermore, when subjects rated their

awareness of palpitations of actual *feeling* of heart beating during the experiment (4-point scale, ranging from "Not at all" to "An intense amount"), the experimental subjects reported experiencing *fewer* palpitations than did the control subjects. This effect was significant for the heart-rate increase versus extraneous-sound comparison (.6 versus 1.10, $p<.05$) and has subsequently been replicated ($p<.06$). Analysis of the data of this replication, which include galvanic skin response and heart-rate measurements, also reveals that subjects exposed to the heart-rate increase and sound increase manipulations react alike physiologically.[5] It is thus likely that the observed effects of bogus heart-rate feedback are primarily a result of cognitive factors and not physiological ones. In fact, the bogus feedback appears to mask veridical feedback by diverting the subject's attention from his actual internal reactions.

The cognitive manipulations and processes which have been emphasized in the present experiment bear some similarity to current techniques and theory concerned with the extinction of maladaptive emotional behavior. Using systematic desensitization therapy (Wolpe, 1958) phobic patients have been treated by teaching them to perform responses to phobic objects that are incompatible with the fear responses usually generated. In an experimental study, Lang and Lazovik (1963) trained snake-phobic subjects in deep muscle relaxation. The subjects were subsequently hypnotized during each of 11 therapeutic sessions and instructed to relax while imagining a number of situations in which a snake was involved. Subjects participating in this treatment were later observed to be less frightened by snakes, and approximately half of them could even be induced to touch or pick up a live snake. The extinction of these well-established behaviors is presumably due to the resulting incompatibility between the induced muscular relaxation and the physiological changes ordinarily accompanying states of fear. Consider the treatment, however, from a subject's point of view. Whereas in the past he has been physiologically upset when

---

[5] S. Valins, unpublished data.

thinking about snakes, he can now think about them without experiencing as many marked internal sensations. His musculature is now completely relaxed and results in his being able to say, "Thinking about snakes no longer affects me internally." Similar cognitions concerning internal events have effectively influenced the labeling of emotional stimuli in the present experiment. It would seem reasonable that such cognitions are also induced during desensitization therapy and might be the primary factor contributing to the successful treatment of phobic patients. If this is so, the rather tedious muscular relaxation procedure could be replaced with another manipulation of the cognitive representation of internal events. It may be possible to eliminate phobic behaviors solely by inducing nonveridical cognitions concerning internal reactions. Such cognitions could be manipulated so that they would be incompatible with the knowledge of how one usually reacts when frightened. Snake-phobic subjects, for example, who are led to believe that thinking about or seeing snakes does not affect them internally, might reevaluate their attitudes toward snakes and become less frightened by them.

REFERENCES

Bramel, D. Selection of a target for defensive projection. *Journal of Abnormal and Social Psychology,* 1963, **66**, 318–324.

Duffy, E. *Activation and behavior.* New York: Wiley, 1962.

Gerard, H., & Rabbie, J. Fear and social comparison. *Journal of Abnormal and Social Psychology,* 1961, **62**, 586–592.

Lang, P. J., & Lazovik, A. D. Experimental desensitization of a phobia. *Journal of Abnormal and Social Psychology,* 1963, **66**, 519–525.

Latané, B., & Schachter, S. Adrenalin and avoidance learning. *Journal of Comparative and Physiological Psychology,* 1962, **65**, 369–372.

Mandler, G. Emotion. In *New directions in psychology.* New York: Holt, Rinehart & Winston, 1962. Pp. 267–343.

Nisbett, R., & Schachter, S. Cognitive manipulation of pain. *Journal of Experimental Social Psychology,* 1966, **2**, 227–236.

Schachter, S. The interaction of cognitive and physiological determinants of emotional state. In L. Berkowitz (Ed.), *Advances in experimental social psychology,* Vol. 1. New York: Academic Press, 1964. Pp. 49–80.

Schachter, S., & Singer, J. E. Cognitive, social, and physiological determinants of emotional state. *Psychological Review,* 1962, **69**, 379–399.

Schachter, S., & Wheeler, L. Epinephrine, chlorpromazine, and amusement. *Journal of Abnormal and Social Psychology,* 1962, **65**, 121–128.

Singer, J. E. Sympathetic activation, drugs, and fright. *Journal of Comparative and Physiological Psychology,* 1963, **56**, 612–615.

Wolpe, J. *Psychotherapy by reciprocal inhibition.* Palo Alto, Calif.: Stanford University Press, 1958.

Woodworth, R. S., & Schlosberg, H. *Experimental psychology.* New York: Holt, Rinehart & Winston, 1962.

Wynne, L. C., & Solomon, R. L. Traumatic avoidance learning: Acquisition and extinction in dogs deprived of normal peripheral autonomic function. *Genetic Psychology Monographs,* 1955, **52**, 241–284.

ARTICLE 36

Some Extraordinary Facts about Obese Humans and Rats[1]

Stanley Schachter

Several years ago, when I was working on the problem of the labeling of bodily states, I first became aware of Stunkard's (Stunkard & Koch, 1964) work on obesity and gastric motility. At that time, my students and I had been working on a series of studies concerned with the interaction of cognitive and physiological determinants of emotional state (Schachter, 1964). Our experiments had all involved manipulating bodily state by injections of adrenaline or placebo and simultaneously manipulating cognitive and situational variables that were presumed to affect a subject's interpretation of his bodily state. In essence, these experiments had demonstrated that cognitive factors play a major role in determining how a subject interprets his bodily feelings. Precisely the same set of physiological symptoms—an adrenaline-induced state of sympathetic arousal—could be interpreted as euphoria, or anger, or anxiety, or indeed as no emotional state at all, depending very largely on our cognitive and situational manipulations. In short, there is not an invariant, one-to-one relationship between a set of physiological symptoms and a psychological state.

This conclusion was based entirely on studies that manipulated bodily state by the exogenous administration of adrenaline or some other agent. My interest in Stunkard's research was generated by the fact that his work suggested that the same

Reprinted from *American Psychologist*, 1971, **26**, 129–144. With permission of the author and the publisher; copyright 1971, American Psychological Association.

[1]The research reported has been supported by National Science Foundation Grant GS 732.

conclusion might be valid for endogenous physiological states. In his study, Stunkard had his subjects do without breakfast and come to his laboratory at 9:00 A.M. They swallowed a gastric balloon, and for the next four hours, Stunkard continuously recorded stomach contractions. Every 15 minutes, he asked his subjects, "Do you feel hungry?" They answered "Yes" or "No," and that is all there was to the study. He has then a record of the extent to which stomach contractions coincide with self-reports of hunger. For normally sized subjects, the two coincide closely. When the stomach contracts, the normal subject is likely to report hunger; when the stomach is quiescent, the normal subject is likely to say that he does not feel hungry. For the obese, on the other hand, there is little correspondence between gastric motility and self-reports of hunger. Whether or not the obese subject describes himself as hungry seems to have almost nothing to do with the state of his gut. There are, then, major individual differences in the extent to which this particular bodily activity—gastric motility—is associated with the feeling state labeled "hunger."

To pursue this lead, we (Schachter, Goldman, & Gordon, 1968) designed an experiment in which we attempted to manipulate gastric motility and the other physiological correlates of food deprivation by the obvious technique of manipulating food deprivation so that some subjects had empty stomachs and others full stomachs before entering an experimental eating situation. The experiment was disguised as a study of taste, and subjects had been asked to do without the meal (lunch or dinner) that preceded the experiment.

When a subject arrived, he was, depending on condition, either fed roast beef sandwiches or fed nothing. He was then seated in front of five bowls of crackers, presented with a long set of rating scales and told, "We want you to judge each cracker on the dimensions (salty, cheesy, garlicky, etc.) listed on these sheets. Taste as many or as few of the crackers of each type as you want in making your judgments; the important thing is that your ratings be as accurate as possible."

The subject then tasted and rated crackers for 15 minutes, under the impression that this was a taste test, and we simply counted the number of crackers that he ate. There were, of course, two types of subjects: obese subjects (from 14% to 75% overweight) and normal subjects (from 8% underweight to 9% overweight).

To review expectations: If it is correct that the obese do not label as hunger the bodily states associated with food deprivation, then this manipulation should have no effect on the amount eaten by obese subjects; on the other hand, the eating behavior of normal subjects should directly parallel the effects of the manipulation on bodily state.

It will be a surprise to no one to learn, from Figure 1, that normal subjects ate considerably

fewer crackers when their stomachs were full of roast beef sandwiches than when their stomachs were empty. The results for obese subjects stand in fascinating contrast. They ate as much—in fact slightly more—when their stomachs were full as when they were empty. Obviously, the actual state of the stomach has nothing to do with the eating behavior of the obese.[2]

In similar studies (Schachter, 1967; Schachter et al., 1968), we have attempted to manipulate bodily state by manipulating fear and by injecting subjects with epinephrine. Both manipulations are based on Cannon's (1915) and Carlson's (1916) demonstrations that both the state of fear and the injection of epinephrine will inhibit gastric motility and increase blood sugar—both peripheral physiological changes associated with low hunger. These manipulations have no effect at all on obese subjects, but do affect the amounts eaten by normal subjects.

It seems clear that the set of bodily symptoms the subject labels "hunger" differs for obese and normal subjects. Whether one measures gastric motility as Stunkard did, or manipulates motility and the other physiological correlates of food deprivation, as I assume my students and I have done, one finds, for normal subjects, a high degree of correspondence between the state of the gut and eating behavior and, for obese subjects, virtually no correspondence.

Whether or not they are responsive to these particular visceral cues, the obese *do* eat, and the search for the cues that trigger obese eating occupied my students' and my attention for a number of years. Since the experimental details of this search have been published (Schachter, 1967, 1968, 1971), and I believe are fairly well known, I will take time now only to summarize our conclusions—eating by the obese seems unrelated to any internal, visceral state, but is determined by external, food-relevant cues such as the sight, smell, and taste of food. Now, obviously, such external cues to some extent affect anyone's eating behavior. However, for normals these exter-

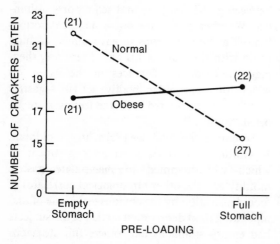

FIGURE 1. The effects of preloading on eating.

[2]The obese subject's failure to regulate when preloaded with sandwiches or some other solid food has now been replicated three times. Pliner's (1970) recent work, however, indicates that the obese will regulate, though not as well as normals, when preloaded with liquid food.

nal factors clearly interact with internal state. They may affect what, where, and how much the normal eats, but chiefly when he is in a state of physiological hunger. For the obese, I suggest, internal state is irrelevant, and eating is determined largely by external cues.

As you may know, there have been a number of experiments testing this hypothesis about the external sensitivity of the obese. To convey some feeling for the nature of the supporting data, I will describe two typical experiments. In one of these, Nisbett (1968a) examined the effects of the sight of food. He reasoned that if the sight of food is a potent cue, the externally sensitive, obese person should eat just as long as food is in sight, and when, in effect, he has consumed all of the available cues, he should stop and make no further attempt to eat. In contrast, the amounts eaten by a normal subject should depend on his physiological needs, not on the quantity of food in sight. Thus, if only a small amount of food is in sight but the subject is given the opportunity to forage for more, the normal subject should eat more than the obese subject. In contrast, if a large amount of food is in sight, the obese should eat more than the normal subject.

To test these expectations, Nisbett provided subjects, who had not eaten lunch, with either one or three roast beef sandwiches. He told them to help themselves and, as he was leaving, pointed to a refrigerator across the room and said, "There are dozens more sandwiches in the refrigerator. Have as many as you want." His results are presented in Table 1. As you can see, obese subjects ate significantly more than normals when presented with three sandwiches, but ate significantly less than normals when presented with only one sandwich.

TABLE 1. Effect of quantity of visible food on amounts eaten.

Subjects	No. sandwiches	
	One	Three
Normal	1.96	1.88
Obese	1.48	2.32

Note.—From Nisbett (1968a).

TABLE 2. Effect of taste on eating.

Subjects	Ounces consumed in	
	Good taste	Bad taste
Normal	10.6	6.4
Obese	13.9	2.6

Note.—From Decke (1971).

In another study, Decke (1971) examined the effects of taste on eating. She reasoned that taste, like the sight or smell of food, is essentially an external cue. Good taste, then, should stimulate the obese to eat more than normals, and bad taste, of course, should have the reverse effect.

In a taste test context, Decke provided her subjects with either a decent vanilla milk shake or with a vanilla milk shake plus quinine. The effects of this taste manipulation are conveyed in Table 2 where, as you can see, obese subjects drank more than normals when the milk shake was good and drank considerably less when the milk shake had been laced with quinine.

Now, anyone who sees Decke's milk shake data and who is familiar with physiological psychology will note that this is precisely what Miller, Bailey, and Stevenson (1950) found and what Teitelbaum (1955) found in the lesioned hyperphagic rat. For those of you who are unfamiliar with this preparation, let me review the facts about this animal. If you make bilateral lesions in the ventromedial nuclei of the hypothalamus, you are likely to get an animal that will eat prodigious amounts of food and will eventually achieve monumental weight—a creature of nightmares. This has been demonstrated for rats, cats, mice, monkeys, rabbits, goats, dogs, and sparrows. Classic descriptions of these preparations portray an animal that immediately after the operation staggers over to its food hopper and shovels in food. For several weeks, this voracious eating continues, and there is, of course, very rapid weight gain. This is called the dynamic phase of hyperphagia. Finally, a plateau is reached, at which point the animal's weight levels off, and its food intake drops to a level only slightly above that of the normal animal. This is called the static phase. During both the static and the dynamic stages, the lesioned animal is also characterized as markedly inactive, and as irascible, emotional, and generally bitchy.

Now it turns out that though the lesioned animal is normally a heavy eater, if you add quinine to its food it drastically decreases its intake to levels far below that of a normal animal's whose food has been similarly tainted. On the other hand, if to its normal food you add dextrose, or lard, or something that is apparently tasty to a rat, the lesioned animal increases its intake to levels considerably above its regular intake and above the intake of a control rat whose food has also been enriched.

The similarity of these facts about the finickiness of the lesioned rat to Decke's findings in her milk shake experiment is, of course, striking, and many people (notably Nisbett, 1968a, 1971) have pointed to this and other similarities between our data on obese humans and the physiologist's data on the obese rat. In order to determine if there was anything more to this than an engaging, occasional resemblance between two otherwise remotely connected sets of data, Judith Rodin and I decided to treat the matter dead seriously and, where possible, to make a point-for-point comparison of every fact we could learn about the hypothalamic, obese rat with every fact we could learn about the obese human. Before describing the results of our work, I would like, however, to be sure that you are aware of the areas of my expertise. I am not a physiological psychologist. Though I am pretty sure that I've eaten a hypothalamus, I doubt that I've ever seen one. When I say something like "bilateral lesions of the ventromedial nuclei of the hypothalamus," you can be sure that I've memorized it. I make this personal confession because of the dilemma that Rodin, also a physiological innocent, and I faced in our work. Though we couldn't have succeeded, we attempted to read *everything* about the ventromedial lesioned rat. If you've ever made this sort of attempt, you may have been seized by the same despair as were we when it sometimes seemed as if there were no such thing as a fact that *someone* had not failed to confirm. (I include in this sweeping generalization, by the way, the apparent fact that a ventromedial lesion produces

a hyperphagic, obese animal—see Reynolds, 1963, and Rabin and Smith, 1968.) And it sometimes seemed as if there were no such thing as an experiment which *someone* had not failed to replicate. Since I happen to have spent my college physics lab course personally disproving most of the laws of physics, I cannot say that I find this particularly surprising, but if one is trying to decide what is the fact, it is a depressing state of affairs. In our own areas of expertise, this probably isn't too serious a problem. Each of us in our specialities knows how to evaluate a piece of work. In a field in which you are not expert, you simply cannot, except in the crudest of cases, evaluate. If several experimenters have different results, you just don't know which to believe. In order to cope with this dilemma, Rodin and I decided to treat each of our facts in batting average terms. For each fact, I will inform you of the number of studies that have been concerned with the fact and the proportion of these studies that work out in a given direction. To be included in the batting average, we required only that a study present all or a substantial portion of its data, rather than report the author's impressions or present only the data of one or two presumably representative cases. I should also note that in all cases we have relied on the data and not on what the experimenter said about the data. It may seem silly to make this point explicit, but it is the case that in a few studies, for some perverse reason, the experimenter's conclusions simply have nothing to do with his data. Finally, I should note that in all comparisons of animal and human data, I will consider the data only for animals in the static phase of obesity, animals who, like our human subjects, are already fat. In general, however, the results for dynamic and static animals are quite similar.

As a shorthand method of making comparisons between studies and species, I shall throughout the rest of this article employ what we can call a Fat to Normal (F/N) ratio in which we simply get an index by dividing the magnitude of the effect for fat subjects by the magnitude of the effect for normal control subjects. Thus, if in a particular study the fat rats ate an average of 15 grams of food and normal rats ate 10 grams, the

F/N ratio would be 1.50, indicating that the fat rats ate 50% more food than normal rats.

To begin our comparisons, let us return to the effects of taste on eating behavior. We know that fat human beings eat more of a good-tasting food than do normal human beings and that they eat less of bad-tasting food than do normals. The physiologists have done almost identical experiments to ours, and in Line 1 of Table 3 we can compare the effects of good-tasting food on lesioned animals and on men. You will notice on the left that Rodin and I found six studies on lesioned animals, in this case largely rats. Batting average: five of the six studies indicate that lesioned, static, obese animals eat more of a good-tasting food than do their normal controls. The average F/N ratio for these six studies is 1.45, indicating that fat rats on the average eat 45% more of good-tasting food than do normal rats. On the right side of the table, you can see that there have been two human studies, and that both of these studies indicate that fat humans eat more of good-tasting food than do normal humans. The average F/N ratio for humans is 1.42, indicating that fat humans eat 42% more of good-tasting food than do normally sized humans.[3]

TABLE 3.   Effects of taste on eating.

Condition	Animals		Humans	
	Batting average	Mean F/N	Mean F/N	Batting average
Good food	5/6	1.45	1.42	2/2
Bad food	3/4	.76	.84	1/2

Note.—F/N = Fat to normal ratio.

Incidentally, please keep in mind throughout this exercise that the left side of each table will always contain the data for lesioned animals, very largely rats, that have been abused by a variety of people named Epstein, and Teitelbaum, and Stellar, and Miller, and so on. The right side of each table will always contain the data for humans,

[3]The technically informed reader undoubtedly will wish to know precisely which studies and what data are included in Tables 3 and 4. There are so many studies involved that, within the context of this paper, it is impossible to supply this information. Dr. Rodin and I are preparing a monograph on this work which will, of course, provide full details on such matters.

mostly Columbia College students, nice boys who go home every Friday night, where, I suppose, they too are abused by a variety of people named Epstein, and Teitelbaum, and Stellar, and Miller.

In line 2 of Table 3, we have the effects of bad taste on consumption. For both animals and men, in all of these studies bad taste was manipulated by the addition of quinine to the food. There are four animal studies; three of the four indicate that fat animals eat less than normal animals, and the average F/N ratio is .76. There are two human studies: one of the two indicates that fats eat considerably less bad food than normals; the other indicates no significant difference between the two groups, and the mean F/N ratio for these two studies is .84. For this particular fact, the data are more fragile than one would like, but the trends for the two species are certainly parallel.

To continue this examination of parallel facts: the eating habits of the lesioned rats have been thoroughly studied, particularly by Teitelbaum and Campbell (1958). It turns out that static obese rats eat on the average slightly, not considerably, more than normal rats. They also eat fewer meals per day, eat more per meal, and eat more rapidly than do normal animals. For each of these facts, we have parallel data for humans. Before presenting these data, I should note that for humans, I have, wherever possible, restricted myself to behavioral studies, studies in which the investigators have actually measured how much their subjects eat. I hope no one will be offended, I assume no one will be surprised, if I say that I am skeptical of the self-reports of fat people about how much they eat or exercise.[4] For those of you who feel that this is high-handed selection of studies, may I remind you of Stunkard's famous chronic fat patients who were fed everything that, in interviews, they admitted to eating daily, and who all steadily lost weight on this diet.

Considering first the average amount eaten per day when on ad-lib feeding of ordinary lab chow or pellets, you will note in Line 1 of Table 4 that consistently static obese rats eat somewhat (19%) more than do their normal counterparts. The data for humans are derived from all of the stud-

[4]In three of four such self-report studies, fat people report eating considerably less food than do normals.

TABLE 4. Eating habits.

Variable	Animals		Humans	
	Batting average	Mean F/N	Mean F/N	Batting average
Amount of food eaten ad lib	9/9	1.19	1.16	2/3
No. meals per day	4/4	.85	.92	3/3
Amount eaten per meal	2/2	1.34	1.29	5/5
Speed of eating	1/1	1.28	1.26	1/1

Note.—F/N = Fat to normal ratio.

ies I know of in which eating is placed in a nosh-ing, or ad-lib, context; that is, a bowl of ordinary food, usually nuts or crackers, is placed in the room, the experiment presumably has nothing to do with eating, and the subject is free to eat or not, as he chooses, just as is a rat in its cage. In two of the three experiments conducted in this context, obese subjects eat slightly more than do normals; in the third experiment, the two groups eat precisely the same number of crackers. For both humans and rats, then, the fat subject eats only slightly more than the normal subject.

Turning next to the number of meals per day, we note on Line 2 of Table 4 that for both rats and humans, fatter subjects consistently eat fewer meals per day. (A rat meal is defined by Teitel-baum and Campbell, 1958, as "any burst of food intake of at least five pellets separated by at least 5 min. from any other burst [p. 138].") For hu-mans, these particular data are based on self-report or interview studies, for I know of no relevant behavioral data. In any case, again the data for the lesioned rat and the obese human correspond very closely indeed.

From the previous two facts, it should, of course, follow that obese subjects will eat more per meal than normal subjects, and, as can be seen in Line 3 of Table 4, this is the case for both lesioned rats and obese humans. The data for rats are based on two experiments that simply recorded the amount of food eaten per eating burst. The data for humans are based on all ex-periments in which a plate of food, usually sand-wiches, is placed before a subject, and he is told to help himself to lunch or dinner.

Our final datum on eating habits is the speed of eating. Teitelbaum and Campbell (1958) sim-

ply recorded the number of pellets their animals ate per minute. Since there is nothing else to do when you are sitting behind a one-way screen watching a subject eat, Nisbett (1968b—data not reported in paper) recorded the number of spoon-fuls of ice cream his subjects ate per minute. The comparison of the two studies is drawn in Line 4 of Table 4, where you will note an unsettling similarity in the rate at which lesioned rats and obese humans outspeed their normal counter-parts.[5]

All told, then, in the existing literature, Rodin and I found a total of six items of behavior on which it is possible to make rather precise com-parisons between lesioned rats and obese humans. These are mostly nonobvious facts, and the com-parisons drawn between the two sets of experi-ments do not attempt to push the analogies beyond the point of common sense. I do not think there can be much debate about pellets versus spoonfuls of ice cream consumed per minute as equivalent measures of eating rate. For all six facts in the existing literature, the parallels be-tween the species are striking. What the lesioned, fat rat does, the obese human does.

In addition to these facts, we identified two other areas of behavior in which it is possible to draw somewhat more fanciful, though still not ridiculous, comparisons between the species. These are the areas of emotionality and of activ-ity. Though there has been little systematic study of emotionality, virtually everyone who has worked with these animals agrees that the le-sioned animals are hyperexcitable, easily startled, overemotional, and generally bitchy to handle. In

[5]Fat rats do not drink more rapidly than do normals. There are no comparable data for humans.

addition, work by Singh (1969) and research on active avoidance learning do generally support this characterization of the lesioned animal as an emotional beast.

For humans, we have two experiments from which it is possible to draw conclusions about emotionality. In one of these (Schachter et al., 1968), we manipulated fear by threat of painful electric shock. On a variety of rating scales, fat subjects acknowledged that they were somewhat more frightened and anxious than did normal subjects. In a second experiment, Rodin (1970) had her subjects listen to an audio tape while they were working at either a monitoring or a proofreading task. The tapes were either neutral (requiring the subject to think about either rain or seashells) or emotionally charged (requiring the subject to think about his own death or about the bombing of Hiroshima). The emotionally charged tapes produced dramatic differences between subjects. On a variety of rating scales, the obese described themselves as considerably more upset and disturbed than did normal subjects; they reported more palpitations and changes in breathing rate than did normals; and performance, at either the proofreading or monitoring tasks, deteriorated dramatically more for obese than for normal subjects. Again, then, the data are consistent, for both the lesioned animal and the obese human seem to react more emotionally than their normal counterparts.

Finally, on activity, numerous studies using stabilimeter cages or activity wheels have demonstrated that the lesioned animal is markedly less active than the normal animal. This is not, I should add, a totally trivial fact indicating only that the lesioned animal has trouble shlepping his immense bulk around the cage, for the dynamic hyperphagic rat—who though not yet fat, will be —is quite as lethargic as his obese counterpart. On the human side, Bullen, Reed, and Mayer (1964) have taken movies of girls at camp during their scheduled periods of swimming, tennis, and volleyball. They categorize each camper for her degree of activity or exertion during these periods, and do find that the normal campers are more active than are the obese girls.

All told, then, Rodin and I found a total of eight facts, indicating a perfect parallel between the behavior of the lesioned rat and the obese human. We have, so far, found no fact on which the two species differ. Now all of this has proved such an engaging exercise that my students and I decided to play "real" scientist, and we constructed a matrix. We simply listed every fact we could find about the lesioned animals and every fact we could find about obese humans. I have told you about those facts for which parallel data exist. There are, however, numerous holes in the matrix—facts for rats for which no parallel human data have yet been collected, and vice versa. For the past year, we have been engaged in filling in these holes—designing for humans, experiments that have no particular rhyme or reason except that someone once did such an experiment on lesioned rats. For example, it is a fact that though lesioned rats will outeat normal rats when food is easily available, they will not lift a paw if they have to work to get food. In a Skinner box setup, Teitelbaum (1957) finds that at FR1, when one press yields one pellet, fat lesioned rats outpress normal. As the payoff decreases, however, fat rats press less and less until at FR256, they do not manage to get a single pellet during a 12-hour experimental session, whereas normal rats are still industriously pressing away. Similarly, Miller et al. (1950) found that though lesioned rats ate more than normal controls when an unweighted lid covered the food dish, they ate less than did the controls when a 75-gram weight was fastened to the lid. They also found that the lesioned rats ran more slowly down an alley to food than controls did and pulled less hard when temporarily restrained by a harness. In short, fat rats will not work to get food.

Since there was no human parallel to these studies, Lucy Friedman and I designed a study in which, when a subject arrived, he was asked simply to sit at the experimenter's desk and fill out a variety of personality tests and questionnaires. Besides the usual student litter, there was a bag of almonds on the desk. The experimenter helped herself to a nut, invited the subject to do the same, and then left him alone with his questionnaires and nuts for 15 minutes. There were two sets of conditions. In one, the nuts had shells on them;

in the other, the nuts had no shells. I assume we agree that eating nuts with shells is considerably more work than eating nuts with no shells.

The top half of Table 5 presents for normal subjects the numbers who do and do not eat nuts in the two conditions. As you can see, shells or no shells has virtually no impact on normal subjects. Fifty-five percent of normals eat nuts without shells, and 50% eat nuts with shells. I am a little self-conscious about the data for obese subjects, for it looks as if I were too stupid to know how to fake data. I know how to fake data, and were I to do so, the bottom half of Table 5 certainly would not look the way it does. When the nuts have no shells, 19 of 20 fat subjects eat nuts. When the nuts have shells on them, 1 out of 20 fat subjects eats. Obviously, the parallel to Miller's and to Teitelbaum's rats is perfect. When the food is easy to get at, fat subjects, rat or human, eat more than normals; when the food is hard to get at, fat subjects eat less than normals.

TABLE 5. Effects of work on the eating behavior of normal and fat subjects.

Nuts have	Number who	
	Eat	Don't eat
Normal subjects		
Shells	10	10
No shells	11	9
Fat subjects		
Shells	1	19
No shells	19	1

Incidentally, as a casual corollary of these and other findings, one could expect that, given acceptable food, fat eaters would be more likely than normals to choose the easiest way of eating. In order to check on this, Lucy Friedman, Joel Handler, and I went to a large number of Chinese and Japanese restaurants, categorized each patron as he entered the restaurant as obese or normal, and then simply noted whether he ate with chopsticks or with silverware. Among Occidentals, for whom chopsticks can be an ordeal, we found that almost five times the proportion of normal eaters ate with chopsticks as did obese eaters—22.4% of normals and 4.7% of the obese ate with chopsticks.

In another matrix-hole-filling experiment, Patricia Pliner (1970) has demonstrated that obese humans, like lesioned rats, do not regulate food consumption when they are preloaded with solids but, again like the rats, do regulate when they are preloaded with liquids.

In addition to these experiments, we are currently conducting studies on pain sensitivity and on passive versus active avoidance learning—all designed to fill in more holes in our human-lesioned rat matrix. To date, we have a total of 12 nonobvious facts in which the behaviors of lesioned rats parallel perfectly the behaviors of obese humans. Though I cannot believe that as our matrix-hole-filling experiments continue, this perfect parallelism will continue, I submit that even now these are mind-boggling data. I would also submit, however, that we have played this enchanting game just about long enough. This is, after all, science through analogy—a sport I recommend with the same qualifications and enthusiasms with which I recommend skiing—and it is time that we asked what on earth does it all mean? To which at this point I can only answer ruefully that I wish to God I really knew.

On its most primitive level, I suppose that I would love to play doctor and issue pronouncements such as, "Madam, you have a very sick hypothalamus." And, indeed, I do know of one case of human obesity (Reeves & Plum, 1969) accompanied by a precisely localized neoplasm that destroyed the ventromedial hypothalamus. This is an astonishing case study, for the lady reads like a lesioned rat—she ate immense amounts of food, as much as 10,000 calories a day, grew impressively fat and was apparently a wildly emotional creature given to frequent outbursts of laughing, crying, and rage. Now I am not, of course, going to suggest that this lady is anything but a pathological extreme. The only vaguely relevant study I know of is a morphological study (Maren, 1955) of the hypothalami of genetically obese mice, an animal whose behavior also resembles the lesioned rat's, which found no structural differences between obese and normal mice.

Mrosovsky (1971) has been developing a more sober hypothesis. Comparing the hibernator and the ventromedial lesioned rat, Mrosovsky has been playing much the same analogical game as have I, and he, too, has noted the marked behavioral similarities of his two species to the obese human. He hypothesizes that the unlesioned, obese animal, rodent or human, has a ventromedial hypothalamus that is functionally quiescent. Though I would be willing to bet that when the appropriate biochemical and electrophysiological studies are done, Mrosovsky will be proven correct, I do not believe that this is a fact which is of fundamental interest to psychologists. Most of us, I suspect, have long been convinced, psychodynamics notwithstanding, that there is *something* biologically responsible for human obesity, and to be able suddenly to point a finger at an offending structure would not really put us much ahead. After all, we've known about the adrenal medulla and emotion for more than 50 years, and I doubt that this particular bit of knowledge has been of much help in our understanding of aggression, or fear, or virtually any other emotional state.

If it is true that the ventromedial hypothalamus is functionally quiescent, for us the question must be, for what function, psychologically speaking, is it quiescent? What processes, or inputs, or outputs are mediated by this particular structure? Speculation and theorizing about the functions of this area have tended to be cautious and modest. Essentially, two suggestions have been made—one that the area is a satiety center, and the other that the area is an emotionality center. Both Miller (1964) and Stellar (1954) have tentatively suggested that the ventromedial area is a satiety center—that in some fashion it monitors the signals indicating a sufficiency of food and inhibits the excitatory (Eat! Eat!) impulses initiated in the lateral hypothalamus. This inhibitory-satiety mechanism can account for the hyperphagia of the lesioned animals and, consequently, for their obesity. It can also account for

most of the facts that I outlined earlier about the daily eating habits of these animals. It cannot by itself, however, account for the finickiness of these animals, nor can it, as I believe I can show, account for the apparent unwillingness of these animals to work for food. Finally, this hypothesis is simply irrelevant to the demonstrated inactivity and hyperemotionality of these animals. This irrelevance, however, is not critical if one assumes, as does Stellar, that discrete neural centers, also located in the ventromedial area, control activity and emotionality. The satiety theory, then, can account for some, but by no means all, of the critical facts about eating, and it has nothing to say about activity or emotionality.

As a theoretically more ambitious alternative, Grossman (1966, 1967) has proposed that the ventromedial area be considered the emotionality center and that the facts about eating be derived from this assumption. By definition, Grossman's hypothesis accounts for the emotionality of these animals, and his own work on active avoidance learning certainly supports the emotionality hypothesis. I must confess, however, that I have difficulty in understanding just why these emotional animals become fat. In essence, Grossman (1966) assumes that "lesions in or near the VMH sharply increase an animal's affective responsiveness to apparently all sensory stimuli [p. 1]." On the basis of this general statement, he suggests that "the 'finickiness' of the ventromedial animal might then reflect a change in its affective response to taste." This could, of course, account for the fact that lesioned animals eat more very good- and less very bad-tasting food than do normals. However, I simply find it hard to believe that this affective hypothesis can account for the basic fact about these animals—that for weeks on end, the lesioned animals eat grossly more of ordinary, freely available lab chow.

Grossman (1967) attributes the fact that lesioned animals will not work for food to their "exaggerated response to handling, the test situation, the deprivation regimen, and the requirement of having to work for their daily bread [p. 358]." I suppose all of this is possible, I simply find it farfetched. At the very least, the response to handling and to the deprivation regime should be just as exaggerated whether the reinforcement schedule is FR1 or FR256 and the lesioned animals do press more than the normals at FR1.

My skepticism, however, is irrelevant, and Grossman may be correct. There are, however, at least two facts with which, it seems to me, Grossman's hypothesis cannot cope. First, it would seem to me that an animal with an affective response to food would be likely to eat more rather than less often per day, as is the fact. Second, it is simply common sense to expect that an animal with strong "affective responsiveness to all sensory stimuli" will be a very active animal indeed, but the lesioned animal is presumably hypoactive.

None of the existing theories, then, can cope with all of the currently available facts. For the remainder of this article, I am going to try my hand at developing a hypothesis that I believe can cope with more of the facts than can the available alternatives. It is a hypothesis that derives entirely from our work on human obesity. I believe, however, that it can explain as many of the facts about ventromedial-lesioned rats as it can about the human obese. If future experimental work on animals proves this correct, it would certainly suggest that science by analogy has merits other than its entertainment value.

The gist of our findings on humans is this—the eating behavior of the obese is under external, rather than internal, control. In effect, the obese seem stimulus-bound. When a food-relevant cue is present, the obese are more likely to eat and to eat a great deal than are normals. When such a cue is absent, the obese are less likely to try to eat or to complain about hunger. Though I have not, in this article, developed this latter point, there is evidence that, in the absence of food-relevant cues, the obese have a far easier time fasting than do normals, while in the presence of such cues, they have a harder time fasting (Goldman, Jaffa, & Schachter, 1968).

Since it is a little hard to believe that such stimulus-binding is limited to food-relevant cues, for some time now my students and I have been concerned with the generalizability of these facts. Given our starting point, this concern has led to some rather odd little experiments. For example, Judith Rodin, Peter Herman, and I have asked subjects to look at slides on which are portrayed 13 objects or words. Each slide is exposed for five seconds, and the subject is then asked to recall what he saw. Fat subjects recall more objects than do normal subjects. The experiment has been replicated, and this appears to be a reliable phenomenon.

In another study, Rodin, Herman, and I compared fat and normal subjects on simple and on complex or disjunctive reaction time. For simple reaction time, they are instructed to lift their finger from a telegraph key as soon as the stimulus light comes on. On this task, there are no differences between obese and normal subjects. For complex reaction time, there are two stimulus lights and two telegraph keys, and subjects are instructed to lift their left finger when the right light comes on and lift their right finger when the left light comes on. Obese subjects respond more rapidly and make fewer errors. Since this was a little hard to believe, this study was repeated three times—each time with the same results—the obese are simply better at complex reaction time than are normals. I do not pretend to understand these results, but they do seem to indicate that, for some reason, the obese are more efficient stimulus or information processors.

At this stage, obviously, this is shotgun research which, in coordination with the results of our eating experiments, seems to indicate that it may be useful to more generally characterize the obese as stimulus-bound and to hypothesize that any stimulus, above a given intensity level, is more likely to evoke an appropriate response from an obese than from a normal subject.

Our first test of implications of this hypothesis in a noneating setting is Rodin's (1970) experiment on the effects of distraction on performance. She reasoned that if the stimulus-binding hypothesis is correct, distracting, irrelevant stimuli should be more disruptive for obese than for normal subjects when they are performing a task requiring concentration. Presumably, the impinging stimulus is more likely to grip the attention of the stimulus-bound obese subject. To test this guess, she had her subjects work at a simple proofreading task. In one condition, the subjects corrected proof with no distractions at all. In the three other conditions, they corrected proof while listening to recorded tapes that varied in the degree to which they were likely to grip a subject's attention, and therefore distract him. The results are presented in Figure 2, where, as you can see, the obese are better at proofreading when undistracted but their performance seriously deteriorates as they are distracted until, at extreme distraction, they are considerably worse than normals. Rodin finds precisely the same pattern of results, by the way, in a similar study in which she uses the complex reaction time task I have already described rather than the proofreading task. For humans, then, there is evidence, outside of the eating context, to support the hypothesis.

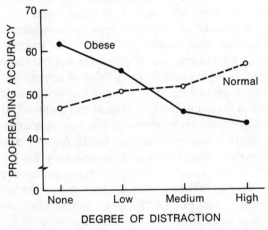

FIGURE 2. The effects of distraction on performance (from Rodin, 1970).

Let us return to consideration of the ventromedial lesioned animal and examine the implications of the hypothesis that any stimulus, above a given intensity level, is more likely to evoke an appropriate response from a lesioned than from an intact animal. This is a hypothesis which is, in many ways, similar to Grossman's hypothesis and, on the face of it, would appear to be vulnerable to exactly the same criticisms as I have leveled at his theory. There are, however, crucial differences that will become evident as I elaborate this notion. I assume it is self-evident that my hypothesis can explain the emotionality of the lesioned

animals and, with the exception of meal frequency—a fact to which I will return—can account for virtually all of our facts about the daily eating habits of these animals. I will, therefore, begin consideration of the hypothesis by examining its implications for those facts that have been most troubling for alternative formulations and by examining those facts that seem to most clearly contradict my own hypothesis.

Let us turn first to the perverse and fascinating fact that though lesioned animals will outeat normals when food is easily available, they simply will not work for food. In my terms, this is an incomplete fact which may prove only that a remote food stimulus will not evoke a food-acquiring response. It is the case that in the experiments concerned with this fact, virtually every manipulation of work has covaried the remoteness or prominence of the food cue. Food at the end of a long alleyway is obviously a more remote cue than food in the animal's food dish. Pellets available only after 256 presses of a lever are certainly more remote food stimuli than pellets available after each press of a lever. If the stimulus-binding hypothesis is correct, it should be anticipated that, in contrast to the results when the food cue is remote, the lesioned animal will work harder than the normal animal when the food stimulus is prominent and compelling. Though the appropriate experiment has not yet been done on rats, to my delight I have learned recently that such an experiment has been done on humans by William Johnson (1970), who independently has been pursuing a line of thought similar to mine.

Johnson seated his subject at a table, fastened his hand in a harness, and, to get food, required the subject for 12 minutes to pull, with his index finger, on a ring that was attached by wire to a seven-pound weight. He received food on a VR50 schedule—that is, on the average, a subject received a quarter of a sandwich for every 50 pulls of the ring. Obviously, this was moderately hard work.

To vary stimulus prominence, Johnson manipulated food visibility and prior taste of food. In "food visible" conditions, he placed beside the subject one desirable sandwich covered in a transparent wrap. In addition, as the subject satisfied the VR requirements, he placed beside him quarter sandwiches similarly wrapped. In "food invisible" conditions, Johnson followed exactly the same procedures, but wrapped the sandwiches in white, nontransparent shelf paper. Subjects, of course, did not eat until they had completed their 12 minutes of labor.

As a second means of varying cue prominence, half of the subjects ate a quarter of a very good sandwich immediately before they began work. The remaining subjects ate a roughly equivalent portion of plain white bread.

In Figure 3, you can see the effects of these manipulations on effort. I have arranged the conditions along the dimension of food cue prominence—ranging from no prominent food cues to two prominent food cues—that is, the subjects ate a quarter sandwich and the food was visible. As you can see, the stimulus prominence manipulations have a marked effect on the obese, for they work far harder when the food cues are prominent and compelling than when they are incon-

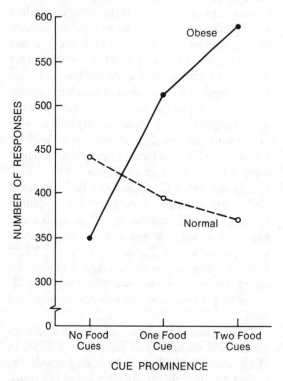

FIGURE 3. The effect of food cue prominence on effort (from Johnson, 1970).

spicuous. In contrast, cue prominence has relatively little effect on normal subjects.

Please note also that these results parallel Miller's and Teitelbaum's results with lesioned rats. When the food cues are remote, the obese human works less hard for food than the normally sized human. The fact that this relationship flips when the cues are prominent is, of course, a delight to me, and wouldn't it be absorbing to replicate this experiment on lesioned rats?

Let us turn next to the fact that lesioned rats are hypoactive. If ever a fact were incompatible with a hypothesis, this one is it. Surely an animal that is more responsive to any stimulus should be hyper-, not hypoactive. Yet this is a most peculiar fact—for it remains a fact only because one rather crucial finding in the literature has been generally overlooked and because the definition of activity seems restricted to measures obtained in running wheels or in stabilimeter-type living cages.

Studies of activity have with fair consistency reported dramatically less activity for lesioned than for normal rats. With one exception, these studies report data in terms of total activity per unit time, making no distinction between periods when the animal room was quiet and undisturbed and periods involving the mild ferment of animal-tending activities. Gladfelter and Brobeck (1962), however, report activity data separately for the "43-hour period when the constant-temperature room was dark and quiet and the rats were undisturbed" and for the "five-hour period when the room was lighted and the rats were cared for [p. 811]." During the quiet time, these investigators find precisely what almost everyone else does—lesioned rats are markedly less active. During the animal-tending period, however, lesioned animals are just about as active as normal animals. In short, when the stimulus field is relatively barren and there is little to react to, the ventromedial animal is inactive; when the field is made up of the routine noises, stirrings, and disturbances involved in tending an animal laboratory, the lesioned animal is just about as active as the normal animal.

Though this is an instructive fact, it hardly proves my hypothesis, which specifies that above a given stimulus intensity the lesioned animal should be *more* reactive than the normal animal. Let us, then, ask—is there any evidence that lesioned animals are more active than normal animals? There is, if you are willing to grant that specific activities such as lever pressing or avoidance behavior are as much "activity" as the gross, overall measures obtained in stabilimeter-mounted living cages.

In his study of activity, Teitelbaum (1957) has distinguished between random and food-directed activity. As do most other investigators, he finds that in their cages, lesioned rats are much less active than are normals. During a 12-hour stint in a Skinner box, however, when on an FR1 schedule, the lesioned animals are more active; that is, they press more than do normals. Thus, when the food cue is salient and prominent, as it is on an FR1 schedule, the lesioned animal is very active indeed. And, as you know, when the food cue is remote, as it is on an FR64 or FR256 schedule, the lesioned animal is inactive.

Since lever pressing is activity in pursuit of food, I suppose one should be cautious in accepting these data as support for my argument. Let us turn, then, to avoidance learning where most of the experiments are unrelated to food.

In overall batting average terms,[6] no area could be messier than this one, for in three of six studies, lesioned animals are better and in three worse at avoidance than normals. However, if one distinguishes between passive and active avoidance, things become considerably more coherent.

In active avoidance studies, a conditioned stimulus, such as a light or buzzer, precedes a noxious event such as electrifying the floor grid. To avoid the shock, the animal must perform some action such as jumping into the nonelectrified compartment of a shuttle box. In three of

four such studies, the lesioned animals learn considerably more rapidly than do normal animals. By this criterion, at least, lesioned animals are more reactive than normal animals.[7] Parenthetically, it is amusing to note that the response latencies of the lesioned animal are smaller (Grossman, 1966) than those of the normal animal, just as in our studies of complex reaction time, obese humans are faster than normal humans.

In contrast to these results, lesioned animals do considerably worse than normal animals in passive avoidance studies. In these studies, the animal's water dish or the lever of a Skinner box are electrified so that if, during the experimental period, the animal touches these objects he receives a shock. In both of the studies we have so far found on passive learning, the lesioned animals do considerably worse than normal animals. They either press the lever or touch the water dish more than do normals and accordingly are shocked far more often. Thus, when the situation requires a response if the animal is to avoid shock, the lesioned animal does better than the normal animal. Conversely, if the situation requires response quiescence if the animal is to avoid shock, the lesioned animal does far worse than the normal animal. This pair of facts, I suggest, provides strong support for the hypothesis that beyond a given stimulus intensity, the lesioned animal is more reactive than the normal animal. I would also suggest that without some variant of this hypothesis, the overall pattern of results on avoidance learning is incoherent.

All in all, then, one can make a case of sorts for the suggestion that there are specifiable circumstances in which lesioned animals will be more active. It is hardly an ideal case, and only an

---

[6]Of all the behavioral areas so far considered, avoidance learning is probably the one for which it makes least sense either to adopt a batting average approach or to attempt to treat the research as a conceptually equivalent set of studies. Except in this area, the great majority of experiments have used, as subjects, rats with electrolytically produced lesions. In the avoidance learning area, the subjects have been mice, rats, and cats; the lesions are variously electrolytically produced, produced by gold thioglucose injections, or are "functional" lesions produced by topical application of atropine or some other agent.

[7]Reactive, yes, but what about activity in the more primitive sense of simply moving or scrambling about the experimental box? Even in this respect, the lesioned animals appear to outmove the normals, for Turner, Sechzer, and Liebelt (1967) report that: "The experimental groups, both mice and rats, emitted strong escape tendencies prior to the onset of shock and in response to shock. Repeated attempts were made to climb out of the test apparatus. This group showed much more vocalization than the control group. . . . In contrast to the behavior of the experimental animals, the control animals appeared to become immobilized or to "freeze" both before and during the shock period. Thus, there was little attempt to escape and little vocalization" [p. 242].

experiment that measures the effects of systematically varied stimulus field richness on gross activity can test the point.

These ruminations on activity do suggest a refinement of the general hypothesis and also, I trust, make clear why I have insisted on inserting that awkward phrase "above a given intensity level" in all statements of the hypothesis. For activity, it appears to be the case that the lesioned animal is less active when the stimulus is remote and more active when the stimulus is prominent. This interaction between reactivity and stimulus prominence is presented graphically in Figure 4. This is a formulation which I believe fits almost all of the available data, on both animals and men, remarkably well. It is also a formulation which for good ad-hoc reasons bears a striking resemblance to almost every relevant set of data I have discussed.

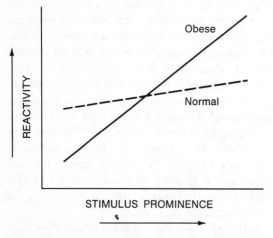

FIGURE 4. Theoretical curves of relationship of reactivity to stimulus prominence.

For human eating behavior, virtually every fact we have supports the assertion that the obese eat more than normals when the food cue is prominent and less when the cue is remote. In Johnson's study of work and cue prominence, the obese do not work as hard as normals when there are no prominent food cues, but work much harder when the food cues are highly salient. In Nisbett's one- and three-sandwich experiment, the obese subjects eat just as long as food cues are prominent—that is, the sandwiches are directly

in front of the subject—but when these immediate cues have been consumed, they stop eating. Thus, they eat more than normals in the three-sandwich condition and less in the one-sandwich condition. We also know that the obese have an easy time fasting in the absence of food cues and a hard time in the presence of such cues, and so on.

About eating habits we know that the obese eat larger meals (what could be a more prominent cue than food on the plate?), but eat fewer meals (as they should if it requires a particularly potent food cue to trigger an eating response). Even the fact that the obese eat more rapidly can be easily derived from this formulation.

For rats, this formulation in general fits what we know about eating habits, but can be considered a good explanation of the various experimental facts only if you are willing to accept my reinterpretation, in terms of cue prominence, of such experiments as Miller et al.'s (1950) study of the effects of work on eating. If, as would I, you would rather suspend judgment until the appropriate experiments have been done on lesioned rats, mark it down as an engaging possibility.

Given the rough state of what we know about emotionality, this formulation seems to fit the data for humans and rats about equally well. The lesioned rats are vicious when handled and lethargic when left alone. In the Rodin (1970) experiment which required subjects to listen to either neutral or emotionally disturbing tapes, obese subjects described themselves (and behaved accordingly) as less emotional than normals when the tapes were neutral and much more emotional than normals when the tapes were disturbing.

All in all, given the variety of species and behaviors involved, it is not a bad ad-hoc hypothesis. So far there has been only one study deliberately designed to test some of the ideas implicit in this formulation. This is Lee Ross's (1969) study of the effects of cue salience on eating. Ross formulated this experiment in the days when we were struggling with some of the data inconsistent with our external-internal theory of eating behavior (see Schachter, 1967). Since the world is full of food cues, it was particularly embarrassing to discover that obese subjects ate less frequently than normals. Short of invoking denial mechanisms, such a fact could be reconciled with the theory only if we assumed that a food cue must be potent in order to trigger an eating response in an obese subject—the difference between a hot dog stand two blocks away and a hot dog under your nose, savory with mustard and steaming with sauerkraut.

To test the effects of cue prominence, Ross simply had his subjects sit at a table covered with a variety of objects among which was a large tin of shelled cashew nuts. Presumably, the subjects were there to take part in a study of thinking. There were two sets of experimental conditions. In high-cue-saliency conditions, the table and the nuts were illuminated by an unshaded table lamp containing a 40-watt bulb. In low-saliency conditions, the lamp was shaded and contained a 7½-watt red bulb. The measure of eating was simply the difference in the weight of the tin of nuts before and after the subject thought his experimentally required thoughts. The results are presented in Figure 5, which, needless to say, though I will say it, bears a marked resemblance to our theoretical curves.

So much for small triumphs. Let us turn now to some of the problems of this formulation. Though I do not intend to detail a catalog of failings, I would like to make explicit some of my discomforts.

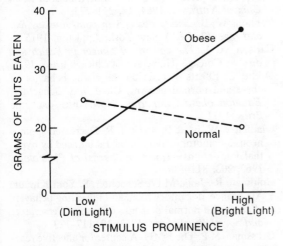

FIGURE 5. The effects of stimulus intensity on amount eaten (from Ross, 1969).

1. Though there has been no direct experimental study of the problem, it seems to be generally thought that the lesioned rat is hyposexual, which, if true, is one hell of a note for a theory which postulates superreactivity. It is the case, however, that gonadal atrophy is frequently a consequence of this operation (Brooks & Lambert, 1946; Hetherington & Ranson, 1940). Possibly, then, we should consider sexual activity as artifactually quite distinct from either gross activity or stimulus-bound activity such as avoidance behavior.

2. I am made uncomfortable by the fact that the obese, both human and rat, eat less bad food than do normals. I simply find it difficult to conceive of nonresponsiveness as a response. I suppose I could conceptually pussyfoot around this difficulty, but I cannot imagine the definition of response that would allow me to cope with both this fact and with the facts about passive avoidance. I take some comfort from the observation that of all of the facts about animals and humans, the fact about bad taste has the weakest batting average. It may yet turn out not to be a fact.

3. Though the fact that obese humans eat less often is no problem, the fact that obese rats also eat less often is awkward, for it is a bit difficult to see how food stimulus intensity can vary for a caged rat on an ad-lib schedule. This may seem farfetched, but there is some experimental evidence that this may be due to the staleness of the food. Brooks, Lockwood, and Wiggins (1946), using mash for food, demonstrated that lesioned rats do not outeat normals when the food is even slightly stale. Only when the food was absolutely fresh and newly placed in the cage did lesioned rats eat conspicuously more than normal rats. It seems doubtful, however, that this could be the explanation for results obtained with pellets.

4. As with food, one should expect from this formulation that the animal's water intake would increase following the lesion. There does not appear to have been much systematic study of the problem, but what data exist are inconsistent from one study to the next. Several studies indicate decreased water intake; at least one study (Krasne, 1964) indicates no change following the operation; and there are even rare occasional case

reports of polydipsia. Possibly my interactional hypothesis can cope with this chaos, and systematically varying the salience of the water cue will systematically affect the water intake of the ventromedial animal. It is also possible that under any circumstance, water, smell-less and tasteless, is a remote cue.

There are, then, difficulties with this formulation. These may be the kinds of difficulties that will ultimately damn the theory, or at least establish its limits. Alternatively, these may mostly be apparent difficulties, and this view of matters may help us clarify inconsistent sets of data, for I suspect that by systematically varying cue prominence we can systematically vary the lesioned animal's reactivity on many dimensions. We shall see. Granting the difficulties, for the moment this view of matters does manage to subsume a surprisingly diverse set of facts about animals and men under one quite simple theoretical scheme.

Since I have presented this article as a more or less personal history of the development of a set of ideas, I would like to conclude by taking a more formal look at this body of data, theory, and speculation, by examining what I believe we now know, what seems to be good guesswork, and what is still out-and-out speculation.

1. With some confidence, we can say that obese humans are externally controlled or stimulus-bound. There is little question that this is true of their eating behavior, and evidence is rapidly accumulating that eating is a special case of the more general state.

I have suggested that stimulus prominence and reactivity are key variables in understanding the realms of behavior with which I have been concerned, and Figure 4 represents a first guess as to the nature of the differential functions involved for obese and normal humans. The specific shapes of the curves are, of course, pure guesswork, and the only absolute requirement that I believe the data impose on the theory is that there be an interaction such that at low levels of stimulus prominence, the obese are less reactive, and at high levels of prominence more reactive, than normals.

2. With considerably less confidence, I believe we can say that this same set of hypotheses may explain many of the differences between the ventromedial lesioned rat and his intact counterpart. This conclusion is based on the fact that so much of the existing data either fit or can be plausibly reinterpreted to fit these ideas. Obviously, the crucial experiments have yet to be done.

3. Finally, and most tentatively, one may guess that the obesity of rats and men has a common physiological locus in the ventromedial hypothalamus. I must emphasize that this guess is based *entirely* on the persistent and tantalizing analogies between lesioned rats and obese humans. There is absolutely no relevant independent evidence. However, should future work support this speculation, I suspect, in light of the evidence already supporting the stimulus-binding hypotheses, that we are in for a radical revision of our notions about the hypothalamus.

REFERENCES

Brooks, C. McC., & Lambert, E. F. A study of the effect of limitation of food intake and the method of feeding on the rate of weight gain during hypothalamic obesity in the albino rat. *American Journal of Physiology,* 1946, **147,** 695–707.

Brooks, C. McC., Lockwood, R. A., & Wiggins, M. L. A study of the effect of hypothalamic lesions on the eating habits of the albino rat. *American Journal of Physiology,* 1946, **147,** 735–741.

Bullen, B. A., Reed, R. B., & Mayer, J. Physical activity of obese and nonobese adolescent girls appraised by motion picture sampling. *American Journal of Clinical Nutrition,* 1964, **14,** 211–223.

Cannon, W. B. *Bodily changes in pain, hunger, fear and rage.* (2nd ed.) New York: Appleton, 1915.

Carlson, A. J. *The control of hunger in health and disease.* Chicago: University of Chicago Press, 1916.

Decke, E. Effects of taste on the eating behavior of obese and normal persons. Cited in S. Schachter, *Emotion, obesity, and crime.* New York: Academic Press, 1971.

Gladfelter, W. E., & Brobeck, J. R. Decreased spontaneous locomotor activity in the rat induced by hypothalamic lesions. *American Journal of Physiology,* 1962, **203,** 811–817.

Goldman, R., Jaffa, M., & Schachter, S. Yom Kippur, Air France, dormitory food, and the eating behavior of obese and normal persons. *Journal of Personality and Social Psychology,* 1968, **10,** 117–123.

Grossman, S. P. The VMH: A center for affective reactions, satiety, or both? *International Journal of Physiology and Behavior,* 1966, **1,** 1–10.

Grossman, S. P. *A textbook of physiological psychology.* New York: Wiley, 1967.

Hetherington, A. W., & Ranson, S. W. Hypothalamic lesions and adiposity in the rat. *Anatomical Record,* 1940, **78,** 149–172.

Johnson, W. G. The effect of prior-taste and food visibility on the food-directed instrumental performance of obese individuals. Unpublished doctoral dissertation, Catholic University of America, 1970.

Krasne, F. B. Unpublished study cited in N. E. Miller, Some psycho-physiological studies of motivation and of the behavioural effects of illness. *Bulletin of the British Psychological Society,* 1964, **17,** 1–20.

Maren, T. H. Cited in J. L. Fuller & G. A. Jacoby, Central and sensory control of food intake in genetically obese mice. *American Journal of Physiology,* 1955, **183,** 279–283.

Miller, N. E. Some psycho-physiological studies of motivation and of the behavioural effects of illness. *Bulletin of the British Psychological Society,* 1964, **17,** 1–20.

Miller, N. E., Bailey, C. J., & Stevenson, J. A. F. Decreased "hunger" but increased food intake resulting from hypothalamic lesions. *Science,* 1950, **112,** 256–259.

Mrosovsky, N. *Hibernation and the hypothalamus.* New York: Appleton-Century-Crofts, 1971.

Nisbett, R. E. Determinants of food intake in human obesity. *Science,* 1968, **159,** 1254–1255. (a)

Nisbett, R. E. Taste, deprivation, and weight determinants of eating behavior. *Journal of Personality and Social Psychology,* 1968, **10,** 107–116. (b)

Nisbett, R. E. Eating and obesity in men and animals. In press, 1971.

Pliner, P. Effects of liquid and solid preloads on the eating behavior of obese and normal persons. Unpublished doctoral dissertation, Columbia University, 1970.

Rabin, B. M., & Smith, C. J. Behavioral comparison of the effectiveness of irritative and non-irritative lesions in producing hypothalamic hyperphagia. *Physiology and Behavior,* 1968, **3,** 417–420.

Reeves, A. G., & Plum, F. Hyperphagia, rage, and dementia accompanying a ventromedial hypothalamic neoplasm. *Archives of Neurology,* 1969, **20,** 616–624.

Reynolds, R. W. Ventromedial hypothalamic lesions with hyperphagia. *American Journal of Physiology,* 1963, **204,** 60–62.

Rodin, J. Effects of distraction on performance of obese and normal subjects. Unpublished doctoral dissertation, Columbia University, 1970.

Ross, L. D. Cue- and cognition-controlled eating among obese and normal subjects. Unpublished doctoral dissertation, Columbia University, 1969.

Schachter, S. The interaction of cognitive and physiological determinants of emotional state. In L. Berkowitz (Ed.), *Advances in experimental social psychology,* Vol. 1. New York: Academic Press, 1964.

Schachter, S. Cognitive effects on bodily functioning: Studies of obesity and eating. In D. C. Glass (Ed.), *Neurophysiology and emotion.* New York: Rockefeller University Press and Russell Sage Foundation, 1967.

Schachter, S. Obesity and eating. *Science,* 1968, **161,** 751–756.

Schachter, S. *Emotion, obesity, and crime.* New York: Academic Press, 1971.

Schachter, S., Goldman, R., & Gordon, A. Effects of fear, food deprivation, and obesity on eating. *Journal of Personality and Social Psychology,* 1968, **10,** 91–97.

Singh, D. Comparison of hyperemotionality caused by lesions in the septal and ventromedial hypothalamic areas in the rat. *Psychonomic Science,* 1969, **16,** 3–4.

Stellar, E. The physiology of motivation. *Psychological Review,* 1954, **61,** 5–22.

Stunkard, A., & Koch, C. The interpretation of gastric motility: I. Apparent bias in the reports of hunger by obese persons. *Archives of General Psychiatry,* 1964, **11,** 74–82.

Teitelbaum, P. Sensory control of hypothalamic hyperphagia. *Journal of Comparative and Physiological Psychology,* 1955, **48,** 156–163.

Teitelbaum, P. Random and food-directed activity in hyperphagic and normal rats. *Journal of Comparative and Physiological Psychology,* 1957, **50,** 486–490.

Teitelbaum, P., & Campbell, B. A. Ingestion patterns in hyperphagic and normal rats. *Journal of Comparative and Physiological Psychology,* 1958, **51,** 135–141.

Turner, S. G., Sechzer, J. A., & Liebelt, R. A. Sensitivity to electric shock after ventromedial hypothalamic lesions. *Experimental Neurology,* 1967, **19,** 236–244.

SECTION SUMMARY

Heider's (1958) general approach to the attribution process has been extended by Harold H. Kelley (1967), by Daryl Bem (1972), and by Edward E. Jones and his colleagues (Jones & Davis, 1965; Jones & Harris, 1967; Jones & Nisbett, 1971). The work of Jones et al. will be discussed here, since it is more relevant to the first article in this section. As that article indicates, Jones and his co-workers are more concerned with personal forces than with environmental forces in the attribution of causes to behavior. They seek *corre-*

spondent inferences, or cases in which a judgment is made by an observer that a disposition (or dispositional characteristic) of a target person is perceived as a *sufficient* explanation of his behavior. For example, a college English professor is faced with the fact that one of his freshmen students continually comes 10 to 15 minutes late to class. If the professor concludes that this behavior is simply the result of the student's attitude of intense dislike for English classes, this attribution would indicate a correspondent inference. Correspondent inference predicts that, if a behavior happens more often, and if it appears to be a matter of free choice rather than forced on the behaver, the observer is more likely to attribute an attitude, or disposition, as the cause of the behavior.

One direction taken by research and speculation on this topic is a study of factors that influence the *confidence* with which such correspondent inferences are made. Why is the faculty member so sure that Eddie "dislikes English classes"? One such influence is the *social desirability* of the behavior, or the degree to which an action conforms to what social norms indicate "should" be done. The greater the social desirability of an action, Jones and Davis propose, the less information it yields about the intentions of the target person. But if an action violates the norms—as "coming late to class" violates norms for students—it is more likely that the action will be attributed to personal forces, or dispositions, than to environmental ones.

A second determinant is the *hedonic relevance* of the action, which concerns itself with the degree to which the target person's action proves rewarding or costly to the observer. An act of strong hedonic relevance is one that has direct and important effects on the observer, and the observer is more likely to rely on such actions as sources in his or her inferring of attributes to the target person. If the professor sees Eddie's late appearance day after day as a deterrent to the effectiveness of his lecture, he will be more confident in attributing a personal cause to the behavior.

Finally, acts of strong *personalism* are more likely to be utilized as bases for inference. Person-

alism refers to the extent to which the presence or the attributes of the observer contribute to the target person's intent to produce certain outcomes. For example, if the observer sees the other's actions as being directed toward him and attempting to influence his state, the observer will utilize personal forces more in the attribution process. If the professor learns that Eddie arrives punctually at all his other courses except English, the professor is more confident in making interpretations of the causes of Eddie's behavior.

So, given this theoretical framework, what types of actions will be most likely to serve as bases for the inference of dispositional attributes of the target person? That is, what types of behavior are most likely to lead you as an observer to feel confident that you can infer what the target person is "really like" or what he "really feels"?

According to Jones and his colleagues, the most fruitful behavior is (1) that which is seen as *not* caused by social norms or other social desirability pressures (that is, not externally caused), (2) that which has real consequences for you (hedonic relevance), and (3) that which is seen as directed intentionally toward you (personalism). Since social desirability pressures are usually toward mature, rational, and positive behaviors, one consequence of this type of analysis is that immature, irrational, or negativistic behaviors will be the ones from which people will draw the most inferences about underlying attributes!

The second and third articles in this section demonstrate that there is also a strong human tendency to seek some attribution or explanation for one's own bodily states. In the second article, male subjects who thought that their heartbeat rates changed in response to their looking at certain *Playboy* nudes came to like *those* photos more than other, similar ones. Thus the subjects used their internal sensations—or what they *thought* to be their internal sensations—as sources of information about the causes of their behavior. We seek in this way to make sense out of our actions.

But there appear to be individual differences in the reliance on internal sensations in attributing causes to our behavior. The thesis of the third article in this section is that, when the concern is eating behavior, obese persons are less responsive to internal factors—and more influenced by environmental forces—than are normal-weight persons. If we may exaggerate, we can say that chronically obese people do not know when they are physiologically hungry. Instead, they eat when the clock says it's mealtime or when food is present. Are there also group differences like these in the responsiveness of subjects to the false information about their heartbeat rates?

In a study subsequent to the one reprinted in this section, Valins (1967) sought to answer this question. He hypothesized that male students who were classified as unemotional on the basis of responses to personality tests would make less use of the information about their heartbeat rates than would male students whose responses to the tests classified them as *emotional*. Two paper-and-pencil measures of emotionality were given to students during freshman orientation meetings. Those who scored in the extreme direction on each of the two measures were selected to participate in the false heart-rate feedback procedure. Just as in the study reprinted in this section, all subjects viewed 10 color slides of *Playboy* nudes. But in the later study *all* subjects were told that the sounds they heard were their heartbeats. For half the subjects, the rate was intensified for certain pictures; for the remaining subjects, the heart rate slowed down when these same photos were viewed.

As in the previous study, male students liked those nudes best to which they thought their heartbeats had reacted. But it was also apparent that the choices of the more emotional subjects were influenced more by the false feedback than were the choices of the less emotional subjects. More emotional subjects chose more of the pictures associated with changed heart rate. For example, given the task of choosing the five most attractive photographs, the average highly emotional subject who had heard his heart rate increase chose 3.7 of those pictures, whereas the less emotional subjects under the same treatment chose 3.2 of those pictures. The same difference in choice occurred for emotional vs. unemotional subjects in the "decreased heart-rate" condition.

Why are certain persons more in tune with their internal sensations than are others? The reasons are still being sought. But Schachter's program of research offers one fascinating hypothesis. It is noteworthy that, when Schachter began his work on the utilization of external cues by obese persons (Schachter, 1964, 1967), environmental causes provided the source for his speculation. Utilizing observations of a psychoanalyst who had worked with obese patients (Bruch, 1961), Schachter at that time wondered if some adults were chronically obese because they had never learned as children, to separate feelings of hunger from feelings of discomfort. According to this explanation, the parents of some infants would respond to every anxious wail by sticking food in the child's mouth. The infant comes to label "almost any aroused state as hunger, or, alternatively, labeling no internal state as hunger" (Schachter, 1967, p. 127).

But more recently Schachter has turned to other possibilities. A major portion of his article in this section documents the striking resemblance of the behaviors of obese humans to those of rats with damage to the ventromedial nuclei of the hypothalamus. Can it be that most cases of chronic human obesity are at least partly caused by some physiological malfunction or defect in the brain? At present it is only an educated guess, as Schachter indicates. The study of this question has only begun. Further research should do the following:

1. Clarify the distinctions between "obese" and "normal-weight" subjects. (So far, Schachter's obese subjects have been chosen simply on the basis of being overweight. It may be that some of these subjects are overweight because of metabolic reasons, whereas others may simply overeat. Additionally, Schachter's pool of "normal-weight" subjects may include some potentially obese persons who keep their weight at a desirable level only through a severe program of self-control.)

2. Make observations of the same subjects over a long period of time in order to illuminate our knowledge of the onset and determinants of obesity. Particularly useful would be studies that begin during infancy, with special attention to feeding habits.

3. Direct the study back into an attributional framework. Schachter's early work dealt with the attribution of emotional and motivational states; in these studies the dependent variable was concerned with how angry or how hungry the subject was. The more recent work, using *eating behavior* rather than feelings of hunger as the response to be studied, makes the research less social psychological in orientation. It remains, of course, of tremendous importance.

REFERENCES

Bem, D. J. The cognitive alteration of feeling states: A discussion. In H. London and R. E. Nisbett (Eds.), *Cognitive alteration of feeling states.* Chicago: Aldine, 1972.

Bruch, H. Transformation of oral impulses in eating disorders: A conceptual approach. *Psychiatric Quarterly,* 1961, **35,** 458–481.

Heider, F. *The psychology of interpersonal relations.* New York: Wiley, 1958.

Jones, E. E., & Davis, K. E. From acts to dispositions. In L. Berkowitz (Ed.), *Advances in experimental social psychology,* Vol. II. New York: Academic Press, 1965. Pp. 219–266.

Jones, E. E., & Harris, V. A. The attribution of attitudes. *Journal of Experimental Social Psychology,* 1967, **3,** 1–24.

Jones, E. E., & Nisbett, R. E. *The actor and the observer: Divergent perceptions of the causes of behavior.* New York: General Learning Corporation, 1971.

Kelly, H. H. Attribution theory in social psychology. In D. Levine (Ed.), *Nebraska symposium on motivation, 1967.* Lincoln: University of Nebraska Press, 1967. Pp. 192–238.

Schachter, S. The interaction of cognitive and physiological determinants of emotional state. In L. Berkowitz (Ed.), *Advances in experimental social psychology,* Vol. I. New York: Academic Press, 1964. Pp. 49–80.

Schachter, S. Cognitive effects on bodily functioning: Studies of obesity and eating. In D. C. Glass (Ed.), *Neurophysiology and emotion.* New York: Rockefeller University Press and Russell Sage Foundation, 1967. Pp. 117–144.

Valins, S. Emotionality and information concerning internal reactions. *Journal of Personality and Social Psychology,* 1967, **6,** 458–463.

SUGGESTED READINGS FOR FURTHER STUDY

Ajzen, I. Attribution of dispositions to an actor: Effects of perceived decision freedom and behavioral utilities. *Journal of Personality and Social Psychology,* 1971, **18,** 144–156.

Barefoot, J. C., & Straub, R. B. Opportunity for information search and the effect of false heart-rate feedback. *Journal of Personality and Social Psychology,* 1971, **17,** 154–157.

Bem, D. J. Self-perception theory. In L. Berkowitz (Ed.), *Advances in experimental social psychology,* Vol. 6. New York: Academic Press, 1972.

Duval, S., & Wicklund, R. *A theory of objective self-awareness.* New York: Academic Press, in press.

Jones, E. E., & Harris, V. A. The attribution of attitudes. *Journal of Experimental Social Psychology,* 1967, **3,** 1–24.

Jones, R. G., & Welsh, J. B. Ability attribution and impression formation in a strategic game: A limiting case of the primacy effect. *Journal of Personality and Social Psychology,* 1971, **20,** 166–175.

Kelley, H. H. Attribution theory in social psychology. In D. Levine (Ed.), *Nebraska symposium on motivation, 1967.* Lincoln: University of Nebraska Press, 1967. Pp. 192–238.

Ross, L., Rodin, J., Zimbardo, P. G. Toward an attribution therapy: The reduction of fear through induced cognitive-emotional misattribution. *Journal of Personality and Social Psychology,* 1969, **12,** 279–288.

Schachter, S. *Emotion, obesity, and crime.* New York: Academic Press, 1971.

Walster, E., & Berscheid, E. Adrenaline makes the heart grow fonder. *Psychology Today,* 1971, **5**(1), 46–50 *ff.*

GLOSSARY

Adrenaline: See Epinephrine.

Aggression: Behavior that is designed to hurt or cause injury or death to another organism or to oneself.

Altruism: Helping behavior; behavior carried out to benefit another person; done without anticipation of rewards from external sources.

Analysis of variance: A statistical test to determine whether the average scores for several groups of subjects (or the average scores resulting from differing treatments) are different enough to permit ruling out chance as a likely cause of the differences. If an analysis of variance is statistically significant, the conclusion is that a true difference exists between groups or treatments. The analysis of variance is expressed by an *F* test.

Anomie: A feeling of being alienated, disoriented, and disassociated from any system of social norms and beliefs.

Anonymity: A condition of urban life in which an individual is surrounded by strangers. This provides freedom from social ties but may also create feelings of alienation and detachment. Similar to deindividuation.

Anthropomorphic: The attribution of human characteristics to inanimate objects or subhuman processes.

Anti-Semitism: A generalized negative attitude toward Jews; may include specific beliefs that are contradictory with each other.

Attitude: The internal response or affect felt for or against a psychological object; usually this affect predisposes its holder toward certain actions. Some researchers see attitudes as having three components —feelings (affect), cognitions (beliefs), and action tendencies.

Attribution theory: A minitheory of social psychology dealing with the causes subjects give to their behavior or the behavior of others. Attribution theory seeks to understand the factors that determine the reasons we give for actions.

Authoritarianism: A basic personality style that includes a set of organized beliefs, values, and preferences, including submission to authority, identification with authority, denial of feelings, cynicism, and others.

Autokinetic effect: The tendency for a stationary light, when viewed in an otherwise completely darkened room, to appear to move; a measure of compliance to norms.

Balance theory: A theory of attitude change that hypothesizes that people like to hold consistent, compatible beliefs and dislike holding inconsistent, incompatible beliefs.

Belief similarity theory: Rokeach's theory that much white rejection of blacks arises not because of race per se but because whites assume that blacks hold values and beliefs very different from their own.

Brainwashing: A massive (and largely unsuccessful)

attitude-change program used on prisoners of war during the Korean War; chiefly utilizes the arousal of guilt and the foot-in-the-door technique.

Catharsis: The unleashing of feelings; the hypothesized reduction in the intensity of an emotion, such as aggression, resulting from the direct or indirect expression of the emotion. In the debate over the effects of witnessing violence on the expression of aggression, the catharsis theory proposes that watching violent acts "drains off" aggression in the viewer.

Cathexis: An attachment to objects that are gratifying or a rejection of those that are unpleasant.

Cautious shift: The situation sometimes observed in which decisions by a group are less risky than those by separate individuals; most likely to occur when negative consequences of failure are particularly great.

Children's Domestic Exchange (CDE): A proposed program in which minority- and majority-group children would live in one another's homes for a period of time; theorized to lead to a reduction in ethnic prejudice.

Choice Dilemmas Questionnaire (CDQ): The instrument used in most research on the risky shift. Subjects are presented with cases in which a person must choose between two courses of action, one of which is more risky than the other but also more rewarding if successful. For each situation the subject must indicate the lowest probability of success that he or she would accept before recommending that the potentially more rewarding alternative be chosen.

Cognitive approach: One that focuses on mental rather than emotional or physiological determinants of behavior.

Cognitive dissonance: The state in which two beliefs are held and one is opposite to, or in conflict with, the other; one theory of attitude change.

Compliance: Overt conformity, or the act of openly acceding to another's wishes; or, the act of doing what another wants you to, whether or not you are aware of the other's wishes.

Confederate: In a psychological experiment, a participant who appears to be a naive subject but who is actually an accomplice of the experimenter.

Conformity: Behavior that is in agreement with that of the others in a group and that is influenced by that of the others.

Counterattitudinal behavior: An individual's behavior that is opposite that which would be predicted from his or her attitude.

Contriently interdependent goals: The case in which, if one person achieves his or her goal, by definition the others are prevented from reaching theirs.

Correlation: An indication of the degree of relationship between two variables in the same population. Correlations can range from +1.00 (perfect positive correlation), through 0.00 (absence of relationship), through −1.00 (perfect negative correlation). The term r is used as a symbol for the Pearson product-moment correlation coefficient.

Debriefing (or dehoaxing): The procedure wherein, at the completion of a study involving deception, the true purpose of the study is explained to each subject, who is given a chance to express his or her feelings.

Decision freedom: The degree to which an experimental subject feels free not to comply with a request to undertake counterattitudinal behavior.

De facto segregation: Racial separation that is not supported by laws but arises because of housing patterns, income differences, and so on.

Deindividuation: A condition of reduced self-identity, whereby conventional restraints are lessened.

De jure segregation: Racial separation that is enforced by law; now illegal in the United States.

Demand characteristics: The expectations that the subjects bring to psychological experiments; the "demands" that they perceive are put upon them to "cooperate," to "look good," and so on.

Diffusion of responsibility: The situation in which the felt responsibility for action may be shared among all participants or onlookers, so that the more participants there are, the less is the amount of responsibility for action felt by any single participant.

Discrimination: Behavior that shows unfair treatment of others and is based on the other person's membership in a specific group rather than on his individual actions or characteristics.

Disposition, or Dispositional Property: An internal characteristic of a person, such as a personality trait or an attitude or an ability, which may be used as an explanation (or partial explanation) of his or her behavior.

Dyad: A two-person group.

Ego: According to Freud, that part of the personality oriented toward acting reasonably and realistically; the "executive" part of personality.

Ego-alien: Irrational; not in tune with what is sensible or realistic or real.

Ego-defensive function: The function of an attitude in which the attitude is a reflection of the holder's unresolved personal problems; often applied to prejudicial attitudes.

Epinephrine: A drug that has the effect of triggering the sympathetic nervous system and causing increased heart rate, increased blood pressure, and other physiological reactions to emotion; also called adrenaline.

Equalitarian view of race differences: The belief that two races do not differ in their innate mental ability.

Equal-status contact: The situation in which ethnic-group members and majority-group members interact in a situation in which their statuses are defined as equal; may lead to a reduction in prejudice.

Equated-environment strategy: In studying racial differences in intelligence, the approach that seeks to find groups that have the same degree of environment yet differ in race. According to this approach, any resultant difference in the average IQ scores of the two groups must be due to differences in heredity.

Equity theory: A minitheory concerned with the tendency to return a favor or comply with the request of a favor-doer because of the norms of social justice and reparation.

Ethnocentrism: A rejection of foreigners, aliens, and all out-groups, accompanied by a belief that one's own group or nationality is the best in all respects.

Ethnic group: A group sharing a common culture, customs, language, religious heritage, or race.

Ethology: The study of the behavior of animals in field situations.

Evaluation apprehension: An experimental subject's fear that his behavior is being observed and evaluated by the experimenter; may lead to changes in behavior within an experiment.

Experimenter expectancy: The ways that experimenters expect their subjects to respond to the experimental manipulation; these expectancies may unconsciously affect the subjects' behaviors.

Expiatory punishment: According to Piaget, the belief held by younger children that a wrongdoer should suffer a punishment that is painful in proportion to the seriousness of the offense but not necessarily related to the offense.

Extrapunitiveness: Attribution of the causes of a frustrating event to some person or object outside oneself; blaming others for one's frustrations.

F test: The statistical test used in conjunction with an analysis of variance. Also used to see if the distributions of two groups are different (*see* Analysis of variance).

Fate control: The degree to which an individual is able, or thinks he is able, to control his own destiny.

Foot-in-the-door technique: The technique wherein the likelihood of an individual's agreeing to a large request is increased by getting him or her to agree to a smaller request first.

Forced-compliance paradigm: The experimental situation in which the subject is pressured to undertake a counterattitudinal behavior. A paradigm used to test the cognitive dissonance theory of attitude change.

Functions of attitudes: Reasons why a person may hold the attitudes he does. Four major functions are theorized: knowledge, social adjustment, ego-defensive, and value-expressive.

Gene: An element that determines, along with other genes, the transmission of hereditary characteristics.

Genotype: An underlying characteristic; often a causal factor.

Hedonic relevance: The degree to which another person's behavior has a rewarding or costly effect on an observer. If an act has hedonic relevance, it has more use in attributing causes to the other person's behavior.

Heritability estimate or coefficient: A measure of the degree to which differences in heredity account for differences in some characteristic; for example, if in a group the heritability coefficient for height is .90, the indication is that 90% of the difference in height between group members is accounted for by differences in their heredity.

Hypothesis of genetic equality: Assumption that two groups (racial groups, for instance) possess equivalent heredities; that is, there is no genetic reason for the groups to differ in measured performance.

Id: According to Freud, a set of drives that is the repository for man's basic unsocialized impulses, including sex and aggression.

Immanent justice: According to Piaget, the belief held by younger children that misdeeds will lead naturally to negative consequences, that punishments emanate automatically from things themselves.

Immigrant analogy: The naive assumption that present-day ethnic-group members (especially blacks) should be able to succeed in the majority culture just as well as European immigrants of past generations.

Incipient attitude: Ethnic attitude of young children (ages 4–8) wherein ethnic concepts and terms are learned but are not yet generalized to all members of the object group.

Identification: The general process by which one person takes on the attributes of another; often involves modeling and imitation.

Independence of judgment: Maintenance and expression of one's true beliefs in the face of the expression of false or contrary beliefs by the other members of the group.

Individual racism: Prejudice toward an ethnic group, usually blacks.

Innate: That which is due to inheritance, as opposed to that which is acquired through learning and the environment.

Innate differences: Those resulting from genetic factors or from different heredities.

Institutional racism: The situation in which major societal institutions are structured to permit or encourage the subjugation or mistreatment of ethnic groups.

Invariant: Irreversible; in only one order.

Knowledge function: The function of an attitude in which it allows the holder to gain new frames of reference or standards for evaluating objects relevant to the attitude.

Latency: The time it takes a person to respond to a stimulus.

Libido: A basic psychic energy. According to Freud,

a person possesses only a certain amount of libido, parts of which he directs toward different concerns.

Likert-type: A specific type of attitude scale in which the format includes a series of definite (that is, not neutral) statements. The subject indicates (usually on a five- or six-point scale) how much he agrees or disagrees with each statement. His answers are summed to give his position or score on this attitude.

Machiavellianism: A set of beliefs held by a person who values the manipulation of others for his or her own purposes.

Mean (or mean score): The average for a set of scores, determined by adding up all the scores and dividing by the number of scores. Symbolized by M or $\bar{X}$.

Mediating variable: One that links two other variables and affects the influence of one on the other.

Mixed-motive games: Games that force the subject to choose between two motives, usually cooperation versus competition.

Modeling: The tendency of persons, particularly children, to imitate the witnessed behavior of others (models).

Monotonic relationship: A linear relationship; one in which, as one variable increases, the other does so correspondingly.

Morale: Extent to which group members find the group personally satisfying and the extent to which they believe the group is successfully progressing toward its goals.

Moral realism: According to Piaget, a belief held by younger children that acts should be judged in terms of consequences, not on the basis of that motive behind the act.

Mores: Cultural standards defining those behaviors that are morally acceptable or unacceptable.

nAff: Need for affiliation; desire to be with others.

Native differences: Differences between racial (or other) groups not attributable to environment or learning but rather innate or hereditary.

Nonconformity: Behavior that is intended to facilitate the attainment of some goal other than that of fulfilling what is seen as the normative group expectations.

Non-zero-sum-game: A two-person game in which the sum of the winnings of the two persons does not have to equal zero—that is, a game in which both can win or both can lose on a particular play.

Normative study: A study that determines how scores are distributed within some representative population of persons.

Overlap: The percentage of black children whose IQs exceed the average IQ of white children. If the two groups are equal in average IQ, we would expect 50% of the black children to have IQs exceeding the average for white children.

Overload: The inability of a person in an urban environment to process inputs from the environment because there are too many inputs or because successive inputs come too rapidly after one another.

p <.05: This statement, read as "probability of less than .05," means that the correlation or mean difference is so great that it could have occurred by chance, or coincidence, fewer than 5 times out of every 100 comparisons. Therefore it is concluded that the relationship or the mean difference is a true one, not simply a coincidental finding.

Paradigm: A specific type of research design or methodology.

Personalism: In attributing causes to the acts of another, personalism deals with the degree to which the presence or the attributes of the observer contribute to the target person's intent to produce certain outcomes.

Phenotype: A surface or observable characteristic; often a resultant rather than a causal factor.

Pilot study: In research, a small study, or series of studies, carried out prior to the actual research, in order to pretest methodology, procedures, and so on.

Pluralistic ignorance: The process by which, in an ambiguous emergency situation, each bystander is led by the apparent lack of concern of the others to interpret the situation as being less serious than he or she would if alone.

Post hoc analysis: A statistical analysis that is decided on and done after the experimental data have been collected; therefore, not a part of the original design or purpose of the experiment.

Prejudice: An unjustified negative attitude toward all members of a group, based on overgeneralization, lack of information, or misinformation about the group.

Principled morality: The two highest stages in Kohlberg's theory of moral judgment, in which adherence to general principles supplants blind adherence to laws and rules.

Promotively interdependent goals: The case in which one person cannot obtain his or her goal unless the other persons achieve theirs.

Prosocial behavior: Behavior toward others that reflects the desired values of one's society (for example, helpfulness, charity, sympathy, dependability).

Psychopathology: Mental disturbance; maladjustment.

r=+.41: This statement, read as "a correlation of plus point forty-one," means that there is a positive relationship between the two variables in this population. Since positive correlations can range from .00 to +1.00, this correlation of +.41 is indicative of a moderate relationship. If the two variables were aggression and obedience, we would conclude that there is a moderate relationship between aggression and obedience—that more aggressive people *tend to be* more obedient.

Race: A population that is geographically contiguous,

that shares certain genes, and whose members breed together.

Racism: A negative orientation toward an ethnic group; differentiated into individual racism and institutional racism.

Reciprocity: According to Piaget, the belief held by older children that punishment should be logically related to the offense.

Reference group: A group with which an individual identifies or aspires to belong.

Risk-as-value hypothesis: The hypothesis that willingness to take a risk is a valued trait in our society and that most people consider themselves at least as risky as others.

Risk-benefit approach: Approach to research ethics wherein the potential risks to the well-being of research participants are weighed against the possible benefits to society of the knowledge that would derive from the research.

Risky shift: The observed tendency for group decisions to be more risky than decisions made separately by comparable individuals.

Role enactment: For urban dwellers, the tendency to deal with one another in highly segmented, functional terms.

S.D.: See Standard deviation.

SES: Socioeconomic status. See Social class.

Selective migration: A point of view that explains the improved IQ performance of Northern black children in terms of tendencies for brighter children to leave the South and emigrate to the North.

Self-attitudes: Attitudes toward, and feelings about, oneself and the ethnic group to which one belongs.

Self-fulfilling prophecy: The situation in which a minority-group member may come to manifest those negative traits constantly applied to him by the majority culture.

Sexism: An attitude or behavior by a person or institution that reflects an unwarranted belief that one sex is inferior to the other.

Sex role: The expectations society holds as to what is acceptable behavior for each sex.

Sims Score Card: A checklist measure of the socioeconomic level of a family.

Social adjustment function: The function of an attitude through which the holder can identify with, or differentiate himself from, various reference groups.

Social class: A grouping of persons who share common values, interests, income level, and educational level.

Social-comparison theory: A point of view that states that one evaluates his or her own attitudes and abilities by comparing them with those of other people similar to himself or herself.

Social Darwinism: The application of Darwin's notion of "survival of the fittest" to cultures and races; seen as a component of racism.

Social desirability: A response set to answer questions about oneself in a manner that makes one look "good" or acceptable.

Social desirability of a behavior: The degree to which a certain action is in keeping with what society in general says is appropriate, right, correct, and so on.

Social-distance scale: A measure of how close (physically, socially, psychologically) one wishes to be to members of a particular ethnic group; a measure of prejudice.

Socialization: A "growing-up" process in which the child acquires his or her distinctive values, attitudes, and personality characteristics.

Social mobility: The extent to which a society permits its members to move upward or downward in the social hierarchy according to their own efforts.

Society for the Psychological Study of Social Issues (SPSSI): An organization of psychologists and other social scientists who are concerned with applying the skills and knowledge from the behavioral sciences to the solution of important human problems.

Span of sympathy: The range of people to whom sympathy is likely to be granted, if appropriate; urban overload may cause a reduction in this range.

Stage theory (of social development): A theory that proposes that a child must pass through a series of stages as he or she develops into adulthood. Each stage has a different set of operations or concerns, and the stages must be passed through in a definite sequence.

Standard deviation (S.D.): A measure of how much variability (or spreading out) is present in a set of scores. A group with a larger standard deviation is more heterogeneous and possesses a wider spread of scores.

Standard error of a score: The amount of inaccuracy (or "error") to be expected in a score a person receives on a mental test. In general, IQ tests have a standard error of five points or more.

Statistically significant: A finding or a difference that is not likely to have been caused by coincidence or chance; hence a true difference.

Stigma: A characteristic that is often taken to indicate that a person is substandard or abnormal.

Superego: According to Freud, the part of personality oriented toward doing what is morally proper; the conscience. The superego also includes one's ego-ideal, or ideal self-image.

Symbolic aggression: Aggression presented through a medium, such as movies or television.

t test: A statistical test to determine whether the average scores for two groups of subjects are different enough to permit ruling out chance as a likely cause of the difference.

True integration: Pettigrew's term for the situation in which interracial togetherness is possible while true personal and group autonomy are maintained.

Value-expressive function: The function of an attitude

wherein the attitude gives expression to the holder's central values and self-concept.

Verbal tests: Those that employ vocabulary and language in their administration or completion.

Yea-sayers: Persons who tend to agree with an attitude statement regardless of the nature of its content.

Zeitgeist: The "spirit of the times."

ARTICLE AUTHOR INDEX

SUBJECT INDEX